Sir William Wilson Hunter

A Comparative Dictionary of the Languages of India and high Asia

With a Dissertation. Based on the Hodgson Lists, offical Records, and...

Sir William Wilson Hunter

A Comparative Dictionary of the Languages of India and high Asia
With a Dissertation. Based on the Hodgson Lists, offical Records, and...

ISBN/EAN: 9783744751766

Printed in Europe, USA, Canada, Australia, Japan

Cover: Foto ©Thomas Meinert / pixelio.de

More available books at **www.hansebooks.com**

OF THE

LANGUAGES OF INDIA AND HIGH ASIA

WITH A DISSERTATION

BASED ON THE HODGSON LISTS, OFFICIAL RECORDS, AND MSS.

BY

W. W. HUNTER, B.A., M.R.A.S.

HON. FEL. ETHNOL. SOC.

OF HER MAJESTY'S BENGAL CIVIL SERVICE

LONDON: TRÜBNER AND CO.

1868

TO HER MOST GRACIOUS MAJESTY

QUEEN VICTORIA,

THIS WORK

IS, WITH HER ROYAL PERMISSION,

DEDICATED.

PREFACE.

IN this book I have brought together the languages of the non-Aryan tribes and peoples who dwell within or border upon the British Empire of India. They form broken and scattered fragments of that unrecorded world which was before the dispersion of the Indo-Germanic stock. On the plains of Hindustan the pre-historic races succumbed so completely beneath the Aryan invaders, as to lose all remembrance of their separate ethnical existence; but, as I endeavoured to show in my *Annals of Rural Bengal*, they have permanently affected the language, religion, and political destiny of the composite Hindus whom they combined with their conquerors to form. On the other hand, among the mountains and lofty plateaux which everywhere abound in India, they have preserved their nationality intact, and during ages waged incessant warfare with the lowland population. The long series of Indian conquerors—Aryan, Affghan, and Moghul—have each in turn laboured to extirpate them. The English are now endeavouring to reclaim them. But in order to civilise, it is necessary first to understand them; and this book, for the first time in the history of India, places the governing race in direct communication with eighty millions of its non-Aryan subjects and neighbours.

While the principal end of my researches has thus been a purely practical one, I am not without a firm hope that they will prove of service to European scholarship. Philology has hitherto concerned herself almost exclusively with Indo-Germanic and Semitic speech; with speech, that is, at a single stage, and perhaps not at its most instructive stage. The study of the non-Aryan tongues of India is destined, I believe, to open the door to the vast linguistic residue, and to furnish the basis of a new science of language, as the study of Sanskrit in India eighty years ago afforded the foundation upon which the present system of philology has been reared. In the following dissertation, the blemishes and probable inaccuracies of this rudimentary effort are carefully set forth. Some of them I hope to remove in the *Comparative Grammar of Non-Aryan Speech*, which I now have in hand; the rest I leave to the generosity of scholars who work at greater leisure and with a fuller knowledge of scientific principles than can be hoped for amid the distractions of Indian official life.

For the convenience of European students and of missionaries, the work is arranged in English, French, German, Russian, and Latin. The five synonyms are placed at the head of each page. Polyglot Prefaces will be found at the beginning, and Alphabetical Indices at the end of the volume.

PRÉFACE.

L'OUVRAGE que je donne aujourd'hui au public contient les éléments des idiomes dont se servent les tribus et peuplades non-Aryennes qui vivent dans l'étendue des possessions Anglaises aux Indes, ou qui se trouvent sur les frontières de cet empire. Ce sont les débris mutilés d'un monde dépourvu d'annales qui précéda la dispersion de la famille Indo-Germanique. Les races ante-historiques succombèrent si complétement dans les plaines de l'Hindustan sous les coups des envahisseurs Aryens qu'elles perdirent tout souvenir de leur origine distincte comme peuple. Cependant, ainsi que j'ai essayé de le démontrer dans mon livre intitulé *Annals of Rural Bengal*, ces races ont affecté d'une manière permanente le langage, la religion et la destinée politique de l'agglomération composite d'Hindous qu'elles concoururent à former en se fusionnant avec leurs vainqueurs. D'un autre côté elles conservèrent leur nationalité intacte dans les montagnes et sur les plateaux élevés qui abondent partout aux Indes ; et firent pendant des siècles une guerre incessante aux populations des basses terres. Aryens, Affghans, et Mongols, les conquérants successifs de ce pays essayèrent tour à tour de les exterminer. Ce sont ces races que les Anglais s'efforcent aujourd'hui de rallier. Mais afin de leur donner les bienfaits de la civilisation, il est indispensable de les comprendre. De là le présent volume qui, pour la première fois, met la race gouvernante en rapports directs avec quatre-vingt millions de ses sujets et de ses voisins d'origine non-Aryenne.

Le but principal de mes recherches a donc été essentiellement pratique : toutefois j'ose espérer qu'elles ne seront pas sans utilité au point de vue de la philologie. Cette science s'est occupée jusqu'ici presqu' exclusivement des idiomes Indo-Germaniques et Semitiques, c'est à dire du langage envisagé dans une seule de ses phases, et non pas la plus intéressante. L'étude des langues non-Aryennes de l'Inde doit, j'en ai la conviction, aboutir au classement d'un vaste résidu linguistique (si je puis m'exprimer ainsi) ; elle fournira les bases d'une nouvelle science du langage, de même qu'il y a quatre-vingt ans l'étude de Sanscrit aux Indes posa les fondements sur lesquels a été élevé le système de philologie qui a cours aujourd'hui. Dans la dissertation suivante, j'ai fait remarquer avec soin les erreurs et les inexactitudes probables de ce premier essai : j'espère pouvoir éliminer les unes dans une Grammaire Comparative des langues non-Aryennes à laquelle je travaille en ce moment. J'abandonne le reste à la générosité des savants qui ont pour leurs recherches ce loisir et cette connaissance complète des principes scientifiques dont on ne saurait espérer de jouir lorsqu'on est plongé, comme je le suis, au milieu des soucis de la vie officielle aux Indes.

Pour la commodité des savants d'Europe, mon vocabulaire est en Anglais, en Français, en Allemand, en Russe, et en Latin. Les synonymes Français sont placés les premiers en tête de chaque page, et à la fin du volume on trouvera un index des mots appartenant à cette langue.

PRÆFATIO LATINA.

IN hoc libro linguas collexi tribuum et populorum, quot sanguinis Aryani non participes aut imperio Britannico apud Indos subjecti sunt aut fines Britannicos accolunt. Monumenta sunt, disjecta sane atque dispersa, temporis obscuri et neque per literas neque per hominum memoriam noti, in quo nondum sede pristina diffuderat sese stirps Indogermanica. In campis quidem Hindusthaniæ ita oppressæ sunt ab immigrantibus Aryanis nationes, quæ ibi antea habitaverant, ut generis diversitatem omnino oblitæ sint: quamvis (quod in Annalibus meis Agri Bengalensis demonstrare conatus sum) linguam, religionem, rei publicæ speciem apud Indos non minime affecerint; Indi enim e vincentium cum victis commixtione progeniti sunt. Sed inter montes et campos editiores, quales per Indiam undique exstant, immutati reperiuntur indigenæ generisque sinceri. Bellum per sæcula cum populis campestribus gesserunt; neque ulli eorum, qui Indiam identidem debellaverunt, Aryani, Affghani, Moghulenses, montanos homines non exstirpare laboraverunt. Angli e contrario nostris temporibus ad cultum atque humanitatem ducere student; quod si facere posse volumus, linguas eorum prius intelligendum est; et primus in serie fastorum Indicorum liber meus quasi interpres in medium prodit inter dominos terræ et octingenties centena millia hominum alienigenarum, qui cum Anglis seu ditione seu vicinitate conjunguntur.

Finem igitur ad quem maxime contendi utilitas hodierna est, et maxime in rebus civilibus; sed valde spero aliquid Europææ eruditioni contulisse. Hactenus vix nisi linguis Indogermanicis et Semiticis incubuit philologia; quæ tamen omnes unius generis sunt, neque ejus, e quo quam plurimum disci potest. Per studium linguarum non Aryanarum porta, ut credo, patebit in congeriem illam indigestam sermonis humani adhuc residui atque neglecti, cujus ad novam scientiam transibimus, non aliter quam ad scientiam, quæ nunc est, philologicam per cognitionem linguæ Sanscriticæ ante octoginta annos admissi sumus. In disputatione, quæ subjecta est, errores, quos suspicor, et vitia operis rudis atque imperfecti diligentissime exhibui: quorum aliqua tollere spero in Grammatica Comparativa sermonis non Aryani, cui nunc intentus sum; cetera viris doctis et æquis relinquo, qui tempore longiore et scientia profundiore fruantur, quam inter distractiones civilium negotiorum ulli apud Indiam competit.

Quinque linguis, ut commodo eruditorum Europæorum inservirem, opus expressi, Anglica, Gallica, Germanica, Russica, Latina. Quintum semper in capite paginarum stat verbum Latinum; et in fine operis indicem Latinum addidi ordine alphabetico exaratum.

Vorwort.

In diesem Buche habe ich die Sprachen der nicht-arischen Stämme und Völker zusammengestellt, die innerhalb des brittischen Reiches in Indien oder an den Grenzen desselben wohnen. Es sind zerstreute Bruchstücke jener historisch nicht verzeichneten Welt, welche der Zerstreuung der indo-germanischen Race vorherging. Auf den Ebenen von Hindostan sind die vorhistorischen Racen den arischen Eroberern so vollständig unterlegen, daß sie jede Erinnerung ihrer eigenen Abstammung verloren haben. Sie haben jedoch, wie ich in meinen Annalen der Dorflandschaften Bengalens zu zeigen versuchte, auf die Sprache, die Religion und die staatliche Entwickelung der Hindus, die aus der Vermischung zwischen ihnen und ihren Eroberern hervorgegangen sind, einen bleibenden Einfluß ausgeübt. Aber auf den zahlreichen Gebirgen und Hochebenen Indiens haben sie sich ihre Nationalität vollständig erhalten und mit der Bevölkerung des Flachlandes während mehrerer Jahrhunderte fortwährend Krieg geführt.

Die lange Reihe indischer Eroberer, Arier, Afghanen und die Großmoguls haben abwechselnd auf die Vertilgung derselben hingearbeitet.

Die Engländer bemühen sich jetzt sie für Gesittung empfänglich zu machen, und durch das gegenwärtige Buch wird zum ersten Male in der Geschichte Indiens die unmittelbare Verständigung der herrschenden Race mit achtzig Millionen ihrer nicht-arischen Unterthanen und Nachbarn angestrebt.

Obwohl nun der Hauptzweck meiner Untersuchungen ein rein praktischer war, darf ich doch zuversichtlich hoffen, daß dieselben der europäischen Sprachforschung von einigem Nutzen sein werden. Die Sprachwissenschaft hat sich bis jetzt fast ausschließlich um die indogermanischen und die semitischen Sprachen, und zwar in einem einzelnen, keineswegs dem lehrreichsten Entwickelungs-Stadium derselben bekümmert.

Das Studium der nicht-arischen Sprachen Indiens ist meines Dafürhaltens dazu bestimmt, das reiche noch übrige Sprachmaterial zu erschließen und die Grundlage einer neuen Sprachwissenschaft abzugeben in eben der Weise, wie vor achtzig Jahren das Sanskritstudium in Indien die Basis lieferte, auf welcher das jetzige Sprachensystem beruht. In der folgenden Abhandlung habe ich die Mängel und etwaigen Ungenauigkeiten dieses Grundrisses sorgfältig angegeben.

Einige derselben hoffe ich in einer vergleichenden Grammatik der nicht-arischen Sprachen, mit deren Ausarbeitung ich jetzt beschäftigt bin, zu beseitigen.

Das Uebrige überlasse ich der milden Beurtheilung der Sprachforscher, die mit mehr Muße und strengerer Wissenschaftlichkeit arbeiten, als man sich unter den Berufsgeschäften des Beamtenlebens in Indien verschaffen kann.

Zum bequemeren Gebrauch für europäische Sprachfreunde ist den Englischen Wörtern eine Französische, Deutsche, Russische und Lateinische Uebersetzung beigegeben. In dem Columnentitel steht jedesmal das deutsche Wort zu zweit, und am Ende des Bandes befindet sich ein alphabetisches deutsches Verzeichniß.

ПРЕДИСЛОВІЕ.

Въ этой книгѣ собраны мною языки не-аріанскихъ народовъ и племенъ, живущихъ въ Англо-индѣйскомъ государствѣ или на границахъ его. Цѣль же всего труда изложена мною подробно въ латинскомъ и нѣмецкомъ предисловіяхъ къ нему, а ошибки, которымъ подверженъ такого рода трудъ, указаны въ разсужденіи, непосредственно слѣдующемъ за предисловіемъ. Для удобства русскихъ читателей, вверху листа, справа каждаго англійскаго слова, помѣщенъ его русскій синонимъ, выраженный латинскими буквами на сколько то возможно близко при разности азбукъ; къ концу же книги приложенъ алфавитный указатель ихъ.

CONTENTS.

PART I.—DISSERTATION.

PART II.—DICTIONARY.

PRONOMINALS.

ROOTS.

APPENDIX.

NOTANDA.

TRANSLITERATION.

a = *u* as in *cut*; *á* = *a* as in *card*.

i = *ee* as in *meet*; *í* = *ee* as in *thee*.

u = *oo* as in *boot*; *ú* = *oo* as in *booth*.

SIGNS.

Dual ([1]); Plural ([2]); Dual Inclusive ([3]); Dual Exclusive ([4]); Plural Inclusive ([5]); Plural Exclusive ([6]).

In Magyar, Turkish, Circassian, or Georgian, an asterisk (*) attached to a word indicates that it is obtained from the '*Gentium Boreo-Orientalium Vulgo Tartarorum Harmonia Linguarum*,' appended to '*A Description of the Northern and Eastern Parts of Europe and Asia*, written in High German by Philip John von Strahlenberg, a Swedish officer, thirteen years captive in those parts,' 4to, 1736, 463 pp. An author not always trustworthy.

In Mongol and Mantshu an asterisk (*) indicates the same thing. The sign † marks an Ostiak word used by the tribes of the river Irtisch in Siberia; ‡ marks Samoyedic words in use among the peoples living between the Yenesei and the Lena; § marks Tungusic words spoken by the races of the Tingus valley in Siberia; || indicate Tungusic or Lamuti words of Kamschatka.

DISSERTATION.

I.—POLITICAL.

AT the close of each year the British Governors of India deliver an account of the provinces entrusted to their care. Their reports are mainly occupied with internal measures, and form monuments of sagacious humanity and the national genius for rule, which no Englishman can contemplate without patriotic pride. But from amid these records of the consolidation of long hostile races into a harmonious empire, one chapter stands out in painful contrast. It is the section which refers to the hill and forest peoples who surround the frontier and inhabit the interior table-lands and mountain ranges of India. No sooner does the narrative enter on this topic, than its whole spirit changes. The deliberate civil strength and calm knowledge which regulate the action of English Governors towards the population of the plains, give place to fitful and violent exertions of armed force. Calculations from ascertained social causes and effects are seldom attempted; the issues of any measure can never be foretold: the only policy discernible is a policy of emergencies; and in place of the sedate forbearance towards the prejudices and weaknesses of the people, little appears save mutual indignation, outrages, reprisals, and a perpetual probability that each cold season will have its highland rising or frontier war.

General statements are feeble when particular illustrations abound. It matters little which province is cited. No population ever made more rapid progress in all that renders life secure, and in all that renders life worth having, than the people of Lower Bengal between 1860 and 1865; and the frontier history of this part of India is certainly not more unsatisfactory than that of its neighbours. The Administration Report for 1860–61 records our dealings with four hill races, two of them situated far within the British boundary. The narrative opens with 'outrages perpetrated on British subjects by the people of Sikhim;' the second section is devoted to military operations against the Kukis; the third to military operations against the Garrows; the fourth relates the sequel of the previous season's military operations against the Cossyahs and Jynteahs. These form the entire record of our intercourse with the hill tribes during the year. But indeed the bare titles of the chapters—titles given, it must be remembered, by an official pen—speak with sufficient clearness as to the character of our administration of the

highland races. The report for 1861–62 contains six short chapters. The first is headed, 'The Cossyah Rebellion;' the second, 'Riot in Nowgong;' the third, 'Excitement in the Sonthal Districts;' the fourth, 'Disturbances in Sumbulpore;' the fifth, 'Disturbances in Boad;' the sixth, 'Booteah Aggressions.' The report for 1862–63 again leads off with 'The Cossyah Rebellion,' and is occupied by the invariable record of outrages and armed pacifications. Next year a lull occurred, but the British power received insults which could be wiped out only by a costly and sanguinary war. The report of 1864–65 accordingly opens with the Bhutan expedition,—an expedition memorable for its disasters not less than for its ultimate triumph; the next section relates a raid into British territory by Tibetans; the third is taken up with a narrative of murder and abduction in British territory by Nepalese; the fourth, with disturbances in Munipur; the fifth is headed 'Naga Raids;' the sixth, 'Garrow Outrages.'

Similar scenes repeat themselves with more or less frequency in every mountainous region of India. The wisdom of British administrators in managing the Hindus and Mussalmans of the plains, seems everywhere turned into folly when dealing with the hill and forest tribes. These tribes approach or exceed two hundred in number; but an impartial historian could not review our intercourse with more than one of them with unmixed pride. It was once customary to lay the blame of our failure on the races themselves; and, without doubt, tribes so far removed from us in their social necessities, habits of thought, and motives of action, are more difficult to deal with than a population which has so much in common with ourselves as the Hindus. Many of the hill races have approved themselves faithful allies, brave soldiers, and peaceful subjects under British rule; and the administrators who know them most intimately, speak most enthusiastically of their manliness and love of truth. But in their political dealings with us, the element of certainty is always wanting. Individual officers can safely rely on them, but the Government cannot; and no length of contented industry or loyal service furnishes a guarantee against sudden risings which cover whole districts with flames.

Indian administrators have accordingly become accustomed to accept the hill races as mysteries, and to look upon their movements, necessities, and animosities, as things beyond the range of political knowledge. But the essence of mystery consists in presenting the effect and concealing the cause. In dealing with the highland tribes, the English have constantly to witness startling results, whose reasons they are unable to perceive. The power of observing and interpreting social indications, by which officers rise to places of trust on the plains, finds no material to act upon among the mountaineers; and frontier administrators are selected less for the qualities which anticipate and avert danger, than for the ready intrepidity which disarms it. The truth is, the English have studied and understand the lowland population as no conquerors ever studied or understood a subject race.

Their history, their habits, their requirements, their very weaknesses and prejudices are known, and furnish a basis for those political inductions, which, under the titles of administrative foresight and timely reform, meet popular movements half-way. The East India Company grudged neither honours nor solid rewards to any meritorious effort to illustrate the peoples whom it ruled. Such efforts led to a series of discoveries which have rolled back the horizon of human knowledge, and brought out in clear relief the ethnical revolutions of a prehistoric world. They have proved that the population of India mainly consists of that Aryan or noble stock which has radiated from Persia to America and Australasia, and is now nearly co-extensive with civilised mankind. At an early period, it became known that another element had entered into the composition of the Indian people; but an ignoble element, destitute of letters, of historical relationship, of religious conceptions, of all that renders the study of a race attractive, and for the most part buried away in forests fatal to European life. The very lustre of Aryan discoveries threw the non-Aryan peoples of India into a deeper shade. Practical usefulness and the gloss of fashion were for once on the same side; and European scholars crowded into a field in which every honest seeker might hope to find some ore, and kept aloof from pursuits in which they could look for little sympathy, and from which they expected no results. While a new science was being erected on the basis furnished by Sanskrit speech, the languages and the very names of the non-Aryan races remained unknown, and Government very properly kept its liberality for those studies which promised most fruit. Every year saw some research into Indo-Aryan history or speech munificently assisted; but during the whole history of the East India Company, it is impossible to adduce a single effort to illustrate the non-Aryan tribes which received efficient support. Until very lately, and perhaps even still, before a man devotes himself to these races, he must make up his mind not merely to dedicate his private fortune to researches which yield no fame, but also to separate himself from the great sympathetic stream of European scholarship.

The practical result now appears. English administrators understand the Aryan, and are almost totally ignorant of the non-Aryan, population of India. They know with remarkable precision how a measure will be received by the higher or purely Aryan ranks of the community; they can foresee with less certainty its effect upon the lower or semi-Aryan classes; but they neither know nor venture to predict the results of any line of action among the non-Aryan tribes. Political calculations are impossible without a knowledge of the people.

But the evil does not stop here. In the void left by ignorance, prejudice has taken up its seat; and the calamity of the non-Aryan races is not merely that they are not understood, but that they are misrepresented. We have gathered our notions concerning them from their immemorial enemies. Nothing can be conceived in a

more malignant spirit, than the epithets which ancient Sanskrit writers apply to them. The Brahminical religion has ever treated them as outcasts, hateful to gods and men; and this traditional and superstitious abhorrence is kept in a glow by the actual necessities of the superior race. The Hindus are an increasing, and consequently an encroaching people. Their advances have to be made at the expense of the hill and forest tribes; and Aryan aggressiveness, mercantile or territorial, has been found to lie at the bottom of almost every non-Aryan rising whose causes have been carefully ascertained. Indian history, indeed, is one long monotonous recital of how the children of the soil have been driven deeper and deeper into the wilds. On the one side is contemptuous detestation, on the other sullen fury; yet frontier investigators have constantly to accept the slanders of the wrong-doers as their sole evidence touching the motives and character of the wronged. What sort of a notion should we arrive at of the Hindus, if our only data had to be gathered among the aborigines? Of most of these unhappy tribes we have not a single portraiture by an impartial hand. The Indian newspapers catch and spread the infection. On more than one occasion, English journalists have so far forgotten their characteristic tenderness to the fallen, as to insult the despairing bravery of hill tribes, to speak of a peasantry fighting for its homesteads as 'adult tigers,' and to propose, as a cure for well-grounded disaffection, the deportation across the seas of a whole race. Within the last fourteen years, Christian gentlemen have penned articles breathing a spirit scarcely less tolerant than that in which the early Sanskrit singers depicted the forest tribes as black, noseless demons, of squat stature, and inarticulate speech.

The strongest proofs of our ignorance of the non-Aryan races, however, are to be found in the works of non-Aryan scholars. I shall cite two writers of unquestionable ability, with regard to whom my remarks cannot be misconstrued into hostile criticism. An admirable lecture, delivered in 1852 before the Royal Asiatic Society of Great Britain and Ireland, stated that a survey officer had 'lately discovered another tribe called Sonthals.' This newly found tribe, it should be observed, had occupied over thirty thousand square miles of British territory during more than half a century, numbered about two million people, had given new land-tenures to adjoining districts, and sent forth colonies to the north and to the east, one of which paid £6803, in the single item of rent, to the British treasury in 1854, and contained at the period of their 'discovery' 82,795 souls. Yet the lecturer was perfectly accurate in speaking of this race—a race equal to the whole rural population of Scotland—as having just been brought to light. Four years later, this unknown race, goaded by wrongs which their English rulers had long failed to understand, and therefore neglected to redress, burst down upon the plains, and during five memorable months devastated the western districts with fire and sword. As soon as order was restored, their complaints were inquired into, and

found to be just. A new system was inaugurated, and they have ever since been the most contented of British subjects. A year ago, the sister society in Bengal put forth an elaborate volume, which endeavoured to bring together all that is known about the non-Aryan peoples. With regard to many of them, scarcely anything appears but their names. Of one important tribe—the Gonds of Bustar and the adjoining countries—the conscientious writer says: 'We know very little except that they are extreme savages—black, ugly, barbarous, and dangerous.' Another—the Kherrias, whose very name, as will subsequently appear, is pregnant with information—are declared to be 'a mystery even to Colonel Dalton,' the most laborious investigator which that section of the aborigines has had.

But while learned men admit and deplore the absence of information, there is a class of writers who are not content to plead ignorance. If Government orders a report on the causes of a frontier raid, a report must be compiled. British officers, however, are scarcely ever able to converse with the offending tribes: no dictionary of their languages has been published, and all that can be found out about them comes through their natural enemies, the Aryan borderers. Extravagant calumnies thus attain to the dignity of State Papers, and are copied from one report into another. The more malignant and striking the caricature, the surer it is of a wide circulation, till, gradually gaining probability by unquestioned iteration, it becomes the materials by which our official dealings are regulated, and on which our political estimate is formed. When it is possible to place such reports side by side by the truth, the result is merely ludicrous; but it is not always possible to do so. And for one calumny that can thus be rendered harmless, a hundred wander forth unrefuted, poisoning public opinion, drying up our natural charity, and, it is to be feared, warping the British policy towards whole races.

It is an invidious, although unfortunately easy, task to select particular instances. In 1854 a long series of misunderstandings and more or less mutual grievances culminated in a war with Bhutan. Here is the official account of the unfortunate race whom it was then found necessary to encounter, and whose untrained valour repelled for a time the resources of civilised war. The description is a sufficiently striking one, and had been transcribed from one Report into another three times before it reached the State Paper from which I excerpt it. The interjections are its own. It sets out by stigmatizing the Bhuteas as 'very quarrelsome and unsociable, *as will be seen from their huts being isolated*,' forgetting that the barrenness of the hills and the necessities of hunting-tribes render large villages on the Hindu plan impracticable. 'They are a very revengeful and sly race, seldom forgetting a wrong done them; the greatest cheats and the most barefaced liars, I may safely say, in India! Morality is not named among them: men and women occupy the same apartment; after a day's work they assemble around one fire, with a large basin full of *murwa* (a spirituous

liquor made from the grain of the same name), which they suck up through narrow bamboo tubes, and eventually all fall about drunk, from the child to the grandsire, unable to rise till the following morning. The women seldom remain true to their husbands. They generally go from one to another, leaving the children, if there are any, with the father!' For this extraordinary picture the colours were mixed, we may be sure, by a lowlander's hand.

It happens that this race is one of those on whom the light of Mr. Brian Hodgson's scholarship has glanced. He discriminates between two branches of the same family; the one considerably advanced in civilisation, the other still rude. With regard to the latter he thus sums up: 'They are, in fact, not noxious, but helpless; not vicious, but aimless, both morally and intellectually; so that one cannot without distress behold their careless, unconscious inaptitude.' Let the reader contrast this touching portraiture of the wildest of the unreclaimed tribes, with the above uncritical denunciation of the whole Bhutea stock; and from its successful calumnies on a people who have formed an object of anxious scrutiny during many years, let him judge of the bold flights of malignancy that are safely ventured upon in delineations of less known races.

Thus ignorance begets misrepresentation, and misrepresentation brings forth bitter political fruits. The non-Aryan element, moreover, is not confined to the hills and forests; it enters largely into the composition of the people of the plains, in some places preponderating over the Aryan, and everywhere forming a thick solid substratum on which the Hindu population rests. Of the lowland aborigines, where they have preserved their nationality, prædial slavery until recently formed the almost universal fate. In some parts of Southern India the intolerant provisions of Manu receive effect at the present day; and the aboriginal castes continue to live apart with their dogs and asses on the outskirts of the village, forbidden to pollute its streets with their processions or their dwellings, or to build any habitation less humble than a thatched mud hut. But in general the non-Aryans of the plains have merged in the composite community; and in my *Annals of Rural Bengal* I have endeavoured, at considerable length, to exhibit the ethnical compromises to which the Aryan element has had to submit, and to illustrate the permanent influence of the aboriginal races on the speech, the religion, the social institutions, and the political destinies of the modern Hindus. It has been my fortune to be brought in several capacities into unusually close contact with both the pure and the mixed non-Aryan population. As an officer for several years upon an ethnical frontier, I was deeply impressed with the almost imperceptible gradations by which the acknowledged non-Aryans of the highlands slid into the low-caste Hindus of the plain. When in charge of the treasury, I had means of learning that the hill races have affected the relation of landlord and tenant in the lowlands to an extent that has not even been conjectured; and that non-Aryan

ideas of property, never recognised by the rulers, but immoveably rooted in the masses of Lower Bengal, had seethed and agitated, and irresistibly worked their way upwards, till they impressed themselves on our most conspicuous piece of rural legislation. As a magistrate, I came in contact with prejudices and traditional convictions, which, however unfounded they may seem to us, nevertheless amount to a sense of duty, and supply motives of action to millions of British subjects; prejudices and convictions for which English criminal justice makes no allowance, yet which, as I shall show, sometimes affect English officers with a sense almost of sickness in administering the law. But it was when in charge of a jail on the ethnical frontier that I really learned of what the Bengali people is made up. In that little captive community each class found itself amply represented. Of four hundred prisoners, one-fourth came from the adjacent highlands, and brought with them the customs, superstitions, and speech of an aboriginal race. The main body consisted of the mixed semi-Aryan Hindus, from the low-caste which eats offal, to the husbandman who in meats and drinks walks after the pattern of the straitest Pundit. Brahmans formed the residue, and illustrated the various gradations in even the purely Aryan element. Men's characters come out in jail as they do on a long voyage; and the not unkindly relations between the prisoners and their non-resident head who sometimes shields them from the harshness of subordinates, whose tempers are tried and whose humanity is impaired by the details of prison discipline, brought me into contact with a hidden world of thought, feeling, and motive, which the ordinary intercourse of life would never have enabled me to reach. Subsequently, in a distant part of the province, it was my office to watch over the emigrants to the tea districts. Every week, bands of hill-men, driven by hunger from the western frontier, embarked for plantations in the extreme north-east. They represented the overflowings of many races, and brought with them tales of disease and chronic starvation, to which their faces and bodies bore touching proof. Still later, when superintending Public Instruction in the south-western division of Bengal, I found that our efforts obtained an adequate success only in the lowland districts. I have had an opportunity of comparing these efforts with the working of State Education in France and Prussia; and I am convinced that the Indian scheme is inferior, neither in its organization nor in its fruits, to the model systems of Europe, while it possesses a single-mindedness and an elasticity all its own. It performs as a solemn obligation a function that has never entered into the ideas or touched the conscience of any other conquering race. It sacrifices nothing of its educational efficiency to political purposes; it is looked upon by neither the rulers nor the people as an engine of government, but keeps itself with cold dignity to its own proper work, and is at this moment increasing by one-third the civilised world. In the Hindu districts, every important village or considerable collection of homesteads has, or will soon

have, an aided school. But within half a day's march beyond the ethnical frontier the scene changes: Government schools can hardly be planted, except in the local capitals, where colonies of Hindu officials and traders have sprung up; and unpaid missionary zeal forms the only educational channel by which the State has found it possible to reach the aboriginal masses. In short, the population of India everywhere divides itself into classes: the preponderating Hinduized section including the whole upper and middle ranks in lowland provinces, with whose languages, habits, and necessities we are perfectly familiar, and to whom British rule is an unmixed blessing; and the aboriginal or semi-aboriginal residue, who form a dense unpenetrated substratum among the population of the plains and the sole inhabitants of mountainous or forest regions,—a residue of whose speech, feelings, and wants we know nothing, whom the English imagination has not yet reached, and for whom the security and prosperity of British rule have, by removing the previous checks on population, only intensified the struggle for life.

Yet these unrealized races have capabilities, both for good and for evil, which it is impossible to overlook. For ages they have formed a difficulty which each succeeding Government of India has been forced to face, and which no Government has been able to get rid of. The Mussalmans dealt with them as with wild beasts, but they have a tenacity to existence which wild beasts do not possess; and the one sorrowful lesson of their history is, that they cannot be exterminated. The most that the Company hoped for, was to keep them quiet; with what success, let the narrative of our dealings with any one among their races, or the events of any single year, attest. The problem which the Queen's Government in India is now called upon to solve, is to utilize them. From time to time, isolated administrators, touched by their miseries and rude virtues, have laboured to acquire their languages and to understand their wants; but such knowledge has hitherto been the property of individuals, and has too often died with its possessors. Even when committed to paper, their researches remain buried in the Government archives, or form scattered and scarcely accessible monographs in the proceedings of learned societies. This book endeavours to render these perishable hoards of individuals the permanent property of the Government, and to place what have hitherto been matters of recondite scholarship, at the disposal of every Indian missionary or administrator who wishes honestly to do his work.

Although we are chiefly acquainted with the non-Aryan peoples as frontier marauders and rebels, their capabilities for good are not unascertained. During the struggle between the worn-out Sanskrit civilisation and the impetuous prime of Islam, the Hindus discovered the value of the aboriginal races. Many chiefs of noble Aryan blood maintained their independence by such alliances; others founded new kingdoms among the forest peoples. To this day some of the tribes exhibit a black original section living side by side with a fair-skinned composite kindred sprung

from the refugees; and the most exalted Hindu princes have to submit to a curious aboriginal rite on their accession to the throne. It was stated before the Royal Asiatic Society in 1852, that the investiture of the Rajput Rajah of Nerwar is not complete, till one of his purely aboriginal subjects, a Mina, paints a round spot on his forehead with blood freshly drawn from the toe of another Mina. Without this formal recognition, his non-Aryan subjects could not be depended upon; when once it has been performed, their fidelity has never been known to waver. They form the treasury and palace guards, hold the personal safety of the prince entirely in their hands, and supply the sole escort to whom he entrusts the honour of his daughters when they go abroad. The Ranah of Udaypur, cited by General Briggs as the highest in rank of all the Hindu sovereigns in India, renders the same homage, however ill it may comport with his caste and personal dignity, to the traditions of his aboriginal subjects. Before he ascends the throne, his forehead must first be marked with the blood of a Bhil. The Hinduized chieftains of Central India receive investiture by the blood of a pure Kol; and so strong a hold has this ceremony on the minds of the people, that among the Cheris—once a great tribe, who defended themselves with honour against Shere Shah and the Imperial army, now reduced to five or six families—the head of the little community is still installed under the title of Rajah, with the token of the round spot of warm aboriginal blood.

But it is not the Hindus alone that have proved the loyalty of these neglected races. Scarcely a single administrator has ruled over them for any length of time, without finding his prejudices conquered, and his heart softened, and leaving on record his sorrow for their present condition, and his belief in their capabilities for good. But lest the traditional tenderness of the Indian Civil Service to the people should weaken the testimony of such witnesses, I shall quote only the words of soldiers—words publicly uttered and printed by veteran servants of the Company or Crown, and never contradicted or impugned. 'They are faithful, truthful, and attached to their superiors,' writes General Briggs; 'ready at all times to lay down their lives for those they serve, and remarkable for their indomitable courage. These qualities have been always displayed in our Service. The aborigines of the Carnatic were the Sepoys of Clive and of Coote. A few companies of the same stock joined the former great captain from Bombay, and fought the battle of Plassey in Bengal, which laid the foundation of our Indian empire. They have since distinguished themselves in the corps of pioneers and engineers, not only in India, but in Ava, in Affghanistan, and in the celebrated defence of Jelalabad. An unjust prejudice against them has grown up in the armies of Madras and Bombay, where they have done best service, produced by the feelings of contempt for them existing among the Hindu and Mahomedan troops. They have no prejudices themselves, are always ready to serve abroad and embark on board ship; and I

believe no instance of mutiny has ever occurred among them.' Colonel Dixon's report, published by the Court of Directors, portrays their character with admirable minuteness. He dilates on their 'fidelity, truth, and honesty,' their determined valour, their simple loyalty, and an extreme and almost touching devotion when put upon their honour. Strong as is the bond of kindred among the Mirs, he vouches for their fidelity in guarding even their own relatives as prisoners when formally entrusted to their care. For centuries they had been known only as exterminators; but beneath the considerate handling of one Englishman who honestly set about understanding them, they became peaceful subjects and well-disciplined soldiers. To the honour of British administrators be it said, the same transformation has taken place in many a remote forest of India; and I fear that, in pleading for the universal and systematic adoption of the policy which has produced such brilliant isolated results, I may have too sparingly acknowledged many noble individual efforts. Every military man who has had anything to do with the aboriginal races, admits that once they admit a claim on their allegiance, nothing tempts them to a treacherous or disloyal act. 'The fidelity to their acknowledged chief,' writes Captain Hunter, 'is very remarkable; and so strong is their attachment, that in no situation or condition, however desperate, can they be induced to betray him. If old and decrepid, they will carry him from place to place, to save him from his enemies.' Their obedience to recognised authority is absolute; and Colonel Tod relates how the wife of an absent chieftain procured for a British messenger safe-conduct and hospitality through the densest forests, by giving him one of her husband's arrows as a token. The very officers who have had to act most sharply against them, speak most strongly, and often not without a noble regret and self-reproach, in their favour. 'It was not war,' Major Vincent Jervis thus writes to me of the operations against the race with which I am best acquainted, 'they did not understand yielding; as long as their national drums beat, the whole party would stand, and allow themselves to be shot down. . . . There was not a Sepoy in the war who did not feel ashamed of himself. The prisoners were for the most part wounded men. They upbraided us with fighting against them; they always said it was with the Bengalis they were at war, not with the English. If a single Englishman had been sent to them who understood their wrongs, and would have redressed them, they declared there would have been no war. It is not true that they used poisoned arrows. They were the most truthful set of men I ever met.'

But why heap up evidence of experts touching a race whose virtues, like their defects, lie on the surface, and are noted in the diaries and itineraries of every passer-by. Bishop Heber knew nothing of their language or their history; but their martial openness, their manliness, their skill as archers, and their habitual bearing of arms, could not escape him; and his imagination, hitting the political truth

of their position nearer than the scholarship of that day divined, carried him back to Robin Hood and the forest communities who stood out against alien encroachments in the oaken fastnesses of England.

The solution of the problem has ceased to be optional. The order and security which the Queen's Government in India has now imperiously imposed, have done away with those cruel checks upon population which seem to be natural and necessary among rude nations. A lowland raid used to be an event which came as punctually as the December harvest; the whole tribe lived at the expense of their neighbours during the cold weather, and the loss of life incident to the annual holiday rendered their own scanty crops sufficient for the survivors during the rest of the year. But all this has now come to an end. Raids, although frequent, have ceased to be either a means of regular profit, or a drain upon the population steady enough to be depended upon. The people, therefore, are increasing, while their former means of subsistence have diminished; and the question of some systematic scheme of dealing with the aboriginal races has been removed from the languid domain of speculation, into the reddened arena in which political necessity and the promptings of self-preservation do their pitiless work.

The remedies are two-fold. The first consists in supplying the place of the old sources of subsistence by new ones; the second, in enabling the people themselves to augment the productiveness of such of the old means of subsistence as remain to them.

I believe that, in attempting to apply the first remedy, the British are yet destined to find a solution for the two great difficulties of their position in India. Their first difficulty is a military one. A vast native army has to be maintained, and this army must be watched by another army with different interests and of a distinct race. The whole burden of supplying the surveillance at present rests upon the population of the British islands,—a population scarcely one-eighth of the Indian people, separated from India by the width of the globe, and by the repugnance which a northern nation has to exile in the tropics; above all, a population who have so much assured comfort and so many avenues to distinction in civil life, as to render military service distasteful. The difficulty will increase to a yet unsuspected intensity, as the effects of co-operation among the lower classes, and of the present tendency of public opinion to a more democratic tone of government, begin to tell. Englishmen will never be wanting in the hour of England's need; but the dull work of holding India will continue, in spite of improvements in the condition of the soldier, to render the army more and more unpopular with working men. From this difficulty the aboriginal tribes of India hold out a means of relief. In interest, in race, in religion, in habits of life, they are cut off from the Hindus and

Mussalmans by a gulf of whose breadth the people of Christian States can form no idea; and their ethnical repugnance is kept in a constant glow by the remembrance of ancient wars and recent wrongs. Sooner would the panther of their native forests herd with the fox of the lowlands, than the hill-men join with the Mussalmans or Hindus. Of the valour of many of their tribes, and that unquestioning fidelity and capacity for discipline which are the raw materials of soldiership, there is no question. It is not needful to add other testimonies to the opinions of the distinguished officers already cited; for the part played by the aboriginal troops during the mutiny is fresh in every Indian statesman's memory. The brilliant actions of Cleveland's Hill Rangers, until enervated by disuse and want of discipline, are matters of history. One of their races, the Bangis, long claimed the honour of leading the forlorn hope in Mussalman sieges. As a military police, they are said to have proved invaluable in Mirwar, Candeish, and wherever they have been employed; and any magistrate in Bengal would rather meet a jail outbreak with a company of Mongolian-cheeked, squat Goorkas, than with a regiment of the tallest and highest caste Sepoys.

It is not as if the experiment had not been tried. It has been tried again and again, and has always succeeded; but routine and our ignorance of the aboriginal races have stood in the way of its systematic application. By extensively employing these tribes as a military police and as soldiers, we should not only relieve the English population of a burden greater than it can permanently bear, but we should offer a livelihood to brave predatory peoples, whom the stern order of British rule has deprived of an important source of subsistence. Their position presents a striking analogy to that of the Scottish Highlanders at the Revolution. A vast reservoir of warlike energy is constantly overflowing on a peaceful lowland people; energy which must find vent in some shape, and which has either to be directed against the Government or utilized by it. During three hundred years, says Hill Burton, the philosophical historian of Scotland, the Stuarts had waged a war of extermination against the mountaineers in vain; to the present dynasty belongs the glory of converting bands of marauders into those disciplined battalions which have reaped honour on every English battle-field during nearly two centuries. The same problem has to be solved for the aboriginal races of India. Their military capacity and energy are undisputed: the only question is, whether this capacity and energy are to be to England a source of weakness or of strength.

The second difficulty of our position in India is a mercantile one. The division of the population into labourers and employers has not taken the trenchant and uncompromising form that it has in England. Sparsely inhabited frontier provinces cannot be peopled from the lowland population, nor can public works of great size be accomplished by them. The aboriginal races supply the want of a

large labouring class among the Hindus. It is they who have constructed our railways, and who are at this moment creating, in tea cultivation, a new source of wealth to India, and a new field for English capital, whose magnitude it is impossible even yet to foresee.

The other means of ameliorating the condition of the non-Aryan tribes, consists in enabling them to augment the legitimate sources of subsistence which remain to them; in one word, to CIVILISE them. For ages they have been unsettled predatory peoples, despising peaceful industry among themselves, and living as much as possible on the peaceful industry of their neighbours. The opportunities for depredation have ceased, but the contempt for steady industry remains. I do not permit myself even to glance at those noble and touching arguments which humanity and the Christian faith suggest for the reclamation of lapsed races. But looking upon the question as one of purely political utility, it seems that in the aboriginal peoples it is possible to find a counterpoise for the great Indian races to whom British rule is at best alien sway. The Hindus regard our accession but as a change of masters; the Mussalmans hate us as conquerors, if not as tyrants. To the aboriginal races alone can we appear in the light of friends and deliverers. They have yet to start on the path of progress. It remains for us to decide whether that path is to lead them to Hinduism, or to the purer faith and civilisation which we represent. Even in their superstitions there is special ground for hope. Anything like conversion *per saltum*, or on a large scale, need not be looked for among races possessed of religious systems so venerable and so nicely adjusted to human instincts as Hinduism and Islam are to the Aryans and Mussalmans of India. We cannot reasonably hope to be the *deus ex machina* to peoples with such august supernal contrivances of their own. But the hill tribes are still in want of everything. Before the conservative inertia of Hinduism, the life of the most earnest Englishman is neither more nor less than a single wave that breaks upon the shore. But from the days of Cleveland downwards, every frontier of India can show some tribe whose destiny has been changed by the energy of individual British administrators. New crops, new villages, new habits, a new mode of life, and bloody rites exchanged for harmless social gatherings,—these are the memorials that any zealous Englishman may hope to leave of his labours among a forest people; and if we glance for a moment at that more solemn side of the human destiny which Indian administrators wisely regard beyond their province, there are instances of little aboriginal communities accepting Christianity in a body, as a protection against witchcraft and those implacable demons whom their fathers had for ages endeavoured to appease with human life.

Our present ignorance of their notions and necessities, and their corresponding inability to understand our system of justice, lead to scenes which no Englishman can contemplate without sorrow. I cite only one instance. The same dread of

witchcraft which in skilful hands makes converts of whole villages, leads to the most appalling outrages. In 1857 the Ho tribes determined to purge themselves of the witches and sorcerers who had grown numerous under our rule. 'The destruction of human life that ensued,' says the official report, 'is too terrible to contemplate. Whole families were put an end to. In some instances, the destroyers, issuing forth in the dusk, and commencing with the denounced wizard and his household, went from house to house, until before the morning dawn they had succeeded in extinguishing, as they thought, the whole race.' For a massacre like this, perpetrated in a settled British district, scarcely a hundred and fifty miles from Calcutta, our system of justice could admit no palliative pleas; but the evident good faith and pitiable ignorance of the criminals almost unnerved the officers of the law. 'The work of retribution was a sad task,' wrote Mr. Justice Campbell eight years later, 'but it was rigorously carried out. It was melancholy to have to condemn men who themselves artlessly detailed every incident of the crime with which they were charged.'

But if our criminal system is sometimes harsh to the aboriginal races, our law of property seems to many of them wholly inexplicable. It is the characteristic of all their tribes, says General Briggs, to consider themselves the rightful owners of their ancient territory. If forcibly driven out, no length of illegal dispossession can bar their claim; their title to plunder the ousters and to appropriate the crops is a precious heirloom that often forms the sole inheritance which one generation has to bequeath to its successor; and this title the lowland borderers in many instances practically acknowledged by the regular payment of blackmail. The English, on the other hand, have been compelled to accept possession as a test of proprietary right in India to a degree unknown to the long settled jurisprudence of Europe. Obsolete claims of ownership have had but small effect in Indian courts, even when eloquently set forth; and the almost sole answer which the aboriginal races have received to their inarticulate pleadings and forcible exertions of fancied rights, consists in burning a few of their villages, or in placing them under a ban, as the Angami Nagas were not many years ago, forbidding them to trade or hold any humanizing intercourse with the plains.

If, instead of seeking refuge in the forests, these unhappy people submitted to the other alternative, and became serfs of the Aryan invaders on the land once their own, they nevertheless do not altogether lose their instinct of *dominium* in the soil. Their Hindu superior may load them with burdens, but under a native government he never ousts them from their hereditary fields. The only way he can get rid of them is by heaping demands and oppressions on them, till they fly to the mountains or forests; and as native government keeps population so low as to render cultivators things to be sought after rather than to be driven away, the hardships of their position are theoretical rather than real, and one generation

after another contentedly repeats the rhythmical proverb, 'Bhagra dhani Raj ho, Bhumra dhani maj ho;' 'The Rajah or Hindu landholder is the owner of his share, but I am the owner of the soil.' The prosperity of British rule has transposed the relation of labour to land. Instead of there being more land than can be cultivated, there are more cultivators than can obtain land. Farms, therefore, have become a subject of keen competition; and, practically, rents can be raised till the poor hereditary tenant, with his rude notions of tillage, is forced off the soil. The theoretical position of the semi-aboriginal or low-caste substratum of the people threatened to become their actual one; and it was not till agrarian agitation had shaken the whole rural economy of Bengal, that a remedy was found in the Land Law of 1859. The historian who calmly reviews that crisis, will acknowledge that the opponents of the measure, with the English Press as their mouthpiece, had the better of the argument, but that the measure itself was both salutary and just. The truth is, that its necessity was visible to every administrator in rural Bengal; but our ignorance of the aboriginal substratum of the population rendered it impossible to get at the fundamental causes. The aboriginal Celts of Western Scotland afford an analogy to the indigenous element in the Indian population, scarcely less striking in their territorial notions than in their military position; and I believe that the difficulty will only be solved by a compromise, not dissimilar in spirit to that which, under William and Mary, clan usages and the undefined patriarchal instinct, wrung from the iron feudalities of the Edinburgh College of Justice.

It may seem that, in speaking so openly of a defect in the British administration, I have forgotten that this book will travel out of England. But the English in India can well afford to have the whole truth told. Their difficulties are the difficulties incident to progress and good government, and could never have arisen under the domination of any other conquering race. I do not cite the French in Algiers, or the Russians in Western Asia; for the exigencies of military nations in such positions are necessarily more cruel than those of a people to whom God has given the English instinct for colonial rule. Nor is more than a passing allusion required to the Dutch in Java, who have lately so far mistaken their interest and their honour, as to suppress a book by one of their own servants, setting forth specific defects in their Eastern policy. But let England's dealings with the Indian races be compared with the same country's conduct towards the aborigines of the New World. I have beside me the whole series of charters granted to the American colonists. I find there the well-set phrases of *habendum, tenendum, et reddendum*, elaborate mention of mines, forests, fisheries, law martial, oaths, wills and domicile, ample securities for the liberties of the settlers, and exhaustive saving-clauses of the claims of the English Crown; but I look in vain for any efficient provision for the rights of the people of the

land. Our children in America have inherited our policy; and the two systems have borne their fruits, in that sympathy with native feelings and sensitiveness in the discharge of self-imposed duties, which form at once the difficulty and the glory of the British administration of India, and in that tale of oppression and blood recently told by the United States Mixed Commission, whose official language no white man can read without a flush of personal remorse and shame.

The aboriginal peoples of India have only to be realized by the British Government, to obtain justice at its hands. In a former work I endeavoured strongly to individualize a single one of their tribes, and to place in bold relief its ethnical peculiarities, its social necessities, and political capabilities for evil or for good. In this book I have hastily and imperfectly brought together materials out of which a comprehensive view of the whole may be constructed. Abler hands than mine will build the edifice; for to the Indian official, scholarship and literary graces are as nothing, excepting in so far as they enable him to understand and to interpret the people. In the Grammar now in progress, I hope to supply a more accurate basis upon which European philology may work; but these vocabularies, notwithstanding their defects, will henceforth enable every frontier administrator to hold direct communication with the races committed to his charge.

If any such Englishman has lost heart amid the daily vexations of dealing with a lapsed people, and takes the Sanskrit view of the incapability of the so-called Serpent Races for better things, let him ponder for a moment on the destiny that awaited the naked, tattooed savages whom Roman mariners found burrowing in the earth, and offering human sacrifices to unknown demons, in Cornwall, —a part of whose island, as Procopius had heard, was peopled with snakes, and sent up poisoned vapours which no man could breathe and live. Or, resting his eye upon a more historic time, let him remember how, not two hundred years ago, Lauzun officially described Ireland to the French Court as a chaos such as he had read of in the book of Genesis; and the keen eyes of Desgrigny could detect in the progenitors of the brilliant Irish nation, only a people hopelessly stupid and brutal,—a race of a noble physical type indeed, but insensible alike to praise or blame, and devoid of the common characteristics of human beings. 'Si bestes qu'ils n'ont presque point d'humanité. Rien ne les emeut. Les menaces ne les estonnent point. L'interest même ne les peut engager au travail.'

II.—LINGUISTIC.

But while the original purpose of these researches was a purely practical and administrative one, I am not without a hope that they may yield some philological fruit. I am aware that, for scientific purposes, the roots of speech afford a less

trustworthy basis than its structure; and I am but too painfully conscious of the defects in the materials which I now submit. Some of these defects were inevitable: for in any attempt to set forth the multitudinous and widely separated tongues of India and High Asia, the labour must be done by many hands, and with many different shades of competency; nor can the editor at the centre hope, except in a few languages, to have the means of checking the work. But many of the blemishes of this book cannot plead this excuse, and are due to my own want of time and limited knowledge. A few months ago, I had no present expectation of putting forth these vocabularies; but on the eve of departing for the East, several scholars urged the inexpediency of again subjecting my collection to the chances of Indian service; and the Royal Asiatic Society of Great Britain and Ireland was pleased to solicit Government to retain me in this country, to bring out the work. Special leave of four months was allowed for moulding the materials into their final shape, passing the book through the press, and returning to India. Had the work been done more slowly, it would have been done better; but the nature of the materials forbade hopes of a high degree of perfection; and, on the whole, it seemed better to do it as best I could, than to risk the chance of never having an opportunity of doing it all.

No available means have been left untried, however, to secure the maximum of accuracy that my opportunities permitted; and the zealous co-operation of the scholars whose kindness I shall afterwards acknowledge in detail, has resulted in a degree of completeness far beyond what I had dared to hope for. In the case of a few of the languages, dictionaries have already been published in an independent form, and I have not always been able to test my lists by comparison with them. But in many instances several lists of the same language were in my possession, and the vocabulary as now printed has been arrived at after careful examination of them all. Some of the vocabularies, indeed, represent several dialects of the same tongue: thus the Gondi is pieced together from three separate lists; the Sgau-karen, as given by the Secretary to the Mission to Ava, includes the results arrived at by four different collectors; and although in the Tibetan I have not been able to copy direct from the original source, the list as now given has been educed from five of Mr. Hodgson's vocabularies, based, I believe, either wholly or chiefly on the researches of De Körös. In two instances, on the other hand, separate lists represent either the same language, or varieties so close as to seem scarcely deserving of separate places. The first is the Toḍuva and Toḍu; the second, the Malabar. But after weighing Mr. Caldwell's statements in his *Dravidian Grammar*, and the considerations which Dr. Rost kindly urged in correspondence, I thought it better to give Malabar a distinct place, as the vocabulary which passes under that name was collected at a period sufficiently remote to allow of dialectic changes between it and the language as now spoken. In this view, it is proper

to add, Professor Max Müller coincided. The process of construction has often been very intricate. The Mantshu and Mongolian lists, for example, were begun by myself, and carried half-way by Mr. Halkett of the Advocates' Library in Edinburgh, working on the materials afforded by Rémusat, J. Schmidt, Klaproth, Gabelentz, translations of the New Testament, and of the Ts'ing Wan K'e Mung (Shanghai, 1855). A small part was added by a reader in the British Museum employed for that purpose, and the whole was completed by the Rev. Charles Malan of Broad Windsor. For the Japanese, again, I had to begin with only a meagre vocabulary printed in Yokohama, and kindly forwarded to me by the Right Hon. E. Hammond, of the Foreign Office. To this, Dr. Rost, the learned Secretary to the Royal Asiatic Society, added a partial list, compiled, I believe, from Mr. Medhurst's work (Batavia, 1853); and a complete vocabulary was ultimately drawn up by Mr. Von Siebold, of Her Majesty's Embassy in Japan. These are fair examples of how many of the lists were done; and so complex a process of construction no doubt opens a door for inconsistencies and errors which might have been avoided had it been possible for me to do them all from my own knowledge.

It may well be conceived, moreover, that, in a dictionary which is the work of so many hands, it was impossible to secure absolute uniformity in transliteration. This difficulty had partly been got over, however, by Mr. Hodgson, from whose lists my book is principally compiled; and with scarcely an important exception, the vowel sounds are regularly represented by the letters set forth in a subsequent page. Short accents and accents over diphthongs are seldom used, saving in the Chinese dialects, in which I had to yield to the necessities of the case, and in the Finnic. To some it may seem that the Russian should have been also exempted from the rule; but to do this, the accents would have required a different meaning in that language from what they have in all the rest, and no system could have perfectly rendered Slavonic words in the English alphabet. It seemed best, therefore, to follow the analogy of transliterations from the Greek, and print the Russian in plain capitals. This plan will be sufficiently clear to those who know the language, and it was scarcely possible to render the Slavonic sounds intelligible to those who do not.

The attempt to represent tones was, after mature consideration, given up. Of the consonants little need be said, except that I have not ventured to improve the apparent accuracy of the book by a manufactured uniformity. The temptation to do so has presented itself on every page. The letters *d*, *ḍ*, *r*, for example, and particularly *ḍ* and *r*, are very often used indiscriminately, some of the compilers of the lists writing *ḍ* generally as *r*, others putting *d* instead of *ḍ*. The truth is, that a European ear can only after careful training catch these Indian niceties of sound. If, indeed, *ḍ* be not in reality the proper *r* sound of the non-Aryan races of India, and adopted into the Sanskrit alphabet from their speech, at any

rate I thought it better, even when it might be clear which was the correct form, to print the words as they stood in my MS. lists, than, for the sake of appearances, to venture on corrections from analogy. The same thing might be remarked regarding the length of vowels. It seems unlikely enough that 'eye' should be *tă* in Siamese and *tá* in the three cognate languages, Ahom, Khamti, and Laos; or that 'father' should be *ăppu* in Ho (Kol), *ápung* in Kol (Singhbhum), *ábá* in Rajmahali, and *abbá* in Khoṇḍ. It would have been easy enough to accent these words in the same way, but it would also have been dangerous to do so. Thus, seeing that the middle syllable in *upŭnia* (four) is short in Bhúmij and Kol (Singhbhum), it might seem safe to infer that *upúnia* in Ho (Kol) is an inaccuracy of the transliterator. But in this, as in many other words, a more extended view discloses traces of a real lengthening and shortening of vowels in cognate dialects. Thus we have *upnia*, shortest of all, in Mundala; *upŭnia*, one stage longer, in Kol and Bhumij; *upúnia*, a second stage, in Ho; and *ponea*, the last and longest vowel form which *u* can assume, in Santali. An honest acknowledgment of uncertainty seemed preferable to a fictitious uniformity; and the only instances in which I ventured upon corrections in languages of which I was ignorant, were such substitutions as *i* for *ee* and *u* for *oo*, where I had ascertained that these were their real sounds. Even the Annamitic *ay* (= *e*) has been left as I received it. Manifest misprints or errors of the transcriber, however, have been set right or marked with a point of interrogation. Thus, Mr. Hodgson's Garo list gives for 'fifty' *rung-ning*, which really means two-scores. I have changed it to the right word *rung-ning-chi*, two-score-ten, like *rung-sha-chi*, thirty, *i.e.* one-score-ten. The reader should remark that *d*, *ḍ*, and *r*; *t* and *ṭ*; *n* and *ṇ*; *l*, *ḷ*, and *zh*, are frequently confounded.

This confusion I chiefly regret, because it has rendered it unsafe to complete what I had hoped would form the most important feature of the book, to wit, a Table of Non-Aryan Phonetic Changes. I expect, however, to be enabled to present this in a trustworthy form in my *Comparative Grammar*, and to exhibit a series of consonant changes of a novel character, and at the same time not less instructive and reliable than those of Indo-Germanic speech. A very curious illustration is to be found in the substitution of *l* for the sibilant and aspirate. The languages of Southern India delight in a sound most correctly expressed by *zh*, but understood to be *l* by the untutored ear, and represented in works of scholarship by *ḷ*. Thus Tamil is properly Tamizh; Tuluva, Tuzhuva, etc. Now it appears that in non-Aryan speech *l* sometimes takes the place of *zh*, *sy*, *s*, *j*, or other sibilant. Thus, to go no further than the numeral four, *si*, Siamese, etc., becomes *li* in the Karens; *zhi*, Bhutani, becomes *li* in the Lepcha *pha-li*, *pha* being a mere prefix, as *pha-li*, four—*pha-gnon*, five; *zhyi*, Serpa, becomes *le* in Súnwár; and in the Kiránti group the *l* completely supersedes the *s*. Many instances might be cited,

as *loddi*, Chentsu, for 'water,' for *jhodi* in Gayeti, or *jodi* in Khond; or *láng-bo* in Serpa, etc., 'elephant' for *siang*, Chinese, probably through the Tibetan *glang-chen* or *lam-boche*. No instance of this occurs in Indo-Germanic languages, but *r* sometimes represents *s*, and *l* and *r* are semi-vowels produced by the same physiological process of articulation, and the one sometimes stands for the other in Aryan speech. Thus the typical Indo-Germanic *l* becomes *r* in Zend. Until a Table of Phonetic Changes is constructed, and its laws ascertained, researches into non-Aryan speech will remain destitute of the exactitude of Indo-Germanic philology; and the present discourse, avoiding anything like generalization, merely endeavours to throw out a few hints which may assist the student of the Lexicon.

For I am much mistaken if the scholar's eye will not decipher upon many of these pages a history far more ancient and not less legible than anything that can be educed from the legends of Greece or Rome, or the rock-inscriptions of India. Chinese has hitherto been looked upon as a language standing by itself, devoid of ethnical kindred or linguistic alliances. But in spite of its inexactitudes, this book proves that China has given its speech not merely to the great islands of the Southern Ocean, but to the whole Eastern Peninsula, to Siam, Tenasserim, Burmah, in a less degree to Central Asia, to many of the Himalayan tribes, and to some of the pre-Aryan peoples of the interior of India. Take in the first case the two numerals in which accidental resemblances are least likely to occur. 'Three' in Chinese is *san* (Nankin) or *sám* (Canton): *a* constantly changes into *u* in non-Aryan speech, in the same way as *u* sometimes takes the place of the Indo-Germanic *a* in Gothic, Old High German, Slavonic, and Lithuanian, and of *á* in Italian, while its lengthened form *o* appears in place of the typical *a* or *á* in every one of the Aryan families excepting Sanskrit and Zend. Bearing this in mind, let the reader turn to page 35, and he will find that the Chinese *san* or *sám* has furnished the third numeral not only to Japan, Siam, Tenasserim, Burmah, Eastern and Northern Bengal, Nepal, the Himalayan tribes, and Tibet, but that it also seems to appear in the Mantshu *sfanga* (respecting which I am doubtful whether it should not be *ssanga*) and *ilan* (*l* replacing *s* in the latter word), in the *thunga* of the tribes of the Yenisei (cf. Burman, *thong*), the *ssuum* of the Dalai-Lama Kalmuks, and even in the *sam-i* of the Georgian and the *han-ku* (*h* = *s*) of the mountaineers of the Caucasus. Let him then pass to p. 41, and remembering that *g* constantly represents *k*, and in its turn is softened to *j* and *y*, he will discover the Chinese *kiu*, *chiu*, or *kau* running through the whole of the non-Aryan languages of Japan, the Eastern Peninsula, Tibet, the Himalayas, and Northern and Eastern Bengal. The same thing may be said of 'I,' p. 48, from which it would seem that the Javanese also, and indeed the whole Malay race, obtained their first pronoun from the Chinese. (*Wo*=*ngo*; *ngo*=*go*; *go*=*ku*, leaning on *á*.)

A very few examples from the nouns will suffice. *Ming*, the Chinese for 'name,'

p. 146, appears to have furnished the first step in social polity, to wit, the act of distinguishing individuals and objects by distinctive designations, to the Tibetan and Himalayan groups, to the Siamese, the Burmese, the Nepalese, the Bhutanese, the Nagas of Eastern Bengal, the Dhimals, Bodos, and Garo hill-men, who have clung to their original word thousands of years after being surrounded by Aryan synonyms. The same may be said of the term for that much higher stage of civil organization represented by the village—the highest, indeed, which the non-Aryans in India seem ever to have attained. Thus, p. 163, Chinese, *hsiang*, *hiang*, *hiuṇ-siá*, *heong;* Tibetan, *thong;* Nepal, Kiranti, *teng;* Tablung and Míthan Nágá, *tying* and *ting;* Pwo-karen, *twan;* Bhuṭani and Lepcha, *kyong;* Pahri, *goṇ;* Kuswar, *gáoṇ;* Garo, *song;* Miri, *long* or *lüng* in *du-long* and *du-lüng;* Vayu, *lung* in *mu-lung*. Amid many variations, the original word every now and again comes in divested of phonetic change. Thus, Nankin, *hiang;* Bhramu, *háng* in *hang-dung;* and with the slight and common change of *g* for *h*, the same word supplies the universal term by which the low-caste semi-aboriginal population of Southern Bengal speak of their homesteads, to wit, *gáng* or *gáong*. If these two words existed by themselves, they might be hypothetically derived from the Sanskrit *gráma;* but when viewed as natural links in a long chain, their origin ceases to be a matter of doubt, and points unmistakeably to a land far to the north-east of the Himalayas. To take two names for the commonest of natural objects. 'Water' in Chinese, p. 164, is *shui;* in Tibetan, *chhú;* in the Nepalese dialects, *chhú*, *kyú*, *kú*, *chúwá*, *cháwá*, *áwá*, *wá;* in Bhuṭani, *chhú;* in Dhimal, *chí;* in Garo, *chóka;* in Deoria Chutia, *ji;* in the Nagas, *zú*, *tsú*, *tü;* in Shou, Kámi, etc., *túi;* in Bodo and Kachári, *doï;* in the Karens and Toung-thu, *hti*, *thi*, or *ti*. *H* is frequently represented by *m:* as, for example, p. 169, 'black'—Chinese, *hak;* Newár, *haku;* Dúmi, *mak-chupu;* Báláli, *mak-thropa*, etc. Bearing this in mind, and turning to p. 123, the word for 'fire' will be found running through the whole of the languages of High Asia, Northern Bengal, and the Eastern Peninsula, down to the Archipelago, bare of accidental wrappings, and with a distinctness not to be hoped for in Aryan speech. Thus: Chinese, Amoy, *he;* Japanese, *hi;* then passing through several aspirated stages—such as Tháksya, *hme;* Magar, *mhe*—into *me* or *mi*, it appears without further change in every group. The proofs, indeed, are wonderfully complete. Thus, as the *he* of the Amoy dialect becomes *me* in India, so the Shanghai *hu* reproduces itself in *mu*, Thulungya. Again we find the *h* of four of the Chinese dialects giving place to the soft labial *f* in the fifth—Canton, *fo*—which in its turn reproduces itself in the Siamese, Ahom, Khámti, and Laos. There are also indications of this soft labial hardening into a mediate one, *hp:* thus, Siamese, etc., *fai;* Shán, *hpihu;* and ultimately, as it would appear, standing out the sharp, clear labial *p*, leaning on the customary vowel prefix, in the Malay *api*.

Passing to the domestic animals, it would almost seem as if roots could be

detected which are common to both the Aryan and non-Aryan languages of mankind. Thus, p. 113, the strong Aryan root for 'cow' is *go*, which appears not less strongly in the Indian than in the Germanic branches of Aryan speech. The strong non-Aryan root appears in the Canton *ngau*, which becomes *gú* in the Amoy; *guo* in Bhuṭani, Khámti, Laos, etc.; *guá* in the Manyak *guá-zi*; *gau* in the Karen *gau-pemo*, etc.; *gou* in the Kol family; *gwaḥ* in Thochu; *ga* in the Tháru *gá-ye*; *gyai* in Dúmi; *gai* in the Himalayan dialects, the tongues of Central India, and in the universal low-caste patois of Bengal. Again, by a common phonetic process, *g* softens in *h*—as *gú*, Amoy; *hu*, Ahom: *h* in its turn hardens into *ph*—as *phou*, Toungh-thu; *phá*, Tibetan, in the spoken dialect *phá-chuk*. *Ph* becomes *b*, as in written Tibetan, *bá*; Takpa, *bah*; Chourásya, *bía*; Súnwár, Dúmi, etc., *bí*. *B* by a regular rule becomes *p*, as in Rodong, *pí*, *píu*, *pa*; Dhimal, *piá*; and this form appears through all the sub-Himalayan dialects. It may be an accident that the semi-aboriginal husbandmen of Beerbhoom call their oxen *beil*, and that the Bask mountaineers of the Pyramees—who frequently drop the letter *l*, as in *belarri* or *bearri*, ear—designate a cow, *bei*; but there can be no accident in the circumstance that the Aryan and the non-Aryan root for 'cow' is so similar, that it requires the utmost care in pronouncing whether the primitive races of India obtained their word *gai* from a Sanskrit or a Chinese source. A similar difficulty exists in deciding whether these peoples have taken their term for 'dog,' p. 116, from the Chinese *kau* (Shanghai, *k'eu*; Sák, *kú*) or from the Sanskrit *kukkura*; and without laying any stress on the similarity of the Arabic *kelb* with the sub-Himalayan *khleb*, *kheb*, etc., which like our own *whelp* may be accidental, I can safely affirm that the pages of this book point to primeval roots common to both Aryan and non-Aryan speech, in a far more definite manner than the similar indications by which scholars have sought to reduce the Semitic and Indo-Germanic families to a cognate source. It is right to add—and the phenomenon may pass for what it is worth—that not only the common substitutions, but the most curious and least accurately ascertained of the Aryan phonetic changes, are reproduced in the speech of the Himalayan and Indian aborigines; and one of the most important features of my Table of Non-Aryan Consonant Displacements will be an examination of the interchanges of *g*, *h*, *ph*, *f*, strangely analogous to the Digamma discussions which have gathered round the glosses of Hesychius.

It is unnecessary to multiply analogies which this book enables every student to find out for himself. The Indian aborigines and the Chinese obtained from a common source not only their terms for common natural objects, and for the civil institutions of a primitive race, but also a part of the nomenclature of tillage, and even such terms of civilisation as 'road.' Thus, p. 166, the Chinese for 'yam' is *ta-shú*, literally *ta*, great, and *shú*, tuber. *Shú* becomes *chú* in the Shanghai dialect, and appears as *tsu* in Japanese; *chu* in Tengsa Nágá; *cho* in Denwar; *zo* in Horpa;

so, sú, or *sá* throughout the whole Nepal; *ho, há, khú, khá,* in North-Eastern Bengal, and down the frontier through all Burmah and Siam to the extremity of the Peninsula. Again, the Horpa *zo* is directly represented by *do* and *tho* of the cognate Tibetan, as *sá* and *há* of the dialects on the south of the Himalayas are by the Bodo *thá*, and it seems questionable whether the non-Aryan replacement of the sibilant by *l* does not give us the word used in modern Sanskrit—*álu*. Thus compare the Tengsa Nágá *chu*, Nowgong Nágá *shi*, with the Sibságar Miri *á-lic*, the Kocch, etc. *á-lu* (the *l*, appearing bare of its prefix in the Dhimál *ling*, as *alu*, Kámi and Kúmi, for 'head,' appears in Khyeng and Mru in its plain form *lu*). A similar connection, allowing for ascertained phonetic changes, between the Chinese and the non-Aryan languages of India can be established in the single tree given in my lists, to wit the plantain, p. 149; and the typical non-Aryan root for 'road' has withstood, during thousands of years, a vast phalanx of Sanskrit synonyms among the whole aboriginal races of High Asia, Bengal, and the Eastern Peninsula.

This is not the place to investigate the relations of individual groups and dialects, but I cannot pass from the subject without referring to the materials which exist for comparing Mongolian and Mantshu with the Chinese and the Indian dialects. I do not refer to isolated phenomena, like the Sokpa colony of pure Mongols, but to distinct series of analogies, such as—Mongolian, *ghar*, hand, p. 129; Sokpa, *kar;* Dúmi, *khar* or *khur;* Dhimál, *khur;* or Mongolian, *ghal*, fire, p. 123; Sokpa, *kwal;* Garo, *wal*. In words like 'father' the one root is probably common to all mankind, but the analogy in the case of the Mongolian and Indian dialects is peculiarly close. Thus, Mongolian, *abu;* Newar, *abú;* Tháksya, Gúrung, Lepcha, *abo;* Chourásya, Báhingya, Angámi Nágá, Kol, etc., *apo* or *apa;* and *aba* or *apa* in as many others. Such instances as Finnic, *puu*, 'tree,' p. 162, Magyar *pa*, Mongolian (Ostcack) *pu*, Deoria Chutia *popoṇ* (a reduplicative), Singpho *phuṇ*, Míthán Nágá and Garo *pan*, Sák *púng-pang* (a reduplicative), Bodo *pháng*, etc., serve to point out a path to generalizations which, in the absence of a comparative grammar, it would be unsafe to enter upon. But indications of analogy in structure are not wanting, even in the most distant branches of non-Aryan speech. Thus the Finnic particle of negation is *E*-, the inseparable prefix which appears in *en, ei, e-pa*, etc., and which probably furnishes the basis of the Bask *ez*. It would scarcely deserve notice that some of the non-Aryan races in India employ a similar particle—*e.d.* Lohorong, *é;* Santali, *e-to*—were it not for a resemblance between the inflections of the negative verb in the first and third persons. Thus, Finnic, 1st person, *e-n;* 2d, *e-t;* 3d, *e-i:* Santali, *e-to-in*, or *e-to-ing;* 2d, *e-to-m;* 3d, *e-to-i*. It is beyond the scope of the present work to examine whether this resemblance be apparent or real.

Passing from the exterior relationships of the non-Aryan peoples of India to their internal polity, I propose to confine my attention to a single group

of the non-Aryan tribes,—the group, that is, of which I can speak from intimate personal knowledge. It has been customary to represent researches into the non-Aryan peoples as necessarily devoid of comprehensive political results, from the isolation in which each race dwells, and its incapability of organization for imperial purposes. But unless I have greatly deceived myself, proofs can be brought forward to show that these now scattered and disjected fragments once formed a great ethnical entity, such as might have produced in prehistoric times a civilisation, a history, and a faith of its own.

Many of the non-Aryan peoples of India take their tribal designations from the word for 'man' in their respective dialects. Thus the Rajmahalis call themselves the Mális, and the very general term *mi* (man) supplies the basis of the race-name to not less than forty ascertained tribes. It generally appears a compound; *mi* furnishing the generic idea of *homo*, and a differentia being obtained from some prefixed and suffixed syllable. Thus, to quote only races whose vocabularies will be found in the Lexicon, the Dú-mi, Kâ-mi, Kú-mi, Angâ-mi Nâgâ, Mí-thân Nâgá, and if we recognise the non-Aryan phonetic displacements of *m* and *l* and *l* and *r*, the list could be indefinitely increased. Indications of such displacements appear even from the single word under examination—thus, p. 139, Sak *lu*, Toung *mrú*, Múrmi *mí*, Thâksya *mli;* and the root *li* affords the generic term *homo* to a whole series of tribal names. Thus, Bálá-li, Mâ-li, Dhimá-li, Santâ-li, Bangá-li, etc., meaning the Bálá people, the Dhimá people, the Bangá people, and so forth. The specific term for 'man' among the section of the aborigines to which I propose to confine my attention is *ha* or *ho*, lengthening through the Visaraga into *haḥ*, *has*, *haḍ* (*har*), *hoḍ* (*hor*). In Santali I have given all the forms as they co-exist at the present day. This word *ho* seems, like other roots in the languages of Central India, to have come from a common origin from the *khon*, *khun*, *kun*, of Siam, and the *ku* of Arrakan. Certain it is that *kh* and *k* constantly stand in these languages for *h;* and indeed the process is visible in a single language, and in the very word under discussion. Thus, the same root furnishes to Santali *haḍ* or *hoḍ*, man, and *koḍa*, a young man; as in Chinese, 'weariness' in Nankin is *k'au-k'oh;* in Pekin, *k'au-ho*, etc. We have therefore a root represented by *ho* and *ko;* the *ho* series shortening into *hu* or *ha*, and the *ko* series into *ku* or *ka*. This root furnishes the specific word for 'man' to the Kol tribes of Central India. We have also a generic root *li*, *homo*, which, as we have seen, is often added to specific terms for man, to form names of aboriginal races.

Ho, indeed, forms one of the oldest and most widely spread roots for man. Mrichhakati gives a reduplicative form of it—*go-ho*—among the words borrowed by the Apabhransa, or vernacular Sanskrit, from the aboriginal races; a form, by the way, curiously analogous to that still in use among the Kúrs near Ellichpore, to wit, *ho-ko*. I have mentioned that, like other words in the languages of Central

India, it seems to have come originally from the other side of the Bay of Bengal, where it appears in the Siamese, Laos, etc., as *khon* or *kun*, the same form that it takes in such tribal names as Khond, etc., in India. The Siamese *khon*, in its turn, appears to be the Chinese *jan* or *yan*, probably through an intermediate form in which the *j* sunk into an *h*. The root *li* is equally widely diffused, and appears in most of the aboriginal languages which I have examined. For example, in Santali, it furnishes the nomenclature connected with the propagation of our species, such as *lai*, *láih*, etc., and appears in *li-ḍih*, a child; *le-ḍaka* or *laḍko*, children; *khi-li* (=*ho-li*), a generation of men; and the hitherto unexplained terms, *che-la*, *che-li* (=*khi-li*, =*ho-li*), for son and daughter, universal among the semi-aboriginal castes of Lower Bengal.

I propose very briefly to inquire what evidence can be found in different parts of India of a primitive race which formed its tribal name from the specific root *ho*, with or without the generic affix *li*. The Ho tribe is now a comparatively small one, on the west of Lower Bengal; but one of the commonest non-Aryan changes of *h* is into *g*, *k*, or *kh*, as I have already shown, and as is visible in the reduplicative form of *ho* already cited, to wit, the Apabhransa *go-ho*, and the *ho-ko* of the tribes near Ellichpore. It must be remembered, too, that the vowel *o* regularly represents *u* or *a*: thus, Santali, *haḍ*, man, Ho, *hoḍa*, or *horo*; Santali, *dam*, Bengali, *dom*, a corpse-bearer; Santali, *paṭá*, the stomach; *poṭeá*, a 'fat-belly.' Again, Kami and Kumi, adjacent tribes in the Eastern Peninsula, *bhági* or *bhugi*, Santali for 'good;' Uriya, Orissa; Santal, Sonthal, etc. Confining our attention to the *ko* form, we find tribal names based upon this root with the generic affix *li*, not only in every part of India, but at all periods of Indian history. Both the Mahabharata and the Vishnu Purana speak of Ko-li tribes in connection with Mi-kalas (cf. the aboriginal root *mi*, man), Dravidas (cf. the Dravidian aborigines of Southern India at the present day), Kirátas (aboriginal tribes still in Nepal), and other of the non-Aryan races existing in modern India. The Sanskrit writers account for them as outcasts of the military clan, the Kshattriyas; but in the same breath the Aitareya Brahmana speaks of them as Dasyus, or aborigines; and the scientific value of their ethnical derivations may be gauged from such sentences as the following, copied from the same source: 'Most of the Dasyus are sprung from Visvamitra.' The Ko-lis generally appear in ancient literature with that epithet attached to them which the Sanskrit race delighted to apply to the aborigines, from the Nagas of North-Eastern Bengal through all India to the indigenous castes of Ceylon, to wit, the Koli-sarpas, Serpent-kols, or Snake-races.

Sanskrit literature refers to other sections of the Kol race under such names as Chol-as, Kul-indas, etc.; and passing to mediæval times, we find in the Arabic geographers and historians evidence that the Kols were co-extensive with the whole explored portion of India. Kulam, 'a large city of India,' stands first in the list

of towns described in the extracts from Al Kazwini. The inhabitants, we are told, ate carrion, as the aborigines did in Sanskrit times and do in our own; they were as destitute of temples or visible idols as the Veda itself describes them; their land was rich in teak; their only articles of commerce were the spontaneous produce of the forest, with the characteristic black pottery which still forms their sole manufacture; and, most curious of all, they chose their king, according to the confused Arabian geography, from China, which no doubt means from among the pure aboriginal tribes on the Indo-Chinese frontier. But I must refrain from amplifications of this sort, and confine myself to a mere list of names taken at random from the Arabian geographers of the tenth to the twelfth centuries. We have in or near Sind, according to Ibn Khurdabda, the province of Kuli, the district and town of Kol, and ($r=l$) Kura at the mouth of the Kolaroon (Coleroon), in Southern India. Al Istakhri speaks of Kalwi or Kallari; Al Idrisi of Kulam-mali, an island near Sind, of Kuli on the Shore, of Kalari in the interior, and then of a district called Kulam, far down on the coast, and north of Malabar. In the Asiatic Society's *Journal* the ancient name for India is stated to have been Kolaria, and turning to the modern map of India, we find indications of the race in every province from Burmah to Malabar: in the Kols of Central India; Kolas of Katwar; the Kolis, inferior husbandmen and a landless clan of Gujarat; the Kolis, obscurely mentioned as helot cultivators on the Simla range; the Kolitas of Northern Bengal and Assam; the Kolami of Central India, classed with the Naikude, etc., in my vocabularies; the Kalars, a robber caste in the Tamil country; the Kalars of Tinevelly: in the Kolis of Bombay; in the names of the Kolarun river in Southern India, of the Koel river, from the Chota Nagpore watershed, of the Culinga and Koladyn rivers, and of many other streams; in Kulna, a district in Bengal; Kulpac, in the Nizam's dominions; Kulalpur, in the Panjab; Kulan and Kola Fort, in the distant north-west; in Kulbunga, town and district, near the Bombay Presidency, within, I believe, the territory of the Nizam; and, to be brief, in such names as the following, scattered over the whole length and breadth of India,—names which the reader may identify in a moment by referring to Dr. Keith Johnston's index to his Map from the Royal Atlas. Kuldah, Kulkeri, Kulianpur in three separate districts, Kullavakurti, Kullean, Kuller-kaher, Kulu district, Kullum, Kullung River, Kullunji, several Kullurs, Kulpani, Kulpi, Kulra, Kulsi. Kolachi, Kolapur town and state, the three Kolars, Kolaspur, Kolbarea, Koli, Kolikod (Calicut), Cola-Bira, Colair, Colgong, Collum (Kayan-kulam), Colur, and Colombo in Ceylon. I would go further, and, if time permitted, could philologically prove the connection of the above with hundreds of other names and places in regular series. For example, writing *d* and *r* indifferently as *r*, and ringing the changes upon the vowels *a*, *u*, and *o*, the first series would present the *h* unchanged, as in Santali, *Har*, man: The Haris, semi-aboriginal tribes of Bengal;

Halgas, semi-aboriginal soldiers in the Maratta armies; the Hunas of the Vishnu Purana; the Hos of Western Bengal and Ho-lar-kas, by which term the Santals call the Kols. In the second series *h* becomes *k* or *kh*. The Khar-wars of the hill-country of Mirzapore; the island of Khar-ak, according to Ibn Khurdabda, near Sindh, and many similar names of places; the Khas, the dominant race in Nepal, outcast military tribes, according to Manu; the Karans, a race of Eastern India, described by Rashidu-d Din as 'barbarians, *i.e.* people whose ears hang down to their shoulders,' and the Karens of Siam at the present day, two of whose dialects I give; the Kurmis, semi-aboriginal cultivators to the south of the Rajputs and Jats; the Kurmis of Manbhum; the Kurumbas, or aboriginal husbandmen of S. Kanara; the Kukis of South-Eastern Bengal, and the Kumis of the Burman frontier; the Kurgs of the south-west coast of India; Korea in Chota-Nagpore; the Koralis, Koras, Khoṇḍs, etc. In the third series *h* becomes *gh* or *g*, as Garrow, Gurka, Gour, the aboriginal capital of Bengal; Gwari, the capital of Nuddea; Gouri, wife of the aboriginal god Siva (cf. Kali); Goa, in Southern India; Goṇdwana, in Central India; Gol-parah (literally Kol-hamlet), on the west of Bengal, etc. In the fourth series *h* becomes *s*, as in Santal, Savara Saka, also one of the outcast military tribes, according to Manu; Sandalia, the semi-aboriginal low-castes, as written by Ibn Khurdabda, or Sandaliya, as Al Idrisi spells it; the Sudras of Brahminical literature; the Sauras, now living with the Oraons; the Sontals, as the word Santal is in some places pronounced; the Sauṇḍikas, whom the Mahabharata classes with Koli-sarpas and Dravidas. In a fifth series the *h* is dropped, as in Uriya, or Uria, and the district Uri-har, according to Rashidu-d Din; the Uras-ir of Ibn Khurdabda, a forest territory abounding in elephants and buffaloes; Orissa; the Oḍras, an outcast military tribe mentioned in Manu; and the Oraons or Oḍaons of the Bengal frontier, whose vocabulary I give.

The pressing necessities of time and space compel me to draw this Dissertation to a close, and forbid me to bring forward my proofs of the above series. But I cannot refrain from selecting the one which will probably be most questioned, and following it out step by step. Many will doubt whether there can be more than a fanciful connection between Ho and Kir-anti, and the proofs to be submitted in this instance form a fair specimen of the general evidence. I write *ḍ* and *r* indifferently as *r*, the distinction seldom being uniformly observed by English collectors of aboriginal words, on whose labours my work is based. The root *har*, man, occurs in Santali as an affix to the names of the seven clans: thus, Nijkasda-har, the Nijkasda clan, etc.; and often with the *h* hardened into *kh*, as Khar-oar or Kher-oar, the name by which the Santals called themselves in ancient times. The first form, Khar-oar, is identical with the Khar-wars, a once numerous race of aborigines living in the distant hill-country of Mirzapore and Rewa to the borders of Benares and Bahar; with the Kor-wahs, one of the wildest of

the Kol tribes; and it furnishes more than a hundred names of places or peoples scattered over India, such as Khar-bu, Khar-dam, the Kar-ens of Burmah, Kar-or or Khar-ur, Kar-u and Kar-i rivers, Kar-natik, Kari-kal, etc. In the other form, Kher-oar, the *e* is represented by the ordinary changes *i* or *ai*, and produces a whole list of its own. Thus the Kher-iahs of Nagpore, who both by their name and their customs are unmistakeably declared an offshoot of the Santal or Ho race. One of the few things we know about them is that they worship their river, the Koel, with rites similar to those with which the Santals adore the Damudah. The root *kher* or *ker*—for English ethnologists transliterate it both ways—appears also in the following names, which may be at once identified from Dr. Keith Johnston's Index: Khera, Kherh district, Kherhi, the two Kheris, Khersiong, Khirki, Kirbassa, Kira, Kiria, Kirinde, Kirpay, Kirtinassa river, the three Khairs and Kheirs, Kheira-garh, and so forth. It also appears in the name of the great ethnical group of the sub-Himalaya, the Kir-antis or Kir-atas, a war-like aboriginal tribe well known to ancient Sanskrit writers; classed by both Manu and the Mahabharata as outcast military peoples, along with the Khasas, Chinas, Dravidas, and other recognised non-Aryan races; and occupying at this day the exact position assigned to them by the Vishnu Purana, to wit, 'the eastern border of Bharatavarsha.' I would go a step further, and prove that the root *chi*, as in Chinas, is only another form of *khi* or *ki*, probably through *k* and *s*, and the substitution is borne out by a whole list of proper names and of non-Aryan words. For example, Chinese, Pekin, *hsieh*, blood, p. 108; the whole Kiranti group, *hi;* Gyami, *sye;* Thulungya, *si-si* (a reduplicative); Garo, *chi;* Bhramu, *chi-wi*. Choli and similar words constantly appear as other forms for Koli; and indeed the very name Kir-bassa, as it is pronounced on the west of the Nepal Mala-bhumi at the foot of the Himalayas, is pronounced and spelt in official documents as Chyebassa in the west of the other Mala-bhumi (now Bishenpore), on the distant south-western frontier of Lower Bengal. The Chinas not only take their name from the same wide-spread root that has furnished race-names to the aboriginal tribes of all India north of the Vindhya range, but they are expressly classed with still existing aboriginal tribes in Manu; and their position can be inferred from Sanskrit authors to be exactly where the Chinese frontier would be at that time, viz. in the extreme east, but further into India than at present. This ancient connection of the Chinas with the Indian aboriginal races is borne out by the mediæval geographer Al Kazwini, who says that the people of Kulam—whose name, habits, and surroundings, as we have seen, mark them unmistakeably as aborigines—'when their king dies, choose another from China;' and I have written this book in vain, if it does not concentrate these scattered indications into positive proof that the aboriginal races of the Eastern Peninsula, Burmah, and India north of the Vindhya range, derived their speech from a source common to themselves and the Chinese.

I turn for a moment from the aboriginal tribes who have maintained their ethnical identity in the forests and mountains of India, to those who were crushed before the Aryan advance, and have merged as serfs into the Hindu population. These unfortunate people appear chiefly under two names in post-Vedic Sanskrit literature—Sudras and Chandalas. Their personal appearance, habits, and occupations, as detailed in ancient writers, mark them as non-Aryan helots; the Sanskrit scheme of society, as Roth well observes, was complete without them; and while the other three natural Aryan castes clearly derive their names from Aryan roots, all attempt to establish a Sanskrit origin for the nomenclature of the fourth or non-Aryan servile caste have failed. Professor Wilson, following the Puranic etymologist, deduces the word *s'údra* from *s'uch*, grieve, and *dru*, run,—a derivation with regard to which Dr. J. Muir writes to me: 'If we are to accept this, we may accept anything.' The truth is, that both S'údra and Cháṇḍála are based upon phonetic modifications of the great aboriginal root *haḍ*, which appears in Ho, Kol, Santal, Sontal, etc. Cháṇḍála becomes, in the mediæval geographers, Sandália (Ibn Khurdabda), or Sandaliya (Al Idrisi), as the Salsas of Rashidu-d Din is the Sanskrit Chelas, a town upon the Indus. This word Sandália is arrived at by the same process as the race-name Santáli, and consists not merely of the specific root *had* ($h = s$), *vir*, but also of the generic root, *li*, *homo*. The insertion of a nasal and dental is a very common feature in tribal designations formed from the root *haḍ*: thus the Khonds and Gondis of Central India, whose languages I give; the Kalindas and Saundikas of the Mahabharata, which appear as outcast military tribes in lists of aboriginal races, such as the Koli-sarpas, Kiratas, Chinas, Dravidas; and in Chandala, Saundika, Khond, Gond, etc., the dotted or aboriginal *ḍ* is uniformly used.

The enslaved Chandals, therefore, were of the same stock, and formed their name from the same universal root, as the aboriginal races of Northern India at the present day. If time permitted, it would be equally easy to follow the process by which Sudra—the Sudaria of the Arabic geographers—and many similar names in Sanskrit literature are evolved from the same base. The fact is, that the whole nomenclature of the helot castes among the mixed Hindus, both in ancient and modern times, is derived from the aborigines. Thus the Ma-lis, gardeners and landless husbandmen in the Hindu community, take their name from the tribal term for man, *male*, p. 139; from which many hill and forest peoples of Northern and Central India, possibly also the whole Malay race of the Archipelago, are called, and the Malavas (cf. Modern Malwa), in the Vishnu Purana. The Doms, or corpse-bearers of the Hinduized lowlands, are the Dams of the Santal hills, and the Dumis, still a well-defined tribe in sub-Himalayan Nepal. The Kharwar helots of Gyah, etc., now perfectly Hinduized, had scarce a century ago a separate language of their own, as the Khar-wars of the Mirzapur highlands, the Kher-

oars or ancient Santals, and the wild 'mysterious' Kher-iahs of Central India, still have. The same may be said of the Chura serfs of the Punjab, the direct descendants of the Chauras or military outcasts of the Mahabharata; of the Coolies (Kulis), hewers of wood and drawers of water through the length and breadth of India; and Hindu speech has enriched itself with a whole vocabulary of abuse from the names of these races. Take, as a single example, the *Haḍis*, a helot caste spread over all Bengal, and called by the bare aboriginal word for man, *haḍ*, and who have supplied such terms as *haḍḍ*, base, low-born; *haḍḍuk*, a sweeper; *huṇḍa*, hog, blockhead, imp; *huḍukka*, a drunken sot, etc. One word in this series tells a peculiarly sad tale of its own. *Haḍi*, in low Bengali *Haḍi-kath*, is the name of a sort of rude fetter or stocks by which the landholder used to confine his serfs until they agreed to his extortions,—a practice within the memory of Indian magistrates still living, and means literally 'the helot's-log.' It was also used for fastening the head of the victim in the bloody oblations which the Aryan religion adopted from the aboriginal races, especially in the human sacrifices to Kali, to which the low-castes even now resort in times of special need. Indeed, so intimately connected is the term with the worship of this ferocious deity, that in the account of the last human offerings, during the famine of 1866—an account given by an English journalist who knew nothing of the aborigines—the word comes to the surface, and we are told that the bleeding head was found fixed in the 'har-cat,' *i.e.* helot's-log.

III.—GENERAL CONCLUSIONS.

The points which I have endeavoured to establish are—

1st, That India is partly peopled by races distinct from the Aryan population,—races whom we have scarcely studied, and whom we do not understand.

2d, That while some of these races have preserved their ethnical identity in sequestered wilds, others have merged as helots or low-castes into the lowland Hindus.

3d, That our ignorance of the first section brings forth incessant risings and frontier wars, and that our imperfect acquaintance with the second forms a serious blot in our internal administration.

4th, That these races are capable of being politically utilized, and by proper measures may be converted from a source of weakness to a source of strength.

5th, That they are also capable of being scientifically investigated, and of furnishing trustworthy materials to European philology.

6th, That indications are not wanting that these now fragmentary peoples form the *débris* of a widely-spread primitive race; and that from the northern shores of the Indian Ocean and the Chinese Sea, traces are here exhumed of

ethnical evolutions and the ebb and flow of human speech, far more ancient, and on a grander scale, than the prehistoric migrations of the Indo-Germanic stock.

IV.—ACKNOWLEDGMENTS.

The construction of a dictionary such as I now submit is a work of compilation rather than of authorship. The main body of the vocabularies are taken from lists printed in the Journals or Proceedings of the Asiatic Societies in Bengal and in England, in the Records of the Government of Bengal, all drawn up by or under the direction of Mr. B. H. Hodgson, late of the Bengal Civil Service, Chevalier of the Legion of Honour, etc. Mr. Hodgson also kindly placed at my disposal two large trunks of manuscripts, amassed during his long and honoured service in the East, and subsequently made over for safe keeping to the India Office. In some respects, therefore, I look upon myself as the editor of materials collected by him rather than as the author of an original work. To the nucleus thus furnished I have added everything that could be obtained from the Government archives, such as the group left by the Rev. Stephen Hislop of Nagpore, and edited with additions by Sir Richard Temple, of the Bengal Civil Service.

I cannot mention Mr. Hislop's name without acknowledging the zealous co-operation which I have received throughout from missionaries of all denominations, both in India and at home. It was to these noble and devoted men that I owed my first materials, and from them I learned that missionary enterprise means not only the propagation of the Christian faith, but also the civilisation of whole races, and the winning back of long lapsed peoples to a new life. No history of the British occupation of India will be complete without the mention of such names as those of Mr. Williamson of Beerbhoom; Mr. Puxley of Rajmahal; the two Phillips, father and son, of Orissa; Dr. Batchelor, who worked the first Santali press at Midnapore; and many others, whose scholarship is warmed from the holy flame of Christian zeal. Some who started with me in these researches have not been permitted to see their fruits; and in my venerable friend Mr. Williamson, who died at Beerbhoom in 1867, after nearly fifty years of missionary service, the world lost one of those lives of calm usefulness which seldom find a biographer here, but which are assuredly written above. In this country I have to thank the London Missionary and Church Missionary Societies in their corporate capacities; the Rev. Dr. Legge for MS. vocabularies of the Nankin, Pekin, and Canton dialects; the Rev. Mr. Muirhead for the Shanghai; and the Rev. W. K. Lea for the Amoy.

To Prince Lucien Bonaparte I am indebted for a MS. Bask vocabulary drawn up by His Highness, and for materials furnished in letters; to the Royal Asiatic Society and its president Viscount Strangford, for obtaining the additional

leave which enabled me to bring out the work, and for valuable materials from the Society's library; to Mr. Hyde Clarke, who long held a responsible office under the Ottoman Government, for MS. lists of Turkish, Magyar, Circassian, and Georgian; to the Rev. Charles Malan of Broad Windsor, and Mr. S. Halkett of the Advocates' Library, Edinburgh, for the Mongolian and Mantshu; to Dr. John Muir, late of the Bengal Civil Service, for portions of the Sanskrit list which I could not myself overtake, and for many valuable suggestions; to the Right Hon. E. Hammond of the Foreign Office for procuring, and to Mr. Von Siebold of the Japanese Mission for drawing up, the Japanese list; to Mr Cull for the Finnic; to Mr. John Hutcheson, formerly of Beyroot, for the Arabic; to Mr. W. Ralston of the British Museum for the Russian, and for another Russian list to Mr. Fiske, the American Consul at Leith; to Mr. J. Purves, Fellow and Lecturer of Balliol, and to Monsieur Gustave Masson of Harrow, eminent as a French *littérateur* and honourably known as an English writer, for the Latin and French prefaces; to Sir Henry Rawlinson, and to Mr Watts of the British Museum, for the suggestion of sporadic affinities which led me to give the three series of Inflecting, Compounding, and Isolating types; to Sir Bartle Frere, for access to his admirable collection of the Bombay Records; to Professor Max Müller, and to General Briggs, for valuable suggestions; to Sir Erskine Perry, for many acts of kindness during the compilation. My obligations to Dr. Rost, the Secretary to the Royal Asiatic Society, for MS. lists drawn up from materials in his library, and for revising the proofs, demand separate mention. But for his generous help, the work could not have been brought out within the time allowed. To my secretary and salaried assistants I have to make my acknowledgments for their fidelity and general accuracy. Many things which ought to have been done by myself had to be entrusted to others; and this list would be incomplete without an acknowledgment of the affectionate industry with which my Wife has corrected proof-sheets and manuscript, of which each page contained five handwritings, and indeed done entire parts of the work, such as the polyglot indices. The Dissertation itself has gone to press without being read over; but I felt that, having once taken in hand to bring out my researches within the four months, it would have been mere cowardice to keep back, through fear of a few verbal slips, ideas that have long been working in my mind, and which I believe capable of doing good for millions of men. If I am right in this belief, I can well afford to let the book go forth with all its faults.

ERRATUM.

On each page of Lexicon.

For 'Nepal (East to West)', *read* 'Nepal (West to East).'

Types.

Group	Language	One
Inflecting.	SANSKRIT,	*Eka.*
	ARABIC, .	*Waḥad.*
Compounding.	BASK, ...	*Bat.*
	FINNIC, ...	*Yksi.*
	MAGYAR, ...	*Egy.*
	TURKISH, ...	*Bir.*
	CIRCASSIAN, ...	*Zi.*
	GEORGIAN, ...	*Erthi, szu.**
	MONGOLIAN, . . .	*Nigen, niken, ith,† gri,‡ um-*
	MANTSHU, ...	*Emou, iga.** [*un,§ om-okon.*‖
	JAVANESE, Ngoko, . .	*Sa.*
	JAVANESE, Krama, . .	*Sa.*
	MALAY, ...	*Sa, sátu.*
Isolating.	CHINESE, Nankin, . .	*Yih.*
	CHINESE, Pekin, . .	*Yi.*
	CHINESE, Canton, . .	*Yat.*
	CHINESE, Shanghai, .	*Ih.*
	AMOY, Colloquial, . .	*Chit.*
	JAPANESE, ...	*Fitots, i-chi, h'to.*
	Brahuí, ...	*Asit.*
Chinese Frontier & Tibet.	Gyámi, ...	*I, iku.*
	Gyárung, ...	*Ka-ti.*
	Tákpa, ...	*Thi.*
	Mányak, ...	*Tá-bi.*
	Thochú, ...	*A'-ri.*
	Sokpa, ...	*Nege.*
	Horpa, ...	*Rá.*
	Tibetan (*written*), . .	*Tschig, gchig.*
	Tibetan (*spoken*), . .	*Chik.*
Nepal (east to west).	Serpa, ...	*Chik.*
	Súnwár, ...	*Ká.*
	Gúrung, ...	*Kri, ri.*
	Múrmi, ...	*Ghrik, rik.*
	Magar, ...	*Kát.*
	Thákysa, ...	*Di.*
	Pákhya, ...	*Yek.*
	Newár, ...	*Chhi.*
	Limbu, ...	*Thit.*
Kiranti Group (East Nepal).	Kiránti, ...	*Ktai, ektai.*
	Rodong, ...	*Aura, itto.*
	Rúngchenbung, . . .	*Eukta, eukchha, eukpop.*
	Chhingtángya, . . .	*Thitta.*
	Náchhereng, ...	*I-bhou.*
	Wáling, ...	*Aktai, akta.*
	Yákha, ...	*Ikko.*
	Chourásya, ...	*Kolo.*
	Kulungya, ...	*Ubum.*
	Thulungya, ...	*Kwong, kong, kole.*
	Báhingya, ...	*Kwong, kong.*
	Lohorong, ...	*Yekko.*
	Lambichhong, . . .	*Thibang, thili.*
	Báláli, ...	*Ikku.*
	Sáng-páng, ...	*Itta, euli, eukla-pang.*
	Dúmi, ...	*Táu, táwa, man-hampo.*
	Kháling, ...	*Tá, táu, táwo.*
	Dungmáli, ...	*Akpo.*
Broken Tribes of Nepal.	Dárhi, ...	*Ek.*
	Denwár, ...	*Ek.*
	Pahri, ...	*Chhi, chhigu.*
	Chepáng, ...	*Yá-zho, ya-zyo.*
	Bhrámu, ...	*De.*
	Váyu, ...	*Ko-lu.*
	Kuswar, ...	*Ek.*
	Kusunda, ...	*Goi-sang.*
	Tháru, ...	*Yek.*
	Lepcha (Sikkim), . .	*Kát.*
	Bhúṭáni v. Lhopa, . .	*Chi.*

Group	Language	One
N.-E. Bengal.	Bodo, ...	*Man-che.*
	Dhimál, ...	*E-long.*
	Kocch, ...	*Ek.*
	Garo, ...	*Go-sha.*
	Káchári, ...	*Man-she, mon-she.*
Eastern Frontier of Bengal.	Munipuri, ...	*Amá.*
	Míthán Nágá, . . .	*A'-ta.*
	Tablung Nágá, . . .	*Chá.*
	Khári Nágá, ...	*A-khet.*
	Angámi Nágá, . . .	*Po.*
	Námsáng Nágá, . . .	*Van-the.*
	Nowgong Nágá, . . .	*Ka-tang.*
	Tengsa Nágá, . . .	*Kha-tu.*
	Abor Miri, ...	*A-ko.*
	Sibságar Miri, . . .	*A-tero.*
	Deoria Chutia, . . .	*Dug-sha.*
	Singpho, ...	*Ai-má.*
Arrakan & Burmah.	Burman (*written*), . .	*Tach.*
	Burman (*spoken*), . .	*Tit, ta.*
	Khyeng v. Shou, . .	*Nhát.*
	Kámi, ...	*Há.*
	Kúmi, ...	*Há.*
	Mrú v. Toung, . . .	*Loung.*
	Sák, ...	*Su-war.*
Siam & Tenasserim.	Talain v. Mon, . . .	*Mway.*
	Sgau-karen, ...	*T'er, hta.*
	Pwo-karen, ...	*Lung.*
	Toungh-thu, ...	*Ta.*
	Shán, ...	*Nein (noung ?).*
	Annamitic, ...	*Mot.*
	Siamese, ...	*Nung, nein.*
	Ahom, ...	*Ling.*
	Khámti, ...	*Nung.*
	Laos, ...	*Nung.*
Central India.	Ho (Kol), ...	*Miad.*
	Kol (Singhbhum), . .	*Mi.*
	Santáli, ...	*Mih, midh.*
	Bhúmij, ...	*Moy.*
	Uráon, ...	*Untá.*
	Mundala, ...	*Miá.*
	Rájmahali, ...	*Ort, ondong, kivong.*
	Gonḍi, ...	*Undi.*
	Gayeti, ...	*Undi.*
	Rutluk, ...	*Wundi.*
	Naikude, ...	*Wákko.*
	Kolami, ...	*Okadu.*
	Mádi, ...	*Undi, wundi, wandi.*
	Mádia, ...	*Udi.*
	Kuri, ...	*Nekor.*
	Keikádi, ...	*Wanu.*
	Khonḍ, ...	*Ronḍi.*
	Sávara, ...	*Aboy.*
	Gadaba, ...	*Vokati.*
	Yerukala, ...	*Vondu (Vondu ?).*
	Chentsu, ...	*Yek.*
Southern India.	Tamiḷ, anc., ...	*Caret.*
	Tamiḷ, mod., ...	*Onṛu.*
	Malayáḷma, anc., . .	*Caret.*
	Malayáḷma, mod., . .	*Onna.*
	Telugu, ...	*Voka.*
	Karṇáṭaka, anc., . .	*Caret.*
	Karṇáṭaka, mod., . .	*Ondu.*
	Tuḷuva, ...	*Onji.*
	Kurgi, ...	*Wondu.*
	Toḍuva, }	*Caret.*
	Toḍa, }	*Vadd.*
	Kóta, ...	*Vodde.*
	Baḍaga, ...	*Vondu.*
	Kuṛumba, ...	*Vondu.*
	Iruḷa, ...	*Vondu.*
	Malabar, ...	*Ondu.*
	Sinhalese, ...	*Ekay.*

Group	Types.	
Inflecting.	SANSKRIT,	*Dwi* (*dwá*).
	ARABIC,	*Ethnán.*
Compounding.	BASK,	*Bi, bia, biga.*
	FINNIC,	*Kaksi.*
	MAGYAR,	*Ketto.*
	TURKISH,	*Iki.*
	CIRCASSIAN,	*Oh.*
	GEORGIAN,	*Ori, gi-gu.**
	MONGOLIAN,	*Khoyar, kaet,*† *siti,*‡ *dzi-un,*§
	MANTSHU,	*Dchoue, lianga.** [*nadan.*‖
	JAVANESE, Ngoko,	*Ro.*
	JAVANESE, Krama,	*Kalih.*
	MALAY,	*Dúa.*
Isolating.	CHINESE, Nankin,	*Urh* (*ár*).
	CHINESE, Pekin,	*Urh.*
	CHINESE, Canton,	*I.*
	CHINESE, Shanghai,	*Ni.*
	AMOY, Colloquial,	*Ng.*
	JAPANESE,	*F'tats, ni, fo.*
	Brahuí,	*Irat.*
Chinese Frontier & Tibet.	Gyámi,	*A'r, liangku.*
	Gyárung,	*Ka-nes.*
	Tákpa,	*Nai.*
	Mányak,	*Ná-bi.*
	Thochú,	*Gná-ri.*
	Sokpa,	*Hoyur.*
	Horpa,	*Gne.*
	Tibetan (*written*),	*Gnyis, nyis.*
	Tibetan (*spoken*),	*Nyi.*
Nepal (east to west).	Serpa,	*Nyi.*
	Súnwár,	*Ni-shi.*
	Gúrung,	*Ni.*
	Múrmi,	*Gni, ni.*
	Magar,	*Nis.*
	Tháksya,	*Gni.*
	Pákhya,	*Dui.*
	Newár,	*Ni.*
	Limbu,	*Nyetsh.*
Kiranti Group (East Nepal).	Kiránti,	*Ha-sat.*
	Rodong,	*Ha-kara.*
	Rúngchenbung,	*Hen-sa, hen-wang.*
	Chhingtángya,	*Hich-che.*
	Náchhereng,	*Nij-bhou.*
	Wáling,	*Ni, ha-sa, ha-sak.*
	Yákha,	*Kich-chi.*
	Chourásya,	*Ni-ksi.*
	Kulungya,	*Nih-chi.*
	Thulungya,	*Ni, ni-chi, na-le.*
	Báhingya,	*Ni-ksi.*
	Lohorong,	*Hich-chi, hi-pang.*
	Lambichhong,	*Hich-chi, hi-pang.*
	Báláli,	*Hich-che.*
	Sáng-páng,	*Hich-chi, hi-sali, hi-slapang.*
	Dúmi,	*Sák-pu.*
	Kháling,	*Sák-po.*
	Dungmáli,	*Hi-chi.*
Broken Tribes of Nepal.	Dárhi,	*Dwi.*
	Denwár,	*Dwi.*
	Pahri,	*Ni, ning-gu.*
	Chepáng,	*Nhi-zho, nhi-zyo.*
	Bhrámu,	*Ni.*
	Váyu,	*Ná-yung.*
	Kuswar,	*Dwi.*
	Kusunda,	*Ghi-gna.*
	Tháru,	*Dui.*
	Lepcha (Sikkim),	*Nyet.*
	Bhútáni v. Lhopa,	*Nyi.*

Group	Language	Two
N.-E. Bengal.	Bodo,	*Man-gne, man-ne.*
	Dhimál,	*Nhe-long, gne-long.*
	Kocch,	*Du.*
	Garo,	*Gi-ning, a-ning.*
	Káchári,	*Man-nai, mu-nai.*
Eastern Frontier of Bengal.	Munipuri,	*Ani.*
	Míthán Nágá,	*A'-nyi.*
	Tablung Nágá,	*Ih.*
	Khári Nágá,	*A-ne.*
	Angámi Nágá,	*Ka-ne.*
	Námsáng Nágá,	*Van-yi.*
	Nowgong Nágá,	*An-na.*
	Tengsa Nágá,	*An-nat.*
	Abor Miri,	*Ani-ko.*
	Sibságar Miri,	*Ngo-ye.*
	Deoria Chutia,	*Duku-ni.*
	Singpho,	*Nkhong.*
Arrakan & Burmah.	Burman (*written*),	*Nhach.*
	Burman (*spoken*),	*Nhit.*
	Khyeng v. Shou,	*Pan-nhi.*
	Kámi,	*Ni.*
	Kúmi,	*Nhu.*
	Mrú v. Toung,	*Pre.*
	Sák,	*Nein.*
Siam & Tenasserim.	Talain v. Mon,	*Pa.*
	Sgau-karen,	*'Ki, khi.*
	Pwo-karen,	*Ne.*
	Toungh-thu,	*Ne.*
	Shán,	*H'tsoung.*
	Annamitic,	*Hai.*
	Siamese,	*Sang, tsoung, song.*
	Ahom,	*Sang.*
	Khámti,	*Song.*
	Laos,	*Song.*
Central India.	Ho (Kol),	*Barria.*
	Kol (Singhbhum),	*Bár-ia.*
	Santáli,	*Bár-ea.*
	Bhúmij,	*Bár-ia.*
	Uráon,	*En-otan.*
	Mundala,	*Bár-ia.*
	Rájmahali,	*Twr* (?), *mákis.*
	Goṇḍi,	*Ranu, rand.*
	Gayeti,	*Rand.*
	Rutluk,	*Rand.*
	Naikude,	*Indi.*
	Kolami,	*Ind-ing.*
	Mádi,	*Randu.*
	Mádia,	*Rand.*
	Kuri,	*Bár-ku.*
	Keikádi,	*Rand.*
	Khoṇḍ,	*Joḍeká.*
	Sávara,	*Bá-gu.*
	Gadaba,	*Renḍu.*
	Yerukala,	*Renḍu.*
	Chentsu,	*Duyi.*
Southern India.	Tamiḷ, anc.,	*Caret.*
	Tamiḷ, mod.,	*Iranḍu.*
	Malayáḷma, anc.,	*Caret.*
	Malayáḷma, mod.,	*Ranḍa.*
	Telugu,	*Renḍu.*
	Karṇáṭaka, anc.,	*Caret.*
	Karṇáṭaka, mod.,	*Eraḍu.*
	Tuḷuva,	*Eraḍ.*
	Kurgi,	*Danḍu.*
	Toḍuva, }	*Caret.*
	Toḍa, }	*Ed, a-ed.*
	Kóta,	*Yeḍe.*
	Baḍaga,	*Yeraḍu.*
	Kuṛumba,	*Yeraḍu.*
	Iruḷa,	*Renḍu, irenḍu.*
	Malabar,	*Iranḍu.*
	Sinhalese,	*Dekay.*

	Types.	
Inflecting.	SANSKRIT,	*Tri* (*tisṛi*).
	ARABIC,	*Thaláthat.*
Compounding.	BASK,	*Iru, hiru, hirur.*
	FINNIC,	*Kolme.*
	MAGYAR,	*Harom.*
	TURKISH,	*U'ch.*
	CIRCASSIAN,	*Shi.*
	GEORGIAN,	*Sami, han-ku.**
	MONGOLIAN,	*Khurban, kollem,*† *nagor,*‡
	MANTSHU,	*Ilan, sfan-ga.** [*il-en,*§
	JAVANESE, Ngoko,	*Telu.* [*dagalk-un.*‖
	JAVANESE, Krama,	*Tiga.*
	MALAY,	*Tiga.*
Isolating.	CHINESE, Nankin,	*San.*
	CHINESE, Pekin,	*San.*
	CHINESE, Canton,	*Sám.*
	CHINESE, Shanghai,	*Saṇ.*
	AMOY, Colloquial,	*Saṇ.*
	JAPANESE,	*Mits, mi, san.*
	Brahuí,	*Musit.*
Chinese Frontier & Tibet.	Gyámi,	*Sán, sang-ku.*
	Gyárung,	*Ka-sám.*
	Tákpa,	*Sám* (*sum* ?).
	Mányak,	*Si-bi.*
	Thochú,	*Kshiri.*
	Sokpa,	*Korbá.*
	Horpa,	*Su.*
	Tibetan (*written*),	*Gsum, sum.*
	Tibetan (*spoken*),	*Sum.*
Nepal (east to west).	Serpa,	*Sum.*
	Súnwár,	*Sáng* (*sung* ?).
	Gúrung,	*Song.*
	Múrmi,	*Som.*
	Magar,	*Song.*
	Tháksya,	*Som.*
	Pákhya,	*Tin.*
	Newár,	*Soṇ.*
	Limbu,	*Syumsh.*
Kiranti Group (East Nepal).	Kiránti,	*Sum-ya.*
	Rodong,	*Sum-ra.*
	Rúngchenbung,	*Sum-yo.*
	Chhingtángya,	*Sum-che.*
	Náchhereng,	*Suk-bhou.*
	Wáling,	*Syum-yak.*
	Yákha,	*Sum-chi.*
	Chourásya,	*Sum-makha.*
	Kulungya,	*Sup-chi.*
	Thulungya,	*Syum, sule.*
	Báhingya,	*Sum* (*sám* ?).
	Lohorong,	*Sum-chi.*
	Lambichhong,	*Sum-chi.*
	Bálálí,	*Sung-che.*
	Sáng-páng,	*Sum-chi.*
	Dúmi,	*Suk-pu.*
	Kháling,	*Suk-po.*
	Dungmáli,	*Sum-chi.*
Broken Tribes of Nepal.	Dárhi,	*Tin.*
	Denwár,	*Tin.*
	Pahri,	*Sung, sung-gu.*
	Chepáng,	*Sung-zho, sung-zyo.*
	Bhrámu,	*Swom.*
	Váyu,	*Chhu-yung.*
	Kuswar,	*Tin.*
	Kusunda,	*Dáha.*
	Tháru,	*Tin.*
	Lepcha (Sikkim),	*Sum* (*sam* ?).
	Bhúṭáni v. Lhopa,	*Sum.*
N.-E. Bengal.	Bodo,	*Man-tham.*
	Dhimál,	*Sum-lang.*
	Kocch,	*Tin.*
	Garo,	*Ga-thám, a-thám.*
	Káchári,	*Man-tang, mung-tung.*
Eastern Frontier of Bengal.	Munipuri,	*Ahum.*
	Míthán Nágá,	*A-zam.*
	Tablung Nágá,	*Lem.*
	Khári Nágá,	*A-sam.*
	Angámi Nágá,	*Su.*
	Námsáng Nágá,	*Van-ram.*
	Nowgong Nágá,	*A-sam.*
	Tengsa Nágá,	*A-sam* (*a-sám* ?).
	Abor Miri,	*Aom-ko.*
	Sibságar Miri,	*Auma.*
	Deoria Chutia,	*Dug-da.*
	Singpho,	*Ma-súm.*
Arrakan & Burmah.	Burman (*written*),	*Sung* (*ṣung* ?).
	Burman (*spoken*),	*Thong, thon.*
	Khyeng v. Shou,	*Thum.*
	Kámi,	*Ka-tun.*
	Kúmi,	*Tum.*
	Mrú v. Toung,	*Shun.*
	Sák,	*Thin.*
Siam & Tenasserim.	Talain v. Mon,	*Pe.*
	Sgau-karen,	*Ther, theh, tho.*
	Pwo-karen,	*Thung.*
	Toungh-thu,	*Thung.*
	Shán,	*H'tsan.*
	Annamitic,	*Ba.*
	Siamese,	*Sám, tsan.*
	Ahom,	*Sam.*
	Khámti,	*Sám.*
	Laos,	*Sám.*
Central India.	Ho (Kol),	*Appiá.*
	Kol (Singhbhum),	*A-piá.*
	Santáli,	*Peá.*
	Bhúmij,	*A-piá.*
	Uráon,	*Man-otan.*
	Mundala,	*A-piá.*
	Rájmahali,	*Tin.*
	Goṇḍi,	*Munu, mund.*
	Gayeti,	*Mund.*
	Rutluk,	*Mund.*
	Naikude,	*Mundi.*
	Kolami,	*Munding.*
	Mádi,	*Mundu.*
	Mádia,	*Mund.*
	Kuri,	*Akor, apkor.*
	Keikádi,	*Múnu.*
	Khoṇḍ,	*Tinigota.*
	Sávara,	*Yági.*
	Gadaba,	*Muḍu.*
	Yerukala,	*Mume.*
	Chentsu,	*Tin.*
Southern India.	Tamiḷ, anc.,	*Caret.*
	Tamiḷ, mod.,	*Múnṟu.*
	Malayáḷma, anc.,	*Caret.*
	Malayáḷma, mod.,	*Múnna.*
	Telugu,	*Múḍu.*
	Karṇáṭaka, anc.,	*Caret.*
	Karṇáṭaka, mod.,	*Múru.*
	Tuḷuva,	*Muji.*
	Kurgi,	*Múndu.*
	Toḍuva, }	*Min.*
	Toda, }	*Muḍu.*
	Kóta,	*Munde* (*muṇḍe* ?).
	Baḍaga,	*Muru* (*muḍu* ?).
	Kuṟumba,	*Muḍu.*
	Iruḷa,	*Muru* (*muḍu* ?).
	Malabar,	*Mundu.*
	Sinhalese,	*Tunai.*

	Types.	
Inflecting.	SANSKṚIT,	*Chatur* (*chatasṛi*).
	ARABIC,	*Arbaat.*
Compounding.	BASK,	*Lau, laur.*
	FINNIC,	*Nelja.*
	MAGYAR,	*Negi.*
	TURKISH,	*Deurt.*
	CIRCASSIAN,	*Tley.*
	GEORGIAN,	*Othkhi, on-ku.**
	MONGOLIAN,	*Turban, nille,*† *ki-eta,*‡ *dig-*[*in,*§ *ullan.*||
	MANTSHU,	*Douin, sfi-gae.**
	JAVANESE, Ngoko,	*Pat, papat.*
	JAVANESE, Krama,	*Sakawan.*
	MALAY,	*Ampat.*
Isolating.	CHINESE, Nankin,	*Sze.*
	CHINESE, Pekin,	*Sze, s'z.*
	CHINESE, Canton,	*Sze.*
	CHINESE, Shanghai,	*Sz.*
	AMOY, Colloquial,	*Si.*
	JAPANESE,	*Yôts, yo, shi.*
	Brahuí,	*Chár.*
Chinese Frontier & Tibet.	Gyámi,	*Si, siku.*
	Gyárung,	*Ka-di.*
	Tákpa,	*Pli.*
	Mányak,	*Re-bi.*
	Thochú,	*Gzháre.*
	Sokpa,	*Tirbá.*
	Horpa,	*Hla.*
	Tibetan (*written*),	Bzhi, *shi.*
	Tibetan (*spoken*),	*Zhyi.*
Nepal (east to west).	Serpa,	*Zhyi.*
	Súnwár,	*Le.*
	Gúrung,	*Pli.*
	Múrmi,	*Bli.*
	Magar,	*Buli.*
	Tháksya,	*Bla.*
	Pákhya,	*Chár.*
	Newár,	*Pi.*
	Limbu,	*Lish.*
Kiranti Group (East Nepal).	Kiránti,	*Laya.*
	Rodong,	*Lyura.*
	Rúngchenbung,	*Láyá.*
	Chhingtángya,	*Caret.*
	Náchhereng,	*Lik-bhou.*
	Wáling,	*Lá-yak.*
	Yákha,	*Li-chi.*
	Chourásya,	*Phi-bakha.*
	Kulungya,	*Li-chi.*
	Thulungya,	*Bli, ble-ule.*
	Báhingya,	*Le.*
	Lohorong,	*Li-chi, ri-chi, le-bang.*
	Lambichhong,	*Caret.*
	Báláli,	*Li-ji.*
	Sáng-páng,	*La-kabo.*
	Dúmi,	*Bhyál.*
	Kháling,	*Bhál.*
	Dungmáli,	*Li-chi, ri-chi.*
Broken Tribes of Nepal.	Dárhi,	*Chár.*
	Denwár,	*Chár.*
	Pahri,	*Pi, ping-gu.*
	Chepáng,	*Ploï-zho, ploï-zyo.*
	Bhrámu,	*Bi.*
	Váyu,	*Bi-ning, bli-ning.*
	Kuswar,	*Chár.*
	Kusunda,	*Pin-jang.*
	Tháru,	*Chár.*
	Lepcha (Sikkim),	*Pha-li.*
	Bhúṭáni v. Lhopa,	*Zhi.*
N.-E. Bengal.	Bodo,	*Man-bre.*
	Dhimál,	*Dia-long.*
	Kocch,	*Chár.*
	Garo,	*Bri.*
	Kácházi,	*Man-buri, mun-buri.*
Eastern Frontier of Bengal.	Munipuri,	*Mari.*
	Míthán Nágá,	*A'-li.*
	Tablung Nágá,	*Pi-li.*
	Khári Nágá,	*Pha-li.*
	Angámi Nágá,	*Deh.*
	Námsáng Nágá,	*Be-li.*
	Nowgong Nágá,	*Pazr.*
	Tengsa Nágá,	*Pha-le.*
	Abor Miri,	*A-pi-ko.*
	Sibságar Miri,	*A-pi-e.*
	Deoria Chutia,	*Dugu-chi.*
	Singpho,	*Me-li.*
Arrakan & Burmah.	Burman (*written*),	*Le.*
	Burman (*spoken*),	*Le, lá.*
	Khyeng v. Shou,	*Lhi.*
	Kámi,	*Ma-li.*
	Kúmi,	*Pa-lu.*
	Mrú v. Toung,	*Ta-li.*
	Sák,	*Pri.*
Siam & Tenasserim.	Talain v. Mon,	*Pou.*
	Sgau-karen,	*Lwi.*
	Pwo-karen,	*Li.*
	Toungh-thu,	*Lit.*
	Shán,	*H'tse.*
	Annamitic,	*Bôn.*
	Siamese,	*Si, tse.*
	Ahom,	*Si.*
	Khámti,	*Si.*
	Laos,	*Si.*
Central India.	Ho (Kol),	*Upúnia.*
	Kol (Singhbhum),	*Upun-ia.*
	Santáli,	*Pon-ea.*
	Bhúmij,	*Upun-ia.*
	Uráon,	*Nákh-otan.*
	Mundala,	*Upnia.*
	Rájmahali,	*Chár.*
	Goṇḍi,	*Nálu, nálung.*
	Gayeti,	*Nálung.*
	Rutluk,	*Nálu.*
	Naikude,	*Chár.*
	Kolami,	*Náling.*
	Mádi,	*Nál.*
	Mádia,	*Nálgu.*
	Kuri,	*Upanku.*
	Keikádi,	*Nál.*
	Khoṇḍ,	*Sári.*
	Sávara,	*Vonji.*
	Gadaba,	*Nálugu.*
	Yerukala,	*Nálu.*
	Chentsu,	*Chár.*
Southern India.	Tamiḷ, anc.,	*Nángu.*
	Tamiḷ, mod.,	*Nálu.*
	Malayáḷma, anc.,	*Caret.*
	Malayáḷma, mod.,	*Nála.*
	Telugu,	*Nálugu.*
	Karṇáṭaka, anc.,	*Caret.*
	Karṇáṭaka, mod.,	*Nálku.*
	Tuḷuva,	*Nálu.*
	Kurgi,	*Nálu.*
	Toḍuva, }	*Nonk.*
	Toḍa, }	*Nánk.*
	Kóta,	*Náke.*
	Baḍaga,	*Nálku.*
	Kuṛumba,	*Nálku.*
	Iruḷa,	*Náku.*
	Malabar,	*Nálu.*
	Sinhalese,	*Hatarai.*

Group	*Types.*	
Inflecting.	SANSKṚIT	*Panchan.*
	ARABIC	*Khamṣat.*
Compounding.	BASK	*Bost, bortz.*
	FINNIC	*Wüsi.*
	MAGYAR	*Öt.*
	TURKISH	*Besh.*
	CIRCASSIAN	*Tpey.*
	GEORGIAN	*Khouthi, tzilo-ku.**
	MONGOLIAN	*Tebun, wet,'† samfolcnka,‡ tunya,§ degen.‖*
	MANTSHU	*Soundcha, u-gae.**
	JAVANESE, Ngoko	*Lima.*
	JAVANESE, Krama	*Gangsal.*
	MALAY	*Lima.*
Isolating.	CHINESE, Nankin	*Wu.*
	CHINESE, Pekin	*Wu.*
	CHINESE, Canton	*'ng.*
	CHINESE, Shanghai	*'ng.*
	AMOY, Colloquial	*Go.*
	JAPANESE	*Its', itsuts', go.*
	Brahuí	*Panj.*
Chinese Frontier & Tibet.	Gyámi	*Wú, wúku.*
	Gyárung	*Kung-gno.*
	Tákpa	*Liá-gno.*
	Mányak	*Gná-bi.*
	Thochú	*Ware.*
	Sokpa	*Thábá.*
	Horpa	*Gwe.*
	Tibetan (*written*)	*Hná.*
	Tibetan (*spoken*)	*Gná.*
Nepal (east to west).	Serpa	*Gná.*
	Súnwár	*Gno.*
	Gúrung	*Gná.*
	Múrmi	*Gná.*
	Magar	*Ba-gná, bangá.*
	Tháksya	*Gná.*
	Pákhya	*Pách.*
	Newár	*Gná.*
	Limbu	*Gnásh.*
Kiránti Group (East Nepal).	Kiránti	*Gná-yá.*
	Rodong	*Gná-ra.*
	Rúngchenbung	*Gná-yá.*
	Chhingtángya	*Caret.*
	Náchhereng	*Gna-kbhou.*
	Wáling	*Gná-yak.*
	Yákha	*Gná-hi.*
	Chourásya	*Caret.*
	Kulungya	*Gná-chi.*
	Thulungya	*Gno, gno-lo.*
	Báhingya	*Gno.*
	Lohorong	*Gná-chi.*
	Lambichhong	*Caret.*
	Báláli	*Gná-ji.*
	Sáng-páng	*Gná-kabo.*
	Dúmi	*Bhuong.*
	Kháling	*Bhong.*
	Dungmáli	*Gná-chi.*
Broken Tribes of Nepal.	Dárhi	*Pánch.*
	Denwár	*Pánch.*
	Pahri	*Gno, gnong-gu.*
	Chepáng	*Puma-zho, puma-zyo.*
	Bhrámu	*Ba-gná.*
	Váyu	*U-ning, kolu-got-kulup.*
	Kuswar	*Panch.*
	Kusunda	*Pa-gnáng-jang.*
	Tháru	*Páche.*
	Lepcha (Sikkim)	*Pha-gnon.*
	Bhúṭáni v. Lhopa	*Gná.*

Group	Language	Five
N.-E. Bengal.	Bodo	*Man-bá.*
	Dhimál	*Ná-long.*
	Kocch	*Pánch.*
	Garo	*Bo-ngá.*
	Káchári	*Man-bá, mun-bá.*
Eastern Frontier of Bengal.	Munipuri	*Mañga.*
	Míthán Nágá	*A'-gá.*
	Tablung Nágá	*Ngá.*
	Khári Nágá	*Pha-ngá.*
	Angámi Nágá	*Pa-ngu.*
	Námsáng Nágá	*Ba-ngá.*
	Nowgong Nágá	*Pu-ngu.*
	Tengsa Nágá	*Phu-ngu.*
	Abor Miri	*Pili-ngo-ko.*
	Sibságar Miri	*U-ngo.*
	Deoria Chutia	*Dugu-mua.*
	Singpho	*Ma-ngá.*
Arrakan & Burmah.	Burman (*written*)	*Ngá (gná).*
	Burman (*spoken*)	*Ngá (gná).*
	Khyeng v. Shou	*Nghau (gnau).*
	Kámi	*Pang-gná.*
	Kúmi	*Pan.*
	Mrú v. Toung	*Ta-ngá.*
	Sák	*Ngá (gná).*
Siam & Tenasserim.	Talain v. Mon	*Pa-tson.*
	Sgau-karen	*Yaï.*
	Pwo-karen	*Yeà.*
	Toungh-thu	*Ngát (gnát).*
	Shán	*Ha (há ?).*
	Annamitic	*Nam.*
	Siamese	*Há, hgná.*
	Ahom	*Há.*
	Khámti	*Há.*
	Laos	*Há.*
Central India.	Ho (Kol)	*Moya.*
	Kol (Singhbhum)	*Moya.*
	Santáli	*Mane (mone ?).*
	Bhúmij	*Monaya.*
	Uráon	*Panje gotang.*
	Mundala	*Moria.*
	Rájmahali	*Pánch.*
	Goṇḍi	*Saijhan, seiung.*
	Gayeti	*Seiyung.*
	Rutluk	*Seiyu.*
	Naikude	*Pánch.*
	Kolami	*Aidu.*
	Mádi	*Aigu, siyu, hium, heingu.*
	Mádia	*Heigi.*
	Kuri	*Maneiku.*
	Keikádi	*Anj.*
	Khoṇḍ	*Pánchu.*
	Sávara	*Mollayi.*
	Gadaba	*Ayidu.*
	Yerukala	*Anju.*
	Chentsu	*Pánch.*
Southern India.	Tamiḷ, anc.	*A'-indu.*
	Tamiḷ, mod.	*Aindu (anju).*
	Malayáḷma, anc.	*Caret.*
	Malayáḷma, mod.	*A'ncha.*
	Telugu	*Aidu.*
	Karṇáṭaka, anc.	*Caret.*
	Karṇáṭaka, mod.	*Aidu.*
	Tuḷuva	*A'yinu.*
	Kurgi	*Anji.*
	Toḍuva, Toḍa	*Yoj. Utsh.*
	Kóta	*Anje.*
	Baḍaga	*Eidu.*
	Kurumba	*Eidu.*
	Iruḷa	*Eindu.*
	Malabar	*Inthu.*
	Sinhalese	*Pahai.*

Types.

Group	Language	Six
Inflecting.	SANSKṚIT,	*Shaṣh.*
	ARABIC,	*Sittat.*
Compounding.	BASK,	*Sei.*
	FINNIC,	*Kuusi.*
	MAGYAR,	*Hat.*
	TURKISH,	*Alti.*
	CIRCASSIAN,	*Shu.*
	GEORGIAN,	*Ekousi, ekwisi, aukal-ga.**
	MONGOLIAN,	*Jhir-goghan, kol',† mot-to,‡ nuc-un,§ gedin.‖*
	MANTSHU,	*Ninggoun, lu-gae.**
	JAVANESE, Ngoko,	*Nem, nenem.*
	JAVANESE, Krama,	*Nem, nenem.*
	MALAY,	*Anam.*
Isolating.	CHINESE, Nankin,	*Lŭh.*
	CHINESE, Pekin,	*Lin.*
	CHINESE, Canton,	*Luk.*
	CHINESE, Shanghai,	*Loh.*
	AMOY, Colloquial,	*Lák.*
	JAPANESE,	*Muts', mu, roku.*
	Brahuí,	*Shash.*
Chinese Frontier & Tibet.	Gyámi,	*Lu, luku.*
	Gyárung,	*Ku-tok.*
	Tákpa,	*Kro.*
	Mányak,	*Tru-bi.*
	Thochú,	*Khatáre.*
	Sokpa,	*Chorka.*
	Horpa,	*Chho.*
	Tibetan (*written*),	*Druk, dug.*
	Tibetan (*spoken*),	*Thu.*
Nepal (east to west).	Serpa,	*Tuk.*
	Súnwár,	*Ruk.*
	Gúrung,	*Tu.*
	Múrmi,	*Dhu.*
	Magar,	*Caret.*
	Tháksya,	*Tu.*
	Pákhya,	*Chha.*
	Newár,	*Khu.*
	Limbu,	*Tuksh.*
Kiranti Group (East Nepal).	Kiránti,	*Tuk-ya.*
	Rodong,	*Tuk-ara.*
	Rúngchenbung,	*Tuk-ya.*
	Chhingtángya,	*Caret.*
	Náchhereng,	*Caret.*
	Wáling,	*Tuk-yak.*
	Yákha,	*Tuk-chi.*
	Chourásya,	*Caret.*
	Kulungya,	*Tuk-chi.*
	Thulungya,	*Ru, ro, ru-le.*
	Báhingya,	*Ruk-ka.*
	Lohorong,	*Tuk-chi.*
	Lambichhong,	*Caret.*
	Báláli,	*Tuk-chi.*
	Sáng-páng,	*Tuk-kabo.*
	Dúmi,	*Rá-wong.*
	Kháling,	*Re.*
	Dungmáli,	*Tuk-chi.*
Broken Tribes of Nepal.	Dárhi,	*Cháh.*
	Denwár,	*Cháh.*
	Pahri,	*Khu, khung-gu.*
	Chepáng,	*Kruk-zho, kruk-zyo.*
	Bhrámu,	*Caret.*
	Váyu,	*Chhu-ning.*
	Kuswar,	*Cháh.*
	Kusunda,	*Caret.*
	Tháru,	*Chha.*
	Lepcha (Sikkim),	*Ta-rok.*
	Bhúṭáni v. Lhopa,	*Dhu.*

Group	Language	Six
N.-E. Bengal.	Bodo,	*Man-do.*
	Dhimál,	*Tu-long.*
	Kocch,	*Choi.*
	Garo,	*Krok.*
	Káchári,	*Man-do, mun-do.*
Eastern Frontier of Bengal.	Munipuri,	*Tarúk.*
	Míthán Nágá,	*A'-rok.*
	Tablung Nágá,	*Vok.*
	Khári Nágá,	*Ta-rok.*
	Angámi Nágá,	*So-ru.*
	Námsáng Nágá,	*I-rok.*
	Nowgong Nágá,	*Ta-rok.*
	Tengsa Nágá,	*The-lok.*
	Abor Miri,	*A-ke-ko.*
	Sibságar Miri,	*A-kunge.*
	Deoria Chutia,	*Dug-uchu.*
	Singpho,	*Kru.*
Arrakan & Burmah.	Burman (*written*),	*Khyok.*
	Burman (*spoken*),	*Khyauk.*
	Khyeng v. Shou,	*Sauk.*
	Kámi,	*Ta-u.*
	Kúmi,	*Ta-ru.*
	Mrú v. Toung,	*Ta-ru.*
	Sák,	*Khyauk.*
Siam & Tenasserim.	Talain v. Mon,	*Ka-roung.*
	Sgau-karen,	*Khú.*
	Pwo-karen,	*Khu.*
	Toungh-thu,	*Ther.*
	Shán,	*Hoht* (*hok ?*).
	Annamitic,	*Sau.*
	Siamese,	*Hok.*
	Ahom,	*Ruk.*
	Khámti,	*Hok.*
	Laos,	*Hok* (*hoht ?*).
Central India.	Ho (Kol),	*Turúia.*
	Kol (Singhbhum),	*Tu-ria.*
	Santáli,	*Tu-ru-i.*
	Bhúmij,	*Tu-ru-ya.*
	Uráon,	*Se-gotan.*
	Mundala,	*Tu-ria.*
	Rájmahali,	*Chah.*
	Goṇḍi,	*Sárong, sárug.*
	Gayeti,	*Sárung.*
	Rutluk,	*Sárug.*
	Naikude,	*Saha* (*sáha ?*).
	Kolami,	*A'r.*
	Mádi,	*Aru, sárum, sáru, hárum.*
	Mádia,	*Harug.*
	Kuri,	*Tu-rei-ku.*
	Keikádi,	*A'r.*
	Khoṇḍ,	*So.*
	Sávara,	*Kudru.*
	Gadaba,	*A'ru.*
	Yerukala,	*A'ru.*
	Chentsu,	*Chhe.*
Southern India.	Tamiḷ, anc.,	*Caret.*
	Tamiḷ, mod.,	*A'ṟu.*
	Malayáḷma, anc.,	*Caret.*
	Malayáḷma, mod.,	*A'ṟa.*
	Telugu,	*A'ru.*
	Karṇáṭaka, anc.,	*Caret.*
	Karṇáṭaka, mod.,	*A'ru.*
	Tuḷuva,	*Aji* (*áji ?*).
	Kurgi,	*A'ru.*
	Toḍuva, } Toḍa, }	*Or.*
		A'r.
	Kóta,	*A're.*
	Baḍaga,	*A'ru.*
	Kuṟumba,	*A'ru.*
	Iruḷa,	*A'ru.*
	Malabar,	*A'ru.*
	Sinhalese,	*Hayai.*

	Types.	
Inflecting.	SANSKRIT,	*Saptan.*
	ARABIC,	*Sabaat.*
Compounding.	BASK,	*Zazpi.*
	FINNIC,	*Seitsemän.*
	MAGYAR,	*Heb.*
	TURKISH,	*Yedi.*
	CIRCASSIAN,	*Dley.*
	GEORGIAN,	*Shwidi, giuht-ku.**
	MONGOLIAN,	*Dologhan, labet',† seiba,‡*
	MANTSHU,	*Nadan, szi-gae.** [*nad-un,*§
	JAVANESE, Ngoko,	*Pitu.* *dgiur.*‖
	JAVANESE, Krama,	*Pitu.*
	MALAY,	*Tújuh.*
Isolating.	CHINESE, Nankin,	*Ts'ih.*
	CHINESE, Pekin,	*Ch'i.*
	CHINESE, Canton,	*Ts'at.*
	CHINESE, Shanghai,	*Ch'ih.*
	AMOY, Colloquial,	*Ch'it.*
	JAPANESE,	*Nanats', nana, schi-chi.*
	Brahuí,	*Haft.*
Chinese Frontier & Tibet.	Gyámi,	*Chhi, chhi-ku.*
	Gyárung,	*Kush-nes.*
	Tákpa,	*Nis.*
	Mányak,	*Skwi-bi.*
	Thochú,	*Stáre.*
	Sokpa,	*Tolo.*
	Horpa,	*Zne.*
	Tibetan (*written*),	*Bdun.*
	Tibetan (*spoken*),	*Dun.*
Nepal (east to west).	Serpa,	*Dyun.*
	Súnwár,	*Cha-ni.*
	Gúrung,	*Nis.*
	Múrmi,	*Nis.*
	Magar,	*Caret.*
	Tháksya,	*Gnes.*
	Pákhya,	*Sát.*
	Newár,	*Nhe.*
	Limbu,	*Nush.*
Kiranti Group (East Nepal).	Kiránti,	*Bhagya.*
	Rodong,	*Rüikara.*
	Rúngchenbung,	*Bhangya.*
	Chhingtángya,	*Caret.*
	Náchhereng,	*Caret.*
	Wáling,	*Caret.*
	Yákha,	*Nuchi.*
	Chourásya,	*Caret.*
	Kulungya,	*Nuchi.*
	Thulungya,	*Ser, seren, serle.*
	Báhingya,	*Chani.*
	Lohorong,	*Nuchi.*
	Lambichhong,	*Caret.*
	Bálálí,	*Nuji.*
	Sáng-páng,	*Nu-kabo.*
	Dúmi,	*Re.*
	Kháling,	*Tar.*
	Dungmáli,	*Caret.*
Broken Tribes of Nepal.	Dárhi,	*Sát.*
	Denwár,	*Sát.*
	Pahri,	*Nhe, nhengu.*
	Chepáng,	*Chana-zho, chana-zyo.*
	Bhrámu,	*Caret.*
	Váyu,	*Caret.*
	Kuswar,	*Sát.*
	Kusunda,	*Caret.*
	Tháru,	*Sat.*
	Lepcha (Sikkim),	*Ka-kyot.*
	Bhúṭáni v. Lhopa,	*Dun.*
N.-E. Bengal.	Bodo,	*Man-sini.*
	Dhimál,	*Nhi-long.*
	Koch,	*Sát.*
	Garo,	*Si-ning.*
	Káchári,	*Man-shini, mun-shini.*
Eastern Frontier of Bengal.	Munipuri,	*Taret.*
	Mithán Nágá,	*A'-nath.*
	Tablung Nágá,	*Nith.*
	Khári Nágá,	*Ta-ni.*
	Angámi Nágá,	*The-ne.*
	Námsáng Nágá,	*I-ngit.*
	Nowgong Nágá,	*Ta-net.*
	Tengsa Nágá,	*Tha-nyet.*
	Abor Miri,	*Ku-nit-ko.*
	Sibságar Miri,	*Ku-nide.*
	Deoria Chutia,	*Dug-uchi (?).*
	Singpho,	*Si-nith.*
Arrakan & Burmah.	Burman (*written*),	*Khwan-nhach.*
	Burman (*spoken*),	*Khun-nith.*
	Khyeng v. Shou,	*S'he.*
	Kámi,	*Sa-ri.*
	Kúmi,	*Sa-ru.*
	Mrú v. Toung,	*Ra-nhit.*
	Sák,	*Tha-ni.*
Siam & Tenasserim.	Talain v. Mon,	*Kha-pau.*
	Sgau-karen,	*Nwi.*
	Pwo-karen,	*Nwaï.*
	Toungh-thu,	*Nwot.*
	Shán,	*T'sit.*
	Annamitic,	*Bay.*
	Siamese,	*T'sit, chet.*
	Ahom,	*T'sit, chet.*
	Khámti,	*T'set.*
	Laos,	*T'set.*
Central India.	Ho (Kol),	*A'ïa.*
	Kol (Singhbhum),	*Iyá.*
	Santáli,	*E-á-e, i-air.*
	Bhúmij,	*Sáth.*
	Uráon,	*Sát-gotang.*
	Mundala,	*Sáth.*
	Rájmahali,	*Sáth.*
	Goṇḍi,	*Yeru, yetu, yedung.*
	Gayeti,	*Yerung.*
	Rutluk,	*Erug.*
	Naikude,	*Caret.*
	Kolami,	*Yed.*
	Mádi,	*Sátte, yedu, eirum.*
	Mádia,	*Sáth.*
	Kuri,	*Yeiku.*
	Keikádi,	*Yal.*
	Khoṇḍ,	*Sáta.*
	Sávara,	*Gulji.*
	Gadaba,	*Yeḍu.*
	Yerukala,	*Yeṛu, vogu.*
	Chentsu,	*Sát.*
Southern India.	Tamiḷ, anc.,	*Ezh.*
	Tamiḷ, mod.,	*Ezhu.*
	Malayáḷma, anc.,	*Caret.*
	Malayáḷma, mod.,	*Ezha.*
	Telugu,	*Yedu.*
	Karṇáṭaka, anc.,	*Caret.*
	Karṇáṭaka, mod.,	*Yeḷu.*
	Tuḷuva,	*Eḷ.*
	Kurgi,	*Eḷu.*
	Toḍuva, }	*El.*
	Toḍa, }	*El.*
	Kóta,	*Yeye.*
	Baḍaga,	*Yellu.*
	Kuṛumba,	*Yellu.*
	Iruḷa,	*Elu.*
	Malabar,	*Elu.*
	Sinhalese,	*Hatai.*

Group	Language	Eight
Types.		
Inflecting.	SANSKRIT,	*Ashtan.*
	ARABIC,	*Thamániat.*
Compounding.	BASK,	*Zortzi.*
	FINNIC,	*Kahdeksăn.*
	MAGYAR,	*Nyolc, nioltz.**
	TURKISH,	*Sekiz.*
	CIRCASSIAN,	*Yi.*
	GEORGIAN,	*Rua, mockbeg-gu.**
	MONGOLIAN,	*Nemen, nilla,† siterčta,‡*
	MANTSHU,	*Dehakon, ba-ya.** [gig-in,§ diár.‖
	JAVANESE, Ngoko,	*Wolu.*
	JAVANESE, Krama,	*Wolu.*
	MALAY,	*Delápan.*
Isolating.	CHINESE, Nankin,	*Păh.*
	CHINESE, Pekin,	*Pa.*
	CHINESE, Canton,	*Pát.*
	CHINESE, Shanghai,	*Peh.*
	AMOY, Colloquial,	*Poeh.*
	JAPANESE,	*Yats', yatsu, ha-chi.*
	Brahuí,	*Hasht.*
Chinese Frontier & Tibet.	Gyámi,	*Pa, ha-ku.*
	Gyárung,	*Oryet.*
	Tákpa,	*Gyet.*
	Mányak,	*Zibi.*
	Thochú,	*Khrare.*
	Sokpa,	*Nema.*
	Horpa,	*Rhi-ćé.*
	Tibetan (*written*),	*Brgyad, gyad, dochad.*
	Tibetan (*spoken*),	*Gye.*
Nepal (east to west).	Serpa,	*Gye.*
	Súnwár,	*Zoh.*
	Gúrung,	*Pre, re.*
	Múrmi,	*Pre.*
	Magar,	*Caret.*
	Tháksya,	*Bhre.*
	Pákhya,	*A'th.*
	Newár,	*Chyá.*
	Limbu,	*Yetsh.*
Kiranti Group (East Nepal).	Kiránti,	*Reya.*
	Rodong,	*Bhok-kara.*
	Rúngchenbung,	*Reya.*
	Chhingtángya,	*Caret.*
	Náchhereng,	*Caret.*
	Wáling,	*Caret.*
	Yákha,	*Yechi.*
	Chourásya,	*Caret.*
	Kulungya,	*Rechi.*
	Thulungya,	*Yen, yet, yetle.*
	Báhingya,	*Yá.*
	Lohorong,	*Yechi.*
	Lambichhong,	*Caret.*
	Báláli,	*Yechi.*
	Sáng-páng,	*Re-kabo.*
	Dúmi,	*Ri.*
	Kháling,	*Rin.*
	Dungmáli,	*Caret.*
Broken Tribes of Nepal.	Dárhi,	*A'th.*
	Denwár,	*A'th.*
	Pahri,	*Chya, chyang-gu.*
	Chepáng,	*Prap-zho, prap-zyo.*
	Bhrámu,	*Caret.*
	Váyu,	*Caret.*
	Kuswar,	*A'th.*
	Kusunda,	*Caret.*
	Tháru,	*A'th.*
	Lepcha (Sikkim),	*Ka-ku.*
	Bhútáni v. Lhopa,	*Gye.*
N.-E. Bengal.	Bodo,	*Man-jot (?).*
	Dhimál,	*Yelong.*
	Kocch,	*A'th.*
	Garo,	*Chet.*
	Káchári,	*Man-jot, mun-jot.*
Eastern Frontier of Bengal.	Munipuri,	*Nipál.*
	Míthán Nágá,	*A'-chet.*
	Tablung Nágá,	*Thath.*
	Khári Nágá,	*Sa-chet.*
	Angámi Nágá,	*The-tha.*
	Námsáng Nágá,	*I-sat.*
	Nowgong Nágá,	*Te.*
	Tengsa Nágá,	*The-sep.*
	Abor Miri,	*Pu-nit-ko.*
	Sibságar Miri,	*Pin-ye.*
	Deoria Chutia,	*Dug-uche.*
	Singpho,	*Mat-sat.*
Arrakan & Burmah.	Burman (*written*),	*Rhach.*
	Burman (*spoken*),	*Shyet, shyit.*
	Khyeng v. Shou,	*Sat.*
	Kámi,	*Kayá.*
	Kúmi,	*Tayá.*
	Mrú v. Toung,	*Riyát.*
	Sák,	*Atseit.*
Siam & Tenasserim.	Talain v. Mon,	*Khasan.*
	Sgau-karen,	*Kho.*
	Pwo-karen,	*Kho.*
	Toungh-thu,	*That.*
	Shán,	*Tet.*
	Annamitic,	*Tam.*
	Siamese,	*Pet, tet.*
	Ahom,	*Pet.*
	Khámti,	*Pet.*
	Laos,	*Pet.*
Central India.	Ho (Kol),	*I'rilia.*
	Kol (Singhbhum),	*Irlia.*
	Santáli,	*Iral.*
	Bhúmij,	*A'th.*
	Uráon,	*A'te.*
	Mundala,	*A'th.*
	Rájmahali,	*A'th.*
	Goṇḍi,	*Anamur, yermud.*
	Gayeti,	*Yermud.*
	Rutluk,	*Armur.*
	Naikude,	*Caret.*
	Kolami,	*A'th.*
	Mádi,	*A'tte, atu, ermadi.*
	Mádia,	*At.*
	Kuri,	*Ilarku, ilariya.*
	Keikádi,	*Yet.*
	Khoṇḍ,	*A'ta (aṭa ?).*
	Sávara,	*Tamuji.*
	Gadaba,	*Yenimide.*
	Yerukala,	*Yeṭṭu, vaṭṭu.*
	Chentsu,	*A'ṭh.*
Southern India.	Tamiḷ, anc.,	*Caret.*
	Tamiḷ, mod.,	*Eṭṭu.*
	Malayáḷma, anc.,	*Caret.*
	Malayáḷma, mod.,	*Eṭṭa.*
	Telugu,	*Enimidi.*
	Karṇáṭaka, anc.,	*Caret.*
	Karṇáṭaka, mod.,	*Yeṇṭu.*
	Tuḷuva,	*Ename.*
	Kurgi,	*Eṭṭu.*
	Toḍuva, }	*Eṭṭ.*
	Toḍa, }	*Eṭṭ.*
	Kóta,	*Yeṭṭe.*
	Baḍaga,	*Yeṭṭu.*
	Kuṟumba,	*Yeṭṭu.*
	Iruḷa,	*Yeṭṭu.*
	Malabar,	*Ettu.*
	Sinhalese,	*Aṭai.*

Group	*Types.*		
Inflecting.	SANSKRIT,	*Navan.*	
	ARABIC,	*Tessaat.*	
Compounding.	BASK,	*Bederatzi, bedratzi.*	
	FINNIC,	*Yhdeksän.*	
	MAGYAR,	*Kilenc.*	
	TURKISH,	*Dokuz.*	
	CIRCASSIAN,	*Bughu.*	
	GEORGIAN,	*Tskhra, utsgu.**	
	MONGOLIAN,	*Yisun, killien,†*	*nayma-*
	MANTSHU,	*Ouyoun, dshugae.**	*tomma.‡*
	JAVANESE, Ngoko,	*Sängä.*	*ziapkun,§*
	JAVANESE, Krama,	*Sängä.*	*dgiur-*
	MALAY,	*Sambilan.*	*diar.‖*
Isolating.	CHINESE, Nankin,	*Kiu.*	
	CHINESE, Pekin,	*Chiu.*	
	CHINESE, Canton,	*Kau.*	
	CHINESE, Shanghai,	*Kiu.*	
	AMOY, Colloquial,	*Káu.*	
	JAPANESE,	*Ku, kokono, kokonots'.*	
	Brahuí,	*Nuh.*	
Chinese Frontier & Tibet.	Gyámi,	*Chyu, chyuku.*	
	Gyárung,	*Kung-gu.*	
	Tákpa,	*Du-gu.*	
	Mányak,	*Gu-bi.*	
	Thochú,	*Rgu-re.*	
	Sokpa,	*Yeso.*	
	Horpa,	*Go.*	
	Tibetan (*written*),	Dgu.	
	Tibetan (*spoken*),	*Guh.*	
Nepal (east to west).	Serpa,	*Guh.*	
	Súnwár,	*Guh.*	
	Gúrung,	*Kuh.*	
	Múrmi,	*Kuh.*	
	Magar,	*Caret.*	
	Tháksya,	*Ku.*	
	Pákhya,	*Nau.*	
	Newár,	*Guṇ.*	
	Limbu,	*Phangsh.*	
Kiránti Group (East Nepal).	Kiránti,	*Phang-ya.*	
	Rodong,	*Kipura.*	
	Rúngchenbung,	*Phang-ya, wang-pop.*	
	Chhingtángya,	*Caret.*	
	Náchhereng,	*Caret.*	
	Wáling,	*Caret.*	
	Yákha,	*Phang-chi.*	
	Chourásya,	*Caret.*	
	Kulungya,	*Bong-chi.*	
	Thulungya,	*Gu, gu-le.*	
	Báhingya,	*Ghu.*	
	Lohorong,	*Báng-chi.*	
	Lambichhong,	*Caret.*	
	Bálálí,	*Báng-ji.*	
	Sáng-páng,	*Caret.*	
	Dúmi,	*Caret.*	
	Kháling,	*Ghu.*	
	Dungmáli,	*Caret.*	
Broken Tribes of Nepal.	Dárhi,	*No-ú.*	
	Denwár,	*No-ú.*	
	Pahri,	*Gun, gun-gu.*	
	Chepáng,	*Taku-zho, taku-zyo.*	
	Bhrámu,	*Caret.*	
	Váyu,	*Caret.*	
	Kuswar,	*No-ú.*	
	Kusunda,	*Caret.*	
	Tháru,	*Nau.*	
	Lepcha (Sikkim),	*Ka-kyot.*	
	Bhúṭáni v. Lhopa,	*Gu.*	

N.-E. Bengal.	Bodo,	*Man-shi-ko (?).*
	Dhimál,	*Kuha-long.*
	Kocch,	*Nau.*
	Garo,	*Ju.*
	Káchári,	*Man-shi-ko, mun-shi-ko.*
Eastern Frontier of Bengal.	Munipuri,	*Mápal.*
	Míthán Nágá,	*A'-ku.*
	Tablung Nágá,	*Thu.*
	Khári Nágá,	*Te-ku.*
	Angámi Nágá,	*Tha-ku.*
	Námsáng Nágá,	*I-khu.*
	Nowgong Nágá,	*Ta-ku.*
	Tengsa Nágá,	*Tha-ku.*
	Abor Miri,	*Ko-nang-ko.*
	Sibságar Miri,	*Ko-nange.*
	Deoria Chutia,	*Dugu-chu-ba.*
	Singpho,	*Tse-khu.*
Arrakan & Burmah.	Burman (*written*),	*Ko.*
	Burman (*spoken*),	*Ko.*
	Khyeng v. Shou,	*Ko.*
	Kámi,	*Ta-ko.*
	Kúmi,	*Ta-kau.*
	Mrú v. Toung,	*Ta-ku.*
	Sák,	*Ta-fu.*
Siam & Tenasserim.	Talain v. Mon,	*Kha-si.*
	Sgau-karen,	*Kwi, hkwi.*
	Pwo-karen,	*Kwi.*
	Toungh-thu,	*Kut.*
	Shán,	*Kaut.*
	Annamitic,	*Kyin.*
	Siamese,	*Kau, kaut.*
	Ahom,	*Kau.*
	Khámti,	*Kau.*
	Laos,	*Kau.*
Central India.	Ho (Kol),	*Arreá.*
	Kol (Singhbhum),	*A'reá.*
	Santáli,	*A're.*
	Bhúmij,	*Nau.*
	Uráon,	*No-gotang.*
	Mundala,	*Noko.*
	Rájmahali,	*Nau.*
	Goṇḍi,	*No, nau.*
	Gayeti,	*Nau.*
	Rutluk,	*Caret.*
	Naikude,	*Caret.*
	Kolami,	*Nau.*
	Mádi,	*Nawe, ermu, tumadi.*
	Mádia,	*Nau.*
	Kuri,	*Areiku.*
	Keikádi,	*Wamberu.*
	Khoṇḍ,	*Nogaṭṭá.*
	Sávara,	*Tinji.*
	Gadaba,	*Tommidi.*
	Yerukala,	*Ombadu.*
	Chentsu,	*Lo, totá.*
Southern India.	Tamiḷ, anc.,	*Onbakadu.*
	Tamiḷ, mod.,	*Onbadu.*
	Malayáḷma, anc.,	*Caret.*
	Malayáḷma, mod.,	*Ombata.*
	Telugu,	*Tommidi.*
	Karṇáṭaka, anc.,	*Caret.*
	Karṇáṭaka, mod.,	*Ombhattu.*
	Tuḷuva,	*Orambo.*
	Kurgi,	*Oyimbadu.*
	Toḍuva, }	*Onbod.*
	Toḍa, }	*Anpath.*
	Kóta,	*Vorupáde.*
	Baḍaga,	*Vombattu.*
	Kuṛumba,	*Vombattu.*
	Iruḷa,	*Vombadu.*
	Malabar,	*Onpathu.*
	Sinhalese,	*Nawanama.*

	Types.	
Inflecting.	SANSKRIT,	*Daşan.*
	ARABIC,	*Aasherat.*
Compounding.	BASK,	*Amar.*
	FINNIC,	*Kymmenen.*
	MAGYAR,	*Tiz.*
	TURKISH,	*On.*
	CIRCASSIAN,	*Tsey.*
	GEORGIAN,	*Aţhi, entzelgu.**
	MONGOLIAN,	*Arban, yang,*† *bi,*‡ *ziun,*§
	MANTSHU,	*Dchouan, schi.** [*entzelgu.*‖
	JAVANESE, Ngoko,	*Sapúluh.*
	JAVANESE, Krama,	*Sadăsă.*
	MALAY,	*Púluh, sapúluh.*
Isolating.	CHINESE, Nankin,	*Shih.*
	CHINESE, Pekin,	*Shih.*
	CHINESE, Canton,	*Shap.*
	CHINESE, Shanghai,	*Seh.*
	AMOY, Colloquial,	*Chấp.*
	JAPANESE,	*Djiu, to, tsuds'.*
	Brahuí,	*Dah.*
Chinese Frontier & Tibet.	Gyámi,	*Ish-sa.*
	Gyárung,	*Sih.*
	Tákpa,	*Pchi.*
	Mányak,	*Che-chi-bi.*
	Thochú,	*Hadure.*
	Sokpa,	*A'rba.*
	Horpa,	*Sga.*
	Tibetan (*written*),	*Bchu, chu-thamba.*
	Tibetan (*spoken*),	*Chuh, chu-thamba.*
Nepal (east to west).	Serpa,	*Chuh.*
	Súnwár,	*Sa-shi.*
	Gúrung,	*Chuh.*
	Múrmi,	*Chi-wai.*
	Magar,	*Caret.*
	Tháksya,	*Chyu.*
	Pákhya,	*Das.*
	Newár,	*Sánho.*
	Limbu,	*Gip, bong, thi-bong.*
Kiranti Group (East Nepal).	Kiránti,	*Kip.*
	Rodong,	*Lip-ura.*
	Rúngchenbung,	*Kip, kip-u, dheuk-ya.*
	Chhingtángya,	*Caret.*
	Náchhereng,	*Caret.*
	Wáling,	*Caret.*
	Yákha,	*I-bong, ik-bong.*
	Chourásya,	*Caret.*
	Kulungya,	*Uk-bong.*
	Thulungya,	*Kong-dyum, kwong-dyum.*
	Báhingya,	*Kol-dyum, kwad-dyum.*
	Lohorong,	*Ip-pong.*
	Lambichhong,	*Íp-pong.*
	Báláli,	*Ip-pong.*
	Sáng-páng,	*Caret.*
	Dúmi,	*Caret.*
	Kháling,	*Tadham.*
	Dungmáli,	*Caret.*
Broken Tribes of Nepal.	Dárhi,	*Das.*
	Denwár,	*Das.*
	Pahri,	*Gi, ging-gu.*
	Chepáng,	*Gyib-zho, gyib-zyo.*
	Bhrámu,	*Caret.*
	Váyu,	*Nayung-got'-khulup, i.e.* two
	Kuswar,	*Das.* [whole hands.
	Kusunda,	*Caret.*
	Tháru,	*Das.*
	Lepcha (Sikkim),	*Kati.*
	Bhúţáni v. Lhopa,	*Cha-tham.*

N.-E. Bengal.	Bodo,	*Man-ji.*
	Dhimál,	*Te-long.*
	Kocch,	*Das.*
	Garo,	*Chi.*
	Káchári,	*Man-ji, mun-ji.*
Eastern Frontier of Bengal.	Munipuri,	*Tará.*
	Míthán Nágá,	*Ban.*
	Tablung Nágá,	*Pan.*
	Khári Nágá,	*Ta-rah.*
	Angámi Nágá,	*Kurr.*
	Námsáng Nágá,	*I-chi.*
	Nowgong Nágá,	*Iarr.*
	Tengsa Nágá,	*The-lu.*
	Abor Miri,	*U-ing-ko.*
	Sibságar Miri,	*U-ying-e.*
	Deoria Chutia,	*Dugu-chuba-dugshe.*
	Singpho,	*Si.*
Arrakan & Burmah.	Burman (*written*),	*Chhe.*
	Burman (*spoken*),	*S'he, ta-s'se, shai.*
	Khyeng v. Shou,	*Há.*
	Kámi,	*Há-suh.*
	Kúmi,	*Hau.*
	Mrú v. Toung,	*Há.*
	Sák,	*Si-su.*
Siam & Tenasserim.	Talain v. Mon,	*T'sau.*
	Sgau-karen,	*Tsi, ta-tsi.*
	Pwo-karen,	*L'tsi.*
	Toungh-thu,	*Tah-si.*
	Shán,	*T'seit.*
	Annamitic,	*Muŏi.*
	Siamese,	*Sip, htseit.*
	Ahom,	*Sip.*
	Khámti,	*Sip.*
	Laos,	*Sip.*
Central India.	Ho (Kol),	*Gel.*
	Kol (Singhbhum),	*Geleá.*
	Santáli,	*Gela.*
	Bhúmij,	*Das.*
	Uráon,	*Das-gotang.*
	Mundala,	*Das-go.*
	Rájmahali,	*Das.*
	Goṇḍi,	*Pada, daha.*
	Gayeti,	*Daha.*
	Rutluk,	*Pad.*
	Naikude,	*Caret.*
	Kolami,	*Daha.*
	Máḍi,	*Daha, dase, pade.*
	Mádia,	*Das.*
	Kuri,	*Gelku.*
	Keikádi,	*Patu.*
	Khoṇḍ,	*Doso.*
	Sávara,	*Gal-iji* (*gel-iji* ?).
	Gadaba,	*Padi.*
	Yerukala,	*Pattu, pottu.*
	Chentsu,	*Das.*
Southern India.	Tamiḷ, anc.,	*Orupakadu.*
	Tamiḷ, mod.,	*Pattu.*
	Malayáḷma, anc.,	*Caret.*
	Malayáḷma, mod.,	*Patta.*
	Telugu,	*Padi.*
	Karṇáṭaka, anc.,	*Pattu.*
	Karṇáṭaka, mod.,	*Hattu.*
	Tuḷuva,	*Pattu.*
	Kurgi,	*Pattu.*
	Toḍuva, }	*Pot.*
	Toḍa, }	*Path.*
	Kóta,	*Patte.*
	Baḍaga,	*Hattu.*
	Kuṛumba,	*Hattu.*
	Iruḷa,	*Pattu.*
	Malabar,	*Pathu.*
	Sinhalese,	*Dahadasa.*

	Types.	
Inflecting.	SANSKṚIT,	*Vinṣati.*
	ARABIC,	*Aasheroun.*
Compounding.	BASK,	*Ogei, ogoi.*
	FINNIC,	*Kaksikymmendă.*
	MAGYAR,	*Husz.*
	TURKISH,	*Yirmi, yighirmi.*
	CIRCASSIAN,	*Ot-shey.*
	GEORGIAN,	*Ot-si, ots, kobbeggu.**
	MONGOLIAN,	*Khorin, sitti-bi.‡*
	MANTSHU,	*Orin, ul-sehi.**
	JAVANESE, Ngoko,	*Rongpúluh likur.*
	JAVANESE, Krama,	*Kalihdăsă likur.*
	MALAY,	*Dúapúluh.*
Isolating.	CHINESE, Nankin,	*Woh-shĭh, ar-shi.*
	CHINESE, Pekin,	*Woh-shih.*
	CHINESE, Canton,	*I-shap.*
	CHINESE, Shanghai,	*Nī-e.*
	AMOY, Colloquial,	*Ji-cháp.*
	JAPANESE,	*Nī-djiu, fatadsi.*
	Brahuí.	*Bist.*
Chinese Frontier & Tibet.	Gyámi,	*Air-sa.*
	Gyárung,	*Kinis-si.*
	Tákpa,	*Khali.*
	Mányak,	*Ná-chábi.*
	Thochú,	*Gnina-so.*
	Sokpa,	*Khore.*
	Horpa,	*Na-ska.*
	Tibetan (*written*),	*Nyi-chuthamba.*
	Tibetan (*spoken*),	*Nyi-chu.*
Nepal (east to west).	Serpa,	*Nyi-shu.*
	Súnwár,	*Khal-ka.*
	Gúrung,	*Kuti.*
	Múrmi,	*Nyi-shu.*
	Magar,	*Caret.*
	Tháksya,	*Gui-yu.*
	Pákhya,	*Bis.*
	Newár,	*Ni-c, sang-sanho.*
	Limbu,	*Ni-bong.*
Kiranti Group (East Nepal).	Kiránti,	*Caret.*
	Rodong,	*Caret.*
	Rúngchenbung,	*Caret.*
	Chhingtángya,	*Caret.*
	Náchhereng,	*Caret.*
	Wáling,	*Caret.*
	Yákha,	*Hi-bong.*
	Chourásya,	*Caret.*
	Kulungya,	*Caret.*
	Thulungya,	*Kong-usang, kwong-usang.*
	Báhingya,	*A'sim, kwong-ásing.*
	Lohorong,	*Nī-bong.*
	Lambichhong,	*Caret.*
	Báláli,	*Caret.*
	Sáng-páng,	*Caret.*
	Dúmi,	*Caret.*
	Kháling,	*Khál, khál-tau, tau-khál.*
	Dungmáli,	*Caret.*
Broken Tribes of Nepal.	Dárhi,	*Bis.*
	Denwár,	*Bis.*
	Pahri,	*Nī.*
	Chepáng,	*Caret.*
	Bhrámu,	*Caret.*
	Váyu,	*Cholok-le-got'-kulup, i.e.* [fingers and toes.
	Kuswar,	*Bis.*
	Kusunda,	*Caret.*
	Tháru,	*Bis.*
	Lepcha (Sikkim),	*Kha-kát.*
	Bhúṭáni v. Lhopa,	*Nyi-sho, khe-chik.*
N.-E. Bengal.	Bodo,	*Chokai-ba, thai-khon, bisha-* [*che.*
	Dhimál,	*Elong-bisha.*
	Kocch,	*Bis.*
	Garo,	*Rung-sha.*
	Káchári,	*Caret.*
Eastern Frontier of Bengal.	Munipuri,	*Kul.*
	Míthán Nágá,	*Chá.*
	Tablung Nágá,	*Caret.*
	Khári Nágá,	*Ma-khi.*
	Angámi Nágá,	*Ma-ku.*
	Námsáng Nágá,	*Ruak-gni.*
	Nowgong Nágá,	*Mat-su.*
	Tengsa Nágá,	*Ma-chi.*
	Abor Miri,	*Ir-ling-ko.*
	Sibságar Miri,	*Uying-anyiko.*
	Deoria Chutia,	*Caret.*
	Singpho,	*Khún.*
Arrakan & Burmah.	Burman (*written*),	*Nhach-chhe.*
	Burman (*spoken*),	*Nhit-t'se, nhit-shai.*
	Khyeng v. Shou,	*Kur.*
	Kámi,	*Ku-suh.*
	Kúmi,	*A-pum-re.*
	Mrú v. Toung,	*Pi-ra-mi.*
	Sák,	*Hun.*
Siam & Tenasserim.	Talain v. Mon,	*Pa-sau.*
	Sgau-karen,	*Ki-si, khi-tsi.*
	Pwo-karen,	*Ni-tsi.*
	Toungh-thu,	*He.*
	Shán,	*Htsoung.*
	Annamitic,	*Hai-muöi.*
	Siamese,	*Ye-sip, ya-t'sit.*
	Ahom,	*Sau.*
	Khámti,	*Sau.*
	Láos,	*Sau-nung.*
Central India.	Ho (Kol),	*Hissi.*
	Kol (Singhbhum),	*Hissi.*
	Santáli,	*Mih-issi.*
	Bhúmij,	*Bis.*
	Uráon,	*Bis.*
	Mundala,	*Bis.*
	Rájmahali,	*Bis.*
	Goṇḍi,	*Bisa.*
	Gayeti,	*Visạ.*
	Rutluk,	*Caret.*
	Naikude,	*Caret.*
	Kolami,	*Vis.*
	Máḍi,	*Bis, visa, irwa.*
	Mádia,	*Bis.*
	Kuri,	*Bis.*
	Keikádi,	*Vis.*
	Khoṇḍ,	*Koḍe.*
	Sávara,	*Bo-koḍi.*
	Gadaba,	*Yiruvai.*
	Yerukala,	*Yiruvadu, yirapottu.*
	Chentsu,	*Bis, panch-ganda.*
Southern India.	Tamiḷ, anc.,	*Irupakuda.*
	Tamiḷ, mod.,	*Irubadu.*
	Malayáḷma, anc.,	*Caret.*
	Malayáḷma, mod.,	*Irupata.*
	Telugu,	*Iruvai.*
	Karṇáṭaka, anc.,	*Caret.*
	Karṇáṭaka, mod.,	*Ippattu.*
	Tuḷuva,	*Irvo.*
	Kurgi,	*Iruvadu.*
	Toḍuva, }	*Irvod.*
	Toḍa, }	*Evoth.*
	Kóta,	*Irváde.*
	Baḍaga,	*Ibbatta.*
	Kuṛumba,	*Ibbattu.*
	Iruḷa,	*Irvadu.*
	Malabar,	*Irupathu.*
	Sinhalese,	*Wisi.*

	Types.	
Inflecting.	SANSKRIT, .	*Triṅṣat.*
	ARABIC, . .	*Thaláthoun.*
Compounding.	BASK, ...	*Ogeit-amar.*
	FINNIC, ...	*Kolmekymmenda.*
	MAGYAR, ...	*Harminc.*
	TURKISH, ...	*Otuz.*
	CIRCASSIAN, ...	*Otsheyrey, hsirey.*
	GEORGIAN, ...	*Otsda-aṭhi, lowergu.**
	MONGOLIAN, ...	*Khuchin, nagor-bi.‡*
	MANTSHU, . . .	*Gósin, sang-schi.**
	JAVANESE, Ngoko, . .	*Telungpúluh.*
	JAVANESE, Krama, . .	*Tigangdásd.*
	MALAV, ...	*Tigapúluh.*
Isolating.	CHINESE, Nankin, . .	*San-shíh.*
	CHINESE, Pekin, . .	*San-shih.*
	CHINESE, Canton, . .	*Sám-shap.*
	CHINESE, Shanghai, . .	*San-sch.*
	AMOV, Colloquial, . .	*San-cháp.*
	JAPANESE, ...	*San-djiu, misodsi.*
Chinese Frontier & Tibet.	Brahui, ...	*Sí.*
	Gyámi, ...	*Sán-sa.*
	Gyárung, ...	*Ka-sam-si.*
	Tákpa, ...	*Caret.*
	Mányak, ...	*Sá-chá-bi.*
	Thochú, ...	*Kshyá-so.*
	Sokpa, ...	*Kochhen.*
	Horpa, ...	*Sús-ka.*
	Tibetan (*written*), .	*Súm-chú-thamba.*
	Tibetan (*spoken*), . .	*Súm-chú.*
Népsl (east to west).	Serpa, ...	*Súm-chú.*
	Súnwár, ...	*Sa-si-sán.*
	Gúrung, ...	*Caret.*
	Múrmi, ...	*Bokal-che-shú.*
	Magar, ...	*Caret.*
	Tháksya, ...	*Som-bu.*
	Pákhya, ...	*Tis.*
	Newár, ...	*Ni-sánho, súye.*
	Limbu, ...	*Sum-bong.*
Kiranti Group (East Népal).	Kiránti, ...	*Caret.*
	Rodong, ...	*Caret.*
	Rúngchenbung, . .	*Caret.*
	Chhingtángya, . . .	*Caret.*
	Náchhereng, . . .	*Caret.*
	Wáling, ...	*Caret.*
	Yákha, ...	*Sum-bong.*
	Chourásya, ...	*Caret.*
	Kulungya, ...	*Caret.*
	Thulungya, ...	*Kwong-usang-kodyum.*
	Báhingya, ...	*Kwong-asing-kot-dyum.*
	Lohorong, ...	*Sum-bong.*
	Lambichhong, . . .	*Caret.*
	Kúláli, ...	*Caret.*
	Sáng-páng, ...	*Caret.*
	Dúmi, ...	*Caret.*
	Kháling, ...	*Taḍham-khál-tau.*
	Dungmáli, ...	*Caret.*
Broken Tribes of Népal.	Dárhi, ...	*Tis.*
	Denwár, ...	*Tis.*
	Pahri, ...	*Suṇ (saṇ ?).*
	Chepáng, ...	*Caret.*
	Bhrámu, ...	*Caret.*
	Váyu, ...	*Caret.*
	Kuswar, ...	*Tis.*
	Kusunda, ...	*Caret.*
	Tháru, ...	*Tis.*
	Lepcha (Sikkim), . .	*Kha-kát-sa-kati.*
	Bhúṭáni v. Lhopa, . .	*Khe-phedáni.*

N.-E. Bengal.	Bodo, ...	*Caret.*
	Dhimál, ...	*Caret.*
	Kocch, ...	*Tis.*
	Garo, ...	*Rung-sha-chi.*
	Káchári, ...	*Caret.*
Eastern Frontier of Bengal.	Munipuri, ...	*Kúnthra.*
	Míthán Nágá, . . .	*Caret.*
	Tablung Nágá, . . .	*Caret.*
	Khári Nágá, ...	*Sam-rá.*
	Angámi Nágá, . . .	*Surr.*
	Námsáng Nágá, . .	*Ruak-ram.*
	Nowgong Nágá, . .	*Caret.*
	Tengsa Nágá, . .	*Machi-li-thelu.*
	Abor Miri, ...	*Uing-aomko.*
	Sibságar Miri, . . .	*Uying-aumko.*
	Deoria Chutia, . . .	*Caret.*
	Singpho, ...	*Tum-si.*
Arakan & Burmah.	Burman (*written*), . .	*Sung-chhe.*
	Burman (*spoken*), . .	*Thong-t'se, thon-shai.*
	Khyeng v. Shou, . .	*Tun-gip.*
	Kámi, ...	*Ru-i-thun.*
	Kúmi, ...	*M'phá-i-re.*
	Mrú v. Toung, . . .	*Tsum-gaum.*
	Sák, ...	*Thon-si.*
Siam & Tenasserim.	Talain v. Mon, . . .	*Pe-tson.*
	Sgau-karen, ...	*Thu-tsi, theh-tsi.*
	Pwo-karen, ...	*Thung-tsi.*
	Toungh-thu, ...	*Thung.*
	Shán, ...	*Iltsan-htsiet.*
	Annamitic, ...	*Ba-muói.*
	Siamese, ...	*Sám-sip.*
	Ahom, ...	*Sam-sip.*
	Khámti, ...	*Sám-sip.*
	Laos, ...	*Sám-sip.*
Central India.	Ho (Kol), . . .	*Dosí.*
	Kol (Singhbhum), . .	*Hissigeleá.*
	Santáli, ...	*Hissi-gel.*
	Bhúmij, ...	*Moy-hissi-dasti.*
	Uráon, ...	*Dedh-kuḍí.*
	Mundala, ...	*Tis.*
	Rájmahali, ...	*Tis.*
	Goṇḍi, ...	*Tis, tisa.*
	Gayeti, ...	*Tisa.*
	Rutluk, ...	*Caret.*
	Naikude, ...	*Caret.*
	Kolami, ...	*Caret.*
	Mádi, ...	*Tis, dedh-visa.*
	Mádia, ...	*Deḍha-koḍi.*
	Kuri, ...	*Tis.*
	Keikádi, ...	*Cannot count above twenty.*
	Khoṇḍ, ...	*Tirisigoṭṭa.*
	Sávara, ...	*Bokoḍigaliji.*
	Gadaba, ...	*Muppai.*
	Yerukala, ...	*Muppadu.*
	Chentsu, ...	*Sát-gandá-doyicha.*
Southern India.	Tamil, anc., ...	*Mupakudu.*
	Tamiḷ, mod., ...	*Muppadu.*
	Malayáḷma, anc., . .	*Caret.*
	Malayáḷma, mod., . .	*Muppata.*
	Telugu, ...	*Muppai.*
	Karṇáṭaka, anc., . .	*Caret.*
	Karṇáṭaka, mod., . .	*Múvattu.*
	Tuḷuva, ...	*Muppo.*
	Kurgi, ...	*Nuppadu.*
	Toḍuva,}	*Mupped.*
	Toḍa, }	*Mubath.*
	Kóta, ...	*Muvatte.*
	Baḍaga, ...	*Muvattu.*
	Kurumba, ...	*Muvattu.*
	Irula, ...	*Mubbadu.*
	Malabar, ...	*Muppathu.*
	Sinhalese, ...	*Tihai, tis.*

Group	Types.	
Inflecting.	SANSKRIT,	*Chatuṡárinṡat.*
	ARABIC,	*Arbaaoun.*
Compounding.	BASK,	*Berrogei.*
	FINNIC,	*Neljánkymmenda.*
	MAGYAR,	*Negyven.*
	TURKISH,	*Keurk.*
	CIRCASSIAN,	*Ot-shitk.*
	GEORGIAN,	*Ormotsi, kokawu.**
	MONGOLIAN,	*Tuchin, tietta-bi.‡*
	MANTSHU,	*Dekhi, sig-schi.**
	JAVANESE, Ngoko,	*Pitangpúluh.*
	JAVANESE, Krama,	*Kawandăsă.*
	MALAY,	*Ampatpúluh.*
Isolating.	CHINESE, Nankin,	*Sze-shih.*
	CHINESE, Pekin,	*Sze-shih.*
	CHINESE, Canton,	*Sze-shap.*
	CHINESE, Shanghai,	*Sz'-seh.*
	AMOY, Colloquial,	*Si-cháp.*
	JAPANESE,	*Si-djiu, shi-jiu, yosodsi.*
	Brahuí,	*Chil.*
Chinese Frontier & Tibet.	Gyámi,	*Syú-sa.*
	Gyárung,	*Kaplis-si.*
	Tákpa,	*Caret.*
	Mányak,	*Zyi-zá-bi.*
	Thochú,	*Ghyi-so.*
	Sokpa,	*Teche.*
	Horpa,	*Les-ká.*
	Tibetan (*written*),	*Bzhib-chu, shi-chu-thamba.*
	Tibetan (*spoken*),	*Hip-chú.*
Nepal (east to west).	Serpa,	*Hip-chú.*
	Súnwár,	*Khák-ne-shi.*
	Gúrung,	*Caret.*
	Múrmi,	*Bokal-nhi.*
	Magar,	*Caret.*
	Tháksya,	*Blib-yu.*
	Pákhya,	*Chális.*
	Newár,	*Su-sánho, hi-ye.*
	Limbu,	*Li-gip.*
Kiranti Group (East Nepal).	Kiránti,	*Caret.*
	Rodong,	*Caret.*
	Rúngchenbung,	*Caret.*
	Chhingtángya,	*Caret.*
	Náchhereng,	*Caret.*
	Wáling,	*Caret.*
	Yákha,	*Li-git.*
	Chourásya,	*Caret.*
	Kulungya,	*Caret.*
	Thulungya,	*Naasang.*
	Báhingya,	*Ni-pachi.*
	Lohorong,	*Rik-pong.*
	Lambichhong,	*Caret.*
	Báláli,	*Caret.*
	Sáng-páng,	*Caret.*
	Dúmi,	*Caret.*
	Kháling,	*Khál-sákpo.*
	Dungmáli,	*Caret.*
Broken Tribes of Nepal.	Dárhi,	*Chális.*
	Denwár,	*Chális.*
	Pahri,	*Pi-i.*
	Chepáng,	*Caret.*
	Bhrámu,	*Caret.*
	Váyu,	*Nayung-cholok.*
	Kuswar,	*Chális.*
	Kusunda,	*Caret.*
	Tháru,	*Chális.*
	Lepcha (Sikkim),	*Kha-nyet.*
	Bhúṭáni v. Lhopa,	*Khe-ni.*
N.-E. Bengal.	Bodo,	*Bisha-gne.*
	Dhimál,	*Nhe-bisa, gne-long-bisha.*
	Kocch,	*Chális.*
	Garo,	*Rung-ning.*
	Káchári,	*Caret.*
Eastern Frontier of Bengal.	Munipuri,	*Niphu.*
	Míthán Nágá,	*Pan-yi.*
	Tablung Nágá,	*Caret.*
	Khári Nágá,	*Li-rah.*
	Angámi Nágá,	*Lhide.*
	Námsáng Nágá,	*Ruak-beli.*
	Nowgong Nágá,	*Li-ri.*
	Tengsa Nágá,	*Mesung-annat.*
	Abor Miri,	*Uing-apie.*
	Sibságar Miri,	*Uying-apiko.*
	Deoria Chutia,	*Caret.*
	Singpho,	*Mli-si.*
Arrakan & Burmah.	Burman (*written*),	*Le-chhe.*
	Burman (*spoken*),	*Le-tse, le-zhai.*
	Khyeng v. Shou,	*Lhi-gip.*
	Kámi,	*Ku-i-mali.*
	Kúmi,	*Wu-palu-ri.*
	Mrú v. Toung,	*Caret.*
	Sák,	*Pri-si.*
Siam & Tenasserim.	Talain v. Mon,	*Pon-tson.*
	Sgau-karen,	*Lwi-si.*
	Pwo-karen,	*Li-tsi.*
	Toungh-thu,	*Lit.*
	Shán,	*Htse-htsiet.*
	Annamitic,	*Bôn-muöi.*
	Siamese,	*Si-sip, tsi-tsit.*
	Ahom,	*Si-sip.*
	Khámti,	*Si-sip.*
	Laos,	*Si-sip.*
Central India.	Ho (Kol),	*Bar-hissi.*
	Kol (Singhbhum),	*Bár-hissi.*
	Santáli,	*Bár-issi.*
	Bhúmij,	*Bár-issi.*
	Uráon,	*Bisend.*
	Mundala,	*Bar-hissi.*
	Rájmahali,	*Chális.*
	Goṇḍi,	*Rand-eisai, chális.*
	Gayeti,	*Caret.*
	Rutluk,	*Caret.*
	Naikude,	*Caret.*
	Kolami,	*Caret.*
	Mádi,	*Rand-visa, chális.*
	Mádia,	*Rand koḍi.*
	Kuri,	*Caret.*
	Keikádi,	*Caret.*
	Khoṇḍ,	*Chalisigoṭṭa.*
	Sávara,	*Bágukoḍi.*
	Gadaba,	*Nalabhai.*
	Yerukala,	*Nalubadu.*
	Chentsu,	*Poun, das-gandá.*
Southern India.	Tamiḷ, anc.,	*Nárpakudu.*
	Tamiḷ, mod.,	*Náṛpadu.*
	Malayáḷma, anc.,	*Caret.*
	Malayáḷma, mod.,	*Nálpata.*
	Telugu,	*Nalubai.*
	Karṇáṭaka, anc.,	*Caret.*
	Karṇáṭaka, mod.,	*Nálvattu.*
	Tuḷuva,	*Nárpo.*
	Kurgi,	*Nápadu.*
	Toḍuva, }	*Nálvod.*
	Toḍa, }	*Narsh-bath.*
	Kóta,	*Nalvatte.*
	Baḍaga,	*Nalvattu.*
	Kuṛumba,	*Nalvattu.*
	Iruḷa,	*Nábadu.*
	Malabar,	*Nátpathu.*
	Sinhalese,	*Hata-lis.*

Group	Language	Fifty
	Types.	
Inflecting.	SANSKRIT,	*Pañchāṣat.*
	ARABIC,	*Khamṣoun.*
Compounding.	BASK,	*Berrogeit-amar.*
	FINNIC,	*Wiisikymmenda.*
	MAGYAR,	*Ötven.*
	TURKISH,	*Elli.*
	CIRCASSIAN,	*Scynuk.*
	GEORGIAN,	*Ormots-da-aṭhi, kikaldans-*
	MONGOLIAN,	*Tchin, samfolenka-bi.‡ [ke.**
	MANTSHU,	*Sousai, ug-schi.**
	JAVANESE, Ngoko,	*Séket.*
	JAVANESE, Krama,	*Séket.*
	MALAY,	*Limapúluh.*
Isolating.	CHINESE, Nankin,	*Wu-shïh.*
	CHINESE, Pekin,	*Wu-shih.*
	CHINESE, Canton,	*'Ng-shap.*
	CHINESE, Shanghai,	*'Ng-seh.*
	AMOY, Colloquial,	*Go-cháp.*
	JAPANESE,	*Go-djiu, isodsi.*
	Brahuí,	*Panjáh.*
Chinese Frontier & Tibet.	Gyámi,	*Wú-sa.*
	Gyárung,	*Kungno-si.*
	Tákpa,	*Caret.*
	Mányak,	*Gna-zá-bi.*
	Thochú,	*Was-so.*
	Sokpa,	*Shá-che.*
	Horpa,	*Gwes-ka.*
	Tibetan (*written*),	*Gna-chúthamba,* luab-*chu.*
	Tibetan (*spoken*),	*Gnap-chú.*
Nepal (east to west).	Serpa,	*Gnap-chu.*
	Súnwár,	*Khak-nishi-sasika.*
	Gúrung,	*Caret.*
	Múrmi,	*Bokal-ni-shú-chú.*
	Magar,	*Caret.*
	Tháksya,	*Gna-syu.*
	Pákhya,	*Pachás.*
	Newár,	*Pi-sánho, gnïá-ye.*
	Limbu,	*Gna-gip.*
Kiránti Group (East Nepal).	Kiránti,	*Caret.*
	Rodong,	*Caret.*
	Rúngchenbung,	*Caret.*
	Chhingtángya,	*Caret.*
	Náchhereng,	*Caret.*
	Wáling,	*Caret.*
	Yákha,	*Gná-gip.*
	Chourásya,	*Caret.*
	Kulungya,	*Caret.*
	Thulungya,	*Naasang-ko-dyum.*
	Báhingya,	*Ni-pachi-kot-dyum.*
	Lohorong,	*Gná-k-pong.*
	Lambichhong,	*Caret.*
	Báláli,	*Caret.*
	Sáng-páng,	*Caret.*
	Dúmi,	*Caret.*
	Kháling,	*Khál-sákpo-taḍham.*
	Dungmáli,	*Caret.*
Broken Tribes of Nepal.	Dárhi,	*Pachás.*
	Denwár,	*Pachás.*
	Pahri,	*Nge-e.*
	Chepáng,	*Caret.*
	Bhrámu,	*Caret.*
	Váyu,	*Caret.*
	Kuswar,	*Pachás.*
	Kusunda,	*Caret.*
	Tháru,	*Pachás.*
	Lepcha (Sikkim),	*Kha-nyet-sa-káti.*
	Bhúṭáni v. Lhopa,	*K'he-pheddángsúm.*

Group	Language	Fifty
N.-E. Bengal.	Bodo,	*Caret.*
	Dhimál,	*Caret.*
	Kocch,	*Pachás.*
	Garo,	*Rung-ning-chi.*
	Káchári,	*Caret.*
Eastern Frontier of Bengal.	Munipuri,	*Yáng-kai.*
	Míthán Nágá,	*Caret.*
	Tablung Nágá,	*Caret.*
	Khári Nágá,	*Ta-nam.*
	Angámi Nágá,	*Ri-pangu.*
	Námsáng Nágá,	*Ruak-bangá.*
	Nowgong Nágá,	*Than-am.*
	Tengsa Nágá,	*Mesung-annat-te-thelu.*
	Abor Miri,	*Caret.*
	Sibságar Miri,	*Ungo-nyingko.*
	Deoria Chutia,	*Caret.*
	Singpho,	*Mangá-si.*
Arrakan & Burmah.	Burman (*written*),	*Ngá-chhe, gá-chhe.*
	Burman (*spoken*),	*Ngá-tse, gá-tse, ngá-zhai.*
	Khyeng v. Shou,	*Nghau-gip.*
	Kámi,	*Ku-i-pang-nga.*
	Kúmi,	*Wi-pá-ri.*
	Mrú v. Toung,	*Caret.*
	Sák,	*Nga-si.*
Siam & Tenasserim.	Talain v. Mon,	*Patsu-tson.*
	Sgau-karen,	*Ya-i-su, yay-tsi.*
	Pwo-karen,	*Yea-tsi.*
	Toungh-thu,	*Ngat.*
	Shán,	*Ha-htsiet.*
	Annamitic,	*Nam-muöi.*
	Siamese,	*Há-sip, há-tsit.*
	Ahom,	*Há-sip.*
	Khámti,	*Há-sip.*
	Laos,	*Há-sip.*
Central India.	Ho (Kol),	*Bar-hissi-gel.*
	Kol (Singhbhum),	*Bár-hissi-gil.*
	Santáli,	*Bár-issi-gel.*
	Bhúmij,	*Bár-hissi-dasti.*
	Uráon,	*Dharihe-koḍi.*
	Mundala,	*Bár-hissi-dasgo.*
	Rájmahali,	*Pachás.*
	Goṇḍi,	*Caret.*
	Gayeti,	*Caret.*
	Rutluk,	*Caret.*
	Naikude,	*Caret.*
	Kolami,	*Caret.*
	Mádi,	*Rand-visa-dahi.*
	Mádia,	*Aḍhei-koḍi.*
	Kuri,	*Caret.*
	Keikádi,	*Caret.*
	Khoṇḍ,	*Panchásо.*
	Sávara,	*Bágukoḍi-galiji.*
	Gadaba,	*Yábhai.*
	Yerukala,	*Anjara-kapottu.*
	Chentsu,	*Bara-ganda-doyicha.*
Southern India.	Tamiḷ, anc.,	*Aimbakudu.*
	Tamiḷ, mod.,	*Aimbadu.*
	Malayáḷma, anc.,	*Caret.*
	Malayáḷma, mod.,	*Ambata.*
	Telugu,	*Yábai.*
	Karṇáṭaka, anc.,	*Caret.*
	Karṇáṭaka, mod.,	*Ayivattu.*
	Tuḷuva,	*Ayiva.*
	Kurgi,	*Eimbadu.*
	Toḍuva, } Toḍa, }	*Erb-bod.* / *Eboth.*
	Kóta,	*Eivatte.*
	Baḍaga,	*Eivattu.*
	Kuṛumba,	*Eivattu.*
	Iruḷa,	*Ambadu.*
	Malabar,	*Aimpathu.*
	Sinhalese,	*Panas.*

	Types.	
Inflecting.	SANSKṚIT, . . .	*Ṣatam.*
	ARABIC, . . .	*Máyat.*
Compounding.	BASK, ...	*Eun.*
	FINNIC, ...	*Sata.*
	MAGYAR, ...	*Szaz.*
	TURKISH, ...	*Yuz.*
	CIRCASSIAN, ...	*Koshed.*
	GEORGIAN, ...	*Asi, nosku.**
	MONGOLIAN, ...	*Saghon, girr.*‡
	MANTSHU, ...	*Tanggô, ibai.**
	JAVANESE, Ngoko, . .	*Sátus.*
	JAVANESE, Krama, . .	*Sátus.*
	MALAY, ...	*Rátus, sàrátus.*
Isolating.	CHINESE, Nankin, . .	*Pih, i-pe.*
	CHINESE, Pekin, . .	*Pai.*
	CHINESE, Canton, . .	*Pák.*
	CHINESE, Shanghai, .	*Ih-pah.*
	AMOY, Colloquial, . .	*Chit-pah.*
	JAPANESE, ...	*Hiaku* (?), *momo.*
	Brahuí, ...	*Sad.*
Chinese Frontier & Tibet.	Gyámi, ...	*I-pe.*
	Gyárung, ...	*Par-ye.*
	Tákpa, ...	*Caret.*
	Mányak, ...	*Teje.*
	Thochú, ...	*Ak-shi.*
	Sokpa, ...	*Cho-vo.*
	Horpa, ...	*Rhyá.*
	Tibetan (*written*), . .	*Tschá-thamba, gyá-thamba.*
	Tibetan (*spoken*), . .	*Gyá, gyá-thámbá.*
Nepal (east to west).	Serpa, ...	*Gyá.*
	Súnwár, ...	*Swai-ká.*
	Gúrung, ...	*Caret.*
	Múrmi, ...	*Bokal-gná.*
	Magar, ...	*Caret.*
	Tháksya, ...	*Bhra.*
	Pákhya, ...	*Saya.*
	Newár, ...	*Gún-sánho, sat-chi.*
	Limbu, ...	*Thi-bong-gip.*
Kiranti Group (East Nepal).	Kiránti, ...	*Caret.*
	Rodong, ...	*Caret.*
	Rúngchenbung, . . .	*Caret.*
	Chhingtángya, . . .	*Caret.*
	Náchhereng, ...	*Caret.*
	Wáling, ...	*Caret.*
	Yákha, ...	*Maknai-bong.*
	Chourásya, ...	*Caret.*
	Kulungya, ...	*Caret.*
	Thulungya, ...	*Gno-sang.*
	Báhingya, ...	*Gno-asing.*
	Lohorong, ...	*Ip-pong-pong.*
	Lambichhong, . . .	*Caret.*
	Báláli, ...	*Caret.*
	Sáng-páng, ...	*Caret.*
	Dúmi, ...	*Caret.*
	Kháling, ...	*Khál-bhong.*
	Dungmáli, ...	*Caret.*
Broken Tribes of Nepal.	Dárhi, ...	*Sou.*
	Denwár, ...	*So.*
	Pahri, ...	*Sá-chi.*
	Chepáng, ...	*Caret.*
	Bhrámu, ...	*Caret.*
	Váyu, ...	*Uning-cholok, kolu-got-cholok,* [*i.e.* one score of hands.
	Kuswar, ...	*Sou.*
	Kusunda, ...	*Caret.*
	Tháru, ...	*Sau.*
	Lepcha (Sikkim), . .	*Khá-phá-gnon.*
	Bhútáni v. Lhopa, . .	*Khe-gná.*

N.-E. Bengal.	Bodo, ...	*Bisha-ba.*
	Dhimál, ...	*Ná-bisa, na-long-bisha.*
	Kocch, ...	*Sau.*
	Garo, ...	*Rung-bonga.*
	Káchári, ...	*Caret.*
Eastern Frontier of Bengal.	Munipuri, ...	*Chámá.*
	Míthán Nágá, . . .	*Pu-gá.*
	Tablung Nágá, . . .	*Caret.*
	Khári Nágá, . . .	*Ru-krá.*
	Angámi Nágá, . . .	*Kre.*
	Námsáng Nágá, . . .	*Chá-the.*
	Nowgong Nágá, . .	*Ro-kru.*
	Tengsa Nágá, . . .	*Mesung-phungu.*
	Abor Miri, ...	*Caret.*
	Sibságar Miri, . . .	*Uying-uyingko.*
	Deoria Chutia, . . .	*Caret.*
	Singpho, ...	*La-tsá.*
Arrakan & Burmah.	Burman (*written*), . .	*Ta-rá.*
	Burman (*spoken*), . . .	*Ta-yi, ta-yá.*
	Khyeng v. Shou, . .	*Kla-át.*
	Kámi, ...	*Ta-rá.*
	Kúmi, ...	*Chum-wá-ri.*
	Mrú v. Toung, . . .	*Caret.*
	Sák, ...	*Ta-yá.*
Siam & Tenasserim.	Talain v. Mon, . . .	*Ka-lun.*
	Sgau-karen, ...	*Tǩzáh, tágáyah.*
	Pwo-karen, ...	*L'yah.*
	Toungh-thu, ...	*Ta-loyen.*
	Shán, ...	*Hpat.*
	Annamitic, ...	*Môt-tram.*
	Siamese, ...	*Roi, róe-nung.*
	Ahom, ...	*Pak.*
	Khámti, ...	*Pák.*
	Laos, ...	*Hoi.*
Central India.	Ho (Kol), ...	*Mi-sau.*
	Kol (Singhbhum), . .	*Moy-hissi.*
	Santáli, ...	*Maṇe-issi.*
	Bhúmij, ...	*Sau.*
	Uráon, ...	*Se.*
	Mundala, ...	*Midso.*
	Rájmahali, ...	*Sau.*
	Goṇḍi, ...	*Nur, so.*
	Gayeti, ...	*Nur.*
	Rutluk, ...	*Caret.*
	Naikude, ...	*Caret.*
	Kolami, ...	*Caret.*
	Mádi, ...	*Nuru.*
	Mádia, ...	*Hein-koḍi.*
	Kuri, ...	*Chovi.*
	Keikádi, ...	*Caret.*
	Khoṇḍ, ...	*Soho.*
	Sávara, ...	*Molloyikoḍi.*
	Gadaba, ...	*Núru.*
	Yerukala, ...	*Pattu padula.*
	Chentsu, ...	*Pánch voḍi* (*pánch koḍi* ?).
Southern India.	Tamiḷ, anc., ...	*Caret.*
	Tamiḷ, mod., ...	*Núṟu.*
	Malayáḷma, anc., . . .	*Caret.*
	Malayáḷma, mod., . . .	*Núra.*
	Telugu, ...	*Núru, vanda.*
	Karṇáṭaka, anc., . . .	*Caret.*
	Karṇáṭaka, mod., . . .	*Núru.*
	Tuḷuva, ...	*Núdu.*
	Kurgi, ...	*Núru.*
	Toḍuva, }	*Onnur.*
	Toḍa, }	*Vaddnúr.*
	Kóta, ...	*Nur.*
	Baḍaga, ...	*Nuru.*
	Kuṟumba, ...	*Nuru.*
	Iruḷa, ...	*Núru.*
	Malabar, ...	*Núru.*
	Sinhalese, ...	*Siya.*

	Types.	
Inflecting.	SANSKRIT,	*Aham (asmat).*
	ARABIC,	*Ana.*
Compounding.	BASK,	*Ni, nik, neu, neuk, neur, [neurk.*
	FINNIC,	*Mina.*
	MAGYAR,	*En.*
	TURKISH,	*Ben.*
	CIRCASSIAN,	*Sayray.*
	GEORGIAN,	*Me.*
	MONGOLIAN,	*Bi.*
	MANTSHU,	*Bi.*
	JAVANESE, Ngoko,	*A'ku.*
	JAVANESE, KRAMA,	*Kúla.*
	MALAY,	*A'ku.*
Isolating.	CHINESE, Nankin,	*Wo.*
	CHINESE, Pekin,	*Wo.*
	CHINESE, Canton,	*Ngo.*
	CHINESE, Shanghai,	*Ngu.*
	AMOY, Colloquial,	*Góa.*
	JAPANESE,	*Ware, washi, ko-chira, [kono-ho.*
	Brahuí,	*I'.*
Chinese Frontier & Tibet.	Gyámi,	*Gnó.*
	Gyárung,	*Gná, gná-yo.*
	Tákpa,	*Gné, nyé.*
	Mányak,	*A'.*
	Thochú,	*Chi, ká.*
	Sokpa,	*Mi, bi, abú.*
	Horpa,	*Gná.*
	Tibetan (*written*),	*Ná.*
	Tibetan (*spoken*),	*Gnyó.*
Nepal (east to west).	Serpa,	*Gná.*
	Súnwár,	*Go.*
	Gúrung,	*Gná.*
	Múrmi,	*Gná.*
	Magar,	*Gná.*
	Tháksya,	*Ghyáng.*
	Pákhya,	*Ma.*
	Newár,	*Ji.*
	Limbu,	*Ingá.*
Kiranti Group (East Nepal).	Kiránti,	*A'nka.*
	Rodong,	*Ka, ka-nga, ing-ka.*
	Rúngchenbung,	*Ang, awka, ung-ka.*
	Chhingtángya,	*A'ká.*
	Náchhereng,	*Ká, ká-gná.*
	Wáling,	*Ing-ka, ang-ka.*
	Yákha,	*Ká.*
	Chourásya,	*Ung-gu.*
	Kulungya,	*Ko-gná.*
	Thulungya,	*Go.*
	Báhingya,	*Go.*
	Lohorong,	*Ká, ká-gná.*
	Lambichhong,	*Ká, ká-gná.*
	Báláli,	*Ká, ká-gná.*
	Sáng-páng,	*Ká-gná.*
	Dúmi,	*Ung, áng-gnu.*
	Kháling,	*Ung.*
	Dungmáli,	*Ang-ka, ing-ka.*
Broken Tribes of Nepal.	Dárhi,	*Má-i.*
	Denwár,	*Mú-i.*
	Pahri,	*Nung, já.*
	Chepáng,	*Ngá.*
	Bhrámu,	*Ngá.*
	Váyu,	*Go.*
	Kuswar,	*Má-ha.*
	Kusunda,	*Chi.*
	Tháru,	*Hang.*
	Lepcha (Sikkim),	*Go.*
	Bhútáni v. Lhopa,	*Gná.*

N.-E. Bengal.	Bodo,	*Ang.*
	Dhimál,	*Ká.*
	Kocch,	*Mu-i.*
	Garo,	*A'ng.*
	Káchári,	*Caret.*
Eastern Frontier of Bengal.	Munipuri,	*Ei.*
	Míthán Nágá,	*Ku.*
	Tablung Nágá,	*Tau.*
	Khári Nágá,	*Ni.*
	Angámi Nágá,	*A'.*
	Námsáng Nágá,	*Ngá.*
	Nowgong Nágá,	*Nyi.*
	Tengsa Nágá,	*Ngai.*
	Abor Miri,	*Ngo.*
	Sibságar Miri,	*Ngo.*
	Deoria Chutia,	*A'n.*
	Singpho,	*Ngai.*
Arrakan & Burmah.	Burman (*written*),	*Ngá.*
	Burman (*spoken*),	*Ngá.*
	Khyeng v. Shou,	*Kyi.*
	Kámi,	*Ká-i.*
	Kúmi,	*Ká-i.*
	Mrú v. Toung,	*Caret.*
	Sák,	*Caret.*
Siam & Tenasserim.	Talain v. Mon,	*Awai.*
	Sgau-karen,	*Yá, yáh.*
	Pwo-karen,	*Yer.*
	Toungh-thu,	*Khwa.*
	Shán,	*Koung.*
	Annamitic,	*Tôi.*
	Siamese,	*Khá.*
	Ahom,	*Kau.*
	Khámti,	*Kau.*
	Laos,	*Ku, ong.*
Central India.	Ho (Kol),	*I'ng.*
	Kol (Singhbhum),	*Aing.*
	Santáli,	*Ing, inge.*
	Bhúmij,	*Ing.*
	Uráon,	*Enan.*
	Mundala,	*Ing.*
	Rájmahali,	*En.*
	Goṇḍi,	*Mánu, anna.*
	Gayeti,	*Nana.*
	Rutluk,	*Nan-na.*
	Naikude,	*An.*
	Kolami,	*An.*
	Mádi,	*Nanna, nau.*
	Mádia,	*Ana.*
	Kuri,	*In (ing?).*
	Keikádi,	*Nanu.*
	Khoṇḍ,	*A'nu.*
	Sávara,	*Gná.*
	Gadaba,	*Nai-sa.*
	Yerukala,	*Ná-nu.*
	Chentsu,	*Há-me, há-mi.*
Southern India.	Tamiḷ, anc.,	*Yán.*
	Tamiḷ, mod.,	*Nán.*
	Malayáḷma, anc.,	*Caret.*
	Malayáḷma, mod.,	*Nyán.*
	Telugu,	*Nénu.*
	Karṇáṭaka, anc.,	*A'n.*
	Karṇáṭaka, mod.,	*Nánu.*
	Tuḷuva,	*En.*
	Kurgi,	*Nánu.*
	Toḍuva, } Toḍa, }	*One.* / *A'nu.*
	Kóta,	*A'ne.*
	Baḍaga,	*Ná, ná-nu.*
	Kuṛumba,	*Ná, nánu.*
	Iruḷa,	*Nánu, ná.*
	Malabar,	*Nán, yán.*
	Sinhalese,	*Ma.*

Types.		
Inflecting.	SANSKRIT,	*Twám* (*twat, yushmat*).
	ARABIC,	*Anta.*
Compounding.	BASK,	*Hi, hik; zu, zuk.*
	FINNIC,	*Sina.*
	MAGYAR,	*Te.*
	TURKISH,	*Sen.*
	CIRCASSIAN,	*Weyru.*
	GEORGIAN,	*Shen.*
	MONGOLIAN,	*Tschi, tchi.*
	MANTSHU,	*Si.*
	JAVANESE, Ngoko,	*Kowe.*
	JAVANESE, Krama,	*Sampeyan.*
	MALAY,	*Angkau.*
Isolating.	CHINESE, Nankin,	*Ni.*
	CHINESE, Pekin,	*Ni.*
	CHINESE, Canton,	*Ni.*
	CHINESE, Shanghai,	*Nung.*
	AMOY, Colloquial,	*Li.*
	JAPANESE,	*Nanji.*
	Brahuí,	*Ni.*
Chinese Frontier & Tibet.	Gyámi,	*Ni.*
	Gyárung,	*Sán-ré.*
	Tákpa,	*I'.*
	Mányak,	*Nö.*
	Thochú,	*Kwá, kwé.*
	Sokpa,	*Chhá.*
	Horpa,	*Ni.*
	Tibetan (*written*),	*Khyod.*
	Tibetan (*spoken*),	*Khé.*
Nepal (east to west).	Serpa,	*Khyo.*
	Súnwár,	*Gai.*
	Gúrung,	*Kén.*
	Múrmi,	*Ai.*
	Magar,	*Náng.*
	Tháksya,	*Gna.*
	Pákhya,	*Ta.*
	Newár,	*Chha.*
	Limbu,	*Khene.*
Kiranti Group (East Nepal).	Kiránti,	*Khaná* (*khána ?*).
	Rodong,	*Khána.*
	Rúngchenbung,	*Khána.*
	Chhingtángya,	*Hána* (*haná ?*).
	Náchhereng,	*A'na.*
	Wáling,	*Hána, khána.*
	Yákha,	*Ing-khi, 'nkhi.*
	Chourásya,	*Gno-me, unu.*
	Kulungya,	*A'na.*
	Thulungya,	*Gána.*
	Báhingya,	*Ga.*
	Lohorong,	*A'na, hána.*
	Lambichhong,	*Khána.*
	Báláli,	*A'na.*
	Sáng-páng,	*A'na.*
	Dúmi,	*In, ánu.*
	Kháling,	*In.*
	Dungmáli,	*Hána.*
Broken Tribes of Nepal.	Dárhi,	*Ta-i.*
	Denwár,	*Tu-i.*
	Pahri,	*Chhung, chhi.*
	Chepáng,	*Náng.*
	Bhrámu,	*Náng.*
	Váyu,	*Gon.*
	Kuswar,	*Tá-ha.*
	Kusunda,	*Nu.*
	Tháru,	*Tong.*
	Lepcha (Sikkim),	*Hau.*
	Bhúṭáni v. Lhopa,	*Chhú.*

N.-E. Bengal.	Bodo,	*Nang.*
	Dhimál,	*Ná.*
	Kocch,	*Tu-i.*
	Garo,	*Nang.*
	Kácharí,	*Caret.*
Eastern Frontier of Bengal.	Munipuri,	*Nung.*
	Míthán Nágá,	*Nang.*
	Tablung Nágá,	*Nang.*
	Khári Nágá,	*Nang.*
	Angámi Nágá,	*No.*
	Námsáng Nágá,	*Nangma.*
	Nowgong Nágá,	*Ná.*
	Tengsa Nágá,	*Nang.*
	Abor Miri,	*No-na.*
	Sibságar Miri,	*No.*
	Deoria Chutia,	*No, áni.*
	Singpho,	*Nang, ni.*
Arrakan & Burmah.	Burman (*written*),	*Nang, mang.*
	Burman (*spoken*),	*Nen, men.*
	Khyeng v. Shou,	*Nang.*
	Kámi,	*Nan.*
	Kúmi,	*Nang.*
	Mrú v. Toung,	*Caret.*
	Sák,	*Caret.*
Siam & Tenasserim.	Talain v. Mon,	*Bai.*
	Sgau-karen,	*Nah, tha.*
	Pwo-karen,	*Ner.*
	Toungh-thu,	*Ná.*
	Shán,	*Moung.*
	Annamitic,	*Anh, máïi.*
	Siamese,	*Ren, tua, mung.*
	Ahom,	*Mo.*
	Khámti,	*Maü.*
	Laos,	*Toa.*
Central India.	Ho (Kol),	*Um.*
	Kol (Singhbhum),	*Um* (*ám ?*).
	Santáli,	*A'm, umge.*
	Bhúmij,	*A'm* (*am ?*).
	Uráon,	*Ni-en.*
	Mundala,	*A'm* (*am ?*)
	Rájmahali,	*Nin.*
	Goṇḍi,	*Imma, imme.*
	Gayeti,	*Ime.*
	Rutluk,	*Imá.*
	Naikude,	*Niwa.*
	Kolami,	*Niwa.*
	Mádi,	*Nima.*
	Mádia,	*Caret.*
	Kuri,	*Am.*
	Keikádi,	*Ninu.*
	Khoṇḍ,	*Yi-nu.*
	Sávara,	*Aman.*
	Gadaba,	*No.*
	Yerukala,	*Ni-nu.*
	Chentsu,	*Yi-ke, tu-myi, tu.*
Southern India.	Tamiḷ, anc.,	*Caret.*
	Tamiḷ, mod.,	*Ni.*
	Malayáḷma, anc.,	*Caret.*
	Malayáḷma, mod.,	*Ni.*
	Telugu,	*Nivu.*
	Karṇáṭaka, anc.,	*Nin.*
	Karṇáṭaka, mod.,	*Ninu.*
	Tuḷuva,	*Ī.*
	Kurgi,	*Nin.*
	Toḍuva, }	*Ni.*
	Toḍa, }	*Ni.*
	Kóta,	*Ni-ye, ni.*
	Baḍaga,	*Ni.*
	Kuṛumba,	*Ni.*
	Iruḷa,	*Ni.*
	Malabar,	*Ni, nir.*
	Sinhalese,	*To.*

Group	Types.	
Inflecting.	SANSKRIT,	*Sas, sá, tat.*
	ARABIC,	*Hou, he.*
Compounding.	BASK,	*Hura, ark.*
	FINNIC,	*Han.*
	MAGYAR,	*Ö.*
	TURKISH,	*O, ol.*
	CIRCASSIAN,	*Sisha.*
	GEORGIAN,	*Igi, iman.*
	MONGOLIAN,	*Tere, ene, tere.*
	MANTSHU,	*Tere, i.*
	JAVANESE, Ngoko,	*Dewe.*
	JAVANESE, Krama,	*Piyambak.*
	MALAY,	*I'ya.*
Isolating.	CHINESE, Nankin,	*Tá.*
	CHINESE, Pekin,	*Tá.*
	CHINESE, Canton,	*K'ü.*
	CHINESE, Shanghai,	*Yi.*
	AMOY, Colloquial,	*I.*
	JAPANESE,	*Kare.*
	Brahuí,	*Dá.*
Chinese Frontier & Tibet.	Gyámi,	*Thá.*
	Gyárung,	*Guá-pos, watú.*
	Tákpa,	*Pé, bé.*
	Mányak,	*Thi.*
	Thochú,	*Kwán-tá-cha.*
	Sokpa,	*Thá.*
	Horpa,	*Ja, jya.*
	Tibetan (*written*),	*Kho.*
	Tibetan (*spoken*),	*Khú.*
Nepal (east to west).	Serpa,	*Khwo.*
	Súnwár,	*Hari.*
	Gúrung,	*Thi.*
	Múrmi,	*Thé.*
	Magar,	*Hos.*
	Tháksya,	*Chana, h'mi.*
	Pákhya,	*U-kya.*
	Newár,	*Wo.*
	Limbu,	*Khúné.*
Kiranti Group (East Nepal).	Kiránti,	*Moko.*
	Rodong,	*Khu, tyáko, hyáko.*
	Rúngchenbung,	*Oko, moko, en-hyáko.*
	Chhingtángya,	*Yoko, mogo, mogwa.*
	Náchhereng,	*Manka, yako.*
	Wáling,	*Aya, hayako, moko.*
	Yákha,	*Ikhi, khena, yona, mona.*
	Chourásya,	*Time, yome, yame.*
	Kulungya,	*Náko, muko, netako.*
	Thulungya,	*Hána.*
	Báhingya,	*Harem, igo, mogo.*
	Lohorong,	*Mi, mo, mo-nu.*
	Lambichhong,	*Ako, mona, yona, toma.*
	Báláli,	*Mo, kho.*
	Sáng-páng,	*Moko, meko.*
	Dúmi,	*Momi, yakám, mam.*
	Kháling,	*Tam, yakám, mam.*
	Dungmáli,	*Mugo.*
Broken Tribes of Nepal.	Dárhi,	*U.*
	Denwár,	*I.*
	Pahri,	*Ho, u.*
	Chepáng,	*U.*
	Bhrámu,	*U.*
	Váyu,	*Mu; wáthi; á, i.*
	Kuswar,	*Hu-lo, há-lo.*
	Kusunda,	*Isi, it, gida (tokpya ?).*
	Tháru,	*U-tu.*
	Lepcha (Sikkim),	*Heu.*
	Bhútáni v. Lhopa,	*Khó.*

N.-E. Bengal.	Bodo,	*Bi.*
	Dhimál,	*Wá.*
	Kocch,	*On-i.*
	Garo,	*U'.*
	Káchári,	*Caret.*
Eastern Frontier of Bengal.	Munipuri,	*Ma.*
	Míthán Nágá,	*Mih.*
	Tablung Nágá,	*Tau-pá.*
	Khári Nágá,	*Pau.*
	Angámi Nágá,	*Me.*
	Námsáng Nágá,	*A'te.*
	Nowgong Nágá,	*Pá.*
	Tengsa Nágá,	*Pá.*
	Abor Miri,	*Bu, no.*
	Sibságar Miri,	*Bu.*
	Deoria Chutia,	*Bare-ni.*
	Singpho,	*Khi.*
Arrakan & Burmah.	Burman (*written*),	*Su.*
	Burman (*spoken*,),	*Thú, tho.*
	Khyeng v. Shou,	*Ni.*
	Kámi,	*Ha-ná-i.*
	Kúmi,	*Hú.*
	Mrú v. Toung,	*Caret.*
	Sák,	*Caret.*
Siam & Tenasserim.	Talain v. Mon,	*Nyá.*
	Sgau-karen,	*Awa-i, au.*
	Pwo-karen,	*Ur.*
	Toungh-thu,	*Wa.*
	Shán,	*Koung-nick.*
	Annamitic,	*A'i, no.*
	Siamese,	*Koung-ni, man.*
	Ahom,	*Heu.*
	Khámti,	*Man.*
	Laos,	*Man, tan.*
Central India.	Ho (Kol),	*A'i, a'io.*
	Kol (Singhbhum),	*Ini.*
	Santáli,	*Huni, uni, ona.*
	Bhúmij,	*Ini.*
	Uráon,	*Asán.*
	Mundala,	*Inni.*
	Rájmahali,	*A'th.*
	Goṇḍi,	*Hore; war; wur..*
	Gayeti,	*Wor; war; wur.*
	Rutluk,	*Ad.*
	Naikude,	*Ound; ad.*
	Kolami,	*Ad.*
	Mádi,	*Woru; oru.*
	Mádia,	*Caret.*
	Kuri,	*Hán.*
	Keikádi,	*Ado.*
	Khoṇḍ,	*Yanju; toliyadu; monju.*
	Sávara,	*Ani.*
	Gadaba,	*Tulokku; tulo; tulo.*
	Yerukala,	*Avanu; avalu, paidi; adu.*
	Chentsu,	*Vu; vamhi; mayáta; vahe.*
Southern India.	Tamiḷ, anc.,	*Akudu.*
	Tamiḷ, mod.,	*Avan; aval; adu.*
	Malayáḷma, anc.,	*Caret.*
	Malayáḷma, mod.,	*Avan; aval; ada.*
	Telugu,	*Vadu; ame; adi.*
	Karṇáṭaka, anc.,	*Avam; aval.*
	Karṇáṭaka, mod.,	*Avanu; avalu; adu.*
	Tuḷuva,	*Aye; aval; av.*
	Kurgi,	*Caret.*
	Toḍuva,	*Caret.*
	Toḍa,	*Adum, avan; aval; adu.*
	Kóta,	*Avane; avale; ade.*
	Baḍaga,	*Ava; avla; adu.*
	Kuṛumba,	*Avanu; avalu; adu.*
	Iruḷa,	*Ava; avla; adu.*
	Malabar,	*Avan, aval, athu.*
	Sinhalese,	*Ohu, aé, eka.*

Group	Language	We
Types.		
Inflecting.	SANSKRIT,	*A'vám,*[1] *vayam.*[2]
	ARABIC,	*Naḥna.*
Compounding.	BASK,	*Gu, Guk.*
	FINNIC,	*Me.*
	MAGYAR,	*Mi.*
	TURKISH,	*Biz.*
	CIRCASSIAN,	*Teyru.*
	GEORGIAN,	*Chwen.*
	MONGOLIAN,	*Bida.*
	MANTSHU,	*Be.*
	JAVANESE, Ngoko,	*Aku.*
	JAVANESE, Krama,	*Kula.*
	MALAY,	*Kámi, kíta.*
Isolating.	CHINESE, Nankin,	*Wo-mên.*
	CHINESE, Pekin,	*Wo-mên.*
	CHINESE, Canton,	*Ngo-ti.*
	CHINESE, Shanghai,	*Ngu-ni.*
	AMOY, Colloquial,	*Lán.*
	JAPANESE,	*Warera.*
	Brahuí,	*Nan.*
Chinese Frontier & Tibet.	Gyámi,	*Gno-me.*
	Gyárung,	*Yŏ.*
	Tákpa,	*Gna-rá.*
	Mányak,	*A-dúr,*[2] *a-ju.*[1]
	Thochú,	*Chúklarchikit*[2] *cheun.*[1]
	Sokpa,	*Mi-ni.*
	Horpa,	*Gna-ni, gna-riggi, rigya.*
	Tibetan (*written*),	*Na-chag.*
	Tibetan (*spoken,*)	*Gná-njo.*
Nepal (east to west).	Serpa,	*Ni-rang.*
	Súnwár,	*Gov-ki.*
	Gúrung,	*Gni-mo.*
	Múrmi,	*Gna-ni.*
	Magar,	*Kan-kúrik.*
	Tháksya,	*Ghyang-si;*[1] *ghyang-cha.*[2]
	Pákhya,	*Caret.*
	Newár,	*Ji-ping.*
	Limbu,	*Anige.*
Kiranti Group (East Nepal).	Kiránti,	*Ankan.*
	Rodong,	*Kai, ka-i;*[5] *ka.*[6]
	Rúngchenbung,	*Ung-kan;*[5] *ung-kanka.*[6]
	Chhingtángya,	*Kana-na, kanga-na.*
	Náchhereng,	*Kai;*[5] *ka.*[6]
	Wáling,	*I-ka,*[5] *u-ka,*[5] *kong-kai-ka.*[6]
	Yákha,	*Kani;*[5] *ka.*[6]
	Chourásya,	*Unggu-ticha.*
	Kulungya,	*Keká-á, ko-i; ko-ni.*
	Thulungya,	*Go-ku;*[5] *go-i.*[5]
	Báhingya,	*Gosi;*[3] *gosuku;*[4] *Go-i;*[5] *go-ku.*[6]
	Lohorong,	*Káchi;*[3] *káchíka;*[4] *káni,*[5] *káningka.*[6]
	Lambichhong,	*Kánchhi,*[3] etc.
	Báláli,	*Káchi;*[3] *káchíka;*[4] *ikin;*[5] *ikka.*[6]
	Sáng-páng,	*Káchi,*[3] etc.; *kayi;*[5] *kani.*[6]
	Dúmi,	*Ichi;*[3] *ochu;*[4] *iki;*[5] *ogue.*[6]
	Kháling,	*Inchi;*[3] *anchu;*[4] *ik;*[5] *ok.*[6]
	Dungmáli,	*Anchá-káche,*[3] etc.; *inkan-ga;*[4] *ankan.*[5]
Broken Tribes of Nepal.	Dárhi,	*Há-mi.*
	Denwár,	*Ha-mi.*
	Pahri,	*Já-di.*
	Chepáng,	*Ngi-lum.*
	Bhrámu,	*Ni.*
	Váyu,	*Go-kháta.*
	Kuswar,	*Há-mi.*
	Kusunda,	*Tok-jhigna;*[1] *cho-baki.*[2]
	Tháru,	*Hang-du;*[1] *hang-log.*[2]
	Lepcha (Sikkim),	*Kayú, ká.*
	Bhútáni v. Lhopa,	*Gná-chá.*
N.-E. Bengal.	Bodo,	*Jong (jong-chur).*
	Dhimál,	*Ky-el.*
	Kocch,	*Hám-i.*
	Garo,	*Ning.*
	Káchári,	*Caret.*
Eastern Frontier of Bengal.	Munipuri,	*Ei-khoi.*
	Míthán Nágá,	*Caret.*
	Tablung Nágá,	*Caret.*
	Khári Nágá,	*Akau.*
	Angámi Nágá,	*Awe.*
	Námsáng Nágá,	*Nimá.*
	Nowgong Nágá,	*Aunok.*
	Tengsa Nágá,	*Akhala.*
	Abor Miri,	*Ngolu.*
	Sibságar Miri,	*Ngosin.*
	Deoria Chutia,	*Jaru-rau.*
	Singpho,	*I.*
Arrakan & Burmah.	Burman (*written*),	*Nga-to.*
	Burman (*spoken*),	*Ngá-do.*
	Khyeng v. Shou,	*Kin-ni.*
	Kámi,	*Ka-chí.*
	Kúmi,	*Ká-i-no.*
	Mrú v. Toung,	*Caret.*
	Sák,	*Caret.*
Siam & Tenasserim.	Talain v. Mon,	*Pwá.*
	Sgau-karen,	*Pwaï.*
	Pwo-karen,	*Pwi-dah.*
	Toungh-thu,	*Ne.*
	Shán,	*Koung-niht.*
	Annamitic,	*Kyung-tôi.*
	Siamese,	*Khá-aen, rău.*
	Ahom,	*Rau.*
	Khámti,	*Hau.*
	Laos,	*Hau.*
Central India.	Ho (Kol),	*A'lle, ábú.*
	Kol (Singhbhum,	*A'ling;*[1] *ále.*[2]
	Santáli,	*A'ling,*[3] *álang;*[4] *ále, ában.*[2]
	Bhúmij,	*A'le* (?).
	Uráon,	*En.*
	Mundala,	*A'llege.*
	Rájmahali,	*Nam, om.*
	Goṇḍi,	*A'mot.*
	Gayeti,	*Mamad.*
	Rutluk,	*Caret.*
	Naikude,	*A'le* (?).
	Kolami,	*Anandun.*
	Mádi,	*Mam.*
	Mádia,	*Caret.*
	Kuri,	*A'le.*
	Keikádi,	*Nang.*
	Khoṇḍ,	*Caret.*
	Sávara,	*Mo-ni.*
	Gadaba,	*Ne-yam.*
	Yerukala,	*Namu, nam-buru.*
	Chentsu,	*Hame.*
Southern India.	Tamiḷ, anc.,	*Yam.*
	Tamiḷ, mod.,	*Nam, nangal.*
	Malayáḷma, anc.,	*Caret.*
	Malayáḷma, mod.,	*Nam, gna-ngal.*
	Telugu,	*Memu, manamu.*
	Karṇáṭaka, anc.,	*Am.*
	Karṇáṭaka, mod.,	*Navu.*
	Tuḷuva,	*Enklu.*
	Kurgi,	*Eng.*
	Toḍuva, }	*Caret.*
	Toḍa, }	*Am, em.*
	Kóta,	*Ye-nge.*
	Badaga,	*Ye-ngal, ye-ngla.*
	Kuṛumba,	*Ye-nga.*
	Iruḷa,	*Navu.*
	Malabar,	*Nám, nangal.*
	Sinhalese,	*Api.*

Group	*Types.*	
Inflecting.	SANSKṚIT,	*Yuvám,*[1] *yúyam.*[2]
	ARABIC,	*Antom.*
Compounding.	BASK,	*Zuek.*
	FINNIC,	*Te.*
	MAGYAR,	*Ti.*
	TURKISH,	*Siz.*
	CIRCASSIAN,	*Sorisher.*
	GEORGIAN,	*Thkwen.*
	MONGOLIAN,	*Ta.*
	MANTSHU,	*Sonwe, soue.*
	JAVANESE, Ngoko,	*Kowe.*
	JAVANESE, Krama,	*Sampeyan.*
	MALAY,	*Kámu.*
Isolating.	CHINESE, Nankin,	*Ni-mên.*
	CHINESE, Pekin,	*Ni-mên.*
	CHINESE, Canton,	*Ni-ti.*
	CHINESE, Shanghai,	*Ná, nung-ná.*
	AMOY, Colloquial,	*Lín.*
	JAPANESE,	*Nanjira.*
	Brahuí,	*Num.*
Chinese Frontier & Tibet.	Gyámi,	*Ni-me.*
	Gyárung,	*Nyo.*
	Tákpa,	*I-rá.*
	Mányak,	*Non-dúr.*
	Thochú,	*Kwéniko, kwa-nik-lar.*
	Sokpa,	*Chhi-ni.*
	Horpa,	*Ni-ni, ni-riggi.*
	Tibetan (*written*),	*Khyod-chag.*
	Tibetan (*spoken*),	*Khe-njo.*
Nepal (east to west).	Serpa,	*Khyo-rang.*
	Súnwár,	*Gaiv-ki.*
	Gúrung,	*Ken-mo.*
	Múrmi,	*Ai-ni.*
	Magar,	*Náng-kúrik.*
	Tháksya,	*Gni-si;*[1] *gna-cha.*[3]
	Pákhya,	*Caret.*
	Newár,	*Chha-ping.*
	Limbu,	*Khenih.*
Kiranti Group (East Nepal).	Kiránti,	*Khananin.*
	Rodong,	*Khána-i, khain-i.*
	Rúngchenbung,	*Kháná-nin; khánâ-na.*
	Chhingtángya,	*Hánâ-nina.*
	Náchhereng,	*A'ná-i, án-nimo.*
	Wáling,	*Háná-ni.*
	Yákha,	*Inkhi-ni, 'nkhi-ni.*
	Chourásya,	*Unu, gnome-ticha.*
	Kulungya,	*A'ná-i, án-i.*
	Thulungya,	*Gán-i.*
	Báhingya,	*Gasi;*[1] *gani.*[2]
	Lohorong,	*Hánáchi;*[1] *hánina.*[2]
	Lambichhong,	*Khánáchi;*[1] *khánáni.*[2]
	Báláli,	*Anáchi;*[1] *ánin.*[3]
	Sáng-páng,	*A'náchi;*[1] *ánáni.*[3]
	Dúmi,	*Yechi;*[1] *áni.*[3]
	Kháling,	*Yechi,*[1] *anchi;*[1] *yen.*[3]
	Dungmáli,	*Hánáche;*[1] *hananin.*[3]
Broken Tribes of Nepal.	Dárhi,	*Ta-he.*
	Denwár,	*To-ho.*
	Pahri,	*Chhá-di.*
	Chepáng,	*Ning-lum.*
	Bhrámu,	*Nung.*
	Váyu,	*Gone-khata.*
	Kuswar,	*Tu-mi.*
	Kusunda,	*Nok-jhigna;*[1] *noki-baki.*[2]
	Tháru,	*Tong-du,*[1] *tu-sal.*[2]
	Lepcha (Sikkim),	*Háyú.*
	Bhúṭáni v. Lhopa,	*Khácha.*

N.-E. Bengal.	Bodo,	*Nang-chur.*
	Dhimál,	*Ny-el.*
	Koech,	*Tum-i.*
	Garo,	*Nan-ok.*
	Káchári,	*Caret.*
Eastern Frontier of Bengal.	Munipuri,	*Nung-khoi.*
	Míthán Nágá,	*Caret.*
	Tablung Nágá,	*Caret.*
	Khári Nágá,	*Ni-khala.*
	Angámi Nágá,	*No-to-leli.*
	Námsáng Nágá,	*Nemá.*
	Nowgong Nágá,	*Na-kara.*
	Tengsa Nágá,	*Na-khala.*
	Abor Miri,	*No-lu.*
	Sibságar Miri,	*No-lu-sin.*
	Deoria Chutia,	*Jákugro-ni.*
	Singpho,	*Ni-theng.*
Arrakan & Burmah.	Burman (*written*),	*Nang-to.*
	Burman (*spoken*),	*Nen-do.*
	Khyeng v. Shou,	*Nang-ni.*
	Kámi,	*Nan-chi.*
	Kúmi,	*Nang-chi-no.*
	Mrú v. Toung,	*Caret.*
	Sák,	*Caret.*
Siam & Tenasserim.	Talain v. Mon,	*Bin-tau.*
	Sgau-karen,	*Thu.*
	Pwo-karen,	*Nwi-dah.*
	Toungh-thu,	*Ná-the.*
	Shán,	*Htsuh-niht.*
	Annamitic,	*Kyung-bay.*
	Siamese,	*Aen, su.*
	Ahom,	*Khau.*
	Khámti,	*Mau-su.*
	Laos,	*Caret.*
Central India.	Ho (Kol),	*A'ppe.*
	Kol (Singhbhum),	*A'pe* (?).
	Santáli,	*Aben;*[1] *ápe.*[2]
	Bhúmij,	*A'pe* (?).
	Uráon,	*A'su.*
	Mundala,	*Inkoghi.*
	Rájmahali,	*Nina.*
	Goṇḍi,	*Unde, immet.*
	Gayeti,	*Im.*
	Rutluk,	*Caret.*
	Naikude,	*A'pe* (?).
	Kolami,	*Niwa.*
	Mádi,	*Mirad.*
	Mádia,	*Caret.*
	Kuri,	*A'pe.*
	Keikádi,	*Ne.*
	Khoṇḍ,	*Caret.*
	Sávara,	*Aman.*
	Gadaba,	*Pen.*
	Yerukala,	*Ning-alu, avaru.*
	Chentsu,	*Te, tu-myi.*
Southern India.	Tamiḷ, anc.,	*Ni-vir.*
	Tamiḷ, mod.,	*Nir, ningal.*
	Malayâḷma, anc.,	*Caret.*
	Malayâḷma, mod.,	*Ning-al.*
	Telugu,	*Mi-ru.*
	Karṇâṭaka, anc.,	*Nim.*
	Karṇâṭaka, mod.,	*Ni-vu.*
	Tuḷuva,	*Inukulu.*
	Kurgi,	*Ning.*
	Toḍuva, }	*Namma.*
	Toḍa, }	*Niv.*
	Kóta,	*Ning-e.*
	Baḍaga,	*Ning-la.*
	Kuṛumba,	*Ning-a.*
	Iruḷa,	*Niv.*
	Malabar,	*Nin-gal.*
	Sinhalese,	*Topi.*

Types.		
Inflecting.	SANSKṚIT,	*Tau,*[1] *te,*[2] *táni.*[3]
	ARABIC,	*Hom.*
Compounding.	BASK,	*Ayek.*
	FINNIC,	*He.*
	MAGYAR,	*Ök.*
	TURKISH,	*Anlar.*
	CIRCASSIAN,	*Arisher.*
	GEORGIAN,	*Igini.*
	MONGOLIAN,	*Ete, etcger, tedet.*
	MANTSHU,	*Tese, t'che.*
	JAVANESE, Ngoko,	*Dewe.*
	JAVANESE, Krama,	*Piyambak.*
	MALAY,	*I'ya.*
Isolating.	CHINESE, Nankin,	*T'a-mên.*
	CHINESE, Pekin,	*T'a-mên.*
	CHINESE, Canton,	*K'ü-ti.*
	CHINESE, Shanghai,	*Yi-láh.*
	AMOY, Colloquial,	*In.*
	JAPANESE,	*Karera.*
	Brahuí,	*Dáfk.*
Chinese Frontier & Tibet.	Gyámi,	*Tha-mé.*
	Gyárung,	*Yapos.*
	Tákpa,	*Pe-rá.*
	Mányak,	*Thi-dúr.*
	Thochú,	*Táho, thák-lar.*
	Sokpa,	*Tha-ni.*
	Horpa,	*Ji-ni, ji-riggi.*
	Tibetan (*written*),	*Kho-chag.*
	Tibetan (*spoken*),	*Khó-njo.*
Nepal (east to west).	Serpa,	*Khwo-rang.*
	Súnwár,	*Harev-ki.*
	Gúrung,	*Thi-mo.*
	Múrmi,	*The-ni.*
	Magar,	*Hos-kúrik.*
	Tháksya,	*H'mi-si,*[1] *H'mi-chá.*[3]
	Pákhya,	*Caret.*
	Newár,	*Wo-ping.*
	Limbu,	*Khúnchi.*
Kiranti Group (East Nepal).	Kiránti,	*Moko-chi.*
	Rodong,	*Khu-i, khu-chu, hay-i.*
	Rúngchenbung,	*Moko.*
	Chhingtángya,	*Yo-go, yo-gwána.*
	Náchhereng,	*Yako-i, maka-i.*
	Wáling,	*Haya-ni, moko-ni, hayak.*
	Yákha,	*Ikhi-ni, yona-ni.*
	Chourásya,	*Yome-ticha.*
	Kulungya,	*Náko-ni.*
	Thulungya,	*Hanom-mim, hanom-nu.*
	Báhingya,	*Haremdá-si;*[1] *haremdá.*[3]
	Lohorong,	*Máhá-chi,*[1] etc.; *miháná.*[3]
	Lambichhong,	*Yona-chi,*[1] etc.; *yokha,* etc.
	Báláli,	*Khochi-hippang;*[1] *khochi.*[3]
	Sáng-páng,	*Mokochi;*[1] *mekoni,*[3] etc.
	Dúmi,	*Yákám-su;*[1] *yakam-ham.*[3]
	Kháling,	*Omsa;*[1] *am-ham.*[3]
	Dungmáli,	*Mu,*[1] *moko-chi;*[1] *mu-kha.*[3]
Broken Tribes of Nepal.	Dárhi,	*U-nin.*
	Denwár,	*U-ho.*
	Pahri,	*U-si, ho-si.*
	Chepáng,	*Wo-mai.*
	Bhrámu,	*Hu-du.*
	Váyu,	*Mü-khata, ko-me, á-me.*
	Kuswar,	*Hu-ri, há-ri, há-ring.*
	Kusunda,	*Gida-jhigna;*[1] *gida-baki.*[3]
	Tháru,	*U-nudu;*[1] *u-sal.*[3]
	Lepcha (Sikkim),	*Hóyú.*
	Bhúṭáni v. Lhopa,	*Khóng.*

N.-E. Bengal.	Bodo,	*Bi-chur.*
	Dhimál,	*U-bal.*
	Kocch,	*Un-i.*
	Garo,	*On-ok, won-ok.*
	Káchári,	*Caret.*
Eastern Frontier of Bengal.	Munipuri,	*Ma-khoi.*
	Míthán Nágá,	*Caret.*
	Tablung Nágá,	*Caret.*
	Khári Nágá,	*Tung-khala.*
	Angámi Nágá,	*To-thete.*
	Námsáng Nágá,	*Sening.*
	Nowgong Nágá,	*Yau.*
	Tengsa Nágá,	*Tebepá.*
	Abor Miri,	*Bulu.*
	Sibságar Miri,	*Ullu-bullu.*
	Deoria Chutia,	*Bario.*
	Singpho,	*Khíni.*
Arrakan & Burmah.	Burman (*written*),	*Su-to,* Thu-to.
	Burman (*spoken*),	Thu-do.
	Khyeng v. Shou,	*Ni-di, ni-li.*
	Kámi,	*Hun-na, ha-ni-chi.*
	Kúmi,	*Caret.*
	Mrú v. Toung,	*Caret.*
	Sák,	*Caret.*
Siam & Tenasserim.	Talain v. Mon,	*Nyi-tau.*
	Sgau-karen,	*Awa-i-tha, ya-we-da.*
	Pwo-karen,	*Athi-we.*
	Toungh-thu,	*Wá-the.*
	Shán,	*Mau-niht.*
	Annamitic,	*Kyung-no.*
	Siamese,	*Loung-ni, khauarai.*
	Ahom,	*Khreu.*
	Khámti,	*Mau-khau.*
	Laos,	*Caret.*
Central India.	Ho (Kol),	*A'ko.*
	Kol (Singhbhum),	*Onko* (?).
	Santáli,	*Onákin;*[1] *onko.*[3]
	Bhúmij,	*Onko* (?).
	Uráon,	*Onko* (?).
	Mundala,	*A'nko.*
	Rájmahali,	*A'sabar, áwar.*
	Goṇḍi,	*Hurk, wurk.*
	Gayeti,	*Wor.*
	Rutluk,	*Ad* (?).
	Naikude,	*Ound* (?).
	Kolami,	*Awar.*
	Mádi,	*Woru.*
	Mádia,	*Caret.*
	Kuri,	*Arko.*
	Keikádi,	*Ado* (?).
	Khoṇḍ,	*Caret.*
	Sávara,	*Ani.*
	Gadaba,	*Mai.*
	Yerukala,	*Tila, avallu.*
	Chentsu,	*Vamhi.*
Southern India.	Tamiḷ, anc.,	*Caret.*
	Tamiḷ, mod.,	*Avar, avargal.*
	Malayáḷma, anc.,	*Caret.*
	Malayáḷma, mod.,	*Avara.*
	Telugu,	*Varu.*
	Karṇáṭaka, anc.,	*Avar.*
	Karṇáṭaka, mod.,	*Avaru.*
	Tuḷuva,	*Akulu.*
	Kurgi,	*Avaru.*
	Toḍuva, }	*Adam.*
	Toḍa, }	*Avar adam.*
	Kóta,	*Avare.*
	Baḍaga,	*Avaka.*
	Kuṛumba,	*Avaru.*
	Iruḷa,	*Aduru.*
	Malabar,	*Averkal, avei.*
	Sinhalese,	*Ovun.*

Group	Types.	
Inflecting.	SANSKRIT,	*Madîya.*
	ARABIC,	*-i.*
Compounding.	BASK,	*Nere.*
	FINNIC,	*Minun.*
	MAGYAR,	*-m.*
	TURKISH,	*-im.*
	CIRCASSIAN,	*Caret.*
	GEORGIAN,	*Cheni.*
	MONGOLIAN,	*Minu, mini.*
	MANTSHU,	*Mini.*
	JAVANESE, Ngoko,	*-ku.*
	JAVANESE, Krama,	*Kula.*
	MALAY,	*A'ku-punya.*
Isolating.	CHINESE, Nankin,	*Wo-tih.*
	CHINESE, Pekin,	*Wo-ti.*
	CHINESE, Canton,	*Ngo-ke.*
	CHINESE, Shanghai,	*Ngu-koh.*
	AMOY, Colloquial,	*Gba-ê.*
	JAPANESE,	*Watakusinoto.*
	Brahuí,	*Kaná.*
Chinese Frontier & Tibet.	Gyámi,	*Gno-ti.*
	Gyárung,	*Gná.*
	Tákpa,	*Gne-ku.*
	Mányak,	*A-i.*
	Thochú,	*Kák-chi.*
	Sokpa,	*Caret.*
	Horpa,	*Gná-á.*
	Tibetan (*written*),	*Nahi, nayi.*
	Tibetan (*spoken*),	*Gnayi.*
Nepal (east to west).	Serpa,	*Gna ti.*
	Súnwár,	*A'ké.*
	Gúrung,	*Gná lá.*
	Múrmi,	*Gná lá.*
	Magar,	*Gnou.*
	Tháksya,	*Ghyang-ge.*
	Pákhya,	*Mero.*
	Newár,	*Ji-gu, ji-mha.*
	Limbu,	*Ingá-in.*
Kiranti Group (East Nepal).	Kiránti,	*Ang-ko.*
	Rodong,	*A', ang, ang-ma.*
	Rúngchenbung,	*Ang, ang-ko.*
	Chhingtángya,	*A', ákwa, ako-o.*
	Nachhereng,	*Ang-mi.*
	Wáling,	*A', áng-pik.*
	Yákha,	*A'-ga.*
	Chourásya,	*A', á-leme.*
	Kulungya,	*Caret.*
	Thulungya,	*A', ámá.*
	Báhingya,	*A', wá, wá-ke.*
	Lohorong,	*Ung, kángá-mi.*
	Lambichhong,	*Ang, um, ung, kákha.*
	Bálálí,	*Um, ung, káng-mi.*
	Sáng-páng,	*A'ṇ, aṇa-mi.*
	Dúmi,	*O, o-po.*
	Khálíng,	*A', á-po.*
	Dungmáli,	*Ang, ang-bi.*
Broken Tribes of Nepal.	Dárhi,	*Me-ro.*
	Denwár,	*Mo-ra.*
	Pahri,	*Nung-gu, já-gu.*
	Chepáng,	*Ngá-ku.*
	Bhrámu,	*Ngá-ku.*
	Váyu,	*Ang, ang-mu.*
	Kuswar,	*Máha-na, -im.*
	Kusunda,	*Chi-yi.*
	Tháru,	*Caret.*
	Lepcha (Sikkim),	*Kascusa.*
	Bhútáni v. Lhopa,	*Gné-gi.*

N.-E. Bengal.	Bodo,	*A'ngni.*
	Dhimál,	*Káng.*
	Kocch,	*Mor, ángni.*
	Garo,	*Caret.*
	Káchári,	*Caret.*
Eastern Frontier of Bengal.	Munipuri,	*Ei-gi.*
	Míthán Nágá,	*Kukuhe.*
	Tablung Nágá,	*Tesei.*
	Khári Nágá,	*Ni.*
	Angámi Nágá,	*Caret.*
	Námsáng Nágá,	*Nga.*
	Nowgong Nágá,	*Ka.*
	Tengsa Nágá,	*Ngaichi.*
	Abor Miri,	*Ngoke.*
	Sibságar Miri,	*Ngoke.*
	Deoria Chutia,	*Aṇyo.*
	Singpho,	*Ngena.*
Arrakan & Burmah.	Burman (*written*),	*Ngái.*
	Burman (*spoken*),	*Ngái.*
	Khyeng v. Shou,	*Ki-ko.*
	Kámi,	*Ká-i-un.*
	Kúmi,	*Caret.*
	Mrú v. Toung,	*Caret.*
	Sák,	*Caret.*
Siam & Tenasserim.	Talain v. Mon,	*Kharu-awái.*
	Sgau-karen,	*Y'waidah.*
	Pwo-karen,	*Y'wadah.*
	Toungh-thu,	*Caret.*
	Shán,	*Khoung-kau.*
	Annamitic,	*Tôi-minh.*
	Siamese,	*Khon-kha.*
	Ahom,	*Au (?), kau.*
	Khámti,	*Kau.*
	Laos,	*Caret.*
Central India.	Ho (Kol),	*Inya.*
	Kol (Singhbhum),	*Iyan.*
	Santáli,	*Ting; ing-reá.*
	Bhúmij,	*Inya.*
	Uráon,	*Enghi.*
	Mundala,	*Jhátaná.*
	Rájmahali,	*Ongki.*
	Goṇḍi,	*Nává ángdo, náwá.*
	Gayeti,	*Idana, awá.*
	Rutluk,	*Náwá.*
	Naikude,	*Anet.*
	Kolami,	*Aneten.*
	Mádi,	*Náwá.*
	Mádia,	*Caret.*
	Kuri,	*Ing.*
	Keikádi,	*Namtu.*
	Khoṇḍ,	*Nánde.*
	Sávara,	*Gránate.*
	Gadaba,	*Noinyo.*
	Yerukala,	*Nunguḍedi, namburudu.*
	Chentsu,	*Hamár.*
Southern India.	Tamil, anc.,	*Caret.*
	Tamil, mod.,	*Enadu, yennudaya.*
	Malayáḷma, anc.,	*Caret.*
	Malayáḷma, mod.,	*Enre.*
	Telugu,	*Nádi, nayokka.*
	Karṇáṭaka, anc.,	*Caret.*
	Karṇaṭaka, mod.,	*Nannadu.*
	Tuḷuva,	*Ennou.*
	Kurgi,	*Caret.*
	Toḍuva, }	*Caret.*
	Toḍa, }	*Yennadu.*
	Kóta,	*Yennade.*
	Baḍaga,	*Yennadu.*
	Kurumba,	*Nanadu, yennadu.*
	Iruḷa,	*Nannadu, yennadu.*
	Malabar,	*Ennudeyathu, enathu.*
	Sinhalese,	*Magé.*

Group	Types.	
Inflecting.	SANSKṚIT, . . .	*Twadiya.*
	ARABIC, ...	*-ak, -ki* (fem.).
Compounding.	BASK, ...	*Hire, zure.*
	FINNIC, ...	*Sinun.*
	MAGYAR, ...	*-d.*
	TURKISH, ...	*-in, -ing.*
	CIRCASSIAN, ...	*Caret.*
	GEORGIAN, ...	*Sheni.*
	MONGOLIAN, ...	*Tschinu, tchini.*
	MANTSHU, ...	*Sini.*
	JAVANESE, Ngoko, . .	*-mu.*
	JAVANESE, Krama, . .	*Sampeyan.*
	MALAY, ...	*Angkau-punya.*
Isolating.	CHINESE, Nankin, . .	*Ni-tih.*
	CHINESE, Pekin, . .	*Ni-ti.*
	CHINESE, Canton, . .	*Ni-ke.*
	CHINESE, Shanghai, .	*Nimg-koh.*
	AMOY, Colloquial, . .	*Li-ê.*
	JAPANESE, ...	*Sonomonoto.*
	Brahuí, ...	*Ná.*
Chinese Frontier & Tibet.	Gyámi, ...	*Ni-ti.*
	Gyárung, ...	*Ni.*
	Tákpa, ...	*I-ku.*
	Mányak, ...	*Nô-i.*
	Thochú, ...	*Kwck chi.*
	Sokpa, ...	*Caret.*
	Horpa, ...	*Ni-i.*
	Tibetan (*written*), . .	*Khyod-kyi.*
	Tibetan (*spoken*), . .	*Khe-yi.*
Nepal (east to west).	Serpa, ...	*Khyô-ti.*
	Súnwár, ...	*I'ke.*
	Gúrung, ...	*Kenlá.*
	Múrmi, ...	*Ai lá.*
	Magar, ...	*Núwo.*
	Tháksya, ...	*Gná-ye.*
	Pákhya, ...	*Tero.*
	Newár, ...	*Chhang-gú.*
	Limbu, ...	*Khene-in.*
Kiranti Group (East Nepal).	Kiránti, ...	*Am-ko.*
	Rodong, ...	*Khá, khá-mo.*
	Rúngchenbung, . . .	*A'm, ám-ko.*
	Chhingtángya, . . .	*Hána, háná-yakwa.*
	Náchhereng, ...	*A'm, ám-mi, án-mi.*
	Wáling, ...	*A'm, ám-pik.*
	Yákha, ...	*In-ga.*
	Chourásya, ...	*I-leme.*
	Kulungya, ...	*Ammi.*
	Thulungya, ...	*I, ye-ma.*
	Báhingya, ...	*I, i-ke.*
	Lohorong, ...	*A'm, háná-mi.*
	Lambichhong, . . .	*A', ám, án, khánâ-kha.*
	Báláli, ...	*A', ám, áp, ám-mi.*
	Sáng-páng, ...	*A'm, ám-mi.*
	Dúmi, ...	*A', á-po.*
	Kháling, ...	*I, in-po.*
	Dungmáli, ...	*A'm, ám-bi.*
Broken Tribes of Nepal.	Dárhi, ...	*Te-ro.*
	Denwár, ...	*To-ra.*
	Pahri, ...	*Chhung-gu.*
	Chepáng, ...	*Náng-ku.*
	Bhrámu, ...	*Nang-ku.*
	Váyu, ...	*Ung, ung-mu.*
	Kuswar, ...	*Taha-na ; -ir.*
	Kusunda, ...	*Niyi.*
	Tháru, ...	*Caret.*
	Lepcha (Sikkim), . .	*Hadosa.*
	Bhúṭáni v. Lhopa, . .	*Chhe-gi.*

N.-E. Bengal.	Bodo, ...	*Náng-ni.*
	Dhimál, ...	*Náng.*
	Kocch, ...	*Tor, nang-ni.*
	Garo, ...	*Nang-ni.*
	Kácharí, ...	*Caret.*
Eastern Frontier of Bengal.	Munipuri, ...	*Nung-gi.*
	Míthán Nágá, . . .	*Caret.*
	Tablung Nágá, . . .	*Caret.*
	Khári Nágá, ...	*-Nang.*
	Angámi Nágá, . . .	*Caret.*
	Námsáng Nágá, . .	*Má.*
	Nowgong Nágá, . .	*Ná.*
	Tengsa Nágá, . . .	*Mechi.*
	Abor Miri, ...	*Noke.*
	Sibságar Miri, . . .	*Noke.*
	Deoria Chutia, . . .	*Niyo.*
	Singpho, ...	*Nána.*
Arrakan & Burmah.	Burman (*written*), . .	*Mangi.*
	Burman (*spoken*), . . .	*Meni.*
	Khyeng v. Shou, . .	*Nang-ko.*
	Kámi, ...	*Nan-un.*
	Kúmi, ...	*Caret.*
	Mrú v. Toung, . . .	*Caret.*
	Sák, ...	*Caret.*
Siam & Tenasserim.	Talain v. Mon, . . .	*Kharu-hpa.*
	Sgau-karen, ...	*N'waïdah.*
	Pwo-karen, ...	*N'wadah.*
	Toungh-thu, ...	*Caret.*
	Shán, ...	*Khoung-moung.*
	Annamitic, ...	*Anh-minh.*
	Siamese, ...	*Khoung-aeng.*
	Ahom, ...	*Mo.*
	Khámti, ...	*Mau.*
	Laos, ...	*Caret.*
Central India.	Ho (Kol), ...	*Umma.*
	Kol (Singhbhum), . .	*Ummá.*
	Santáli, ...	*Tám ; ám-rea (ámi ?).*
	Bhúmij, ...	*Ummá.*
	Uráon, ...	*Ni-enghi.*
	Mundala, ...	*A'má-tana.*
	Rájmahali, ...	*Ning-ki.*
	Goṇḍi, ...	*Nidvu-triand, niwá.*
	Gayeti, ...	*Niwá.*
	Rutluk, ...	*Niwá.*
	Naikude, ...	*Inet.*
	Kolami, ...	*Ineten.*
	Mádi, ...	*Niwá.*
	Mádia, ...	*Caret.*
	Kuri, ...	*A'ma.*
	Keikádi, ...	*Nimtu.*
	Khoṇḍ, ...	*Minde.*
	Sávara, ...	*Ammanate.*
	Gadaba, ...	*Nenne.*
	Yerukala, ...	*Ningaḍeo, ninaḍidi.*
	Chentsu, ...	*Thor.*
Southern India.	Tamiḷ, anc., ...	*Ninadu.*
	Tamiḷ, mod., ...	*Unadu, unnudaya.*
	Malayáḷma, anc., . .	*Caret.*
	Malayáḷma, mod., . .	*Ninra.*
	Telugu, ...	*Nidi, niyokka.*
	Karṇáṭaka, anc., . .	*Caret.*
	Karṇáṭaka, mod., . .	*Ninnadu.*
	Tuḷuva, ...	*Innou.*
	Kurgi, ...	*Caret.*
	Toḍuva, }	*Caret.*
	Toḍa, }	*Ninnadu.*
	Kóta, ...	*Ninnade.*
	Baḍaga, ...	*Ninnadu.*
	Kuṛumba, ...	*Ninnadu.*
	Iruḷa, ...	*Ninnadu.*
	Malabar, ...	*Ummudiathu, umathu.*
	Sinhalese, ...	*Tôge.*

Group	Types.	
Inflecting.	SANSKRIT,	*Tadiya.*
	ARABIC,	*Ho.*
Compounding.	BASK,	*Bere, aren.*
	FINNIC,	*Hanen.*
	MAGYAR,	*-ja, -je.*
	TURKISH,	*-i.*
	CIRCASSIAN,	*Caret.*
	GEORGIAN,	*Thwyesi.*
	MONGOLIAN,	*Ta.*
	MANTSHU,	*Terei, ini.*
	JAVANESE, Ngoko,	*-e.*
	JAVANESE, Krama,	*-ipun.*
	MALAY,	*I'ya-punya.*
Isolating.	CHINESE, Nankin,	*Ta-tih.*
	CHINESE, Pekin,	*Ta-ti.*
	CHINESE, Canton,	*Kü-kê.*
	CHINESE, Shanghai,	*Yi-koh.*
	AMOY, Colloquial,	*I-ê.*
	JAPANESE,	*Anofitonoto.*
	Brahuí,	*Dáná.*
Chinese Frontier & Tibet.	Gyámi,	*Tha-ti.*
	Gyárung,	*Wá.*
	Tákpa,	*Pé-ku.*
	Mányak,	*Thi-o.*
	Thochú,	*Thákchi, kwanákchi.*
	Sokpa,	*Caret.*
	Horpa,	*Jyá-a.*
	Tibetan (*written*),	*Khó-yi, khó-hi.*
	Tibetan (*spoken*),	*Khó-yi.*
Nepal (east to west).	Serpa,	*Khwo-ti.*
	Súnwár,	*Hareá-ke, mere-ke.*
	Gúrung,	*Thi-lá.*
	Múrmi,	*The-lá.*
	Magar,	*Ho-chú.*
	Tháksya,	*Hmi-ye.*
	Pákhya,	*Usai-ko.*
	Newár,	*Waya-gú.*
	Limbu,	*Khúne-in.*
Kiranti Group (East Nepal).	Kiránti,	*Mósó.*
	Rodong,	*U, o, um, khu-mo.*
	Rúngchenbung,	*U, o, mo-so, ya-u-so.*
	Chhingtángya,	*U, mo-gwa-sekkwa.*
	Náchhereng,	*U, um, yak-mi, manka-mi.*
	Wáling,	*Hayek-pik.*
	Yákha,	*I, i-ga, yona-ga.*
	Chourásya,	*Gneme-leme.*
	Kulungya,	*Wa, nakwa-mi.*
	Thulungya,	*U, o-kam, hanom-kam.*
	Báhingya,	*A', a-ke, harem-ke.*
	Lohorong,	*Um, mo-mi, meyem-mi.*
	Lambichhong,	*Im, ako-im, yona-gnákha.*
	Báláli,	*U, o, mom, khomi.*
	Sáng-páng,	*Um, me-kum, me-komi.*
	Dúmi,	*U, mom, mom-po.*
	Kháling,	*U, yákám, yákám-po.*
	Dungmáli,	*I-gem, mo-gom, mo-gombi.*
Broken Tribes of Nepal.	Dárhi,	*U-ker.*
	Denwár,	*Wok-rak.*
	Pahri,	*Hong-gu, hwang-gu.*
	Chepáng,	*U-ku.*
	Bhrámu,	*U-ku. [minung-mu.*
	Váyu,	*A', á-mu; wathim-mu;*
	Kuswar,	*Hulo-kara; -ik.*
	Kusunda,	*Gida-yi.*
	Tháru,	*Caret.*
	Lepcha (Sikkim),	*Heusa.*
	Bhútáni v. Lhopa,	*Kheugi.*

N.-E. Bengal.	Bodo,	*Bi-ni.*
	Dhimál,	*Wang, oko-wang.*
	Kocch,	*Or.*
	Garo,	*U-ni.*
	Káchári,	*Caret.*
Eastern Frontier of Bengal.	Munipuri,	*Ma-gi.*
	Míthán Nágá,	*Caret.*
	Tablung Nágá,	*Caret.*
	Khári Nágá,	*Caret.*
	Angámi Nágá,	*Caret.*
	Námsáng Nágá,	*Ate.*
	Nowgong Nágá,	*Pá.*
	Tengsa Nágá,	*Páchi.*
	Abor Miri,	*Büke.*
	Sibságar Miri,	*Büke.*
	Deoria Chutia,	*Biyo.*
	Singpho,	*Khina.*
Arrakan & Burmah.	Burman (*written*),	*Sui.*
	Burman (*spoken*),	Th*ui*, th*u-ha.*
	Khyeng v. Shou,	*Ni-ko.*
	Kámi,	*Ha-na-i-un.*
	Kúmi,	*Caret.*
	Mrú v. Toung,	*Caret.*
	Sák,	*Caret.*
Siam & Tenasserim.	Talain v. Mon,	*Kharu-nyung.*
	Sgau-karen,	*A-waïdah.*
	Pwo-karen,	*A-wadah.*
	Toungh-thu,	*Caret.*
	Shán,	*Khoung-pen.*
	Annamitic,	*A'i-minh.*
	Siamese,	*Khoung-troung.*
	Ahom,	*Heu.*
	Khámti,	*Man.*
	Laos,	*Caret.*
Central India.	Ho (Kol),	*Aï-á.*
	Kol (Singhbhum),	*Inni.*
	Santáli,	*Tìi; hun-rea (un-ea ?).*
	Bhúmij,	*Aige.*
	Uráon,	*A'sghi.*
	Mundala,	*Annerá-tana.*
	Rájmahali,	*A'hiki.*
	Goṇḍi,	*Oná, honá.*
	Gayeti,	*Oná.*
	Rutluk,	*Waná.*
	Naïkude,	*Awanet, yennet.*
	Kolami,	*Awanel.*
	Mádi,	*Woná, hatundu.*
	Mádia,	*Woná.*
	Kuri,	*Caret.*
	Keikádi,	*Atuti.*
	Khoṇḍ,	*Yevánetara.*
	Sávara,	*Ani-nate.*
	Gadaba,	*Mayino.*
	Yerukala,	*Avanudu, attamuḍidi.*
	Chentsu,	*Vahár.*
Southern India.	Tamiḷ, anc.,	*Caret.*
	Tamiḷ, mod.,	*Avanadu, avanudaya.*
	Malayáḷma, anc.,	*Caret.*
	Malayáḷma, mod.,	*Avanre.*
	Telugu,	*Váḍidi, vaḍiokka.*
	Karṇáṭaka, anc.,	*Caret.*
	Karṇáṭaka, mod.,	*Avana.*
	Tuḷuva,	*Ayanou.*
	Kurgi,	*Caret.*
	Toḍuva, }	*Caret.*
	Toḍa, }	*Avandu.*
	Kóta,	*Avanade.*
	Baḍaga,	*Avanadu.*
	Kurumba,	*Avanadu.*
	Iruḷa,	*Avanudu.*
	Malabar,	*Avanudeyathu.*
	Sinhalese,	*Ohuge.*

Group	Types.	
Inflecting.	SANSKRIT,	*Asmadiya.*
	ARABIC,	*-na.*
Compounding.	BASK,	*Gure, geure, geren.*
	FINNIC,	*Meidan.*
	MAGYAR,	*-nk.*
	TURKISH,	*-imiz.*
	CIRCASSIAN,	*Caret.*
	GEORGIAN,	*Chweni.*
	MONGOLIAN,	*Manu, bidanu.*
	MANTSHU,	*Meni, musei.*
	JAVANESE, Ngoko,	*-ku.*
	JAVANESE, Krama,	*Kula.*
	MALAY,	*Kámi-puña, kita-puña, -ku.*
Isolating.	CHINESE, Nankin,	*Wo-mên-tih.*
	CHINESE, Pekin,	*Wo-mên-ti.*
	CHINESE, Canton,	*Ngo-ti-ke.*
	CHINESE, Shanghai,	*Ngu-ni-kŭh.*
	AMOY, Colloquial,	*Lán-ê.*
	JAPANESE,	*Wataks-domonoto.*
	Brahuí,	*Nána.*
Chinese Frontier & Tibet.	Gyámi,	*Gnomé-ti.*
	Gyárung,	*Caret.*
	Tákpa,	*Gnará-ku.*
	Mányak,	*Adur-i.*
	Thochú,	*Chikúk.*
	Sokpa,	*Caret.*
	Horpa,	*Gnúárigya.*
	Tibetan (*written*),	*Nachag-gi.*
	Tibetan (*spoken*),	*Gnáajo-yi.*
Nepal (east to west).	Serpa,	*Nirá-ti.*
	Súnwár,	*Go-ain-ke.*
	Gúrung,	*Gnimo-lo.*
	Múrmi,	*Inná.*
	Magar,	*Kan kúrikúm.*
	Tháksya,	*Ghyang-si-ye;*[1] *ghyang-cha-ye.*[2]
	Pákhya,	*Caret.*
	Newár,	*Jiping-gú.*
	Limbu,	*Anigen-in.*
Kiranti Group (East Nepal).	Kiránti,	*A' in ko.*
	Rodong,	*I-mo, ái-mo.*
	Rúngchenbung,	*A'in-kwa.*
	Chhingtángya,	*Kánu-gnaikkwa.*
	Náchhereng,	*Woki-mi.*
	Wáling,	*Ang-kapik.*
	Yákha,	*Aen-ga.*
	Chourásya,	*Iki-leme.*
	Kulungya,	*Wokhi-mi.*
	Thulungya,	*A'ki-ma, iki-ma.*
	Báhingya,	*I-si,*[3] *wa-si;*[4] *ikke,*[5] *wake.*[6]
	Lohorong,	*Ká-chim,*[3] *ká-chikam.*[4]
	Lambichhong,	*Kán-chhi;*[3] *kan-chhigna.*[4]
	Báláli,	*Ká-chim,*[3] *ká-chigam;*[4] *i-king.*[5]
	Sáng-páng,	*U-chu,*[3] *an-chu,*[4] *ye.*[5]
	Dúmi,	*I-chi,*[3] *o-chu;*[4] *in-ki.*[5]
	Kháling,	*Is,*[3] *os;*[4] *ik,*[5] *ok.*[6]
	Dungmáli,	*An-cha,*[3] *an-chaga;*[4] *an-ga.*[5]
Broken Tribes of Nepal.	Dárhi,	*Ham-ro.*
	Denwár,	*Ham-rai.*
	Pahri,	*Já-gu.*
	Chepáng,	*Ngi-ku.*
	Bhrámu,	*Ni-ku.*
	Váyu,	*Ang-ki, ang-chimo.*
	Kuswar,	*Ham-ára.*
	Kusunda,	*Tok-jhigna-yi;*[1] *chobaki-yida.*[2]
	Tháru,	*Hamarnu-hye;*[1] *ham-log-kau.*[2]
	Lepcha (Sikkim),	*Kayú-pongsa.*
	Bhútáni v. Lhopa,	*Gnáchégi.*
N.-E. Bengal.	Bodo,	*Jong-ni.*
	Dhimál,	*King.*
	Kocch,	*Hám-aro.*
	Garo,	*Ning-ni.*
	Káchári,	*Caret.*
Eastern Frontier of Bengal.	Munipuri,	*Eikhoi-gi.*
	Míthán Nágá,	*Caret.*
	Tablung Nágá,	*Caret.*
	Khári Nágá,	*Caret.*
	Angámi Nágá,	*Caret.*
	Námsáng Nágá,	*Caret.*
	Nowgong Nágá,	*Asáu.*
	Tengsa Nágá,	*Akhali.*
	Abor Miri,	*Caret.*
	Sibságar Miri,	*Ngo-luke.*
	Deoria Chutia,	*Caret.*
	Singpho,	*Caret.*
Arrakan & Burmah.	Burman (*written*),	*Ngá-toi.*
	Burman (*spoken*),	*Ngá-doi.*
	Khyeng v. Shou,	*Kini-ko.*
	Kámi,	*Kachi-un.*
	Kúmi,	*Caret.*
	Mrú v. Toung,	*Caret.*
	Sák,	*Caret.*
Siam & Tenasserim.	Talain v. Mon,	*Kharu-away-tau.*
	Sgau-karen,	*P'waïdah.*
	Pwo-karen,	*P'wadah.*
	Toungh-thu,	*Caret.*
	Shán,	*Khoung-houng.*
	Annamitic,	*Kyung-tôi-minh.*
	Siamese,	*Khoukha-tsoung.*
	Ahom,	*Rau.*
	Khámti,	*Hau.*
	Laos,	*Caret.*
Central India.	Ho (Kol),	*Alléa, abúá.*
	Kol (Singhbhum),	*Alle-á.*
	Santáli,	*Táling;*[1] *tále, taban,*[2] [*(alleá ?)*.
	Bhúmij,	*A'busa-ban.*
	Urâon,	*Emhi.*
	Mundala,	*Ahuá-tana.*
	Rájmahali,	*Emki, nám-ki.*
	Gondi,	*Mábaï, mawa.*
	Gayeti,	*Idana, awa.*
	Rutluk,	*Mawa.*
	Naikude,	*A'med.*
	Kolami,	*Anet.*
	Mádi,	*Mawa, adunawand.*
	Mádia,	*Caret.*
	Kuri,	*Nan.*
	Keikádi,	*Caret.*
	Khond,	*Caret.*
	Sávara,	*Moni-nate.*
	Gadaba,	*Niyyino.*
	Yerukala,	*Namburudu.*
	Chentsu,	*Hamár.*
Southern India.	Tamil, anc.,	*Emadu.*
	Tamil, mod.,	*Namadu, yengaludaiya.*
	Malayálma, anc.,	*Caret.*
	Malayálma, mod.,	*Nammute, nangngalute.*
	Telugu,	*Mádi, má-yokka.*
	Karnátaka, anc.,	*Caret.*
	Karnátaka, mod.,	*Nammadu.*
	Tuluva,	*Enkulanou.*
	Kurgi,	*Yengada, nangada.*
	Toduva, }	*Caret.*
	Toda, }	*Yemmadu, nammadu.*
	Kóta,	*Nangude.*
	Badaga,	*Yengadu, nammadu.*
	Kurumba,	*Yengadu.*
	Irula,	*Nammudu.*
	Malabar,	*Engaludeyathu, emathu.*
	Sinhalese,	*Apé.*

Group	*Types.*	
Inflecting.	SANSKṚIT,	*Yushmadíya.*
	ARABIC, .	*-kom.*
Compounding.	BASK, ...	*Zuen, zeuen, zeren.*
	FINNIC, ...	*Teidan.*
	MAGYAR, ...	*-tok, -tek.*
	TURKISH, ...	*-iniz.*
	CIRCASSIAN, ...	*Caret.*
	GEORGIAN, ...	*Thkweni.*
	MONGOLIAN, ...	*Tanu.*
	MANTSHU, ...	*Sueni.*
	JAVANESE, Ngoko, . .	*-mu.*
	JAVANESE, Krama, . .	*Sampeyan.*
	MALAY, ...	*Kámu-puña, -mu.*
Isolating.	CHINESE, Nankin, . .	*Ni-mên-tih.*
	CHINESE, Pekin, . .	*Ni-mên-ti.*
	CHINESE, Canton, . .	*Ni-ti-ké.*
	CHINESE, Shanghai, .	*Na-kŭh.*
	AMOY, Colloquial, . .	*Lín-ê.*
	JAPANESE, ...	*Nanjiranoto.*
	Brahuí, ...	*Numá.*
Chinese Frontier & Tibet.	Gyámi, ...	*Nimê-ti.*
	Gyárung, ...	*Caret.*
	Tákpa, ...	*Irá-ku.*
	Mányak, ...	*Nondur-í.*
	Thochú, ...	*Kwánikúk.*
	Sokpa, ...	*Caret.*
	Horpa, ...	*Nürigya.*
	Tibetan (*written*), . .	*Kyhodchag-gi.*
	Tibetan (*spoken*), . .	*Khenjo-yi.*
Nepal (east to west).	Serpa, ...	*Khyorá-ti.*
	Súnwár, ...	*Gai-ain-ke, in-ke.*
	Gúrung, ...	*Kememo-lo.*
	Múrmi, ...	*Anná.*
	Magar, ...	*Nang-kúrikúm.*
	Tháksya, ...	*Eni-si-ye;*[1] *gna-cha-ye.*[2]
	Pákhya, ...	*Caret.*
	Newár, ...	*Chhaping-gú.*
	Limbu, ...	*Khenih' in.*
Kiranti Group (East Nepal).	Kiránti, ...	*A'mno.*
	Rodong, ...	*Kha-mo, khái-mo.*
	Rúngchenbung, . . .	*A'mno.*
	Chhingtángya, . . .	*Háni-yakkwa.*
	Náchhereng, ...	*Amni-mowá.*
	Wáling, ...	*Haye-kapik.*
	Yákha, ...	*Ning-ga.*
	Chourásya, ...	*Muyem-leme.*
	Kulungya, ...	*Amni-mi.*
	Thulungya, ...	*Ini-má.*
	Báhingya, ...	*I-si,*[1] *i-sike;*[1] *i-ni.*[2]
	Lohorong, ...	*Am-chi;*[1] *am-ni.*[2]
	Lambichhong, . . .	*Khána-chhi;*[1] *khánani.*[2]
	Báláli, ...	*A'ná-chim;*[1] *áninim.*[2]
	Sáng-páng, ...	*A'm-chu;*[1] *amnu.*[2]
	Dúmi, ...	*An-chi;*[1] *anni.*[2]
	Kháling, ...	*Yés;*[1] *yén.*[2]
	Dungmáli, ...	*Am-cha;*[1] *amga.*[2]
Broken Tribes of Nepal.	Dárhi, ...	*Taharo (tumharo?).*
	Denwár, ...	*Caret.*
	Pahri, ...	*Chhá-gu.*
	Chepáng, ...	*Ning-ku.*
	Bhrámu, ...	*Nung-ku.*
	Váyu, ...	*Ung-chimu;*[1] *un-nimu.*[2]
	Kuswar, ...	*Tum-árá.*
	Kusunda, ...	*Nok-jhigna-yi; nokibaki-yida.*[2]
	Tháru, ...	*Tahárasa-bake.*
	Lepcha (Sikkim), . .	*Hayú-pongsa.*
	Bhúṭáni v. Lhopa, . .	*Khen-chêgi.*

N.-E. Bengal.	Bodo, ...	*Nangchur-ni.*
	Dhimál, ...	*Ning.*
	Kocch, ...	*Tum-aro.*
	Garo, ...	*Nanok-ni.*
	Káchári, ...	*Caret.*
Eastern Frontier of Bengal.	Munipuri, . .	*Nungkhoi-gi.*
	Míthán Nágá, . .	*Caret.*
	Tablung Nágá, . . .	*Caret.*
	Khári Nágá, ...	*Caret.*
	Angámi Nágá, . . .	*Caret.*
	Námsáng Nágá, . .	*Caret.*
	Nowgong Nágá, . .	*Nü.*
	Tengsa Nágá, . . .	*Nákhali.*
	Abor Miri, . . .	*Caret.*
	Sibságar Miri, . . .	*No-luke.*
	Deoria Chutia, . . .	*Caret.*
	Singpho, ...	*Caret.*
Arrakan & Burmah.	Burman (*written*), . .	*Mang-toi.*
	Burman (*spoken*), . . .	*Men-doi.*
	Khyeng v. Shou, . .	*Nangni-ko.*
	Kámi, ...	*Nanchi-un.*
	Kúmi, ...	*Caret.*
	Mrú v. Toung, . . .	*Caret.*
	Sák, ...	*Caret.*
Siam & Tenasserim.	Talain v. Mon, . . .	*Kharu-hpay-tau.*
	Sgau-karen, ...	*Thu-waïdah.*
	Pwo-karen, ...	*N'thi-wadah.*
	Toungh-thu, ...	*Caret.*
	Shán, ...	*Khoung-moung-pen.*
	Annamitic, ...	*Kyung-bay-minh.*
	Siamese, ...	*Khrong-tsoung-aen.*
	Ahom, ...	*Khau.*
	Khámti, ...	*Mau-su.*
	Laos, ...	*Caret.*
Central India.	Ho (Kol), ...	*Appêa.*
	Kol (Singhbhum), . .	*Appea.*
	Santáli, ...	*Táben;*[1] *tápe;*[2] *(appe?).*
	Bhúmij, ...	*(A'ppe, tápe?)*
	Uráon, ...	*A'ssghi.*
	Mundala, ...	*A'piá-tana.*
	Rájmahali, ...	*Nimki.*
	Goṇḍi, ...	*Nia-hille, niwa, miwa.*
	Gayeti, ...	*Ida-woonan.*
	Rutluk, ...	*Miwa.*
	Naikude, ...	*Imed.*
	Kolami, ...	*Yeinnaton.*
	Mádi, ...	*Miwa, adumiwand.*
	Mádia, ...	*Caret.*
	Kuri, ...	*Caret.*
	Keikádi, ...	*Miwa?*
	Khoṇḍ, ...	*Caret.*
	Sávara, ...	*Amannate.*
	Gadaba, ...	*Caret.*
	Yerukala, ...	*Ningalide, nine-bududu.*
	Chentsu, ...	*Thor.*
Southern India.	Tamiḻ, anc., ...	*Numadu.*
	Tamiḻ, mod., ...	*Umadu, ungaḷuḍai.*
	Malayáḷma, anc., . .	*Caret.*
	Malayáḷma, mod., . .	*Ningngaḷuṭe.*
	Telugu, ...	*Mídi, míyokka.*
	Karṇáṭaka, anc., . .	*Caret.*
	Karṇáṭaka, mod., . .	*Nimmadu.*
	Tuḷuva, ...	*Inkulanou.*
	Kurgi, ...	*Ningaḍa.*
	Toḍuva, }	*Caret.*
	Toḍa, }	*Nimmadu, ningadu.*
	Kóta, ...	*Ningude.*
	Baḍaga, ...	*Ningadu.*
	Kuṛumba, ...	*Ningadu.*
	Iruḷa, ...	*Nimmudu.*
	Malabar, ...	*Ungaludeyathu, umathu.*
	Sinhalese, ...	*Topê.*

Group	Types.	
Inflecting.	SANSKRIT,	*Tadiya.*
	ARABIC,	*-hom.*
Compounding.	BASK,	*Beren, ayen, aen, en.*
	FINNIC,	*Heidan.*
	MAGYAR,	*-jök.*
	TURKISH,	*-lare.*
	CIRCASSIAN,	*Caret.*
	GEORGIAN,	*Mathi.*
	MONGOLIAN,	*Edenu.*
	MANTSHU,	*T'cheni.*
	JAVANESE, Ngoko,	*-e.*
	JAVANESE, Krama,	*-ipun.*
	MALAY,	*I'ya-puña, -ña.*
Isolating.	CHINESE, Nankin,	*Tá-mên-tih.*
	CHINESE, Pekin,	*Tá-mên-ti.*
	CHINESE, Canton,	*K'ü-ki-ké.*
	CHINESE, Shanghai,	*Yi-la-kŭh.*
	AMOY, Colloquial,	*In-ê.*
	JAPANESE,	*Kareranoto.*
	Brahuí,	*Dáfta.*
Chinese Frontier & Tibet.	Gyámi,	*Thamê-ti.*
	Gyárung,	*Caret.*
	Tákpa,	*Pérá-ku.*
	Mányak,	*Thidur-i.*
	Thochú,	*Thakúk.*
	Sokpa,	*Caret.*
	Horpa,	*Jaa-rigya.*
	Tibetan (*written*),	*Khochag-gi.*
	Tibetan (*spoken*),	*Khonjo-yi.*
Népal (east to west).	Serpa,	*Khwora-ti.*
	Súnwár,	*Hariain-ké.*
	Gúrung,	*Thamê-la.*
	Múrmi,	*Thenná.*
	Magar,	*Akúrikúm.*
	Tháksya,	*Hmi-si-ye;[1] hmi-cha-ye.[2]*
	Pákhya,	*Caret.*
	Newár,	*Waping-gú.*
	Limbu,	*Khúnchi-in.*
Kiranti Group (East Népal).	Kiránti,	*Myaucho, mayo-so.*
	Rodong,	*Khu-mo, khu-i-mo.*
	Rúngchenbung,	*Myá-u-cho.*
	Chhingtángya,	*Hung-cheikkwa.*
	Náchhereng,	*Yakmo-mi.*
	Wáling,	*Kayau-kapik.*
	Yákha,	*Ichi-ga.*
	Chourásya,	*Gono-maticha-leme.*
	Kulungya,	*Kwachi-mi, na-kwachimi.*
	Thulungya,	*Hanom-mikam.*
	Báhingya,	*A'sike;[1] áni.[2]*
	Lohorong,	*Mahachim;[1] mihachim.[2]*
	Lambichhong,	*Akochhi;[1] aokha.[2]*
	Báláli,	*Michim;[1] mochim.[2]*
	Sáng-páng,	*Me-ko-chim.[2]*
	Dúmi,	*Yákám-supo;[1] man-hám.[2]*
	Kháling,	*Unsu;[1] yákám.[2]*
	Dungmáli,	*Mugum;[1] mugum-ga.[2]*
Broken Tribes of Népal.	Dárhi,	*Un-karo.*
	Denwár,	*Wal-ko.*
	Pahri,	*Asya-gu.*
	Chepáng,	*Umai-ku.*
	Bhrámu,	*Un-ku.*
	Váyu,	*A'chimu,[1] wáthim-nak-pomu.[1]*
	Kuswar,	*Háring-kara.*
	Kusunda,	*Gida-jhigna-yi;[1] gidabaki-yida.[2]*
	Tháru,	*Udu-wonko;[1] una-kara.[2]*
	Lepcha (Sikkim),	*Hoyú-pongsa.*
	Bhúṭáni v. Lhopa,	*Khong-gi.*
N.-E. Bengal.	Bodo,	*Bichur-ni.*
	Dhimál,	*Ubal-ko.*
	Kocch,	*Un-nár.*
	Garo,	*Onok-ni.*
	Káchári,	*Caret.*
Eastern Frontier of Bengal.	Munipuri,	*Makhoi-gi.*
	Míthán Nágá,	*Caret.*
	Tablung Nágá,	*Caret.*
	Khári Nágá,	*Caret.*
	Angámi Nágá,	*Caret.*
	Námsáng Nágá,	*Caret.*
	Nowgong Nágá,	*Pá-ri.*
	Tengsa Nágá,	*Pá-li.*
	Abor Miri,	*Bulu-ke.*
	Sibságar Miri,	*Bulu-ke.*
	Deoria Chutia,	*Caret.*
	Singpho,	*Caret.*
Arrakan & Burmah.	Burman (*written*),	*Su-toi.*
	Burman (*spoken*),	*Thu-doi.*
	Khyeng v. Shou,	*Nidi-ko.*
	Kámi,	*Hanichi-nu.*
	Kúmi,	*Caret.*
	Mrú v. Toung,	*Caret.*
	Sák,	*Caret.*
Siam & Tenasserim.	Talain v. Mon,	*Kharum-yin-tau.*
	Sgau-karen,	*Awaïtha-waïdah.*
	Pwo-karen,	*Athi-wadah.*
	Toungh-thu,	*Caret.*
	Shán,	*Khoung-houng-pen.*
	Annamitic,	*Kyung-no-minh.*
	Siamese,	*Khonkha-tsoung-aen.*
	Ahom,	*Khreu.*
	Khámti,	*Man-khau.*
	Laos,	*Caret.*
Central India.	Ho (Kol),	*Akoá.*
	Kol (Singhbhum),	*En-koá.*
	Santáli,	*Tákin;[1] táko[2] (unkúre?).*
	Bhúmij,	*Táko (?).*
	Uráon,	*Caret.*
	Mundala,	*Ankoá-tana.*
	Rájmahali,	*A'sá-beriki.*
	Goṇḍi,	*Oná-ánd, hon, wora, wura.*
	Gayeti,	*Ada-wonan.*
	Rutluk,	*Hade-nae.*
	Naikude,	*Awaned.*
	Kolami,	*Awareten.*
	Mádi,	*Wona, adun-monandana.*
	Mádia,	*Caret.*
	Kuri,	*Caret.*
	Keikádi,	*Wora?*
	Khoṇḍ,	*Caret.*
	Sávara,	*Aninate.*
	Gadaba,	*Mayyino.*
	Yerukala,	*Avanudu.*
	Chentsu,	*Vahár.*
Southern India.	Tamiḷ, anc.,	*Avaradu.*
	Tamiḷ, mod.,	*Avaradu, avargaḷuḍaiya.*
	Malayáḷma, anc.,	*Caret.*
	Malayáḷma, mod.,	*Avaruṭe.*
	Telugu,	*Váridi, vánḍla.*
	Karṇáṭaka, anc.,	*Caret.*
	Karṇáṭaka, mod.,	*Avaradu.*
	Tuḷuva,	*Akulunou.*
	Kurgi,	*Ayanḍa, adanḍa.*
	Toḍuva, }	*Caret.*
	Toḍa, }	*Avardu.*
	Kóta,	*Avarade.*
	Baḍaga,	*Avaradu, avakaradu.*
	Kuṛumba,	*Avaradu.*
	Iruḷa,	*Avarudu.*
	Malabar,	*Oné.*
	Sinhalese,	*Ungé.*

Group	Types.	
Inflecting.	SANSKRIT,	*Eshas (etad), ayam, idam.*
	ARABIC,	*Háza.*
Compounding.	BASK,	*Au, onek, oyek;*[3] *auk, oek.*[4]
	FINNIC,	*Tama.*
	MAGYAR,	*Ez.*
	TURKISH,	*Bu.*
	CIRCASSIAN,	*Wusey.*
	GEORGIAN,	*Es.*
	MONGOLIAN,	*Ene.*
	MANTSHU,	*Ere.*
	JAVANESE, Ngoko,	*Iki.*
	JAVANESE, Krama,	*Punniki.*
	MALAY,	*I'ni.*
Isolating.	CHINESE, Nankin,	*Che-ko.*
	CHINESE, Pekin,	*Che-ko.*
	CHINESE, Canton,	*Li-ko.*
	CHINESE, Shanghai,	*Ti-kuh.*
	AMOY, Colloquial,	*Chit-ê.*
	JAPANESE,	*Kore, kono.*
	Brahuí,	*Dád.*
Chinese Frontier & Tibet.	Gyámi,	*Thikou.*
	Gyárung,	*Chidi.*
	Tákpa,	*Wochú.*
	Mányak,	*Thú.*
	Thochú,	*Chá.*
	Sokpa,	*Ani, yeni.*
	Horpa,	*U'de.*
	Tibetan (*written*),	*Hade.*
	Tibetan (*spoken*),	*Di.*
Nepal (east to west).	Serpa,	*Diráng.*
	Súnwár,	*Yekwe.*
	Gúrung,	*Chun-yo.*
	Múrmi,	*Chún.*
	Magar,	*Ise-ná.*
	Tháksya,	*Pa-áng-kyungpa.*
	Pákhya,	*Yehi, yó.*
	Newár,	*Tho.*
	Limbu,	*Kon.*
Kiránti Group (East Nepal).	Kiránti,	*Wo.*
	Rodong,	*Hyá, hyá-ko.*
	Rúngchenbung,	*O, oko.*
	Chhingtángya,	*Oko, bago, nago.*
	Náchhereng,	*Unu, ang-na.*
	Wáling,	*Ogná, oko, ipigna.*
	Yákha,	*Khena, ná, ná-má, á-me.*
	Chourásya,	*Caret.*
	Kulungya,	*Ing-kong, inkopi.*
	Thulungya,	*Wo, woram; wochi;*[1] *wo-mim.*[2]
	Báhingya,	*Yam, yem.*
	Lohorong,	*I'go.*
	Lambichhong,	*Ná, nárok.*
	Balálí,	*Ko-ó.*
	Sáng-páng,	*Noko, nokogná.*
	Dúmi,	*Tem, temgna.*
	Kháling,	*Tomgná.*
	Dungmáli,	*Igo.*
Broken Tribes of Népal.	Dárhi,	*U.*
	Denwár,	*I.*
	Pahri,	*U, ho.*
	Chepáng,	*U.*
	Bhrámu,	*U.*
	Váyu,	*I.*
	Kuswar,	*Hu-lo, há-lo.*
	Kusunda,	*Tá-i, tá.*
	Tháru,	*Caret.*
	Lepcha (Sikkim),	*Aré.*
	Bhúṭáni v. Lhopa,	*Di, didi.*

N.-E. Bengal.	Bodo,	*Imbe, imbo.*
	Dhimál,	*I'thoi, iti, idong.*
	Kocch,	*Yáhi.*
	Garo,	*I'mara.*
	Káchári,	*Caret.*
Eastern Frontier of Bengal.	Munipuri,	*Yo.*
	Míthán Nágá,	*Hi-ha.*
	Tablung Nágá,	*Thoi-nan.*
	Khári Nágá,	*Pio.*
	Angámi Nágá,	*Hawe.*
	Námsáng Nágá,	*A'ra.*
	Nowgong Nágá,	*Yá-e.*
	Tengsa Nágá,	*Igákú.*
	Abor Miri,	*Si, issi.*
	Sibságar Miri,	*Shidebulu.*
	Deoria Chutia,	*Taihoni.*
	Singpho,	*Ndai.*
Arrakan & Burmah.	Burman (*written*),	*I, sin.*
	Burman (*spoken*),	*I, thi.*
	Khyeng v. Shou,	*Ni, i-ni.*
	Kámi,	*Hi.*
	Kúmi,	*Caret.*
	Mrú v. Toung,	*Caret.*
	Sák,	*Caret.*
Siam & Tenasserim.	Talain v. Mon,	*Enan.*
	Sgau-karen,	*Tah-i.*
	Pwo-karen,	*A'yu.*
	Toungh-thu,	*Yo.*
	Shán,	*Tso-niht.*
	Annamitic,	*Näi.*
	Siamese,	*Ni-lai, ni.*
	Ahom,	*Iu.*
	Khámti,	*An-nai.*
	Laos,	*Ni.*
Central India.	Ho (Kol),	*Ni.*
	Kol (Singhbhum),	*Nea.*
	Santáli,	*Nu-i, nu-á, ni-á.*
	Bhúmij,	*Ni.*
	Uráon,	*Edah.*
	Mundala,	*Nia.*
	Rájmahali,	*Ih.*
	Goṇḍi,	*Yer* (mas.), *id* (fem.).
	Gayeti,	*Id* (?).
	Rutluk,	*Id* (?).
	Naikude,	*Id.*
	Kolami,	*Idda.*
	Mádi,	*Veru, viru, attu.*
	Mádia,	*Caret.*
	Kuri,	*Caret.*
	Keikádi,	*Kite.*
	Khoṇḍ,	*Caret.*
	Sávara,	*Ani.*
	Gadaba,	*Caret.*
	Yerukala,	*Avanu.*
	Chentsu,	*Vahare, vu.*
Southern India.	Tamiḷ, anc.,	*Ivan, ivaḷ, idu.*
	Tamiḷ, mod.,	*Ivan, ivaḷ, idu.*
	Malayáḷma, anc.,	*Caret.*
	Malayáḷma, mod.,	*Ivan, ivaḷ, ita.*
	Telugu,	*Viḍu, idi.*
	Karṇáṭaka, anc.,	*Caret.*
	Karṇáṭaka, mod.,	*Ivanv, ivaḷu, idu.*
	Tuḷuva,	*A'yino.*
	Kurgi,	*Ivu, iva, idu.*
	Toḍuva, } Toḍa, }	*Caret.* / *Avan.*
	Kóta,	*Avane.*
	Baḍaga,	*Avana.*
	Kurumba,	*Avana.*
	Iruḷa,	*Ava.*
	Malabar,	*Avanudeva.*
	Sinhalese,	*Mé.*

Group	Types.	
Inflecting.	SANSKRIT,	*Asau (adas, amu), etad.*
	ARABIC,	*Zálik.*
Compounding.	BASK,	*Ori, orrek, oriek;[1] hura, ark, ayek;[1] ak, aek.[1]*
	FINNIC,	*Tuo.*
	MAGYAR,	*Az.*
	TURKISH,	*Ol, o.*
	CIRCASSIAN,	*S'z'showah.*
	GEORGIAN,	*Is.*
	MONGOLIAN,	*Tere.*
	MANTSHU,	*Tere.*
	JAVANESE, Ngoko,	*Ika.*
	JAVANESE, Krama,	*Punnika.*
	MALAY,	*I'tu.*
Isolating.	CHINESE, Nankin,	*Na-ko.*
	CHINESE, Pekin,	*Na-ko.*
	CHINESE, Canton,	*Ko-ko.*
	CHINESE, Shanghai,	*Ku-kuh.*
	AMOY, Colloquial,	*Hit-ê.*
	JAPANESE,	*Sore, sono.*
	Brahuí,	*Od, ed.*
Chinese Frontier & Tibet.	Gyámi,	*Lakou.*
	Gyárung,	*Hadi.*
	Tákpa,	*Wotho.*
	Mányak,	*Quathú.*
	Thochú,	*Thá.*
	Sokpa,	*Theni.*
	Horpa,	*Outhá, ye.*
	Tibetan (*written*),	*Dé.*
	Tibetan (*spoken*),	*Phi-di.*
Nepal (east to west).	Serpa,	*Phi-dirúng.*
	Súnwár,	*Makwe.*
	Gúrung,	*Ho-chún-yo.*
	Múrmi,	*Ho-chan.*
	Magar,	*O-se-ná.*
	Tháksya,	*Cha, khapami.*
	Pákhya,	*Wóhi ú.*
	Newár,	*Wo.*
	Limbu,	*Khen.*
Kiranti Group (East Nepal).	Kiránti,	*Mo.*
	Rodong,	*Tya, tya-ko.*
	Rúngchenbung,	*Mo, mo-ko, kho-kho.*
	Chhingtángya,	*Kho-kho, mo-go.*
	Náchhereng,	*Khán-ko-u; yak-gua.*
	Wáling,	*Khog-ná, kho-ko, haya-ya.*
	Yákha,	*Yo-na, yo-námá, ime.*
	Chourásya,	*Caret.*
	Kulungya,	*Mung-kong, ná-kong, na-kopi.*
	Thulungya,	*Myo, myo-rám, han-úm.*
	Báhingya,	*Myám, mem-harem.*
	Lohorong,	*Mo.*
	Lambichhong,	*Yoná, yonarok, áko.*
	Báláli,	*Mo-ó.*
	Sáng-páng,	*Moko, mokogná.*
	Dúmi,	*Momi, yákám, yakamgna.*
	Kháling,	*Mámgná.*
	Dungmáli,	*Mú-go.*
Broken Tribes of Nepal.	Dárhi,	*U.*
	Denwár,	*I.*
	Pahri,	*U, ho.*
	Chepáng,	*U.*
	Bhrámu,	*U.*
	Váyu,	*Wáthi, mi (mu?).*
	Kuswar,	*Hu-lo, há-lo.*
	Kusunda,	*Issi, it.*
	Tháru,	*U.*
	Lepcha (Sikkim),	*Oré.*
	Bhútáni v. Lhopa,	*Phe, phedi.*

N.-E. Bengal.	Bodo,	*Obe, hobo.*
	Dhimál,	*Uthoi, uti, udong.*
	Kocch,	*Vohi.*
	Garo,	*Omara.*
	Káchári,	*Caret.*
Eastern Frontier of Bengal.	Munipuri,	*Ta-hlon.*
	Míthán Nágá,	*Hi-ha.*
	Tablung Nágá,	*Thoi-theo.*
	Khári Nágá,	*Poicho chu.*
	Angámi Nágá,	*Liwe.*
	Námsáng Nágá,	*I'rapá.*
	Nowgong Nágá,	*Aunchika.*
	Tengsa Nágá,	*Ochika.*
	Abor Miri,	*Iüna.*
	Sibságar Miri,	*Ütlübullu.*
	Deoria Chutia,	*Bare.*
	Singpho,	*Orawá.*
Arrakan & Burmah.	Burman (*written*),	*Tho, ho.*
	Burman (*spoken*),	*Tho, ho.*
	Khyeng v. Shou,	*Oni.*
	Kámi,	*Ma-há.*
	Kúmi,	*Caret.*
	Mrú v. Toung,	*Caret.*
	Sák,	*Caret.*
Siam & Tenasserim.	Talain v. Mon,	*Tai-kau.*
	Sgau-karen,	*Tah-nu, a-ná.*
	Pwo-karen,	*A'nau.*
	Toungh-thu,	*Ta-hlon.*
	Shán,	*Tso-nan.*
	Annamitic,	*Kia.*
	Siamese,	*Nan-lai, nan.*
	Ahom,	*Heu.*
	Khámti,	*An-nan.*
	Laos,	*Nan.*
Central India.	Ho (Kol),	*En.*
	Kol (Singhbhum),	*Enó.*
	Santáli,	*Uni, háná, honá, oná.*
	Bhúmij,	*Caret.*
	Uráon,	*Húdah.*
	Mundala,	*A'ná.*
	Rájmahali,	*A'h.*
	Goṇḍi,	*Hud, war, wor.*
	Gayeti,	*Wor.*
	Rutluk,	*Wor.*
	Naikude,	*Ad.*
	Kolami,	*Atol.*
	Mádi,	*Woru, oru, attu.*
	Mádia,	*Caret.*
	Kuri,	*Handi.*
	Keikádi,	*Ture.*
	Khoṇḍ,	*Yerivi.*
	Sávara,	*Ani.*
	Gadaba,	*Tono.*
	Yerukala,	*Adu.*
	Chentsu,	*Vahe, ke.*
Southern India.	Tamiḷ, anc.,	*Avan, avaḷ, adu.*
	Tamiḷ, mod.,	*Avan, avaḷ, adu.*
	Malayâḷma, anc.,	*Caret.*
	Malayâḷma, mod.,	*Avan, avaḷ, ata.*
	Telugu,	*Vâḍu, adi.*
	Karṇâṭaka, anc.,	*Caret.*
	Karṇâṭaka, mod.,	*Avanu, avaḷu, adu.*
	Tuḷuva,	*Avu.*
	Kurgi,	*Avu, ava, adu.*
	Toḍuva,	*Ad.*
	Toḍa,	*Adu.*
	Kóta,	*Adu.*
	Baḍaga,	*Adu.*
	Kurumba,	*Adu.*
	Iruḷa,	*Adu.*
	Malabar,	*Ah thu, athu.*
	Sinhalese,	*Ara.*

Group	Types.	
Inflecting.	SANSKRIT,	*Yas, yá, yat.*
	ARABIC,	*Illazi.*
Compounding.	BASK,	*Zeñ, zeña, zeñak; zein, zeina.*
	FINNIC,	*Joka* (root = *jo*).
	MAGYAR,	*Melly.*
	TURKISH,	*Caret.*
	CIRCASSIAN,	*Terrahrey.*
	GEORGIAN,	*Caret.*
	MONGOLIAN,	*Caret.*
	MANTSHU,	*Caret.*
	JAVANESE, Ngoko,	*Sing, kang* (rel. and correl.).
	JAVANESE, Krama,	*Ingkang, kang* (rel. and cor.).
	MALAY,	*Yang* (rel. and correl.).
Isolating.	CHINESE, Nankin,	*So, sho.*
	CHINESE, Pekin,	*So, sho.*
	CHINESE, Canton,	*So, sho.*
	CHINESE, Shanghai,	*Su.*
	AMOY, Colloquial,	*So.*
	JAPANESE,	*Dore, dochi, dono.*
	Brahuí,	*Arà.*
Chinese Frontier & Tibet.	Gyámi,	*Hi-me* (rel.), *la'-me* (corr.).
	Gyárung,	*Caret.*
	Tákpa,	*Caret.*
	Mányak,	*Caret.*
	Thochú,	*Caret.*
	Sokpa,	*Caret.*
	Horpa,	*Caret.*
	Tibetan (*written*),	*Caret* (rel.).
	Tibetan (*spoken*),	*Thinda* (rel.), *the* (corr.).
Nepal (east to west).	Serpa,	*Swán* (rel.), *thi-dáng* (corr.).
	Súnwár,	*Tékwé* (rel.), *mekwé* (corr.).
	Gúrung,	*Su* (rel.), *thi* (corr.).
	Múrmi,	*Khó-chuá* (rl.), *ho-chua* (cor.).
	Magar,	*Kos* (rel.), *hos* (corr.).
	Tháksya,	*Khanáng-pemhi, khaju-hemhi.*
	Pákhya,	*Jimanchha, jaunamánchha.*
	Newár,	*Gú, sú* (rel.), *wo* (corr.).
	Limbu,	*A'ti* (rel.), *khen* (corr.).
Kiranti Group (East Nepal).	Kiránti,	*Sá* (rel.), *kho* (corr.).
	Rodong,	*Tyo-so; tya-kwa, chi.*
	Rúngchenbung,	*Sáng; khog-ná.*
	Chhingtángya,	*Hokkogo; ho-en.*
	Náchhereng,	*A's; khan.*
	Wáling,	*Khá-ú; khog-ná.*
	Yákha,	*Isá; ikhi.*
	Chourásya,	*Thámé; eme.*
	Kulungya,	*A'sá; kho.*
	Thulungya,	*Uhem; myo.*
	Báhingya,	*Mém.*
	Lohorong,	*Caret.*
	Lambichhong,	*U'ndok.*
	Báláli,	*Khosá, khosálo.*
	Sáng-páng,	*Khogná.*
	Dúmi,	*Mom.*
	Kháling,	*Caret.*
	Dungmáli,	*Há-go.*
Broken Tribes of Nepal.	Dárhi,	*I-sek, u-sek* (rel.).
	Denwár,	*I* (rel.), *U'* (corr.).
	Pahri,	*A'rkhyá-gu* (rel.), *hórkhyá-gu* (corr.).
	Chepáng,	*Caret.*
	Bhrámu,	*Hétu* (rel.), *ho-tu* (corr.).
	Váyu,	*Súdo* (rel.), *mido* (corr.).
	Kuswar,	*Jé* (rl.), *húle* (cor.).
	Kusunda,	*Hágim-ya-hák, hágit, nataim-ya-hak.*
	Tháru,	*Kun-manai, um-manai.*
	Lepcha (Sikkim),	*Sare* (rel.), *ware* (corr.).
	Bhútáni v. Lhopa,	*Kádi* (rel.), *ádi* (corr.).
N.-E. Bengal.	Bodo,	*Jé, jai* (rel.), *bi* (corr.), *háshu.*
	Dhimál,	*Jédong* (rel.), *kódong* (corr.).
	Kocch,	*Je* (rel.), *so-i* (corr.).
	Garo,	*Jon* (rel.), *won* (corr.).
	Káchári,	*Caret.*
Eastern Frontier of Bengal.	Munipuri,	*Lisa-may-nay.*
	Míthán Nágá,	*Caret.*
	Tablung Nágá,	*Caret.*
	Khári Nágá,	*Kubai.*
	Angámi Nágá,	*Kiuru.*
	Námsáng Nágá,	*Mapá.*
	Nowgong Nágá,	*Yákung.*
	Tengsa Nágá,	*Kachi.*
	Abor Miri,	*Ing-kono.*
	Sibságar Miri,	*Okolone.*
	Deoria Chutia,	*Boroshini.*
	Singpho,	*Gadenud.*
Arrakan & Burmah.	Burman (*written*),	*Abhe.*
	Burman (*spoken*),	*Abhe.*
	Khyeng v. Shou,	*I-ni-a-ka.*
	Kámi,	*Na-ná-i.*
	Kúmi,	*Caret.*
	Mrú v. Toung,	*Caret.*
	Sák,	*Caret.*
Siam & Tenasserim.	Talain v. Mon,	*I-la-rau.*
	Sgau-karen,	*Lir-la-i, pai-lai-ga-lai.*
	Pwo-karen,	*Ler-lai.*
	Toungh-thu,	*Lisa-may-nay.*
	Shán,	*An-loung-lai.*
	Annamitic,	*Ke* (rel.), *ki* (corr.).
	Siamese,	*Nihn-louk, khon-dai.*
	Ahom,	*Panku.*
	Khámti,	*An-naü.*
	Laos,	*Caret.*
Central India.	Ho (Kol),	*Chikana.*
	Kol (Singhbhum),	*Caret.*
	Santáli,	*Jáháng-e.*
	Bhúmij,	*Caret.*
	Uráon,	*Ikrah.*
	Mundala,	*Okah.*
	Rájmahali,	*Caret.*
	Gondi,	*Bad.*
	Gayeti,	*Bad.*
	Rutluk,	*Bako.*
	Naikude,	*Yand.*
	Kolami,	*Yetten.*
	Mádi,	*B-ona, patenind.*
	Mádia,	*Caret.*
	Kuri,	*Caret.*
	Keikádi,	*Caret.*
	Khond,	*Yes tanju.*
	Sávara,	*Vongá.*
	Gadaba,	*Bhulóm.*
	Yerukala,	*Yedu.*
	Chentsu,	*Kahá.*
Southern India.	Tamil, anc.,	*Yádu.*
	Tamil, mod.,	*Edu, yedu.*
	Malayálma, anc.,	*Caret.*
	Malayálma, mod.,	*Eda.*
	Telugu,	*Edi, yedi.*
	Karnátaka, anc.,	*Caret.*
	Karnátaka, mod.,	*Yáv-adu.*
	Tuluva,	*Erno.*
	Kurgi,	*Caret.*
	Toduva, }	*Caret.*
	Toda, }	*Yádu.*
	Kóta,	*Yede.*
	Badaga,	*Yeadu.*
	Kurumba,	*Y-av-adu.*
	Irula,	*Yedu.*
	Malabar,	*Thu* (rel.).
	Sinhalese,	*Kó-koda.*

	Types.	
Inflecting.	SANSKRIT,	*Kas, ká.*
	ARABIC,	*Man.*
Compounding.	BASK,	*Nor, nork; zeñ, zein.*
	FINNIC,	*Ken.*
	MAGYAR,	*Ki.*
	TURKISH,	*Kim.*
	CIRCASSIAN,	*Shet.*
	GEORGIAN,	*Win.*
	MONGOLIAN,	*Ken.*
	MANTSHU,	*We.*
	JAVANESE, Ngoko,	*Sapa.*
	JAVANESE, Krama,	*Sinten.*
	MALAY,	*Siápa.*
Isolating.	CHINESE, Nankin,	*Shin-mo-jin.*
	CHINESE, Pekin,	*Shen-mo-jen.*
	CHINESE, Canton,	*Mat-shui.*
	CHINESE, Shanghai,	*Sá-niang.*
	AMOY, Colloquial,	*Chi-chúi.*
	JAPANESE,	*Dare, tare.*
	Brahuí,	*Der.*
Chinese Frontier & Tibet.	Gyámi,	*Syá, hima.*
	Gyárung,	*Su.*
	Tákpa,	*Su.*
	Mányak,	*Su.*
	Thochú,	*Su.*
	Sokpa,	*Caret.*
	Horpa,	*Su, lo.*
	Tibetan (*written*),	*Sú, kha.*
	Tibetan (*spoken*),	*Khangi, sú.*
Nepal (east to west).	Serpa,	*Sú.*
	Súnwár,	*Súká.*
	Gúrung,	*Sú.*
	Múrmi,	*Khá.*
	Magar,	*Súra, hira.*
	Tháksya,	*Tá.*
	Pákhya,	*Kaunamanchha.*
	Newár,	*Sú.*
	Limbu,	*Hát.*
Kiranti Group (East Nepal).	Kiránti,	*Di.*
	Rodong,	*Sa.*
	Rúngchenbung,	*Sáng.*
	Chhingtángya,	*Hokkogo, sáló.*
	Náchhereng,	*A's.*
	Wáling,	*Dei.*
	Yákha,	*Hétnámá, hét-ná.*
	Chourásya,	*A'-chú.*
	Kulungya,	*A'sé.*
	Thulungya,	*Syú, úhem.*
	Báhingya,	*Syú.*
	Lohorong,	*A'sá.*
	Lambichhong,	*Sé-ong.*
	Báláli,	*A'sálo, ásá.*
	Sáng-páng,	*A'sá, asále.*
	Dúmi,	*Syúgo, syú.*
	Kháling,	*Khám.*
	Dungmáli,	*Ság, khigo.*
Broken Tribes of Nepal.	Dárhi,	*Kb-no.*
	Denwár,	*Kb-hik.*
	Pahri,	*Gú-gú, gu-huo.*
	Chepáng,	*Caret.*
	Bhrámu,	*Hai.*
	Váyu,	*Sú.*
	Kuswar,	*Ke.*
	Kusunda,	*Nátát.*
	Tháru,	*Kaunmanai.*
	Lepcha (Sikkim),	*To.*
	Bhúṭáni v. Lhopa,	*Ká.*

N.-E. Bengal.	Bodo,	*Chúr.*
	Dhimál,	*Héti, háshu.*
	Kocch,	*Ká-i.*
	Garo,	*Cháng.*
	Káchári,	*Caret.*
Eastern Frontier of Bengal.	Munipuri,	*Pá-may-nay.*
	Míthán Nágá,	*Oveh.*
	Tablung Nágá,	*Owai.*
	Khári Nágá,	*Sui.*
	Angámi Nágá,	*Soru.*
	Námsáng Nágá,	*Hand.*
	Nowgong Nágá,	*Sirau.*
	Tengsa Nágá,	*Sine.*
	Abor Miri,	*Seko.*
	Sibságar Miri,	*Seko.*
	Deoria Chutia,	*Bas-ani.*
	Singpho,	*Gadaimá.*
Arrakan & Burmah.	Burman (*written*),	*Bhesú.*
	Burman (*spoken*),	*Bhethú.*
	Khyeng v. Shou,	*U'-li-am.*
	Kámi,	*A-pá-i-mé.*
	Kúmi,	*Caret.*
	Mrú v. Toung,	*Caret.*
	Sák,	*Caret.*
Siam & Tenasserim.	Talain v. Mon,	*Nyay-gau-rau.*
	Sgau-karen,	*M'tah-tghah-la-i.*
	Pwo-karen,	*Ma-paw-lai.*
	Toungh-thu,	*Pá-may-nay.*
	Shán,	*Hpoung.*
	Annamitic,	*Ai.*
	Siamese,	*Níhn-loung, khrai, sung.*
	Ahom,	*Phreu.*
	Khámti,	*Phau.*
	Laos,	*Khai, phai.*
Central India.	Ho (Kol),	*Okoï.*
	Kol (Singhbhum),	*Caret.*
	Santáli,	*Oko-e, chele.*
	Bhúmij,	*Caret.*
	Uráon,	*Ekoa.*
	Mundala,	*O'-kówé.*
	Rájmahali,	*Ik.*
	Goṇḍi,	*Bor, boni.*
	Gayeti,	*Bor, boni.*
	Rutluk,	*Bor.*
	Naikude,	*Yenendiv.*
	Kolami,	*Níveniv.*
	Mádi,	*Boru, poninda.*
	Mádia,	*Bor.*
	Kuri,	*Tine, eiye.*
	Keikádi,	*Yedu.*
	Khoṇḍ,	*Yestánju, yinu.*
	Sávara,	*Bote.*
	Gadaba,	*Láyi.*
	Yerukala,	*Yáru.*
	Chentsu,	*Ke, vuhe.*
Southern India.	Tamiḷ, anc.,	*Yár.*
	Tamiḷ, mod.,	*A'r.*
	Malayáḷma, anc.,	*Caret.*
	Malayáḷma, mod.,	*A'ra.*
	Telugu,	*Evaḍu, yevaḍu.*
	Karṇáṭaka, anc.,	*Caret.*
	Karṇáṭaka, mod.,	*Yávanu.*
	Tuḷuva,	*Evanda.*
	Kurgi,	*Yevu.*
	Toḍuva, }	*In.*
	Toḍa, }	*A'r.*
	Kóta,	*A're.*
	Baḍaga,	*Y-áru.*
	Kuṛumba,	*Y-aru.*
	Iruḷa,	*Aru.*
	Malabar,	*Y-ar, evcr.*
	Sinhalese,	*Kauda.*

	Types.	
Inflecting.	SANSKṚIT,	*Kim (kat), ke,*[1] *káni.*[2]
	ARABIC,	*Aï, ayyon.*
Compounding.	BASK,	*Zer, ze.*
	FINNIC,	*Mika, kuka.*
	MAGYAR,	*Mi.*
	TURKISH,	*Neh.*
	CIRCASSIAN,	*Papshey.*
	GEORGIAN,	*Ra.*
	MONGOLIAN,	*Yaghon.*
	MANTSHU,	*Ai, ai-gese.*
	JAVANESE, Ngoko,	*Apa.*
	JAVANESE, Krama,	*Punnapa.*
	MALAY,	*A'pa.*
Isolating.	CHINESE, Nankin,	*Shin-motung-si.*
	CHINESE, Pekin,	*Shen-motung-si.*
	CHINESE, Canton,	*Mat-ye-mat-kin.*
	CHINESE, Shanghai,	*Sá-neh-sz.*
	AMOY, Colloquial,	*Siâ-mih.*
	JAPANESE,	*Nani.*
	Brahuí,	*Ant, der.*
Chinese Frontier & Tibet.	Gyámi,	*Syácha, hima.*
	Gyárung,	*Thú.*
	Tákpa,	*Si.*
	Mányak,	*Háno.*
	Thochú,	*Sú.*
	Sokpa,	*Caret.*
	Horpa,	*Achin.*
	Tibetan (*written*),	*Chi.*
	Tibetan (*spoken*),	*Khâng.*
Nepal (east to west).	Serpa,	*Khâng.*
	Súnwár,	*Maro.*
	Gúrung,	*Tá.*
	Múrmi,	*Tigi.*
	Magar,	*Hi.*
	Tháksya,	*Khajupero.*
	Pákhya,	*Kyá.*
	Newár,	*Chhú.*
	Limbu,	*Thé.*
Kiranti Group (East Nepal).	Kiránti,	*Di, dè.*
	Rodong,	*Dakô.*
	Rúngchenbung,	*Diyè.*
	Chhingtángya,	*Thêm.*
	Náchhereng,	*U'lè.*
	Wáling,	*Tikwa.*
	Yákha,	*I, e.*
	Chourásya,	*A'-má.*
	Kulungya,	*Usó, úi.*
	Thulungya,	*Hám.*
	Báhingya,	*Mara.*
	Lohorong,	*Imang.*
	Lambichhong,	*Thiya.*
	Bálálí,	*U'kha.*
	Sáng-páng,	*Yen.*
	Dúmi,	*Mimgna.*
	Khâling,	*Mangga.*
	Dungmáli,	*Tigo.*
Broken Tribes of Nepal.	Dárhi,	*Ko-no.*
	Denwár,	*Ko-hik.*
	Pahri,	*Gu-gu, gu-hmo.*
	Chepáng,	*Caret.*
	Bhrámu,	*Hai.*
	Váyu,	*Sú.*
	Kuswar,	*Ke.*
	Kusunda,	*Nátáng.*
	Tháru,	*Ká.*
	Lepcha (Sikkim),	*Shu.*
	Bhúṭáni v. Lhopa,	*Kang-chi, kan.*

N.-E. Bengal.	Bodo,	*Má.*
	Dhimál,	*Hai.*
	Kocch,	*Ki.*
	Garo,	*A'to.*
	Kácháni,	*Caret.*
Eastern Frontier of Bengal.	Munipuri,	*Pá-may-nay.*
	Míthán Nágá,	*Tem.*
	Tablung Nágá,	*Toi-nan.*
	Khári Nágá,	*Chabau.*
	Angámi Nágá,	*Kaje.*
	Námsáng Nágá,	*Chená.*
	Nowgong Nágá,	*Kachisür.*
	Tengsa Nágá,	*Chaba.*
	Abor Miri,	*Ingkua, ong-kokko.*
	Sibságar Miri,	*Okko.*
	Deoria Chutia,	*Damdarini.*
	Singpho,	*Phakaimá.*
Arrakan & Burmah.	Burman (*written*),	*Abhe.*
	Burman (*spoken*),	*Abhe, bhá.*
	Khyeng v. Shou,	*I'ni-hám.*
	Kámi,	*A-pa-i-me.*
	Kúmi,	*Caret.*
	Mrú v. Toung,	*Caret.*
	Sák,	*Caret.*
Siam & Tenasserim.	Talain v. Mon,	*Mu-gau-rau.*
	Sgau-karen,	*M'tah-tghah-la-i.*
	Pwo-karen,	*Ma-paw-lai.*
	Toungh-thu,	*Lo-may-nay.*
	Shán,	*Ka-tsan-lay.*
	Annamitic,	*Shi, yi.*
	Siamese,	*Ayo-loung, arai.*
	Ahom,	*Re.*
	Khámti,	*Sang.*
	Laos,	*Sang.*
Central India.	Ho (Kol),	*Chiá.*
	Kol (Singhbhum),	*Caret.*
	Santáli,	*Chet.*
	Bhúmij,	*Caret.*
	Uráon,	*Indrári.*
	Mundala,	*Chikina.*
	Rájmahali,	*Ik.*
	Goṇḍi,	*Bará-ánd, bang.*
	Gayeti,	*Badánga.*
	Rutluk,	*Badáng.*
	Naikude,	*Táne.*
	Kolami,	*Táneten.*
	Mádi,	*Bara.*
	Mádia,	*Bara.*
	Kuri,	*Tune, yo.*
	Keikádi,	*Yendu.*
	Khoṇḍ,	*Anná.*
	Sávara,	*Vongáḍo.*
	Gadaba,	*Caret.*
	Yerukala,	*Y-anna, yemmatuku.*
	Chentsu,	*Ki, kochcher.*
Southern India.	Tamiḷ, anc.,	*Yedu, yádu.*
	Tamiḷ, mod.,	*Enna, yenna.*
	Malayáḷma, anc.,	*Caret.*
	Malayáḷma, mod.,	*Enta.*
	Telugu,	*Emi, edi.*
	Karṇáṭaka, anc.,	*Caret.*
	Karṇáṭaka, mod.,	*Yenu.*
	Tuḷuva,	*Jána.*
	Kurgi,	*Yennu.*
	Toḍuva, }	*In.*
	Toḍa, }	*En.*
	Kóta,	*Yena.*
	Baḍaga,	*Yena.*
	Kuṛumba,	*Yenu.*
	Iruḷa,	*Yenna.*
	Malabar,	*Enna, entha.*
	Sinhalese,	*Mokada.*

Types.

Inflecting.	SANSKṚIT, . . .	*Kaşchit, káchit.*
	ARABIC, ...	*Kol waḥid, fulán.*
Compounding.	BASK, ...	*Norbait, iñor.*
	FINNIC, ...	*Caret.*
	MAGYAR, ...	*Volamelly.*
	TURKISH, ...	*Kimseh.*
	CIRCASSIAN, ...	*Zaypit.*
	GEORGIAN, ...	*Caret.*
	MONGOLIAN, ...	*Ali-yaghon.*
	MANTSHU, ...	*Caret.*
	JAVANESE, Ngoko, . .	*Sapa-sapa.*
	JAVANESE, Krama, . .	*Sinten-sinten.*
	MALAY, ...	*Bárang saorang.*
Isolating.	CHINESE, Nankin, . .	*Puh-lun-shin-mo-jin.*
	CHINESE, Pekin, . .	*Puh-lun-shen-mo-jen.*
	CHINESE, Canton, . .	*Mo-lun-mat-shin.*
	CHINESE, Shanghai, . .	*Sui-bien-sa-niang.*
	AMOY, Colloquial, . .	*Put-lun-sian-mih-lang.*
	JAPANESE, ...	*Daredemo, taremo.*
	Brahuí, . .	*Khadr-bandagh.*
Chinese Frontier & Tibet.	Gyámi, ...	*Ohki, hiong.*
	Gyárung, ...	*Sú.*
	Tákpa, ...	*Sirang.*
	Mányak, ...	*Súye.*
	Thochú, ...	*Ning-wan, song-wang.*
	Sokpa, ...	*Caret.*
	Horpa, ...	*Súyo.*
	Tibetan (*written*), . .	*Súzhig, khachig.*
	Tibetan (*spoken*), . .	*Sú-in.*
Nepal (east to west).	Serpa, ...	*Súi-náng.*
	Súnwár, ...	*Súká.*
	Gúrung, ...	*Súzáng.*
	Múrmi, ...	*Khá-láï.*
	Magar, ...	*Súr.*
	Tháksya, ...	*Sabadhyángpá.*
	Pákhya, ...	*Kohimánchhá.*
	Newár, ...	*Súng.*
	Limbu, ...	*Hát-lo.*
Kiranti Group (East Nepal).	Kiránti, ...	*Aktai (ak-táï ?).*
	Rodong, ...	*Isáma, söï.*
	Rúngchenbung, . . .	*Sángchháng.*
	Chhingtángya, . . .	*Sáló-yáng.*
	Náchhereng, ...	*A'sa.*
	Wáling, ...	*Asakchhú.*
	Yákha, ...	*Isáchá.*
	Chourásya, ...	*A'-chú-yé.*
	Kulungya, ...	*A'so, ás.*
	Thulungya, ...	*Syubwa.*
	Báhingya, ...	*Syúye.*
	Lohorong, ...	*A'sá-sáng (mette !).*
	Lambichhong, . . .	*Sichhá.*
	Bálálí, ...	*A'sáne.*
	Sáng-páng, ...	*A'sá-sáng.*
	Dúmi, ...	*Syúyo.*
	Kháling, ...	*Súi-yo.*
	Dungmáli, ...	*Ságchhang.*
Broken Tribes of Nepal.	Dárhi, ...	*Kolho-pun.*
	Denwár, ...	*Kolhu.*
	Pahri, ...	*Súnung.*
	Chepáng, ...	*Caret.*
	Bhrámu, ...	*Súng.*
	Váyu, ...	*Súna.*
	Kuswar, ...	*Ke-hu.*
	Kusunda, ...	*Nataim 'yahak* vel *hyak.*
	Tháru, ...	*Konamanai.*
	Lepcha (Sikkim), . .	*Tólá.*
	Bhútáni v. Lhopa, . .	*Káyé, ka-imchi.*

N.-E. Bengal.	Bodo, ...	*Chur, jishláp.*
	Dhimál, ...	*Háshu, hete.*
	Kocch, ...	*Káho.*
	Garo, ...	*Já-tá.*
	Káchári, ...	*Caret.*
Eastern Frontier of Bengal.	Munipuri, ...	*Caret.*
	Míthán Nágá, . . .	*Caret.*
	Tablung Nágá, . . .	*Caret.*
	Khári Nágá, ...	*Koi-murh.*
	Angámi Nágá, . . .	*Chakra-paru.*
	Námsáng Nágá, . . .	*Caret.*
	Nowgong Nágá, . .	*Caret.*
	Tengsa Nágá, . . .	*Caret.*
	Abor Miri, ...	*Caret.*
	Sibságar Miri, . . .	*Sekodi.*
	Deoria Chutia, . . .	*Shámádu.*
	Singpho, ...	*Caret.*
Arrakan & Burmah.	Burman (*written*), . .	*Bhesúmhya.*
	Burman (*spoken*), . . .	*Bhethúnahya.*
	Khyeng v. Shou, . .	*Caret.*
	Kámi, ...	*A-pá-i-me.*
	Kúmi, ...	*Caret.*
	Mrú v. Toung, . . .	*Caret.*
	Sák, ...	*Caret.*
Siam & Tenasserim.	Talain v. Mon, . . .	*Kha-ra-tan-mwai-mwai.*
	Sgau-karen, ...	*Caret.*
	Pwo-karen, ...	*Caret.*
	Toungh-thu, ...	*Caret.*
	Shán, ...	*Pen-htsaytsó-tsó.*
	Annamitic, ...	*Hé-ai.*
	Siamese, ...	*Hpayla-righn.*
	Ahom, ...	*Pheu.*
	Khámti, ...	*Kau-phong.*
	Laos, ...	*Caret.*
Central India.	Ho (Kol), ...	*Amba.*
	Kol (Singhbhum), . .	*Oko-ho.*
	Santáli, ...	*Tínd, tináng, okuren-horh.*
	Bhúmij, ...	*Okoji.*
	Uráon, ...	*E'ko-árten.*
	Mundala, ...	*Oko-waihi.*
	Rájmahali, ...	*Né-góté.*
	Goṇḍi, ...	*Vóndi-ándi.*
	Gayeti, ...	*Bore, bati.*
	Rutluk, ...	*Bore.*
	Naikude, ...	*Yanna-katir.*
	Kolami, ...	*Amdenen.*
	Mádi, ...	*Bortadi.*
	Mádia, ...	*Caret.*
	Kuri, ...	*Caret.*
	Keikádi, ...	*Yedagas.*
	Khoṇḍ, ...	*Yestánáte.*
	Sávara, ...	*Bote, botegáni.*
	Gadaba, ...	*Loyis-á.*
	Yerukala, ...	*Yeduayiná.*
	Chentsu, ...	*Kevu, jehaive.*
Southern India.	Tamiḷ, anc., ...	*A'ráyinum.*
	Tamiḷ, mod., ...	*A'rágilum.*
	Malayáḷma, anc., . .	*Caret.*
	Malayáḷma, mod., . .	*Yádaruttorum.*
	Telugu, ...	*Ev-araina.*
	Karṇáṭaka, anc., . .	*Caret.*
	Karṇáṭaka, mod., . .	*Yárádarú.*
	Tuḷuva, ...	*Caret.*
	Kurgi, ...	*Caret.*
	Toḍuva, }	*Caret.*
	Toḍa, }	*Caret.*
	Kóta, ...	*Caret.*
	Baḍaga, ...	*Caret.*
	Kuṛumba, ...	*Caret.*
	Iruḷa, ...	*Caret.*
	Malabar, ...	*Everayenum, yarunum.*
	Sinhalese, ...	*Kauru-wat.*

Group	Types.	
Inflecting.	SANSKṚIT, ...	*Kinchit, kechit,*[1] *kánichit.*[2]
	ARABIC, ...	*Kol shaï.*
Compounding.	BASK, ...	*Zerbait, zeredozer.*
	FINNIC, ...	*Caret.*
	MAGYAR, ...	*Volamelli.*
	TURKISH, ...	*Kimseh.*
	CIRCASSIAN, ...	*Zaypit.*
	GEORGIAN, ...	*Caret.*
	MONGOLIAN, ...	*Ali-ken.*
	MANTSHU, ...	*Caret.*
	JAVANESE, Ngoko, . .	*Apa-apa.*
	JAVANESE, Krama, . .	*Punnapa-punnapa.*
	MALAY, ...	*Bárang-ápa.*
Isolating.	CHINESE, Nankin, . .	*Pu-lun-shin-mo-tungsi.*
	CHINESE, Pekin, . .	*Pu-lun-shen-mo-tungsi.*
	CHINESE, Canton, . .	*Mo-lun-mat-ye-mat-kin.*
	CHINESE, Shanghai, .	*Sui-bien-sá-meh-sz.*
	AMOY, Colloquial, . .	*Put-lun-sian-mih.*
	JAPANESE, ...	*Nanimo, arumono.*
	Brahuí, ...	*Khadr-gidá.*
Chinese Frontier & Tibet.	Gyámi, ...	*Hiong.*
	Gyárung, ...	*Tenzi, tizze.*
	Tákpa, ...	*Sirang.*
	Mányak, ...	*Táká.*
	Thochú, ...	*Ning.*
	Sokpa, ...	*Caret.*
	Horpa, ...	*A'ke.*
	Tibetan (*written*), . .	*Chizhig.*
	Tibetan (*spoken*), . .	*Khá-in.*
Nepal (east to west).	Serpa, ...	*Khai-náng.*
	Súnwár, ...	*Márká.*
	Gúrung, ...	*Tayáng.*
	Múrmi, ...	*Tigi.*
	Magar, ...	*Hihi-ko.*
	Thákṣya, ...	*Khajang-pemhi.*
	Pákhya, ...	*Kehi-bastu.*
	Newár, ...	*Chhung.*
	Limbu, ...	*The-re.*
Kiránti Group (East Nepal).	Kiránti, ...	*Dimin.*
	Rodong, ...	*De-i, dyen, nyú.*
	Rúngchenbung, . . .	*Dichháng.*
	Chhingtángya, . . .	*Them-yáng.*
	Náchhereng, ...	*Usa.*
	Wáling, ...	*Ti-ikchhú.*
	Yákha, ...	*Iehá.*
	Chourásya, ...	*A'má-yé.*
	Kulungya, ...	*U'so.*
	Thulungya, ...	*Hambwa.*
	Báhingya, ...	*Máráye.*
	Lohorong, ...	*Imáng-sang.*
	Lambichhong, . . .	*Thichhá.*
	Bálálí, ...	*U'k-háng.*
	Sáng-páng, ...	*Yon-sáng.*
	Dúmi, ...	*Máng-yó.*
	Kháling, ...	*Máng-yó.*
	Dungmáli, ...	*Tichhang.*
Broken Tribes of Nepal.	Dárhi, ...	*Kyá-hú-je.*
	Denwár, ...	*Ki-chhu.*
	Pahri, ...	*Chala.*
	Chepáng, ...	*Caret.*
	Bhrámu, ...	*Hang.*
	Váyu, ...	*Mis-che.*
	Kuswar, ...	*Ke-hu.*
	Kusunda, ...	*Nataum-'ya-hágit.*
	Tháru, ...	*Kunbastu.*
	Lepcha (Sikkim), . .	*Shúri, tham.*
	Bhúṭáni v. Lhopa, . .	*Kándochi.*

N.-E. Bengal.	Bodo, ...	*Múngbó, jishlap.*
	Dhimál, ...	*Hété, haidong.*
	Kocch, ...	*Kucch.*
	Garo, ...	*Harj-múrj.*
	Káchári, ...	*Caret.*
Eastern Frontier of Bengal.	Munipuri, ...	*Caret.*
	Míthán Nágá, . . .	*Caret.*
	Tablung Nágá, . . .	*Caret.*
	Khári Nágá, . . .	*Kuiai.*
	Angámi Nágá, . . .	*Kajipuru.*
	Námsáng Nágá, . . .	*Caret.*
	Nowgong Nágá, . .	*Caret.*
	Tengsa Nágá, . . .	*Caret.*
	Abor Miri, ...	*Anjoko.*
	Sibságar Miri, . . .	*Okko.*
	Deoria Chutia, . . .	*Damasirini.*
	Singpho, ...	*Caret.*
Arrakan & Burmah.	Burman (*written*), . .	*Bhemhya.*
	Burman (*spoken*), . .	*Bhámhya.*
	Khyeng v. Shou, . .	*Caret.*
	Kámi, ...	*Ta-u-i.*
	Kúmi, ...	*Caret.*
	Mrú v. Toung, . . .	*Caret.*
	Sák, ...	*Caret.*
Siam & Tenasserim.	Talain v. Mon, . . .	*Mway-theik-payai.*
	Sgau-karen, ...	*Caret.*
	Pwo-karen, ...	*Caret.*
	Toungh-thu, ...	*Caret.*
	Shán, ...	*Pen-hts-aytso-tso.*
	Annamitic, ...	*Dêu-gì.*
	Siamese, ...	*Hpayla, arai.*
	Ahom, ...	*Caret.*
	Khámti, ...	*Caret.*
	Laos, ...	*Asang.*
Central India.	Ho (Kol), ...	*Chikanna.*
	Kol (Singhbhum), . .	*Oko-bitte.*
	Santáli, ...	*Chet-hong, oka-dhon.*
	Bhúmij, ...	*Ako-dhon.*
	Uráon, ...	*Indara.*
	Mundala, ...	*Jáha, nági.*
	Rájmahali, ...	*Indarbadi.*
	Goṇḍi, ...	*Bittichij, bore.*
	Gayeti, ...	*Bore.*
	Rutluk, ...	*Bore.*
	Naikude, ...	*Yanna-kátir.*
	Kolami, ...	*Amdenen.*
	Mádi, ...	*Bánataki.*
	Mádia, ...	*Caret.*
	Kuri, ...	*Caret.*
	Keikádi, ...	*Yedagao.*
	Khoṇḍ, ...	*Annátiki.*
	Sávara, ...	*Yetagani, jitagani.*
	Gadaba, ...	*Máḍisá.*
	Yerukala, ...	*Yemmadainá.*
	Chentsu, ...	*Kichu, jehaive.*
Southern India.	Tamiḷ, anc., ...	*Yádákilum, yedágilum.*
	Tamiḷ, mod., ...	*Edákilum.*
	Malayáḷma, anc., . .	*Caret.*
	Malayáḷma, mod., . .	*Yádonnengil.*
	Telugu, ...	*Edaina, vedaina.*
	Karṇáṭaka, anc., . .	*Caret.*
	Karṇáṭaka, mod., . .	*Yávadádarú.*
	Tuḷuva, ...	*Eránda.*
	Kurgi, ...	*Caret.*
	Toḍuva, }	*Caret.*
	Toḍa, }	*Caret.*
	Kóta, ...	*Caret.*
	Baḍaga, ...	*Caret.*
	Kuṛumba, ...	*Caret.*
	Iruḷa, ...	*Caret.*
	Malabar, ...	*Ethum.*
	Sinhalese, ...	*Monawáda.*

Group	Types.	
Inflecting.	SANSKRIT,	*Upari.*
	ARABIC,	*Fauk.*
Compounding.	BASK,	*Goyan, goyen, goiti, gora.*
	FINNIC,	*Päällinen.*
	MAGYAR,	*Fent.*
	TURKISH,	*Ust, yokaru.*
	CIRCASSIAN,	*Ahpsey.*
	GEORGIAN,	*Maghla.*
	MONGOLIAN,	*Caret.*
	MANTSHU,	*Dergi.*
	JAVANESE, Ngoko,	*Ing-duwur.*
	JAVANESE, Krama,	*Nginggil.*
	MALAY,	*Didtas.*
Isolating.	CHINESE, Nankin,	*Shang.*
	CHINESE, Pekin,	*Shang.*
	CHINESE, Canton,	*Sheong.*
	CHINESE, Shanghai,	*Zong-deu.*
	AMOY, Colloquial,	*Teng.*
	JAPANESE,	*Uyeni, uye.*
	Brahuí,	*Burzá.*
Chinese Frontier & Tibet.	Gyámi,	*Syáng-thou.*
	Gyárung,	*U'rkyé.*
	Tákpa,	*Gáng.*
	Mányak,	*Chú.*
	Thochú,	*Tikh.*
	Sokpa,	*Téré.*
	Horpa,	*Chhá.*
	Tibetan (*written*),	*Stengna.*
	Tibetan (*spoken*),	*Teng, ché, yégi.*
Nepal (east to west).	Serpa,	*Tyáng.*
	Súnwár,	*Ri.*
	Gúrung,	*Túnri.*
	Múrmi,	*Toyáng.*
	Magar,	*Dhénam.*
	Tháksya,	*Caret.*
	Pákhya,	*Hapra.*
	Newár,	*Cho.*
	Limbu,	*Tháng.*
Kiranti Group (East Nepal).	Kiránti,	*Madhani.*
	Rodong,	*Dhála, dhálo.*
	Rúngchenbung,	*Euchokda, euchongda, eukhukda.*
	Chhingtángya,	*Uténbe.*
	Náchhereng,	*Itwa ta, itó-ta.*
	Wáling,	*Itá, adháni, angyúni.*
	Yákha,	*Tö.*
	Chourásya,	*Bháta, imtóla.*
	Kulungya,	*U'mdúptu, metwáka, metyoka.*
	Thulungya,	*Denda.*
	Báhingya,	*Hátyu, apiye-di.*
	Lohorong,	*Songpittú, mittu, mito.*
	Lambichhong,	*Itemdu, to.*
	Báláli,	*Múttú.*
	Sáng-páng,	*Mitáni.*
	Dúmi,	*Túkálá.*
	Kháling,	*Túká.*
	Dungmáli,	*Háté-dá.*
Broken Tribes of Nepal.	Dárhi,	*U'para.*
	Denwár,	*Akásai.*
	Pahri,	*Cho-gu-tha.*
	Chepáng,	*Caret.*
	Bhrámu,	*Hú-khai.*
	Váyu,	*Wa-ne.*
	Kuswar,	*U'para.*
	Kusunda,	*Drasuok.*
	Tháru,	*Upara.*
	Lepcha (Sikkim),	*Atún, tal, aplóng.*
	Bhúṭáni v. Lhopa,	*Tén-khá, téng.*

N.-E. Bengal.	Bodo,	*Chhá.*
	Dhimál,	*Rhútá.*
	Kocch,	*Rhútá (?).*
	Garo,	*Pirvai.*
	Káchári,	*Sa.*
Eastern Frontier of Bengal.	Munipuri,	*Mathuk.*
	Míthán Nágá,	*Ding.*
	Tablung Nágá,	*Kawang.*
	Khári Nágá,	*Tamachingu.*
	Angámi Nágá,	*Bale.*
	Námsáng Nágá,	*A'khònang.*
	Nowgong Nágá,	*Talak.*
	Tengsa Nágá,	*Tathak.*
	Abor Miri,	*Taleng.*
	Sibságar Miri,	*Taluto.*
	Deoria Chutia,	*Picho.*
	Singpho,	*Ning-tsang.*
Arrakan & Burmah.	Burman (*written*),	*Apo-mhá.*
	Burman (*spoken*),	*Apo-mhá, a-htet-ma.*
	Khyeng v. Shou,	*Ada-ma-ka.*
	Kámi,	*A-koung-bé.*
	Kúmi,	*I'-klún.*
	Mrú v. Toung,	*Caret.*
	Sák,	*Caret.*
Siam & Tenasserim.	Talain v. Mon,	*Atotá.*
	Sgau-karen,	*A'pawko.*
	Pwo-karen,	*A'pangku, ler-tah.*
	Toungh-thu,	*Enké.*
	Shán,	*Pamon.*
	Annamitic,	*Trên.*
	Siamese,	*Ti-nan-bon.*
	Ahom,	*Nu.*
	Khámti,	*Kanlu.*
	Laos,	*Pin.*
Central India.	Ho (Kol),	*Sirma-ré.*
	Kol (Singhbhum),	*Sirma.*
	Santáli,	*Sirma, muchát-re.*
	Bhúmij,	*Sirma.*
	Uráon,	*Meyah.*
	Mundala,	*Chaitan.*
	Rájmahali,	*Meche.*
	Goṇḍi,	*Kis, parro.*
	Gayeti,	*Caret.*
	Rutluk,	*Caret.*
	Naikude,	*Caret.*
	Kolami,	*Caret.*
	Mádi,	*Caret.*
	Mádia,	*Caret.*
	Kuri,	*Caret.*
	Keikádi,	*Mele.*
	Khoṇḍ,	*Caret.*
	Sávara,	*Lanka.*
	Gadaba,	*Tommá.*
	Yerukala,	*Mene.*
	Chentsu,	*Vupár, vuparot.*
Southern India.	Tamiḷ, anc.,	*Misei.*
	Tamiḷ, mod.,	*Mél, méle.*
	Malayáḷma, anc.,	*Caret.*
	Malayáḷma, mod.,	*Méle, mite.*
	Telugu,	*Payina, midá.*
	Karṇáṭaka, anc.,	*Caret.*
	Karṇáṭaka, mod.,	*Méle.*
	Tuḷuva,	*Mett.*
	Kurgi,	*-méke, -koḍi.*
	Toḍuva,	*Caret.*
	Toḍa,	*Mel.*
	Kóta,	*Mele.*
	Baḍaga,	*Mele, vodega.*
	Kuṛumba,	*Mele.*
	Iruḷa,	*Mele, moke.*
	Malabar,	*Melei, uyara.*
	Sinhalese,	*Ihala.*

	Types.	
Inflecting.	SANSKṚIT,	*Cha, api.*
	ARABIC,	*Wa, fa, thomma.*
Compounding.	BASK,	*Ere, bere.*
	FINNIC,	*Ja, myos.*
	MAGYAR,	*Caret.*
	TURKISH,	*Caret.*
	CIRCASSIAN,	*Caret.*
	GEORGIAN,	*Caret.*
	MONGOLIAN,	*Tshu.*
	MANTSHU,	*Geli.*
	JAVANESE, Ngoko,	*Lan.*
	JAVANESE, Krama,	*Kaliyan.*
	MALAY,	*Dan.*
Isolating.	CHINESE, Nankin,	*Ho.*
	CHINESE, Pekin,	*Ho.*
	CHINESE, Canton,	*T'ung.*
	CHINESE, Shanghai,	*Yá, loh.*
	AMOY, Colloquial,	*Iú.*
	JAPANESE,	*Soste, -mo.*
	Brahuí,	*U.*
Chinese Frontier & Tibet.	Gyámi,	*Orcha.*
	Gyárung,	*Caret.*
	Tákpa,	*Caret.*
	Mányak,	*Caret.*
	Thochú,	*Tah, dah.*
	Sokpa,	*Pichhé.*
	Horpa,	*Ré.*
	Tibetan (*written*),	*Yáng.*
	Tibetan (*spoken*),	*Yáng.*
Nepal (east to west).	Serpa,	*Dáng, ang.*
	Súnwár,	*Nú.*
	Gúrung,	*Yé.*
	Múrmi,	*Yen, den.*
	Magar,	*Ra.*
	Tháksya,	*Bikigang.*
	Pákhya,	*Ra.*
	Newár,	*Ang, nang.*
	Limbu,	*Ang.*
Kiranti Group (East Nepal).	Kiránti,	*Ning.*
	Rodong,	*Pini, pitigno.*
	Rúngchenbung,	*Ning, chháng.*
	Chhingtángya,	*Yé. nang, yáng.*
	Náchhereng,	*Sa, ló.*
	Wáling,	*Chha.*
	Yákha,	*Yó, áng.*
	Chourásya,	*Yé.*
	Kulungya,	*Só.*
	Thulungya,	*Nung, bó.*
	Báhingya,	*Yó.*
	Lohorong,	*Sá, song.*
	Lambichhong,	*Chha.*
	Báláli,	*Sáng.*
	Sáng-páng,	*Sáng.*
	Dúmi,	*Yó.*
	Kháling,	*Núng-yo.*
	Dungmáli,	*Chhang.*
Broken Tribes of Nepal.	Dárhi,	*Ra, pún* (?).
	Denwár,	*Sa, sua* (?).
	Pahri,	*Khá* (?).
	Chepáng,	*Caret.*
	Bhrámu,	*Wóng.*
	Váyu,	*Lé.*
	Kuswar,	*Gyú.*
	Kusunda,	*Caret.*
	Tháru,	*Ká.*
	Lepcha (Sikkim),	*Lá.*
	Bhúṭáni v. Lhopa,	*Dá.*
N.-E. Bengal.	Bodo,	*Bi, bo.*
	Dhimál,	*Edong.*
	Kocch,	*Evong, o, áro.*
	Garo,	*Bá.*
	Káchári,	*Caret.*
Eastern Frontier of Bengal.	Munipuri,	*Súng, ama-súlei.*
	Míthán Nágá,	*Caret.*
	Tablung Nágá,	*O* (?).
	Khári Nágá,	*Caret.*
	Angámi Nágá,	*Caret.*
	Námsáng Nágá,	*O, áro* (?).
	Nowgong Nágá,	*Caret.*
	Tengsa Nágá,	*Caret.*
	Abor Miri,	*Ain.*
	Sibságar Miri,	*Caret.*
	Deoria Chutia,	*Caret.*
	Singpho,	*Caret.*
Arrakan & Burmah.	Burman (*written*),	*Lin-kong.*
	Burman (*spoken*),	*Ligaung, yuay.*
	Khyeng v. Shou,	*Caret.*
	Kámi,	*Caret.*
	Kúmi,	*Caret.*
	Mrú v. Toung,	*Caret.*
	Sák,	*Caret.*
Siam & Tenasserim.	Talain v. Mon,	*Young.*
	Sgau-karen,	*Dau, daw, sa-kaw.*
	Pwo-karen,	*Dai.*
	Toungh-thu,	*La.*
	Shán,	*Caret.*
	Annamitic,	*Vá.*
	Siamese,	*Le, kap, tak.*
	Ahom,	*Caret.*
	Khámti,	*Caret.*
	Laos,	*Le.*
Central India.	Ho (Kol),	*Ando, aṇdo* (?).
	Kol (Singhbhum),	*U'ndo.*
	Santáli,	*A'do, ar, rehong.*
	Bhúmij,	*Ar.*
	Uráon,	*Aur.*
	Mundala,	*Inni.*
	Rájmahali,	*Inseki.*
	Goṇḍi,	*Uṇḍe, úḍé.*
	Gayeti,	*Caret.*
	Rutluk,	*O* (?), *ar.*
	Naikude,	*Caret.*
	Kolami,	*O* (?), *ado.*
	Mádi,	*Caret.*
	Mádia,	*O* (?).
	Kuri,	*Caret.*
	Keikádi,	*Caret.*
	Khoṇḍ,	*Caret.*
	Sávara,	*Caret.*
	Gadaba,	*Tonnó.*
	Yerukala,	*Num.*
	Chentsu,	*Ke, ye.*
Southern India.	Tamiḷ, anc.,	*Caret.*
	Tamiḷ, mod.,	*-um.*
	Malayáḷma, anc.,	*Caret.*
	Malayáḷma, mod.,	*-um, num.*
	Telugu,	*-nni, -nnu, -nunnú.*
	Karṇáṭaka, anc.,	*Caret.*
	Karṇáṭaka, mod.,	*-ú.*
	Tuḷuva,	*No.*
	Kurgi,	*-ú.*
	Toḍuva, }	*Caret.*
	Toḍa, }	*O* (?).
	Kóta,	*Caret.*
	Baḍaga,	*O* (?).
	Kuṛumba,	*Caret.*
	Iruḷa,	*Caret.*
	Malabar,	*Um, thanum.*
	Sinhalese,	*-ta, -da.*

Group	Types.	
Inflecting.	SANSKRIT,	*Yathá.*
	ARABIC,	*K* (insep. prefix).
Compounding.	BASK,	*Bezala, bezela, bekela, legez, laso.*
	FINNIC,	*Nünkuin.*
	MAGYAR,	*Mint.*
	TURKISH,	*Gebi.*
	CIRCASSIAN,	*Beddeh.*
	GEORGIAN,	*Mebr.*
	MONGOLIAN,	*Caret.*
	MANTSHU,	*Caret.*
	JAVANESE, Ngoko,	*Sapolah.*
	JAVANESE, Krama,	*Satingkah.*
	MALAY,	*Saparti.*
Isolating.	CHINESE, Nankin,	*Che-yang.*
	CHINESE, Pekin,	*Che-yang.*
	CHINESE, Canton,	*Kom-yeong.*
	CHINESE, Shanghai,	*Ki-zeṇ; zü-dung.*
	AMOY, Colloquial,	*Ná.*
	JAPANESE,	*Yoni.*
	Brahui,	*Handunos.*
Chinese Frontier & Tibet.	Gyámi,	*Ah-men-ti.*
	Gyárung,	*Caret.*
	Tákpa,	*Dantang.*
	Mányak,	*Mi.*
	Thochú,	*Tek.*
	Sokpa,	*Caret.*
	Horpa,	*Naya.*
	Tibetan (*written*),	*Hadêtsúg.*
	Tibetan (*spoken*),	*Khánda.*
Nepal (east to west).	Serpa,	*Kándê.*
	Súnwár,	*Dódio.*
	Gúrung,	*Khaga-liyon.*
	Múrmi,	*Khájú.*
	Magar,	*Kúdángcha.*
	Tháksya,	*Khajibá.*
	Pákhya,	*Caret.*
	Newár,	*Gathing.*
	Limbu,	*Aphádong-bá.*
Kiranti Group (East Nepal).	Kiránti,	*Khâin súko.*
	Rodong,	*Caret.*
	Rúngchenbung,	*Caret.*
	Chhingtángya,	*Hókhyakkha* (?).
	Náchhereng,	*Dákhtó* (?).
	Wáling,	*Hagnê kagna.*
	Yákha,	*Irok-ha.*
	Chourásya,	*A'sijokcho.*
	Kulungya,	*Dátúkwa.*
	Thulungya,	*Heka, hêkgnám.*
	Báhingya,	*Gekho* (?).
	Lohorong,	*Mantok* (?).
	Lambichhong,	*Caret.*
	Báláli,	*Caret.*
	Sáng-páng,	*Caret.*
	Dúmi,	*Caret.*
	Kháling,	*Caret.*
	Dungmáli,	*Caret.*
Broken Tribes of Nepal.	Dárhi,	*Ja-sai.*
	Denwár,	*Já-nhê.*
	Pahri,	*Gê-rê.*
	Chepáng,	*Caret.*
	Bhrámu,	*Jún.*
	Váyu,	*Háng-nga.*
	Kuswar,	*Jásege.*
	Kusunda,	*Natiya.*
	Tháru,	*Jaisan.*
	Lepcha (Sikkim),	*Salom.*
	Bhúṭáni v. Lhopa,	*Kate.*

N.-E. Bengal.	Bodo,	*Jirin.*
	Dhimál,	*Jedong.*
	Kocch,	*Jenon.*
	Garo,	*Jegándá.*
	Káchári,	*Caret.*
Eastern Frontier of Bengal.	Munipuri,	*Asundouna.*
	Mithán Nágá,	*Caret.*
	Tablung Nágá,	*Caret.*
	Khári Nágá,	*Caret.*
	Angámi Nágá,	*Caret.*
	Námsáng Nágá,	*Caret.*
	Nowgong Nágá,	*Caret.*
	Tengsa Nágá,	*Caret.*
	Abor Miri,	*Caret.*
	Sibságar Miri,	*Caret.*
	Deoria Chutia,	*Caret.*
	Singpho,	*Caret.*
Arrakan & Burmah.	Burman (*written*),	*Keso.*
	Burman (*spoken*),	*Geṭho, Kai-ṭho.*
	Khyeng v. Shou,	*Caret.*
	Kámi,	*Hi-ná-i.*
	Kúmi,	*Caret.*
	Mrú v. Toung,	*Caret.*
	Sák,	*Caret.*
Siam & Tenasserim.	Talain v. Mon,	*Nwaytseik-nau.*
	Sgau-karen,	*De-i, di-ne.*
	Pwo-karen,	*Bayi.*
	Toungh-thu,	*Nay-yó.*
	Shán,	*Neik-youk.*
	Annamitic,	*Nhu'.*
	Siamese,	*Ni.*
	Ahom,	*Caret.*
	Khámti,	*Caret.*
	Laos,	*Caret.*
Central India.	Ho (Kol),	*Umchileka.*
	Kol (Singhbhum),	*Nuá-leko.*
	Santáli,	*Iná-leko, nung-ká.*
	Bhúmij,	*Nuṇ-ká.*
	Uráon,	*Caret.*
	Mundala,	*Nimnú.*
	Rájmahali,	*Nung-ká.*
	Goṇḍi,	*Inchur mandá.*
	Gayeti,	*Caret.*
	Rutluk,	*Caret.*
	Naikude,	*Caret.*
	Kolami,	*Nuṇ-ká* (?).
	Mádi,	*Caret.*
	Mádia,	*Caret.*
	Kuri,	*Caret.*
	Keikádi,	*Caret.*
	Khoṇḍ,	*Caret.*
	Sávara,	*Caret.*
	Gadaba,	*Caret.*
	Yerukala,	*Caret.*
	Chentsu,	*Lakha.*
Southern India.	Tamiḷ, anc.,	*Kaḍuppa.*
	Tamiḷ, mod.,	*-póla.*
	Malayáḷma, anc.,	*Caret.*
	Malayáḷma, mod.,	*-pol.*
	Telugu,	*Vale.*
	Karṇáṭaka, anc.,	*-pol.*
	Karṇáṭaka, mod.,	*-háge.*
	Tuḷuva,	*Anchane.*
	Kurgi,	*Caret.*
	Toḍuva,	*Caret.*
	Toḍa,	*Yingei.*
	Kóta,	*Yete.*
	Baḍaga,	*Hyinge, yetate.*
	Kuṛumba,	*Yetate.*
	Iruḷa,	*Yepaḍi.*
	Malabar,	*Pól, ena.*
	Sinhalese,	*-wágê.*

	Types.	
Inflecting.	SANSKRIT,	*Adhas.*
	ARABIC,	*Taḥt.*
Compounding.	BASK,	*Azpian, azpira, bean.*
	FINNIC,	*Alla.*
	MAGYAR,	*Lent-ala.*
	TURKISH,	*Alt, ashagh.*
	CIRCASSIAN,	*Caret.*
	GEORGIAN,	*Dabla.*
	MONGOLIAN,	*Caret.*
	MANTSHU,	*Fedshergi.*
	JAVANESE, Ngoko,	*Ngisor.*
	JAVANESE, Krama,	*Ngaṇḍap.*
	MALAY,	*Dibáwah.*
Isolating.	CHINESE, Nankin,	*Hia.*
	CHINESE, Pekin,	*Hià.*
	CHINESE, Canton,	*Ha.*
	CHINESE, Shanghai,	*O-dew.*
	AMOY, Colloquial,	*E-bin, e-toe.*
	JAPANESE,	*Sta, sita.*
	Brahuí,	*Shef.*
Chinese Frontier & Tibet.	Gyámi,	*Ti syá.*
	Gyárung,	*Wáki.*
	Tákpa,	*Wá.*
	Mányak,	*Zyé.*
	Thochú,	*Köl.*
	Sokpa,	*Törö.*
	Horpa,	*Wö.*
	Tibetan (*written*),	*Ho-gna.*
	Tibetan (*spoken*),	*Wö, syú, magi.*
Nepal (east to west).	Serpa,	*Wag.*
	Súnwár,	*Yú.*
	Gúrung,	*Muṇri.*
	Múrmi,	*Moyang.*
	Magar,	*Mháka.*
	Tháksya,	*Masi.*
	Pákhya,	*Tala.*
	Newár,	*Ko.*
	Limbu,	*Mó.*
Kiranti Group (East Nepal).	Kiránti,	*Mbyúni.*
	Rodong,	*Hila, hwilo.*
	Rúngchenbung,	*Múpúni, uyuni.*
	Chhingtángya,	*Móba.*
	Nachhereng,	*U'yúyu.*
	Wáling,	*Itú, akhúkyu.*
	Yákha,	*Mó.*
	Chourásya,	*Bháya, bhayola.*
	Kulungya,	*U'mdhókpu, núkka-ah.*
	Thulungya,	*Goyu.*
	Báhingya,	*Háyu, apum-di.*
	Lohorong,	*Khúkmemo, mik-mú.*
	Lambichhong,	*Ikhúk-bé-mó.*
	Báláli,	*Múk-mu.*
	Sáng-páng,	*Mú-yúni.*
	Dúmi,	*Yúkálá.*
	Kháling,	*Yúká.*
	Dungmáli,	*Ungk-hok-mo.*
Broken Tribes of Nepal.	Dárhi,	*Hét.*
	Denwár,	*Hé-then.*
	Pahri,	*Ko-gú-thá.*
	Chepáng,	*Caret.*
	Bhrámu,	*Hu-mai.*
	Váyu,	*Hu-the.*
	Kuswar,	*Hét.*
	Kusunda,	*Tumái.*
	Tháru,	*Tare.*
	Lepcha (Sikkim),	*Achúm, cheul, sadom.*
	Bhúṭáni v. Lhopa,	*Wóh.*

N.-E. Bengal.	Bodo,	*Sying.*
	Dhimál,	*Létó.*
	Kocch,	*Letá, adhar (?).*
	Garo,	*Churik vai.*
	Káchári,	*Sin.*
Eastern Frontier of Bengal.	Munipuri,	*Makha.*
	Míthán Nágá,	*Hopang.*
	Tablung Nágá,	*Opang.*
	Khári Nágá,	*Tamoksing.*
	Angámi Nágá,	*Chakise.*
	Námsáng Nágá,	*Akhannang.*
	Nowgong Nágá,	*Tasung.*
	Tengsa Nágá,	*Tachung.*
	Abor Miri,	*Rumking.*
	Sibságar Miri,	*Rumkube.*
	Deoria Chutia,	*Kumo.*
	Singpho,	*Katai.*
Arrakan & Burmah.	Burman (*written*),	*Okmha.*
	Burman (*spoken*),	*Aukmha.*
	Khyeng v. Shou,	*De-kan.*
	Kámi,	*Thing-be.*
	Kúmi,	*I-klot.*
	Mrú v. Toung,	*Caret.*
	Sák,	*Caret.*
Siam & Tenasserim.	Talain v. Mon,	*Kha-ta-ta.*
	Sgau-karen,	*A'pawlah.*
	Pwo-karen,	*A'punglah.*
	Toungh-thu,	*Enla.*
	Shán,	*Palon.*
	Annamitic,	*Dwoï.*
	Siamese,	*Khan-la, ti.*
	Ahom,	*Lep.*
	Khámti,	*Caret.*
	Laos,	*Lum.*
Central India.	Ho (Kol),	*Suba-ré.*
	Kol (Singhbhum),	*Súbá.*
	Santáli,	*Pheḍ, butáre, látárate.*
	Bhúmij,	*Athé.*
	Uráon,	*Kiyah.*
	Mundala,	*Látin.*
	Rájmahali,	*Pissi.*
	Goṇḍi,	*Naiti, sir, khálai, mandar.*
	Gayeti,	*Caret.*
	Rutluk,	*Caret.*
	Naikude,	*Caret.*
	Kolami,	*Caret.*
	Mádi,	*Caret.*
	Mádia,	*Caret.*
	Kuri,	*Caret.*
	Keikádi,	*Digu.*
	Khoṇḍ,	*Neḍe.*
	Sávara,	*Jayitá.*
	Gadaba,	*Alóm.*
	Yerukala,	*Tallen.*
	Chentsu,	*Tolot, tól.*
Southern India.	Tamiḷ, anc.,	*Kizhakku, kiḷakku.*
	Tamiḷ, mod.,	*Kízh, kízhe.*
	Malayáḷma, anc.,	*Caret.*
	Malayáḷma, mod.,	*Tázhe, tázhe.*
	Telugu,	*Kinda.*
	Karṇáṭaka, anc.,	*Caret.*
	Karṇaṭaka, mod.,	*Keḷage.*
	Tuḷuva,	*Sett.*
	Kurgi,	*-kida.*
	Toḍuva, }	*Caret.*
	Toḍa, }	*Erg, neshg*
	Kóta,	*Kriyage.*
	Baḍaga,	*Kria.*
	Kuṛumba,	*Kelage.*
	Iruḷa,	*Kálake.*
	Malabar,	*Kelei.*
	Sinhalese,	*Pahala.*

	Types.	
Inflecting.	SANSKRIT,	*Antar.*
	ARABIC,	*Bein.*
Compounding.	BASK,	*Artean, artera, arte.*
	FINNIC,	*Waihella.*
	MAGYAR,	*Caret.*
	TURKISH,	*Caret.*
	CIRCASSIAN,	*Et-katsh.*
	GEORGIAN,	*Caret.*
	MONGOLIAN,	*Caret.*
	MANTSHU,	*Sidende.*
	JAVANESE, Ngoko,	*Selan.*
	JAVANESE, Krama,	*Selan.*
	MALAY,	*Ditangah.*
Isolating.	CHINESE, Nankin,	*Chung-kien.*
	CHINESE, Pekin,	*Chung-chien.*
	CHINESE, Canton,	*Chung-kan.*
	CHINESE, Shanghai,	*Tong-tsung.*
	AMOY, Colloquial,	*Tiong-ng.*
	JAPANESE,	*Aida, naka.*
	Brahui,	*Caret.*
Chinese Frontier & Tibet.	Gyámi,	*Túng-jen.*
	Gyárung,	*Ule, tile.*
	Tákpa,	*Bút-ká, képá.*
	Mányak,	*Onglhe.*
	Thochú,	*Tigú.*
	Sokpa,	*Toung dú.*
	Horpa,	*Kyúkú.*
	Tibetan (*written*),	*Bar, du.*
	Tibetan (*spoken*),	*Bhar.*
Nepal (east to west).	Serpa,	*Par.*
	Súnwár,	*Daté.*
	Gúrung,	*Khionri.*
	Múrmi,	*Gúngari.*
	Magar,	*Mi khiáng.*
	Tháksya,	*Kung ri.*
	Pákhya,	*Májha.*
	Newár,	*Dathú.*
	Limbu,	*Kúlúm.*
Kiranti Group (East Nepal).	Kiránti,	*Lúndi.*
	Rodong,	*Mrá, máru.*
	Rúngchenbung,	*Lumda, rádoa.*
	Chhingtángya,	*Urhábe.*
	Náchhereng,	*Umlam.*
	Wáling,	*Umrápe, arádha, adhung-ya.*
	Yákha,	*Ilúm.*
	Chourásya,	*Khácki, khachilo, gota.*
	Kulungya,	*Umrápi.*
	Thulungya,	*Théte.*
	Báhingya,	*A'lyo, aleu-da.*
	Lohorong,	*Lúmbe, lúmpi.*
	Lambichhong,	*Ilúm-bé.*
	Bálálí,	*Májhábi, lúli'pi.*
	Sáng-páng,	*Ammrápi.*
	Dúmi,	*Májhábi.*
	Kháling,	*O'lipphibi.*
	Dungmáli,	*U'mrá, úmrábi.*
Broken Tribes of Nepal.	Dárhi,	*Májhai.*
	Denwár,	*Majhen.*
	Pahri,	*Dári.*
	Chepáng,	*Caret.*
	Bhrámu,	*A-sal.*
	Váyu,	*Mádúm-be.*
	Kuswar,	*Manjhi.*
	Kusunda,	*Gijhágda.*
	Tháru,	*Biche.*
	Lepcha (Sikkim),	*Abik, achúk.*
	Bhútáni v. Lhopa,	*Páná.*

N.-E. Bengal.	Bodo,	*Gejer.*
	Dhimál,	*Majhata.*
	Kocch,	*Antar (?).*
	Garo,	*Majár-vai.*
	Káchári,	*Caret.*
Eastern Frontier of Bengal.	Munipuri,	*Moyaida.*
	Mithán Nágá,	*Caret.*
	Tablung Nágá,	*Caret.*
	Khári Nágá,	*Tiong.*
	Angámi Nágá,	*Caret.*
	Námsáng Nágá,	*Caret.*
	Nowgong Nágá,	*Kimá.*
	Tengsa Nágá,	*Ulam.*
	Abor Miri,	*Radang.*
	Sibságar Miri,	*A'ráso.*
	Deoria Chutia,	*Caret.*
	Singpho,	*Caret.*
Arrakan & Burmah.	Burman (*written*),	*Akrámhá.*
	Burman (*spoken*),	*Akyámhá-alay-mha.*
	Khyeng v. Shou,	*A-lhá-ka-ku.*
	Kámi,	*Thin-be, u-thin-á.*
	Kúmi,	*Si-lá.*
	Mrú v. Toung,	*Caret.*
	Sák,	*Caret.*
Siam & Tenasserim.	Talain v. Mon,	*Adho.*
	Sgau-karen,	*A'bersir.*
	Pwo-karen,	*A'bong-tsung.*
	Toungh-thu,	*Akha.*
	Shán,	*Akhun.*
	Annamitic,	*Yiu'a.*
	Siamese,	*Khalan, wang.*
	Ahom,	*Klang.*
	Khámti,	*Caret.*
	Laos,	*Caret.*
Central India.	Ho (Kol),	*Caret.*
	Kol (Singhbhum),	*Talaré.*
	Santáli,	*Táláre.*
	Bhúmij,	*Talaré.*
	Uráon,	*Majin.*
	Mundala,	*Talar.*
	Rájmahali,	*Máji.*
	Goṇḍi,	*Nuddum, bichte mandar.*
	Gayeti,	*Caret.*
	Rutluk,	*Caret.*
	Naikude,	*Caret.*
	Kolami,	*Caret.*
	Mádi,	*Caret.*
	Mádia,	*Caret.*
	Kuri,	*Caret.*
	Keikádi,	*Naduwa.*
	Khoṇḍ,	*Madde.*
	Sávara,	*Lanka.*
	Gadaba,	*Vomiḍi.*
	Yerukala,	*Neduve.*
	Chentsu,	*Mayidhit, móyid.*
Southern India.	Tamiḷ, anc.,	*Náppan.*
	Tamiḷ, mod.,	*-naḍu, -naḍuve.*
	Malayáḷma, anc.,	*Caret.*
	Malayáḷma, mod.,	*Naṭukke, naṭuvil.*
	Telugu,	*-naḍama, -naduma.*
	Karṇáṭaka, anc.,	*Caret.*
	Karṇáṭaka, mod.,	*-maḍuve.*
	Tuḷuva,	*-naḍu.*
	Kurgi,	*Caret.*
	Toḍuva, }	*Caret.*
	Toda, }	*Nárth, -kúshi.*
	Kóta,	*-naḍle.*
	Baḍaga,	*-naḍuve.*
	Kurumba,	*-naḍuve.*
	Iruḷa,	*-naḍuve.*
	Malabar,	*-údei, -idiyil.*
	Sinhalese,	*-atare.*

Group	Types.	
Inflecting.	SANSKRIT,	*-á, -bhyám,*[1] *-bhis*[2] (instr.).
	ARABIC,	*B-* (insep. prefix).
Compounding.	BASK,	*-z, -zas.*
	FINNIC,	*Caret.*
	MAGYAR,	*-a, -rol.*
	TURKISH,	*-dan.*
	CIRCASSIAN,	*Caret.*
	GEORGIAN,	*-gan.*
	MONGOLIAN,	*-yer, -ber.*
	MANTSHU,	*Caret.*
	JAVANESE, Ngoko,	*Dene.*
	JAVANESE, Krama,	*Dening.*
	MALAY,	*U'lih.*
Isolating.	CHINESE, Nankin,	*Yung.*
	CHINESE, Pekin,	*Yung.*
	CHINESE, Canton,	*Yung.*
	CHINESE, Shanghai,	*Táng.*
	AMOY, Colloquial,	*Eng.*
	JAPANESE,	*-de, motte.*
	Brahuí,	*-ene.*
Chinese Frontier & Tibet.	Gyámi,	*La.*
	Gyárung,	*Gi.*
	Tákpa,	*Gi.*
	Mányak,	*Lé.*
	Thochú,	*I'.*
	Sokpa,	*Rá.*
	Horpa,	*Khá, wú.*
	Tibetan (*written*),	*Kyis, gis, his, yis.*
	Tibetan (*spoken*),	*I'.*
Nepal (east to west).	Serpa,	Elongation of terminal vowel.
	Súnwár,	*Mi.*
	Gúrung,	*Ji.*
	Múrmi,	*Syé.*
	Magar,	*Ye, i.*
	Tháksya,	*Kau.*
	Pákhya,	*Le.*
	Newár,	*Ang.*
	Limbu,	*Illé, nú.*
Kiranti Group (East Nepal).	Kiránti,	*Yá.*
	Rodong,	*Wá.*
	Rúngchenbung,	*Ya, á.*
	Chhingtángya,	*Gná.*
	Náchhereng,	*A'.*
	Wáling,	*A'.*
	Yákha,	*Gná.*
	Chourásya,	*Kho.*
	Kulungya,	*A'.*
	Thulungya,	*Ká.*
	Báhingya,	*Mi.*
	Lohorong,	*E, yé.*
	Lambichhong,	*Gná.*
	Báláli,	*Gná.*
	Sáng-páng,	*A'.*
	Dúmi,	*A', gná.*
	Kháling,	*A'.*
	Dungmáli,	*A'.*
Broken Tribes of Nepal.	Dárhi,	*Caret.*
	Denwár,	*Caret.*
	Pahri,	*Caret.*
	Chepáng,	*Caret.*
	Bhrámu,	*Caret.*
	Váyu,	*Caret.*
	Kuswar,	*Caret.*
	Kusunda,	*A'i.*
	Tháru,	*Le.*
	Lepcha (Sikkim),	*Nan, sa.*
	Bhúṭáni v. Lhopa,	*Ki, dá.*
N.-E. Bengal.	Bodo,	*Jong.*
	Dhimál,	*Dong, ow, sho.*
	Kocch,	*Diyá.*
	Garo,	*Man.*
	Káchári,	*Caret.*
Eastern Frontier of Bengal.	Munipuri,	*Na.*
	Míthán Nágá,	*Caret.*
	Tablung Nágá,	*Caret.*
	Khári Nágá,	*Caret.*
	Angámi Nágá,	*Caret.*
	Námsáng Nágá,	*Caret.*
	Nowgong Nágá,	*Wá.*
	Tengsa Nágá,	*Nu.*
	Abor Miri,	*Umnus.*
	Sibságar Miri,	*Appunge.*
	Deoria Chutia,	*Caret.*
	Singpho,	*Caret.*
Arrakan & Burmah.	Burman (*written*),	*Phrang.*
	Burman (*spoken*),	*Phyen.*
	Khyeng v. Shou,	*Caret.*
	Kámi,	*Má.*
	Kúmi,	*Caret.*
	Mrú v. Toung,	*Caret.*
	Sák,	*Caret.*
Siam & Tenasserim.	Talain v. Mon,	*Nakeu.*
	Sgau-karen,	*A'ghaw'ti.*
	Pwo-karen,	*Boh-koh.*
	Toungh-thu,	*Tome.*
	Shán,	*Caret.*
	Annamitic,	*Tu.*
	Siamese,	*Caret.*
	Ahom,	*Caret.*
	Khámti,	*Caret.*
	Laos,	*Caret.*
Central India.	Ho (Kol),	*-té.*
	Kol (Singhbhum),	*Jete.*
	Santáli,	*-iyáte, -iáte, -hatete.*
	Bhúmij,	By affix.
	Uráon,	By affix.
	Mundala,	*A'tam.*
	Rájmahali,	By affix.
	Gondi,	*Igat, turse, durse.*
	Gayeti,	*Caret.*
	Rutluk,	*Caret.*
	Naikude,	*Caret.*
	Kolami,	*Caret.*
	Mádi,	*Caret.*
	Mádia,	*Caret.*
	Kuri,	*Caret.*
	Keikádi,	*Caret.*
	Khond,	*Caret.*
	Sávara,	*Sitholo.*
	Gadaba,	*Rom.*
	Yerukala,	*Valla.*
	Chentsu,	*Soyi.*
Southern India.	Tamil, anc.,	*-án.*
	Tamil, mod.,	*-ál, -nale.*
	Malayáḷma, anc.,	*Caret.*
	Malayáḷma, mod.,	*-ál, -konda.*
	Telugu,	*-valla, -walla, -chéta.*
	Karṇáṭaka, anc.,	*Caret.*
	Karṇáṭaka, mod.,	*-inda.*
	Tuḷuva,	*-ath.*
	Kurgi,	*-gondu.*
	Toḍuva, }	*Caret.*
	Toḍa, }	*-ind, ar.*
	Kóta,	*-inde.*
	Baḍaga,	*-inda.*
	Kuṛumba,	*-inda.*
	Iruḷa,	*-irinda, inda.*
	Malabar,	*-kondu, ál.*
	Sinhalese,	*-wisin.*

Types.		
Inflecting.	SANSKRIT,	*Dúram, paras.*
	ARABIC,	*Baaîd.*
Compounding.	BASK,	*Urruti, urrun.*
	FINNIC,	*Kaukainen.*
	MAGYAR,	*Messze.*
	TURKISH,	*Uzak.*
	CIRCASSIAN,	*Tshihshey.*
	GEORGIAN,	*Kide.*
	MONGOLIAN,	*Khola.*
	MANTSHU,	*Goro.*
	JAVANESE, Ngoko,	*Adoh.*
	JAVANESE, Krama,	*Tebih.*
	MALAY,	*Dakat.*
Isolating.	CHINESE, Nankin,	*Yuen.*
	CHINESE, Pekin,	*Yüan.*
	CHINESE, Canton,	*Ün.*
	CHINESE, Shanghai,	*Yüṇ.*
	AMOY, Colloquial,	*Hñg.*
	JAPANESE,	*Toku.*
	Brahuí,	*Caret.*
Chinese Frontier & Tibet.	Gyámi,	*Ywén.*
	Gyárung,	*Ka-sri.*
	Tákpa,	*Ringbú.*
	Mányak,	*Rassá.*
	Thochú,	*Grikho.*
	Sokpa,	*Khóló.*
	Horpa,	*Chéchi.*
	Tibetan (*written*),	*Né, nyé.*
	Tibetan (*spoken*),	*Tháring.*
Népal (east to west).	Serpa,	*Rimbo.*
	Súnwár,	*Gnani.*
	Gúrung,	*Rhémó.*
	Múrmi,	*Tháring.*
	Magar,	*Lós.*
	Tháksya,	*Chari.*
	Pákhya,	*Táhi.*
	Newár,	*Tápá.*
	Limbu,	*Mánkhó.*
Kiranti Group (East Népal).	Kiránti,	*Mángsá.*
	Rodong,	*Mokhá, mise, mose.*
	Rúngchenbung,	*Mángsa, mangkhiyada,*
	Chhingtángya,	*Mángmwa, mangno.* [*mang.*
	Náchhereng,	*Chhiburu.*
	Wáling,	*Mángkhaya.*
	Yákha,	*Mangdúna.*
	Chourásya,	*Bhána.*
	Kulungya,	*Chhúgri.*
	Thulungya,	*Chhyubat.*
	Báhingya,	*Brába, hare.*
	Lohorong,	*Wó, miyo.*
	Lambichhong,	*Mánglok.*
	Báláli,	*Túrho.*
	Sáng-páng,	*Chhúsi.*
	Dúmi,	*Chhyú.*
	Kháling,	*Chhy-úpá.*
	Dungmáli,	*Máng, mang-khá-yá.*
Broken Tribes of Népal.	Dárhi,	*Tárho.*
	Denwár,	*Tar-hai.*
	Pahri,	*Ta-pa-le.*
	Chepáng,	*Dyáng-to.*
	Bhrámu,	*Ka-loh.*
	Váyu,	*Ho-lám.*
	Kuswar,	*Dú-re.*
	Kusunda,	*Isinha.*
	Thárú,	*Uhá.*
	Lepcha (Sikkim),	*Maram.*
	Bhútáni v. Lhopa,	*Tháring.*

N.-E. Bengal.	Bodo,	*Gajáng.*
	Dhimál,	*Dúre.*
	Koch,	*Dúr.*
	Garo,	*Pijáng.*
	Káchári,	*Caret.*
Eastern Frontier of Bengal.	Munipuri,	*Arápa.*
	Míthán Nágá,	*Atai.*
	Tablung Nágá,	*Kátike.*
	Khári Nágá,	*Uragu.*
	Angámi Nágá,	*Chawé.*
	Námsáng Nágá,	*Háló.*
	Nowgong Nágá,	*Talang.*
	Tengsa Nágá,	*Langla.*
	Abor Miri,	*Caret.*
	Sibságar Miri,	*Modo.*
	Deoria Chutia,	*As-aiṇ.*
	Singpho,	*Tsan.*
Arrakan & Burmah.	Burman (*written*),	*Wé.*
	Burman (*spoken*),	*Wé, a-wá-mha.*
	Khyeng v. Shou,	*Tsua-alau-ame.*
	Kámi,	*Khán-lá.*
	Kúmi,	*Pi-lú-pa-i.*
	Mrú v. Toung,	*Caret.*
	Sák,	*Caret.*
Siam & Tenasserim.	Talain v. Mon,	*Nu-ma-way.*
	Sgau-karen,	*Yi, yizi.*
	Pwo-karen,	*Yaing.*
	Toungh-thu,	*Hyá.*
	Shán,	*An-kehn.*
	Annamitic,	*Xa.*
	Siamese,	*Ka-rihn, kli.*
	Ahom,	*Jau, sai.*
	Khámti,	*Kai.*
	Laos,	*Kai.*
Central India.	Ho (Kol),	*Sanging.*
	Kol (Singhbhum),	*Sánging, sánginiya.*
	Santáli,	*Sánging.*
	Bhúmij,	*Sánginiya.*
	Uráon,	*Gécha.*
	Mundala,	*Sángin.*
	Rájmahali,	*Géchi.*
	Goṇḍi,	*Lak, langkak mandar.*
	Gayeti,	*Lak.*
	Rutluk,	*Lab.*
	Naikude,	*Daw.*
	Kolami,	*Peredáw.*
	Mádi,	*Vilak, jeku.*
	Mádia,	*Lap.*
	Kuri,	*Atár.*
	Keikádi,	*Dúram.*
	Khoṇḍ,	*Aṭumané.*
	Sávara,	*Sangayi.*
	Gadaba,	*Sulóm.*
	Yerukala,	*Túra, kiṭṭe.*
	Chentsu,	*Dúr.*
Southern India.	Tamiḷ, anc.,	*Scimei.*
	Tamiḷ, mod.,	*Tulei, dúram.*
	Malayáḷma, anc.,	*Caret.*
	Malayáḷma, mod.,	*Akale.*
	Telugu,	*Davvu, dúramu.*
	Karṇáṭaka, anc.,	*Caret.*
	Karṇáṭaka, mod.,	*Caret.*
	Tuḷuva,	*Caret.*
	Kurgi,	*Caret.*
	Toḍuva, }	*Caret.*
	Toḍa, }	*Podthdshi.*
	Kóta,	*Durame.*
	Baḍaga,	*Dura.*
	Kuṛumba,	*Dúra.*
	Iruḷa,	*Dúra.*
	Malabar,	*Thúra.*
	Sinhalese,	*Dura.*

Group	Types.	
Inflecting.	SANSKRIT,	*-as, -bhyám,*[1] *-bhyas*[2] (abl.).
	ARABIC,	*Min.*
Compounding.	BASK,	*-dik, -tik, -gandik, -ganik.*
	FINNIC,	*-lta.*
	MAGYAR,	*-rol, -bol.*
	TURKISH,	*-dan.*
	CIRCASSIAN,	*Caret.*
	GEORGIAN,	*-sagan, -sgan.*
	MONGOLIAN,	*Etse.*
	MANTSHU,	*-tchi.*
	JAVANESE, Ngoko,	*Teka, saka.*
	JAVANESE, Krama,	*Sangking, saking.*
	MALAY,	*Dari.*
Isolating.	CHINESE, Nankin,	*Ts'ung.*
	CHINESE, Pekin,	*Ts'ung, kheu.*
	CHINESE, Canton,	*Ts'ung.*
	CHINESE, Shanghai,	*Dzyung.*
	AMOY, Colloquial,	*Lùi.*
	JAPANESE,	*-yori, kara.*
	Brahuí,	*-áng, -aṇ.*
Chinese Frontier & Tibet.	Gyámi,	*Li.*
	Gyárung,	*Shis, -s.*
	Tákpa,	*I'.*
	Mányak,	*Tha, ni.*
	Thochú,	*-k, to, gé.*
	Sokpa,	*Gásá.*
	Horpa,	*Lháno, gha.*
	Tibetan (*written*),	*Nas, las.*
	Tibetan (*spoken*),	*Né, diné.*
Nepal (east to west).	Serpa,	*Nébá.*
	Súnwár,	*Gná.*
	Gúrung,	*Wájé.*
	Múrmi,	*Yanché.*
	Magar,	*In.*
	Tháksya,	*Kyáche.*
	Pákhya,	*Báto.*
	Newár,	*Ni shyang, ang, yákén.*
	Limbu,	*Nú, manú.*
Kiranti Group (East Nepal).	Kiránti,	*Dánká.*
	Rodong,	*Dáká, dano.*
	Rúngchenbung,	*Dángká.*
	Chhingtángya,	*Gná.*
	Náchhereng,	*A'm.*
	Wáling,	*Pangkwa.*
	Yákha,	*Bwang.*
	Chourásya,	*Lo-gno.*
	Kulungya,	*Gna, á, piká.*
	Thulungya,	*D-ang, káng.*
	Báhingya,	*Ding.*
	Lohorong,	*Báng, páng.*
	Lambichhong,	*Behong.*
	Báláli,	*Páng, pi.*
	Sáng-páng,	*Piká.*
	Dúmi,	*Biká.*
	Kháling,	*Biká.*
	Dungmáli,	*Bang, ibangá.*
Broken Tribes of Nepal.	Dárhi,	*Nhé.*
	Denwár,	*Súṇ.*
	Pahri,	*Ang.*
	Chepáng,	*I.*
	Bhrámu,	*Jáng, gáng.*
	Váyu,	*Khen.*
	Kuswar,	*Batho, dékhi.*
	Kusunda,	*Jang, jai.*
	Tháru,	*Paidádekhalbat.*
	Lepcha (Sikkim),	*Nan, liang.*
	Bhúṭáni v. Lhopa,	*Nálé, le chálé.*

N.-E. Bengal.	Bodo,	*-phra.*
	Dhimál,	*-sho.*
	Kocch,	*-hoïte* (?).
	Garo,	*Prá.*
	Kácheri,	*Caret.*
Eastern Frontier of Bengal.	Munipuri,	*Di gi.*
	Míthán Nágá,	*Caret.*
	Tablung Nágá,	*Caret.*
	Khári Nágá,	*Bine.*
	Angámi Nágá,	*Caret.*
	Námsáng Nágá,	*Caret.*
	Nowgong Nágá,	*Caret.*
	Tengsa Nágá,	*Caret.*
	Abor Miri,	*Odankang.*
	Sibságar Miri,	*Lokke.*
	Deoria Chutia,	*Caret.*
	Singpho,	*Caret.*
Arrakan & Burmah.	Burman (*written*),	*Ka.*
	Burman (*spoken*),	*Ga.*
	Khyeng v. Shou,	*Lá.*
	Kámi,	*Ná-i.*
	Kúmi,	*Caret.*
	Mrú v. Toung,	*Caret.*
	Sák,	*Caret.*
Siam & Tenasserim.	Talain v. Mon,	*Nu.*
	Sgau-karen,	*Ler.*
	Pwo-karen,	*Ler.*
	Toungh-thu,	*A.*
	Shán,	*Kohn.*
	Annamitic,	*Boï.*
	Siamese,	*Tway, -té.*
	Ahom,	*Caret.*
	Khámti,	*Luk.*
	Laos,	*Caret.*
Central India.	Ho (Kol),	*-te.*
	Kol (Singhbhum),	*Te (-te ?).*
	Santáli,	*-thenkhon, -khond, -khon.*
	Bhúmij,	*-khon.*
	Uráon,	*Té.*
	Mundala,	*Sé.*
	Rájmahali,	*-khon* (?).
	Goṇḍi,	*-te* (?).
	Gayeti,	*Caret.*
	Rutluk,	*Caret.*
	Naikude,	*Caret.*
	Kolami,	*Caret.*
	Máḍi,	*Caret.*
	Mádia,	*Caret.*
	Kuri,	*Caret.*
	Keikádi,	*Caret.*
	Khoṇḍ,	*Caret.*
	Sávara,	*Sitholo.*
	Gadaba,	*Rom.*
	Yerukala,	*Nunche.*
	Chentsu,	*Singa.*
Southern India.	Tamiḷ, anc.,	*-il.*
	Tamiḷ, mod.,	*-ninru.*
	Malayáḷma, anc.,	*Caret.*
	Malayáḷma, mod.,	*-ninna, -ilninna.*
	Telugu,	*-nunchi.*
	Karṇáṭaka, anc.,	*Caret.*
	Karṇáṭaka, mod.,	*-inda, -deseyinda.*
	Tuḷuva,	*Caret.*
	Kurgi,	*-chellitu.*
	Toḍuva,	*-n.*
	Toḍa,	*-ind, ar.*
	Kóta,	*-inde.*
	Baḍaga,	*-inda.*
	Kuṟumba,	*-inda.*
	Iruḷa,	*-irinda, inda.*
	Malabar,	*-ál, irunthu.*
	Sinhalese,	*-gen.*

Types.		
Inflecting	SANSKRIT, ...	*Iha, atra.*
	ARABIC, ...	*Honá, háhoná.*
Compounding	BASK, ...	*Emen, ona, onara, onat, unat.*
	FINNIC, ...	*Tasa.*
	MAGVAR, ...	*It.*
	TURKISH, ...	*Buraya.*
	CIRCASSIAN, . . .	*Medehshey (?).*
	GEORGIAN, ...	*Aka.*
	MONGOLIAN, ...	*Ende.*
	MANTSHU, ...	*Ubade.*
	JAVANESE, Ngoko, .	*Kene.*
	JAVANESE, Krama, .	*Ngriki.*
	MALAV, ...	*Distni.*
Isolating	CHINESE, Nankin, . .	*Che-li.*
	CHINESE, Pekin, . .	*Che-li.*
	CHINESE, Canton, .	*Ni-chü.*
	CHINESE, Shanghai, .	*Ti-teh.*
	AMOV, Colloquial, .	*Chí-tau, tí-chia.*
	JAPANESE, ...	*Kokoni, koko.*
	Brahuí, ...	*Dáde.*
Chinese Frontier & Tibet	Gyámi, ...	*Thi-mé.*
	Gyárung, ...	*Chidú.*
	Tákpa, ...	*Wo cho.*
	Mányak, ...	*Khopú, dait.*
	Thochú, ...	*Cho, kúzgá, chaksi, thaksi.*
	Sokpa, ...	*Indé.*
	Horpa, ...	*U'dú.*
	Tibetan (*written*), .	*Hadina.*
	Tibetan (*spoken*), .	*Dicho.*
Nepal (east to west)	Serpa, ...	*Dirú.*
	Súnwár, ...	*Watha.*
	Gúrung, ...	*Chúri.*
	Múrmi, ...	*Jyásé.*
	Magar, ...	*Ilak.*
	Tháksya, ...	*Kesichosi.*
	Pákhya, ...	*Ytá.*
	Newár, ...	*Thúké.*
	Limbu, ...	*Kót-ná.*
Kiranti Group (East Nepal)	Kiránti, ...	*Wadá.*
	Rodong, ...	*Wada.*
	Rúngchenbung, . .	*Oḍa.*
	Chhingtángya, . .	*Báye, báyétni.*
	Náchhereng, . . .	*Ik, yéksa.*
	Wáling, ...	*I'yák, wada, waya.*
	Yákha, ...	*Khé, núkhé.*
	Chourásya, . . .	*Alo, amna, alvi.*
	Kulungya, ...	*Yiksa, ingkwápi.*
	Thulungya, . . .	*A'no, ási, asinda.*
	Bdhingya, ...	*Yákáre, éke, yeke.*
	Lohorong, ...	*Igobe, igiyú, kiyú.*
	Lambichhong, . .	*Nábe, nate.*
	Báláli, ...	*Kobi, koyú.*
	Sáng-páng, . . .	*Nopyá, nopi.*
	Dúmi, ...	*Tébi.*
	Kháling, ...	*Tábi, tábigná.*
	Dungmáli, ...	*Ibi, yák.*
Broken Tribes of Nepal	Dárhi, ...	*I'-chi.*
	Denwár, ...	*Yé-ti.*
	Pahri, ...	*Thúgu-thá.*
	Chepáng, ...	*Caret.*
	Bhrámu, ...	*Hi-di.*
	Váyu, ...	*I-ne, i-the.*
	Kuswar, ...	*Achi-na.*
	Kusunda, ...	*Tau-wa.*
	Tháru, ...	*Yehara.*
	Lepcha (Sikkim), . .	*Alim, aba.*
	Bhújáni v. Lhopa, . .	*Di té.*

N.-E. Bengal	Bodo, ...	*Imbo.*
	Dhimál, ...	*I'sho.*
	Kocch, ...	*Yahán.*
	Garo, ...	*Yaydu.*
	Káchári, ...	*Caret.*
Eastern Frontier of Bengal	Munipuri, ...	*Asída.*
	Míthán Nágá, . . .	*Caret.*
	Tablung Nágá, . .	*Caret.*
	Khári Nágá, . . .	*Nikó.*
	Angámi Nágá, . .	*Haki.*
	Námsáng Nágá, . .	*Anang.*
	Nowgong Nágá, . .	*Yóng.*
	Tengsa Nágá, . .	*Iga.*
	Abor Miri, ...	*Sho.*
	Sibságar Miri, . .	*So.*
	Deoria Chutia, . .	*Lohore.*
	Singpho, ...	*Nade.*
Arrakan & Burmah	Burman (*written*), .	*Simhá.*
	Burman (*spoken*), .	*Thimha.*
	Khyeng v. Shou, .	*Ní-ám.*
	Kámi, ...	*Illa, ya.*
	Kúmi, ...	*Hi-bang.*
	Mrú v. Toung, . .	*Caret.*
	Sák, ...	*Caret.*
Siam & Tenasserim	Talain v. Mon, . .	*Kha-na-nau.*
	Sgau-karen, . . .	*'Pali.*
	Pwo-karen, . . .	*Taung-yu.*
	Toungh-thu, . . .	*Yo.*
	Shán, ...	*Kaniht.*
	Annamitic, ...	*Dáï.*
	Siamese, ...	*Hta-ni, ni.*
	Ahom, ...	*U, tinai.*
	Khámti, ...	*Phe, thai.*
	Laos, ...	*Ni.*
Central India	Ho (Kol), ...	*Nendre.*
	Kol (Singhbhum), .	*Nethá.*
	Santáli, ...	*Nante.*
	Bhúmij, ...	*Nethai.*
	Uráon, ...	*Isan.*
	Mundala, ...	*Nithi.*
	Rájmahali, ...	*Ino.*
	Goṇḍi, ...	*Ingabará.*
	Gayeti, ...	*Caret.*
	Rutluk, ...	*Caret.*
	Naikude, ...	*Caret.*
	Kolami, ...	*Caret.*
	Mádi, ...	*Caret.*
	Mádia, ...	*Caret.*
	Kuri, ...	*Caret.*
	Keikádi, ...	*Caret.*
	Khoṇḍ, ...	*Caret.*
	Sávara, ...	*Tenne.*
	Gadaba, ...	*Tennó.*
	Yerukala, ...	*Yatukire, yinge.*
	Chentsu, ...	*I'haná, yechhiṇi.*
Southern India	Tamil, anc., . . .	*Ivan.*
	Tamil, mod., . . .	*I'ngu.*
	Malayáḷma, anc., .	*Caret.*
	Malayáḷma, mod., .	*Ivite.*
	Telugu, ...	*Ikkaḍa.*
	Karṇáṭaka, anc., .	*Caret.*
	Karṇáṭaka, mod., .	*Illi.*
	Tuḷuva, ...	*Inchi.*
	Kurgi, ...	*Illi.*
	Toḍuva, }	*Itt.*
	Toḍa, }	*It, ing.*
	Kóta, ...	*Iyóne.*
	Baḍaga, ...	*Illi.*
	Kurumba, ...	*Illi.*
	Irula, ...	*Inge.*
	Malabar, ...	*Ingá.*
	Sinhalese, ...	*Mehé.*

Group	Types.	
Inflecting.	SANSKRIT,	*Katham.*
	ARABIC,	*Keif.*
Compounding.	BASK,	*Nola, zelan.*
	FINNIC,	*Kuinka.*
	MAGYAR,	*Hogy.*
	TURKISH,	*Nasl.*
	CIRCASSIAN,	*Sidu shit.*
	GEORGIAN,	*Kith.*
	MONGOLIAN,	*Yaghon-yer.*
	MANTSHU,	*Adarame.*
	JAVANESE, Ngoko,	*Kapriye.*
	JAVANESE, Krama,	*Kadospundi.*
	MALAY,	*Bagimána.*
Isolating.	CHINESE, Nankin,	*Tsen-mo-yang.*
	CHINESE, Pekin,	*Tsen-mo-yang.*
	CHINESE, Canton,	*Tim-yeong.*
	CHINESE, Shanghai,	*Na-năng.*
	AMOY, Colloquial,	*Chiah-iuṇ.*
	JAPANESE,	*Doste, ikan.*
	Brahui,	*Kán.*
Chinese Frontier & Tibet.	Gyámi,	*Thi-má.*
	Gyárung,	*Thigúpso, this-pé.*
	Tákpa,	*Katin-gyá.*
	Mányak,	*Hanus-moh.*
	Thochú,	*Nikanjú, nikachan.*
	Sokpa,	*Caret.*
	Horpa,	*A'chibi.*
	Tibetan (*written*),	*Tsug, chitsug.*
	Tibetan (*spoken*),	*Khá-ché, khanda.*
Nepal (east to west).	Serpa,	*Kánde, kándá.*
	Súnwár,	*Dódiv.*
	Gúrung,	*Khaga liyon.*
	Múrmi,	*Khátpá.*
	Magar,	*Kúdáng-cha.*
	Tháksya,	*Khajulába.*
	Pákhya,	*Caret.*
	Newár,	*Gathé, gé.*
	Limbu,	*A'pha.*
Kiranti Group (East Nepal).	Kiránti,	*A'insúko.*
	Rodong,	*Dáskwa, dásókwa.*
	Rúngchenbung,	*Khainsaki, kháinse.*
	Chhingtángya,	*Hókhyakkha.*
	Náchhereng,	*Dákhtó.*
	Wáling,	*Hagnékagna.*
	Yákha,	*Náhók.*
	Chourásya,	*A'si chokcho.*
	Kulungya,	*U'ddim, dáim.*
	Thulungya,	*Hésaka, heka, hé.*
	Báhingya,	*Gekho, gekhom.*
	Lohorong,	*Mantok, mantok'ye.*
	Lambichhong,	*Hende-khá.*
	Báláli,	*A'pto.*
	Sáng-páng,	*Yán-tako.*
	Dúmi,	*Hemphem.*
	Kháling,	*Hemphem.*
	Dungmáli,	*Tete.*
Broken Tribes of Nepal.	Dárhi,	*Ká-sai.*
	Denwár,	*Ka-nhe.*
	Pahri,	*Gi-re.*
	Chepáng,	*Caret.*
	Bhrámu,	*Hé-tu.*
	Váyu,	*Húng-ngá.*
	Kuswar,	*Ká-sege.*
	Kusunda,	*Natuwan.*
	Tháru,	*Caret.*
	Lepcha (Sikkim),	*Salom.*
	Bhútáni v. Lhopa,	*Káte-bé.*

N.-E. Bengal.	Bodo,	*Bre.*
	Dhimál,	*He-sá, he-dong.*
	Kocch,	*Kemon.*
	Garo,	*Bigándá.*
	Káchári,	*Caret.*
Eastern Frontier of Bengal.	Munipuri,	*Kurumtouna.*
	Míthán Nágá,	*Caret.*
	Tablung Nágá,	*Caret.*
	Khári Nágá,	*Kotisau.*
	Angámi Nágá,	*Nokidihika.*
	Námsáng Nágá,	*Caret.*
	Nowgong Nágá,	*Kotau.*
	Tengsa Nágá,	*Katikiang.*
	Abor Miri,	*Káppida.*
	Sibságar Miri,	*Kapu.*
	Deoria Chutia,	*Dakang.*
	Singpho,	*Caret.*
Arrakan & Burmah.	Burman (*written*),	*Bheso.*
	Burman (*spoken*),	*Bhetho.*
	Khyeng v. Shou,	*I'ban.*
	Kámi,	*Ná-ha-bé.*
	Kúmi,	*Caret.*
	Mrú v. Toung,	*Caret.*
	Sák,	*Caret.*
Siam & Tenasserim.	Talain v. Mon,	*Tson-la.*
	Sgau-karen,	*Di-lai.*
	Pwo-karen,	*Baithele.*
	Toungh-thu,	*Leu-may.*
	Shán,	*Tso-hu.*
	Annamitic,	*Thê-nào.*
	Siamese,	*Ran-rihu, thau phra het.*
	Ahom,	*Caret.*
	Khámti,	*Caret.*
	Laos,	*Caret.*
Central India.	Ho (Kol),	*Chialeka.*
	Kol (Singhbhum),	*Chi-lika.*
	Santáli,	*Chet-leko.*
	Bhúmij,	*Chi-lika.*
	Uráon,	*Yékassi.*
	Mundala,	*Chilke.*
	Rájmahali,	*Ikna.*
	Gondi,	*Báhún.*
	Gayeti,	*Caret.*
	Rutluk,	*Caret.*
	Naikude,	*Caret.*
	Kolami,	*Caret.*
	Mádi,	*Caret.*
	Mádia,	*Caret.*
	Kuri,	*Caret.*
	Keikádi,	*Yedanu.*
	Khond,	*Caret.*
	Sávara,	*Yengá.*
	Gadaba,	*Yerándi.*
	Yerukala,	*Yate.*
	Chentsu,	*Kemune.*
Southern India.	Tamil, anc.,	*Caret.*
	Tamil, mod.,	*Eppadi, yeppadi.*
	Malayálma, anc.,	*Caret.*
	Malayálma, mod.,	*Engine.*
	Telugu,	*Etlá, yetlá.*
	Karnátaka, anc.,	*Caret.*
	Karnátaka, mod.,	*Hyánge, yentu.*
	Tuluva,	*Caret.*
	Kurgi,	*Yennane.*
	Toduva,	*Caret.*
	Toda,	*Hyage.*
	Kóta,	*Yége.*
	Badaga,	*Yitete, hyage.*
	Kurumba,	*Yetate.*
	Irula,	*Yepadi.*
	Malabar,	*Eppadi, evocthamaka.*
	Sinhalese,	*Kohomada.*

Group	Language	How much?
	Types.	
Inflecting.	SANSKRIT,	*Kiyat.*
	ARABIC,	*Kam.*
Compounding.	BASK,	*Zembat, zeimbeste.*
	FINNIC,	*Kuinka paljo.*
	MAGYAR,	*Mennyivel.*
	TURKISH,	*Kach.*
	CIRCASSIAN,	*Yet-shash.*
	GEORGIAN,	*Raoden.*
	MONGOLIAN,	*Kedür-tsineghen.*
	MANTSHU,	*Udu.*
	JAVANESE, Ngoko,	*Pira.*
	JAVANESE, Krama,	*Pinten.*
	MALAY,	*Barápa.*
Isolating.	CHINESE, Nankin,	*Yu-to-shaou.*
	CHINESE, Pekin,	*Yu-to-shaou.*
	CHINESE, Canton,	*Ki-to.*
	CHINESE, Shanghai,	*Ki-ho.*
	AMOY, Colloquial,	*Joá-choe.*
	JAPANESE,	*Dono gurai, ikura.*
	Brahuí,	*Akhadr.*
Chinese Frontier & Tibet.	Gyámi,	*Tö syó.*
	Gyárung,	*This-ti.*
	Tákpa,	*Gó.*
	Mányak,	*Trimni.*
	Thochú,	*Nikal.*
	Sokpa,	*In chhin yúbi.*
	Horpa,	*Haisyi.*
	Tibetan (*written*),	*Tsam, tsoma.*
	Tibetan (*spoken*),	*Khá chwé.*
Nepal (east to west).	Serpa,	*Kajó.*
	Súnwár,	*Gisi.*
	Gúrung,	*Ká té.*
	Múrmi,	*Gádé.*
	Magar,	*Kúdit.*
	Tháksya,	*Kang nya.*
	Pákhya,	*Kati.*
	Newár,	*Guli.*
	Limbu,	*A'khen.*
Kiranti Group (East Nepal).	Kiránti,	*Dê móyé.*
	Rodong,	*Dúm no.*
	Rúngchenbung,	*Dém ye.*
	Chhingtángya,	*A'suk.*
	Náchhereng,	*Dél.*
	Wáling,	*Tem, dem.*
	Yákha,	*Ingkhóg ha.*
	Chourásya,	*A'skwalo.*
	Kulungya,	*Déiye-Déi.*
	Thulungya,	*Hala, hayu, hamko.*
	Báhingya,	*Gisko.*
	Lohorong,	*Yeh-wa.*
	Lambichhong,	*Caret.*
	Báláli,	*Aptoklo.*
	Sáng-páng,	*Dáhile.*
	Dúmi,	*Hebe.*
	Kháling,	*Hebe.*
	Dungmáli,	*Tem.*
Broken Tribes of Nepal.	Dárhi,	*Kat-ha.*
	Denwár,	*Kat-ha.*
	Pahri,	*Gu-pi.*
	Chepáng,	*Caret.*
	Bhrámu,	*Ku-wa.*
	Váyu,	*Há-thá.*
	Kuswar,	*Katak.*
	Kusunda,	*A'sina.*
	Tháru,	*Ketaná.*
	Lepcha (Sikkim),	*Satet.*
	Bhútáni v. Lhopa,	*Kájéu.*
N.-E. Bengal.	Bodo,	*Bechi-chibáng.*
	Dhimál,	*He-jokho.*
	Kocch,	*Koto, kiti.*
	Garo,	*Bipáng.*
	Káchári,	*Caret.*
Eastern Frontier of Bengal.	Munipuri,	*Caret.*
	Mithán Nágá,	*Caret.*
	Tablung Nágá,	*Caret.*
	Khári Nágá,	*Kuia.*
	Angámi Nágá,	*Kichuru.*
	Námsáng Nágá,	*Chento.*
	Nowgong Nágá,	*Kayuka.*
	Tengsa Nágá,	*Katekat.*
	Abor Miri,	*Eritko.*
	Sibságar Miri,	*Uduko.*
	Deoria Chutia,	*Amcha.*
	Singpho,	*Gadéma.*
Arrakan & Burmah.	Burman (*written*),	*Bhelok.*
	Burman (*spoken*),	*Bhelauk.*
	Khyeng v. Shou,	*Hyau-ûm.*
	Kámi,	*Ha-yë-to.*
	Kúmi,	*Caret.*
	Mrú v. Toung,	*Caret.*
	Sák,	*Caret.*
Siam & Tenasserim.	Talain v. Mon,	*Ma-tsi.*
	Sgau-karen,	*Si-ah-lai, tse-ah.*
	Pwo-karen,	*Tsai-ah-lai.*
	Toungh-thu,	*Kháng hmay.*
	Shán,	*Hta-noung.*
	Annamitic,	*Mây.*
	Siamese,	*Htau-riht, ki lem.*
	Ahom,	*Caret.*
	Khámti,	*Caret.*
	Laos,	*Kilam.*
Central India.	Ho (Kol),	*Cheminang.*
	Kol (Singhbhum),	*Chimiáng.*
	Santáli,	*Tin, tinâh, tintiri.*
	Bhúmij,	*Chimiáng.*
	Uráon,	*Yúngpagi.*
	Mundala,	*Chimna.*
	Rájmahali,	*Ina.*
	Goṇḍi,	*Bachola, banchur.*
	Gayeti,	*Caret.*
	Rutluk,	*Caret.*
	Naikude,	*Caret.*
	Kolami,	*Caret.*
	Mádi,	*Caret.*
	Mádia,	*Caret.*
	Kuri,	*Caret.*
	Keikádi,	*Yentabaru.*
	Khoṇḍ,	*Mesóni.*
	Sávara,	*Dite.*
	Gadaba,	*Àḍḍisugó.*
	Yerukala,	*Yiṭṭana.*
	Chentsu,	*Ketta, kettagulá.*
Southern India.	Tamiḷ, anc.,	*Ettunei.*
	Tamiḷ, mod.,	*Evaḷavu, yevvaḷavu.*
	Malayáḷma, anc.,	*Caret.*
	Malayáḷma, mod.,	*Etra.*
	Telugu,	*Enta, yenta.*
	Karṇáṭaka, anc.,	*Caret.*
	Karṇáṭaka, mod.,	*Estitu.*
	Tuḷuva,	*Ett.*
	Kurgi,	*Caret.*
	Toḍuva,	*Caret.*
	Toḍa,	*Yet.*
	Kóta,	*Yëje.*
	Baḍaga,	*Yëja.*
	Kuṛumba,	*Yesaga.*
	Iruḷa,	*Yettani.*
	Malabar,	*Evvalovu.*
	Sinhalese,	*Koccharada.*

	Types.	
Inflecting.	SANSKRIT,	*-i, -os,*[1] *-su*[2] (loc.).
	ARABIC,	*Fi.*
Compounding.	BASK,	*-n, -barrenen, -gan.*
	FINNIC,	*-ssa.*
	MAGYAR,	*-ban.*
	TURKISH,	*-deh.*
	CIRCASSIAN,	*Ehkotz.*
	GEORGIAN,	*-shin.*
	MONGOLIAN,	*Tur, dur.*
	MANTSHU,	*Dolo, dorgi.*
	JAVANESE, Ngoko,	*Jero.*
	JAVANESE, Krama,	*Lebet.*
	MALAY,	*Di.*
Isolating.	CHINESE, Nankin,	*Tsái.*
	CHINESE, Pekin,	*Tsái.*
	CHINESE, Canton,	*Hai.*
	CHINESE, Shanghai,	*Leh-lah.*
	AMOY, Colloquial,	*Ti.*
	JAPANESE,	*-ni.*
	Brahuí,	*-tí.*
Chinese Frontier & Tibet.	Gyámi,	*Lá.*
	Gyárung,	*-s, pri.*
	Tákpa,	*Ná.*
	Mányak,	*Khú, choh.*
	Thochú,	*Kúkú, tik, ti.*
	Sokpa,	*Thú, tú.*
	Horpa,	*Ná, no, chá.*
	Tibetan (*written*),	*Lá, na.*
	Tibetan (*spoken*),	*Lá.*
Nepal (east to west).	Serpa,	*Lá.*
	Súnwár,	*Mi.*
	Gúrung,	*Ri.*
	Múrmi,	*Ri.*
	Magar,	*Yáng, ang.*
	Tháksya,	*Hisono.*
	Pákhya,	*Beli.*
	Newár,	*E', tè.*
	Limbu,	*Mo, khep-mo, kúthung-tho.*
Kiranti Group (East Nepal).	Kiránti,	*Dá.*
	Rodong,	*Dá.*
	Rúngchenbung,	*Dá.*
	Chhingtángya,	*Be, pe.*
	Náchhereng,	*Pi.*
	Wáling,	*Inan, da, ida.*
	Yákha,	*Be, songbe.*
	Chourásya,	*Lo.*
	Kulungya,	*Pá, pi, gopá, pitú, themtú.*
	Thulungya,	*Ná, dá, dú, duda.*
	Báhingya,	*Di, bóre, gware.*
	Lohorong,	*Be, bi.*
	Lambichhong,	*Be.*
	Báláli,	*Pi, chapittu.*
	Sáng-páng,	*Pi.*
	Dúmi,	*Yo, bi.*
	Kháling,	*Bi.*
	Dungmáli,	*Pi, yá.*
Broken Tribes of Nepal.	Dárhi,	*Yer, her.*
	Denwár,	*In.*
	Pahri,	*Gar-hi-né.*
	Chepáng,	*Háng.*
	Bhrámu,	*Thá-chi.*
	Váyu,	*Be.*
	Kuswar,	*Kana.*
	Kusunda,	*Tái.*
	Tháru,	*Bákinahi.*
	Lepcha (Sikkim),	*Ká, plóng.*
	Bhúṭáni v. Lhopa,	*Ná.*

N.-E. Bengal.	Bodo,	*-há, -ou, -chou, -nou.*
	Dhimál,	*-tá, -rhutá.*
	Kocch,	*-te* (?).
	Garo,	*Pumvai.*
	Káchári,	*Caret.*
Eastern Frontier of Bengal.	Munipuri,	*Da.*
	Míthán Nágá,	*Khá.*
	Tablung Nágá,	*Sah.*
	Khári Nágá,	*Gu.*
	Angámi Nágá,	*Kinu.*
	Námsáng Nágá,	*Hum-nyu.*
	Nowgong Nágá,	*Lóng.*
	Tengsa Nágá,	*Atap.*
	Abor Miri,	*A'rang.*
	Sibságar Miri,	*A'rálo.*
	Deoria Chutia,	*Chikimo.*
	Singpho,	*Katai.*
Arrakan & Burmah.	Burman (*written*),	*Nhaik.*
	Burman (*spoken*),	*Nhaik, a-htamha.*
	Khyeng v. Shou,	*Dúka.*
	Kámi,	*Yá.*
	Kúmi,	*Caret.*
	Mrú v. Toung,	*Caret.*
	Sák,	*Caret.*
Siam & Tenasserim.	Talain v. Mon,	*Atway.*
	Sgau-karen,	*A'pu.*
	Pwo-karen,	*Ler-pung.*
	Toungh-thu,	*Pu.*
	Shán,	*Kanoung.*
	Annamitic,	*Trong.*
	Siamese,	*Khan-ná, nai.*
	Ahom,	*Khau.*
	Khámti,	*Kanuu.*
	Laos,	*Nai.*
Central India.	Ho (Kol),	*-re.*
	Kol (Singhbhum),	*-re.*
	Santáli,	*-tálire, -re.*
	Bhúmij,	*Bhitar, re* (?).
	Uráon,	*U'lá.*
	Mundala,	*Bhitar* (within).
	Rájmahali,	*-tálare* (?).
	Goṇḍi,	*Imitté.*
	Gayeti,	*Caret.*
	Rutluk,	*Caret.*
	Naikude,	*Caret.*
	Kolami,	*Caret.*
	Mádi,	*Caret.*
	Mádia,	*Caret.*
	Kuri,	*Caret.*
	Keikádi,	*Caret.*
	Khoṇḍ,	*Caret.*
	Sávara,	*Logna.*
	Gadaba,	*Ra* (?).
	Yerukala,	*Kore, koku.*
	Chentsu,	*Gant, ta.*
Southern India.	Tamiḷ, anc.,	*-kan.*
	Tamiḷ, mod.,	*-il.*
	Malayáḷma, anc.,	*Caret.*
	Malayáḷma, mod.,	*-il.*
	Telugu,	*-lo, -andu.*
	Karṇáṭaka, anc.,	*-ol.*
	Karṇáṭaka, mod.,	*-olage, -alli.*
	Tuḷuva,	*-olai-idu.*
	Kurgi,	*-lu, -pakka.*
	Toḍuva,	*-ol.*
	Toḍa,	*-ult.*
	Kóta,	*-vollage.*
	Baḍaga,	*-vollage.*
	Kuṛumba,	*-vollage.*
	Iruḷa,	*-úlle.*
	Malabar,	*-il, ul.*
	Sinhalese,	*-atulé.*

Group	Types.	
Inflecting.	SANSKṚIT,	*Alpa.*
	ARABIC,	*Ḳalil.*
Compounding.	BASK,	*Guchi, gichi, guti.*
	FINNIC,	*Waha.*
	MAGYAR,	*Caret.*
	TURKISH,	*Az.*
	CIRCASSIAN,	*Caret.*
	GEORGIAN,	*Caret.*
	MONGOLIAN,	*Utsoghen teduï, tsüghen.*
	MANTSHU,	*Madchighe, kheni.*
	JAVANESE, Ngoko,	*Saṭiṭik.*
	JAVANESE, Krama,	*Saṭeḍik.*
	MALAY,	*Sadikit.*
Isolating.	CHINESE, Nankin,	*Shaou.*
	CHINESE, Pekin,	*Shaou.*
	CHINESE, Canton,	*Shiú.*
	CHINESE, Shanghai,	*Siaw.*
	AMOY, Colloquial,	*Soe.*
	JAPANESE,	*Skoshi, sukoshi.*
	Brahuí,	*Maih.*
Chinese Frontier & Tibet.	Gyámi,	*Syóti.*
	Gyárung,	*Kúh-ché.*
	Tákpa,	*Chúti.*
	Mányak,	*Tameh.*
	Thochú,	*Khwini.*
	Sokpa,	*Bágá.*
	Horpa,	*A'mohé.*
	Tibetan (*written*),	*Nyung.*
	Tibetan (*spoken*),	*Nigúva.*
Nepal (east to west).	Serpa,	*Chúyak chik.*
	Súnwár,	*Iská.*
	Gúrung,	*Chigi-dé.*
	Múrmi,	*Udit.*
	Magar,	*Chék-já.*
	Thaksya,	*Chipri.*
	Pákhya,	*Yokai, thokái.*
	Newár,	*Bhati.*
	Limbu,	*Mi-sa.*
Kiranti Group (East Nepal).	Kiránti,	*Chichi.*
	Rodong,	*Pichhe.*
	Rúngchenbung,	*Chi-chi.*
	Chhingtángya,	*Mih-mo.*
	Náchhereng,	*Chichha.*
	Wáling,	*A'chichi, achi.*
	Yákha,	*Misyáha.*
	Chourásya,	*Chig-nápu.*
	Kulungya,	*Chichha, gichha.*
	Thulungya,	*Kichwe.*
	Báhingya,	*Ká-chi.*
	Lohorong,	*Mig'-mo.*
	Lambichhong,	*Miyo.*
	Báláli,	*Mechhúk.*
	Sáng-páng,	*U'ttú-chhe.*
	Dúmi,	*Tibichyo.*
	Kháling,	*Tibiche.*
	Dungmáli,	*Achichi.*
Broken Tribes of Nepal.	Dárhi,	*Chút-hi.*
	Denwár,	*Chút-ek-pe.*
	Pahri,	*Bhá-chá.*
	Chepáng,	*Caret.*
	Bhrámu,	*Són-bi.*
	Váyu,	*Iti-bang.*
	Kuswar,	*Thóre.*
	Kusunda,	*Dyoro.*
	Tháru,	*Thoro.*
	Lepcha (Sikkim),	*Amán.*
	Bhúṭáni v. Lhopa,	*Nyúng-bo.*
N.-E. Bengal.	Bodo,	*Tisi, kitisi.*
	Dhimál,	*A'toisá.*
	Kocch,	*Gutik.*
	Garo,	*Kiték si.*
	Káchári,	*Caret.*
Eastern Frontier of Bengal.	Munipuri,	*Yámde.*
	Míthán Nágá,	*Ohipia.*
	Tablung Nágá,	*Echinghá.*
	Khári Nágá,	*Ichadango.*
	Angámi Nágá,	*Katuno.*
	Námsáng Nágá,	*Achá.*
	Nowgong Nágá,	*Ishika.*
	Tengsa Nágá,	*Tesu.*
	Abor Miri,	*Caret.*
	Sibságar Miri,	*Ajo-da.*
	Deoria Chutia,	*Poiani.*
	Singpho,	*Katsi.*
Arrakan & Burmah.	Burman (*written*),	*Chhitkhalé.*
	Burman (*spoken*),	*Seik-khalé.*
	Khyeng v. Shou,	*A-lák-chá-i.*
	Kámi,	*Tsei-dú-to.*
	Kúmi,	*A-htan.*
	Mrú v. Toung,	*Caret.*
	Sák,	*Caret.*
Siam & Tenasserim.	Talain v. Mon,	*Sut.*
	Sgau-karen,	*'Si-ku, tse, atjhe.*
	Pwo-karen,	*Re-pu.*
	Toungh-thu,	*Pa.*
	Shán,	*Aït.*
	Annamitic,	*It.*
	Siamese,	*Net-ta-ró, leknoi.*
	Ahom,	*Chut.*
	Khámti,	*Lek kye.*
	Laos,	*Caret.*
Central India.	Ho (Kol),	*Anga.*
	Kol (Singhbhum),	*Huḍing.*
	Santáli,	*A'dhan, charakoï-chakoïh.*
	Bhúmij,	*Huḍing.*
	Uráon,	*Sani.*
	Mundala,	*Huḍing.*
	Rájmahali,	*Jóká.*
	Goṇḍi,	*Thodko, jarásó mandar.*
	Gayeti,	*Caret.*
	Rutluk,	*Thor.*
	Naikude,	*Torra.*
	Kolami,	*Turra.*
	Mádi,	*Ichun, huduk.*
	Mádia,	*Hudu, ugunam.*
	Kuri,	*Thani.*
	Keikádi,	*Tode.*
	Khoṇḍ,	*Yike.*
	Sávara,	*Tete.*
	Gadaba,	*Khanḍiki.*
	Yerukala,	*Rútana.*
	Chentsu,	*Ráj, chone.*
Southern India.	Tamiḷ, anc.,	*Caret.*
	Tamiḷ, mod.,	*Siṛiya, chinna.*
	Malayāḷma, anc.,	*Caret.*
	Malayāḷma, mod.,	*Kora, kuṛe.*
	Telugu,	*Kásta, konchemu.*
	Karṇáṭaka, anc.,	*Caret.*
	Karṇáṭaka, mod.,	*Tus-a, tho-ḍe.*
	Tuḷuva,	*Onda.*
	Kurgi,	*Chennang.*
	Toḍuva,	*Caret.*
	Toḍa,	*Yeddi, kinud.*
	Kóta,	*Kunade.*
	Baḍaga,	*Kuna, konji.*
	Kuṛumba,	*Vósi.*
	Iruḷa,	*Konja.*
	Malabar,	*Siru, konjam.*
	Sinhalese,	*Tika.*

	Types.	
Inflecting.	SANSKRIT,	*Bahu.*
	ARABIC,	*Kathir.*
Compounding.	BASK,	*Asko, aski, lar, gei, geyegi.*
	FINNIC,	*Paljo.*
	MAGYAR,	*Sok.*
	TURKISH,	*Chok.*
	CIRCASSIAN,	*Bedded.*
	GEORGIAN,	*Bekri.*
	MONGOLIAN,	*Olan, teduïghen.*
	MANTSHU,	*Labdu.*
	JAVANESE, Ngoko,	*Akeh.*
	JAVANESE, Krama,	*Katah.*
	MALAY,	*Bañak.*
Isolating.	CHINESE, Nankin,	*To.*
	CHINESE, Pekin,	*To.*
	CHINESE, Canton,	*To.*
	CHINESE, Shanghai,	*Tu.*
	AMOY, Colloquial,	*Choe.*
	JAPANESE,	*Takusan, tanto.*
	Brahuí,	*Báz.*
Chinese Frontier & Tibet.	Gyámi,	*Tá-ti.*
	Gyárung,	*Kak-ti.*
	Tákpa,	*Shibo.*
	Mányak,	*Tabrá.*
	Thochú,	*Brobo.*
	Sokpa,	*Ehvik.*
	Horpa,	*Kagaré.*
	Tibetan (*written*),	*Máng, tumo.*
	Tibetan (*spoken*),	*Má-gúá (mángná ?).*
Nepal (east to west).	Serpa,	*A'lá.*
	Súnwár,	*Itch-ká.*
	Gúrung,	*Lhéyó.*
	Múrmi,	*Lhánú.*
	Magar,	*Dhér.*
	Tháksya,	*Dhau-há.*
	Pákhya,	*Mauti.*
	Newár,	*Apá.*
	Limbu,	*Yorik.*
Kiranti Group (East Nepal).	Kiránti,	*Badho.*
	Rodong,	*Kébha.*
	Rúngchenbung,	*Bad-dho.*
	Chhingtángya,	*Dhéra, bádhe.*
	Náchhereng,	*Antkhópa.*
	Wáling,	*Dhéráng, badhe.*
	Yákha,	*Pyág-ha.*
	Chourásya,	*Yétikhótse.*
	Kulungya,	*Waddétwa, wadetto.*
	Thulungya,	*Dhékóng.*
	Báhingya,	*Yáko.*
	Lohorong,	*Dhe-rok, dilik, khwa, chopmo.*
	Lambichhong,	*Badhebák.*
	Báláli,	*Dúklo.*
	Sáng-páng,	*Otto, wotto.*
	Dúmi,	*Thobe.*
	Kháling,	*Thebe, gole.*
	Dungmáli,	*Nirdám-má.*
Broken Tribes of Nepal.	Dárhi,	*Dhérai.*
	Denwár,	*Dhéré.*
	Pahri,	*Chó-hong.*
	Chepáng,	*Jhó.*
	Bhrámu,	*Búd-he.*
	Váyu,	*Ching-ngak, sing-ye.*
	Kuswar,	*Dhére.*
	Kusunda,	*Mang-gni.*
	Tháru,	*Bahut.*
	Lepcha (Sikkim),	*Ag-yáp.*
	Bhútáni v. Lhopa,	*Máng-bo.*

N.-E. Bengal.	Bodo,	*Gab-áng, gobáng.*
	Dhimál,	*Eshúto.*
	Kocch,	*Bhelela.*
	Garo,	*Takkri.*
	Káchári,	*Caret.*
Eastern Frontier of Bengal.	Munipuri,	*Yame.*
	Míthán Nágá,	*Taihu.*
	Tablung Nágá,	*Eselai.*
	Khári Nágá,	*Kwalangau.*
	Angámi Nágá,	*Hyapur.*
	Námsáng Nágá,	*A'já.*
	Nowgong Nágá,	*Ayuka.*
	Tengsa Nágá,	*Tebe.*
	Abor Miri,	*Caret.*
	Sibságar Miri,	*A'b-ako.*
	Deoria Chutia,	*Poini.*
	Singpho,	*Lo.*
Arrakan & Burmah.	Burman (*written*),	*Myá.*
	Burman (*spoken*),	*Myá, apon.*
	Khyeng v. Shou,	*A-pá-lúk.*
	Kámi,	*Pa, ong-je.*
	Kúmi,	*No-i.*
	Mrú v. Toung,	*Caret.*
	Sák,	*Caret.*
Siam & Tenasserim.	Talain v. Mon,	*Hbau.*
	Sgau-karen,	*Ah, ahmah.*
	Pwo-karen,	*Ahmah.*
	Toungh-thu,	*A.*
	Shán,	*Taima.*
	Annamitic,	*Nhieu.*
	Siamese,	*Hton, lai, bundá.*
	Ahom,	*Rá.*
	Khámti,	*Nam.*
	Laos,	*Nak, lái.*
Central India.	Ho (Kol),	*Pura, essu.*
	Kol (Singhbhum),	*E'sú.*
	Santáli,	*Udi, udi-utár, ater, atua,*
	Bhúmij,	*Bara (udi ?). [ákutá, ámdá.*
	Uráon,	*Udi, dhér.*
	Mundala,	*Dhér (ámdá ?).*
	Rájmahali,	*Gáuri.*
	Gondi,	*Wale, pharol, balè mandar.*
	Gayeti,	*Wale.*
	Rutluk,	*Walle.*
	Naikude,	*Dagár.*
	Kolami,	*Kub.*
	Mádi,	*Velle.*
	Mádia,	*Bel.*
	Kuri,	*Galetakig.*
	Keikádi,	*Wanrási.*
	Khond,	*Púrá-áte.*
	Sávara,	*Bari.*
	Gadaba,	*Burre.*
	Yerukala,	*Mettá.*
	Chentsu,	*Bhóri.*
Southern India.	Tamil, anc.,	*Mikka.*
	Tamil, mod.,	*Mikunda, michamana.*
	Malayálma, anc.,	*Caret.*
	Malayálma, mod.,	*Valara.*
	Telugu,	*Nindá, mikkili.*
	Karnátaka, anc.,	*Caret.*
	Karnátaka, mod.,	*Bahala.*
	Tuluva,	*Dinja.*
	Kurgi,	*Perta.*
	Toduva, }	*Uppom.*
	Toda, }	*Upam.*
	Kóta,	*Yeddame.*
	Badaga,	*Thumba, appara.*
	Kurumba,	*Appara.*
	Irula,	*Thumba.*
	Malabar,	*Met-tha.*
	Sinhalese,	*Bohoma.*

Group	Language	Near
	Types.	
Inflecting.	SANSKRIT,	*Antikam.*
	ARABIC,	*Karib.*
Compounding.	BASK,	*Aldean, alboan, urbill, arras.*
	FINNIC,	*Lahi, -lasna.*
	MAGYAR,	*Közel.*
	TURKISH,	*Yakin.*
	CIRCASSIAN,	*Tlagha.*
	GEORGIAN,	*Akhlo.*
	MONGOLIAN,	*Oira.*
	MANTSHU,	*Khantchi.*
	JAVANESE, Ngoko,	*Cherak.*
	JAVANESE, Krama,	*Chelak.*
	MALAY,	*Jáuh.*
Isolating.	CHINESE, Nankin,	*Kin.*
	CHINESE, Pekin,	*Chin.*
	CHINESE, Canton,	*Kan.*
	CHINESE, Shanghai,	*Kiäng.*
	AMOY, Colloquial,	*Kún.*
	JAPANESE,	*Chikaku.*
	Brahuí,	*Musti.*
Chinese Frontier & Tibet.	Gyámi,	*Jhin.*
	Gyárung,	*Kaching.*
	Tákpa,	*Thúngbú.*
	Mányak,	*Rini.*
	Thochú,	*Grin, grinista.*
	Sokpa,	*Nangui.*
	Horpa,	*Tháne.*
	Tibetan (*written*),	*Ring.*
	Tibetan (*spoken*),	*Tháni.*
Nepal (east to west).	Serpa,	*Thak-nimbo.*
	Súnwár,	*Nétthá.*
	Gúrung,	*Kéndo.*
	Múrmi,	*Jyat-na.*
	Magar,	*Khwep.*
	Tháksya,	*Nyese.*
	Pákhya,	*Nesai.*
	Newár,	*Satti.*
	Limbu,	*Neng dáng.*
Kiranti Group (East Nepal).	Kiránti,	*Nektá.*
	Rodong,	*Gnan', gnan'ge, nenge.*
	Rúngchenbung,	*Nek-ta, nekkhida, neck.*
	Chhingtángya,	*Tanghe, tangne.*
	Náchhereng,	*Caret.*
	Wáling,	*Mumikgná, nek-yang.*
	Yákha,	*Ningdáng.*
	Chourásya,	*A'mna.*
	Kulungya,	*Nén-kha.*
	Thulungya,	*Gnépa.*
	Báhingya,	*Neng-tha, pumbi.*
	Lohorong,	*Nen, ning-láng.*
	Lambichhong,	*Tang-neklok.*
	Báláli,	*Netá.*
	Sáng-páng,	*Neti, yúbhi.*
	Dúmi,	*Mebigná.*
	Kháling,	*Néphám.*
	Dungmáli,	*Nek, nektáng.*
Broken Tribes of Nepal.	Dárhi,	*Ná-gák.*
	Denwár,	*Yén-chi.*
	Pahri,	*Nhyár-ke.*
	Chepáng,	*Lok-to.*
	Bhrámu,	*Ka-nyák.*
	Váyu,	*Khé-wa.*
	Kuswar,	*Pas-yong.*
	Kusunda,	*Ista.*
	Tháru,	*Ihyá.*
	Lepcha (Sikkim),	*Athol.*
	Bhútáni v. Lhopa,	*Thá-ni.*
N.-E. Bengal.	Bodo,	*Khátai.*
	Dhimál,	*Cheng-so.*
	Kocch,	*Nag-ich.*
	Garo,	*Katai.*
	Káchári,	*Caret.*
Eastern Frontier of Bengal.	Munipuri,	*Nugle.*
	Míthán Nágá,	*Hole.*
	Tablung Nágá,	*Otike.*
	Khári Nágá,	*Anhagu.*
	Angámi Nágá,	*Chaguno.*
	Námsáng Nágá,	*Therkó.*
	Nowgong Nágá,	*Tats-aka.*
	Tengsa Nágá,	*Annanghi.*
	Abor Miri,	*Aninda.*
	Sibságar Miri,	*Anünse.*
	Deoria Chutia,	*Buttigaiṇ.*
	Singpho,	*Ni.*
Arrakan & Burmah.	Burman (*written*),	*Ní.*
	Burman (*spoken*),	*Ni, a-ni-mha.*
	Khyeng v. Shou,	*A-shyo-zo-yan.*
	Kámi,	*Nei.*
	Kúmi,	*Ki-sá.*
	Mrú v. Toung,	*Caret.*
	Sák,	*Caret.*
Siam & Tenasserim.	Talain v. Mon,	*Tsouk.*
	Sgau-karen,	*Bu.*
	Pwo-karen,	*Boh.*
	Toungh-thu,	*Lau.*
	Shán,	*An-san.*
	Annamitic,	*Gán.*
	Siamese,	*Kará, klai.*
	Ahom,	*Klai.*
	Khámti,	*Kan.*
	Laos,	*Kai.*
Central India.	Ho (Kol),	*Nálte.*
	Kol (Singhbhum),	*Nia.*
	Santáli,	*Phed, ṭháh, ṭhen, ṭhenare.*
	Bhúmij,	*Járéyá.*
	Uráon,	*Hédi.*
	Mundala,	*Najik, nagich.*
	Rájmahali,	*Atgi.*
	Goṇḍi,	*Karum, múntosa mandar.*
	Gayeti,	*Karum.*
	Rutluk,	*Karúm.*
	Naikude,	*Daia.*
	Kolami,	*Madawattan.*
	Mádi,	*Vere, here.*
	Mádia,	*Hor.*
	Kuri,	*Merá.*
	Keikádi,	*Kitte.*
	Khoṇḍ,	*Caret.*
	Sávara,	*Tuya.*
	Gadaba,	*Tantel.*
	Yerukala,	*Kíṭṭa, kiṭṭáyi.*
	Chentsu,	*Lág.*
Southern India.	Tamiḷ, anc.,	*Aṇmei.*
	Tamiḷ, mod.,	*Kitta.*
	Malayáḷma, anc.,	*Caret.*
	Malayáḷma, mod.,	*Aṭukke.*
	Telugu,	*Dápu, daggera.*
	Karṇáṭaka, anc.,	*Caret.*
	Karṇáṭaka, mod.,	*Hattara, sáre.*
	Tuḷuva,	*Khayi, tob.*
	Kurgi,	*Pakka.*
	Toḍuva, }	*Keguri.*
	Toḍa, }	*Kéhuri.*
	Kóta,	*Vottle.*
	Badaga,	*Vottura, sári.*
	Kurumba,	*Pakkaru.*
	Iruḷa,	*Kitta.*
	Malabar,	*Kiṭṭa.*
	Sinhalese,	*Langa.*

	Types.	
Inflecting.	SANSKRIT,	*Na* (*má* = not).
	ARABIC,	*La, lam, leis.*
Compounding.	BASK,	*Ez.*
	FINNIC,	*En, et, ei,* etc. (neg. particle [= *e*).
	MAGYAR,	*Sem.*
	TURKISH,	*Yok.*
	CIRCASSIAN,	*Shgeb.*
	GEORGIAN,	*Nu.*
	MONGOLIAN,	*Ugei.*
	MANTSHU,	*Ako.*
	JAVANESE, Ngoko,	*Ora.*
	JAVANESE, Krama,	*Boten.*
	MALAY,	*Búkan.*
Isolating.	CHINESE, Nankin,	*Puh-shi.*
	CHINESE, Pekin,	*Pu-shih.*
	CHINESE, Canton,	*'M-hai.*
	CHINESE, Shanghai,	*Veh.*
	AMOY, Colloquial,	*Bô, -'m-si.*
	JAPANESE,	*Nai, iya, iye.*
	Brahuí,	*Ahá.*
Chinese Frontier & Tibet.	Gyámi,	*Púsitiéyó.*
	Gyárung,	*Dimek.*
	Tákpa,	*Men.*
	Mányak,	*Má-zyi.*
	Thochú,	*Mángwá, mang.*
	Sokpa,	*Bi-si.*
	Horpa,	*Nyẽr.*
	Tibetan (*written*),	*Má, mi.*
	Tibetan (*spoken*),	*Men.*
Nepal (east to west).	Serpa,	*Men.*
	Súnwár,	*Ma-mai.*
	Gúrung,	*A'ni.*
	Múrmi,	*A'nin.*
	Magar,	*Málé.*
	Tháksya,	*Ai.*
	Pákhya,	*A'sin.*
	Newár,	*Makhú, mai, ahang.*
	Limbu,	*Men, ná.*
Kiranti Group (East Nepal).	Kiránti,	*Máng.*
	Rodong,	*Ai-na.*
	Rúngchenbung,	*Má-áng.*
	Chhingtángya,	*Máhá.*
	Náchhereng,	*Má, má-á.*
	Wáling,	*Máin, máang.*
	Yákha,	*Múnna, imúnna.*
	Chourásya,	*A'tti.*
	Kulungya,	*Má.*
	Thulungya,	*Mẽẽ.*
	Báhingya,	*Máh'-á.*
	Lohorong,	*Caret.*
	Lambichhong,	*Máhá, mále.*
	Báláli,	*Hé-gnane.*
	Sáng-páng,	*Máná.*
	Dúmi,	*Mo-ó.*
	Kháling,	*Ma-aṇ.*
	Dungmáli,	*Mán, jé, soh'.*
Broken Tribes of Nepal.	Dárhi,	*Hói-né.*
	Denwár,	*Boy-in.*
	Pahri,	*Makhi.*
	Chepáng,	*Caret.*
	Bhrámu,	*Mami, alik.*
	Váyu,	*Má, ma-nom.*
	Kuswar,	*Ná.*
	Kusunda,	*A'yewá.*
	Tháru,	*Náhi.*
	Lepcha (Sikkim),	*Má né.*
	Bhúṭáni v. Lhopa,	*Mé-túp, men.*

N.-E. Bengal.	Bodo,	*Ongá, geyá.*
	Dhimál,	*Má, mánthú.*
	Kocch,	*Nah, nahin.*
	Garo,	*Ahá.*
	Káchári,	*Caret.*
Eastern Frontier of Bengal.	Munipuri,	*Nate.*
	Mithán Nágá,	*Mantai.*
	Tablung Nágá,	*Mang-cha.*
	Khári Nágá,	*Nongó.*
	Angámi Nágá,	*Mowe.*
	Námsáng Nágá,	*Má.*
	Nowgong Nágá,	*Mau, nonga.*
	Tengsa Nágá,	*Nongo.*
	Abor Miri,	*Mámá.*
	Sibságar Miri,	*Má.*
	Deoria Chutia,	*Hóya.*
	Singpho,	*Galai.*
Arrakan & Burmah.	Burman (*written*),	*Mahut.*
	Burman (*spoken*),	*Mahok, mahot-bú.*
	Khyeng v. Shou,	*Hi-a.*
	Kámi,	*Na-u-ká.*
	Kúmi,	*Na-o.*
	Mrú v. Toung,	*Caret.*
	Sák,	*Caret.*
Siam & Tenasserim.	Talain v. Mon,	*Ha-tsen.*
	Sgau-karen,	*T'mabah, tho-mi-bah.*
	Pwo-karen,	*Mwai-al.*
	Toungh-thu,	*Ta-mwá-tu.*
	Shán,	*Ma-tsouk.*
	Annamitic,	*Không.*
	Siamese,	*Mai-htsa, michi.*
	Ahom,	*Bukhewo.*
	Khámti,	*Ma-tsau.*
	Laos,	*Bo-tsai.*
Central India.	Ho (Kol),	*Banno.*
	Kol (Singhbhum),	*Báno.*
	Santáli,	*Ah, báng, bái, bánu,* = is not.
	Bhúmij,	*Báno.*
	Uráon,	*Málá.*
	Mundala,	*Báno.*
	Rájmahali,	*Mallá.*
	Goṇḍi,	*Halli, hillé.*
	Gayeti,	*Caret.*
	Rutluk,	*Caret.*
	Naikude,	*Caret.*
	Kolami,	*Caret.*
	Mádi,	*Caret.*
	Mádia,	*Caret.*
	Kuri,	*Caret.*
	Keikádi,	*Illa.*
	Khoṇḍ,	*Caret.*
	Sávara,	*Yajja.*
	Gadaba,	*Vure.*
	Yerukala,	*Yillá.*
	Chentsu,	*Nahi.*
Southern India.	Tamiḷ, anc.,	*Caret.*
	Tamiḷ, mod.,	*Illei, alla.*
	Malayáḷma, anc.,	*Caret.*
	Malayáḷma, mod.,	*Illa, alla.*
	Telugu,	*Lédu.*
	Karṇáṭaka, anc.,	*Caret.*
	Karṇáṭaka, mod.,	*Illa, alla.*
	Tuḷuva,	*Iddi.*
	Kurgi,	*Alla.*
	Toḍuva, }	*Caret.*
	Toḍa, }	*A'.*
	Kóta,	*Illa.*
	Baḍaga,	*Illei.*
	Kuṛumba,	*Illa.*
	Iruḷa,	*Ille.*
	Malabar,	*Alla, illei.*
	Sinhalese,	*Næ.*

Group	Types.	
Inflecting.	SANSKRIT,	*Má.*
	ARABIC,	*Lá.*
Compounding.	BASK,	*Ez.*
	FINNIC,	*E-* (insep. particle as in *en*, [*ei*, *epa*, etc.).
	MAGYAR,	*Sem.*
	TURKISH,	*Yok.*
	CIRCASSIAN,	*Shgeb.*
	GEORGIAN,	*Ara.*
	MONGOLIAN,	*Ugei.*
	MANTSHU,	*Ako.*
	JAVANESE, Ngoko,	*Aja.*
	JAVANESE, Krama,	*Sampun.*
	MALAY,	*Jángan.*
Isolating.	CHINESE, Nankin,	*Puh-yaou.*
	CHINESE, Pekin,	*Pu-yaou.*
	CHINESE, Canton,	*'M-ho.*
	CHINESE, Shanghai,	*Veh-yau-tsu.*
	AMOY, Colloquial,	*'M-t'ang.*
	JAPANESE,	*Suruna, na.*
	Brahuí,	*Mat* (*-fa*, *-pa*, infixed).
Chinese Frontier & Tibet.	Gyámi,	*Púsyo.*
	Gyárung,	*Met.*
	Tákpa,	*Ma, magyá.*
	Mányak,	*Thá.*
	Thochú,	*Chi.*
	Sokpa,	*Puthi-ké.*
	Horpa,	*Má, di.*
	Tibetan (*written*),	*Caret.*
	Tibetan (*spoken*),	*Má.*
Nepal (east to west).	Serpa,	*Má.*
	Súnwár,	*Mo.*
	Gúrung,	*A', waché.*
	Múrmi,	*Thá.*
	Magar,	*Má.*
	Tháksya,	*Kino.*
	Pákhya,	*Na.*
	Newár,	*Ma-te.*
	Limbu,	*Ma-ne.*
Kiranti Group (East Nepal).	Kiránti,	*Man.*
	Rodong,	*Mi, mai, dá.*
	Rúngchenbung,	*Man.*
	Chhingtángya,	*Má, thá.*
	Náchhereng,	*Nó.*
	Wáling,	*Má-yé, mái.*
	Yákha,	*An.*
	Chourásya,	*A', nó.*
	Kulungya,	*Na.*
	Thulungya,	*Mé.*
	Báhingya,	*Ma.*
	Lohorong,	*E'.*
	Lambichhong,	*Ang-, -n* (*ang* before, *n* after [the word).
	Báláli,	*Ná.*
	Sáng-páng,	*Na.*
	Dúmi,	*Mú.*
	Kháling,	*Mó.*
	Dungmáli,	*Man'-to.*
Broken Tribes of Nepal.	Dárhi,	*Jún.*
	Denwár,	*Jú-nú.*
	Pahri,	*Mi-re.*
	Chepáng,	*Caret.*
	Bhrámu,	*Man.*
	Váyu,	*Thá.*
	Kuswar,	*Má-má.*
	Kusunda,	*Hyá.*
	Tháru,	*Rahare.*
	Lepcha (Sikkim),	*Má-nan.*
	Bhúṭáni v. Lhopa,	*Má.*

N.-E. Bengal.	Bodo,	*Dá.*
	Dhimál,	*Má.*
	Kocch,	*Mat.*
	Garo,	*Tá.*
	Káchári,	*Caret.*
Eastern Frontier of Bengal.	Munipuri,	*Nate.*
	Míthán Nágá,	*Caret.*
	Tablung Nágá,	*Caret.*
	Khári Nágá,	*Tá.*
	Angámi Nágá,	*Caret.*
	Námsáng Nágá,	*Nak.*
	Nowgong Nágá,	(*Tok*) *u'* (*shi*).
	Tengsa Nágá,	(*Tha*) *m'* (*thi*).
	Abor Miri,	*Ioka.*
	Sibságar Miri,	*Yoka.*
	Deoria Chutia,	*Dá.*
	Singpho,	*Ng, phung.*
Arrakan & Burmah.	Burman (*written*),	*Ma* (*pru*) *nhang.*
	Burman (*spoken*),	*Ma* (*pya*) *nhen, ma-lot- ú.*
	Khyeng v. Shou,	*Né-é.*
	Kámi,	*Na, nan.*
	Kúmi,	*Caret.*
	Mrú v. Toung,	*Caret.*
	Sák,	*Caret.*
Siam & Tenasserim.	Talain v. Mon,	*Hó-ka-lon.*
	Sgau-karen,	*T'mabah, tho-mi-bah.*
	Pwo-karen,	*Mwai-ai.*
	Toungh-thu,	*Caret.*
	Shán,	*Ma-het-a.*
	Annamitic,	*Dú'ng*
	Siamese,	*Mai-htan, mi, yá.*
	Ahom,	*Bu, ma.*
	Khámti,	*Le, tak.*
	Laos,	*Bo, mai, yá.*
Central India.	Ho (Kol),	*Ká.*
	Kol (Singhbhum),	*Aha* (*alam ?*).
	Santáli,	*Ah, álo-, eto-, bánu-.*
	Bhúmij,	*Aham, alape.*
	Uráon,	*Ampá.*
	Mundala,	*Alú, aha.*
	Rájmahali,	*Aha.*
	Goṇḍi,	*Hillé bará.*
	Gayeti,	*Caret.*
	Rutluk,	*Caret.*
	Naikude,	*Caret.*
	Kolami,	*Caret.*
	Mádi,	*Caret.*
	Mádia,	*Caret.*
	Kuri,	*Caret.*
	Keikádi,	*Caret.*
	Khoṇḍ,	*Kunámá.*
	Sávara,	*Tiggo.*
	Gadaba,	*Ayide.*
	Yerukala,	*Mánu, Yikkara.*
	Chentsu,	*Kámnai, kámnahi.*
Southern India.	Tamiḷ, anc.,	*Caret.*
	Tamiḷ, mod.,	*Venḍá.*
	Malayáḷma, anc.,	*Caret.*
	Malayáḷma, mod.,	*Venḍá.*
	Telugu,	*Vaddu.*
	Karṇáṭaka, anc.,	*Caret.*
	Karṇáṭaka, mod.,	*Béḍa.*
	Tuḷuva,	*Botri.*
	Kurgi,	*Caret.*
	Toḍuva, }	*Caret.*
	Toḍa, }	*Achadi.*
	Kóta,	*Véḍa.*
	Baḍaga,	*Béḍa.*
	Kuṛumba,	*Boḍa.*
	Iruḷa,	*Vánḍa.*
	Malabar,	*Seyathéi.*
	Sinhalese,	*Apá.*

Group	Language	Now
	Types.	
Inflecting.	Sanskṛit	*Idá, idánîm, etarhi.*
	Arabic	*Elán.*
Compounding.	Bask	*Oran, orain.*
	Finnic	*Nyt.*
	Magyar	*Most.*
	Turkish	*Shimdi.*
	Circassian	*Heg-gi.*
	Georgian	*Akhla, ats.*
	Mongolian	*Eduke.*
	Mantshu	*Te.*
	Javanese, Ngoko	*Sahiki.*
	Javanese, Krama	*Sapunnika.*
	Malay	*Sakárang.*
Isolating.	Chinese, Nankin	*Che-shi.*
	Chinese, Pekin	*Che-shi.*
	Chinese, Canton	*Ni-shi.*
	Chinese, Shanghai	*Yen-ze.*
	Amoy, Colloquial	*Chit-sí.*
	Japanese	*Ima.*
	Brahuí	*Dásá.*
Chinese Frontier & Tibet.	Gyámi	*Chhá-yé.*
	Gyárung	*Púz-dúi.*
	Tákpa	*Dá.*
	Mányak	*Milé.*
	Thochú	*Patino.*
	Sokpa	*Otó, nótó.*
	Horpa	*Habdeu.*
	Tibetan (*written*)	*Déngtsé, da, deng.*
	Tibetan (*spoken*)	*Thándá.*
Nepal (east to west).	Serpa	*Tángdá.*
	Súnwár	*I'chi.*
	Gúrung	*Tasso.*
	Múrmi	*Dande.*
	Magar	*Chamlán.*
	Tháksya	*Ghyángchye.*
	Pákhya	*Yeso.*
	Newár	*A'.*
	Limbu	*Alo.*
Kiranti Group (East Nepal).	Kiránti	*Handé.*
	Rodong	*Wôs-ara, wospa.*
	Rúngchenbung	*Hangde, hande.*
	Chhingtángya	*Bágári.*
	Náchhereng	*Ha.*
	Wáling	*Is-ghâring.*
	Yákha	*Akku.*
	Chourásya	*Bokkémse, bokemmo.*
	Kulungya	*Wadolo, wolló.*
	Thulungya	*Athá.*
	Báhingya	*Ye-khona.*
	Lohorong	*Hog'nok, honok.*
	Lambichhong	*Hálik.*
	Bálálí	*Hogno.*
	Sáng-páng	*Otolo, wotolo.*
	Dúmi	*Tholo.*
	Kháling	*A'nagná.*
	Dungmáli	*Ighári.*
Broken Tribes of Nepal.	Dárhi	*Yéhe.*
	Denwár	*Akhan.*
	Pahri	*Alaga.*
	Chepáng	*Caret.*
	Bhrámu	*Tha-chi.*
	Váyu	*U'm-be.*
	Kuswar	*Já-khen.*
	Kusunda	*Ipwaji.*
	Tháru	*Amai, abhai.*
	Lepcha (Sikkim)	*Along.*
	Bhúṭáni v. Lhopa	*Dháto.*
N.-E. Bengal.	Bodo	*Dánó.*
	Dhimál	*E'lang.*
	Kocch	*Abhi* (?).
	Garo	*Tayan.*
	Káchári	*Caret.*
Eastern Frontier of Bengal.	Munipuri	*Huchik.*
	Míthán Nágá	*Atha.*
	Tablung Nágá	*Chάha.*
	Khári Nágá	*Hiku.*
	Angámi Nágá	*Akihawe.*
	Námsáng Nágá	*Dokko.*
	Nowgong Nágá	*Tang.*
	Tengsa Nágá	*Thong.*
	Abor Miri	*Supáb.*
	Sibságar Miri	*Su.*
	Deoria Chutia	*Derereni.*
	Singpho	*Yá.*
Arrakan & Burmah.	Burman (*written*)	*Yakhu.*
	Burman (*spoken*)	*Yakhu.*
	Khyeng v. Shou	*Tú-a.*
	Kámi	*Avá-i.*
	Kúmi	*Wá-i-mé.*
	Mrú v. Toung	*Caret.*
	Sák	*Caret.*
Siam & Tenasserim.	Talain v. Mon	*La-mod.*
	Sgau-karen	*Kalkinal, kaikane.*
	Pwo-karen	*Rongniang-yu.*
	Toungh-thu	*Ngá-khayen.*
	Shán	*Mayóknihn.*
	Annamitic	*Nay.*
	Siamese	*Pá-tu-ni, reu, than-chai.*
	Ahom	*Tinai.*
	Khámti	*Tsang, ngai.*
	Laos	*Leng.*
Central India.	Ho (Kol)	*Ná.*
	Kol (Singhbhum)	*Na.*
	Santáli	*Nit, nito, nita-bade, nitoh-do,* [*nit-ge.*
	Bhúmij	*Nit* (?).
	Uráon	*U'kú.*
	Mundala	*Náhá.*
	Rájmahali	*Aneké.*
	Gonḍi	*Inga.*
	Gayeti	*Caret.*
	Rutluk	*Caret.*
	Naikude	*Caret.*
	Kolami	*Caret.*
	Mádi	*Caret.*
	Mádia	*Caret.*
	Kuri	*Caret.*
	Keikádi	*Ipo.*
	Khonḍ	*Iddáli.*
	Sávara	*Nami.*
	Gadaba	*A'.*
	Yerukala	*Yeppudu.*
	Chentsu	*Yekhán, yechiṇi.*
Southern India.	Tamiḷ, anc.	*Ippozhudu.*
	Tamiḷ, mod.	*Ippodu, ippo.*
	Malayáḷma, anc.	*Caret.*
	Malayáḷma, mod.	*Ippoḷ.*
	Telugu	*Ippuḍu.*
	Karṇáṭaka, anc.	*Caret.*
	Karṇáṭaka, mod.	*I'ga.*
	Tuḷuva	*Itteu.*
	Kurgi	*Ikkale.*
	Toḍuva	*Itwan.*
	Toḍa	*Eni.*
	Kóta	*Innale.*
	Baḍaga	*Iga.*
	Kuṛumba	*Igale.*
	Iruḷa	*I'pá.*
	Malabar	*Ippothu.*
	Sinhalese	*Dán.*

Types.

Inflecting.	SANSKRIT,	*-as, -os,*[1] *-ám*[2] (gen. case).
Inflecting.	ARABIC,	*-i.*
Compounding.	BASK,	*-en, -n.*
Compounding.	FINNIC,	*-n.*
Compounding.	MAGYAR,	*-a.*
Compounding.	TURKISH,	*-in, -un.*
Compounding.	CIRCASSIAN,	*Caret.*
Compounding.	GEORGIAN,	*-is, -isa, -as, -asi.*
Compounding.	MONGOLIAN,	*-i.*
Compounding.	MANTSHU,	*-i, -ni.*
Compounding.	JAVANESE, Ngoko,	*Caret.*
Compounding.	JAVANESE, Krama,	*Caret.*
Compounding.	MALAY,	*Caret.*
Isolating.	CHINESE, Nankin,	*Tih.*
Isolating.	CHINESE, Pekin,	*Ti.*
Isolating.	CHINESE, Canton,	*Ke.*
Isolating.	CHINESE, Shanghai,	*Koh.*
Isolating.	AMOY, Colloquial,	*E.*
Isolating.	JAPANESE,	*-no.*
	Brahuí,	*-ná, -tá.*
Chinese Frontier & Tibet.	Gyámi,	*Ti.*
Chinese Frontier & Tibet.	Gyárung,	*Caret. Um* (?).
Chinese Frontier & Tibet.	Tákpa,	*Kú.*
Chinese Frontier & Tibet.	Mányak,	*I'.*
Chinese Frontier & Tibet.	Thochú,	*K.*
Chinese Frontier & Tibet.	Sokpa,	*Na, né.*
Chinese Frontier & Tibet.	Horpa,	*I. Dang* (?).
Chinese Frontier & Tibet.	Tibetan (*written*),	*Kyi, gi, hi, yi.*
Chinese Frontier & Tibet.	Tibetan (*spoken*),	*Gi.*
Népal (east to west).	Serpa,	*Ti.*
Népal (east to west).	Súnwár,	*Kwé, kyé.*
Népal (east to west).	Gúrung,	*Yé, lá, bó.*
Népal (east to west).	Múrmi,	*Lá.*
Népal (east to west).	Magar,	*Yó, wó.*
Népal (east to west).	Tháksya,	*Cháye.*
Népal (east to west).	Pákhya,	*Ko.*
Népal (east to west).	Newár,	*Yá.*
Népal (east to west).	Limbu,	*Le, in.*
Kiránti Group (East Népal).	Kiránti,	*Wó.*
Kiránti Group (East Népal).	Rodong,	*Mi, mo.*
Kiránti Group (East Népal).	Rúngchenbung,	*Caret.*
Kiránti Group (East Népal).	Chhingtángya,	*O.*
Kiránti Group (East Népal).	Náchhereng,	*Mi.*
Kiránti Group (East Népal).	Wáling,	*O.*
Kiránti Group (East Népal).	Yákha,	*I, ga.*
Kiránti Group (East Népal).	Chourásya,	*Lema.*
Kiránti Group (East Népal).	Kulungya,	*Mi.*
Kiránti Group (East Népal).	Thulungya,	*Kam.*
Kiránti Group (East Népal).	Báhingya,	*Ké, kem, dim.*
Kiránti Group (East Népal).	Lohorong,	*Mi.*
Kiránti Group (East Népal).	Lambichhong,	*I, khá, im, gná, ka.*
Kiránti Group (East Népal).	Báláli,	*'M, mi (-m ?).*
Kiránti Group (East Népal).	Sáng-páng,	*Mi.*
Kiránti Group (East Népal).	Dúmi,	*Pó.*
Kiránti Group (East Népal).	Kháling,	*Pó.*
Kiránti Group (East Népal).	Dungmáli,	*Bi, úm.*
Broken Tribes of Népal.	Dárhi,	*Ko.*
Broken Tribes of Népal.	Denwár,	*I'k, ák.*
Broken Tribes of Népal.	Pahri,	*Yá, yágu.*
Broken Tribes of Népal.	Chepáng,	*Kú.*
Broken Tribes of Népal.	Bhrámu,	*Kú.*
Broken Tribes of Népal.	Váyu,	*Mu, mo, mi.*
Broken Tribes of Népal.	Kuswar,	*Na, kara.*
Broken Tribes of Népal.	Kusunda,	*Nata igin.*
Broken Tribes of Népal.	Tháru,	*Keha.*
	Lepcha (Sikkim),	*Sa.*
	Bhúṭáni v. Lhopa,	*Gi, yé.*

N.-E. Bengal.	Bodo,	*-ni.*
N.-E. Bengal.	Dhimál,	*-ko.*
N.-E. Bengal.	Kocch,	*-ro, -r.*
N.-E. Bengal.	Garo,	*Ni.*
N.-E. Bengal.	Káchári,	*Caret.*
Eastern Frontier of Bengal.	Munipuri,	*Caret.*
Eastern Frontier of Bengal.	Míthán Nágá,	*Caret.*
Eastern Frontier of Bengal.	Tablung Nágá,	*Caret.*
Eastern Frontier of Bengal.	Khári Nágá,	*Caret.*
Eastern Frontier of Bengal.	Angámi Nágá,	*Caret.*
Eastern Frontier of Bengal.	Námsáng Nágá,	*Caret.*
Eastern Frontier of Bengal.	Nowgong Nágá,	*Caret.*
Eastern Frontier of Bengal.	Tengsa Nágá,	*Caret.*
Eastern Frontier of Bengal.	Abor Miri,	*Met.*
Eastern Frontier of Bengal.	Sibságar Miri,	*Caret.*
Eastern Frontier of Bengal.	Deoria Chutia,	*Caret.*
Eastern Frontier of Bengal.	Singpho,	*Na.*
Arrakan & Burmah.	Burman (*written*),	*I.*
Arrakan & Burmah.	Burman (*spoken*),	*I.*
Arrakan & Burmah.	Khyeng v. Shou,	*Caret.*
Arrakan & Burmah.	Kámi,	*U'n.*
Arrakan & Burmah.	Kúmi,	*Caret.*
Arrakan & Burmah.	Mrú v. Toung,	*Caret.*
Arrakan & Burmah.	Sák,	*Caret.*
Siam & Tenasserim.	Talain v. Mon,	*Mkeu.*
Siam & Tenasserim.	Sgau-karen,	*Bah-khah, ah.*
Siam & Tenasserim.	Pwo-karen,	*Ler.*
Siam & Tenasserim.	Toungh-thu,	*A.*
Siam & Tenasserim.	Shán,	*Caret.*
Siam & Tenasserim.	Annamitic,	*Caret.*
Siam & Tenasserim.	Siamese,	*Thi.*
Siam & Tenasserim.	Ahom,	*Caret.*
Siam & Tenasserim.	Khámti,	*Caret.*
Siam & Tenasserim.	Laos,	*Caret.*
Central India.	Ho (Kol),	*-á.*
Central India.	Kol (Singhbhum),	*-rinih.*
Central India.	Santáli,	*-rinih, -renkin, -renko.*
Central India.	Bhúmij,	*-reá.*
Central India.	Uráon,	*Ye.*
Central India.	Mundala,	*Ki.*
Central India.	Rájmahali,	*By affix.*
Central India.	Goṇḍi,	*Orá, bará.*
Central India.	Gayeti,	*Caret.*
Central India.	Rutluk,	*Caret.*
Central India.	Naikude,	*Caret.*
Central India.	Kolami,	*Caret.*
Central India.	Mádi,	*Caret.*
Central India.	Mádia,	*Caret.*
Central India.	Kuri,	*Caret.*
Central India.	Keikádi,	*Caret.*
Central India.	Khoṇḍ,	*Caret.*
Central India.	Sávara,	*Ti.*
Central India.	Gadaba,	*Móyi.*
Central India.	Yerukala,	*Vakka.*
Central India.	Chentsu,	*Vór.*
Southern India.	Tamiḷ, anc.,	*-adu.*
Southern India.	Tamiḷ, mod.,	*-uḍeiya.*
Southern India.	Malayáḷma, anc.,	*Caret.*
Southern India.	Malayáḷma, mod.,	*-uṭe.*
Southern India.	Telugu,	*-yokka.*
Southern India.	Karṇáṭaka, anc.,	*Caret.*
Southern India.	Karṇáṭaka, mod.	*-na, -da.*
Southern India.	Tuḷuva,	*-no, -du.*
Southern India.	Kurgi,	*-ḍa, -anḍu.*
Southern India.	Toḍuva, Toḍa,	*Caret.* / *-na.*
Southern India.	Kóta,	*-na.*
Southern India.	Baḍaga,	*-ya, -na.*
Southern India.	Kuṛumba,	*-ya, -na.*
Southern India.	Iruḷa,	*-no.*
Southern India.	Malabar,	*-in, -uḍeya, -thu.*
Southern India.	Sinhalese,	*-é, -gé.*

Types.		
Inflecting.	SANSKṚIT,	-*i*, -*os*,[1] -*su*[2] (loc. case).
	ARABIC,	*Aala.*
Compounding.	BASK,	*Gañean, gañera, gaindi.*
	FINNIC,	*Păällă.*
	MAGYAR,	*Ra.*
	TURKISH,	*Uzere.*
	CIRCASSIAN,	*Caret.*
	GEORGIAN,	*Isa.*
	MONGOLIAN,	*Deghora.*
	MANTSHU,	*Derghi.*
	JAVANESE, Ngoko,	*Ing.*
	JAVANESE, Krama,	*Ing.*
	MALAY,	*Diátas.*
Isolating.	CHINESE, Nankin,	*Shang.*
	CHINESE, Pekin,	*Shang.*
	CHINESE, Canton,	*Sheong.*
	CHINESE, Shanghai,	*Lah-long.*
	AMOY, Colloquial,	*Ti.*
	JAPANESE,	*Uyeni, -uye, -ni.*
	Brahuí,	*Swár, -ai.*
Chinese Frontier & Tibet.	Gyámi,	*La.*
	Gyárung,	*S, pri.*
	Tákpa,	*Ná.*
	Mányak,	*Khú, choḳ.*
	Thochú,	*Kúkú, tik, ti.*
	Sokpa,	*Thú, tu.*
	Horpa,	*Ná, no, chá.*
	Tibetan (*written*),	*Ná, la.*
	Tibetan (*spoken*),	*Lá.*
Nepal (east to west).	Serpa,	*Lá.*
	Súnwár,	*Mi.*
	Gúrung,	*Ri.*
	Múrmi,	*Ri.*
	Magar,	*Yáng, ang.*
	Tháksya,	*Caret.*
	Pákhya,	*Caret.*
	Newár,	*E, té.*
	Limbu,	*Mo, khep-mo, kúthung-tho.*
Kiranti Group (East Nepal).	Kiránti,	*Dá.*
	Rodong,	*Cho-top.*
	Rúngchenbung,	*Chokdo, dungda.*
	Chhingtángya,	*Caret.*
	Náchhereng,	*Caret.*
	Wáling,	*Caret.*
	Yákha,	*Caret.*
	Chourásya,	*Caret.*
	Kulungya,	*Caret.*
	Thulungya,	*Caret.*
	Báhingya,	*Tóre, taure.*
	Lohorong,	*Wettú, songpi, sokbe.*
	Lambichhong,	*Temdú.*
	Báláli,	*Chápittu.*
	Sáng-páng,	*Chhopi.*
	Dúmi,	*Cho-tu, tyu, teyo.*
	Kháling,	*Ti.*
	Dungmáli,	*Chokpi, chokyá.*
Broken Tribes of Nepal.	Dárhi,	*Her, úpare.*
	Denwár,	*In, úpare.*
	Pahri,	*Gar-hi-ne.*
	Chepáng,	*Háng.*
	Bhrámu,	*Thá-chi, gái.*
	Váyu,	*Bé, nane.*
	Kuswar,	*Kana, -te, -e.*
	Kusunda,	*Caret.*
	Tháru,	*Caret.*
	Lepcha (Sikkim),	*Ká, plóng.*
	Bhúṭáni v. Lhopa,	*Ná.*

N.-E. Bengal.	Bodo,	*-há, ou, chou.*
	Dhimál,	*-rhutá.*
	Kocch,	*-te.*
	Garo,	*Pirvai.*
	Káchári,	*Caret.*
Eastern Frontier of Bengal.	Munipuri,	*Thuk.*
	Mithán Nágá,	*Caret.*
	Tablung Nágá,	*Caret.*
	Khári Nágá,	*Tamnge.*
	Angámi Nágá,	*Caret.*
	Námsáng Nágá,	*A'khónang.*
	Nowgong Nágá,	*Talak.*
	Tengsa Nágá,	*Tathak.*
	Abor Miri,	*Teó-só.*
	Sibságar Miri,	*Talulo.*
	Deoria Chutia,	*Pichoni.*
	Singpho,	*Lethá.*
Arrakan & Burmah.	Burman (*written*),	*Pomhá.*
	Burman (*spoken*),	*Bomha, apau.*
	Khyeng v. Shou,	*Há-nang.*
	Kámi,	*A-koung-be.*
	Kúmi,	*Caret.*
	Mrú v. Toung,	*Caret.*
	Sák,	*Caret.*
Siam & Tenasserim.	Talain v. Mon,	*Atu.*
	Sgau-karen,	*A'pau 'ko.*
	Pwo-karen,	*A'paingu.*
	Toungh-thu,	*Long.*
	Shán,	*Ka-nouk.*
	Annamitic,	*Trên.*
	Siamese,	*Khau-mon, bón.*
	Ahom,	*Nu.*
	Khámti,	*Nau.*
	Laos,	*Nu.*
Central India.	Ho (Kol),	*-re.*
	Kol (Singhbhum),	*-re, chitán.*
	Santáli,	*Chetan, -re, -tálare.*
	Bhúmij,	*-re* (?).
	Uráon,	*U'lá.*
	Mundala,	*-te* (?), *upar* (?).
	Rájmahali,	*By affix, -re* (?).
	Goṇḍi,	*Imitté.*
	Gayeti,	*Caret.*
	Rutluk,	*Caret.*
	Naikude,	*Caret.*
	Kolami,	*Caret.*
	Mádi,	*Caret.*
	Mádia,	*Caret.*
	Kuri,	*Caret.*
	Keikádi,	*Caret.*
	Khoṇḍ,	*Séndó.*
	Sávara,	*Lanka.*
	Gadaba,	*Te.*
	Yerukala,	*Paini.*
	Chentsu,	*Vuparbru, vuparot.*
Southern India.	Tamiḷ, anc.,	*Caret.*
	Tamiḷ, mod.,	*-mél.*
	Malayâḷma, anc.,	*Caret.*
	Malayâḷma, mod.,	*-mél, -méle.*
	Telugu,	*-mida, -paina.*
	Karṇâṭaka, anc.,	*Caret.*
	Karṇâṭaka, mod.,	*-méle.*
	Tuḷuva,	*-mittu.*
	Kurgi,	*-méle.*
	Toḍuva, }	*Caret.*
	Toḍa, }	*-mel, -mok.*
	Kóta,	*-melte.*
	Baḍaga,	*-mele.*
	Kuṛumba,	*-mele.*
	Iruḷa,	*-mele.*
	Malabar,	*-mél, -péril.*
	Sinhalese,	*-piṭa.*

Types.		
Inflecting.	SANSKṚIT,	*Vá.*
	ARABIC,	*Aou.*
Compounding.	BASK,	*Edo.*
	FINNIC,	*Tahi, taikka.*
	MAGYAR,	*Vagy.*
	TURKISH,	*Yoksa.*
	CIRCASSIAN,	*Caret.*
	GEORGIAN,	*Amu.*
	MONGOLIAN,	*Esepsu.*
	MANTSHU,	*Ememu.*
	JAVANESE, Ngoko,	*Utawa.*
	JAVANESE, Krama,	*Utawi.*
	MALAY,	*Atáu.*
Isolating.	CHINESE, Nankin,	*Hwoh-che.*
	CHINESE, Pekin,	*Hwo-che.*
	CHINESE, Canton,	*Wak-che.*
	CHINESE, Shanghai,	*Ohsz'.*
	AMOY, Colloquial,	*A'.*
	JAPANESE,	*Matawa, ya.*
	Brahuí,	*Yá.*
Chinese Frontier & Tibet.	Gyámi,	*Tháng.*
	Gyárung,	*Kö, wövé.*
	Tákpa,	*Na, iná.*
	Mányak,	*Lé.*
	Thochú,	*Gnóá.*
	Sokpa,	*Caret.*
	Horpa,	*Ná.*
	Tibetan (*written*),	*Caret.*
	Tibetan (*spoken*),	*Mo.*
Nepal (east to west).	Serpa,	*Nam, inam.*
	Súnwár,	*Dé.*
	Gúrung,	*Bani, gi.*
	Múrmi,	*Wá.*
	Magar,	*Ki.*
	Tháksya,	*Howochuchhyáng.*
	Pákhya,	*Caret.*
	Newár,	*Lá.*
	Limbu,	*Bi.*
Kiranti Group (East Nepal).	Kiránti,	*Hé.*
	Rodong,	*Wö.*
	Rúngchenbung,	*Hé.*
	Chhingtángya,	*Yáng.*
	Náchhereng,	*Lé.*
	Wáling,	*Hé.*
	Yákha,	*E.*
	Chourásya,	*Ké.*
	Kulungya,	*Yo.*
	Thulungya,	*Dé.*
	Báhingya,	*Ki.*
	Lohorong,	*Dú, do* (?).
	Lambichhong,	*A'* (?).
	Báláli,	*Caret.*
	Sáng-páng,	*Lé* (?).
	Dúmi,	*Yé.*
	Kháling,	*Yé.*
	Dungmáli,	*Hé.*
Broken Tribes of Nepal.	Dárhi,	*Ti.*
	Denwár,	*Láne, né.*
	Pahri,	*Ki, lá.*
	Chepáng,	*Caret.*
	Bhrámu,	*Ke.*
	Váyu,	*Ki.*
	Kuswar,	*Na.*
	Kusunda,	*Caret.*
	Tháru,	*Ihe.*
	Lepcha (Sikkim),	*Yáng, eu.*
	Bhúṭáni v. Lhopa,	*Yáng, mo.*

N.-E. Bengal.	Bodo,	*Ná.*
	Dhimál,	*Ná.*
	Kocch,	*Ki.*
	Garo,	*Ná.*
	Káchári,	*Caret.*
Eastern Frontier of Bengal.	Munipuri,	*Caret.*
	Míthán Nágá,	*Caret.*
	Tablung Nágá,	*Caret.*
	Khári Nágá,	*Caret.*
	Angámi Nágá,	*Caret.*
	Námsáng Nágá,	*Caret.*
	Nowgong Nágá,	*Caret.*
	Tengsa Nágá,	*Caret.*
	Abor Miri,	*Caret.*
	Sibságar Miri,	*Caret.*
	Deoria Chutia,	*Caret.*
	Singpho,	*Caret.*
Arrakan & Burmah.	Burman (*written*),	*Sómahut.*
	Burman (*spoken*),	Thómahók.
	Khyeng v. Shou,	*Caret.*
	Kámi,	*Caret.*
	Kúmi,	*Caret.*
	Mrú v. Toung,	*Caret.*
	Sák,	*Caret.*
Siam & Tenasserim.	Talain v. Mon,	*Ho-to-tseik-ko.*
	Sgau-karen,	*Magha, má-t-má.*
	Pwo-karen,	*A'L'muaibah.*
	Toungh-thu,	*Caret.*
	Shán,	*Tso-neik-ma-tsouk.*
	Annamitic,	*Hay-lá.*
	Siamese,	*Mai-pen-yau.*
	Ahom,	*Caret.*
	Khámti,	*Caret.*
	Laos,	*Caret.*
Central India.	Ho (Kol),	*Bandreto.*
	Kol (Singhbhum),	*Nado.*
	Santáli,	*Se.*
	Bhúmij,	*Se.*
	Uráon,	*I's.*
	Mundala,	*Ani.*
	Rájmahali,	*Malé.*
	Goṇḍi,	*Idaré.*
	Gayeti,	*Caret.*
	Rutluk,	*Caret.*
	Naikude,	*Caret.*
	Kolami,	*Caret.*
	Mádi,	*Caret.*
	Mádia,	*Caret.*
	Kuri,	*Caret.*
	Keikádi,	*Caret.*
	Khoṇḍ,	*Caret.*
	Sávara,	*Caret.*
	Gadaba,	*Vúre.*
	Yerukala,	*Taradote.*
	Chentsu,	*Nahi.*
Southern India.	Tamiḷ, anc.,	*Caret.*
	Tamiḷ, mod.,	*Alladu.*
	Malayáḷma, anc.,	*Caret.*
	Malayáḷma, mod.,	*Engkil, adalla, allengkil.*
	Telugu,	*Léka.*
	Karṇáṭaka, anc.,	*Caret.*
	Karṇáṭaka, mod.,	*A'darú, illavi.*
	Tuḷuva,	*Andala.*
	Kurgi,	*Allengi.*
	Toḍuva, } Toḍa, }	*Caret.*
		Illade.
	Kóta,	*Illave.*
	Baḍaga,	*Illave, illadhóle.*
	Kuṛumba,	*Innadhole.*
	Iruḷa,	*Illavitta.*
	Malabar,	*Allathu.*
	Sinhalese,	*Nohot.*

Group	*Types.*	
Inflecting.	SANSKRIT,	*Bahis.*
	ARABIC,	*Birra.*
Compounding.	BASK,	*Kampoan, landan, lekora.*
	FINNIC,	*Ulkoinen.*
	MAGYAR,	*Ki.*
	TURKISH,	*Dicheru.*
	CIRCASSIAN,	*Caret.*
	GEORGIAN,	*Gali.*
	MONGOLIAN,	*Ghadana.*
	MANTSHU,	*Toulergi.*
	JAVANESE, Ngoko,	*Ingjaba.*
	JAVANESE, Krama,	*Ingjawi.*
	MALAY,	*Dilúar.*
Isolating.	CHINESE, Nankin,	*Wai.*
	CHINESE, Pekin,	*Wai.*
	CHINESE, Canton,	*Ngoi.*
	CHINESE, Shanghai,	*Ngá-dew.*
	AMOY, Colloquial,	*Goá-bin.*
	JAPANESE,	*Soto, so-toni.*
	Brahuí,	*Peshan.*
Chinese Frontier & Tibet.	Gyámi,	*Wai-thú.*
	Gyárung,	*Wonpo.*
	Tákpa,	*Phit-ka.*
	Mányak,	*Nwá.*
	Thochú,	*Khanyis.*
	Sokpa,	*Gáchá.*
	Horpa,	*Pheu-so.*
	Tibetan (*written*),	*Phyi, rohna.*
	Tibetan (*spoken*),	*Chi.*
Nepal (east to west).	Serpa,	*Yáng.*
	Súnwár,	*Báhir.*
	Gúrung,	*Hú-jéri.*
	Múrmi,	*Mang-gyér.*
	Magar,	*Báhar.*
	Tháksya,	*Phelori.*
	Pákhya,	*Báhira.*
	Newár,	*Pine.*
	Limbu,	*Báhar.*
Kiranti Group (East Nepal).	Kiránti,	*Udúng-yá.*
	Rodong,	*Búng-ya.*
	Rúngchenbung,	*Ubungya, udungya, huviya.*
	Chhingtángya,	*Báhari.*
	Náchhereng,	*Pákhá.*
	Wáling,	*Hibu, bungkháya.*
	Yákha,	*Caret.*
	Chourásya,	*Bhánà, twala.*
	Kulungya,	*Hochho, pótél, hachhópa.*
	Thulungya,	*Chépnóa.*
	Báhingya,	*A'tola.*
	Lohorong,	*Song-bé, úng-phú.*
	Lambichhong,	*A'yó.*
	Báláli,	*Pákha yú.*
	Sáng-páng,	*Amkonpó.*
	Dúmi,	*Ghobai, ghoyo.*
	Kháling,	*Pátel.*
	Dungmáli,	*Kúbú-yá.*
Broken Tribes of Nepal.	Dárhi,	*Báhir.*
	Denwár,	*Báhir.*
	Pahri,	*Pen-há.*
	Chepáng,	*Caret.*
	Bhrámu,	*Am-bu.*
	Váyu,	*Tongma, lok.*
	Kuswar,	*Báhir.*
	Kusunda,	*Bang-jo.*
	Tháru,	*Bahera.*
	Lepcha (Sikkim),	*Póng.*
	Bhútáni v. Lhopa,	*Phi.*

N.-E. Bengal.	Bodo,	*Báhiron.*
	Dhimál,	*Báhiro.*
	Kocch,	*Báhir.*
	Garo,	*Báhir-vai.*
	Káchári,	*Shotla.*
Eastern Frontier of Bengal.	Munipuri,	*Mapál.*
	Míthán Nágá,	*Caret.*
	Tablung Nágá,	*Caret.*
	Khári Nágá,	*Takigu.*
	Angámi Nágá,	*Kite.*
	Námsáng Nágá,	*Vákánang.*
	Nowgong Nágá,	*Tamá.*
	Tengsa Nágá,	*Ma.*
	Abor Miri,	*Lulo.*
	Sibságar Miri,	*Rongongolo.*
	Deoria Chutia,	*Bajuni.*
	Singpho,	*Caret.*
Arrakan & Burmah.	Burman (*written*),	*Prangmha.*
	Burman (*spoken*),	*Pyen-mhá.*
	Khyeng v. Shou,	*Kláng-á-me.*
	Kámi,	*A-kham-be.*
	Kúmi,	*A-ngám.*
	Mrú v. Toung,	*Caret.*
	Sák,	*Caret.*
Siam & Tenasserim.	Talain v. Mon,	*Ma-ngá.*
	Sgau-karen,	*A'klor, ler-ko.*
	Pwo-karen,	*Ler-kaung.*
	Toungh-thu,	*Ta-h'tann.*
	Shán,	*Ka-nouk.*
	Annamitic,	*Ngoai.*
	Siamese,	*Khan-nouk, thi-nok.*
	Ahom,	*Bi.*
	Khámti,	*Caret.*
	Laos,	*Caret.*
Central India.	Ho (Kol),	*Caret.*
	Kol (Singhbhum),	*Ráchárc.*
	Santáli,	*Udung-re, ráchále.*
	Bhúmij,	*Ráchárè (ráchále ?).*
	Uráon,	*Báhari.*
	Mundala,	*Báhari.*
	Rájmahali,	*Dwárè.*
	Goṇḍi,	*Bahro, bahiro mandar.*
	Gayeti,	*Caret.*
	Rutluk,	*Caret.*
	Naikude,	*Caret.*
	Kolami,	*Caret.*
	Mádi,	*Caret.*
	Mádia,	*Caret.*
	Kuri,	*Caret.*
	Keikádi,	*Beilu.*
	Khoṇḍ,	*Caret.*
	Sávara,	*Vo-ḍite.*
	Gadaba,	*Valumúsá.*
	Yerukala,	*Bele.*
	Chentsu,	*Bahar.*
Southern India.	Tamiḷ, anc.,	*Caret.*
	Tamiḷ, mod.,	*Veḷiyil, veḷiyé, tavira.*
	Malayáḷma, anc.,	*Caret.*
	Malayáḷma, mod.,	*Puṛame, puṛatta.*
	Telugu,	*Bayiṭa, beiṭa, vinó.*
	Karṇáṭaka, anc.,	*Caret.*
	Karṇáṭaka, mod.,	*Horage.*
	Tuḷuva,	*Pedi.*
	Kurgi,	*Porame.*
	Toḍuva, Toḍa, }	*Parmutak.*
		Pormud.
	Kóta,	*Porenje.*
	Baḍaga,	*Horasu.*
	Kuṛumba,	*Honage.*
	Iruḷa,	*Valli.*
	Malabar,	*Veliye, purámbér.*
	Sinhalese,	*Piṭata, bahir.*

Group	Types.	
Inflecting.	SANSKṚIT, ...	*Tathá.*
	ARABIC, ...	*Hákaza.*
Compounding.	BASK, ...	*Ala, onela, alan, onla, aiñ.*
	FINNIC, ...	*Nüu.*
	MAGYAR, ...	*Ugy.*
	TURKISH, ...	*Beuileh.*
	CIRCASSIAN, ...	*Arahrey.*
	GEORGIAN, ...	*Ats.*
	MONGOLIAN, ...	*Dayiu.*
	MANTSHU, ...	*Tuttu.*
	JAVANESE, Ngoko, . .	*Mangkana.*
	JAVANESE, Krama, . .	*Mangkaten.*
	MALAY, ...	*Bagitu.*
Isolating.	CHINESE, Nankin, . .	*Ye-che-yang.*
	CHINESE, Pekin, . .	*Ye-che-yang.*
	CHINESE, Canton, . .	*Yau-kom-yeong.*
	CHINESE, Shanghai, .	*Seh-kah-nang.*
	AMOY, Colloquial, . .	*A'n-ni, ân-hiun.*
	JAPANESE, ...	*Sayoni.*
	Brahuí, ...	*Handunos.*
Chinese Frontier & Tibet.	Gyámi, ...	*Lá-menti.*
	Gyárung, ...	*Caret.*
	Tákpa, ...	*Dantarang.*
	Mányak, ...	*Thúzyo.*
	Thochú, ...	*Stíká.*
	Sokpa, ...	*Yenichin.*
	Horpa, ...	*Nyú.*
	Tibetan (*written*), . .	*Dtesúg.*
	Tibetan (*spoken*), . .	*Thendá.*
Nepal (east to west).	Serpa, ...	*Phánde.*
	Súnwár, ...	*Modiv.*
	Gúrung, ...	*Húchúga-líyon.*
	Múrmi, ...	*Waspa.*
	Magar, ...	*Adáng-cha.*
	Thaksya, ...	*Khapribá khaju.*
	Pákhya, ...	*Caret.*
	Newár, ...	*Athing.*
	Limbu, ...	*Khem-phá-dong-ba.*
Kiranti Group (East Nepal).	Kiránti, ...	*Khoïn-súko.*
	Rodong, ...	*Kyaskwa, kyasokwa* (?).
	Rúngchenbung, . . .	*Khoïnsa* (?).
	Chhingtángya, . . .	*Hungkhyakkha.*
	Náchhereng, ...	*Khángtokgná.*
	Wáling, ...	*Múgnek.*
	Yákha, ...	*Ikhbkha.*
	Chourásya, ...	*Insimegná.*
	Kulungya, ...	*Khúntúkwa.*
	Thulungya, ...	*Mehomka, mihopmá, ohopma.*
	Báhingya, ...	*Mekho.*
	Lohorong, ...	*Mado-knok.*
	Lambichhong, . . .	*Natte.*
	Bálálí, ...	*Caret.*
	Sáng-páng, ...	*Caret.*
	Dúmi, ...	*Caret.*
	Kháling, ...	*Caret.*
	Dungmáli, ...	*Caret.*
Broken Tribes of Nepal.	Dárhi, ...	*Wo-sai.*
	Denwár, ...	*Tú-nhe.*
	Pahri, ...	*He-re.*
	Chepáng, ...	*Caret.*
	Bhrámu, ...	*U'chi.*
	Váyu, ...	*Me-má.*
	Kuswar, ...	*Há-sege.*
	Kusunda, ...	*Nápawai.*
	Thárú, ...	*Wunaisan.*
	Lepcha (Sikkim), . .	*Olom.*
	Bhúṭáni v. Lhopa, . .	*Ote.*

N.-E. Bengal.	Bodo, ...	*U'rin.*
	Dhimál, ...	*Kodong.*
	Kocch, ...	*Temon.*
	Garo, ...	*U'gánda.*
	Káchári, ...	*Caret.*
Eastern Frontier of Bengal.	Munipuri, ...	*Asundouna.*
	Míthán Nágá, . . .	*Caret.*
	Tablung Nágá, . . .	*Caret.*
	Khári Nágá, ...	*Itango.*
	Angámi Nágá, . . .	*Tsawe.*
	Námsáng Nágá, . . .	*A'rarang.*
	Nowgong Nágá, . .	*A'nyakang.*
	Tengsa Nágá, . . .	*A'nyakong.*
	Abor Miri, ...	*Depu, au.*
	Sibságar Miri, . . .	*Sempidang.*
	Deoria Chutia, . . .	*Lakireni.*
	Singpho, ...	*Ndaisat.*
Arrakan & Burmah.	Burman (*written*), . .	*Lo, so.*
	Burman (*spoken*), . .	*Lo, tho.*
	Khyeng v. Shou, . .	*Caret.*
	Kámi, ...	*Ka.*
	Kúmi, ...	*Caret.*
	Mrú v. Toung, . . .	*Caret.*
	Sák, ...	*Caret.*
Siam & Tenasserim.	Talain v. Mon, . . .	*Nyoung-tseik-kau.*
	Sgau-karen, ...	*De-i, de-ne.*
	Pwo-karen, ...	*Bayi.*
	Toungh-thu, ...	*Nay-yo.*
	Shán, ...	*Tso-neik-youk.*
	Annamitic, ...	*Vây.*
	Siamese, ...	*Ram-ni.*
	Ahom, ...	*Caret.*
	Khámti, ...	*Ce.*
	Laos, ...	*Caret.*
Central India.	Ho (Kol), ...	*Enleka.*
	Kol (Singhbhum), . .	*I'nlikate.*
	Santáli, ...	*Nangká, onaká, nunáh, onakáge.*
	Bhúmij, ...	*Nangká.*
	Uráon, ...	*Yeli.*
	Mundala, ...	*Se.*
	Rájmahali, ...	*Indeki.*
	Goṇḍi, ...	*Arobara.*
	Gayeti, ...	*Caret.*
	Rutluk, ...	*Caret.*
	Naikude, ...	*Caret.*
	Kolami, ...	*Caret.*
	Mádi, ...	*Caret.*
	Mádia, ...	*Caret.*
	Kuri, ...	*Caret.*
	Keikádi, ...	*Caret.*
	Khoṇḍ, ...	*Caret.*
	Sávara, ...	*Kaninásan.*
	Gadaba, ...	*Vottu.*
	Yerukala, ...	*Aṭe.*
	Chentsu, ...	*Vu, vumane.*
Southern India.	Tamiḷ, anc., ...	*Caret.*
	Tamiḷ, mod., ...	*Appaḍi.*
	Malayáḷma, anc., . .	*Caret.*
	Malayáḷma, mod., . .	*Angngine.*
	Telugu, ...	*Atla.*
	Karṇáṭaka, anc., . .	*Caret.*
	Karṇáṭaka, mod., . .	*Háge.*
	Tuḷuva, ...	*Do.*
	Kurgi, ...	*Annane.*
	Toḍuva, }	*Caret.*
	Toḍa, }	*Ingei.*
	Kóta, ...	*A'te.*
	Baḍaga, ...	*Hinge.*
	Kuṛumba, ...	*Hage.*
	Iruḷa, ...	*Ipaḍi.*
	Malabar, ...	*Appaḍie, avoannam.*
	Sinhalese, ...	*Mese.*

	Types.	
Inflecting.	SANSKRIT,	*Tadá, tadánim, tarhi.*
	ARABIC,	*Hiná izen.*
Compounding.	BASK,	*Orduan.*
	FINNIC,	*Sitte.*
	MAGYAR,	*Akhor.*
	TURKISH,	[By circumlocution.]
	CIRCASSIAN,	[Id.]
	GEORGIAN,	*Misha.*
	MONGOLIAN,	*Detsighe.*
	MANTSHU,	*Utkhai.*
	JAVANESE, Ngoko,	*Nuli.*
	JAVANESE, Krama,	*Nunten.*
	MALAY,	*Tatkála-itu.*
Isolating.	CHINESE, Nankin,	*Na-shi.*
	CHINESE, Pekin,	*Na-shi.*
	CHINESE, Canton,	*Ko-shi.*
	CHINESE, Shanghai,	*Na-koh-sz-en.*
	AMOY, Colloquial,	*Hit-si.*
	JAPANESE,	*Sonotoki, anotoki.*
	Brahuí,	*O-wakt.*
Chinese Frontier & Tibet.	Gyámi,	*Lá-khún.*
	Gyárung,	*Tis-dúi.*
	Tákpa,	*Tene.*
	Mányak,	*Thile.*
	Thochú,	*Stáka, hatús.*
	Sokpa,	*Caret.*
	Horpa,	*Tábdeu.*
	Tibetan (*written*),	*De-t'se.*
	Tibetan (*spoken*),	*Thi-dwi.*
Nepal (east to west).	Serpa,	*Támá.*
	Súnwár,	*Méná.*
	Gúrung,	*Chok-lene.*
	Múrmi,	*Jámá.*
	Magar,	*Arnau.*
	Tháksya,	*Khaghángchye.*
	Pákhya,	*Caret.*
	Newár,	*Wala.*
	Limbu,	*Khem-phalé.*
Kiranti Group (East Nepal).	Kiránti,	*Khwomlo.*
	Rodong,	*Khonglo, tespa.*
	Rúngchenbung,	*Khomlo, khollo.*
	Chhingtángya,	*Uilhe.*
	Náchhereng,	*Khontalo.*
	Wáling,	*Húlong.*
	Yákha,	*Ikhoning.*
	Chourásya,	*Ingyelo.*
	Kulungya,	*Khodolo.*
	Thulungya,	*Mehomlo.*
	Báhingya,	*Mekhona.*
	Lohorong,	*Mokloua, wanok.*
	Lambichhong,	*U'ndena.*
	Báláli,	*Mudoklo.*
	Sáng-páng,	*Khotolo, kholo.*
	Dúmi,	*Melo.*
	Kháling,	*Mebelo.*
	Dungmáli,	*Ughári.*
Broken Tribes of Nepal.	Dárhi,	*Wohe.*
	Denwár,	*Takhen.*
	Pahri,	*Welhe.*
	Chepáng,	*Caret.*
	Bhrámu,	*Wá-lhe.*
	Váyu,	*Me-the.*
	Kuswar,	*A-khen.*
	Kusunda,	*Nhu.*
	Thárú,	*Nabhai, thabhai.*
	Lepcha (Sikkim),	*Othá.*
	Bhúṭáni v. Lhopa,	*O'de, odi-gáng.*
N.-E. Bengal.	Bodo,	*Obelá.*
	Dhimál,	*Kolá.*
	Kocch,	*Te, te-khong.*
	Garo,	*Te-eng.*
	Káchári,	*Caret.*
Eastern Frontier of Bengal.	Munipuri,	*Asai.*
	Míthán Nágá,	*Caret.*
	Tablung Nágá,	*Caret.*
	Khári Nágá,	*Jiku.*
	Angámi Nágá,	*Lilitiha.*
	Námsáng Nágá,	*Caret.*
	Nowgong Nágá,	*Tas-au.*
	Tengsa Nágá,	*Kab-áng.*
	Abor Miri,	*Caret.*
	Sibságar Miri,	*Kojo.*
	Deoria Chutia,	*Deremai.*
	Singpho,	*Caret.*
Arrakan & Burmah.	Burman (*written*),	*Tho-akhá.*
	Burman (*spoken*),	*Tho-akhá.*
	Khyeng v. Shou,	*Ni-kho-á.*
	Kámi,	*Ho-ná-i-gán.*
	Kúmi,	*Caret.*
	Mrú v. Toung,	*Caret.*
	Sák,	*Caret.*
Siam & Tenasserim.	Talain v. Mon,	*Akha.*
	Sgau-karen,	*Tu'nuts'u.*
	Pwo-karen,	*Taungnaut-pung.*
	Toungh-thu,	*Moung-ma.*
	Shán,	*Chyain-huigh.*
	Annamitic,	*Thi.*
	Siamese,	*Hpa-la, mua.*
	Ahom,	*Tamnai.*
	Khámti,	*Caret.*
	Laos,	*Caret.*
Central India.	Ho (Kol),	*Emindré.*
	Kol (Singhbhum),	*En.*
	Santáli,	*Unare, un-khona, endng,*
	Bhúmij,	*En* (?). [*inakhánage.*
	Uráon,	*Pis-á.*
	Mundala,	*I'nam.*
	Rájmahali,	*Ani.*
	Goṇḍi,	*Anni, ada.*
	Gayeti,	*Caret.*
	Rutluk,	*Caret.*
	Naikude,	*Caret.*
	Kolami,	*Caret.*
	Mádi,	*Caret.*
	Mádia,	*Caret.*
	Kuri,	*Caret.*
	Keikádi,	*Apo.*
	Khoṇḍ,	*Caret.*
	Sávara,	*Namóde.*
	Gadaba,	*Appuḍu.*
	Yerukala,	*Appuḍu.*
	Chentsu,	*Tekhán, areghoḍi.*
Southern India.	Tamiḷ, anc.,	*Appozhuḍu* (*appoḷaḍu*).
	Tamiḷ, mod.,	*Appoḍu, appo.*
	Malayáḷma, anc.,	*Caret.*
	Malayáḷma, mod.,	*Appoḷ* (*appozh*).
	Telugu,	*Appuḍu.*
	Karṇáṭaka, anc.,	*Caret.*
	Karṇáṭaka, mod.,	*A'ga, andu.*
	Tuḷuva,	*Apaḷ* (*apazh*).
	Kurgi,	*Anda, akka.*
	Toḍuva, } Toḍa, }	*Atwan.* / *A'ni.*
	Kóta,	*Annale.*
	Baḍaga,	*Aga.*
	Kuṟumba,	*Agale.*
	Iruḷa,	*Apaḷe* (*apazhe*).
	Malabar,	*Appothu.*
	Sinhalese,	*Ewita.*

Group	Language	There
	Types.	
Inflecting.	SANSKṚIT,	*Tatra, amutra.*
	ARABIC,	*Honák, honálek.*
Compounding.	BASK,	*An, or, hor, ara, orrat.*
	FINNIC,	*Siella.*
	MAGYAR,	*Ott.*
	TURKISH,	*Orda.*
	CIRCASSIAN,	*Medehshey* (?).
	GEORGIAN,	*Ik.*
	MONGOLIAN,	*Tende.*
	MANTSHU,	*Tubade.*
	JAVANESE, Ngoko,	*Kono.*
	JAVANESE, Krama,	*Ngrika.*
	MALAY,	*Disitu.*
Isolating.	CHINESE, Nankin,	*Na-li.*
	CHINESE, Pekin,	*Na-li.*
	CHINESE, Canton,	*Ko-ch'ü.*
	CHINESE, Shanghai,	*Ku-teh.*
	AMOY, Colloquial,	*Hi-tau, ti-hia.*
	JAPANESE,	*Asoko, as-koni.*
	Brahui,	*Ode.*
Chinese Frontier & Tibet.	Gyámi,	*Lá-mé.*
	Gyárung,	*Hadú.*
	Tákpa,	*Wo-tho.*
	Mányak,	*Thúngá-pu, kwonait.*
	Thochú,	*Háto.*
	Sokpa,	*Yá-bú.*
	Horpa,	*Oúthú.*
	Tibetan (*written*),	*Héna.*
	Tibetan (*spoken*),	*Hácho.*
Nepal (east to west).	Serpa,	*Chúrú.*
	Súnwár,	*Yéré.*
	Gúrung,	*Kyúri.*
	Múrmi,	*Kersyé.*
	Magar,	*Alak.*
	Tháksya,	*Khatáikhanti.*
	Pákhya,	*U'ta.*
	Newár,	*Uké.*
	Limbu,	*Na.*
Kiránti Group (East Nepal).	Kiránti,	*Miyánú.*
	Rodong,	*Túkhe, túku.*
	Rúngchenbung,	*Euhyana, endhako, moda, miyanung.*
	Chhingtángya,	*Yotni.*
	Náchhereng,	*Méksa, miyaya.*
	Wáling,	*Múyák, modo, moya.*
	Yákha,	*Yona, yokhyá.*
	Chourásya,	*Bhanala, bhána, gnóna.*
	Kulungya,	*Meksa, nakwápa, náya.*
	Thulungya,	*Háno, hanopna.*
	Báhingya,	*Nekare, meke, hare.*
	Lohorong,	*Miyú, mobe, hákiyu.*
	Lambichhong,	*Yo.*
	Báláli,	*Mobi, moyú.*
	Sáng-páng,	*Meni, mopyá.*
	Dúmi,	*Yákámbi.*
	Kháling,	*Yakámbi.*
	Dungmáli,	*Háyeyá, múhyák.*
Broken Tribes of Nepal.	Dárhi,	*U'chi.*
	Denwár,	*Wo-ti.*
	Pahri,	*Hong-tha.*
	Chepáng,	*Caret.*
	Bhrámu,	*Hú-di.*
	Váyu,	*Mi-ne, wa-the.*
	Kuswar,	*U'-chi-na.*
	Kusunda,	*Isága.*
	Tháru,	*Uhara.*
	Lepcha (Sikkim),	*Pil, woba.*
	Bhúṭáni v. Lhopa,	*Phá-te.*

Group	Language	There
N.-E. Bengal.	Bodo,	*Hobo.*
	Dhimál,	*U'sho.*
	Kocch,	*Tahán.*
	Garo,	*Wáng (táng ?).*
	Káchári,	*Caret.*
Eastern Frontier of Bengal.	Munipuri,	*Asomda.*
	Míthán Nágá,	*Caret.*
	Tablung Nágá,	*Caret.*
	Khári Nágá,	*Wadengu oju.*
	Angámi Nágá,	*Lithe.*
	Námsáng Nágá,	*Dinang.*
	Nowgong Nágá,	*Aunchi.*
	Tengsa Nágá,	*O'tiga.*
	Abor Miri,	*Caret.*
	Sibságar Miri,	*Ulo.*
	Deoria Chutia,	*Hobong.*
	Singpho,	*Tode.*
Arrakan & Burmah.	Burman (*written*),	*Homhá.*
	Burman (*spoken*),	*Homhá.*
	Khyeng v. Shou,	*Tsú-á.*
	Kámi,	*Há-bhe.*
	Kúmi,	*Caret.*
	Mrú v. Toung,	*Caret.*
	Sák,	*Caret.*
Siam & Tenasserim.	Talain v. Mon,	*Kha-na-ko.*
	Sgau-karen,	*'Palna.*
	Pwo-karen,	*Taung-nau.*
	Toungh-thu,	*Ea-h'su.*
	Shán,	*Ka-po.*
	Annamitic,	*Dó.*
	Siamese,	*Hainan, thi-nau.*
	Ahom,	*Tet.*
	Khámti,	*Hanpun.*
	Laos,	*Caret.*
Central India.	Ho (Kol),	*Endré.*
	Kol (Singhbhum),	*Entai.*
	Santáli,	*Háṇḍe, hándre, entege, ante.*
	Bhúmij,	*Eta thái.*
	Uráon,	*Háhá.*
	Mundala,	*Unthi.*
	Rájmahali,	*Ano.*
	Goṇḍi,	*Hukkai.*
	Gayeti,	*Caret.*
	Rutluk,	*Caret.*
	Naikude,	*Caret.*
	Kolami,	*Caret.*
	Mádi,	*Caret.*
	Mádia,	*Caret.*
	Kuri,	*Caret.*
	Keikádi,	*Akada.*
	Khoṇḍ,	*Caret.*
	Sávara,	*Voḍite.*
	Gadaba,	*Tonno.*
	Yerukala,	*Aṭukire, ange.*
	Chentsu,	*Unhaná, vuha.*
Southern India.	Tamiḷ, anc.,	*Avan.*
	Tamiḷ, mod.,	*Angu, ange.*
	Malayáḷma, anc.,	*Caret.*
	Malayáḷma, mod.,	*Aviṭe.*
	Telugu,	*Akkaḍa.*
	Karṇáṭaka, anc.,	*Caret.*
	Karṇáṭaka, mod.,	*Alli.*
	Tuḷuva,	*Anchi.*
	Kurgi,	*Caret.*
	Toḍuva,	*Caret.*
	Toḍa,	*At, ang.*
	Kóta,	*Able.*
	Baḍaga,	*Alli.*
	Kuṟumba,	*Alli.*
	Iruḷa,	*Ange.*
	Malabar,	*Angei.*
	Sinhalese,	*Ehe.*

Group	Types.	
Inflecting.	SANSKRIT,	*Evam, ittham.*
	ARABIC,	*Kizá.*
Compounding.	BASK,	*Orrela, orla, orlatan, orlanka.*
	FINNIC,	*Nün.*
	MAGYAR,	*Ugy.*
	TURKISH,	*Euileh.*
	CIRCASSIAN,	*Arahrey.*
	GEORGIAN,	*Ats.*
	MONGOLIAN,	*Degautsilen.*
	MANTSHU,	*Teuteke.*
	JAVANESE, Ngoko,	*Mangkana.*
	JAVANESE, Krama,	*Mangkaten.*
	MALAY,	*Bagini.*
Isolating.	CHINESE, Nankin,	*Cháou-che-yang.*
	CHINESE, Pekin,	*Cháou-che-yang.*
	CHINESE, Canton,	*Chiu-kom-yeong.*
	CHINESE, Shanghai,	*Seh-keh.*
	AMOY, Colloquial,	*A'n-ni, án-hlun.*
	JAPANESE,	*Chodo, koste.*
	Brahuí,	*Handoan.*
Chinese Frontier & Tibet.	Gyámi,	*Thi-men-ti.*
	Gyárung,	*Caret.*
	Tákpa,	*Ustúm.*
	Mányak,	*Thúsú, moh.*
	Thochú,	*Cheu.*
	Sokpa,	*Yenichhin.*
	Horpa,	*Wode.*
	Tibetan (*written*),	*Jitsúng.*
	Tibetan (*spoken*),	*Dindá.*
Nepal (east to west).	Serpa,	*Dinde.*
	Súnwár,	*Akko.*
	Gúrung,	*Chúga-liyon.*
	Múrmi,	*Chuspá.*
	Magar,	*I'dáng-cha.*
	Tháksya,	*Ho-alába.*
	Pákhya,	*Caret.*
	Newár,	*Tha-thing.*
	Limbu,	*Kon-pha-dong-ba.*
Kiranti Group (East Nepal).	Kiránti,	*Woïn súko.*
	Rodong,	*Tyaskwa ngo.*
	Rúngchenbung,	*Wöïnsa.*
	Chhingtángya,	*Bákhyakkha.*
	Náchhereng,	*Antok-gná.*
	Wáling,	*Múgnek.*
	Yákha,	*Naktog-ha, ná.*
	Chourásya,	*Ansi-me.*
	Kulungya,	*Wántwa, wadommo.*
	Thulungya,	*Ohom.*
	Báhingya,	*Yekho, mekho.*
	Lohorong,	*Idok, mo-dok.*
	Lambichhong,	*Natte-khá, khá.*
	Bálali,	*Kodokpá.*
	Sáng-páng,	*Otá.*
	Dúmi,	*Temphem.*
	Kháling,	*Támphem.*
	Dungmáli,	*Ignego.*
Broken Tribes of Nepal.	Dárhi,	*Ye-sai.*
	Denwár,	*Ye-nhe.*
	Pahri,	*Ye-re.*
	Chepáng,	*Caret.*
	Bhrámu,	*He, khákső.*
	Váyu,	*I'-ma.*
	Kuswar,	*I'-sege.*
	Kusunda,	*Tantan.*
	Tháru,	*Háṇ.*
	Lepcha (Sikkim),	*A'lom.*
	Bhúṭáni v. Lhopa,	*Ode, de.*

N.-E. Bengal.	Bodo,	*Worin, risha, idi, úrin.*
	Dhimál,	*U'dong, usáng.*
	Kocch,	*Weo-mon, temon.*
	Garo,	*U'gándá.*
	Kácharí,	*Caret.*
Eastern Frontier of Bengal.	Munipuri,	*Asundouna.*
	Míthán Nágá,	*Caret.*
	Tablung Nágá,	*Caret.*
	Khári Nágá,	*Itango.*
	Angámi Nágá,	*Tsawe.*
	Námsáng Nágá,	*A'rarang.*
	Nowgong Nágá,	*A'nyakáng.*
	Tengsa Nágá,	*Atti.*
	Abor Miri,	*Pua.*
	Sibságar Miri,	*Umpe.*
	Deoria Chutia,	*Lakireni.*
	Singpho,	*Ndaisat.*
Arrakan & Burmah.	Burman (*written*),	*Thoso.*
	Burman (*spoken*),	*Tho-tho, the-né.*
	Khyeng v. Shou,	*Caret.*
	Kámi,	*Ka.*
	Kúmi,	*Caret.*
	Mrú v. Toung,	*Caret.*
	Sák,	*Caret.*
Siam & Tenasserim.	Talain v. Mon,	*Top-peun.*
	Sgau-karen,	*De-i, de-ne.*
	Pwo-karen,	*Bayi.*
	Toungh-thu,	*Nay-yo.*
	Shán,	*Tso-na-youk.*
	Annamitic,	*Väi.*
	Siamese,	*Men-ran-ni, yang nan, chen.*
	Ahom,	*Plai.*
	Khámti,	*Nang nai.*
	Laos,	*Caret.*
Central India.	Ho (Kol),	*Enleka.*
	Kol (Singhbhum),	*I'nlikate.*
	Santáli,	*Nangká, oṇko, huṇkate, iná-leko, neṇkán.*
	Bhúmij,	*Nekagia.*
	Uráon,	*Yeli.*
	Mundala,	*Nikemeh.*
	Rájmahali,	*Indeki.*
	Goṇḍi,	*I'hún.*
	Gayeti,	*Caret.*
	Rutluk,	*Caret.*
	Naikude,	*Caret.*
	Kolami,	*Caret.*
	Mádi,	*Caret.*
	Mádia,	*Caret.*
	Kuri,	*Caret.*
	Keikádi,	*Caret.*
	Khoṇḍ,	*Yisingi.*
	Sávara,	*Yettená.*
	Gadaba,	*Vokke.*
	Yerukala,	*Yiṭe.*
	Chentsu,	*Yi, yemune.*
Southern India.	Tamiḷ, anc.,	*Caret.*
	Tamiḷ, mod.,	*Ippaḍi.*
	Malayáḷma, anc.,	*Caret.*
	Malayáḷma, mod.,	*Ingngine.*
	Telugu,	*Ittá.*
	Karṇáṭaka, anc.,	*Caret.*
	Karṇáṭaka, mod.,	*Hige, intu.*
	Tuḷuva,	*Inchene.*
	Kurgi,	*Innane.*
	Toḍuva,	*Iggas.*
	Toḍa,	*Ingei, angei.*
	Kóta,	*A'te, angei.*
	Baḍaga,	*Háge.*
	Kuṟumba,	*Háge.*
	Iruḷa,	*Ippaḍi.*
	Malabar,	*Ippaḍi, avoethamaka.*
	Sinhalese,	*Mesi.*

Types.

Inflecting.	SANSKRIT,	*-e, -bhyám,*[1] *-bhyas*[2] (dat.).
	ARABIC,	*Ila, l* (insep. prefix).
Compounding.	BASK,	*-ra, -rat ; gana, ganat.*
	FINNIC,	*-lle.*
	MAGYAR,	*-ra, -ba.*
	TURKISH,	*-ah, -eh.*
	CIRCASSIAN,	*Caret.*
	GEORGIAN,	*-sa.*
	MONGOLIAN,	*-to, -tu, -do, -du.*
	MANTSHU,	*-de.*
	JAVANESE, Ngoko,	*Marang.*
	JAVANESE, Krama,	*Dateng.*
	MALAY,	*Ka, ákan.*
Isolating.	CHINESE, Nankin,	*Kih.*
	CHINESE, Pekin,	*Kei.*
	CHINESE, Canton,	*Kwo.*
	CHINESE, Shanghai,	*Taw.*
	AMOY, Colloquial,	*Kàu.*
	JAPANESE,	*-ni.*
	Brahuí,	*-ne, -te.*
Chinese Frontier & Tibet.	Gyámi,	*Khá.*
	Gyárung,	*Caret.*
	Tákpa,	*Syá, la.*
	Mányak,	*We.*
	Thochú,	*Shil.*
	Sokpa,	*Tú.*
	Horpa,	*Gi* (?), *da.*
	Tibetan (*written*),	*Lá, tú, dú, ra, sú.*
	Tibetan (*spoken*),	*Lá.*
Nepal (east to west).	Serpa,	*Lá.*
	Súnwár,	*Kali.*
	Gúrung,	*De.*
	Múrmi,	*Dá.*
	Magar,	*Kí.*
	Tháksya,	*Dhyári.*
	Pákhya,	*La.*
	Newár,	*Yáta.*
	Limbu,	*Mo, nin.*
Kiranti Group (East Nepal).	Kiránti,	*Caret.*
	Rodong,	*Caret.*
	Rúngchenbung,	*Caret.*
	Chhingtángya,	*Lagi.*
	Náchhereng,	*Caret.*
	Wáling,	*Caret.*
	Yákha,	*A'.*
	Chourásya,	*Caret.*
	Kulungya,	*Caret.*
	Thulungya,	*Caret.*
	Báhingya,	*Caret.*
	Lohorong,	*Caret.*
	Lambichhong,	*Caret.*
	Báláli,	*Caret.*
	Sáng-páng,	*Caret.*
	Dúmi,	*Caret.*
	Kháling,	*Caret.*
	Dungmáli,	*Caret.*
Broken Tribes of Nepal.	Dárhi,	*Lai.*
	Denwár,	*Ki.*
	Pahri,	*Yá-ta.*
	Chepáng,	*Sái.*
	Bhrámu,	*Tú.*
	Váyu,	*Caret.*
	Kuswar,	*Lái.*
	Kusunda,	*Lái.*
	Tháru,	*Keráke.*
	Lepcha (Sikkim),	*Ká, rem.*
	Bhútáni v. Lhopa,	*Lö.*
N.-E. Bengal.	Bodo,	*-no.*
	Dhimál,	*-eng.*
	Kocch,	*-ko, -no* (?).
	Garo,	*Ná.*
	Káchári,	*Caret.*
Eastern Frontier of Bengal.	Munipuri,	*Da* (*na* ?).
	Míthán Nágá,	*Caret.*
	Tablung Nágá,	*Caret.*
	Khári Nágá,	*Ná.*
	Angámi Nágá,	*Caret.*
	Námsáng Nágá,	*Nang.*
	Nowgong Nágá,	*Tang.*
	Tengsa Nágá,	*Nai.*
	Abor Miri,	*Telópu.*
	Sibságar Miri,	*Lope.*
	Deoria Chutia,	*Caret.*
	Singpho,	*Fe.*
Arrakan & Burmah.	Burman (*written*),	*A'.*
	Burman (*spoken*),	*A', go.*
	Khyeng v. Shou,	*A'.*
	Kámi,	*A'.*
	Kúmi,	*Caret.*
	Mrú v. Toung,	*Caret.*
	Sák,	*Caret.*
Siam & Tenasserim.	Talain v. Mon,	*Pway.*
	Sgau-karen,	*Su.*
	Pwo-karen,	*Tsu.*
	Toungh-thu,	*En.*
	Shán,	*Caret.*
	Annamitic,	*Kyo.*
	Siamese,	*Ke.*
	Ahom,	*Caret.*
	Khámti,	*Hang, ti.*
	Laos,	*Caret.*
Central India.	Ho (Kol),	*-té.*
	Kol (Singhbhum),	*Té* (*then* ?).
	Santáli,	*Seh* (in compos.), *-the, -then, -phed.*
	Bhúmij,	*the.*
	Uráon,	*Gai.*
	Mundala,	*Ko.*
	Rájmahali,	*-the* (?).
	Goṇḍi,	*Baina.*
	Gayeti,	*Caret.*
	Rutluk,	*Caret.*
	Naikude,	*Caret.*
	Kolami,	*Caret.*
	Mádi,	*Caret.*
	Mádia,	*Caret.*
	Kuri,	*Caret.*
	Keikádi,	*Ku.*
	Khoṇḍ,	*Caret.*
	Sávara,	*Tí.*
	Gadaba,	*No.*
	Yerukala,	*Ku.*
	Chentsu,	*Ku.*
Southern India.	Tamiḻ, anc.,	*Caret.*
	Tamiḻ, mod.,	*-ku, -gu.*
	Malayáḷma, anc.,	*Caret.*
	Malayáḷma, mod.,	*-kka, -nna.*
	Telugu,	*Ku, ki.*
	Karṇáṭaka, anc.,	*Caret.*
	Karṇáṭaka, mod.,	*Ge, kke.*
	Tuḷuva,	*Ku, ge.*
	Kurgi,	*-ku, -gu.*
	Toḍuva,	*K.*
	Toḍa,	*Ge.*
	Kóta,	*Ge.*
	Baḍaga,	*Ga.*
	Kurumba,	*Ge, ke.*
	Iruḷa,	*Ke.*
	Malabar,	*Ku.*
	Sinhalese,	*-ṭa.*

	Types.	
Inflecting.	SANSKRIT,	*Adya.*
	ARABIC,	*Ilyoum.*
Compounding.	BASK,	*Gaur, egun.*
	FINNIC,	*Tanapana.*
	MAGYAR,	*Ma.*
	TURKISH,	*Bugun.*
	CIRCASSIAN,	*Nep.*
	GEORGIAN,	*Dghes.*
	MONGOLIAN,	*Ene, edur.*
	MANTSHU,	*Enenggi.*
	JAVANESE, Ngoko,	*Dinna-iki.*
	JAVANESE, Krama,	*Dinten-punniki.*
	MALAY,	*Harini.*
Isolating.	CHINESE, Nankin,	*Kin-jih.*
	CHINESE, Pekin,	*Chin-jih.*
	CHINESE, Canton,	*Kam-yat.*
	CHINESE, Shanghai,	*Kiang-tsaw.*
	AMOY, Colloquial,	*Kin-ná-jit.*
	JAPANESE,	*Kon-nichi.*
	Brahuí,	*Ainú.*
Chinese Frontier & Tibet.	Gyámi,	*Chin-the.*
	Gyárung,	*Pish-nyi.*
	Tákpa,	*Tashi.*
	Mányak,	*Tanyúr.*
	Thochú,	*Pashi.*
	Sokpa,	*In dúr.*
	Horpa,	*Pas-ni.*
	Tibetan (*written*),	*Dering.*
	Tibetan (*spoken*),	*Thiring.*
Nepal (east to west).	Serpa,	*Táring.*
	Súnwár,	*Mún-láti.*
	Gúrung,	*Tíní.*
	Múrmi,	*Tíní.*
	Magar,	*Chini.*
	Tháksya,	*Námá.*
	Pákhya,	*A'ja.*
	Newár,	*Thawon.*
	Limbu,	*Ain.*
Kiranti Group (East Nepal).	Kiránti,	*Ai.*
	Rodong,	*A'i, ále.*
	Rúngchenbung,	*Aya, ái.*
	Chhingtángya,	*Páyam.*
	Náchhereng,	*A'se.*
	Wáling,	*A'ilo, áyo.*
	Yákha,	*Hoh'yen.*
	Chourásya,	*Tianso.*
	Kulungya,	*Yese.*
	Thulungya,	*Anep.*
	Báhingya,	*A'na.*
	Lohorong,	*A'yu.*
	Lambichhong,	*Hálok.*
	Báláli,	*I-sin.*
	Sáng-páng,	*Yese.*
	Dúmi,	*A'nyol.*
	Kháling,	*Anyalo.*
	Dungmáli,	*A'-i.*
Broken Tribes of Nepal.	Dárhi,	*A'ju.*
	Denwár,	*A'-ju.*
	Pahri,	*Tha-ra.*
	Chepáng,	*Ten.*
	Bhrámu,	*Ti-ya.*
	Váyu,	*Ti-ri.*
	Kuswar,	*A'-ja.*
	Kusunda,	*Itwaji, ipwaji.*
	Tháru,	*Aju.*
	Lepcha (Sikkim),	*Sarong.*
	Bhúṭáni v. Lhopa,	*Dharing.*

N.-E. Bengal.	Bodo,	*Dine.*
	Dhimál,	*Nani.*
	Kocch,	*Aj, adhya* (?).
	Garo,	*Tingni.*
	Kácháni,	*Dinesanché.*
Eastern Frontier of Bengal.	Munipuri,	*Ashi.*
	Míthán Nágá,	*Anyi.*
	Tablung Nágá,	*Tinyi.*
	Khári Nágá,	*Thani.*
	Angámi Nágá,	*Teje.*
	Námsáng Nágá,	*Tajá.*
	Nowgong Nágá,	*Tannu.*
	Tengsa Nágá,	*Thanglu.*
	Abor Miri,	*Silo.*
	Sibságar Miri,	*Silo.*
	Deoria Chutia,	*Dinineni.*
	Singpho,	*Daini.*
Arrakan & Burmah.	Burman (*written*),	*Yane.*
	Burman (*spoken*),	*Yane, thu-khana.*
	Khyeng v. Shou,	*Tun-ap.*
	Kámi,	*Wei-ni.*
	Kúmi,	*Wá-i-ni.*
	Mrú v. Toung,	*Caret.*
	Sák,	*Caret.*
Siam & Tenasserim.	Talain v. Mon,	*Thang waynau.*
	Sgau-karen,	*M'sah, m'tsai.*
	Pwo-karen,	*L'ni-yu.*
	Toungh-thu,	*Hau-ne.*
	Shán,	*Ma-hniht.*
	Annamitic,	*Hôm-nay.*
	Siamese,	*Wan-ni, wan ni.*
	Ahom,	*Banai.*
	Khámti,	*Caret.*
	Laos,	*Wanni.*
Central India.	Ho (Kol),	*Tising.*
	Kol (Singhbhum),	*Ná.*
	Santáli,	*Teheng.*
	Bhúmij,	*Tising.*
	Uráon,	*Inam.*
	Mundala,	*Tihin.*
	Rájmahali,	*Ine.*
	Goṇḍi,	*Naind, naiú.*
	Gayeti,	*Caret.*
	Rutluk,	*Caret.*
	Naikude,	*Caret.*
	Kolami,	*Caret.*
	Mádi,	*Caret.*
	Mádia,	*Caret.*
	Kuri,	*Caret.*
	Keikádi,	*Iuanu.*
	Khoṇḍ,	*Nenju.*
	Sávara,	*Nangadini.*
	Gadaba,	*Yinchá.*
	Yerukala,	*I'mán.*
	Chentsu,	*Ayije, ajko.*
Southern India.	Tamiḷ, anc.,	*Ittai.*
	Tamiḷ, mod.,	*Inṟu, innaki.*
	Malayáḷma, anc.,	*Caret.*
	Malayáḷma, mod.,	*Inna.*
	Telugu,	*Neḍu.*
	Karṇáṭaka, anc.,	*Caret.*
	Karṇaṭaka, mod.,	*I'hottu.*
	Tuḷuva,	*Ini.*
	Kurgi,	*Indu.*
	Toḍuva, }	*Iḍḍ.*
	Toḍa, }	*E'du.*
	Kóta,	*Inde.*
	Baḍaga,	*Indu.*
	Kuṟumba,	*Indu.*
	Iruḷa,	*Indu.*
	Malabar,	*Indu, indeikku.*
	Sinhalese,	*Ada.*

Group	Language	To-morrow
	Types.	
Inflecting.	SANSKṚIT,	*'Svaḥ.*
	ARABIC,	*Bukra, ghadá.*
Compounding.	BASK,	*Bigar, biar.*
	FINNIC,	*Huomenna.*
	MAGYAR,	*Kolnap.*
	TURKISH,	*Yarin.*
	CIRCASSIAN,	*Caret.*
	GEORGIAN,	*Khkal.*
	MONGOLIAN,	*Managhai.*
	MANTSHU,	*Chimakha, chimari.*
	JAVANESE, Ngoko,	*Sěsok.*
	JAVANESE, Krama,	*Benjing-enjing.*
	MALAY,	*Esok-hári.*
Isolating.	CHINESE, Nankin,	*Ming-jïh.*
	CHINESE, Pekin,	*Ming-jih.*
	CHINESE, Canton,	*Ming-yat.*
	CHINESE, Shanghai,	*Ming-tsaw.*
	AMOY, Colloquial,	*Bin-ná-jït, bin-ná-chài.*
	JAPANESE,	*Myonichi, meo-nichi.*
	Brahuí,	*Pagí.*
Chinese Frontier & Tibet.	Gyámi,	*Min the.*
	Gyárung,	*Sos-nyi.*
	Tákpa,	*Nogor.*
	Mányak,	*Sorúḥ.*
	Thochú,	*Sozyú.*
	Sokpa,	*Mágár.*
	Horpa,	*Khasi.*
	Tibetan (*written*),	*Sang, thore.*
	Tibetan (*spoken*),	*Sáng.*
Nepal (east to west).	Serpa,	*Thoráng.*
	Súnwár,	*Dis.*
	Gúrung,	*Nhá gá.*
	Múrmi,	*Nangar.*
	Magar,	*Pyúngúra.*
	Tháksya,	*Tila.*
	Pákhya,	*Bholi.*
	Newár,	*Ka-nhai.*
	Limbu,	*Tándik.*
Kiránti Group (East Nepal).	Kiránti,	*Mang-koleng.*
	Rodong,	*Seṇ-la, seṇ-lam.*
	Rúngchenbung,	*Mángkolen.*
	Chhingtángya,	*Wárangda.*
	Náchhereng,	*Sála.*
	Wáling,	*Hámáye, mangkolen.*
	Yákha,	*Wáng' di.*
	Chourásya,	*Dis'-na.*
	Kulungya,	*Desa ali'.*
	Thulungya,	*Dika.*
	Báhingya,	*Dil'la.*
	Lohorong,	*Weng-dá.*
	Lambichhong,	*Wáring.*
	Báláli,	*Selmá.*
	Sáng-páng,	*Selámá.*
	Dúmi,	*Dis'yá.*
	Kháling,	*Disá-á.*
	Dungmáli,	*Hàmá-young.*
Broken Tribes of Nepal.	Dárhi,	*Kálú.*
	Denwár,	*Ka-lhi, ka-l-hi.*
	Pahri,	*Kin-chi.*
	Chepáng,	*Syáng.*
	Bhrámu,	*Wo-gai.*
	Váyu,	*Nu-kana.*
	Kuswar,	*Kál-hi.*
	Kusunda,	*Gorak.*
	Tháru,	*Kálhi.*
	Lepcha (Sikkim),	*Lúk.*
	Bhúṭáni v. Lhopa,	*Nábah.*

Group	Language	To-morrow
N.-E. Bengal.	Bodo,	*Gábún.*
	Dhimál,	*Júmni.*
	Kocch,	*Kal, kalya* (?).
	Garo,	*Gánáp.*
	Káchári,	*Kapun sanche.*
Eastern Frontier of Bengal.	Munipuri,	*Aráng.*
	Míthán Nágá,	*Nai-ni.*
	Tablung Nágá,	*Ngai-ni.*
	Khári Nágá,	*Asang.*
	Angámi Nágá,	*Thedu.*
	Námsáng Nágá,	*Ninap.*
	Nowgong Nágá,	*Asong.*
	Tengsa Nágá,	*A'sang.*
	Abor Miri,	*Iampo.*
	Sibságar Miri,	*Yampo.*
	Deoria Chutia,	*Disuini.*
	Singpho,	*Mphoni.*
Arrakan & Burmah.	Burman (*written*),	*Nakphan.*
	Burman (*spoken*),	*Netphán.*
	Khyeng v. Shou,	*Nhát-ta.*
	Kámi,	*Cha-khon.*
	Kúmi,	*Qui-dám.*
	Mrú v. Toung,	*Caret.*
	Sák,	*Caret.*
Siam & Tenasserim.	Talain v. Mon,	*Li-ya.*
	Sgau-karen,	*'Kai-ghaw.*
	Pwo-karen,	*Ke-ghau-koh.*
	Toungh-thu,	*Mu-reu.*
	Shán,	*Má-hpot.*
	Annamitic,	*Ngay-mai.*
	Siamese,	*Hpunei phrungni.*
	Ahom,	*Sang-manai.*
	Khámti,	*Maphok.*
	Laos,	*Phuk.*
Central India.	Ho (Kol),	*Gappa.*
	Kol (Singhbhum),	*Gúphá.*
	Santáli,	*Gápá* (declined with *-ko*, *-b*, [*-pe*]).
	Bhúmij,	*Gúphá.*
	Uráon,	*Nelá.*
	Mundala,	*Gápá.*
	Rájmahali,	*Lele.*
	Goṇḍi,	*Nadi, ningnai.*
	Gayeti,	*Caret.*
	Rutluk,	*Caret.*
	Naikude,	*Caret.*
	Kolami,	*Caret.*
	Mádi,	*Caret.*
	Mádia,	*Caret.*
	Kuri,	*Caret.*
	Keikádi,	*Nalaka.*
	Khoṇd,	*Rosi.*
	Sávara,	*Biyo.*
	Gadaba,	*Beyyar.*
	Yerukala,	*Nesú.*
	Chentsu,	*Kayil.*
Southern India.	Tamiḷ, anc.,	*Pinrei.*
	Tamiḷ, mod.,	*Nálei, náḷeikku.*
	Malayáḷma, anc.,	*Caret.*
	Malayáḷma, mod.,	*Náḷe.*
	Telugu,	*Elli* (anc.), *repu* (mod.).
	Karṇáṭaka, anc.,	*Caret.*
	Karṇáṭaka, mod.,	*Náḷe.*
	Tuḷuva,	*Elli.*
	Kurgi,	*Náḷe.*
	Toḍuva, } Toḍa, }	*Mokol.* / *Belkash.*
	Kóta,	*Nalke.*
	Baḍaga,	*Nale.*
	Kuṛumba,	*Nale.*
	Iruḷa,	*Nale.*
	Malabar,	*Nálei.*
	Sinhalese,	*Heta.*

Group	Language	When?
	Types.	
Inflecting.	SANSKRIT,	*Kadá, karhi.*
	ARABIC,	*Lamma, mata, iza.*
Compounding.	BASK,	*Noiz.*
	FINNIC,	*Koska.*
	MAGYAR,	*Mikor.*
	TURKISH,	*Caret.*
	CIRCASSIAN,	*Caret.*
	GEORGIAN,	*Odes.*
	MONGOLIAN,	*Ghetsighe.*
	MANTSHU,	*Atanggi.*
	JAVANESE, Ngoko,	*Kapan.*
	JAVANESE, Krama,	*Kapan.*
	MALAY,	*Kápan.*
Isolating.	CHINESE, Nankin,	*Shin-mo-shi.*
	CHINESE, Pekin,	*Shen-mo-shih.*
	CHINESE, Canton,	*Ki-shi.*
	CHINESE, Shanghai,	*Ki-sz'.*
	AMOY, Colloquial,	*Ti-si.*
	JAPANESE,	*Itsugoro, itsu.*
	Brahuí,	*Chi-wakt.*
Chinese Frontier & Tibet.	Gyámi,	*Ná-khún.*
	Gyárung,	*This-dûi, kwástra.*
	Tákpa,	*Kashú.*
	Mányak,	*Ninkhe.*
	Thochú,	*Thisni.*
	Sokpa,	*Khech-che.*
	Horpa,	*Sa-deu.*
	Tibetan (*written*),	*Gang-tse, nam.*
	Tibetan (*spoken*),	*Kha-dwi.*
Nepal (east to west).	Serpa,	*Tanam.*
	Súnwár,	*Gená.*
	Gúrung,	*Kái-mo.*
	Múrmi,	*Kái-ma.*
	Magar,	*Syen.*
	Tháksya,	*Tigni.*
	Pákhya,	*Caret.*
	Newár,	*Gola.*
	Limbu,	*A'phále.*
Kiranti Group (East Nepal).	Kiránti,	*Demkhe.*
	Rodong,	*Delo.*
	Rúngchenbung,	*Demkhe.*
	Chhingtángya,	*A'nám.*
	Náchhereng,	*A'dem.*
	Wáling,	*Demkha, khinam.*
	Yákha,	*Hetning, heh'ning.*
	Chourásya,	*A'selo.*
	Kulungya,	*Hádolo, hádemiye.*
	Thulungya,	*Hám-syuká.*
	Báhingya,	*Gyána.*
	Lohorong,	*A'nám, hánám.*
	Lambichhong,	*Hembína.*
	Bálálí,	*Hádemlo.*
	Sáng-páng,	*Hallo.*
	Dúmi,	*Helo.*
	Kháling,	*Hebelo.*
	Dungmálí,	*Khinám.*
Broken Tribes of Nepal.	Dárhi,	*Káhe.*
	Denwár,	*Kaṇhin.*
	Pahri,	*Gwe-the.*
	Chepáng,	*Caret.*
	Bhrámu,	*Kai-lhe.*
	Váyu,	*Há-ke.*
	Kuswar,	*Ka-khen.*
	Kusunda,	*A'sahi.*
	Tháru,	*Kabahu.*
	Lepcha (Sikkim),	*Sathá.*
	Bhúṭáni v. Lhopa,	*Nam.*
N.-E. Bengal.	Bodo,	*Mábelá.*
	Dhimál,	*Helou.*
	Kocch,	*Kab.*
	Garo,	*Bibá.*
	Káchári,	*Caret.*
Eastern Frontier of Bengal.	Munipuri,	*Horen.*
	Míthán Nágá,	*Caret.*
	Tablung Nágá,	*Caret.*
	Khári Nágá,	*Kuim.*
	Angámi Nágá,	*Tadzune.*
	Námsáng Nágá,	*Matu suanta.*
	Nowgong Nágá,	*Kodang.*
	Tengsa Nágá,	*Kápá.*
	Abor Miri,	*Caret.*
	Sibságar Miri,	*Udilo.*
	Deoria Chutia,	*Dumoni.*
	Singpho,	*Yango.*
Arrakan & Burmah.	Burman (*written*),	*Bhesokhá.*
	Burman (*spoken*),	*Bheṭhokhá.*
	Khyeng v. Shou,	*I'kho-á.*
	Kámi,	*Há-ni-kán.*
	Kúmi,	*Má-na-ká.*
	Mrú v. Toung,	*Caret.*
	Sák,	*Caret.*
Siam & Tenasserim.	Talain v. Mon,	*A-khalarau.*
	Sgau-karen,	*Tu, kai-lai.*
	Pwo-karen,	*Taung.*
	Toungh-thu,	*Tu-ma.*
	Shán,	*Chyain-lu.*
	Annamitic,	*Khi-nao.*
	Siamese,	*Hpalahighu, nua-dai.*
	Ahom,	*Phreu-nai.*
	Khámti,	*Caret.*
	Laos,	*Caret.*
Central India.	Ho (Kol),	*Chooila.*
	Kol (Singhbhum),	*Chúilá.*
	Santáli,	*Tin-joho, tinare, okáhiláh, tisah.*
	Bhúmij,	*Caret.*
	Uráon,	*Eká here.*
	Mundala,	*Chielo, chimto.*
	Rájmahali,	*I-kono.*
	Goṇḍi,	*Baska, vang-pur.*
	Gayeti,	*Caret.*
	Rutluk,	*Caret.*
	Naikude,	*Caret.*
	Kolami,	*Caret.*
	Mádi,	*Caret.*
	Mádia,	*Caret.*
	Kuri,	*Caret.*
	Keikádi,	*Yepo.*
	Khoṇḍ,	*Yeseká.*
	Sávara,	*Yenga.*
	Gadaba,	*Yiṇḍoyi.*
	Yerukala,	*Yeppuḍu.*
	Chentsu,	*Kekhau, kekkoṇeki.*
Southern India.	Tamiḷ, anc.,	*Eppozhudu.*
	Tamiḷ, mod.,	*Eppoḍu, yeppo.*
	Malayáḷma, anc.,	*Caret.*
	Malayáḷma, mod.,	*Eppol.*
	Telugu,	*Eppuḍu, yeppuḍu.*
	Karṇáṭaka, anc.,	*Caret.*
	Karṇáṭaka, mod.,	*Yávága.*
	Tuḷuva,	*Epag.*
	Kurgi,	*Ekka.*
	Toḍuva,	*Caret.*
	Toḍa,	*Etvan.*
	Kóta,	*Yennale.*
	Baḍaga,	*Yegva.*
	Kuṛumba,	*Yega.*
	Iruḷa,	*Yepa.*
	Malabar,	*Eppothu.*
	Sinhalese,	*Kawadá.*

Group	Language	Where?
	Types.	
Inflecting.	SANSKRIT,	*Kva, kutra.*
	ARABIC,	*Ayn, haith.*
Compounding.	BASK,	*Non, nun.*
	FINNIC,	*Kusa.*
	MAGYAR,	*Hol.*
	TURKISH,	*Nereye.*
	CIRCASSIAN,	*Tehduey.*
	GEORGIAN,	*Kidre.*
	MONGOLIAN,	*Ali.*
	MANTSHU,	*Aibide.*
	JAVANESE, Ngoko,	*Endi.*
	JAVANESE, Krama,	*Pundi.*
	MALAY,	*Dimána.*
Isolating.	CHINESE, Nankin,	*Shin-mo-ti-fang, na-li.*
	CHINESE, Pekin,	*Shen-mo-ti-fang, na-li.*
	CHINESE, Canton,	*Pinchü.*
	CHINESE, Shanghai,	*Há-li.*
	AMOY, Colloquial,	*Ta-loh-úi.*
	JAPANESE,	*Doko, do-koni.*
	Brahuí,	*Aráde.*
Chinese Frontier & Tibet.	Gyámi,	*Lá-li.*
	Gyárung,	*Katú.*
	Tákpa,	*Gá, gáhá.*
	Mányak,	*Khade.*
	Thochú,	*Tano.*
	Sokpa,	*Thyerthor.*
	Horpa,	*Lore.*
	Tibetan (*written*),	*Gangna.*
	Tibetan (*spoken*),	*Khácho.*
Nepal (east to west).	Serpa,	*Káni.*
	Súnwár,	*Dotha, getha.*
	Gúrung,	*Khanirí.*
	Múrmi,	*Kháin.*
	Magar,	*Kúlak.*
	Tháksya,	*Tomi.*
	Pákhya,	*Kota.*
	Newár,	*Gúkhe.*
	Limbu,	*Atáng.*
Kiranti Group (East Nepal).	Kiránti,	*Khádánú.*
	Rodong,	*Khoda.*
	Rúngchenbung,	*Kháda, kháda-nung.*
	Chhingtángya,	*Hoket.*
	Náchhereng,	*Háppa, hápbále.*
	Wáling,	*Khini, kháda.*
	Yákha,	*Heli'na, henuche.*
	Chourásya,	*Thálo.*
	Kulungya,	*Hápise, hákwade.*
	Thulungya,	*Báte, bánte.*
	Báhingya,	*Gyála, a-júju-di.*
	Lohorong,	*Hángbe, hámpe.*
	Lambichhong,	*Hetne.*
	Báláli,	*Hápábi, hápáng.*
	Sáng-páng,	*Há-pi.*
	Dúmi,	*Khebi.*
	Kháling,	*Khábi.*
	Dungmáli,	*Khibi, khibiyá.*
Broken Tribes of Nepal.	Dárhi,	*Ká-chi.*
	Denwár,	*Ká-chi.*
	Pahri,	*Gu-thá.*
	Chepáng,	*Caret.*
	Bhrámu,	*Ku-nai.*
	Váyu,	*Há-ne.*
	Kuswar,	*Ka-chi-na.*
	Kusunda,	*A'naka.*
	Tháru,	*Kápha.*
	Lepcha (Sikkim),	*Saba, sabi.*
	Bhútáni v. Lhopa,	*Kánú-te.*

Group	Language	Where?
N.-E. Bengal.	Bodo,	*Mouha.*
	Dhimál,	*Hesho.*
	Kocch,	*Kahán.*
	Garo,	*Bil.*
	Káchári,	*Caret.*
Eastern Frontier of Bengal.	Munipuri,	*Keida.*
	Míthán Nágá,	*Pau-pu.*
	Tablung Nágá,	*Taw-wai.*
	Khári Nágá,	*Kuchi.*
	Angámi Nágá,	*Kiraporú.*
	Námsáng Nágá,	*Makoa.*
	Nowgong Nágá,	*Kong.*
	Tengsa Nágá,	*Otiga.*
	Abor Miri,	*Ungkolo.*
	Sibságar Miri,	*Okolon.*
	Deoria Chutia,	*Borong.*
	Singpho,	*Gadegui.*
Arrakan & Burmah.	Burman (*written*),	*Bhemhá.*
	Burman (*spoken*),	*Bhemhá.*
	Khyeng v. Shou,	*Iniám.*
	Kámi,	*Ná-ná-be.*
	Kúmi,	*Má-mo.*
	Mrú v. Toung,	*Caret.*
	Sák,	*Caret.*
Siam & Tenasserim.	Talain v. Mon,	*Alorau.*
	Sgau-karen,	*Pai-lai.*
	Pwo-karen,	*Shaing-te.*
	Toungh-thu,	*Eu-hmay.*
	Shán,	*Kalau.*
	Annamitic,	*Dâu.*
	Siamese,	*Kalau, thi-nai.*
	Ahom,	*Ho.*
	Khámti,	*Thau.*
	Laos,	*Tinai.*
Central India.	Ho (Kol),	*Okoïré.*
	Kol (Singhbhum),	*Okotai.*
	Santáli,	*Ukuri, okáre, okále, okathen.*
	Bhúmij,	*Oko-tháï.*
	Uráon,	*Eksan.*
	Mundala,	*U'thi.*
	Rájmahali,	*Ikeno.*
	Gondi,	*Bugga, vagá.*
	Gayeti,	*Caret.*
	Rutluk,	*Caret.*
	Naikude,	*Caret.*
	Kolami,	*Caret.*
	Mádi,	*Caret.*
	Mádia,	*Caret.*
	Kuri,	*Caret.*
	Keikádi,	*Yekada.*
	Khond,	*Caret.*
	Sávara,	*Tengá.*
	Gadaba,	*Ammano.*
	Yerukala,	*Yite, yenge.*
	Chentsu,	*Kuhaná, kahá.*
Southern India.	Tamil, anc.,	*Evan.*
	Tamil, mod.,	*Engu, yengé.*
	Malayálma, anc.,	*Caret.*
	Malayálma, mod.,	*Evite.*
	Telugu,	*Ekkada, éda.*
	Karnátaka, anc.,	*Caret.*
	Karnátaka, mod.,	*Elli.*
	Tuluva,	*Odeke.*
	Kurgi,	*Yelli.*
	Toduva, }	*Ett.*
	Toda, }	*Et.*
	Kóta,	*Yeye.*
	Badaga,	*Yelli.*
	Kurumba,	*Yelli.*
	Irula,	*Yenge.*
	Malabar,	*Engei.*
	Sinhalese,	*Kohéda.*

	Types.	
Inflecting.	SANSKRIT,	*Kim-artham.*
	ARABIC,	*Limáza, laish.*
Compounding.	BASK,	*Zergatik, zegaiti, zeren.*
	FINNIC,	*Mita.*
	MAGYAR,	*Caret.*
	TURKISH,	*Nichun.*
	CIRCASSIAN,	*Sida.*
	GEORGIAN,	*Rad.*
	MONGOLIAN,	*Yahonotola.*
	MANTSHU,	*Ainu.*
	JAVANESE, Ngoko,	*Punnapaha.*
	JAVANESE, Krama,	*Yagénné.*
	MALAY,	*A'pakárana.*
Isolating.	CHINESE, Nankin,	*Wei-shin-mo.*
	CHINESE, Pekin,	*Wei-shen-mo.*
	CHINESE, Canton,	*Wai-mat-ye.*
	CHINESE, Shanghai,	*Wei-sah.*
	AMOY, Colloquial,	*Sian-sú.*
	JAPANESE,	*Nazhe, nase.*
	Brahuí,	*Antai.*
Chinese Frontier & Tibet.	Gyámi,	*Syá-chú.*
	Gyárung,	*Thús-pe.*
	Tákpa,	*Sagyak.*
	Mányak,	*Hámile.*
	Thochú,	*Niblin, nishi.*
	Sokpa,	*Tharichhin.*
	Horpa,	*A'chú-gno.*
	Tibetan (*written*),	*Caret.*
	Tibetan (*spoken*),	*Khá-in.*
Nepal (east to west).	Serpa,	*Káng.*
	Súnwár,	*Mara.*
	Gúrung,	*Ta.*
	Múrmi,	*Tik.*
	Magar,	*Kútta.*
	Thákysa,	*Caret.*
	Pákhya,	*Caret.*
	Newár,	*Chhá.*
	Limbu,	*The-jokma, the-áng.*
Kiránti Group (East Nepal).	Kiránti,	*Khâïnse.*
	Rodong,	*Dema.*
	Rúngchenbung,	*Dena, dene.*
	Chhingtángya,	*Mechchhá.*
	Náchhereng,	*U'mú.*
	Wáling,	*Dehá-ná.*
	Yákha,	*Irok-há, irok.*
	Chourásya,	*A'se, ámá.*
	Kulungya,	*Dái, dátúkwa.*
	Thulungya,	*Hágna, hamta.*
	Báhingya,	*Marcho, martha.*
	Lohorong,	*Imang-musi, manthoug.*
	Lambichhong,	*Thimmá.*
	Bálálí,	*U'khálo.*
	Sáng-páng,	*Yánpi.*
	Dúmi,	*Mápúne.*
	Kháling,	*Mábi.*
	Dungmálí,	*Tená.*
Broken Tribes of Nepal.	Dárhi,	*Caret.*
	Denwár,	*Caret.*
	Pahri,	*Caret.*
	Chepáng,	*Caret.*
	Bhrámu,	*Caret.*
	Váyu,	*Mis-pa.*
	Kuswar,	*Kyú-hún.*
	Kusunda,	*Caret.*
	Thárú,	*Caret.*
	Lepcha (Sikkim),	*Shú-mat.*
	Bhúṭáni v. Lhopa,	*Kám-be.*
N.-E. Bengal.	Bodo,	*Máno.*
	Dhimál,	*Hai-páli.*
	Kocch,	*Ki-táne.*
	Garo,	*A'táng.*
	Káchári,	*Caret.*
Eastern Frontier of Bengal.	Munipuri,	*Karigi-tumuk.*
	Mithán Nágá,	*Caret.*
	Tablung Nágá,	*Caret.*
	Khári Nágá,	*Chibatsawi.*
	Angámi Nágá,	*Kaji.*
	Námsáng Nágá,	*Reto.*
	Nowgong Nágá,	*Kashia.*
	Tengsa Nágá,	*Kado.*
	Abor Miri,	*Okkiduna.*
	Sibságar Miri,	*Kappu.*
	Deoria Chutia,	*Damno.*
	Singpho,	*Fari.*
Arrakan & Burmah.	Burman (*written*),	*Bheprulo.*
	Burman (*spoken*),	*Bhepyulo.*
	Khyeng v. Shou,	*I'-na-to-ám.*
	Kámi,	*Ta-ú-sá-n'e.*
	Kúmi,	*Caret.*
	Mrú v. Toung,	*Caret.*
	Sák,	*Caret.*
Siam & Tenasserim.	Talain v. Mon,	*Mu-parau.*
	Sgau-karen,	*M'nulai, mu-lai.*
	Pwo-karen,	*Nau-lai.*
	Toungh-thu,	*H'twa-may.*
	Shán,	*Pen-htsau.*
	Annamitic,	*Lám-sao.*
	Siamese,	*Hta mihn, phra aurai.*
	Ahom,	*Wá.*
	Khámti,	*Caret.*
	Laos,	*Caret.*
Central India.	Ho (Kol),	*Chikan-menté.*
	Kol (Singhbhum),	*Chikan-minte.*
	Santáli,	*Chéh, chedá, chetlágih.*
	Bhúmij,	*Chi-lika.*
	Uráon,	*Indari.*
	Mundala,	*Chikanle.*
	Rájmahali,	*Indrik.*
	Goṇḍi,	*Bass-áti, bárad, barri.*
	Gayeti,	*Caret.*
	Rutluk,	*Caret.*
	Naikude,	*Caret.*
	Kolami,	*Caret.*
	Mádi,	*Caret.*
	Mádia,	*Caret.*
	Kuri,	*Caret.*
	Keikádi,	*Yenátuku.*
	Khoṇḍ,	*Annáḍeki.*
	Sávara,	*Jitásamgná.*
	Gadaba,	*Caret.*
	Yerukala,	*Yemmatuku, phaláyá.*
	Chentsu,	*Kissóle.*
Southern India.	Tamiḷ, anc.,	*Ennei.*
	Tamiḷ, mod.,	*En, yédu.*
	Malayáḷma, anc.,	*Caret.*
	Malayáḷma, mod.,	*Entina.*
	Telugu,	*E'la, yenduku.*
	Karṇáṭaka, anc.,	*Caret.*
	Karṇáṭaka, mod.,	*Yátake, yáke.*
	Tuḷuva,	*Jayekk.*
	Kurgi,	*Caret.*
	Toḍuva, }	*Caret.*
	Toḍa, }	*A'ed.*
	Kóta,	*Yendea.*
	Baḍaga,	*Yeka.*
	Kuṛumba,	*Yeka.*
	Iruḷa,	*Yenna.*
	Malabar,	*En, ethukkuka.*
	Sinhalese,	*Äyi.*

Group	Language	With
	Types.	
Inflecting.	SANSKRIT,	*Sam-, sa-, saha.*
	ARABIC,	*Maa.*
Compounding.	BASK,	*-gaz, -kin, -ki.*
	FINNIC,	*Kanssa.*
	MAGYAR,	*-val.*
	TURKISH,	*-ileh.*
	CIRCASSIAN,	*Caret.*
	GEORGIAN,	*-tha.*
	MONGOLIAN,	*Logha, tula.*
	MANTSHU,	*Sasa.*
	JAVANESE, Ngoko,	*Sambi, kambi.*
	JAVANESE, Krama,	*Kalayan.*
	MALAY,	*Dangan.*
Isolating.	CHINESE, Nankin,	*T'ung.*
	CHINESE, Pekin,	*T'ung.*
	CHINESE, Canton,	*T'ung.*
	CHINESE, Shanghai,	*Teh-tsz', ho.*
	AMOY, Colloquial,	*Kap.*
	JAPANESE,	*-to, tomoni.*
	Brahuí,	*-to.*
Chinese Frontier & Tibet.	Gyámi,	*Kháng-chhen.*
	Gyárung,	*Kri, khyás.*
	Tákpa,	*Núm-lang.*
	Mányak,	*Pháe.*
	Thochú,	*Ong.*
	Sokpa,	*Thángdi.*
	Horpa,	*A'che.*
	Tibetan (*written*),	*Lhanchig.*
	Tibetan (*spoken*),	*Lá, dá.*
Nepal (east to west).	Serpa,	*Táng.*
	Súnwár,	*Núh.*
	Gúrung,	*De, deye.*
	Múrmi,	*Ta.*
	Magar,	*Le-tháng, kháta.*
	Tháksya,	*Gnáyero.*
	Pákhya,	*Saga.*
	Newár,	*Yaken, nápo.*
	Limbu,	*Nú, teng.*
Kiranti Group (East Nepal).	Kiránti,	*Dá.*
	Rodong,	*Pida.*
	Rúngchenbung,	*It'nan.*
	Chhingtángya,	*Núng.*
	Náchhereng,	*Gnáng, máng.*
	Wáling,	*Pi, edá, inan.*
	Yákha,	*Núng.*
	Chourásya,	*Bilo.*
	Kulungya,	*Gámpi, lo.*
	Thulungya,	*Nung.*
	Báhingya,	*Nung.*
	Lohorong,	*Nung.*
	Lambichhong,	*Lok.*
	Báláli,	*Lung.*
	Sáng-páng,	*Pi.*
	Dúmi,	*Bi, ke.*
	Kháling,	*Pobi, kolo.*
	Dungmáli,	*Bit'pi, náng*
Broken Tribes of Nepal.	Dárhi,	*Súi.*
	Denwár,	*I'n.*
	Pahri,	*Nang.*
	Chepáng,	*I.*
	Bhrámu,	*Chon.*
	Váyu,	*Nong.*
	Kuswar,	*Sin.*
	Kusunda,	*Tangche.*
	Tháru,	*Saga.*
	Lepcha (Sikkim),	*Sá, tyol.*
	Bhúṭáni v. Lhopa,	*Chá, dá, cháro.*
N.-E. Bengal.	Bodo,	*Lago, jong.*
	Dhimál,	*Dopá, dosá.*
	Kocch,	*Dosor, sáthe.*
	Garo,	*Mon.*
	Káchári,	*Caret.*
Eastern Frontier of Bengal.	Munipuri,	*Loi-nit-na.*
	Míthán Nágá,	*Caret.*
	Tablung Nágá,	*Caret.*
	Khári Nágá,	*Ashe.*
	Angámi Nágá,	*Caret.*
	Námsáng Nágá,	*Caret.*
	Nowgong Nágá,	*Yasu.*
	Tengsa Nágá,	*Suga.*
	Abor Miri,	*Caret.*
	Sibságar Miri,	*Logolo.*
	Deoria Chutia,	*Caret.*
	Singpho,	*Caret.*
Arrakan & Burmah.	Burman (*written*),	*Nhang.*
	Burman (*spoken*),	*Nhen, hnen.*
	Khyeng v. Shou,	*Yung.*
	Kámi,	*Há-i.*
	Kúmi,	*Caret.*
	Mrú v. Toung,	*Caret.*
	Sák,	*Caret.*
Siam & Tenasserim.	Talain v. Mon,	*Ku.*
	Sgau-karen,	*Dau, atho.*
	Pwo-karen,	*Dai.*
	Toungh-thu,	*Caret.*
	Shán,	*Han.*
	Annamitic,	*Kung.*
	Siamese,	*Kha, duei.*
	Ahom,	*Chum.*
	Khámti,	*Caret.*
	Laos,	*Caret.*
Central India.	Ho (Kol),	*Lo, teinredo.*
	Kol (Singhbhum),	*Tote.*
	Santáli,	*Gáte, túlui, saüngte.*
	Bhúmij,	*Tului (?).*
	Uráon,	*Sang.*
	Mundala,	*Gatt, minna.*
	Rájmahali,	*Guni.*
	Goṇḍi,	*Sang.*
	Gayeti,	*Caret.*
	Rutluk,	*Caret.*
	Naikude,	*Caret.*
	Kolami,	*Caret.*
	Mádi,	*Caret.*
	Mádia,	*Caret.*
	Kuri,	*Caret.*
	Keikádi,	*Caret.*
	Khoṇḍ,	*Caret.*
	Sávara,	*Ruhá.*
	Gadaba,	*Bonom.*
	Yerukala,	*Tote.*
	Chentsu,	*Sang.*
Southern India.	Tamiḷ, anc.,	*Caret.*
	Tamiḷ, mod.,	*-ōḍu, -kúḍa.*
	Malayáḷma, anc.,	*Caret.*
	Malayáḷma, mod.,	*-oṭe, -kúṭe.*
	Telugu,	*-to.*
	Karṇáṭaka, anc.,	*Caret.*
	Karṇáṭaka, mod.,	*-kúḍa, -sangaḍa.*
	Tuḷuva,	*-ottugu.*
	Kurgi,	*-kúḍe.*
	Toḍuva, }	*Caret.*
	Toḍa, }	*Caret.*
	Kóta,	*-sengaḍa.*
	Baḍaga,	*-koḍa.*
	Kuṛumba,	*-sangaḍa.*
	Iruḷa,	*-kúḍa.*
	Malabar,	*-udan, odu, idat-thu.*
	Sinhalese,	*-samaga.*

Group	Types.	
Inflecting.	SANSKRIT,	*Antar.*
	ARABIC,	*Jouá.*
Compounding.	BASK,	*Barruan, barrena, barrura, barnen.*
	FINNIC,	*Sisainen.*
	MAGYAR,	*Be.*
	TURKISH,	*Ich.*
	CIRCASSIAN,	*Caret.*
	GEORGIAN,	*Caret.*
	MONGOLIAN,	*Todova.*
	MANTSHU,	*Dorgi.*
	JAVANESE, Ngoko,	*Sajero.*
	JAVANESE, Krama,	*Salebetting.*
	MALAY,	*Didálam.*
Isolating.	CHINESE, Nankin,	*Néi.*
	CHINESE, Pekin,	*Néi.*
	CHINESE, Canton,	*Noi.*
	CHINESE, Shanghai,	*Li-hiang.*
	AMOY, Colloquial,	*Lái-bin.*
	JAPANESE,	*Uchi, naka.*
	Brahuí,	*Fahti.*
Chinese Frontier & Tibet.	Gyámi,	*Lithú.*
	Gyárung,	*Ugú, wogú.*
	Tákpa,	*Nengá.*
	Mányak,	*Khú.*
	Thochú,	*Kúkú.*
	Sokpa,	*Totar.*
	Horpa,	*Náng.*
	Tibetan (*written*),	*Náng, ná.*
	Tibetan (*spoken*),	*Náng.*
Nepal (east to west).	Serpa,	*Náng.*
	Súnwár,	*A'gá.*
	Gúrung,	*Nhori.*
	Múrmi,	*Tung-gyer.*
	Magar,	*Bhitar.*
	Tháksya,	*Nhári.*
	Pákhya,	*Bhitra.*
	Newár,	*Dúne.*
	Limbu,	*Kúsi-gang, hong.*
Kiranti Group (East Nepal).	Kiránti,	*Ukúng-yá.*
	Rodong,	*Kung-ya. kongda.*
	Rúngchenbung,	*Ukonghud'ya, ukongva,*
	Chhingtángya,	*Ukúmbe, khimbáyu.*
	Náchhereng,	*Khimgwa, khimgo.*
	Wáling,	*Khimko, akungya.*
	Yákha,	*Caret.*
	Chourásya,	*Kudukwáya, koya.*
	Kulungya,	*Gopa.*
	Thulungya,	*Gona, ngwa-ana.*
	Báhingya,	*Agwádi, agwa-la.*
	Lohorong,	*Hongsiyú.*
	Lambichhong,	*Ichhite.*
	Báláli,	*Hoksyúyú.*
	Sáng-páng,	*Hoptáṇ.*
	Dúmi,	*U'tong.*
	Kháling,	*Ugo-ya.*
	Dungmáli,	*Um-kong-ya.*
Broken Tribes of Nepal.	Dárhi,	*Bhitar.*
	Denwár,	*Bhitar.*
	Pahri,	*Dohoṇ.*
	Chepáng,	*Caret.*
	Bhrámu,	*Tṛka, náng.*
	Váyu,	*Neng, bek.*
	Kuswar,	*Bhitar.*
	Kusunda,	*Wáha.*
	Tháru,	*Bhitra.*
	Lepcha (Sikkim),	*Sagong.*
	Bhúṭáni v. Lhopa,	*Náng.*

N.-E. Bengal.	Bodo,	*Singou, sing.*
	Dhimál,	*Lipta.*
	Kocch,	*Bhitar.*
	Garo,	*Púmavai.*
	Káchári,	*Nú noishing.*
Eastern Frontier of Bengal.	Munipuri,	*Yimung.*
	Míthán Nágá,	*Caret.*
	Tablung Nágá,	*Caret.*
	Khári Nágá,	*Tisinge.*
	Angámi Nágá,	*Kinu.*
	Námsáng Nágá,	*Caret.*
	Nowgong Nágá,	*Talong.*
	Tengsa Nágá,	*Atap.*
	Abor Miri,	*A'ráso.*
	Sibságar Miri,	*Araso.*
	Deoria Chutia,	*Chikimi.*
	Singpho,	*Caret.*
Arrakan & Burmah.	Burman (*written*),	*Atwang.*
	Burman (*spoken*),	*Atwen, a-hlay-mha.*
	Khyeng v. Shou,	*Dúgáme.*
	Kámi,	*A'-thum-be.*
	Kúmi,	*Thúm.*
	Mrú v. Toung,	*Caret.*
	Sák,	*Caret.*
Siam & Tenasserim.	Talain v. Mon,	*Kha-tway.*
	Sgau-karen,	*A'-pu, len-pu.*
	Pwo-karen,	*Ler-a-pung.*
	Toungh-thu,	*En-pu.*
	Shán,	*Ka-noung.*
	Annamitic,	*Trong.*
	Siamese,	*Khannoung, thmai.*
	Ahom,	*Khauju.*
	Khámti,	*Tinau.*
	Laos,	*Caret.*
Central India.	Ho (Kol),	*Tallaré.*
	Kol (Singhbhum),	*Bhitar.*
	Santáli,	*Bhitár, bhitarite.*
	Bhúmij,	*Bhitar.*
	Uráon,	*U'lá.*
	Mundala,	*Bhitar.*
	Rájmahali,	*U'le.*
	Goṇḍi,	*Rappu, núpá mandar.*
	Gayeti,	*Caret.*
	Rutluk,	*Caret.*
	Naikude,	*Caret.*
	Kolami,	*Caret.*
	Mádi,	*Caret.*
	Mádia,	*Caret.*
	Kuri,	*Caret.*
	Keikádi,	*Wulle.*
	Khoṇd,	*Caret.*
	Sávara,	*Alogna.*
	Gadaba,	*Vomiḍi.*
	Yerukala,	*Vulle.*
	Chentsu,	*Bhitar.*
Southern India.	Tamiḷ, anc.,	*Caret.*
	Tamiḷ, mod.,	*-uḷḷé.*
	Malayáḷma, anc.,	*Caret.*
	Malayáḷma, mod.,	*Akatta.*
	Telugu,	*Lopala, logá.*
	Karṇáṭaka, anc.,	*Caret.*
	Karṇáṭaka, mod.,	*Oḷage.*
	Tuḷuva,	*Oli.*
	Kurgi,	*Caret.*
	Toḍuva,	*Ulhu.*
	Toḍa,	*Ulf.*
	Kóta,	*U'luli.*
	Baḍaga,	*Volage.*
	Kuṛumba,	*Vollage.*
	Iruḷa,	*Ulle.*
	Malabar,	*Ullé.*
	Sinhalese,	*Ätulé.*

Group	Types.	
Inflecting.	SANSKRIT,	*Viná.*
	ARABIC,	*Belá.*
Compounding.	BASK,	*-gabe, -ke; gabe, baga bake, [-bake.*
	FINNIC,	*Tta.*
	MAGYAR,	*-nelkül.*
	TURKISH,	*-siz.*
	CIRCASSIAN,	*Weyrey, burey.*
	GEORGIAN,	*Thwienier.*
	MONGOLIAN,	*Ügheï, üghëi-bar.*
	MANTSHU,	*De ako.*
	JAVANESE, Ngoko,	*Ora-nganggo.*
	JAVANESE, Krama,	*Boten-ngangge.*
	MALAY,	*Korang.*
Isolating.	CHINESE, Nankin,	*Püh-yu.*
	CHINESE, Pekin,	*Mei-yu.*
	CHINESE, Canton,	*Mo.*
	CHINESE, Shanghai,	*Veh-yu, veh-i-daw.*
	AMOY, Colloquial,	*Bo.*
	JAPANESE,	*Foka, nakute.*
	Brahuí,	*Baghar.*
Chinese Frontier & Tibet.	Gyámi,	*Momá, meyú-má.*
	Gyárung,	*Kamei.*
	Tákpa,	*Ma-nona.*
	Mányak,	*Májú.*
	Thochú,	*Marúk.*
	Sokpa	*U'g-gwe.*
	Horpa,	*Máchú.*
	Tibetan (*written*),	*Caret.*
	Tibetan (*spoken*),	*Thána.*
Nepal (east to west).	Serpa,	*Me-tála.*
	Súnwár,	*Mabáthú.*
	Gúrung,	*Ar-esyá.*
	Múrmi,	*A'dá-ná.*
	Magar,	*Mámúle.*
	Tháksya,	*A'robhoja.*
	Pákhya,	*Bholi.*
	Newár,	*Madaya-kang.*
	Limbu,	*Menne.*
Kiránti Group (East Nepal).	Kiránti,	*Mádang.*
	Rodong,	*Madang.*
	Rúngchenbung,	*Madang, mandang.*
	Chhingtángya,	*Mángchi.*
	Náchhereng,	*Mángdi.*
	Wáling,	*Mochhi.*
	Yákha,	*Mánnúng, metning.*
	Chourásya,	*Sokho.*
	Kulungya,	*Mándi.*
	Thulungya,	*Mánthi.*
	Báhingya,	*Mánthi.*
	Lohorong,	*Meddin'g.*
	Lambichhong,	*Mángchhi.*
	Báláli,	*Medding.*
	Sáng-páng,	*Mand, mán.*
	Dúmi,	*Mánthine, mandi.*
	Kháling,	*Máng-thá.*
	Dungmáli,	*Mánchhi.*
Broken Tribes of Nepal.	Dárhi,	*Báhir.*
	Denwár,	*Báhir.*
	Pahri,	*Pen-há.*
	Chepáng,	*Caret.*
	Bhrámu,	*Am-bu.*
	Váyu,	*Tongma, lok.*
	Kuswar,	*Báhir.*
	Kusunda,	*Káuthá-i.*
	Tháru,	*Nahiho-i.*
	Lepcha (Sikkim),	*Ti.*
	Bhútáni v. Lhopa,	*Te-lo.*

N.-E. Bengal.	Bodo,	*O'ngá, geya.*
	Dhimál,	*Mánthú.*
	Kocch,	*Bine.*
	Garo,	*Thong chani gamang.*
	Káchári,	*Caret.*
Eastern Frontier of Bengal.	Munipuri,	*Caret.*
	Míthán Nágá,	*Caret.*
	Tablung Nágá,	*Caret.*
	Khári Nágá,	*Caret.*
	Angámi Nágá,	*Caret.*
	Námsáng Nágá,	*Caret.*
	Nowgong Nágá,	*Caret.*
	Tengsa Nágá,	*Caret.*
	Abor Miri,	*Caret.*
	Sibságar Miri,	*Caret.*
	Deoria Chutia,	*Caret.*
	Singpho,	*Caret.*
Arrakan & Burmah.	Burman (*written*),	*Ba.*
	Burman (*spoken*),	*Caret.*
	Khyeng v. Shou,	*Caret.*
	Kámi,	*Caret.*
	Kúmi,	*Caret.*
	Mrú v. Toung,	*Caret.*
	Sák,	*Caret.*
Siam & Tenasserim.	Talain v. Mon,	*Hpa.*
	Sgau-karen,	*Ler-koung* (?).
	Pwo-karen,	*Ler-koung.*
	Toungh-thu,	*Caret.*
	Shán,	*Mai.*
	Annamitic,	*Kyang-ko.*
	Siamese,	*Caret.*
	Ahom,	*Caret.*
	Khámti,	*Caret.*
	Laos,	*Caret.*
Central India.	Ho (Kol),	*Kaï-tainredo.*
	Kol (Singhbhum),	*Bánoá.*
	Santáli,	*Bánuh* (= is not), *begar.*
	Bhúmij,	*Caret.*
	Uráon,	*Ni.*
	Mundala,	*Sámá.*
	Rájmahali,	*Walo.*
	Goṇḍi,	*Bahro, bigúr.*
	Gayeti,	*Caret.*
	Rutluk,	*Caret.*
	Naikude,	*Caret.*
	Kolami,	*Caret.*
	Mádi,	*Caret.*
	Mádia,	*Caret.*
	Kuri,	*Caret.*
	Keikádi,	*Beilu.*
	Khoṇḍ,	*Caret.*
	Sávara,	*Y'ejja.*
	Gadaba,	*Vuregusu.*
	Yerukala,	*Yilladote.*
	Chentsu,	*Navunánai.*
Southern India.	Tamiḻ, anc.,	*-anri.*
	Tamiḻ, mod.,	*-illámal.*
	Malayáḷma, anc.,	*Caret.*
	Malayáḷma, mod.,	*-illáte, -kúṭáte.*
	Telugu,	*-lěkuṇḍá.*
	Karṇáṭaka, anc.,	*Caret.*
	Karṇáṭaka, mod.,	*-illade.*
	Tuḷuva,	*-horata.*
	Kurgi,	*Caret.*
	Toḍuva, }	*Caret.*
	Toḍa, }	*-allade.*
	Kóta,	*-allade.*
	Baḍaga,	*-allade.*
	Kuṛumba,	*-allade.*
	Iruḷa,	*-adalla.*
	Malabar,	*-vittu, allathu, indi.*
	Sinhalese,	*-nătua.*

	Types.	
Inflecting.	SANSKṚIT,	*Báḍham.*
	ARABIC,	*Naam, eiwa, bela.*
Compounding.	BASK,	*Bai.*
	FINNIC,	*On* (= it is).
	MAGYAR,	*Igen.*
	TURKISH,	*Evet.*
	CIRCASSIAN,	*Wayhi.*
	GEORGIAN,	*He.*
	MONGOLIAN,	*Mün.*
	MANTSHU,	*Inu.*
	JAVANESE, Ngoko,	*Iya.*
	JAVANESE, Krama,	*Inggih.*
	MALAY,	*Behkan.*
Isolating.	CHINESE, Nankin,	*Shi.*
	CHINESE, Pekin,	*Shih.*
	CHINESE, Canton,	*Hai.*
	CHINESE, Shanghai,	*Sz̀.*
	AMOY, Colloquial,	*Sí, chián-sí.*
	JAPANESE,	*He, hai, ha.*
	Brahuí,	*Handon.*
Chinese Frontier & Tibet.	Gyámi,	*Syo.*
	Gyárung,	*Do-mos.*
	Tákpa,	*In.*
	Mányak,	*Zyi.*
	Thochú,	*Gnowá, gno.*
	Sokpa,	*Bi.*
	Horpa,	*Gnor.*
	Tibetan (*written*),	*Caret.*
	Tibetan (*spoken*),	*I'ṇ.*
Nepal (east to west).	Serpa,	*In.*
	Súnwár,	*Mai.*
	Gúrung,	*Woi.*
	Múrmi,	*Minná, yá.*
	Magar,	*Ho, le-au.*
	Thíksya,	*Hin.*
	Pákhya,	*Hoho.*
	Newár,	*Khau, da-ang.*
	Limbu,	*Ok.*
Kiranti Group (East Nepal).	Kiránti,	*Angá.*
	Rodong,	*Ou, ai.*
	Rúngchenbung,	*Ang-gna.*
	Chhingtángya,	*Ye, yet.*
	Náchhereng,	*Le, ho.*
	Wáling,	*Hanaṇ, o, á.*
	Yákha,	*Ihhi.*
	Chourásya,	*Time.*
	Kulungya,	*Ye.*
	Thulungya,	*Misi, bú.*
	Báhingya,	*Moko.*
	Lohorong,	*Ye.*
	Lambichhong,	*Ye.*
	Báláli,	*Hegne.*
	Sáng-páng,	*Ye, inchhúng, ingná.*
	Dúmi,	*Aṇná.*
	Kháling,	*Go, ant má.*
	Dungmáli,	*Han-aṇ, go, imchang-bá.*
Broken Tribes of Nepal.	Dárhi,	*Ho.*
	Denwár,	*Te.*
	Pahri,	*Khyú.*
	Chepáng,	*Caret.*
	Bhrámu,	*Mo, lik.*
	Váyu,	*Dik-sa, nom.*
	Kuswar,	*Ah, an.*
	Kusunda,	*A'yábakiho.*
	Tháru,	*Náhibá.*
	Lepcha (Sikkim),	*Ah, euk.*
	Bhúṭáni v. Lhopa,	*Túp, in.*
N.-E. Bengal.	Bodo,	*Ongo, ong-thárgo.*
	Dhimál,	*He, jeng.*
	Kocch,	*Hen.*
	Garo,	*Há.*
	Káchári,	*Caret.*
Eastern Frontier of Bengal.	Munipuri,	*Hoi.*
	Míthán Nágá,	*Vai.*
	Tablung Nágá,	*Aiya.*
	Khári Nágá,	*Hau.*
	Angámi Nágá,	*E.*
	Námsáng Nágá,	*Idanga.*
	Nowgong Nágá,	*Au.*
	Tengsa Nágá,	*Ho.*
	Abor Miri,	*Iu.*
	Sibságar Miri,	*U.*
	Deoria Chutia,	*Hoi.*
	Singpho,	*Raia.*
Arrakan & Burmah.	Burman (*written*),	*Hotkhe.*
	Burman (*spoken*),	*Hokhe, hot-kai.*
	Khyeng v. Shou,	*A-hi.*
	Kámi,	*Ta-ko-ká.*
	Kúmi,	*Nán.*
	Mrú v. Toung,	*Caret.*
	Sák,	*Caret.*
Siam & Tenasserim.	Talain v. Mon,	*Tot-kwai.*
	Sgau-karen,	*Ma, ma-li, meye.*
	Pwo-karen,	*Mwai.*
	Toungh-thu,	*Mwá.*
	Shán,	*Htsouk-hi.*
	Annamitic,	*Phai.*
	Siamese,	*Tsen, khá.*
	Ahom,	*Khewo.*
	Khámti,	*Tsau.*
	Laos,	*Tsai, men.*
Central India.	Ho (Kol),	*Eya.*
	Kol (Singhbhum),	*Haṇ, ho.*
	Santáli,	*Hung, ho, ho-i, hong-már.*
	Bhúmij,	*Hong.*
	Uráon,	*Háh.*
	Mundala,	*Háh, ho.*
	Rájmahali,	*Onon, ho.*
	Goṇḍi,	*Hingi, inge.*
	Gayeti,	*Caret.*
	Rutluk,	*Caret.*
	Naikude,	*Caret.*
	Kolami,	*Caret.*
	Mádi,	*Caret.*
	Mádia,	*Caret.*
	Kuri,	*Caret.*
	Keikádi,	*A'mbo.*
	Khoṇḍ,	*Vujje.*
	Sávara,	*Jáḍite.*
	Gadaba,	*Vom.*
	Yerukala,	*Ambo.*
	Chentsu,	*Schchhá, hoyyá.*
Southern India.	Tamiḷ, anc.,	*Caret.*
	Tamiḷ, mod.,	*A'm.*
	Malayáḷma, anc.,	*Caret.*
	Malayáḷma, mod.,	*Ate, úvva.*
	Telugu,	*Avunu.*
	Karṇáṭaka, anc.,	*Caret.*
	Karṇáṭaka, mod.,	*Haudu.*
	Tuḷuva,	*And.*
	Kurgi,	*Akku.*
	Toḍuva, }	*Caret.*
	Toḍa, }	*Ha.*
	Kóta,	*Ha.*
	Baḍaga,	*Ha.*
	Kuṛumba,	*Haudu.*
	Iruḷa,	*A'ma.*
	Malabar,	*A'm, om.*
	Sinhalese,	*Ou.*

Group	Language	Yesterday
	Types.	
Inflecting.	SANSKRIT,	*Hyaḥ.*
	ARABIC,	*Ams, imbárich.*
Compounding.	BASK,	*Atzo.*
	FINNIC,	*Eilen.*
	MAGYAR,	*Tegnap.*
	TURKISH,	*Dun.*
	CIRCASSIAN,	*Boghaz.*
	GEORGIAN,	*Gushin.*
	MONGOLIAN,	*Ütsek-edur.*
	MANTSHU,	*Sikse.*
	JAVANESE, Ngoko,	*Wingi.*
	JAVANESE, Krama,	*Wingi.*
	MALAY,	*Kalamári.*
Isolating.	CHINESE, Nankin,	*Tsŏh-jih.*
	CHINESE, Pekin,	*Tso-jih.*
	CHINESE, Canton,	*Tsok-yat.*
	CHINESE, Shanghai,	*Dzo-nieh.*
	AMOY, Colloquial,	*Chá-jit.*
	JAPANESE,	*Saku-dsitsu, sakusichu.*
	Brahuí,	*Daro.*
Chinese Frontier & Tibet.	Gyámi,	*Hou-the.*
	Gyárung,	*Púsyúr.*
	Tákpa,	*Dáng.*
	Mányak,	*Yáhá.*
	Thochú,	*Narr.*
	Sokpa,	*Nokhor.*
	Horpa,	*Naga, áwesni.*
	Tibetan (*written*),	*Mdáng.*
	Tibetan (*spoken*),	*Dáng.*
Nepal (east to west).	Serpa,	*Dáng.*
	Súnwár,	*Sináti.*
	Gúrung,	*Tela.*
	Múrmi,	*Tilá.*
	Magar,	*Tisyengmi.*
	Tháksya,	*Kemichuri.*
	Pákhya,	*Hijo.*
	Newár,	*Mhigo.*
	Limbu,	*Meh'ma.*
Kiranti Group (East Nepal).	Kiránti,	*Akhománg.*
	Rodong,	*A'se.*
	Rúngchenbung,	*A'khománg.*
	Chhingtángya,	*A'sinda.*
	Náchhereng,	*A'spa.*
	Wáling,	*A'se, akomang.*
	Yákha,	*A'chhen.*
	Chourásya,	*Saiso.*
	Kulungya,	*Is'pa.*
	Thulungya,	*Básta.*
	Báhingya,	*Sanam'ti.*
	Lohorong,	*A'-seï, ásen, a-sye.*
	Lambichhong,	*A'sen.*
	Bálálí,	*Ye-má.*
	Sáng-páng,	*A'-thepá.*
	Dúmi,	*A'meski.*
	Kháling,	*Amiske.*
	Dungmáli,	*A'se.*
Broken Tribes of Nepal.	Dárhi,	*Kálú.*
	Denwár,	*Ká-lú.*
	Pahri,	*Mi-zye.*
	Chepáng,	*Yon.*
	Bhrámu,	*Mi-lya.*
	Váyu,	*Ti-jong.*
	Kuswar,	*Kal-hai.*
	Kusunda,	*Binágá.*
	Tháru,	*Byáhan.*
	Lepcha (Sikkim),	*Tasso.*
	Bhútáni v. Lhopa,	*Khácha.*
N.-E. Bengal.	Bodo,	*Mia.*
	Dhimál,	*Anji.*
	Kocch,	*Kal-gata-kalya* (?).
	Garo,	*Mi-vai.*
	Káchári,	*Mia-sanche.*
Eastern Frontier of Bengal.	Munipuri,	*Hai-yeng.*
	Míthán Nágá,	*Manyi.*
	Tablung Nágá,	*Manyi.*
	Khári Nágá,	*Hashi.*
	Angámi Nágá,	*Koshe.*
	Námsáng Nágá,	*Maja.*
	Nowgong Nágá,	*Yashi.*
	Tengsa Nágá,	*Osi.*
	Abor Miri,	*Milo.*
	Sibságar Miri,	*Melobo.*
	Deoria Chutia,	*Dupuroni.*
	Singpho,	*Mani.*
Arrakan & Burmah.	Burman (*written*),	*Yamanne.*
	Burman (*spoken*),	*Yamanne, ma-na-ga.*
	Khyeng v. Shou,	*Yam-tú.*
	Kámi,	*Ya-dúm.*
	Kúmi,	*Caret.*
	Mrú v. Toung,	*Caret.*
	Sák,	*Caret.*
Siam & Tenasserim.	Talain v. Mon,	*Let-ka-na.*
	Sgau-karen,	*M'hah.*
	Pwo-karen,	*Ler-mu-gah.*
	Toungh-thu,	*Má-ha.*
	Shán,	*Ma-wa.*
	Annamitic,	*Hôm-qua.*
	Siamese,	*Ma-wa-ni, wa, wan.*
	Ahom,	*Poi.*
	Khámti,	*Mangá.*
	Laos,	*Caret.*
Central India.	Ho (Kol),	*Holá.*
	Kol (Singhbhum),	*Halá.*
	Santáli,	*Halá, haláng.*
	Bhúmij,	*Halá.*
	Uráon,	*Chelo:*
	Mundala,	*Halá* (*hola ?*).
	Rájmahali,	*Chewr.*
	Gondi,	*Nadi, nara, khai.*
	Gayeti,	*Caret.*
	Rutluk,	*Caret.*
	Naikude,	*Caret.*
	Kolami,	*Caret.*
	Mádi,	*Caret.*
	Mádia,	*Caret.*
	Kuri,	*Caret.*
	Keikádi,	*Ninná.*
	Khond,	*Caret.*
	Sávara,	*Amanni.*
	Gadaba,	*Minde.*
	Yerukala,	*Nesu yennáyi.*
	Chentsu,	*Káyil, porusú.*
Southern India.	Tamiḷ, anc.,	*Nerunal.*
	Tamiḷ, mod.,	*Néttu.*
	Malayáḷma, anc.,	*Caret.*
	Malayáḷma, mod.,	*Innale.*
	Telugu,	*Ninna.*
	Karṇáṭaka, anc.,	*Caret.*
	Karṇáṭaka, mod.,	*Ninne.*
	Tuḷuva,	*Kode.*
	Kurgi,	*Nenne, ninnándu.*
	Toduva,	*Enner.*
	Toda,	*Enner.*
	Kóta,	*Ner.*
	Badaga,	*Ninne.*
	Kuṛumba,	*Ninne.*
	Iruḷa,	*Nettu.*
	Malabar,	*Nettu.*
	Sinhalese,	*I'yé.*

Types.

Inflecting.

SANSKRIT,	*Antariksha, vyoman, váyu, gagana, ákása.*
ARABIC,	*Hawá.*

Compounding.

BASK,	*Aire.*
FINNIC,	*Ilma.*
MAGYAR,	*Leg.*
TURKISH,	*Caret.*
CIRCASSIAN,	*Shuey.*
GEORGIAN,	*Caret.*
MONGOLIAN,	*Ki, keï.*
MANTSHU,	*Sukdun, apka.*
JAVANESE, Ngoko,	*Angin.*
JAVANESE, Krama,	*Angin.*
MALAY,	*Angin.*

Isolating.

CHINESE, Nankin,	*K'i.*
CHINESE, Pekin,	*Ch'i.*
CHINESE, Canton,	*Hi.*
CHINESE, Shanghai,	*Ti-chi* (earth-air).
AMOY, Colloquial,	*K'i.*
JAPANESE,	*Kuki, kaza.*

Brahuí,	*Caret.*

Chinese Frontier & Tibet.

Gyámi,	*Sphún.*
Gyárung,	*Tali.*
Tákpa,	*Rhot.*
Mányak,	*Merdah.*
Thochú,	*Mozyú.*
Sokpa,	*Sálki.*
Horpa,	*Púryú.*
Tibetan (*written*),	*Rsungma, rlungma.*
Tibetan (*spoken*),	*Shákpá, lhakpá.*

Nepal (east to west).

Serpa,	*Lúngbo.*
Súnwár,	*Phase.*
Gúrung,	*Náng mro.*
Múrmi,	*Lhábá.*
Magar,	*Namsú.*
Tháksya,	*Nammar.*
Pákhya,	*Bayálo.*
Newár,	*Phai.*
Limbu,	*Sammit.*

Kiranti Group (East Nepal).

Kiránti,	*Hak.*
Rodong,	*Hyú.*
Rúngchenbung,	*Hik, hak.*
Chhingtángya,	*Him'ma.*
Náchhereng,	*Hi, i.*
Wáling,	*Him'ma, hak.*
Yákha,	*Hig'wa-phák, hik'gwa.*
Chourásya,	*Phúrim.*
Kulungya,	*Hik-pa.*
Thulungya,	*Ju.*
Báhingya,	*Ju.*
Lohorong,	*Hiwá-bá, higwá-phak.*
Lambichhong,	*Him-má.*
Báláli,	*Húwápa, híwá-ma.*
Sáng-páng,	*Him'má, heu.*
Dúmi,	*Húk'-ú, hú'-u.*
Kháling,	*Jhúng.*
Dungmáli,	*Heuk, himma.*

Broken Tribes of Nepal.

Dárhi,	*Batás.*
Denwár,	*Bátás.*
Pahri,	*Phú-sá.*
Chepáng,	*Má-rú.*
Bhrámu,	*A-sí.*
Váyu,	*Hujum, hojum.*
Kuswar,	*Batás.*
Kusunda,	*Kái.*
Tháru,	*Bayár.*

Lepcha (Sikkim),	*Sagmat.*
Bhúṭáni v. Lhopa,	*Lúng.*

N.-E. Bengal.

Bodo,	*Bár, nokhorong.*
Dhimál,	*Birima, bhirma.*
Kocch,	*Batás.*
Garo,	*Lampár.*
Káchári,	*Bar.*

Eastern Frontier of Bengal.

Munipuri,	*Núngsit.*
Míthán Nágá,	*Rangben.*
Tablung Nágá,	*Wang-yak.*
Khári Nágá,	*Aning.*
Angámi Nágá,	*Tikhe.*
Námsáng Nágá,	*Pong.*
Nowgong Nágá,	*Mabung.*
Tengsa Nágá,	*Mapung.*
Abor Miri,	*Asar.*
Sibságar Miri,	*Esár.*
Deoria Chutia,	*Beni.*
Singpho,	*M'bung.*

Arrakan & Burmah.

Burman (*written*),	*Le.*
Burman (*spoken*),	*Le, lá.*
Khyeng v. Shou,	*Kee.*
Kámi,	*Ga-li.*
Kúmi,	*A-li.*
Mrú v. Toung,	*Ra-li.*
Sák,	*Mwi-ya-he.*

Siam & Tenasserim.

Talain v. Mon,	*Kya.*
Sgau-karen,	*Káli, kli.*
Pwo-karen,	*Li.*
Toungh-thu,	*Ta-li.*
Shán,	*Lonma.*
Annamitic,	*Khi.*
Siamese,	*Lon, lom.*
Ahom,	*Lom.*
Khámti,	*Lom.*
Laos,	*Lom.*

Central India.

Ho (Kol),	*Hoyo.*
Kol (Singhbhum),	*Hoiyo.*
Santáli,	*Hoye, chaṭ* (sky), *haedát* (wind).
Bhúmij,	*Hoyo.*
Uráon,	*Thákká.*
Mundala,	*Hoyoh.*
Rájmahali,	*Táke, táphe.*
Goṇḍi,	*Báribá itá, wadi.*
Gayeti,	*Wadi.*
Rutluk,	*Wadi-wadi.*
Naikude,	*Gáli.*
Kolami,	*Gáli.*
Mádi,	*Wadi wadigu.*
Mádia,	*Wadi.*
Kuri,	*Koyo.*
Keikádi,	*Gáli.*
Khoṇḍ,	*Billu.*
Sávara,	*Ringe.*
Gadaba,	*Gamváyi.*
Yerukala,	*Gáli.*
Chentsu,	*Batás.*

Southern India.

Tamiḷ, anc.,	*Kál.*
Tamiḷ, mod.,	*Káṭṭu, wáyu.*
Malayáḷma, anc.,	*Caret.*
Malayáḷma, mod.,	*Káṭṭa.*
Telugu,	*Gáli.*
Karṇáṭaka, anc.,	*Elaru.*
Karṇáṭaka, mod.,	*Gháḷi.*
Tuḷuva,	*Gháli.*
Kurgi,	*Bána, káttu.*
Toḍuva, Toḍa,	*Kott. Kátu.*
Kóta,	*Gále.*
Baḍaga,	*Glai.*
Kurumba,	*Gáli.*
Iruḷa,	*Kátu.*
Malabar,	*Akayam.*
Sinhalese,	*Bhúvana.*

Group	Types.	
Inflecting.	SANSKRIT,	*Pipílíká, vamrí.*
	ARABIC,	*Naml.*
Compounding.	BASK,	*Chingurri, chindurri, inurri.*
	FINNIC,	*Muurainen.*
	MAGYAR,	*Hangya.*
	TURKISH,	*Karinja.*
	CIRCASSIAN,	*Caret.*
	GEORGIAN,	*Caret.*
	MONGOLIAN,	*Sirgoltchin.*
	MANTSHU,	*Caret.*
	JAVANESE, Ngoko,	*Semut.*
	JAVANESE, Krama,	*Semut.*
	MALAY,	*Samút.*
Isolating.	CHINESE, Nankin,	*I'.*
	CHINESE, Pekin,	*I'.*
	CHINESE, Canton,	*Ngai.*
	CHINESE, Shanghai,	*Mō-ni.*
	AMOY, Colloquial,	*Kaú-hiá.*
	JAPANESE,	*Ari.*
	Brahuí,	*Caret.*
Chinese Frontier & Tibet.	Gyámi,	*Mai-thún.*
	Gyárung,	*Ko-rok.*
	Tákpa,	*Rhok-po.*
	Mányak,	*Ba-rah.*
	Thochú,	*Tú-khrá.*
	Sokpa,	*Khoro-khwe.*
	Horpa,	*Skhro.*
	Tibetan (*written*),	*Grogma.*
	Tibetan (*spoken*),	*Thomá.*
Nepal (east to west).	Serpa,	*Rhúnmá.*
	Súnwár,	*Ragmachi.*
	Gúrung,	*Chiji.*
	Múrmi,	*Syouri.*
	Magar,	*Mhár.*
	Tháksya,	*Naṭo.*
	Pákhya,	*Krimula.*
	Newár,	*Imo.*
	Limbu,	*Sikchemba.*
Kiranti Group (East Nepal).	Kiránti,	*Sáchakáva.*
	Rodong,	*Chikarepa.*
	Rúngchenbung,	*Sáchakáwa, chikyang.*
	Chhingtángya,	*Pongkharok.*
	Náchhereng,	*Chhámpalyú.*
	Wáling,	*Chhikyáng.*
	Yákha,	*Khelek, khelem.*
	Chourásya,	*Po urung'ma, pworum'm.*
	Kulungya,	*Khálem.*
	Thulungya,	*Khálim.*
	Báhingya,	*Gága chimmo, gágáchingmo.*
	Lohorong,	*Pong-khorok, yangkhrepá.*
	Lambichhong,	*Pong khorok, ya-khrepá.*
	Báláli,	*Yá khlepa.*
	Sáng-páng,	*Chhámphalú, champa-leu.*
	Dúmi,	*Chiká-repú.*
	Kháling,	*Grákmo.*
	Dungmáli,	*Chig-yáng.*
Broken Tribes of Nepal.	Dárhi,	*Cheunta, t-seu-n-ta.*
	Denwár,	*Cheu-ti, t-seu-ti.*
	Pahri,	*Mig-za.*
	Chepáng,	*Túl-ti.*
	Bhrámu,	*A-nap.*
	Váyu,	*Chiki-bulla.*
	Kuswar,	*Kimili.*
	Kusunda,	*Pyai-ki.*
	Tháru,	*Doká.*
	Lepcha (Sikkim),	*Takphyúl.*
	Bhúṭáni v. Lhopa,	*Kyomá.*

N.-E. Bengal.	Bodo,	*Hásá-brai, mocha-rám.*
	Dhimál,	*Nhá-muí.*
	Kocch,	*Nuti-pipara.*
	Garo,	*Gongá, sámbúr.*
	Káchári,	*Caret.*
Eastern Frontier of Bengal.	Munipuri,	*Kukcheng.*
	Mithán Nágá,	*Tiksá.*
	Tablung Nágá,	*Tikhá.*
	Khári Nágá,	*Hung-zah.*
	Angámi Nágá,	*Hache.*
	Námsáng Nágá,	*Tsip-chak.*
	Nowgong Nágá,	*Mochá.*
	Tengsa Nágá,	*Mathán.*
	Abor Miri,	*Mirang.*
	Sibságar Miri,	*Meráng.*
	Deoria Chutia,	*Chi-mechi.*
	Singpho,	*Gagin.*
Arrakan & Burmah.	Burman (*written*),	*Parwak-chhit.*
	Burman (*spoken*),	*Paynet-seik, parwet.*
	Khyeng v. Shou,	*Lhing-sá-mi.*
	Kámi,	*Ba-lin.*
	Kúmi,	*Pa-lin.*
	Mrú v. Toung,	*Loung-tsa-ring-já.*
	Sák,	*Phun-si-gyá.*
Siam & Tenasserim.	Talain v. Mon,	*Khamol.*
	Sgau-karen,	*Ter, ta-ghi-sau.*
	Pwo-karen,	*Tung.*
	Toungh-thu,	*H'tung.*
	Shán,	*Mot.*
	Annamitic,	*Kién.*
	Siamese,	*Mot.*
	Ahom,	*Nyuchu.*
	Khámti,	*Mot.*
	Laos,	*Mot, puak.*
Central India.	Ho (Kol),	*Nidír.*
	Kol (Singhbhum),	*Mui.*
	Santáli,	*Muih, muṇi, upi* (white and winged).
	Bhúmij,	*Mue.*
	Uráon,	*Poh.*
	Mundala,	*Munj.*
	Rájmahali,	*Pok.*
	Goṇḍi,	*Patte* (black); *Udeli* (white).
	Gayeti,	*Pate* (bl.); *alu* (wh.).
	Rutluk,	*Diwar* (wh.).
	Naikude,	*Simál* (bl.); *sedal* (wh.).
	Kolami,	*Shimel* (bl.); *sedal* (wh).
	Mádi,	*Chutti* (bl.); *yelam, nusu* (w.).
	Mádia,	*Caret.*
	Kuri,	*Cháti* (bl.); *ninder* (wh.).
	Keikádi,	*Caret.*
	Khoṇḍ,	*Caret.*
	Sávara,	*Bobo.*
	Gadaba,	*Gusálá.*
	Yerukala,	*Chima.*
	Chentsu,	*Peppiḍi.*
Southern India.	Tamiḷ, anc.,	*Uravi.*
	Tamiḷ, mod.,	*Erumbu* (bl.); *karaiyán* (w.).
	Malayáḷma, anc.,	*Caret.*
	Malayáḷma, mod.,	*Irumba.*
	Telugu,	*Chíma* (bl.); *chedullu* (wh.).
	Karnáṭaka, anc.,	*Caret.*
	Karnáṭaka, mod.,	*Irivi.*
	Tuḷuva,	*Pijin.*
	Kurgi,	*Caret.*
	Toḍuva,	*Erbb.*
	Toḍa,	*Erb.*
	Kóta,	*Irbe.*
	Baḍaga,	*Irupu.*
	Kurumba,	*Irupu.*
	Iruḷa,	*Irumbu.*
	Malabar,	*Erumbu.*
	Sinhalese,	*Kumbiyá.*

Group	Language	Arrow
	Types.	
Inflecting.	SANSKṚIT,	*Sáyaka, báṇa, ṣara, ishu.*
Inflecting.	ARABIC,	*Sahm.*
Compounding.	BASK,	*Guezi, isto, sayeta, lutzi* [*tragaz.*
Compounding.	FINNIC,	*Nuoli.*
Compounding.	MAGYAR,	*Nyil.*
Compounding.	TURKISH,	*Ok.*
Compounding.	CIRCASSIAN,	*Bzey.*
Compounding.	GEORGIAN,	*Isari.*
Compounding.	MONGOLIAN,	*Somon.*
Compounding.	MANTSHU,	*Niru.*
Compounding.	JAVANESE, Ngoko,	*Pannah.*
Compounding.	JAVANESE, Krama,	*Jemparing.*
Compounding.	MALAY,	*A'nak-pánah.*
Isolating.	CHINESE, Nankin,	*Tsien.*
Isolating.	CHINESE, Pekin,	*Chien.*
Isolating.	CHINESE, Canton,	*Tsin.*
Isolating.	CHINESE, Shanghai,	*Tsieṇ.*
Isolating.	AMOY, Colloquial,	*Chìṇ.*
Isolating.	JAPANESE,	*Ya.*
	Brahuí,	*Sum.*
Chinese Frontier & Tibet.	Gyámi,	*Chen.*
Chinese Frontier & Tibet.	Gyárung,	*Ki-pi.*
Chinese Frontier & Tibet.	Tákpa,	*Mlá.*
Chinese Frontier & Tibet.	Mányak,	*Má.*
Chinese Frontier & Tibet.	Thochú,	*Jáḥ.*
Chinese Frontier & Tibet.	Sokpa,	*Selime.*
Chinese Frontier & Tibet.	Horpa,	*Ldá.*
Chinese Frontier & Tibet.	Tibetan (*written*),	*Mdha, ṃdáh.*
Chinese Frontier & Tibet.	Tibetan (*spoken*),	*Da.*
Nepal (east to west).	Serpa,	*Dá.*
Nepal (east to west).	Súnwár,	*Blá.*
Nepal (east to west).	Gúrung,	*Myá.*
Nepal (east to west).	Múrmi,	*Myá.*
Nepal (east to west).	Magar,	*Myá.*
Nepal (east to west).	Tháksya,	*Tume.*
Nepal (east to west).	Pákhya,	*Káḍha.*
Nepal (east to west).	Newár,	*Bálá.*
Nepal (east to west).	Limbu,	*Tong.*
Kiránti Group (East Nepal).	Kiránti,	*Me.*
Kiránti Group (East Nepal).	Rodong,	*Bhe.*
Kiránti Group (East Nepal).	Rúngchenbung,	*Bhye, bhe, ubhe.*
Kiránti Group (East Nepal).	Chhingtángya,	*Phesik, phesw-k.*
Kiránti Group (East Nepal).	Náchhereng,	*Be-i.*
Kiránti Group (East Nepal).	Wáling,	*Be, bhe.*
Kiránti Group (East Nepal).	Yákha,	*Pisik', pishik'.*
Kiránti Group (East Nepal).	Chourásya,	*Blo.*
Kiránti Group (East Nepal).	Kulungya,	*Beï, be-i.*
Kiránti Group (East Nepal).	Thulungya,	*Ne ple.*
Kiránti Group (East Nepal).	Báhingya,	*Blá.*
Kiránti Group (East Nepal).	Lohorong,	*Phe, thúk-lá, nobe.*
Kiránti Group (East Nepal).	Lambichhong,	*Thuk-la, phet, phek'.*
Kiránti Group (East Nepal).	Báláli,	*Thuk-lá.*
Kiránti Group (East Nepal).	Sáng-páng,	*Sebi.*
Kiránti Group (East Nepal).	Dúmi,	*Númá-á, no-mo-wo.*
Kiránti Group (East Nepal).	Khálíng,	*Selmo.*
Kiránti Group (East Nepal).	Dungmáli,	*Pe.*
Broken Tribes of Nepal.	Dárhi,	*Káṇr.*
Broken Tribes of Nepal.	Denwár,	*Káṇr.*
Broken Tribes of Nepal.	Pahri,	*Bá-rá.*
Broken Tribes of Nepal.	Chepáng,	*Lá.*
Broken Tribes of Nepal.	Bhrámu,	*Pá-rá.*
Broken Tribes of Nepal.	Váyu,	*Sár, blo.*
Broken Tribes of Nepal.	Kuswar,	*Sár.*
Broken Tribes of Nepal.	Kusunda,	*Muyu.*
Broken Tribes of Nepal.	Tháru,	*Khánḍha.*
	Lepcha (Sikkim),	*Chong.*
	Bhúṭáni v. Lhopa,	*Dá.*

Group	Language	Arrow
N.-E. Bengal.	Bodo,	*Balá.*
N.-E. Bengal.	Dhimál,	*Kher, tir.*
N.-E. Bengal.	Kocch,	*Tir.*
N.-E. Bengal.	Garo,	*Phe-e.*
N.-E. Bengal.	Káchári,	*Bola-kárai.*
Eastern Frontier of Bengal.	Munipuri,	*Tel.*
Eastern Frontier of Bengal.	Míthán Nágá,	*Sán.*
Eastern Frontier of Bengal.	Tablung Nágá,	*Lá-han.*
Eastern Frontier of Bengal.	Khári Nágá,	*Takaba.*
Eastern Frontier of Bengal.	Angámi Nágá,	*Thiwu.*
Eastern Frontier of Bengal.	Námsáng Nágá,	*Latchan.*
Eastern Frontier of Bengal.	Nowgong Nágá,	*Lasang.*
Eastern Frontier of Bengal.	Tengsa Nágá,	*Lasan.*
Eastern Frontier of Bengal.	Abor Miri,	*Epuk.*
Eastern Frontier of Bengal.	Sibságar Miri,	*Epug.*
Eastern Frontier of Bengal.	Deoria Chutia,	*A'tá.*
Eastern Frontier of Bengal.	Singpho,	*Pelá.*
Arrakan & Burmah.	Burman (*written*),	Mra.
Arrakan & Burmah.	Burman (*spoken*),	Myá, *hmya.*
Arrakan & Burmah.	Khyeng v. Shou,	*Thwá.*
Arrakan & Burmah.	Kámi,	*Li.*
Arrakan & Burmah.	Kúmi,	*Li-tá-i.*
Arrakan & Burmah.	Mrú v. Toung,	*Sa, qwá-i.*
Arrakan & Burmah.	Sák,	*To-li-malá.*
Siam & Tenasserim.	Talain v. Mon,	*Lau.*
Siam & Tenasserim.	Sgau-karen,	*Plah, khli.*
Siam & Tenasserim.	Pwo-karen,	*Plah.*
Siam & Tenasserim.	Toungh-thu,	*Pla.*
Siam & Tenasserim.	Shán,	*Pen.*
Siam & Tenasserim.	Annamitic,	*Tên.*
Siam & Tenasserim.	Siamese,	*Tsán, luk-son.*
Siam & Tenasserim.	Ahom,	*Lem.*
Siam & Tenasserim.	Khámti,	*Lim.*
Siam & Tenasserim.	Laos,	*Lem-pür.*
Central India.	Ho (Kol),	*Sar.*
Central India.	Kol (Singhbhum),	*Sárh.*
Central India.	Santáli,	*Sár, jhampá.*
Central India.	Bhúmij,	*Sárh.*
Central India.	Uráon,	*Chár.*
Central India.	Mundala,	*Sáár.*
Central India.	Rájmahali,	*Chár.*
Central India.	Goṇḍi,	*Tir, jiyatúr.*
Central India.	Gayeti,	*Tir.*
Central India.	Rutluk,	*Caret.*
Central India.	Naikude,	*Tir.*
Central India.	Kolami,	*Murre.*
Central India.	Máḍi,	*Káḍi, káni.*
Central India.	Mádia,	*Káḍi.*
Central India.	Kuri,	*Tir.*
Central India.	Keikádi,	*Tirkamtá.*
Central India.	Khoṇḍ,	*Pinju.*
Central India.	Sávara,	*Am.*
Central India.	Gadaba,	*Sonai.*
Central India.	Yerukala,	*Yikke.*
Central India.	Chentsu,	*Konḍu, kánḍ.*
Southern India.	Tamiḷ, anc.,	*Kanei.*
Southern India.	Tamiḷ, mod.,	*Ambu.*
Southern India.	Malayáḷma, anc.,	*Caret.*
Southern India.	Malayáḷma, mod.,	*Amba.*
Southern India.	Telugu,	*Báṇamu, ambu.*
Southern India.	Karṇáṭaka, anc.,	*Saralu.*
Southern India.	Karṇáṭaka, mod.,	*Ambu.*
Southern India.	Tuḷuva,	*Biru.*
Southern India.	Kurgi,	*Caret.*
Southern India.	Toḍuva, }	*Caret.*
Southern India.	Toḍa, }	*Abu.*
Southern India.	Kóta,	*Ambe.*
Southern India.	Baḍaga,	*Ambu.*
Southern India.	Kuṛumba,	*Ambu.*
Southern India.	Iruḷa,	*Ambu.*
Southern India.	Malabar,	*Ambu, kanri, at-thiram,* [*pasam.*
Southern India.	Sinhalese,	*Sara, igaha.*

	Types.	
Inflecting.	SANSKRIT,	*Vi* (vedic), *vayas, pakshin.*
	ARABIC,	*Táyir.*
Compounding.	BASK,	*Chori, egazti, pizti.*
	FINNIC,	*Lintu.*
	MAGYAR,	*Madar.*
	TURKISH,	*Kush.*
	CIRCASSIAN,	*Bzu.*
	GEORGIAN,	*Tsilo, prinweli.*
	MONGOLIAN,	*Sibghon.*
	MANTSHU,	*Gaskha.*
	JAVANESE, Ngoko,	*Manut.*
	JAVANESE, Krama,	*Petsi.*
	MALAY,	*Búrung.*
Isolating.	CHINESE, Nankin,	*Niáou.*
	CHINESE, Pekin,	*Niáou.*
	CHINESE, Canton,	*Niu.*
	CHINESE, Shanghai,	*Tiau-niau.*
	AMOY, Colloquial,	*Chiáu.*
	JAPANESE,	*Tori.*
	Brahuí,	*Chuk.*
Chinese Frontier & Tibet.	Gyámi,	*Sphúi-chher.*
	Gyárung,	*Pye-pye.*
	Tákpa,	*Pyá.*
	Mányak,	*Há.*
	Thochú,	*Marwo.*
	Sokpa,	*Thá-kol.*
	Horpa,	*Gyo.*
	Tibetan (*written*),	*Byu.*
	Tibetan (*spoken*),	*Chyá.*
Nepal (east to west).	Serpa,	*Jhá.*
	Súnwár,	*Chívá, chi-vá.*
	Gúrung,	*Nemyá.*
	Múrmi,	*Námyá.*
	Magar,	*Gwájá.*
	Tháksya,	*Nom'ya.*
	Pákhya,	*Cháḍa.*
	Newár,	*Jhango, jhá-ngo.*
	Limbu,	*Bú.*
Kiránti Group (East Nepal).	Kiránti,	*Chongwá.*
	Rodong,	*Wása.*
	Rúngchenbung,	*Chhongwa.*
	Chhingtángya,	*Wása.*
	Náchhereng,	*Chho wa.*
	Wáling,	*Chhong wá.*
	Yákha,	*Núa, nuawachi.*
	Chourásya,	*Chak bwa.*
	Kulungya,	*Chhowa.*
	Thulungya,	*Chakpu.*
	Báhingya,	*Chik-ba.*
	Lohorong,	*Song-wá.*
	Lambichhong,	*Nowa.*
	Balálí,	*Chhong-wa.*
	Sáng-páng,	*Chhon-wá.*
	Dúmi,	*Sal-pu.*
	Kháling,	*Sal-po.*
	Dungmáli,	*Chhong-wá.*
Broken Tribes of Nepal.	Dárhi,	*Chári.*
	Denwár,	*Chárái.*
	Pahri,	*Bu-khlucha, bu-khin-cha.*
	Chepáng,	*Wá, mo-á, mo-wá.*
	Bhrámu,	*Jyá-ling.*
	Váyu,	*Chin-chi.*
	Kuswar,	*Chári.*
	Kusunda,	*Kotau.*
	Tháru,	*Chirai.*
	Lepcha (Sikkim),	*Pho.*
	Bhúṭáni v. Lhopa,	*Bhyá.*

N.-E. Bengal.	Bodo,	*Dou-chen.*
	Dhimál,	*Jihá.*
	Kocch,	*Pokhi.*
	Garo,	*Tou-chap.*
	Káchári,	*Dao tao sen.*
Eastern Frontier of Bengal.	Munipuri,	*U'chek.*
	Míthán Nágá,	*O.*
	Tablung Nágá,	*Ou-há.*
	Khári Nágá,	*Ozah.*
	Angámi Nágá,	*Pará.*
	Námsáng Nágá,	*Vo.*
	Nowgong Nágá,	*Üzz.*
	Tengsa Nágá,	*Uso.*
	Abor Miri,	*Pettang.*
	Sibságar Miri,	*Pátáng.*
	Deoria Chutia,	*Duá.*
	Singpho,	*Wu.*
Arrakan & Burmah.	Burman (*written*),	*Nghak.*
	Burman (*spoken*),	*Nghet, hnget.*
	Khyeng v. Shou,	*Hau.*
	Kámi,	*Ka-vá, ta-vá.*
	Kúmi,	*Ta-wú.*
	Mrú v. Toung,	*Ta-wá.*
	Sák,	*Wá-si.*
Siam & Tenasserim.	Talain v. Mon,	*Kha-ten.*
	Sgau-karen,	*To, hto, hthu.*
	Pwo-karen,	*Tu, htoh.*
	Toungh-thu,	*A-wa.*
	Shán,	*H'not.*
	Annamitic,	*Shim.*
	Siamese,	*H'not, nok.*
	Ahom,	*Nuktu.*
	Khámti,	*Nok.*
	Laos,	*Nok.*
Central India.	Ho (Kol),	*Oé.*
	Kol (Singhbhum),	*Oe.*
	Santáli,	*Cheṇe.*
	Bhúmij,	*Chene* (*cheṇe ?*).
	Uráon,	*Orak.*
	Mundala,	*Ure.*
	Rájmahali,	*Puj.*
	Goṇḍi,	*Itte, pitte.*
	Gayeti,	*Pitte.*
	Rutluk,	*Pithe.*
	Naikude,	*Pittá.*
	Kolami,	*Sidemugi.*
	Mádi,	*Pittá, paritta.*
	Mádia,	*Pidhe.*
	Kuri,	*Tilit.*
	Keikádi,	*Piská, kunju.*
	Khoṇḍ,	*Propá-manneru.*
	Sávara,	*Onti.*
	Gadaba,	*Piti.*
	Yerukala,	*Kokku, sogiḍe, kunju.*
	Chentsu,	*Chodai.*
Southern India.	Tamiḷ, anc.,	*Pul.*
	Tamiḷ, mod.,	*Paṛavei, kuruvi.*
	Malayáḷma, anc.,	*Paṛva.*
	Malayáḷma, mod.,	*Pakshi, paṛava.*
	Telugu,	*Piṭṭa.*
	Karṇáṭaka, anc.,	*Carei.*
	Karṇáṭaka, mod.,	*Hakki.*
	Tuḷuva,	*Pakki.*
	Kurgi,	*Pakki.*
	Toḍuva,	*Pull.*
	Toḍa,	*Bilti.*
	Kóta,	*Peke* (*pakhi ?*).
	Badaga,	*Hakibu.*
	Kuṛumba,	*Hakibu.*
	Iruḷa,	*Pákhi.*
	Malabar,	*Kuruvi, pullu.*
	Sinhalese,	*Kurullá.*

	Types.	
Inflecting.	SANSKRIT,	*Asṛij, rudhira, lohita, [śoṇita.*
	ARABIC,	*Dumm.*
Compounding.	BASK,	*Odol.*
	FINNIC,	*Weri.*
	MAGYAR,	*Ver.*
	TURKISH,	*Kan.*
	CIRCASSIAN,	*Kleh.*
	GEORGIAN,	*Siskhli.*
	MONGOLIAN,	*Tchison.*
	MANTSHU,	*Senggi.*
	JAVANESE, Ngoko,	*Getih.*
	JAVANESE, Krama,	*Erah.*
	MALAY,	*Dárah.*
Isolating.	CHINESE, Nankin,	*Hiueh.*
	CHINESE, Pekin,	*Hsieh.*
	CHINESE, Canton,	*Hüt.*
	CHINESE, Shanghai,	*Hüüh.*
	AMOY, Colloquial,	*Huih.*
	JAPANESE,	*Chi, tshi.*
	Brahuí,	*Ditar.*
Chinese Frontier & Tibet.	Gyámi,	*Sye.*
	Gyárung,	*Tá-shi.*
	Tákpa,	*Khrá.*
	Mányak,	*Sháḥ.*
	Thochú,	*Sáḥ.*
	Sokpa,	*Khoro-give.*
	Horpa,	*Sye, seh.*
	Tibetan (*written*),	*Khrág, khrag.*
	Tibetan (*spoken*),	*Thak.*
Nepal (east to west).	Serpa,	*Thák.*
	Súnwár,	*U'si.*
	Gúrung,	*Koh.*
	Múrmi,	*Ká.*
	Magar,	*Hyú.*
	Tháksya,	*Ká.*
	Pákhya,	*Ragat.*
	Newár,	*Hi.*
	Limbu,	*Makhi.*
Kiranti Group (East Nepal).	Kiránti,	*Hau.*
	Rodong,	*Hi, háa.*
	Rúngchenbung,	*Há, héu.*
	Chhingtángya,	*Há-li.*
	Náchhereng,	*Hi.*
	Wáling,	*Hi, há.*
	Yákha,	*He-l'la, he-l'wa.*
	Chourásya,	*Usú.*
	Kulungya,	*Hi.*
	Thulungya,	*Sisi.*
	Báhingya,	*Húsi.*
	Lohorong,	*Hári.*
	Lambichhong,	*Háli.*
	Báláli,	*Hellu-wa, helwa.*
	Sáng-páng,	*Hi.*
	Dúmi,	*Hi.*
	Kháling,	*Hi.*
	Dungmáli,	*Hi.*
Broken Tribes of Nepal.	Dárhi,	*Rágát.*
	Denwár,	*Ráktái.*
	Pahri,	*Hi.*
	Chepáng,	*Wé-i, wi.*
	Bhrámu,	*Chi-wi.*
	Váyu,	*Vi.*
	Kuswar,	*Rakti.*
	Kusunda,	*Uyú.*
	Tháru,	*Lohu.*
	Lepcha (Sikkim),	*Vi.*
	Bhúṭáni v. Lhopa,	*Thyak.*

N.-E. Bengal.	Bodo,	*Thoi.*
	Dhimál,	*Hiki, hitti.*
	Kocch,	*Lohu.*
	Garo,	*Chi.*
	Kácharí,	*Thai.*
Eastern Frontier of Bengal.	Munipuri,	*I'.*
	Míthán Nágá,	*A'ji.*
	Tablung Nágá,	*Ih.*
	Khári Nágá,	*Ai.*
	Angámi Nágá,	*Uuhi.*
	Námsáng Nágá,	*He.*
	Nowgong Nágá,	*Azü.*
	Tengsa Nágá,	*A'i.*
	Abor Miri,	*Yilpi-ui.*
	Sibságar Miri,	*Iye.*
	Deoria Chutia,	*Chui.*
	Singpho,	*Sai.*
Arrakan & Burmah.	Burman (*written*),	*Swe.*
	Burman (*spoken*),	*Thwe.*
	Khyeng v. Shou,	*Ka-thi.*
	Kámi,	*A-thi.*
	Kúmi,	*A-thi.*
	Mrú v. Toung,	*Wi.*
	Sák,	*The.*
Siam & Tenasserim.	Talain v. Mon,	*H'tsein.*
	Sgau-karen,	*Athui, thwi.*
	Pwo-karen,	*Thwi.*
	Toungh-thu,	*Thway.*
	Shán,	*Lit.*
	Annamitic,	*Máu.*
	Siamese,	*Lit (le-et ?), leuat.*
	Ahom,	*Let.*
	Khámti,	*Lüt.*
	Laos,	*Leut.*
Central India.	Ho (Kol),	*Myúm.*
	Kol (Singhbhum),	*Myun.*
	Santáli,	*Máyám (páchate* = to bleed).
	Bhúmij,	*Myun.*
	Uráon,	*Khens.*
	Mundala,	*Myun.*
	Rájmahali,	*Kesu.*
	Goṇḍi,	*Nattur, natur.*
	Gayeti,	*Natur.*
	Rutluk,	*Natur.*
	Naikude,	*Netur.*
	Kolami,	*Natur.*
	Mádi,	*Netur.*
	Mádia,	*Kanhántue.*
	Kuri,	*Pachua.*
	Keikádi,	*Natho.*
	Khoṇḍ,	*Rakko.*
	Sávara,	*Míyamo.*
	Gadaba,	*Yignam.*
	Yerukala,	*Regam, vudaram.*
	Chentsu,	*Lahu.*
Southern India.	Tamiḷ, anc.,	*Sennir.*
	Tamiḷ, mod.,	*Udiram, irattam.*
	Malayáḷma, anc.,	*Caret.*
	Malayáḷma, mod.,	*Chora.*
	Telugu,	*Netturu.*
	Karṇáṭaka, anc.,	*Kennīru.*
	Karṇáṭaka, mod.,	*Netturu.*
	Tuḷuva,	*Nettar.*
	Kurgi,	*Chore.*
	Toḍuva, }	*Caret.*
	Toḍa, }	*Bách.*
	Kóta,	*Netra.*
	Baḍaga,	*Netru.*
	Kuṛumba,	*Netaru.*
	Iruḷa,	*Latta.*
	Malabar,	*Irat-tham, kuruthi.*
	Sinhalese,	*Lé.*

Group	Language	Boat
	Types.	
Inflecting.	SANSKRIT,	*Uḍupa, plava, nau, kola, bhela.*
	ARABIC,	*Merkab.*
Compounding.	BASK,	*Barka, barko, bote.*
	FINNIC,	*Wenhet.*
	MAGYAR,	*Csajka, ladik.*
	TURKISH,	*Sandal, kaïk.*
	CIRCASSIAN,	*Caret.*
	GEORGIAN,	*Navi.*
	MONGOLIAN,	*Onghotcha, omo.*
	MANTSHU,	*Yakhoda, weikku.*
	JAVANESE, Ngoko,	*Prâu.*
	JAVANESE, Krama,	*Bahita.*
	MALAY,	*Sampan, prâu.*
Isolating.	CHINESE, Nankin,	*Siáou ch'uen.*
	CHINESE, Pekin,	*Hsiáou ch'uen.*
	CHINESE, Canton,	*Shün-tsai.*
	CHINESE, Shanghai,	*Siau-zeṇ.*
	AMOY, Colloquial,	*Chûn.*
	JAPANESE,	*Fune, kobune.*
	Brahuí,	*Bedí.*
Chinese Frontier & Tibet.	Gyámi,	*Sí-thú.*
	Gyárung,	*Brú.*
	Tákpa,	*Grú.*
	Mányak,	*Gú.*
	Thochú,	*Phyá.*
	Sokpa,	*Sákersú.*
	Horpa,	*Grá.*
	Tibetan (*written*),	*Gru.*
	Tibetan (*spoken*),	*Koá, syen.*
Nepal (east to west).	Serpa,	*Thú.*
	Súnwár,	*Dúngá.*
	Gúrung,	*Plava.*
	Múrmi,	*Dúngá.*
	Magar,	*Dúngá.*
	Tháksya,	*P'saba.*
	Pákhya,	*Dúga.*
	Newár,	*Donga.*
	Limbu,	*Khombe.*
Kiranti Group (East Nepal).	Kiránti,	*Náva.*
	Rodong,	*Náwa.*
	Rúngchenbung,	*Náwa.*
	Chhingtángya,	*Dong'ga.*
	Náchhereng,	*Dúng'ga.*
	Wáling,	*Dúng'ga.*
	Yákha,	*Dúng'ga.*
	Chourásya,	*Ghág.*
	Kulungya,	*Bo-kho.*
	Thulungya,	*Dúng'ga.*
	Báhingya,	*Dúnga.*
	Lohorong,	*Dúngga.*
	Lambichhong,	*Dúnggá.*
	Báláli,	*Dúnggá.*
	Sáng-páng,	*Bakhou.*
	Dúmi,	*Bákhopú.*
	Kháling,	*Pokham.*
	Dungmáli,	*Dunga.*
Broken Tribes of Nepal.	Dárhi,	*Dúngo, dun-go.*
	Denwár,	*Dúnga, dun-ga.*
	Pahri,	*Don-ga.*
	Chepáng,	*Dún-ga.*
	Bhrámu,	*Dún-gá.*
	Váyu,	*Dun-ga.*
	Kuswar,	*Dun-ga.*
	Kusunda,	*Wai, wou.*
	Tháru,	*Náu.*
	Lepcha (Sikkim),	*Navar.*
	Bhúṭáni v. Lhopa,	*Drú, tú.*

Group	Language	Boat
N.-E. Bengal.	Bodo,	*Nau, jhák, sorongo.*
	Dhimál,	*Náwár.*
	Kocch,	*Nau, ghornau, soronga.*
	Garo,	*Rung.*
	Káchári,	*Nao.*
Eastern Frontier of Bengal.	Munipuri,	*Hi.*
	Míthán Nágá,	*Khoa.*
	Tablung Nágá,	*Iseng.*
	Khári Nágá,	*Arong.*
	Angámi Nágá,	*Ru.*
	Námsáng Nágá,	*Khuon-kho.*
	Nowgong Nágá,	*Su-rung.*
	Tengsa Nágá,	*Lung.*
	Abor Miri,	*El-long.*
	Sibságar Miri,	*Ol-lungá.*
	Deoria Chutia,	*Nu.*
	Singpho,	*Li.*
Arrakan & Burmah.	Burman (*written*),	*Lhe.*
	Burman (*spoken*),	*Lhe, hlá.*
	Khyeng v. Shou,	*Loung.*
	Kámi,	*M'loung.*
	Kúmi,	*P"loung.*
	Mrú v. Toung,	*Loung.*
	Sák,	*Hau.*
Siam & Tenasserim.	Talain v. Mon,	*H'lo.*
	Sgau-karen,	*Kli, hkali.*
	Pwo-karen,	*Kli.*
	Toungh-thu,	*Phray.*
	Shán,	*Ho.*
	Annamitic,	*Ghe.*
	Siamese,	*Ro, reua.*
	Ahom,	*Ru.*
	Khámti,	*Hü.*
	Laos,	*Heu.*
Central India.	Ho (Kol),	*Ḍhanga, ḍunga.*
	Kol (Singhbhum),	*Dungá.*
	Santáli,	*Ḍhangá.*
	Bhúmij,	*Ḍungá.*
	Uráon,	*Dongá.*
	Mundala,	*Dongá.*
	Rájmahali,	*Náve.*
	Goṇḍi,	*Dongo.*
	Gayeti,	*Caret.*
	Rutluk,	*Caret.*
	Naikude,	*Caret.*
	Kolami,	*Caret.*
	Mádi,	*Caret.*
	Mádia,	*Caret.*
	Kuri,	*Caret.*
	Keikádi,	*Caret.*
	Khoṇḍ,	*Tekkinga.*
	Sávara,	*Voḍá.*
	Gadaba,	*Dona.*
	Yerukala,	*Paḍava.*
	Chentsu,	*Lá.*
Southern India.	Tamiḷ, anc.,	*Pakada.*
	Tamiḷ, mod.,	*Oḍam, paḍagu.*
	Malayáḷma, anc.,	*Caret.*
	Malayáḷma, mod.,	*Vanji, vaḷḷam.*
	Telugu,	*Paḍava.*
	Karṇáṭaka, anc.,	*Páru.*
	Karṇáṭaka, mod.,	*Dóṇi.*
	Tuḷuva,	*Oḍa.*
	Kurgi,	*Caret.*
	Toḍuva, }	*Caret.*
	Toḍa, }	*Caret.*
	Kóta,	*Caret.*
	Baḍaga,	*Caret.*
	Kuṟumba,	*Caret.*
	Iruḷa,	*Caret.*
	Malabar,	*Thoni, odam, morak-kalam.*
	Sinhalese,	*Orua.*

	Types.	
Inflecting.	SANSKRIT,	*Asthi, kíkasa, kulya.*
	ARABIC,	*Aazm.*
Compounding.	BASK,	*Ezur, azur.*
	FINNIC,	*Luu.*
	MAGYAR,	*Ksontok.*
	TURKISH,	*Kemik.*
	CIRCASSIAN,	*Psha, kutsha.*
	GEORGIAN,	*Dswali.*
	MONGOLIAN,	*Yason.*
	MANTSHU,	*Gizenggi.*
	JAVANESE, Ngoko,	*Balung.*
	JAVANESE, Krama,	*Balung.*
	MALAY,	*Tulang.*
Isolating.	CHINESE, Nankin,	*Kuh.*
	CHINESE, Pekin,	*Kú.*
	CHINESE, Canton,	*Kwat.*
	CHINESE, Shanghai,	*Kweh-den.*
	AMOY, Colloquial,	*Kut.*
	JAPANESE,	*Hone.*
	Brahuí,	*Caret.*
Chinese Frontier & Tibet.	Gyámi,	*Kútho.*
	Gyárung,	*Syárhú.*
	Tákpa,	*Rospá.*
	Mányak,	*Rúkhú.*
	Thochú,	*Ripat.*
	Sokpa,	*Yá so.*
	Horpa,	*Rerá.*
	Tibetan (*written*),	*Ruspa.*
	Tibetan (*spoken*),	*Ruko.*
Nepal (east to west).	Serpa,	*Rúbá.*
	Súnwár,	*Rúshe.*
	Gúrung,	*Nágri.*
	Múrmi,	*Nákhú.*
	Magar,	*Misyá ros.*
	Tháksya,	*Nati.*
	Pákhya,	*Háḍ.*
	Newár,	*Kwe.*
	Limbu,	*Sayet.*
Kiránti Group (East Nepal).	Kiránti,	*Saiba.*
	Rodong,	*Sar'wa, sárúwa.*
	Rúngchenbung,	*Sáyuba, yúwá.*
	Chhingtángya,	*Sárúk-wa.*
	Náchhereng,	*Tuprú, tupru.*
	Wáling,	*Sar'wa, salwa.*
	Yákha,	*Seng-khok'wa, seng-khog'we.*
	Chourásya,	*Rúsú.*
	Kulungya,	*Taprí, tapri.*
	Thulungya,	*Sasar.*
	Báhingya,	*Rise, ri-sye.*
	Lohorong,	*Syákowa.*
	Lambichhong,	*Rúk-wa.*
	Báláli,	*Sátuprú.*
	Sáng-páng,	*Tum-bu-rup, sá-túmburú.*
	Dúmi,	*Salú, solo.*
	Kháling,	*Solo.*
	Dungmáli,	*Súr-wá, sá-rú-wá.*
Broken Tribes of Nepal.	Dárhi,	*Haḍ.*
	Denwár,	*Háḍ.*
	Pahri,	*Ku-sá.*
	Chepáng,	*Rhu-s.*
	Bhrámu,	*Wot.*
	Váyu,	*Rú.*
	Kuswar,	*Haḍh.*
	Kusunda,	*Gou.*
	Tháru,	*Háḍ.*
	Lepcha (Sikkim),	*Arhet.*
	Bhúṭáni v. Lhopa,	*Rutok.*
N.-E. Bengal.	Bodo,	*Begeng.*
	Dhimál,	*Hara, hár (háḍ ?).*
	Kocch,	*Harwá (haḍwá ?).*
	Garo,	*Kereng.*
	Káchári,	*Caret.*
Eastern Frontier of Bengal.	Munipuri,	*Surru.*
	Míthán Nágá,	*Rha.*
	Tablung Nágá,	*Wan.*
	Khári Nágá,	*Caret.*
	Angámi Nágá,	*Uru.*
	Námsáng Nágá,	*A'ráh.*
	Nowgong Nágá,	*Terap.*
	Tengsa Nágá,	*Telet.*
	Abor Miri,	*A'long.*
	Sibságar Miri,	*A'long.*
	Deoria Chutia,	*Pichong.*
	Singpho,	*Nráng.*
Arrakan & Burmah.	Burman (*written*),	*Aro.*
	Burman (*spoken*),	*Ayo.*
	Khyeng v. Shou,	*Ka-yok.*
	Kámi,	*Ahu.*
	Kúmi,	*Ahu.*
	Mrú v. Toung,	*Ahot.*
	Sák,	*Amza.*
Siam & Tenasserim.	Talain v. Mon,	*H'tsot.*
	Sgau-karen,	*Khi, akhhui.*
	Pwo-karen,	*Khwi.*
	Toungh-thu,	*H'tsot.*
	Shán,	*Sot.*
	Annamitic,	*Xu'o'ng.*
	Siamese,	*Katot, kaduk.*
	Ahom,	*Tau.*
	Khámti,	*Nuk.*
	Laos,	*Duk.*
Central India.	Ho (Kol),	*Jang.*
	Kol (Singhbhum),	*Jáng.*
	Santáli,	*Jáng.*
	Bhúmij,	*Jáng.*
	Uráon,	*Khochal.*
	Mundala,	*Jáng.*
	Rájmahali,	*Kochal.*
	Goṇḍi,	*Haḍa, padeka.*
	Gayeti,	*Padeká.*
	Rutluk,	*Haḍa, padeká.*
	Naikude,	*Bokkál.*
	Kolami,	*Bokka.*
	Mádi,	*Bokairo, padeká.*
	Mádia,	*Atká.*
	Kuri,	*Haḍi.*
	Keikádi,	*Zamká.*
	Khoṇḍ,	*Pásu.*
	Sávara,	*Ajágna.*
	Gadaba,	*Vonḍrám-goyi.*
	Yerukala,	*Yamaka.*
	Chentsu,	*Haḍ.*
Southern India.	Tamiḷ, anc.,	*Enpu.*
	Tamiḷ, mod.,	*Elumbu.*
	Malayáḷma, anc.,	*Caret.*
	Malayáḷma, mod.,	*Ella.*
	Telugu,	*Emuka, bokka.*
	Karṇáṭaka, anc.,	*Elume.*
	Karṇáṭaka, mod.,	*Eluvu.*
	Tuḷuva,	*Elu.*
	Kurgi,	*Caret.*
	Toḍuva,	*Caret.*
	Toḍa,	*Elf.*
	Kóta,	*Yelave.*
	Badaga,	*Yellu, illu.*
	Kurumba,	*Zellu.*
	Iruḷa,	*Zellambu.*
	Malabar,	*Elumbu, at-thi.*
	Sinhalese,	*Äṭe.*

Group	Language	Buffalo
	Types.	
Inflecting.	SANSKRIT,	*Mahisha, kásara, sairibha, [luláya.*
	ARABIC,	*Jámous.*
Compounding.	BASK,	*Idi, zezen.*
	FINNIC,	*Metsaharka.*
	MAGYAR,	*Bival.*
	TURKISH,	*Manda.*
	CIRCASSIAN,	*Caret.*
	GEORGIAN,	*Kanbichi.*
	MONGOLIAN,	*Khaïnokh.*
	MANTSHU,	*Ikhan.*
	JAVANESE, Ngoko,	*Kebo.*
	JAVANESE, Krama,	*Mahesa.*
	MALAY,	*Karbau.*
Isolating.	CHINESE, Nankin,	*Shwui-niú.*
	CHINESE, Pekin,	*Shui-niú.*
	CHINESE, Canton,	*Shui-ngau.*
	CHINESE, Shanghai,	*S'-nieu.*
	AMOY, Colloquial,	*Súi-gu* (water-cow).
	JAPANESE,	*Sai, sui-gui.*
	Brahuí,	*Caret.*
Chinese Frontier & Tibet.	Gyámi,	*Swi-nyú.*
	Gyárung,	*Caret.*
	Tákpa,	*Caret.*
	Mányak,	*Dingmi.*
	Thochú,	*Caret.*
	Sokpa,	*Caret.*
	Horpa,	*Caret.*
	Tibetan (*written*),	*Máhi.*
	Tibetan (*spoken*),	*Máhe.*
Nepal (east to west).	Serpa,	*Meshi.*
	Súnwár,	*Mesye.*
	Gúrung,	*Máï.*
	Múrmi,	*Mahi.*
	Magar,	*Bhainsa.*
	Tháksya,	*Mai.*
	Pákhya,	*Bhaínsa.*
	Newár,	*Me.*
	Limbu,	*Sáwet.*
Kiranti Group (East Nepal).	Kiránti,	*Sáwwá.*
	Rodong,	*Báhira, maisi.*
	Rúngchenbung,	*Sángwa.*
	Chhingtángya,	*Sáŋgwa.*
	Náchhereng,	*Meisá, meis.*
	Wáling,	*Sáng wa.*
	Yákha,	*Sáŋ wa.*
	Chourásya,	*Be-í-so.*
	Kulungya,	*Mesi.*
	Thulungya,	*Mesi.*
	Báhingya,	*Mese.*
	Lohorong,	*Sáŋ-wa.*
	Lambichhong,	*Sáng-wa.*
	Báláli,	*Sáng-wa'.*
	Sáng-páng,	*Mesi.*
	Dúmi,	*Mes.*
	Kháling,	*Mes.*
	Dungmáli,	*Sang-wá.*
Broken Tribes of Nepal.	Dárhi,	*Bhainsa.*
	Denwár,	*Bhainsi.*
	Pahri,	*Me-sá.*
	Chepáng,	*Mi-syá, mi-sha.*
	Bhrámu,	*Bhai-sa.*
	Váyu,	*Mechho.*
	Kuswar,	*Bhaiŋsa.*
	Kusunda,	*Mahi.*
	Tháru,	*Bhaisa.*
	Lepcha (Sikkim),	*Mahí.*
	Bhúṭáni v. Lhopa,	*Mahi.*

Group	Language	Buffalo
N.-E. Bengal.	Bodo,	*Mai-sho.*
	Dhimál,	*Diá.*
	Kocch,	*Bhainsa, rángá, sáral, dhenu.*
	Garo,	*Maishi.*
	Káchári,	*Maisho.*
Eastern Frontier of Bengal.	Munipuri,	*Iroi.*
	Míthán Nágá,	*Loi.*
	Tablung Nágá,	*Tek.*
	Khári Nágá,	*Apang.*
	Angámi Nágá,	*Rali.*
	Námsáng Nágá,	*Le.*
	Nowgong Nágá,	*Chang.*
	Tengsa Nágá,	*Tyang* (*iyang ?*).
	Abor Miri,	*Menjek.*
	Sibságar Miri,	*Menjeg.*
	Deoria Chutia,	*Me.*
	Singpho,	*Ngá.*
Arrakan & Burmah.	Burman (*written*),	*Kwye.*
	Burman (*spoken*),	*Kyue, kúwai.*
	Khyeng v. Shou,	*Nau.*
	Kámi,	*Ma-na.*
	Kúmi,	*Pan-no.*
	Mrú v. Toung,	*Na.*
	Sák,	*Kro.*
Siam & Tenasserim.	Talain v. Mon,	*Paren.*
	Sgau-karen,	*P'nah, paná, penná.*
	Pwo-karen,	*P'nah, páná.*
	Toungh-thu,	*Paynay.*
	Shán,	*Kwihn.*
	Annamitic,	*Trâu.*
	Siamese,	*Khwa, khwái.*
	Ahom,	*Khrai.*
	Khámti,	*Khwai.*
	Laos,	*Khwái.*
Central India.	Ho (Kol),	*Karra* (*káḍa ?*).
	Kol (Singhbhum),	*Keḍá.*
	Santáli,	*Káḍá, báyár, bit-kil, sáïl [(wild).*
	Bhúmij,	*Keḍa.*
	Uráon,	*Mánkhá.*
	Mundala,	*Bhitkil.*
	Rájmahali,	*Mánge.*
	Goṇḍi,	*Háliyá, boda* (m.); *yedmi* (f.).
	Gayeti,	*Boda* (m.); *zedmi* (f.).
	Rutluk,	*Bodal* (m.); *ádami* (f.).
	Naikude,	*Helyá* (m.); *chir* (f.).
	Kolami,	*Sir* (f.).
	Mádi,	*Zeligál* (m.); *zermi* (f.).
	Mádia,	*Adami.*
	Kuri,	*Butkil.*
	Keikádi,	*Hate* (m.); *Baremádu* (f.).
	Khoṇḍ,	*Koḍu.*
	Sávara,	*Bognátel.*
	Gadaba,	*Vontsani.*
	Yerukala,	*Barre.*
	Chentsu,	*Mohis.*
Southern India.	Tamiḷ, anc.,	*Káḍán.*
	Tamiḷ, mod.,	*Erumei.*
	Malayáḷma, anc.,	*Caret.*
	Malayáḷma, mod.,	*Eruma.*
	Telugu,	*Enumu, barre, gède.*
	Karṇáṭaka, anc.,	*Caret.*
	Karṇáṭaka, mod.,	*Emme, koṇa.*
	Tuḷuva,	*Erme.*
	Kurgi,	*Póri.*
	Toḍuva,	*Ir.*
	Toḍa,	*Caret.*
	Kóta,	*Caret.*
	Baḍaga,	*Caret.*
	Kurumba,	*Caret.*
	Iruḷa,	*Caret.*
	Malabar,	*Erumei.*
	Sinhalese,	*Míharaká.*

	Types.	
Inflecting.	SANSKRIT,	*Otu, márjára, viḍála.*
	ARABIC,	*Kiṭṭ.*
Compounding.	BASK,	*Katu.*
	FINNIC,	*Kissa.*
	MAGYAR,	*Makska.*
	TURKISH,	*Kedi.*
	CIRCASSIAN,	*Kettu.*
	GEORGIAN,	*Pati.*
	MONGOLIAN,	*Mighoi.*
	MANTSHU,	*Kesike.*
	JAVANESE, Ngoko,	*Kuching.*
	JAVANESE, Krama,	*Kuching.*
	MALAY,	*Kúching.*
Isolating.	CHINESE, Nankin,	*Máou.*
	CHINESE, Pekin,	*Máou.*
	CHINESE, Canton,	*Máou.*
	CHINESE, Shanghai,	*Mau.*
	AMOY, Colloquial,	*Niauṇ.*
	JAPANESE,	*Nekko.*
	Brahuí,	*Pishí.*
Chinese Frontier & Tibet.	Gyámi,	*Mau, myau.*
	Gyárung,	*Tarhú.*
	Tákpa,	*Syimbú.*
	Mányak,	*Macheu.*
	Thochú,	*Lochi.*
	Sokpa,	*Simí.*
	Horpa,	*Chúlaḥ.*
	Tibetan (*written*),	*Byila.*
	Tibetan (*spoken*),	*Simi.*
Nepal (east to west).	Serpa,	*Bermo.*
	Súnwár,	*Bermo.*
	Gúrung,	*Nawár.*
	Múrmi,	*Tháwar.*
	Magar,	*Súthú.*
	Tháksya,	*Nobar.*
	Pákhya,	*Billo.*
	Newár,	*Bhon.*
	Limbu,	*Myong.*
Kiránti Group (East Nepal).	Kiránti,	*Myong.*
	Rodong,	*Bera.*
	Rúngchenbung,	*Sur'ma, minima.*
	Chhingtángya,	*Púsú.*
	Náchhereng,	*Manimá.*
	Wáling,	*Múnimá.*
	Yákha,	*Púsúma.*
	Chourásya,	*Bir'mo.*
	Kulungya,	*Biráli.*
	Thulungya,	*Bir'má, ubirma.*
	Báhingya,	*Bir'ma.*
	Lohorong,	*Myouma.*
	Lambichhong,	*Múnumá.*
	Báláli,	*Minimá.*
	Sáng-páng,	*Mánimá.*
	Dúmi,	*Birmá, múni.*
	Kháling,	*Birme.*
	Dungmáli,	*Mánimá.*
Broken Tribes of Nepal.	Dárhi,	*Birálo.*
	Denwár,	*Mai-ni.*
	Pahri,	*Bhi.*
	Chepáng,	*Birál.*
	Bhrámu,	*Manzy.*
	Váyu,	*Dána.*
	Kuswar,	*Birálo.*
	Kusunda,	*Birálo.*
	Tháru,	*Birála.*
	Lepcha (Sikkim),	*Aleu.*
	Bhuṭáni v. Lhopa,	*Pilli.*

N.-E. Bengal.	Bodo,	*Mouji.*
	Dhimál,	*Menkhou.*
	Kocch,	*Bilai.*
	Garo,	*Myou.*
	Káchári,	*Bilai.*
Eastern Frontier of Bengal.	Munipuri,	*Houdong.*
	Míthán Nágá,	*Miáh.*
	Tablung Nágá,	*Ami.*
	Khári Nágá,	*Mochi.*
	Angámi Nágá,	*Nunno.*
	Námsáng Nágá,	*Miang.*
	Nowgong Nágá,	*Tanu.*
	Tengsa Nágá,	*Meyau.*
	Abor Miri,	*Mendari.*
	Sibságar Miri,	*Menkuri.*
	Deoria Chutia,	*Midige.*
	Singpho,	*Ningyau.*
Arrakan & Burmah.	Burman (*written*),	*Krong.*
	Burman (*spoken*),	*Kyaung.*
	Khyeng v. Shou,	*Min.*
	Kámi,	*Mim-bo-i.*
	Kúmi,	*Min-cho.*
	Mrú v. Toung,	*Ta-myin.*
	Sák,	*Heing.*
Siam & Tenasserim.	Talain v. Mon,	*Pakway.*
	Sgau-karen,	*Thah-menyaw, mengaw.*
	Pwo-karen,	*Maing-yaw.*
	Toungh-thu,	*Nyen.*
	Shán,	*Myoung.*
	Annamitic,	*Meo.*
	Siamese,	*May, meau.*
	Ahom,	*Men.*
	Khámti,	*Miau.*
	Laos,	*Meau.*
Central India.	Ho (Kol),	*Púsí, billye.*
	Kol (Singhbhum),	*Bilai.*
	Santáli,	*Puṣi, ṭoṭoh* (wild).
	Bhúmij,	*Bilai.*
	Uráon,	*Birkha, kudurám* (wild).
	Mundala,	*Pusi.*
	Rájmahali,	*Berge.*
	Goṇḍi,	*Bilál.*
	Gayeti,	*Bilál.*
	Rutluk,	*Bilál.*
	Naikude,	*Pilli.*
	Kolami,	*Pilli.*
	Mádi,	*Biláli, pusál.*
	Mádia,	*Bilái.*
	Kuri,	*Minnu.*
	Keikádi,	*Puná.*
	Khoṇḍ,	*Miyo.*
	Sávara,	*Rámegná.*
	Gadaba,	*Girem.*
	Yerukala,	*Púna.*
	Chentsu,	*Billeyi.*
Southern India.	Tamiḷ, anc.,	*Púsei.*
	Tamiḷ, mod.,	*Púnei.*
	Malayáḷma, anc.,	*Caret.*
	Malayáḷma, mod.,	*Púchcha.*
	Telugu,	*Pilli.*
	Karṇáṭaka, anc.,	*Caret.*
	Karṇáṭaka, mod.,	*Bekku.*
	Tuḷuva,	*Puchche.*
	Kurgi,	*Caret.*
	Toḍuva, }	*Caret.*
	Toḍa, }	*Koti.*
	Kóta,	*Pise.*
	Baḍaga,	*Koti.*
	Kuṛumba,	*Koti.*
	Iruḷa,	*Púne.*
	Malabar,	*Púnei.*
	Sinhalese,	*Balalá.*

Group	Types.	
Inflecting.	SANSKṚIT,	*Go, usrá.*
	ARABIC,	*Baḳrat.*
Compounding.	BASK,	*Bei.*
	FINNIC,	*Lehma.*
	MAGYAR,	*Tehen.*
	TURKISH,	*Inek.*
	CIRCASSIAN,	*Shkah.*
	GEORGIAN,	*Puri, zrokha.*
	MONGOLIAN,	*Üniyan, unnewon.*§
	MANTSHU,	*Iban khekhe, unin.*
	JAVANESE, Ngoko,	*Sápi.*
	JAVANESE, Krama,	*Lembu.*
	MALAY,	*Lambu.*
Isolating.	CHINESE, Nankin,	*Niú.*
	CHINESE, Pekin,	*Niú.*
	CHINESE, Canton,	*Ngau.*
	CHINESE, Shanghai,	*Nieu.*
	AMOY, Colloquial,	*Gú.*
	JAPANESE,	*Ushi, meusi.*
	Brahuí,	*Dagí.*
Chinese Frontier & Tibet.	Gyámi,	*Neu, nyeu.*
	Gyárung,	*Nye-nye.*
	Tákpa,	*Báḥ.*
	Mányak,	*Womi; gndzi* (bull).
	Thochú,	*Gwaḥ; zyah* (bull).
	Sokpa,	*Sá-lo.*
	Horpa,	*Gnaumeḥ.*
	Tibetan (*written*),	*Bá.*
	Tibetan (*spoken*),	*Phá-chúk.*
Nepal (east to west).	Serpa,	*Chú-ma.*
	Súnwár,	*Bi.*
	Gúrung,	*Myau.*
	Múrmi,	*Mhe.*
	Magar,	*Nhet.*
	Tháksya,	*Hmemama.*
	Pákhya,	*Gái.*
	Newár,	*Sá.*
	Limbu,	*Bit.*
Kiránti Group (East Nepal).	Kiránti,	*Pit.*
	Rodong,	*Piu pa, pi.*
	Rúngchenbung,	*Pit, pik'.*
	Chhingtángya,	*Pit.*
	Náchhereng,	*Pi.*
	Wáling,	*Gái.*
	Yákha,	*I'machha pik'.*
	Chourásya,	*Bia, biya, ámo-bia.*
	Kulungya,	*Pi-imma, ummapi.*
	Thulungya,	*Gai.*
	Báhingya,	*A'mo-bing.*
	Lohorong,	*Pik, pi úmma, ummruma-pi'.*
	Lambichhong,	*Pik', imma-o-pik'.*
	Báláli,	*Pik', oma-pik'.*
	Sáng-páng,	*U'mma-pi.*
	Dúmi,	*Gyai, bi.*
	Kháling,	*Gai.*
	Dungmáli,	*U'mmá-pit'.*
Broken Tribes of Nepal.	Dárhi,	*Gai.*
	Denwár,	*Gai.*
	Pahri,	*Mo-sá.*
	Chepáng,	*Mo-syá, mo-shyá.*
	Bhrámu,	*Syá.*
	Váyu,	*Gai.*
	Kuswar,	*Gai.*
	Kusunda,	*Nokmwa gimi.*
	Tháru,	*Gáye.*
	Lepcha (Sikkim),	*Bik.*
	Bhúṭáni v. Lhopa,	*Guo.*
N.-E. Bengal.	Bodo,	*Musho.*
	Dhimál,	*Piá.*
	Kocch,	*Gai, goru, ándhia, báchru.*
	Garo,	*Mashu.*
	Káchári,	*Moshu.*
Eastern Frontier of Bengal.	Munipuri,	*Sul.*
	Míthán Nágá,	*Máhu.*
	Tablung Nágá,	*Máhu.*
	Khári Nágá,	*Masu.*
	Angámi Nágá,	*Mithu.*
	Námsáng Nágá,	*Mán.*
	Nowgong Nágá,	*Nasi.*
	Tengsa Nágá,	*Mási.*
	Abor Miri,	*Gúrúshameh.*
	Sibságar Miri,	*Goru.*
	Deoria Chutia,	*Mosu.*
	Singpho,	*Kansú.*
Arrakan & Burmah.	Burman (*written*),	Nwá.
	Burman (*spoken*),	Nuá, *nwau.*
	Khyeng v. Shou,	*Sharh.*
	Kámi,	*Kha-bo-i.*
	Kúmi,	*Si-rá.*
	Mrú v. Toung,	*Tsi-yá.*
	Sák,	*Tha-múk.*
Siam & Tenasserim.	Talain v. Mon,	*Karau.*
	Sgau-karen,	*Ghaw'pi, klau, gaupemo.*
	Pwo-karen,	*Tsernung-mu.*
	Toungh-thu,	*Phou.*
	Shán,	*Wo.*
	Annamitic,	*Bò-kái.*
	Siamese,	*Ngwau, woa, ngoa.*
	Ahom,	*Hu.*
	Khámti,	*Ngo.*
	Laos,	*Ngoa.*
Central India.	Ho (Kol),	*Gou.*
	Kol (Singhbhum),	*Gundi.*
	Santáli,	*Gai, gunḍi, gaṭ* = herd.
	Bhúmij,	*Gaï.*
	Uráon,	*Uḍu.*
	Mundala,	*Uḍi.*
	Rájmahali,	*Oi.*
	Gonḍi,	*Dhoriyal, tali, muḍa.*
	Gayeti,	*Muḍá.*
	Rutluk,	*Muḍa.*
	Naikude,	*Ku-te.*
	Kolami,	*Ku-te.*
	Mádi,	*Muḍi, muḍa.*
	Mádia,	*Caret.*
	Kuri,	*Gai.*
	Keikádi,	*Potamadu.*
	Khonḍ,	*Kháyi.*
	Sávara,	*Tangli.*
	Gadaba,	*Banḍi.*
	Yerukala,	*Alamádu, púṭamáḍu.*
	Chentsu,	*Gáyi.*
Southern India.	Tamiḷ, anc.,	*A', pettam.*
	Tamiḷ, mod.,	*Pasu, pasu-máḍu.*
	Malayáḷma, anc.,	*Caret.*
	Malayáḷma, mod.,	*Paśu.*
	Telugu,	*A'vu, áu.*
	Karṇáṭaka, anc.,	*A'vu.*
	Karṇáṭaka, mod.,	*Hasuvu, ákaḷu.*
	Tuḷuva,	*Petta.*
	Kurgi,	*Payyu.*
	Toḍuva,	*Tanma.*
	Toḍa,	*Dánám.*
	Kóta,	*A've.*
	Baḍaga,	*Dana, hasu.*
	Kuṛumba,	*Dana.*
	Iruḷa,	*Mádu.*
	Malabar,	*Pasú, au.*
	Sinhalese,	*Eladena.*

Group	Types.	
Inflecting.	SANSKRIT, ...	*Káka, váyasa, karaṭa, dhváṅksha.*
	ARABIC, ...	*Kaaḳ.*
Compounding.	BASK, ...	*Belzurda.*
	FINNIC, ...	*Wares.*
	MAGYAR, ...	*Varju.*
	TURKISH, ...	*Kargha.*
	CIRCASSIAN, ...	*Caret.*
	GEORGIAN, ...	*Qvavi.*
	MONGOLIAN, . . .	*Khong gerüa, kerisa.*
	MANTSHU, ...	*Kara gaskha.*
	JAVANESE, Ngoko, . .	*Gágak.*
	JAVANESE, Krama, . .	*Gágak.*
	MALAY, ...	*Gágak.*
Isolating.	CHINESE, Nankin, . .	*Láou-yá.*
	CHINESE, Pekin, . .	*Láou-yá.*
	CHINESE, Canton, . .	*Lò-á.*
	CHINESE, Shanghai, .	*Lau-o.*
	AMOY, Colloquial, . .	*A'.*
	JAPANESE, ...	*Karasu.*
	Brahuí, ...	*Khakho.*
Chinese Frontier & Tibet.	Gyámi, ...	*Láwa.*
	Gyárung, ...	*Ta-brok.*
	Tákpa, ...	*A'kpo.*
	Mányak, ...	*Kali.*
	Thochú, ...	*Nyágwo.*
	Sokpa, ...	*Khere.*
	Horpa, ...	*Kale.*
	Tibetan (*written*), . .	*Kháta.*
	Tibetan (*spoken*), . . .	*Ablak.*
Nepal (east to west).	Serpa, ...	*Ká lak.*
	Súnwár, ...	*Khad.*
	Gúrung, ...	*Mlongyá.*
	Múrmi, ...	*Káwá.*
	Magar, ...	*Kág.*
	Tháksya, ...	*Ghábráng.*
	Pákhya, ...	*Kág.*
	Newár, ...	*Ko.*
	Limbu, ...	*A'hwá.*
Kiranti Group (East Nepal).	Kiránti, ...	*Káhwá.*
	Rodong, ...	*Oúwá.*
	Rúngchenbung, . . .	*Kága, kah' wá, gah' wá.*
	Chhingtángya, . . .	*Ghák-wa.*
	Náchhereng, ...	*Gogok-pá.*
	Wáling, ...	*Gowá.*
	Yákha, ...	*A'k'-gwá, ag-wa.*
	Chourásya, ...	*Gág-bo.*
	Kulungya, ...	*Gágáh'-po.*
	Thulungya, ...	*Gápwa, gá-po.*
	Báhingya, ...	*Gá-gákba.*
	Lohorong, ...	*A'rá-wá.*
	Lambichhong, . . .	*Gáh'-wá, gak-wa.*
	Báláli, ...	*A'ra'-wá.*
	Sáng-páng, ...	*Ar'-wá.*
	Dúmi, ...	*Gápo, gagak.*
	Kháling, ...	*Gágakpo.*
	Dungmáli, ...	*Gah'-wá.*
Broken Tribes of Nepal.	Dárhi, ...	*Káwá.*
	Denwár, ...	*Kowa.*
	Pahri, ...	*Ko-ko.*
	Chepáng, ...	*Kág, ka, kuwá.*
	Bhrámu, ...	*Káng-kang.*
	Váyu, ...	*Gá-gin.*
	Kuswar, ...	*Kág-le.*
	Kusunda, ...	*Kaúwa.*
	Tháru, ...	*Kaúwa.*
	Lepcha (Sikkim), . .	*Alok.*
	Bhúṭáni v. Lhopa, . .	*O'lá.*

N.-E. Bengal.	Bodo, ...	*Doukhá.*
	Dhimál, ...	*Kawá.*
	Kocch, ...	*Kág, kowá, kawá.*
	Garo, ...	*Koura.*
	Káchári, ...	*Daoku.*
Eastern Frontier of Bengal.	Munipuri, ...	*Kwák.*
	Míthán Nágá, . . .	*Okhá.*
	Tablung Nágá, . . .	*Ausapa.*
	Khári Nágá, ...	*Waru.*
	Angámi Nágá, . . .	*Chejá.*
	Námsáng Nágá, . .	*Vakhá.*
	Nowgong Nágá, . .	*Waru.*
	Tengsa Nágá, . . .	*Walo.*
	Abor Miri, ...	*Piák.*
	Sibságar Miri, . . .	*Püag.*
	Deoria Chutia, . . .	*Duká.*
	Singpho, ...	*Kokhá.*
Arrakan & Burmah.	Burman (*written*), . .	*Kyí.*
	Burman (*spoken*), . .	*Kyí, kyí-gan.*
	Khyeng v. Shou, . .	*A'ng-au.*
	Kámi, ...	*Wa-á.*
	Kúmi, ...	*O'-á.*
	Mrú v. Toung, . . .	*Wa-á.*
	Sák, ...	*Wúk-ká.*
Siam & Tenasserim.	Talain v. Mon, . . .	*Khatat.*
	Sgau-karen, ...	*Sowah-khah, tsoa-khah.*
	Pwo-karen, ...	*Klah.*
	Toungh-thu, ...	*Zank-ay.*
	Shán, ...	*Ka.*
	Annamitic, ...	*Shim-khásh.*
	Siamese, ...	*Ka.*
	Ahom, ...	*Ka.*
	Khámti, ...	*Ka.*
	Laos, ...	*Ka.*
Central India.	Ho (Kol), ...	*Ká.*
	Kol (Singhbhum), . .	*Ka.*
	Santáli, ...	*Kahu, kahung.*
	Bhúmij, ...	*Ková.*
	Uráon, ...	*Khákhá.*
	Mundala, ...	*Ková.*
	Rájmahali, ...	*Káki.*
	Goṇḍi, ...	*Káwá, kawal.*
	Gayeti, ...	*Kawal.*
	Rutluk, ...	*Caret.*
	Naikude, ...	*Kawala.*
	Kolami, ...	*Káka.*
	Mádi, ...	*Kákadi, kákari.*
	Mádia, ...	*Kabal.*
	Kuri, ...	*Caret.*
	Keikádi, ...	*Koi.*
	Khoṇḍ, ...	*Káka.*
	Sávara, ...	*Káká.*
	Gadaba, ...	*Guggá.*
	Yerukala, ...	*Selán, káka.*
	Chentsu, ...	*Kovvá.*
Southern India.	Tamiḷ, anc., ...	*Karumpillei.*
	Tamiḷ, mod., ...	*Kákkei.*
	Malayáḷma, anc., . .	*Caret.*
	Malayáḷma, mod., . .	*Kákka.*
	Telugu, ...	*Káki.*
	Karṇáṭaka, anc., . .	*Caret.*
	Karṇáṭaka, mod., . .	*Kági, káki.*
	Tuḷuva, ...	*Khákke.*
	Kurgi, ...	*Caret.*
	Toḍuva, ...	*Kak.*
	Toḍa, ...	*Kák.*
	Kóta, ...	*Káke.*
	Baḍaga, ...	*Káke.*
	Kuṛumba, ...	*Kake.*
	Iruḷa, ...	*Káke.*
	Malabar, ...	*Kákam, kakkei.*
	Sinhalese, ...	*Kapuṭá, kakká.*

Types.		
Inflecting.	SANSKRIT,	*Ahan, vásara, ghasra, [divasa, dina.*
	ARABIC,	*Youm.*
Compounding.	BASK,	*Egun.*
	FINNIC,	*Pairva.*
	MAGYAR,	*Nap.*
	TURKISH,	*Gun.*
	CIRCASSIAN,	*Mahpey, akini.**
	GEORGIAN,	*Dghe, bigula.**
	MONGOLIAN,	*Edor.*
	MANTSHU,	*Inenggi.*
	JAVANESE, Ngoko,	*Dina.*
	JAVANESE, Krama,	*Dinten.*
	MALAY,	*A'ri.*
Isolating.	CHINESE, Nankin,	*Jih.*
	CHINESE, Pekin,	*Jih.*
	CHINESE, Canton,	*Yat.*
	CHINESE, Shanghai,	*Nieh-tsz'.*
	AMOY, Colloquial,	*Jit.*
	JAPANESE,	*Hi, nichi, fi.*
	Brahuí,	*Caret.*
Chinese Frontier & Tibet.	Gyámi,	*Peth-yan.*
	Gyárung,	*Pish-né, nye.*
	Tákpa,	*Nyenti.*
	Mányak,	*Nashchâh.*
	Thochú,	*Styáklo.*
	Sokpa,	*Wúndúr.*
	Horpa,	*Nye-le.*
	Tibetan (*written*),	*Nyin-mo.*
	Tibetan (*spoken*),	*Nyi-mo.*
Nepal (east to west).	Serpa,	*Nimo.*
	Súnwár,	*Náthi.*
	Gúrung,	*Dini.*
	Múrmi,	*Dini.*
	Magar,	*Na-msin.*
	Tháksya,	*Sar.*
	Pákhya,	*Diüso.*
	Newár,	*Nhi.*
	Limbu,	*Lendik.*
Kiranti Group (East Nepal).	Kiránti,	*Len.*
	Rodong,	*Khole.*
	Rúngchenbung,	*Ukholen.*
	Chhingtángya,	*Nám.*
	Náchhereng,	*Mlepa.*
	Wáling,	*Wo-khole, nam-diya.*
	Yákha,	*Leh'ni.*
	Chourásya,	*Duk so.*
	Kulungya,	*Lepá.*
	Thulungya,	*Nemphú.*
	Báhingya,	*Nám' ti.*
	Lohorong,	*Lentá, len.*
	Lambichhong,	*Ilemba.*
	Báláli,	*Letta.*
	Sáng-páng,	*Lépa, úmlépa.*
	Dúmi,	*U'nyol, núlu.*
	Kháling,	*U'nyol.*
	Dungmáli,	*Lento, lentok, umlentok, [umlento.*
Broken Tribes of Nepal.	Dárhi,	*Din.*
	Denwár,	*Di-ni.*
	Pahri,	*Nhi-na-ko.*
	Chepáng,	*Nyi, ngi, gni.*
	Bhrámu,	*Di-ná.*
	Váyu,	*Nu-ma, no-mo.*
	Kuswar,	*Di-ní.*
	Kusunda,	*Dina.*
	Tháru,	*Dina.*
	Lepcha (Sikkim),	*Sakni.*
	Bhútáni v. Lhopa,	*Nyim.*

N.-E. Bengal.	Bodo,	*Shyán, shán.*
	Dhimál,	*Nyi-tima, nhitima.*
	Kocch,	*Din.*
	Garo,	*Rasán, sán.*
	Káchári,	*Chân-dung.*
Eastern Frontier of Bengal.	Munipuri,	*Númit.*
	Míthán Nágá,	*Anyi.*
	Tablung Nágá,	*Tini.*
	Khári Nágá,	*Asonga.*
	Angámi Nágá,	*Tiso.*
	Námsáng Nágá,	*Rangyi.*
	Nowgong Nágá,	*Caret.*
	Tengsa Nágá,	*Tünglú.*
	Abor Miri,	*Longeh.*
	Sibságar Miri,	*Longko.*
	Deoria Chutia,	*Sánjá.*
	Singpho,	*Ningthoi.*
Arrakan & Burmah.	Burman (*written*),	*Ne.*
	Burman (*spoken*),	*Ne, na.*
	Khyeng v. Shou,	*Ko-nup.*
	Kámi,	*Ma-ni.*
	Kúmi,	*Ka-ni twun.*
	Mrú v. Toung,	*Ni.*
	Sák,	*Yat-ta.*
Siam & Tenasserim.	Talain v. Mon,	*Ta-ngway.*
	Sgau-karen,	*Ni, mu-khni.*
	Pwo-karen,	*Ni.*
	Toungh-thu,	*Mo-yay.*
	Shán,	*Kawon.*
	Annamitic,	*Ngày.*
	Siamese,	*Wan.*
	Ahom,	*Bán.*
	Khámti,	*Wan.*
	Laos,	*Wan.*
Central India.	Ho (Kol),	*Má.*
	Kol (Singhbhum),	*Sugi, ma.*
	Santáli,	*Sing, máhá (ma ?).*
	Bhúmij,	*Din.*
	Uráon,	*Ullah.*
	Mundala,	*Sing.*
	Rájmahali,	*Dine.*
	Goṇḍi,	*Patti, din.*
	Gayeti,	*Din.*
	Rutluk,	*Piyál.*
	Naikude,	*Pod.*
	Kolami,	*Páte.*
	Mádi,	*Peyál.*
	Mádia,	*Biyár.*
	Kuri,	*Din.*
	Keikádi,	*Pugdu, poddu.*
	Khoṇḍ,	*Vujjyágu.*
	Sávara,	*Tambá.*
	Gadaba,	*Simmyá.*
	Yerukala,	*Pammárú, pangámáru.*
	Chentsu,	*Din.*
Southern India.	Tamiḷ, anc.,	*El.*
	Tamiḷ, mod.,	*Pagal, dinam, náḷ.*
	Malayáḷma, anc.,	*Caret.*
	Malayáḷma, mod.,	*Pakal.*
	Telugu,	*Pagalu, dinamu.*
	Karṇáṭaka, anc.,	*Pagalu.*
	Karṇáṭaka, mod.,	*Hagalu.*
	Tuḷuva,	*Pagil.*
	Kurgi,	*Pogal.*
	Toḍuva, } Toḍa, }	*Pokhal. Nál.*
	Kóta,	*Nále.*
	Baḍaga,	*Dina, jina.*
	Kuṛumba,	*Dina.*
	Iruḷa,	*Nalu.*
	Malabar,	*Naul, thenam.*
	Sinhalese,	*Dawasa, dina.*

Types.		
Inflecting.	SANSKṚIT,	*S'van, bhashaka, kukkura.*
	ARABIC,	*Kelb.*
Compounding.	BASK,	*Chakur, zakur, potzo, ora.*
	FINNIC,	*Koira.*
	MAGYAR,	*Kutya.*
	TURKISH,	*Keupek.*
	CIRCASSIAN,	*Khah, schy,* koy.**
	GEORGIAN,	*Tsaghli.*
	MONGOLIAN,	*Nokhai, nochai, kalziakan,§*
	MANTSHU,	*Indakhon.* [*tollokin.*‖
	JAVANESE, Ngoko,	*A'su.*
	JAVANESE, Krama,	*Segáwon.*
	MALAY,	*Anjing.*
Isolating.	CHINESE, Nankin,	*Kau.*
	CHINESE, Pekin,	*Kau.*
	CHINESE, Canton,	*Kau.*
	CHINESE, Shanghai,	*K'eu.*
	AMOY, Colloquial,	*Kaú.*
	JAPANESE,	*Inu.*
	Brahuí,	*Kuchak.*
Chinese Frontier & Tibet.	Gyámi,	*Kou.*
	Gyárung,	*Khi.*
	Tákpa,	*Khi.*
	Mányak,	*Kshaḥ.*
	Thochú,	*Khwaḥ.*
	Sokpa,	*Nokhwe.*
	Horpa,	*Katáḥ.*
	Tibetan (*written*),	*Khyi.*
	Tibetan (*spoken*),	*Uyo.*
Nepal (east to west).	Serpa,	*Khí.*
	Súnwár,	*Kúchúng.*
	Gúrung,	*Nagyú.*
	Múrmi,	*Nángi.*
	Magar,	*Chhyú.*
	Tháksya,	*Nága, nak'yu.*
	Pákhya,	*Kyatáí.*
	Newár,	*Khí-chá.*
	Limbu,	*Khiá.*
Kiranti Group (East Nepal).	Kiránti,	*Kochú.*
	Rodong,	*Khlí.*
	Rúngchenbung,	*Kochúwá.*
	Chhingtángya,	*Kochúwá.*
	Náchhereng,	*Haga.*
	Wáling,	*Kotima, kochuwá.*
	Yákha,	*Kochúma.*
	Chourásya,	*Cháli.*
	Kulungya,	*Kheb.*
	Thulungya,	*Khlebá.*
	Báhingya,	*Khlícha.*
	Lohorong,	*Hú wá.*
	Lambichhong,	*Kochú.*
	Báláli,	*Kochúmá.*
	Sáng-páng,	*Há-ága, hoga.*
	Dúmi,	*Khleb, khlibu.*
	Kháling,	*Khleb.*
	Dungmáli,	*Kúti-má.*
Broken Tribes of Nepal.	Dárhi,	*Kúkúr.*
	Denwár,	*Kú-kúr.*
	Pahri,	*Ku-ju, ku.*
	Chepáng,	*Kwí, kúí.*
	Bhrámu,	*A-kyá.*
	Váyu,	*Urí.*
	Kuswar,	*Ku-kol.*
	Kusunda,	*Agai.*
	Tháru,	*Kútta.*
	Lepcha (Sikkim),	*Kazeu.*
	Bhúṭáni v. Lhopa,	*Khi.*
N.-E. Bengal.	Bodo,	*Choïma, chikú.*
	Dhimál,	*Khiá.*
	Kocch,	*Kúkúr, kúhok.*
	Garo,	*Kai.*
	Káchári,	*Shoima, shíma.*
Eastern Frontier of Bengal.	Munipuri,	*Hwí.*
	Míthán Nágá,	*Hi.*
	Tablung Nágá,	*Kui.*
	Khári Nágá,	*Ai.*
	Angámi Nágá,	*Tasü.*
	Námsáng Nágá,	*Hú.*
	Nowgong Nágá,	*Azz.*
	Tengsa Nágá,	*Arh.*
	Abor Miri,	*Eki.*
	Sibságar Miri,	*Iki.*
	Deoria Chutia,	*Shi.*
	Singpho,	*Gúi.*
Arrakan & Burmah.	Burman (*written*),	*Khwe.*
	Burman (*spoken*),	*Khwe, khwá.*
	Khyeng v. Shou,	*U-i.*
	Kámi,	*U-i.*
	Kúmi,	*U-i.*
	Mrú v. Toung,	*Ta-kwi.*
	Sák,	*Kú.*
Siam & Tenasserim.	Talain v. Mon,	*Kalá.*
	Sgau-karen,	*'Twi, htwi.*
	Pwo-karen,	*Twi.*
	Toungh-thu,	*Htwe.*
	Shán,	*Ma.*
	Annamitic,	*Sho.*
	Siamese,	*Ma.*
	Ahom,	*Má.*
	Khámti,	*Má.*
	Laos,	*Má.*
Central India.	Ho (Kol),	*Seta.*
	Kol (Singhbhum),	*Setá.*
	Santáli,	*Setá.*
	Bhúmij,	*Setá.*
	Uráon,	*Alla.*
	Mundala,	*Setá.*
	Rájmahali,	*Allay.*
	Goṇḍi,	*Nāi, nei.*
	Gayeti,	*Nai.*
	Rutluk,	*Nei.*
	Naikude,	*A'tte.*
	Kolami,	*A'tte.*
	Mádi,	*Neiyu, nei-o.*
	Mádia,	*Nei.*
	Kuri,	*Chita, seta.*
	Keikádi,	*Nai.*
	Khoṇḍ,	*Nahuḍi.*
	Sávara,	*Kencho.*
	Gadaba,	*Guso.*
	Yerukala,	*Náyi.*
	Chentsu,	*Kukkúr.*
Southern India.	Tamiḷ, anc.,	*Caret.*
	Tamiḷ, mod.,	*Náyi, muḍuval.*
	Malayáḷma, anc.,	*Caret.*
	Malayáḷma, mod.,	*Náya, paṭṭi.*
	Telugu,	*Kukka.*
	Karṇáṭaka, anc.,	*Caret.*
	Karṇáṭaka, mod.,	*Náyi.*
	Tuḷuva,	*Náyi.*
	Kurgi,	*Náyi.*
	Toḍuva,	*Náyi.*
	Toḍa,	*Noi.*
	Kóta,	*Nai.*
	Baḍaga,	*Nai.*
	Kuṛumba,	*Nai.*
	Iruḷa,	*Nai.*
	Malabar,	*Noy, suv-anam.*
	Sinhalese,	*Ballá.*

Types.

Group	Language	Ear
Inflecting.	Sanskrit,	*Karṇa.*
	Arabic,	*Uzn.*
Compounding.	Bask,	*Belarri, bearri.*
	Finnic,	*Korwa.*
	Magyar,	*Fül.*
	Turkish,	*Kulak.*
	Circassian,	*Takhum.*
	Georgian,	*Kuri.*
	Mongolian,	*Chikin, tsighin; bucha.*‖
	Mantshu,	*Shan; udak.**
	Javanese, Ngoko,	*Kúping.*
	Javanese, Krama,	*Tali ngan.*
	Malay,	*Talinga.*
Isolating.	Chinese, Nankin,	*Urh.*
	Chinese, Pekin,	*Urh.*
	Chinese, Canton,	*Urh.*
	Chinese, Shanghai,	*Ni-tu.*
	Amoy, Colloquial,	*Hi.*
	Japanese,	*Mimi.*
	Brahuí,	*Khaff.*
Chinese Frontier & Tibet.	Gyámi,	*Airto.*
	Gyárung,	*Tir-ne.*
	Tákpa,	*Nehláp.*
	Mányak,	*Nápi.*
	Thochú,	*Núkh.*
	Sokpa,	*Khikhe.*
	Horpa,	*Nyo.*
	Tibetan (*written*),	Rna.
	Tibetan (*spoken*),	*Amcho.*
Nepal (east to west).	Serpa,	*Am-chúk.*
	Súnwár,	*Nophá.*
	Gúrung,	*Nábe.*
	Múrmi,	*Nápe.*
	Magar,	*Ná-kyep.*
	Tháksya,	*Hna, nha.*
	Pákhya,	*Kán.*
	Newár,	*Nhai-pong.*
	Limbu,	*Nekho.*
Kiranti Group (East Nepal).	Kiránti,	*Nábá.*
	Rodong,	*Nápro.*
	Rúngchenbung,	*Nába.*
	Chhingtángya,	*Nárek.*
	Náchhereng,	*Nábá.*
	Wáling,	*Náphák.*
	Yákha,	*Náphák.*
	Chourásya,	*Dobú.*
	Kulungya,	*Nobwa, no-bo.*
	Thulungya,	*Nokphla.*
	Báhingya,	*Sámá-nyeú.*
	Lohorong,	*Nábak, nába.*
	Lambichhong,	*Noro.*
	Báláli,	*Naba.*
	Sáng-páng,	*Naba.*
	Dúmi,	*Necho.*
	Kháling,	*Necho.*
	Dungmáli,	*Náphak.*
Broken Tribes of Nepal.	Dárhi,	*Kán.*
	Denwár,	*Kán.*
	Pahri,	*Nhúa-puru.*
	Chepáng,	*Ne, no.*
	Bhrámu,	*Ká-ná.*
	Váyu,	*Nak-chú, nok-chung.*
	Kuswar,	*Kán.*
	Kusunda,	*Chyáü.*
	Tháru,	*Kán.*
	Lepcha (Sikkim),	*Anyor.*
	Bhúṭáni v. Lhopa,	*Navo.*

Group	Language	Ear
N.-E. Bengal.	Bodo,	*Khoma.*
	Dhimál,	*Nhá-tong, náháthong.*
	Kocch,	*Kán.*
	Garo,	*Máchor.*
	Káchári,	*Khoma.*
Eastern Frontier of Bengal.	Munipuri,	*Na.*
	Míthán Nágá,	*Ná.*
	Tablung Nágá,	*Ná.*
	Khári Nágá,	*Tenhaung.*
	Angámi Nágá,	*Anye.*
	Námsáng Nágá,	*Ná.*
	Nowgong Nágá,	*Tenaung.*
	Tengsa Nágá,	*Telánnu.*
	Abor Miri,	*Norong.*
	Sibságar Miri,	*Yerung.*
	Deoria Chutia,	*Yáku.*
	Singpho,	*Ná.*
Arrakan & Burmah.	Burman (*written*),	Ná.
	Burman (*spoken*),	*Ná, nau.*
	Khyeng v. Shou,	*Ka-nhau.*
	Kámi,	*A-ga-ná.*
	Kúmi,	*Ka-no.*
	Mrú v. Toung,	*Pa-rám.*
	Sák,	*A-ka-ná.*
Siam & Tenasserim.	Talain v. Mon,	*Khato.*
	Sgau-karen,	*Nah, na-khu.*
	Pwo-karen,	*Nah.*
	Toungh-thu,	*Nau.*
	Shán,	*Hu.*
	Annamitic,	*Tai.*
	Siamese,	*Hú.*
	Ahom,	*Pik.*
	Khámti,	*Hú.*
	Laos,	*Hú.*
Central India.	Ho (Kol),	*Lútur.*
	Kol (Singhbhum),	*Lutúr.*
	Santáli,	*Lutúr, húpa* = side of ear.
	Bhúmij,	*Lutúr.*
	Uráon,	*Khebda.*
	Mundala,	*Lutúr.*
	Rájmahali,	*Khetway.*
	Goṇḍi,	*Kavi.*
	Gayeti,	*Kavi.*
	Rutluk,	*Kavi.*
	Naikude,	*Kewal* (pl.).
	Kolami,	*Kavval* (pl.).
	Mádi,	*Chouku, kewoku* (pl.).
	Mádia,	*Kavi.*
	Kuri,	*Lutur.*
	Keikádi,	*Suvi.*
	Khoṇḍ,	*Kirru.*
	Sávara,	*Luv.*
	Gadaba,	*Nintiri.*
	Yerukala,	*Soyi.*
	Chentsu,	*Kán.*
Southern India.	Tamiḻ, anc.,	*Sevi.*
	Tamiḻ, mod.,	*Kádu, sevi.*
	Malayáḷma, anc.,	*Caret.*
	Malayáḷma, mod.,	*Káta, chevi.*
	Telugu,	*Chevi.*
	Karṇáṭaka, anc.,	*Caret.*
	Karṇáṭaka, mod.,	*Kivi, kimi.*
	Tuḷuva,	*Kebi.*
	Kurgi,	*Kemi.*
	Toḍuva, }	*Kavi.*
	Toḍa, }	*Kevvi.*
	Kóta,	*Kive.*
	Badaga,	*Kive.*
	Kurumba,	*Kive.*
	Iruḷa,	*Kádu.*
	Malabar,	*Káthu, sevi.*
	Sinhalese,	*Kana.*

Group	Language	Earth
	Types.	
Inflecting.	SANSKRIT,	*Bhú, bhúmi, go, prithiví.*
	ARABIC,	*Arḍ.*
Compounding.	BASK,	*Lur.*
	FINNIC,	*Maa.*
	MAGYAR,	*Föld.*
	TURKISH,	*Yer, toprak.*
	CIRCASSIAN,	*Yattah, wahtey.*
	GEORGIAN,	*Mitsa, musa.**
	MONGOLIAN,	*Küsar, ghazar; daradu.§*
	MANTSHU,	*Na, usin.*
	JAVANESE, Ngoko,	*Bumi.*
	JAVANESE, Krama,	*Bumi.*
	MALAY,	*Tánah.*
Isolating.	CHINESE, Nankin,	*Tí, ni-t'ú,* i.e. soil.
	CHINESE, Pekin,	*Tí, ni-t'ú,* i.e. soil.
	CHINESE, Canton,	*Tí, nai-t'o,* i.e. soil.
	CHINESE, Shanghai,	*Ti-bi, ni,* i.e. mud.
	AMOY, Colloquial,	*Toe.*
	JAPANESE,	*Tsuchi.*
	Brahuí,	*Caret.*
Chinese Frontier & Tibet.	Gyámi,	*Tí, thou.*
	Gyárung,	*Seḥ.*
	Tákpa,	*Sáḥ.*
	Mányak,	*Mali, mlí.*
	Thochú,	*Zip.*
	Sokpa,	*Wonnish.*
	Horpa,	*Kcha.*
	Tibetan (*written*),	*Ná, sa.*
	Tibetan (*spoken*),	*Sá.*
Nepal (east to west).	Serpa,	*Sá.*
	Súnwár,	*Kha-pi.*
	Gúrung,	*Sa, nhe.*
	Múrmi,	*Sá.*
	Magar,	*Jhá.*
	Tháksya,	*Sa.*
	Pákhya,	*Máto.*
	Newár,	*Chá.*
	Limbu,	*Kham.*
Kiranti Group (East Nepal).	Kiránti,	*Bákhá.*
	Rodong,	*Bokhá.*
	Rúngchenbung,	*Bákhá, henkhama.*
	Chhingtángya,	*Khám.*
	Náchhereng,	*Baha.*
	Wáling,	*Pákhá.*
	Yákha,	*Khám.*
	Chourásya,	*Káṇksi.*
	Kulungya,	*Boho.*
	Thulungya,	*Kwá.*
	Báhingya,	*Wáleko.*
	Lohorong,	*Bá khá.*
	Lambichhong,	*Khamhangtangba.*
	Báláli,	*Bali kha.*
	Sáng-páng,	*Báhá.*
	Dúmi,	*Caret.*
	Kháling,	*Caret.*
	Dungmáli,	*Wálikha.*
Broken Tribes of Nepal.	Dárhi,	*Máti.*
	Denwár,	*Máto.*
	Pahri,	*Chá.*
	Chepáng,	*Sá.*
	Bhrámu,	*Ná-sá.*
	Váyu,	*Ko.*
	Kuswar,	*Mati.*
	Kusunda,	*Doma.*
	Tháru,	*Máti.*
	Lepcha (Sikkim),	*Phat.*
	Bhúṭáni v. Lhopa,	*Sáh.*
N.-E. Bengal.	Bodo,	*Há, hásharhá.*
	Dhimál,	*Bhonoï.*
	Kocch,	*Bhúmi, máti.*
	Garo,	*Há.*
	Kácháhri,	*Há.*
Eastern Frontier of Bengal.	Munipuri,	*Laipák.*
	Míthán Nágá,	*Háwán.*
	Tablung Nágá,	*Katok.*
	Khári Nágá,	*Ali.*
	Angámi Nágá,	*Kije.*
	Námsáng Nágá,	*Há.*
	Nowgong Nágá,	*A'li.*
	Tengsa Nágá,	*A'li.*
	Abor Miri,	*A'mong.*
	Sibságar Miri,	*A'mong.*
	Deoria Chutia,	*Yá.*
	Singpho,	*Nggá.*
Arrakan & Burmah.	Burman (*written*),	*Mre.*
	Burman (*spoken*),	*Mye, myá-ghí.*
	Khyeng v. Shou,	*Det.*
	Kámi,	*Ka-lái-hong.*
	Kúmi,	*Ka-loung.*
	Mrú v. Toung,	*Kroung.*
	Sák,	*Ká.*
Siam & Tenasserim.	Talain v. Mon,	*Te.*
	Sgau-karen,	*Hawks, hau-hko.*
	Pwo-karen,	*Gon-ku.*
	Toungh-thu,	*Ham-tan.*
	Shán,	*Sen.*
	Annamitic,	*Dát.*
	Siamese,	*Tĕin, phendin.*
	Ahom,	*Din.*
	Khámti,	*Langmin.*
	Laos,	*Din.*
Central India.	Ho (Kol),	*Ote, hassa.*
	Kol (Singhbhum),	*Ote.*
	Santáli,	*Hásá, atha* = the earth,
	Bhúmij,	*Ote.* (*ḍáḍá* = paddock,
	Uráon,	*Khekhel.* *ḍhalák* = clod,
	Mundala,	*Wathe.* *dëma* = plain.)
	Rájmahali,	*Kekal.*
	Gonḍi,	*Dharti, dhartri.*
	Gayeti,	*Dhartri.*
	Rutluk,	*Dhartri.*
	Naikude,	*El.*
	Kolami,	*El.*
	Mádi,	*Dartri.*
	Mádia,	*Neli.*
	Kuri,	*Ote, wote.*
	Keikádi,	*Nard.*
	Khonḍ,	*Táṇá.*
	Sávara,	*Labo.*
	Gadaba,	*Caret.*
	Yerukala,	*Tarra.*
	Chentsu,	*Bhúyi.*
Southern India.	Tamiḷ, anc.,	*Caret.*
	Tamiḷ, mod.,	*Nilam, ulagam.*
	Malayáḷma, anc.,	*Caret.*
	Malayáḷma, mod.,	*Nilam, maṇṇa.*
	Telugu,	*Puḍami, nela, mannu.*
	Karṇáṭaka, anc.,	*Caret.*
	Karṇáṭaka, mod.,	*Poḍavi.*
	Tuḷuva,	*Nela.*
	Kurgi,	*Caret.*
	Toḍuva, }	*Nelan.*
	Toḍa, }	*Búmi.*
	Kóta,	*Búmi.*
	Baḍaga,	*Búmi.*
	Kuṛumba,	*Mannu, búmi.*
	Iruḷa,	*Bumi.*
	Malabar,	*Púmi, puvi, prithivi.*
	Sinhalese,	*Polawa.*

Group	Language	Egg
	Types.	
Inflecting.	SANSKRIT,	*Aṇḍa.*
	ARABIC,	*Beiḍ.*
Compounding.	BASK,	*Arraultz.*
	FINNIC,	*Muna.*
	MAGYAR,	*Tojas.*
	TURKISH,	*Yumurta.*
	CIRCASSIAN,	*Kanghey, tshankey.*
	GEORGIAN,	*Kwertskhi.*
	MONGOLIAN,	*Ümdoken, ümtuke.*
	MANTSHU,	*Umhan, tchoko-i-umakha.*
	JAVANESE, Ngoko,	*Endog.*
	JAVANESE, Krama,	*Tigan.*
	MALAY,	*Talor.*
Isolating.	CHINESE, Nankin,	*Tán.*
	CHINESE, Pekin,	*Tán.*
	CHINESE, Canton,	*Tán.*
	CHINESE, Shanghai,	*Ki-daṇ.*
	AMOY, Colloquial,	*Nñg.*
	JAPANESE,	*Tamago.*
	Brahuí,	*Caret.*
Chinese Frontier & Tibet.	Gyámi,	*Chitun.*
	Gyárung,	*Ki-tan.*
	Tákpa,	*Khálúm.*
	Mányak,	*Rácha.*
	Thochú,	*Kiwost.*
	Sokpa,	*Caret.*
	Horpa,	*Sgangá.*
	Tibetan (*written*),	*Sgonga.*
	Tibetan (*spoken*),	*Gong-ná.*
Nepal (east to west).	Serpa,	*Gongná.*
	Súnwár,	*Bá-phú.*
	Gúrung,	*Phúng.*
	Múrmi,	*Phúm.*
	Magar,	*Rhú.*
	Tháksya,	*Chhyárkyaphúm.*
	Pákhya,	*Phul.*
	Newár,	*Khyen, khen.*
	Limbu,	*Thín, thín.*
Kiranti Group (East Nepal).	Kiránti,	*U'ding.*
	Rodong,	*Dai, da-i.*
	Rúngchenbung,	*U'-ding, wá-din.*
	Chhingtángya,	*U'-thin.*
	Náchhereng,	*Di-i.*
	Wáling,	*Dim.*
	Yákha,	*In, wá-in.*
	Chourásya,	*Bábáng'ya.*
	Kulungya,	*U'mdi, wádi, di.*
	Thulungya,	*Di-i.*
	Báhingya,	*Di, bá-di.*
	Lohorong,	*Wehdiṇ, we-din.*
	Lambichhong,	*Thin, ithin.*
	Bálálí,	*Wádin.*
	Sáng-páng,	*Di.*
	Dúmi,	*U'ti, ti.*
	Kháling,	*Phátte.*
	Dungmáli,	*U'mting, ting.*
Broken Tribes of Nepal.	Dárhi,	*Anda.*
	Denwár,	*Dimba.*
	Pahri,	*Khen-ja.*
	Chepáng,	*Wá-kúm, lum.*
	Bhrámu,	*Hom.*
	Váyu,	*Chálung.*
	Kuswar,	*Dimba.*
	Kusunda,	*Goä, gwa.*
	Thárú,	*Anda.*
	Lepcha (Sikkim),	*Ati.*
	Bhúṭáni v. Lhopa,	*Gong-do.*
N.-E. Bengal.	Bodo,	*Dau-doï.*
	Dhimál,	*Tüi.*
	Kocch,	*Dima.*
	Garo,	*Touchi.*
	Káchári,	*Caret.*
Eastern Frontier of Bengal.	Munipuri,	*Caret.*
	Míthán Nágá,	*Oti.*
	Tablung Nágá,	*Kek.*
	Khári Nágá,	*Ansü.*
	Angámi Nágá,	*Podzü.*
	Námsáng Nágá,	*Ati.*
	Nowgong Nágá,	*Antsü.*
	Tengsa Nágá,	*Utü.*
	Abor Miri,	*A'piu.*
	Sibságar Miri,	*Apü.*
	Deoria Chutia,	*Dujá.*
	Singpho,	*U'di.*
Arrakan & Burmah.	Burman (*written*),	*U.*
	Burman (*spoken*),	*U, o-o.*
	Khyeng v. Shou,	*To-i.*
	Kámi,	*Du.*
	Kúmi,	*Dú-i.*
	Mrú v. Toung,	*Dú-i.*
	Sák,	*Wa-ti.*
Siam & Tenasserim.	Talain v. Mon,	*Khmatsan.*
	Sgau-karen,	*Di, hdi, dhi.*
	Pwo-karen,	*Di.*
	Toungh-thu,	*De.*
	Shán,	*Khiht.*
	Annamitic,	*Trú'ng.*
	Siamese,	*Khu, khai.*
	Ahom,	*Khrai.*
	Khámti,	*Khai.*
	Laos,	*Khai.*
Central India.	Ho (Kol),	*Petto, billi.*
	Kol (Singhbhum),	*Pittü.*
	Santáli,	*Bele.*
	Bhúmij,	*Pito.*
	Uráon,	*Bi.*
	Mundala,	*Billi.*
	Rájmahali,	*Kirpan.*
	Goṇḍi,	*Mej, mes.*
	Gayeti,	*Caret.*
	Rutluk,	*Caret.*
	Naikude,	*Caret.*
	Kolami,	*Caret.*
	Mádi,	*Caret.*
	Mádia,	*Caret.*
	Kuri,	*Caret.*
	Keikádi,	*Caret.*
	Khoṇḍ,	*Vaṭánga.*
	Sávara,	*Are.*
	Gadaba,	*Mittá.*
	Yerukala,	*Muṭṭa.*
	Chentsu,	*Dimma.*
Southern India.	Tamiḷ, anc.,	*Sinei.*
	Tamiḷ, mod.,	*Muṭṭei.*
	Malayáḷma, anc.,	*Caret.*
	Malayáḷma, mod.,	*Muṭṭa.*
	Telugu,	*Guḍḍu.*
	Karṇáṭaka, anc.,	*Caret.*
	Karṇáṭaka, mod.,	*Tatti, moṭṭe, guḍḍu.*
	Tuḷuva,	*Muṭṭe, teṭṭi.*
	Kurgi,	*Caret.*
	Toḍuva, }	*Mukshu.*
	Toḍa, }	*Moṭṭe.*
	Kóta,	*Moṭṭe.*
	Badaga,	*Moṭṭe.*
	Kurumba,	*Moṭṭe.*
	Iruḷa,	*Moṭṭu.*
	Malabar,	*Muttei.*
	Sinhalese,	*Bijja.*

Types.

Inflecting.	SANSKRIT,	*Várana, hastin.*
	ARABIC,	*Fil.*
Compounding.	BASK,	*Elefandi.*
	FINNIC,	*Norsu.*
	MAGYAR,	*Caret.*
	TURKISH,	*Caret.*
	CIRCASSIAN,	*Caret.*
	GEORGIAN,	*Caret.*
	MONGOLIAN,	*Dsakhan, saghan.*
	MANTSHU,	*Sufan.*
	JAVANESE, Ngoko,	*Gajah.*
	JAVANESE, Krama,	*Gajah.*
	MALAY,	*Gajah.*
Isolating.	CHINESE, Nankin,	*Siang.*
	CHINESE, Pekin,	*Hsiang.*
	CHINESE, Canton,	*Tseong.*
	CHINESE, Shanghai,	*Siáng.*
	AMOY, Colloquial,	*Chiún.*
	JAPANESE,	*Zô.*
	Brahuí,	*Caret.*
Chinese Frontier & Tibet.	Gyámi,	*Syáng.*
	Gyárung,	*Láng-chhen.*
	Tákpa,	*Lang-chhen.*
	Mányak,	*Caret.*
	Thochú,	*Caret.*
	Sokpa,	*Lhábochc.*
	Horpa,	*Lámochhen.*
	Tibetan (*written*),	*Glángchen.*
	Tibetan (*spoken*),	*Lámboche.*
Nepal (east to west).	Serpa,	*Lángbo.*
	Súnwár,	*So-da.*
	Gúrung,	*Hathi.*
	Múrmi,	*Háthi.*
	Magar,	*Hathi.*
	Tháksya,	*Lam'bochhe.*
	Pákhya,	*Hátti.*
	Newár,	*Kisi.*
	Limbu,	*Hetti.*
Kiranti Group (East Nepal).	Kiránti,	*Háthi.*
	Rodong,	*Hátti.*
	Rúngchenbung,	*Háti.*
	Chhingtángya,	*Háti.*
	Náchhereng,	*Háthi.*
	Wáling,	*Háthi.*
	Yákha,	*Hátti.*
	Chourásya,	*Hátti.*
	Kulungya,	*Hátti.*
	Thulungya,	*Háti.*
	Báhingya,	*Hátti.*
	Lohorong,	*Hátti.*
	Lambichhong,	*Hátti.*
	Báláli,	*Hátti.*
	Sáng-páng,	*Bon-lan.*
	Dúmi,	*Hátti.*
	Kháling,	*Hádi.*
	Dungmáli,	*Hátti.*
Broken Tribes of Nepal.	Dárhi,	*Hathi.*
	Denwár,	*Hatti.*
	Pahri,	*Ki-si.*
	Chepáng,	*Há-thi.*
	Bhrámu,	*Caret.*
	Váyu,	*Hati.*
	Kuswar,	*Hathi.*
	Kusunda,	*Hátti-gyá.*
	Tháru,	*Hathi.*
	Lepcha (Sikkim),	*Tyanmo.*
	Bhútáni v. Lhopa,	*Langchen.*
N.-E. Bengal.	Bodo,	*Moï-gedet, moidet.*
	Dhimál,	*Nária.*
	Kocch,	*Háthi.*
	Garo,	*Náplo.*
	Káchári,	*Megadett.*
Eastern Frontier of Bengal.	Munipuri,	*Sámu.*
	Míthán Nágá,	*Loak.*
	Tablung Nágá,	*Lok-niu.*
	Khári Nágá,	*Sati.*
	Angámi Nágá,	*Tsu.*
	Námsáng Nágá,	*Puok.*
	Nowgong Nágá,	*Shiti.*
	Tengsa Nágá,	*Suti.*
	Abor Miri,	*Sita.*
	Sibságar Miri,	*Site.*
	Deoria Chutia,	*Meu.*
	Singpho,	*Magui.*
Arrakan & Burmah.	Burman (*written*),	*Chhang.*
	Burman (*spoken*),	*Shen, tsheng.*
	Khyeng v. Shou,	*Mwí.*
	Kámi,	*Ka-sái.*
	Kúmi,	*Ka-sá-i.*
	Mrú v. Toung,	*Nga-s'háit.*
	Sák,	*U-kú.*
Siam & Tenasserim.	Talain v. Mon,	*Tsing.*
	Sgau-karen,	*K'saw, ka-sau, kah-tsau.*
	Pwo-karen,	*K'sang.*
	Toungh-thu,	*Hsan.*
	Shán,	*Tsan.*
	Annamitic,	*Voi.*
	Siamese,	*Htsanu, chang.*
	Ahom,	*Tyáng.*
	Khámti,	*Tsáng.*
	Laos,	*Tsang.*
Central India.	Ho (Kol),	*Caret.*
	Kol (Singhbhum),	*Háthi.*
	Santáli,	*Háthi, sunda* = the trunk.
	Bhúmij,	*Háthi.*
	Uráon,	*Háthi.*
	Mundala,	*Háthi.*
	Rájmahali,	*A'thi.*
	Gondi,	*Yeje, yani.*
	Gayeti,	*Caret.*
	Rutluk,	*Caret.*
	Naikude,	*Caret.*
	Kolami,	*Caret.*
	Mádi,	*Caret.*
	Mádia,	*Caret.*
	Kuri,	*Caret.*
	Keikádi,	*Caret.*
	Khond,	*Hattanga.*
	Sávara,	*Ra.*
	Gadaba,	*Kom.*
	Yerukala,	*A'na.*
	Chentsu,	*H'ate.*
Southern India.	Tamil, anc.,	*Kaliru.*
	Tamil, mod.,	*A'nei, yánei.*
	Malayálma, anc.,	*Caret.*
	Malayálma, mod.,	*A'na.*
	Telugu,	*Yénuga.*
	Karnátaka, anc.,	*Caret.*
	Karnátaka, mod.,	*A'ne.*
	Tuluva,	*A'ne.*
	Kurgi,	*A'ne.*
	Toduva, }	*A'n.*
	Toda, }	*A'n.*
	Kóta,	*Caret.*
	Badaga,	*A'ne.*
	Kurumba,	*A'ne.*
	Irula,	*A'ne.*
	Malabar,	*Yanei, kunjaram, varanam.*
	Sinhalese,	*Ätá.*

Types.		
Inflecting.	SANSKRIT,	*Akshi, chakshus, netra.*
	ARABIC,	*Aayn.*
Compounding.	BASK,	*Begui.*
	FINNIC,	*Silma.*
	MAGYAR,	*Szem.*
	TURKISH,	*Geuz.*
	CIRCASSIAN,	*Neh.*
	GEORGIAN,	*Thwali.*
	MONGOLIAN,	*Nidon.*
	MANTSHU,	*Yasa.*
	JAVANESE, Ngoko,	*Máta.*
	JAVANESE, Krama,	*Maripat.*
	MALAY,	*Máta.*
Isolating.	CHINESE, Nankin,	*Yen.*
	CHINESE, Pekin,	*Yen.*
	CHINESE, Canton,	*Ngán.*
	CHINESE, Shanghai,	*Ngan-tsing.*
	AMOY, Colloquial,	*Bák.*
	JAPANESE,	*Me.*
	Brahuí,	*Khan.*
Chinese Frontier & Tibet.	Gyámi,	*Yen-chin.*
	Gyárung,	*Tai-myek, tam-myek.*
	Tákpa,	*Melong.*
	Mányak,	*Mni.*
	Thochú,	*Kan.*
	Sokpa,	*Nútú.*
	Horpa,	*Mo.*
	Tibetan (*written*),	*Mig.*
	Tibetan (*spoken*),	*Mik.*
Nepal (east to west).	Serpa,	*Mik.*
	Súnwár,	*Mi-chi.*
	Gúrung,	*Mi.*
	Múrmi,	*Mi.*
	Magar,	*Mik.*
	Tháksya,	*Mi.*
	Pákhya,	*A'nkhá.*
	Newár,	*Mi-khá.*
	Limbu,	*Mik.*
Kiranti Group (East Nepal).	Kiránti,	*Mak.*
	Rodong,	*Michak.*
	Rúngchenbung,	*Mak, maák.*
	Chhingtángya,	*Mak.*
	Náchhereng,	*Mik'-sa.*
	Wáling,	*Mak.*
	Yákha,	*Mik.*
	Chourásya,	*Bisi.*
	Kulungya,	*Muk'-si.*
	Thulungya,	*Mik'-si.*
	Báhingya,	*Michi.*
	Lohorong,	*Mik'*, (pl.) *mi' chi.*
	Lambichhong,	*Mik, mik'.*
	Báláli,	*Múik, muk'.*
	Sáng-páng,	*Mák, múk'.*
	Dúmi,	*Mas, miksi.*
	Kháling,	*Mash.*
	Dungmáli,	*Mak.*
Broken Tribes of Nepal.	Dárhi,	*A'nkhi.*
	Denwár,	*A'nkhá.*
	Pahri,	*Mi-gi.*
	Chepáng,	*Mi, mi-k.*
	Bhrámu,	*Mi-k.*
	Váyu,	*Me-k.*
	Kuswar,	*A'nkhi.*
	Kusunda,	*Chining.*
	Tháru,	*A'ṇkh.*
	Lepcha (Sikkim),	*Amik.*
	Bhúṭáni v. Lhopa,	*Mido.*
N.-E. Bengal.	Bodo,	*Mogon.*
	Dhimál,	*Mi.*
	Kocch,	*Chakhu.*
	Garo,	*Makar.*
	Káchári,	*Mogun.*
Eastern Frontier of Bengal.	Munipuri,	*Mit.*
	Míthán Nágá,	*Mik.*
	Tablung Nágá,	*Mik.*
	Khári Nágá,	*Tenik.*
	Angámi Nágá,	*Amhi.*
	Námsáng Nágá,	*Mit.*
	Nowgong Nágá,	*Tenok.*
	Tengsa Nágá,	*Tenyik.*
	Abor Miri,	*A'mik.*
	Sibságar Miri,	*Amik.*
	Deoria Chutia,	*Mukuti.*
	Singpho,	*Mi.*
Arrakan & Burmah.	Burman (*written*),	*Myakchi.*
	Burman (*spoken*),	*Myetsi, myet-se.*
	Khyeng v. Shou,	*Mi-ú-i.*
	Kámi,	*A-mi.*
	Kúmi,	*Me.*
	Mrú v. Toung,	*Min.*
	Sák,	*A-mi.*
Siam & Tenasserim.	Talain v. Mon,	*Mot.*
	Sgau-karen,	*Me, maï.*
	Pwo-karen,	*Mit-thah.*
	Toungh-thu,	*May.*
	Shán,	*Mat-ta.*
	Annamitic,	*Mat.*
	Siamese,	*Ta.*
	Ahom,	*Tá.*
	Khámti,	*Tá.*
	Laos,	*Tá.*
Central India.	Ho (Kol),	*Met.*
	Kol (Singhbhum),	*Met.*
	Santáli,	*Meh.*
	Bhúmij,	*Met.*
	Uráon,	*Khán.*
	Mundala,	*Med.*
	Rájmahali,	*Káne.*
	Goṇḍi,	*Kán* (sing.), *kank* (pl.).
	Gayeti,	*Kark* (pl.).
	Rutluk,	*Kanak, kadak* (pl.).
	Naikude,	*Kandlu* (pl.).
	Kolami,	*Kanul* (pl.).
	Mádi,	*Kondá.*
	Mádia,	*Kodá.*
	Kuri,	*Met, med.*
	Keikádi,	*Kán.*
	Khoṇḍ,	*Kannuka.*
	Sávara,	*Amu.*
	Gadaba,	*Ollo.*
	Yerukala,	*Supán.*
	Chentsu,	*A'yenkhi.*
Southern India.	Tamiḷ, anc.,	*Náṭṭam.*
	Tamiḷ, mod.,	*Kaṇ.*
	Malayáḷma, anc.,	*Caret.*
	Malayáḷma, mod.,	*Kaṇṇa.*
	Telugu,	*Kannu.*
	Karṇáṭaka, anc.,	*Caret.*
	Karṇáṭaka, mod.,	*Kaṇṇu.*
	Tuḷuva,	*Kann.*
	Kurgi,	*Kann.*
	Toḍuva, }	*Konn.*
	Toḍa, }	*Kaṇṇ.*
	Kóta,	*Kaṇṇu.*
	Baḍaga,	*Kaṇṇu.*
	Kuṛumba,	*Kaṇṇu.*
	Iruḷa,	*Kaṇṇu.*
	Malabar,	*Kan, vilzi, net-theram.*
	Sinhalese,	*Aha, äsa.*

Group	Types.	
Inflecting.	SANSKṚIT,	*Pitṛi.*
	ARABIC,	*Ab.*
Compounding.	BASK,	*Aita.*
	FINNIC,	*Isa.*
	MAGYAR,	*Atya.*
	TURKISH,	*Baba.*
	CIRCASSIAN,	*Taht, iyat.*
	GEORGIAN,	*Mama.*
	MONGOLIAN,	*Etsigha, etsige, abu.*
	MANTSHU,	*Ama.*
	JAVANESE, Ngoko,	*Bápa.*
	JAVANESE, Krama,	*Káma.*
	MALAY,	*Bápa.*
Isolating.	CHINESE, Nankin,	*Fu-ts'in.*
	CHINESE, Pekin,	*Fu-ts'in.*
	CHINESE, Canton,	*Fu-ts'an.*
	CHINESE, Shanghai,	*Yá, áh-tiáh.*
	AMOY, Colloquial,	*Pe.*
	JAPANESE,	*Oya, tchi-tchi.*
	Brahuí,	*Báv.*
Chinese Frontier & Tibet.	Gyámi,	*Dhá-dá.*
	Gyárung,	*Ta-pe.*
	Tákpa,	*A'pá.*
	Mányak,	*A'pá.*
	Thochú,	*Ai.*
	Sokpa,	*I'chiki.*
	Horpa,	*A'pá.*
	Tibetan (*written*),	*Phá.*
	Tibetan (*spoken*),	*Púlá.*
Nepal (east to west).	Serpa,	*A'bá.*
	Súnwár,	*Báve.*
	Gúrung,	*Abo.*
	Múrmi,	*A'pá.*
	Magar,	*Bai.*
	Tháksya,	*A'bo.*
	Pákhya,	*Babaï.*
	Newár,	*Abú.*
	Limbu,	*Amba.*
Kiranti Group (East Nepal).	Kiránti,	*Opa-eupa.*
	Rodong,	*Ú'm' pa.*
	Rúngchenbung,	*Eu-pa, wa-pa, opa.*
	Chhingtángya,	*U'pá.*
	Náchhereng,	*U'pa.*
	Wáling,	*A' pá, pápá.*
	Yákha,	*I'pa.*
	Chourásya,	*A'po.*
	Kulungya,	*Um' pá.*
	Thulungya,	*Páp, úpáp.*
	Báhingya,	*A'-po.*
	Lohorong,	*Um-pa.*
	Lambichhong,	*Impá.*
	Báláli,	*O'pa.*
	Sáng-páng,	*Um' pa.*
	Dúmi,	*Upyap, ipyáp, upú.*
	Kháling,	*Upáp.*
	Dungmáli,	*Umpa.*
Broken Tribes of Nepal.	Dárhi,	*Búbo.*
	Denwár,	*Bábá.*
	Pahri,	*Bá.*
	Chepáng,	*Ba-bú.*
	Bhrámu,	*Ba-bái.*
	Váyu,	*U'-pá, úpú.*
	Kuswar,	*Bábáik.*
	Kusunda,	*Páï.*
	Tháru,	*Bábá.*
	Lepcha (Sikkim),	*Abo.*
	Bhúṭáni v. Lhopa,	*Appá.*

N.-E. Bengal.	Bodo,	*Bipha.*
	Dhimál,	*Abá.*
	Kocch,	*Bap.*
	Garo,	*A'bá.*
	Káchári,	*Apa.*
Eastern Frontier of Bengal.	Munipuri,	*Ipá.*
	Míthán Nágá,	*Apá.*
	Tablung Nágá,	*Opáh.*
	Khári Nágá,	*Tabá.*
	Angámi Nágá,	*Apo.*
	Námsáng Nágá,	*Vá.*
	Nowgong Nágá,	*Upá.*
	Tengsa Nágá,	*Apu.*
	Abor Miri,	*Yiai.*
	Sibságar Miri,	*Bábá.*
	Deoria Chutia,	*Tsipá.*
	Singpho,	*Wá.*
Arrakan & Burmah.	Burman (*written*),	*Phae.*
	Burman (*spoken*),	*Phá-e, ahpa.*
	Khyeng v. Shou,	*Pau.*
	Kámi,	*Pá-ei.*
	Kúmi,	*Am-po.*
	Mrú v. Toung,	*Pá.*
	Sák,	*Abá.*
Siam & Tenasserim.	Talain v. Mon,	*Má.*
	Sgau-karen,	*Pah, bah.*
	Pwo-karen,	*Pah.*
	Toungh-thu,	*Pha.*
	Shán,	*Pau.*
	Annamitic,	*Sha.*
	Siamese,	*Hpau, po.*
	Ahom,	*Po.*
	Khámti,	*Po.*
	Laos,	*Po.*
Central India.	Ho (Kol),	*Appu.*
	Kol (Singhbhum),	*A'pung.*
	Santáli,	*Bábá, áp-* (with *-at, -ting, -um* affixed).
	Bhúmij,	*Bábu.*
	Uráon,	*Bábe.*
	Mundala,	*A'púng.*
	Rájmahali,	*A'bá.*
	Goṇḍi,	*Wáwo, bába, dáda.*
	Gayeti,	*Bába.*
	Rutluk,	*Báwo, dáda.*
	Naikude,	*Tág.*
	Kolami,	*Báo.*
	Mádi,	*Bába.*
	Mádia,	*Bakdalta.*
	Kuri,	*Ba-abba.*
	Keikádi,	*Eiya, bába.*
	Khoṇḍ,	*Abbá.*
	Sávara,	*Uwá.*
	Gadaba,	*Abbá.*
	Yerukala,	*A'va.*
	Chentsu,	*Bá.*
Southern India.	Tamiḷ, anc.,	*Endei.*
	Tamiḷ, mod.,	*Tandei, tagappan, appan.*
	Malayáḷma, anc.,	*Caret.*
	Malayáḷma, mod.,	*Appan.*
	Telugu,	*Tandri, abba.*
	Karṇáṭaka, anc.,	*Caret.*
	Karṇáṭaka, mod.,	*Appa, tande.*
	Tuḷuva,	*Amme.*
	Kurgi,	*Caret.*
	Toḍuva, }	*Eyyan.*
	Toḍa, }	*Eyan, eiyan.*
	Kóta,	*Eyan, eiyane.*
	Baḍaga,	*Appa, tande.*
	Kuṛumba,	*Tande.*
	Iruḷa,	*A'mme, amma.*
	Malabar,	*Tahappen, pitha, thathei.*
	Sinhalese,	*Piyá, appá.*

	Types.	
Inflecting.	SANSKRIT,	*Agni.*
	ARABIC,	*Nár.*
Compounding.	BASK,	*Su.*
	FINNIC,	*Tuli.*
	MAGYAR,	*Tüz.*
	TURKISH,	*Atesh.*
	CIRCASSIAN,	*Mahzwa.*
	GEORGIAN,	*Tsetskhli.*
	MONGOLIAN,	*Ghel, ghal.*
	MANTSHU,	*Tua.*
	JAVANESE, Ngoko,	*Genni.*
	JAVANESE, Krama,	*Latu.*
	MALAY,	*Api.*
Isolating.	CHINESE, Nankin,	*Ho.*
	CHINESE, Pekin,	*Ho.*
	CHINESE, Canton,	*Fo.*
	CHINESE, Shanghai,	*Hu.*
	AMOY, Colloquial,	*He.*
	JAPANESE,	*Hi.*
	Brahuí,	*Khákhar.*
Chinese Frontier & Tibet.	Gyámi,	*Ak-khá.*
	Gyárung,	*Tími.*
	Tákpa,	*Meh.*
	Mányak,	*Sa-meh.*
	Thochú,	*Meh.*
	Sokpa,	*Kwál.*
	Horpa,	*U-mak.*
	Tibetan (*written*),	*Má.*
	Tibetan (*spoken*),	*Me.*
Nepal (east to west).	Serpa,	*Me.*
	Súnwár,	*Mi.*
	Gúrung,	*Mi.*
	Múrmi,	*Me.*
	Magar,	*Mhe.*
	Tháksya,	*Hme.*
	Pákhya,	*A'go.*
	Newár,	*Mi.*
	Limbu,	*Me.*
Kiranti Group (East Nepal).	Kiránti,	*Mi.*
	Rodong,	*Mi.*
	Rúngchenbung,	*Mi.*
	Chhingtángya,	*Mi.*
	Náchhereng,	*Mi.*
	Wáling,	*Mi.*
	Yákha,	*Mi.*
	Chourásya,	*Mi.*
	Kulungya,	*Mi.*
	Thulungya,	*Mú.*
	Báhingya,	*Mi.*
	Lohorong,	*Mi.*
	Lambichhong,	*Mi.*
	Báláli,	*Mi.*
	Sáng-páng,	*Mi.*
	Dúmi,	*Mi.*
	Kháling,	*Mi.*
	Dungmáli,	*Mi.*
Broken Tribes of Nepal.	Dárhi,	*A'ge.*
	Denwár,	*Agi.*
	Pahri,	*Mi.*
	Chepáng,	*Me, mi.*
	Bhrámu,	*Má-i.*
	Váyu,	*Me.*
	Kuswar,	*A'ghi.*
	Kusunda,	*Já.*
	Tháru,	*A'gi.*
	Lepcha (Sikkim),	*Mi.*
	Bhúṭáni v. Lhopa,	*Mi.*

N.-E. Bengal.	Bodo,	*Wat.*
	Dhimál,	*Me.*
	Kocch,	*Agni.*
	Garo,	*Ver, wal.*
	Káchári,	*Od.*
Eastern Frontier of Bengal.	Munipuri,	*Mei.*
	Míthán Nágá,	*Van.*
	Tablung Nágá,	*A'h.*
	Khári Nágá,	*Matsü.*
	Angámi Nágá,	*Mi.*
	Námsáng Nágá,	*Van.*
	Nowgong Nágá,	*Mi.*
	Tengsa Nágá,	*Masi.*
	Abor Miri,	*Eme.*
	Sibságar Miri,	*Umme.*
	Deoria Chutia,	*Nye.*
	Singpho,	*Wan.*
Arrakan & Burmah.	Burman (*written*),	Mí.
	Burman (*spoken*),	Mí.
	Khyeng v. Shou,	*Mi.*
	Kámi,	*Má-i.*
	Kúmi,	*Mhá-i.*
	Mrú v. Toung,	*Má-i.*
	Sák,	*Bá-in.*
Siam & Tenasserim.	Talain v. Mon,	*Ka-mol.*
	Sgau-karen,	*May-u, má-u, mi-uh.*
	Pwo-karen,	*Mi.*
	Toungh-thu,	*May.*
	Shán,	*Hpihn.*
	Annamitic,	*Lửa.*
	Siamese,	*Thwa, fai.*
	Ahom,	*Fai.*
	Khámti,	*Fai.*
	Laos,	*Fai.*
Central India.	Ho (Kol),	*Sengel.*
	Kol (Singhbhum),	*Sengel.*
	Santáli,	*Sengel.*
	Bhúmij,	*Sengel.*
	Uráon,	*Chik.*
	Mundala,	*Singil.*
	Rájmahali,	*Chi-che.*
	Goṇḍi,	*Kis.*
	Gayeti,	*Kis.*
	Rutluk,	*Kis.*
	Naikude,	*Kich.*
	Kolami,	*Kis.*
	Mádi,	*Kis.*
	Mádia,	*Kis.*
	Kuri,	*Singal.*
	Keikádi,	*Narpu.*
	Khoṇḍ,	*Náḍi.*
	Sávara,	*Togo.*
	Gadaba,	*Sungol.*
	Yerukala,	*Nerupu.*
	Chentsu,	*Agin.*
Southern India.	Tamiḷ, anc.,	*Azhal.*
	Tamiḷ, mod.,	*Neruppu, ti.*
	Malayáḷma, anc.,	*Caret.*
	Malayáḷma, mod.,	*Tí.*
	Telugu,	*Nippu.*
	Karṇáṭaka, anc.,	*Caret.*
	Karṇáṭaka, mod.,	*Benki.*
	Tuḷuva,	*Tu.*
	Kurgi,	*Caret.*
	Toḍuva, }	*Caret.*
	Toḍa, }	*Nebb, dilth.*
	Kóta,	*Dije.*
	Baḍaga,	*Kichchu.*
	Kuṟumba,	*Kichchu.*
	Iruḷa,	*Tü, ti.*
	Malabar,	*Neruppu, thee, kanali.*
	Sinhalese,	*Gini.*

	Types.	
Inflecting.	SANSKRIT,	*Matsya, mína, jhasha.*
	ARABIC,	*Samak.*
Compounding.	BASK,	*Arrai, arrain.*
	FINNIC,	*Kala.*
	MAGYAR,	*Hal.*
	TURKISH,	*Baluk.*
	CIRCASSIAN,	*Zeyshí, tzey.*
	GEORGIAN,	*Thev-zi.*
	MONGOLIAN,	*Dshigason.*
	MANTSHU,	*Nimakha.*
	JAVANESE, Ngoko,	*Iwak.*
	JAVANESE, Krama,	*Ulam.*
	MALAY,	*Ikan.*
Isolating.	CHINESE, Nankin,	*Yu.*
	CHINESE, Pekin,	*Yü.*
	CHINESE, Canton,	*Ü.*
	CHINESE, Shanghai,	*'Ng.*
	AMOY, Colloquial,	*Hi.*
	JAPANESE,	*Siwo.*
	Brahui,	*Caret.*
Chinese Frontier & Tibet.	Gyámi,	*Yüe.*
	Gyárung,	*Chú-ngyo.*
	Tákpa,	*Gná, nyá.*
	Mányak,	*Yú.*
	Thochú,	*Izháḥ.*
	Sokpa,	*Khele.*
	Horpa,	*Hyá.*
	Tibetan (*written*),	*Nyá.*
	Tibetan (*spoken*),	*Gná.*
Nepal (east to west).	Serpa,	*Gná.*
	Súnwár,	*Gnau.*
	Gúrung,	*Tángná.*
	Múrmi,	*Tarnya.*
	Magar,	*Dishe.*
	Tháksya,	*Trang-gná.*
	Pákhya,	*Máchhá.*
	Newár,	*Nyá.*
	Limbu,	*Gna.*
Kiranti Group (East Nepal).	Kiránti,	*Gna.*
	Rodong,	*Gná-sa.*
	Rúngchenbung,	*Gná.*
	Chhingtángya,	*Gná-sa.*
	Náchhereng,	*Gná.*
	Wáling,	*Gná.*
	Yákha,	*Gná-sa.*
	Chourásya,	*Gno-so.*
	Kulungya,	*Gná.*
	Thulungya,	*Gno-sa, gno-swe.*
	Báhingya,	*Gná.*
	Lohorong,	*Gná-sa.*
	Lambichhong,	*Gná-sá.*
	Báláli,	*Gná.*
	Sáng-páng,	*Gná.*
	Dúmi,	*Gno.*
	Kháling,	*Gno.*
	Dungmáli,	*Gná.*
Broken Tribes of Nepal.	Dárhi,	*Má-chha.*
	Denwár,	*Ma-chhe.*
	Pahri,	*Nyo-já.*
	Chepáng,	*Nyá, nga.*
	Bhrámu,	*Ná-ngá.*
	Váyu,	*Ho.*
	Kuswar,	*Jhá-in.*
	Kusunda,	*Gná-sa.*
	Tháru,	*Machheri.*
	Lepcha (Sikkim),	*Gno.*
	Bhúṭáni v. Lhopa,	*Gnyá.*

N.-E. Bengal.	Bodo,	*Ná, gná.*
	Dhimál,	*Haiyá, hiyá.*
	Kocch,	*Mátch.*
	Garo,	*Ná.*
	Káchári,	*Ná.*
Eastern Frontier of Bengal.	Munipuri,	*Caret.*
	Míthán Nágá,	*Ngiá.*
	Tablung Nágá,	*Nyále.*
	Khári Nágá,	*Anghá.*
	Angámi Nágá,	*Kho.*
	Námsáng Nágá,	*Ngá.*
	Nowgong Nágá,	*Angu.*
	Tengsa Nágá,	*Angu.*
	Abor Miri,	*Engo.*
	Sibságar Miri,	*Orgo.*
	Deoria Chutia,	*Tsingá.*
	Singpho,	*Nga.*
Arrakan & Burmah.	Burman (*written*),	Ngá.
	Burman (*spoken*),	Ngá.
	Khyeng v. Shou,	*Ngau.*
	Kámi,	*Mo-i.*
	Kúmi,	*Ngho.*
	Mrú v. Toung,	*Dám.*
	Sák,	*Pan-ná.*
Siam & Tenasserim.	Talain v. Mon,	*Ka.*
	Sgau-karen,	*Caret.*
	Pwo-karen,	*Caret.*
	Toungh-thu,	*Lita.*
	Shán,	*Pa.*
	Annamitic,	*Ká.*
	Siamese,	*Para, pla.*
	Ahom,	*Plá.*
	Khámti,	*Pá.*
	Laos,	*Pá.*
Central India.	Ho (Kol),	*Haku.*
	Kol (Singhbhum),	*Háku.*
	Santáli,	*Kárselá, háku, utu* (relish).
	Bhúmij,	*Hai.*
	Uráon,	*Injo.*
	Mundala,	*Háku.*
	Rájmahali,	*Min.*
	Goṇḍi,	*Min.*
	Gayeti,	*Min.*
	Rutluk,	*Caret.*
	Naikude,	*Keiye.*
	Kolami,	*Kei.*
	Mádi,	*Min.*
	Mádia,	*Min.*
	Kuri,	*Kaku.*
	Keikádi,	*Min.*
	Khoṇḍ,	*Mininga.*
	Sávara,	*A'yo.*
	Gadaba,	*Aḍḍám.*
	Yerukala,	*Minu.*
	Chentsu,	*Matstso.*
Southern India.	Tamiḷ, anc.,	*Puzhal.*
	Tamiḷ, mod.,	*Min.*
	Malayáḷma, anc.,	*Caret.*
	Malayáḷma, mod.,	*Min.*
	Telugu,	*Minu,* (mod.) *chepa.*
	Karṇáṭaka, anc.,	*Caret.*
	Karṇáṭaka, mod.,	*Minu.*
	Tuḷuva,	*Min.*
	Kurgi,	*Caret.*
	Toḍuva,	*Caret.*
	Toda,	*Min.*
	Kóta,	*Mine.*
	Baḍaga,	*Minu.*
	Kuṛumba,	*Minu.*
	Iruḷa,	*Minu.*
	Malabar,	*Min, matcham.*
	Sinhalese,	*Matsia.*

Types.

Group	Language	Flower
Inflecting.	SANSKRIT,	*Pushpa.*
	ARABIC,	*Zahr.*
Compounding.	BASK,	*Lore, lora.*
	FINNIC,	*Kukka.*
	MAGYAR,	*Virag.*
	TURKISH,	*Chichek.*
	CIRCASSIAN,	*S'oreke.*
	GEORGIAN,	*Qvavili.*
	MONGOLIAN,	*Tsitshik.*
	MANTSHU,	*Ilkha.*
	JAVANESE, Ngoko,	*Kĕmbang.*
	JAVANESE, Krama,	*Sĕkar.*
	MALAY,	*Búnga.*
Isolating.	CHINESE, Nankin,	*Hwá.*
	CHINESE, Pekin,	*Hwá.*
	CHINESE, Canton,	*Fá.*
	CHINESE, Shanghai,	*Hwo.*
	AMOY, Colloquial,	*Hoe.*
	JAPANESE,	*Hana.*
	Brahuí,	*Pulle.*
Chinese Frontier & Tibet.	Gyámi,	*Khwá.*
	Gyárung,	*Tau-den.*
	Tákpa,	*Mento.*
	Mányak,	*Mento.*
	Thochú,	*Lámpáḥ.*
	Sokpa,	*Chichúk.*
	Horpa,	*Meto.*
	Tibetan (*written*),	*Metog.*
	Tibetan (*spoken*),	*Mentok.*
Nepal (east to west).	Serpa,	*Mendok.*
	Súnwár,	*Phu.*
	Gúrung,	*Táh.*
	Múrmi,	*Mendú.*
	Magar,	*Sár.*
	Tháksya,	*Ro.*
	Pákhya,	*Phul.*
	Newár,	*Swong.*
	Limbu,	*Phúng.*
Kiranti Group (East Nepal).	Kiránti,	*Búngwai.*
	Rodong,	*Búngná.*
	Rúngchenbung,	*Búngwai.*
	Chhingtángya,	*Phúng.*
	Náchhereng,	*Bú.*
	Wáling,	*Búng.*
	Yákha,	*Phúng.*
	Chourásya,	*Phúri.*
	Kulungya,	*Búng.*
	Thulungya,	*Búng'ma.*
	Báhingya,	*Phúng.*
	Lohorong,	*Búng.*
	Lambichhong,	*Phúng.*
	Bálálí,	*Bung, búng-wa.*
	Sáng-páng,	*Búṇ-wa.*
	Dúmi,	*Púmmá.*
	Kháling,	*Púngmá.*
	Dungmálí,	*Púng.*
Broken Tribes of Nepal.	Dárhi,	*Phúl.*
	Denwár,	*Phúl.*
	Pahri,	*So-no.*
	Chepáng,	*Do, ro.*
	Bhrámu,	*A-wai.*
	Váyu,	*Púm-mí, pung-mi.*
	Kuswar,	*Phúl.*
	Kusunda,	*Gipodu.*
	Tháru,	*Phul.*
	Lepcha (Sikkim),	*Rip.*
	Bhúṭáni v. Lhopa,	*Meṇtog.*
N.-E. Bengal.	Bodo,	*Bibár.*
	Dhimál,	*Lhep.*
	Kocch,	*Phúl.*
	Garo,	*Parr.*
	Káchári,	*Dolong piper.*
Eastern Frontier of Bengal.	Munipuri,	*Lei.*
	Míthán Nágá,	*Maipoa.*
	Tablung Nágá,	*Chupeng.*
	Khári Nágá,	*Taben.*
	Angámi Nágá,	*Popu.*
	Námsáng Nágá,	*Chongpo.*
	Nowgong Nágá,	*Naru.*
	Tengsa Nágá,	*Nolong.*
	Abor Miri,	*A'pun.*
	Sibságar Miri,	*A'pun.*
	Deoria Chutia,	*Ibá.*
	Singpho,	*Siban.*
Arrakan & Burmah.	Burman (*written*),	Pau.
	Burman (*spoken*),	Pán.
	Khyeng v. Shou,	*Pa-pá.*
	Kámi,	*A-pá.*
	Kúmi,	*Ka-shyoung.*
	Mrú v. Toung,	*Pá-ou.*
	Sák,	*A-pán.*
Siam & Tenasserim.	Talain v. Mon,	*Koung.*
	Sgau-karen,	*Paw, phoh.*
	Pwo-karen,	*Paw.*
	Toungh-thu,	*Ken.*
	Shán,	*Mau.*
	Annamitic,	*Hoa.*
	Siamese,	*Towkma, dokmai.*
	Ahom,	*Blok.*
	Khámti,	*Mok.*
	Laos,	*Dok.*
Central India.	Ho (Kol),	*Bah.*
	Kol (Singhbhum),	*Bowh.*
	Santáli,	*Buhá.*
	Bhúmij,	*Baha.*
	Uráon,	*Phup.*
	Mundala,	*Baha.*
	Rájmahali,	*Pup.*
	Goṇḍi,	*Phul, pungár.*
	Gayeti,	*Pungár.*
	Rutluk,	*Pungár.*
	Naikude,	*Putá.*
	Kolami,	*Phuel.*
	Mádi,	*Pungár, pungári, puitá.*
	Mádia,	*Pungár.*
	Kuri,	*Phul.*
	Keikádi,	*Phuo.*
	Khoṇḍ,	*Sáru.*
	Sávara,	*Taraba.*
	Gadaba,	*Sari.*
	Yerukala,	*Puvvu.*
	Chentsu,	*Phúl.*
Southern India.	Tamiḷ, anc.,	*Alar.*
	Tamiḷ, mod.,	*Pú.*
	Malayáḷma, anc.,	*Caret.*
	Malayáḷma, mod.,	*Pú.*
	Telugu,	*Puvvu, púvu.*
	Karṇáṭaka, anc.,	*Puvvu, pú.*
	Karṇáṭaka, mod.,	*Huvvu, húvu.*
	Tuḷuva,	*Pu.*
	Kurgi,	*Caret.*
	Toḍuva,	*Puvvu.*
	Toḍa,	*Púf.*
	Kóta,	*Púve.*
	Baḍaga,	*Húvu.*
	Kuṛumba,	*Huv.*
	Iruḷa,	*Pu.*
	Malabar,	*Pu, putpam.*
	Sinhalese,	*Mala.*

	Types.	
Inflecting.	SANSKRIT, ...	*Pád, pad.*
	ARABIC, ...	*Rijl, ḳadam.*
Compounding.	BASK, ...	*Oñ, oiñ.*
	FINNIC, ...	*Jalka.*
	MAGYAR, ...	*Lab.*
	TURKISH, ...	*Ayak.*
	CIRCASSIAN, ...	*Tlako.*
	GEORGIAN, ...	*Perhi, peli.*
	MONGOLIAN, ...	*Ölmai, kül.*
	MANTSHU, ...	*Betkhe.*
	JAVANESE, Ngoko, . .	*Sikil.*
	JAVANESE, Krama, . .	*Suku.*
	MALAY, ...	*Kaki.*
Isolating.	CHINESE, Nankin, . .	*Kioh.*
	CHINESE, Pekin, . .	*Chio.*
	CHINESE, Canton, . .	*Keuk.*
	CHINESE, Shanghai, .	*Kiáh.*
	AMOY, Colloquial, . .	*K'a.*
	JAPANESE, ...	*Ashi.*
	Brahuí, ...	*Nath.*
Chinese Frontier & Tibet.	Gyámi, ...	*Chya-a.*
	Gyárung, ...	*Támi.*
	Tákpa, ...	*Lemi.*
	Mányak, ...	*Lipchheḥ.*
	Thochú, ...	*Jáko.*
	Sokpa, ...	*Khoil.*
	Horpa, ...	*Ko.*
	Tibetan (*written*), . .	*Rkangpa.*
	Tibetan (*spoken*), . .	*Kángo.*
Népal (east to west).	Serpa, ...	*Kángo.*
	Súnwár, ...	*Khweli.*
	Gúrung, ...	*Bhale.*
	Múrmi, ...	*Bale.*
	Magar, ...	*Mihil.*
	Tháksya, ...	*Malethin, male.*
	Pákhya, ...	*Caret.*
	Newár, ...	*Páli.*
	Limbu, ...	*Langdaphe.*
Kiranti Group (East Népal).	Kiránti, ...	*U'khúro.*
	Rodong, ...	*Philú.*
	Rúngchenbung, . . .	*Langtemma, wukhuro, ukhuro.*
	Chhingtángya, . . .	*L'ang.*
	Náchhereng, ...	*La, lophoma.*
	Wáling, ...	*Lángkutem.*
	Yákha, ...	*Lang-tápi.*
	Chourásya, ...	*Losu.*
	Kulungya, ...	*Long.*
	Thulungya, ...	*Phemkhel.*
	Báhingya, ...	*Kholi-blem.*
	Lohorong, ...	*Láng phokma.*
	Lambichhong, . . .	*Temmaláng.*
	Báláli, ...	*Lák' phekma.*
	Sáng-páng, ...	*Lán-pháma.*
	Dúmi, ...	*Syáb, yú.*
	Kháling, ...	*Syál.*
	Dungmáli, ...	*Láng.*
Broken Tribes of Népal.	Dárhi, ...	*Goḍ.*
	Denwár, ...	*Goḍ.*
	Pahri, ...	*Li.*
	Chepáng, ...	*La.*
	Bhrámu, ...	*U'n-zik.*
	Váyu, ...	*Le.*
	Kuswar, ...	*Goṛ.*
	Kusunda, ...	*Chán.*
	Tháru, ...	*Pángo goḍa.*
	Lepcha (Sikkim), . .	*Diangliok.*
	Bhúṭáni v. Lhopa, . .	*Kánglep.*

N.-E. Bengal.	Bodo, ...	*Yáppá.*
	Dhimál, ...	*Khokoï.*
	Kocch, ...	*Bhori.*
	Garo, ...	*Chaplap.*
	Káchári, ...	*Atheng.*
Eastern Frontier of Bengal.	Munipuri, ...	*Khúng-pa.*
	Míthán Nágá, . . .	*Tchyá.*
	Tablung Nágá, . . .	*Yah-lan.*
	Khári Nágá, ...	*Tachang.*
	Angámi Nágá, . . .	*Uphi.*
	Námsáng Nágá, . . .	*Dá.*
	Nowgong Nágá, . .	*Tatsüng.*
	Tengsa Nágá, . . .	*Taching.*
	Abor Miri, ...	*A'le.*
	Sibságar Miri, . . .	*A'le.*
	Deoria Chutia, . . .	*Yápásu.*
	Singpho, ...	*Lagóng.*
Arrakan & Burmah.	Burman (*written*), . .	*Khre.*
	Burman (*spoken*), . . .	*Khye, khyá-hlouk.*
	Khyeng v. Shou, . .	*Ka-ko.*
	Kámi, ...	*A-kho.*
	Kúmi, ...	*Khou.*
	Mrú v. Toung, . . .	*Khouk.*
	Sák, ...	*A-tar.*
Siam & Tenasserim.	Talain v. Mon, . . .	*Htsihu.*
	Sgau-karen, ...	*Kaw.*
	Pwo-karen, ...	*Kang.*
	Toungh-thu, ...	*Khan.*
	Shán, ...	*Ten.*
	Annamitic, ...	*Sho'n.*
	Siamese, ...	*Tenn, tin.*
	Ahom, ...	*Tin.*
	Khámti, ...	*Tin.*
	Laos, ...	*Tín.*
Central India.	Ho (Kol), ...	*Katta.*
	Kol (Singhbhum), . .	*Kátá.*
	Santáli, ...	*Jánga, kurá, supti-jánga.*
	Bhúmij, ...	*Kátá.*
	Uráon, ...	*Dappe.*
	Mundala, ...	*Kátá.*
	Rájmahali, ...	*Kev.*
	Goṇḍi, ...	*Kalk, kal.*
	Gayeti, ...	*Kal.*
	Rutluk, ...	*Kal.*
	Naikude, ...	*Talgatta.*
	Kolami, ...	*Taral.*
	Mádi, ...	*Kal.*
	Mádia, ...	*Kal, erpwugi.*
	Kuri, ...	*Jang.*
	Keikádi, ...	*Kal.*
	Khoṇḍ, ...	*Vestámu.*
	Sávara, ...	*Aji.*
	Gadaba, ...	*Adugesenánu.*
	Yerukala, ...	*Medapán, keru.*
	Chentsu, ...	*Khoju.*
Southern India.	Tamiḷ, anc., ...	*Kazhal.*
	Tamiḷ, mod., ...	*Aḍi, pádam.*
	Malayáḷma, anc., . .	*Caret.*
	Malayáḷma, mod., . .	*Aḍi.*
	Telugu, ...	*Adugu, pádamu, kálu.*
	Karṇáṭaka, anc., . .	*Aḍi.*
	Karṇaṭaka, mod., . .	*Hejje.*
	Tuḷuva, ...	*Hajji.*
	Kurgi, ...	*Caret.*
	Toḍuva, ...	*Orri.*
	Toḍa, ...	*Kál.*
	Kóta, ...	*Káln.*
	Baḍaga, ...	*Kálu.*
	Kuṛumba, ...	*Kálu.*
	Iruḷa, ...	*Kálu.*
	Malabar, ...	*Kál, pátham, thál, ade.*
	Sinhalese, ...	*Paya.*

	Types.	
Inflecting.	SANSKRIT,	*Chhága.*
	ARABIC,	*Maaz.*
Compounding.	BASK,	*Auntz.*
	FINNIC,	*Kauris.*
	MAGYAR,	*Keoske.*
	TURKISH,	*Kechi.*
	CIRCASSIAN,	*Tshenney.*
	GEORGIAN,	*Ṭhkhavi.*
	MONGOLIAN,	*Ilmaghan, imaghan.*
	MANTSHU,	*Niman.*
	JAVANESE, Ngoko,	*Wĕdus.*
	JAVANESE, Krama,	*Mendă.*
	MALAY,	*Kambing.*
Isolating.	CHINESE, Nankin,	*Shán-yang.*
	CHINESE, Pekin,	*Shán-yang.*
	CHINESE, Canton,	*Shán-yeong.*
	CHINESE, Shanghai,	*Saṇ-yáng.*
	AMOY, Colloquial,	*Iúṇ.*
	JAPANESE,	*Yagi.*
	Brahuí,	*Caret.*
Chinese Frontier & Tibet.	Gyámi,	*Chúlyú.*
	Gyárung,	*Kús-so.*
	Tákpa,	*Rá.*
	Mányak,	*Tsáh.*
	Thochú,	*Tsáh.*
	Sokpa,	*Yá-má.*
	Horpa,	*Chhe.*
	Tibetan (*written*),	*Rá.*
	Tibetan (*spoken*),	*Rá.*
Nepal (east to west).	Serpa,	*Rá.*
	Súnwár,	*Charsye.*
	Gúrung,	*Ra.*
	Múrmi,	*Rá.*
	Magar,	*Rha.*
	Tháksya,	*Rámo.*
	Pákhya,	*Boko.*
	Newár,	*Chole.*
	Limbu,	*Menda.*
Kiranti Group (East Nepal).	Kiránti,	*Chhengár.*
	Rodong,	*Chhong-gara.*
	Rúngchenbung,	*Chheng-gara.*
	Chhingtángya,	*Mendiba.*
	Náchhereng,	*Chhángara.*
	Wáling,	*Bákara.*
	Yákha,	*Mengthibak.*
	Chourásya,	*Sángara.*
	Kulungya,	*Chháng-gara.*
	Thulungya,	*Chhwáṇra.*
	Báhingya,	*Song' gara.*
	Lohorong,	*Mithuba.*
	Lambichhong,	*Mendi.*
	Báláli,	*Mithibá.*
	Sáng-páng,	*Chhán'-gara.*
	Dúmi,	*Grot, chan'gur.*
	Kháling,	*Grodyú.*
	Dungmáli,	*Chhágar.*
Broken Tribes of Nepal.	Dárhi,	*Chág-ri, cha-g-ri.*
	Denwár,	*Chá-gár, cha-ga-r.*
	Pahri,	*Chá-lá.*
	Chepáng,	*Me-syá, mi-chá.*
	Bhrámu,	*Mi-chha, mi-ch-ya.*
	Váyu,	*Chi-li.*
	Kuswar,	*Chá-gari, cha-ga-ri.*
	Kusunda,	*Mijha.*
	Tháru,	*Chhegadi.*
	Lepcha (Sikkim),	*Saar.*
	Bhúṭáni v. Lhopa,	*Ráh.*

N.-E. Bengal.	Bodo,	*Búrmá.*
	Dhimál,	*E' echá.*
	Kocch,	*Chágol, bákri, pátha.*
	Garo,	*Púrún.*
	Káchári,	*Borma.*
Eastern Frontier of Bengal.	Munipuri,	*Humeng.*
	Míthán Nágá,	*Ron.*
	Tablung Nágá,	*Yun.*
	Khári Nágá,	*Nabong.*
	Angámi Nágá,	*Tanü.*
	Námsáng Nágá,	*Kien.*
	Nowgong Nágá,	*Nabung.*
	Tengsa Nágá,	*Nabung.*
	Abor Miri,	*Shuben.*
	Sibságar Miri,	*Ságoli.*
	Deoria Chutia,	*Lipeduru.*
	Singpho,	*Bainam.*
Arrakan & Burmah.	Burman (*written*),	*Chhit.*
	Burman (*spoken*),	*Sheik, hlsiet.*
	Khyeng v. Shou,	*Ma.*
	Kámi,	*Tso-be.*
	Kúmi,	*Mi-e.*
	Mrú v. Toung,	*Ta-rau-a.*
	Sák,	*Ki-bi.*
Siam & Tenasserim.	Talain v. Mon,	*Khapa.*
	Sgau-karen,	*Maï-taï-laï, mi-tel-leh.*
	Pwo-karen,	*Bi.*
	Toungh-thu,	*Bay.*
	Shán,	*Pá.*
	Annamitic,	*Dê.*
	Siamese,	*Hpá, pe.*
	Ahom,	*Pengá.*
	Khámti,	*Pe.*
	Laos,	*Pe.*
Central India.	Ho (Kol),	*Merom.*
	Kol (Singhbhum),	*Meram.*
	Santáli,	*Merom, bodá* (male), *chaḍi* (bridal gift).
	Bhúmij,	*Meram.*
	Uráon,	*Era.*
	Mundala,	*Meram.*
	Rájmahali,	*Kre.*
	Goṇḍi,	*Bokra, bokadal* (m.); *yetti* (f.).
	Gayeti,	*Bokadal* (m.); *yeti, here* (f.).
	Rutluk,	*Bukaral* (m.); *edi* (f.).
	Naikude,	*Meka.*
	Kolami,	*Meke.*
	Mádi,	*Bokada* (m.); *yatti* (f.).
	Mádia,	*Edhi.*
	Kuri,	*Bongara, siri.*
	Keikádi,	*Ad.*
	Khoṇḍ,	*Vodangá.*
	Sávara,	*Kime.*
	Gadaba,	*Yimme.*
	Yerukala,	*A'ḍú.*
	Chentsu,	*Chheli.*
Southern India.	Tamiḷ, anc.,	*Veḷḷei.*
	Tamiḷ, mod.,	*A'ḍu.*
	Malayáḷma, anc.,	*Caret.*
	Malayáḷma, mod.,	*Veḷḷáṭa.*
	Telugu,	*Meka.*
	Karṇáṭaka, anc.,	*Caret.*
	Karṇáṭaka, mod.,	*Kuri.*
	Tuḷuva,	*E'du.*
	Kurgi,	*Kuri.*
	Toḍuva, }	*A'ḍr.*
	Toḍa, }	*A'ḍu.*
	Kóta,	*A'ḍu.*
	Baḍaga,	*Aḍu.*
	Kurumba,	*A'ḍu.*
	Iruḷa,	*A'ḍu.*
	Malabar,	*Adu, velladu.*
	Sinhalese,	*Eḷuá.*

Group	Language	Hair
	Types.	
Inflecting.	SANSKRIT,	*Keśa.*
	ARABIC,	*Shaar.*
Compounding.	BASK,	*Ille, ule, bilo.*
	FINNIC,	*Hiwus.*
	MAGYAR,	*Hajak.*
	TURKISH,	*Sach.*
	CIRCASSIAN,	*Shatzey, skahtsi.*
	GEORGIAN,	*Thma.*
	MONGOLIAN,	*Üson, üsun.*
	MANTSHU,	*Funiyekhe.*
	JAVANESE, Ngoko,	*Rambut.*
	JAVANESE, Krama,	*Rema.*
	MALAY,	*Rambut.*
Isolating.	CHINESE, Nankin,	*Fah, máou.*
	CHINESE, Pekin,	*Fá, máou.*
	CHINESE, Canton,	*Fát, mò.*
	CHINESE, Shanghai,	*Deu-feh.*
	AMOY, Colloquial,	*Mñg.*
	JAPANESE,	*Kami, ke.*
	Brahuí,	*Pishkou.*
Chinese Frontier & Tibet.	Gyámi,	*Thou-phwá.*
	Gyárung,	*Tar-ní.*
	Tákpa,	*Pu; krá* (of the head).
	Mányak,	*Múi; tsi* (of the head).
	Thochú,	*Hompá, grong; kachu* (of the head).
	Sokpa,	*Kechige.*
	Horpa,	*Spú.*
	Tibetan (*written*),	*Skrá, spu.*
	Tibetan (*spoken*),	*Tá, krá.*
Nepal (east to west).	Serpa,	*Tá.*
	Súnwár,	*Chang.*
	Gúrung,	*Moi.*
	Múrmi,	*Krá.*
	Magar,	*Chham.*
	Tháksya,	*Chham.*
	Pákhya,	*Ráwa.*
	Newár,	*Song.*
	Limbu,	*Thagi.*
Kiranti Group (East Nepal).	Kiránti,	*Moá.*
	Rodong,	*Mus'ya, twong.*
	Rúngchenbung,	*Má-a.*
	Chhingtángya,	*Tang' phúkwa.*
	Náchhereng,	*Taa sám.*
	Wáling,	*Táng-múwa.*
	Yákha,	*Táng-pháng-wa.*
	Chourásya,	*Som.*
	Kulungya,	*Múi, tosúm.*
	Thulungya,	*Sem, swem.*
	Báhingya,	*Chám, súng.*
	Lohorong,	*Tagna', mih'.*
	Lambichhong,	*Múng, tang-phúkwa.*
	Báláli,	*Tagná, chámi, mung.*
	Sáng-páng,	*Mú-wa, támusám.*
	Dúmi,	*Dosúm, usom.*
	Khálingr,	*Umarsam, dosamúsam.*
	Dungmáli,	*Mú-a.*
Broken Tribes of Nepal.	Dárhi,	*Bár.*
	Denwár,	*Bár.*
	Pahri,	*Son.*
	Chepáng,	*Men.*
	Bhrámu,	*Syám.*
	Váyu,	*Song, swom.*
	Kuswar,	*Bár.*
	Kusunda,	*Gyai-i.*
	Tháru,	*Bár.*
	Lepcha (Sikkim),	*Achom, a-chom.*
	Bhúṭáni v. Lhopa,	*Kya.*
N.-E. Bengal.	Bodo,	*Khanai, khomon.*
	Dhimál,	*Múi-tu, moishu, hoshom.*
	Kocch,	*Chuli, rom.*
	Garo,	*Kamau, houru.*
	Káchári,	*Kumun.*
Eastern Frontier of Bengal.	Munipuri,	*Thum.*
	Míthán Nágá,	*Kho.*
	Tablung Nágá,	*Min, su.*
	Khári Nágá,	*Kwá.*
	Angámi Nágá,	*Atsüthá.*
	Námsáng Nágá,	*Kacho.*
	Nowgong Nágá,	*Ko.*
	Tengsa Nágá,	*Ku.*
	Abor Miri,	*Dumit.*
	Sibságar Miri,	*Dumed.*
	Deoria Chutia,	*Kin.*
	Singpho,	*Kará.*
Arrakan & Burmah.	Burman (*written*),	*Chhangbang.*
	Burman (*spoken*),	*S'haben, htsaben.*
	Khyeng v. Shou,	*Lu-sám.*
	Kámi,	*A-s'hám.*
	Kúmi,	*S'hám.*
	Mrú v. Toung,	*S'hám.*
	Sák,	*Kumi.*
Siam & Tenasserim.	Talain v. Mon,	*Swet.*
	Sgau-karen,	*Ko-thu, kho-thu.*
	Pwo-karen,	*Ku-thu.*
	Toungh-thu,	*Ta-lu.*
	Shán,	*Khon-ho.*
	Annamitic,	*Tok.*
	Siamese,	*Hpohn, phom.*
	Ahom,	*Phrum.*
	Khámti,	*Phom.*
	Laos,	*Phom.*
Central India.	Ho (Kol),	*U'p.*
	Kol (Singhbhum),	*Ub.*
	Santáli,	*Ub, up, hátá.*
	Bhúmij,	*Ub.*
	Uráon,	*Chutti.*
	Mundala,	*Up.*
	Rájmahali,	*Tali.*
	Goṇḍi,	*Robáng, chuti.*
	Gayeti,	*Chuti.*
	Rutluk,	*Roba-chuti.*
	Naikude,	*Til.*
	Kolami,	*Til.*
	Mádi,	*Kelku.*
	Mádia,	*Kalak.*
	Kuri,	*Katha.*
	Keikádi,	*Meir.*
	Khoṇḍ,	*Tlámberakha.*
	Sávara,	*Avu.*
	Gadaba,	*Jarli.*
	Yerukala,	*Vonḍu, mogurú.*
	Chentsu,	*Kems.*
Southern India.	Tamiḷ, anc.,	*Kuzhal.*
	Tamiḷ, mod.,	*Mayir, meir.*
	Malayáḷma, anc.,	*Caret.*
	Malayáḷma, mod.,	*Talamuṭi.*
	Telugu,	*Venṭruka.*
	Karṇáṭaka, anc.,	*Caret.*
	Karṇáṭaka, mod.,	*Kúdalu.*
	Tuḷuva,	*Kúdalu.*
	Kurgi,	*Orama.*
	Toḍuva,	*Mir.*
	Toḍa,	*Mir.*
	Kóta,	*Mire.*
	Baḍaga,	*Manḍe, kúdalu.*
	Kuṟumba,	*Kúdalu.*
	Iruḷa,	*Meiru.*
	Malabar,	*Mayir, romam.*
	Sinhalese,	*Kes.*

Group	Types.	
Inflecting.	SANSKRIT,	*Hasta, páṇi.*
	ARABIC,	*Yidd.*
Compounding.	BASK,	*Escu.*
	FINNIC,	*Kasi.*
	MAGYAR,	*Kez.*
	TURKISH,	*Yel.*
	CIRCASSIAN,	*Euyg, eh.*
	GEORGIAN,	*Heli, kheli.*
	MONGOLIAN,	*Ghar.*
	MANTSHU,	*Gala.*
	JAVANESE, Ngoko,	*Tangan.*
	JAVANESE, Krama,	*Tangan.*
	MALAY,	*Tángan.*
Isolating.	CHINESE, Nankin,	*Shau.*
	CHINESE, Pekin,	*Shau.*
	CHINESE, Canton,	*Shau.*
	CHINESE, Shanghai,	*Seu.*
	AMOY, Colloquial,	*C'hiú.*
	JAPANESE,	*Te.*
	Brahuí,	*Dú.*
Chinese Frontier & Tibet.	Gyámi,	*Syú, syeu.*
	Gyárung,	*Ta-yak.*
	Tákpa,	*Lá.*
	Mányak,	*Láp-cheḥ.*
	Thochú,	*Jipaḥ.*
	Sokpa,	*Kar.*
	Horpa,	*Lhá.*
	Tibetan (*written*),	*Lág-pá.*
	Tibetan (*spoken*),	*Lángo.*
Nepal (east to west).	Serpa,	*Lángo.*
	Súnwár,	*Table, gwi.*
	Gúrung,	*Laptá.*
	Múrmi,	*Yá.*
	Magar,	*Hút-piák.*
	Tháksya,	*Yáyáthin.*
	Pákhya,	*Hatkela.*
	Newár,	*Pa-láhá.*
	Limbu,	*Húktáphe.*
Kiránti Group (East Nepal).	Kiránti,	*Chúkúphemá.*
	Rodong,	*Chhúku-phema.*
	Rúngchenbung,	*Chhúkhu-phema.*
	Chhingtángya,	*Múk.*
	Náchhereng,	*Húú.*
	Wáling,	*Chhúk.*
	Yákha,	*Múktápi.*
	Chourásya,	*Lá.*
	Kulungya,	*Húh' pháma.*
	Thulungya,	*Lwáblem.*
	Báhingya,	*Gúblem.*
	Lohorong,	*Húk'-phekma.*
	Lambichhong,	*Temma-múk.*
	Báláli,	*Húphek'-ma.*
	Sáng-páng,	*Huk'-pháma.*
	Dúmi,	*Khar, khúr.*
	Kháling,	*Phlemkhar.*
	Dungmáli,	*Chhúk.*
Broken Tribes of Nepal.	Dárhi,	*Hát.*
	Denwár,	*Háth.*
	Pahri,	*Lá.*
	Chepáng,	*Kút-t, kú-t-pa.*
	Bhrámu,	*Bhi-t.*
	Váyu,	*Got.*
	Kuswar,	*Háth.*
	Kusunda,	*Gipan.*
	Tháru,	*Tar-hatti.*
	Lepcha (Sikkim),	*Kaliok.*
	Bhúṭáni v. Lhopa,	*Láppa.*

N.-E. Bengal.	Bodo,	*Akhai, nákhai.*
	Dhimál,	*Khúr.*
	Kocch,	*Háth.*
	Garo,	*Chákreng.*
	Káchári,	(palm) *nashitola, nashi naka.*
Eastern Frontier of Bengal.	Munipuri,	*Khút-pák.*
	Míthán Nágá,	*Chak.*
	Tablung Nágá,	*Yak.*
	Khári Nágá,	*Tak-het.*
	Angámi Nágá,	*Abi.*
	Námsáng Nágá,	*Dak.*
	Nowgong Nágá,	*Tekhá.*
	Tengsa Nágá,	*Tekhát.*
	Abor Miri,	*A'lák.*
	Sibságar Miri,	*Elág.*
	Deoria Chutia,	*O'tuṇ.*
	Singpho,	*Lettá.*
Arrakan & Burmah.	Burman (*written*),	*Lak.*
	Burman (*spoken*),	*Let.*
	Khyeng v. Shou,	*Kuth.*
	Kámi,	*A-ku.*
	Kúmi,	*Ka.*
	Mrú v. Toung,	*Rut.*
	Sák,	*Ta-ku.*
Siam & Tenasserim.	Talain v. Mon,	*Tway.*
	Sgau-karen,	*Su, tsu.*
	Pwo-karen,	*Su.*
	Toungh-thu,	*Su.*
	Shán,	*Mi.*
	Annamitic,	*Tay.*
	Siamese,	*Mo, mü.*
	Ahom,	*Khá.*
	Khámti,	*Mü.*
	Laos,	*Mü.*
Central India.	Ho (Kol),	*Tí.*
	Kol (Singhbhum),	*Thi.*
	Santáli,	*Tí, lulá, tálakhá* = palms.
	Bhúmij,	*Thi.*
	Uráon,	*Khekháh.*
	Mundala,	*Tihi.*
	Rájmahali,	*Sesu.*
	Goṇḍi,	*Kaik, kyk.*
	Gayeti,	*Caret.*
	Rutluk,	*Caret.*
	Naikude,	*Caret.*
	Kolami,	*Caret.*
	Mádi,	*Caret.*
	Mádia,	*Caret.*
	Kuri,	*Caret.*
	Keikádi,	*Caret.*
	Khoṇḍ,	*Káju.*
	Sávara,	*Asi.*
	Gadaba,	*Titi.*
	Yerukala,	*Kayi, ki.*
	Chentsu,	*Hát.*
Southern India.	Tamiḷ, anc.,	*Tol* (?).
	Tamiḷ, mod.,	*Kai.*
	Malayáḷma, anc.,	*Caret.*
	Malayáḷma, mod.,	*Kai.*
	Telugu,	*Cheyyi.*
	Karṇáṭaka, anc.,	*Tol* (?).
	Karṇáṭaka, mod.,	*Kayi.*
	Tuḷuva,	*Kai.*
	Kurgi,	*Kei.*
	Toḍuva, }	*Kayi.*
	Toḍa, }	*Koi.*
	Kóta,	*Kei.*
	Baḍaga,	*Kei.*
	Kuṛumba,	*Kei.*
	Iruḷa,	*Kei.*
	Malabar,	*Kai, karam, at-tham.*
	Sinhalese,	*Ata.*

Group	Language	Head
Types.		
Inflecting.	SANSKṚIT,	*'Siras.*
	ARABIC,	*Rás.*
Compounding.	BASK,	*Buru.*
	FINNIC,	*Pää.*
	MAGYAR,	*Fej.*
	TURKISH,	*Bash.*
	CIRCASSIAN,	*Tshkha.*
	GEORGIAN,	*Thavi.*
	MONGOLIAN,	*Tologhai.*
	MANTSHU,	*Udshu, utshu.*
	JAVANESE, Ngoko,	*Enḍas.*
	JAVANESE, Krama,	*Sirah.*
	MALAY,	*Kapála.*
Isolating.	CHINESE, Nankin,	*T'au.*
	CHINESE, Pekin,	*T'au.*
	CHINESE, Canton,	*T'au.*
	CHINESE, Shanghai,	*Deu.*
	AMOY, Colloquial,	*T'aú.*
	JAPANESE,	*Atama.*
	Brahuí,	*Kátumb.*
Chinese Frontier & Tibet.	Gyámi,	*Thau.*
	Gyárung,	*Ta-ko.*
	Tákpa,	*Gok-ti.*
	Mányak,	*Wúlli.*
	Thochú,	*Kapat.*
	Sokpa,	*Tholá-gwe.*
	Horpa,	*Gho.*
	Tibetan (*written*),	Mgo.
	Tibetan (*spoken*),	*Go.*
Nepal (east to west).	Serpa,	*Go.*
	Súnwár,	*Piyá.*
	Gúrung,	*Krá.*
	Múrmi,	*Thobo.*
	Magar,	*Mi-tálú.*
	Tháksya,	*Ta.*
	Pákhya,	*Manto.*
	Newár,	*Chhon.*
	Limbu,	*Thagek.*
Kiránti Group (East Nepal).	Kiránti,	*Táng.*
	Rodong,	*Táklo, tak-lo.*
	Rúngchenbung,	*Táng, eu-táng.*
	Chhingtángya,	*Táng.*
	Náchhereng,	*Ták-lo.*
	Wáling,	*Táng.*
	Yákha,	*Tukh-rúk, tukhurúk, tú khrúk.*
	Chourásya,	*Phútiri.*
	Kulungya,	*Tong.*
	Thulungya,	*Búi.*
	Báhingya,	*Piya.*
	Lohorong,	*Tákhrok', ning-tang-wa, ummruma.*
	Lambichhong,	*Táng.*
	Báláli,	*Tákh-lo.*
	Sáng-páng,	*Tákhúlo.*
	Dúmi,	*Dhong, dakhlok.*
	Kháling,	*U-dhong.*
	Dungmáli,	*Táng, um-táng.*
Broken Tribes of Nepal.	Dárhi,	*Múd.*
	Denwár,	*Mú-dek.*
	Pahri,	*Chhe.*
	Chepáng,	*Tá-to-long.*
	Bhrámu,	*Ká-pá.*
	Váyu,	*Pú-chhi.*
	Kuswar,	*Ká-pá.*
	Kusunda,	*Chipi.*
	Tháru,	*Muḍi.*
	Lepcha (Sikkim),	*Athiak.*
	Bhúṭáni v. Lhopa,	*Gútoh.*

Group	Language	Head
N.-E. Bengal.	Bodo,	*Khoro.*
	Dhimál,	*Puring.*
	Kocch,	*Mura.*
	Garo,	*Dakam.*
	Káchári,	*Khoro, koro.*
Eastern Frontier of Bengal.	Munipuri,	*Moko.*
	Míthán Nágá,	*Khang.*
	Tablung Nágá,	*Sáng.*
	Khári Nágá,	*Telim.*
	Angámi Nágá,	*Atsü.*
	Námsáng Nágá,	*Kho.*
	Nowgong Nágá,	*Takolák.*
	Tengsa Nágá,	*Teko.*
	Abor Miri,	*Tuku, mittuk.*
	Sibságar Miri,	*Mittub.*
	Deoria Chutia,	*Gubong.*
	Singpho,	*Bong.*
Arrakan & Burmah.	Burman (*written*),	Khong.
	Burman (*spoken*),	Ghaung, *o-hkaung.*
	Khyeng v. Shou,	*Lu.*
	Kámi,	*A-lu.*
	Kúmi,	*A-lu.*
	Mrú v. Toung,	*Lu.*
	Sák,	*A-khu.*
Siam & Tenasserim.	Talain v. Mon,	*Katau.*
	Sgau-karen,	*Ko, hko.*
	Pwo-karen,	*Ko.*
	Toungh-thu,	*Katu.*
	Shán,	*Ho.*
	Annamitic,	*Dâu.*
	Siamese,	*Kamon, hoa.*
	Ahom,	*Ru.*
	Khámti,	*Ho.*
	Laos,	*Ho.*
Central India.	Ho (Kol),	*Bo.*
	Kol (Singhbhum),	*Bu.*
	Santáli,	*Buho, baha.*
	Bhúmij,	*Buho.*
	Uráon,	*Kuk.*
	Mundala,	*Bhuo.*
	Rájmahali,	*Kupe.*
	Goṇḍi,	*Talla, talú.*
	Gayeti,	*Talá.*
	Rutluk,	*Talá.*
	Naikude,	*Tal.*
	Kolami,	*Kupál.*
	Mádi,	*Talá, talai.*
	Mádia,	*Talá.*
	Kuri,	*Dui.*
	Keikádi,	*Talkai.*
	Khoṇḍ,	*Tláva.*
	Sávara,	*Abobumv, abumv.*
	Gadaba,	*Bo.*
	Yerukala,	*Vonḍu, talayi.*
	Chentsu,	*Múnḍ.*
Southern India.	Tamiḷ, anc.,	*Senni.*
	Tamiḷ, mod.,	*Talei.*
	Malayáḷma, anc.,	*Caret.*
	Malayáḷma, mod.,	*Tala.*
	Telugu,	*Tala.*
	Karṇáṭaka, anc.,	*Caret.*
	Karṇáṭaka, mod.,	*Tale.*
	Tuḷuva,	*Tare.*
	Kurgi,	*Manḍe.*
	Toḍuva, }	*Muḍḍ.*
	Toḍa, }	*Maḍḍ.*
	Kóta,	*Manḍe.*
	Baḍaga,	*Manḍe, tále.*
	Kuṛumba,	*Manḍe.*
	Iruḷa,	*Tele.*
	Malabar,	*Thalei, siram.*
	Sinhalese,	*Oḷua.*

Types.		
Inflecting.	SANSKRIT,	*'Súkara.*
	ARABIC,	*Khanzír.*
Compounding.	BASK,	*Cherri, charri, yerri, urde.*
	FINNIC,	*Orasa.*
	MAGYAR,	*Malac.*
	TURKISH,	*Domuz.*
	CIRCASSIAN,	*Koh.*
	GEORGIAN,	*Gori.*
	MONGOLIAN,	*Khaban.*
	MANTSHU,	*Ulghiyan.*
	JAVANESE, Ngoko,	*Babi.*
	JAVANESE, Krama,	*Babi.*
	MALAY,	*Bábi.*
Isolating.	CHINESE, Nankin,	*Chú.*
	CHINESE, Pekin,	*Chú.*
	CHINESE, Canton,	*Chü.*
	CHINESE, Shanghai,	*Tsz'-lu.*
	AMOY, Colloquial,	*Ti.*
	JAPANESE,	*Butta.*
	Brahuí,	*Caret.*
Chinese Frontier & Tibet.	Gyámi,	*Dhú.*
	Gyárung,	*Ki.*
	Tákpa,	*Phá.*
	Mányak,	*Wáh.*
	Thochú,	*Pi.*
	Sokpa,	*Khá-khai.*
	Horpa,	*Váh.*
	Tibetan (*written*),	*Phag.*
	Tibetan (*spoken*),	*Phak-pa, phak.*
Nepal (east to west).	Serpa,	*Phak.*
	Súnwár,	*Po.*
	Gúrung,	*Tili.*
	Múrmi,	*Dhwá.*
	Magar,	*Wak.*
	Tháksya,	*Tili.*
	Pákhya,	*Har'ra.*
	Newár,	*Pha.*
	Limbu,	*Phag.*
Kiránti Group (East Nepal).	Kiránti,	*Bhag.*
	Rodong,	*Bo.*
	Rúngchenbung,	*Bá, yángbá* (wild hog).
	Chhingtángya,	*Phak.*
	Náchhereng,	*Bo-o.*
	Wáling,	*Bok, phá, khong.*
	Yákha,	*Phák.*
	Chourásya,	*Pá.*
	Kulungya,	*Bo-o.*
	Thulungya,	*Bwá, bo.*
	Báhingya,	*Po.*
	Lohorong,	*Ba', bak, bag'.*
	Lambichhong,	*Phák.*
	Báláli,	*Báh'.*
	Sáng-páng,	*Bhá.*
	Dúmi,	*Po, pwo.*
	Kháling,	*Po.*
	Dungmáli,	*Pák, pá.*
Broken Tribes of Nepal.	Dárhi,	*Sú-er.*
	Denwár,	*Sú-gúr.*
	Pahri,	*Pho.*
	Chepáng,	*Pyá, pyák.*
	Bhrámu,	*Pak-syá.*
	Váyu,	*Pog, pok.*
	Kuswar,	*Sú-ri.*
	Kusunda,	*Hi, yasa.*
	Tháru,	*Suwar.*
	Lepcha (Sikkim),	*Mon.*
	Bhúṭáni v. Lhopa,	*Phagpo.*

N.-E. Bengal.	Bodo,	*Yoma.*
	Dhimál,	*Páyá.*
	Kocch,	*Súvar, pangár, pathi* (sow).
	Garo,	*Vak.*
	Káchári,	*Oma.*
Eastern Frontier of Bengal.	Munipuri,	*Ok.*
	Míthán Nágá,	*Vak.*
	Tablung Nágá,	*Ak.*
	Khári Nágá,	*Auk.*
	Angámi Nágá,	*Thavo.*
	Námsáng Nágá,	*Vak.*
	Nowgong Nágá,	*A'k.*
	Tengsa Nágá,	*A'k.*
	Abor Miri,	*Yúek.*
	Sibságar Miri,	*Eyeg.*
	Deoria Chutia,	*Chu.*
	Singpho,	*Wá.*
Arrakan & Burmah.	Burman (*written*),	*Wak.*
	Burman (*spoken*),	*Wet.*
	Khyeng v. Shou,	*Weuk.*
	Kámi,	*O.*
	Kúmi,	*A-ou.*
	Mrú v. Toung,	*Ta-pák.*
	Sák,	*Vák.*
Siam & Tenasserim.	Talain v. Mon,	*Kalet.*
	Sgau-karen,	*To, tho.*
	Pwo-karen,	*Toh, htu.*
	Toungh-thu,	*Htau.*
	Shán,	*Mu.*
	Annamitic,	*Heo.*
	Siamese,	*Mu.*
	Ahom,	*Mu.*
	Khámti,	*Mu.*
	Laos,	*Mu.*
Central India.	Ho (Kol),	*Sukri.*
	Kol (Singhbhum),	*Sukri.*
	Santáli,	*Kuḍu, sukuri.*
	Bhúmij,	*Sukri.*
	Uráon,	*Kis.*
	Mundala,	*Sukri.*
	Rájmahali,	*Kis.*
	Goṇḍi,	*Paddi, padi.*
	Gayeti,	*Caret.*
	Rutluk,	*Padi.*
	Naikude,	*Turre.*
	Kolami,	*Turre.*
	Mádi,	*Paddi, patti.*
	Mádia,	*Pahi.*
	Kuri,	*Chukadi.*
	Keikádi,	*Pani.*
	Khoṇḍ,	*Pajji.*
	Sávara,	*Kimbo.*
	Gadaba,	*Gibbi.*
	Yerukala,	*Panḍri.*
	Chentsu,	*Suwar, ghusiri.*
Southern India.	Tamiḷ, anc.,	*Kezhal.*
	Tamiḷ, mod.,	*Panri, panni.*
	Malayáḷma, anc.,	*Caret.*
	Malayáḷma, mod.,	*Panni.*
	Telugu,	*Pandi.*
	Karṇáṭaka, anc.,	*Pandi.*
	Karṇáṭaka, mod.,	*Handi.*
	Tuḷuva,	*Panji.*
	Kurgi,	*Panḍi.*
	Toḍuva,	*Caret.*
	Toḍa,	*Pandij.*
	Kóta,	*Panje.*
	Baḍaga,	*Handij.*
	Kuṛumba,	*Handij.*
	Iruḷa,	*Pani, panni.*
	Malabar,	*Pandi, súkaram.*
	Sinhalese,	*Urá.*

Types.

Inflecting.	SANSKRIT,	*'Sṛinga.*
	ARABIC,	*Ḳorn.*
Compounding.	BASK,	*Adar.*
	FINNIC,	*Sarwi.*
	MAGYAR,	*Caret.*
	TURKISH,	*Caret.*
	CIRCASSIAN,	*Caret.*
	GEORGIAN,	*Caret.*
	MONGOLIAN,	*Eber.*
	MANTSHU,	*Uikhe, uihe.*
	JAVANESE, Ngoko,	*Sungu.*
	JAVANESE, Krama,	*Singat.*
	MALAY,	*Tanduḳ.*
Isolating.	CHINESE, Nankin,	*Koh.*
	CHINESE, Pekin,	*Ko.*
	CHINESE, Canton,	*Kok.*
	CHINESE, Shanghai,	*Koh.*
	AMOY, Colloquial,	*Kak.*
	JAPANESE,	*Tsŭno.*
	Brahuí,	*Caret.*
Chinese Frontier & Tibet.	Gyámi,	*Tiko.*
	Gyárung,	*Ta-rú.*
	Tákpa,	*Rú-ba.*
	Mányak,	*Rú-bu.*
	Thochú,	*Rak.*
	Sokpa,	*Ye-bour.*
	Horpa,	*K'-rum-bo.*
	Tibetan (*written*),	*Rá.*
	Tibetan (*spoken*),	*Rájo.*
Nepal (east to west).	Serpa,	*Arkyok.*
	Súnwár,	*Gúro.*
	Gúrung,	*Ru.*
	Múrmi,	*Rhú.*
	Magar,	*Mirháng.*
	Tháksya,	*Ru.*
	Pákhya,	*Sing.*
	Newár,	*Nekú.*
	Limbu,	*Tang.*
Kiranti Group (East Nepal).	Kiránti,	*Us-ángá.*
	Rodong,	*Rúng, tong, um-tong.*
	Rúngchenbung,	*Usang'ga.*
	Chhingtángya,	*Sing'ga.*
	Náchhereng,	*Tá-á.*
	Wáling,	*Khú-úng-táng, tammi khak.*
	Yákha,	*Itáng.*
	Chourásya,	*Roso.*
	Kulungya,	*U'mpitta, pitta.*
	Thulungya,	*Ráng, um ráng.*
	Báhingya,	*G-ro-ng, grong.*
	Lohorong,	*Tang, kisa tang* (deer's).
	Lambichhong,	*Singa.*
	Báláli,	*Sátáng.*
	Sáng-páng,	*Tán, umtán.*
	Dúmi,	*Grong, gro.*
	Kháling,	*Ughrong.*
	Dungmáli,	*Khúkmútáng.*
Broken Tribes of Nepal.	Dárhi,	*Sing.*
	Denwár,	*Sing.*
	Pahri,	*Mhú-ní.*
	Chepáng,	*Ro-ng.*
	Bhrámu,	*U'-nyá, ún-yú.*
	Váyu,	*Ru-ng.*
	Kuswar,	*Sing-ek.*
	Kusunda,	*Iping-jing.*
	Thárú,	*Sing.*
	Lepcha (Sikkim),	*Arong, a-rong.*
	Bhúṭáni v. Lhopa,	*Rou.*
N.-E. Bengal.	Bodo,	*Gong.*
	Dhimál,	*Dáng.*
	Kocch,	*Singh, khág* (of a rhinoceros).
	Garo,	*Korong* (*khorong ?*).
	Káchári,	*Gong.*
Eastern Frontier of Bengal.	Munipuri,	*Suji.*
	Míthán Nágá,	*Rong.*
	Tablung Nágá,	*Wong.*
	Khári Nágá,	*Tíh.*
	Angámi Nágá,	*Pokhye.*
	Námsáng Nágá,	*Rong.*
	Nowgong Nágá,	*Tazzü.*
	Tengsa Nágá,	*Tai.*
	Abor Miri,	*A'reng.*
	Sibságar Miri,	*A'reng.*
	Deoria Chutia,	*Nu.*
	Singpho,	*Rung.*
Arrakan & Burmah.	Burman (*written*),	*Khyo.*
	Burman (*spoken*),	*Ghyo, gyo.*
	Khyeng v. Shou,	*A-kyi.*
	Kámi,	*At-ta-ki.*
	Kúmi,	*Ta-ki.*
	Mrú v. Toung,	*A-náng.*
	Sák,	*A-rúng.*
Siam & Tenasserim.	Talain v. Mon,	*Kareng.*
	Sgau-karen,	*Nir, ner, tha-nah.*
	Pwo-karen,	*Nong.*
	Toungh-thu,	*Nung.*
	Shán,	*Khoung.*
	Annamitic,	*Sŭ'ng.*
	Siamese,	*Khoung, khau.*
	Ahom,	*Khau.*
	Khámti,	*Khau.*
	Laos,	*Khau.*
Central India.	Ho (Kol),	*Sakwa.*
	Kol (Singhbhum),	*Dring.*
	Santáli,	*Dereng, daring.*
	Bhúmij,	*Derring.*
	Uráon,	*Márag.*
	Mundala,	*Daring.*
	Rájmahali,	*Márg.*
	Goṇḍi,	*Singh, kor; kokak* (pl.).
	Gayeti,	*Kor; kohak* (pl.).
	Rutluk,	*Singi-kor.*
	Naikude,	*Komul.*
	Kolami,	*Pedata.*
	Mádi,	*Kor, korru; kohak, baraya* (pl.).
	Mádia,	*Caret.*
	Kuri,	*Singi.*
	Keikádi,	*Caret.*
	Khoṇḍ,	*Kosko.*
	Sávara,	*Ajigna.*
	Gadaba,	*Nirri.*
	Yerukala,	*Kommu.*
	Chentsu,	*Sing.*
Southern India.	Tamiḻ, anc.,	*Kōḍu.*
	Tamiḻ, mod.,	*Kombu.*
	Malayáḻma, anc.,	*Caret.*
	Malayáḻma, mod.,	*Komba.*
	Telugu,	*Kommu.*
	Karṇáṭaka, anc.,	*Caret.*
	Karṇáṭaka, mod.,	*Kōḍu, kombu.*
	Tuḷuva,	*Kombu.*
	Kurgi,	*Caret.*
	Toḍuva,	*Kurr.*
	Toḍa,	*Kuar.*
	Kóta,	*Khobe* (*kobe ?*).
	Baḍaga,	*Khodu, khombu* (*kodu ?*).
	Kuṛumba,	*Khombu* (*kombu ?*).
	Iruḷa,	*Khombu* (*kombu ?*).
	Malabar,	*Kombu, kodu* (*khombu ?*).
	Sinhalese,	*Anga.*

Types.

Inflecting.	SANSKRIT,	*Aśva.*
	ARABIC,	*Hiṣân, faras* = mare.
Compounding.	BASK,	*Zaldi.*
	FINNIC,	*Hepo.*
	MAGYAR,	*Lo.*
	TURKISH,	*At.*
	CIRCASSIAN,	*Shey, tziu,* ascia,* belgan.**
	GEORGIAN,	*Tskheni.*
	MONGOLIAN,	*Morin, junta,‡ kinakin.‖*
	MANTSHU,	*Mori, junta.**
	JAVANESE, Ngoko,	*Jâran.*
	JAVANESE, Krama,	*Kapal.*
	MALAY,	*Kûda.*
Isolating.	CHINESE, Nankin,	*Má.*
	CHINESE, Pekin,	*Má.*
	CHINESE, Canton,	*Má.*
	CHINESE, Shanghai,	*Mo.*
	AMOY, Colloquial,	*Be.*
	JAPANESE,	*M'ma.*
	Brahuí,	*Huli.*
Chinese Frontier & Tibet.	Gyámi,	*Má.*
	Gyárung,	*Bo-roḥ.*
	Tákpa,	*Teḥ.*
	Mányak,	*Bo-roh, broh.*
	Thochú,	*Roḥ.*
	Sokpa,	*Má-ri.*
	Horpa,	*Rhí, ryi.*
	Tibetan (*written*),	*Rtá.*
	Tibetan (*spoken*),	*Tá.*
Nepal (east to west).	Serpa,	*Tá.*
	Súnwár,	*Ghora.*
	Gúrung,	*Ghora.*
	Múrmi,	*Tá.*
	Magar,	*Ghora.*
	Tháksya,	*Caret.*
	Pákhya,	*Caret.*
	Newár,	*Sala.*
	Limbu,	*On.*
Kiranti Group (East Nepal).	Kiránti,	*Ghora.*
	Rodong,	*Ghoḍá.*
	Rúngchenbung,	*Ghoḍá.*
	Chhingtángya,	*Ghoḍá.*
	Náchhereng,	*Ghoḍá.*
	Wáling,	*Ghoḍá.*
	Yákha,	*O'n.*
	Chourásya,	*Ghoḍá.*
	Kulungya,	*Ghoḍa.*
	Thulungya,	*Ghoḍá.*
	Báhingya,	*Ghoḍa.*
	Lohorong,	*En.*
	Lambichhong,	*Ghoḍa.*
	Báláli,	*Yen, eún.*
	Sáng-páng,	*Phúṇ, yempa.*
	Dúmi,	*Ghoḍa.*
	Kháling,	*Ghora.*
	Dungmáli,	*Ghoḍa.*
Broken Tribes of Nepal.	Dárhi,	*Ghoro.*
	Denwár,	*Ghora.*
	Pahri,	*Sa-ro.*
	Chepáng,	*Se-rang.*
	Bhrámu,	*Caret.*
	Váyu,	*Caret.*
	Kuswar,	*Ghora.*
	Kusunda,	*Caret.*
	Tháru,	*Caret.*
	Lepcha (Sikkim),	*On.*
	Bhúṭáni v. Lhopa,	*Táh.*

N.-E. Bengal.	Bodo,	*Korai.*
	Dhimál,	*Onhyá.*
	Kocch,	*Ghora.*
	Garo,	*Ghora.*
	Kácharí,	*Ghorai.*
Eastern Frontier of Bengal.	Munipuri,	*Sagol.*
	Míthán Nágá,	*Man, mok.*
	Tablung Nágá,	*Kowai.*
	Khári Nágá,	*Kungri.*
	Angámi Nágá,	*Chekwir.*
	Námsáng Nágá,	*Mok.*
	Nowgong Nágá,	*Kor.*
	Tengsa Nágá,	*Kuri.*
	Abor Miri,	*Gore.*
	Sibságar Miri,	*Gure.*
	Deoria Chutia,	*Gori.*
	Singpho,	*Gu-mrang.*
Arrakan & Burmah.	Burman (*written*),	*Mrang.*
	Burman (*spoken*),	*Myen, myin.*
	Khyeng v. Shou,	*S'he.*
	Kámi,	*Ta-phu.*
	Kúmi,	*Koung-ngu.*
	Mrú v. Toung,	*Ko-ra-ngá.*
	Sák,	*Sapu.*
Siam & Tenasserim.	Talain v. Mon,	*Chway.*
	Sgau-karen,	*K'tha, kathay, kathi.*
	Pwo-karen,	*Thi.*
	Toungh-thu,	*Thay.*
	Shán,	*Ma.*
	Annamitic,	*Ngu'a.*
	Siamese,	*Má.*
	Ahom,	*Má.*
	Khámti,	*Má.*
	Laos,	*Má.*
Central India.	Ho (Kol),	*Sádom.*
	Kol (Singhbhum),	*Sadham.*
	Santáli,	*Sádom, sadham.*
	Bhúmij,	*Sadham.*
	Uráon,	*Ghoro.*
	Mundala,	*Sadam.*
	Rájmahali,	*Goro.*
	Goṇḍi,	*Koṇdand* (?), *kodá.*
	Gayeti,	*Kodá.*
	Rutluk,	*Kodá.*
	Naikude,	*Gurram.*
	Kolami,	*Gurram.*
	Mádi,	*Kodá, gudá.*
	Mádia,	*Kodá.*
	Kuri,	*Ghoji.*
	Keikádi,	*Kudara.*
	Khoṇḍ,	*Goḍá.*
	Sávara,	*Kuḍata.*
	Gadaba,	*Kirtyám.*
	Yerukala,	*Kudara.*
	Chentsu,	*Ghoḍo.*
Southern India.	Tamiḷ, anc.,	*Páymá.*
	Tamiḷ, mod.,	*Kudirei.*
	Malayâḷma, anc.,	*Caret.*
	Malayâḷma, mod.,	*Kutira.*
	Telugu,	*Gurramu.*
	Karṇáṭaka, anc.,	*Caret.*
	Karṇáṭaka, mod.,	*Kudure.*
	Tuḷuva,	*Kudare.*
	Kurgi,	*Kudre.*
	Toḍuva, } Toḍa, }	*Kadar.* *Kadurae.*
	Kóta,	*Kudare.*
	Baḍaga,	*Kudure.*
	Kurumba,	*Kudure.*
	Iruḷa,	*Kudure.*
	Malabar,	*Kutherei, pari, asuvam.*
	Sinhalese,	*Aswayá.*

	Types.	
Inflecting.	SANSKRIT,	*Griha, vástu, veś'man.*
	ARABIC,	*Beit.*
Compounding.	BASK,	*Eche, iche.*
	FINNIC,	*Huonet.*
	MAGYAR,	*Haz.*
	TURKISH,	*Ev.*
	CIRCASSIAN,	*Wuney, ruck,* kall.**
	GEORGIAN,	*Sakhli, pathat.**
	MONGOLIAN,	*Ger, baising, iueran.‖*
	MANTSHU,	*Boo, fanfa.**
	JAVANESE, Ngoko,	*Umah.*
	JAVANESE, Krama,	*Griya.*
	MALAY,	*Rúmah.*
Isolating.	CHINESE, Nankin,	*Uh.*
	CHINESE, Pekin,	*Wú.*
	CHINESE, Canton,	*Uk.*
	CHINESE, Shanghai,	*Vong-tsz'.*
	AMOY, Colloquial,	*Ch'ú.*
	JAPANESE,	*Iye.*
	Brahuí,	*Urá.*
Chinese Frontier & Tibet.	Gyámi,	*Shhangcha.*
	Gyárung,	*Chhem.*
	Tákpa,	*Khem.*
	Mányak,	*Nyeh.*
	Thochú,	*Kih.*
	Sokpa,	*Pá-syáng.*
	Horpa,	*Hyo.*
	Tibetan (*written*),	*Khyim.*
	Tibetan (*spoken*),	*Náng.*
Nepal (east to west).	Serpa,	*Khángbá.*
	Súnwár,	*Khí.*
	Gúrung,	*Tin.*
	Múrmi,	*Dhim.*
	Magar,	*Yúm.*
	Tháksya,	*Ghim.*
	Pákhya,	*Ghar.*
	Newár,	*Chhen.*
	Limbu,	*Him.*
Kiranti Group (East Nepal).	Kiránti,	*Khim.*
	Rodong,	*Khim.*
	Rúngchenbung,	*Khim.*
	Chhingtángya,	*Khim.*
	Náchhereng,	*Khim.*
	Wáling,	*Khim.*
	Yákha,	*Páng.*
	Chourásya,	*Kúdú.*
	Kulungya,	*Khim.*
	Thulungya,	*Nem.*
	Báhingya,	*Khim.*
	Lohorong,	*Khim.*
	Lambichhong,	*Khim.*
	Báláli,	*Khim.*
	Sáng-páng,	*Khim.*
	Dúmi,	*Kám, kim.*
	Kháling,	*Kám.*
	Dungmáli,	*Khim.*
Broken Tribes of Nepal.	Dárhi,	*Ghar.*
	Denwár,	*Ghar.*
	Pahri,	*Chen.*
	Chepáng,	*Tim, kyim.*
	Bhrámu,	*Nam.*
	Váyu,	*Kim, kem.*
	Kuswar,	*Ghara.*
	Kusunda,	*Báhi.*
	Tháru,	*Ghar.*
	Lepcha (Sikkim),	*Lí.*
	Bhútáni v. Lhopa,	*Khyim.*

N.-E. Bengal.	Bodo,	*No-o, nü.*
	Dhimál,	*Chá, sá.*
	Kocch,	*Ghor.*
	Garo,	*Nagou.*
	Káchári,	*Nau.*
Eastern Frontier of Bengal.	Munipuri,	*Yim.*
	Míthán Nágá,	*Ham, hum.*
	Tablung Nágá,	*Nok.*
	Khári Nágá,	*Aki.*
	Angámi Nágá,	*Ki.*
	Námsáng Nágá,	*Hum.*
	Nowgong Nágá,	*Ki.*
	Tengsa Nágá,	*Ki.*
	Abor Miri,	*Ekum.*
	Sibságar Miri,	*Ekum.*
	Deoria Chutia,	*Nyá.*
	Singpho,	*N'tá.*
Arrakan & Burmah.	Burman (*written*),	*Im.*
	Burman (*spoken*),	*Eing, seng.*
	Khyeng v. Shou,	*Im.*
	Kámi,	*In.*
	Kúmi,	*Um.*
	Mrú v. Toung,	*Kin.*
	Sák,	*Kyin.*
Siam & Tenasserim.	Talain v. Mon,	*Hnyi.*
	Sgau-karen,	*He, hhi.*
	Pwo-karen,	*Yaing, gayn.*
	Toungh-thu,	*Sam.*
	Shán,	*Hen.*
	Annamitic,	*Nhà.*
	Siamese,	*Rau, reu-an.*
	Ahom,	*Ren.*
	Khámti,	*Hün.*
	Laos,	*Heun.*
Central India.	Ho (Kol),	*Oá.*
	Kol (Singhbhum),	*Oá.*
	Santáli,	*Odáh, bákhol, kudiá, kumlá.*
	Bhúmij,	*Orá.*
	Uráon,	*Erpá.*
	Mundala,	*Urá-a.*
	Rájmahali,	*Avá.*
	Gondi,	*Ron.*
	Gayeti,	*Ron.*
	Rutluk,	*Ron.*
	Naikude,	*Ella.*
	Kolami,	*Ella.*
	Mádi,	*Lon.*
	Mádia,	*Lon.*
	Kuri,	*Ura (uda ?).*
	Keikádi,	*Ud (ud ?).*
	Khond,	*Yiddu.*
	Sávara,	*Sugna.*
	Gadaba,	*Deyyon.*
	Yerukala,	*Vúdu.*
	Chentsu,	*Ghor.*
Southern India.	Tamil, anc.,	*Illam.*
	Tamil, mod.,	*Manei, vídu.*
	Malayálma, anc.,	*Carei.*
	Malayálma, mod.,	*Vita, illam.*
	Telugu,	*Illu.*
	Karnátaka, anc.,	*Caret.*
	Karnátaka, mod.,	*Mane.*
	Tuluva,	*Illa.*
	Kurgi,	*Caret.*
	Toduva, }	*Arra.*
	Toda, }	*Arsh, kuat, daë-ryh-alti.*
	Kóta,	*Pei.*
	Badaga,	*Mane.*
	Kurumba,	*Mane.*
	Irula,	*Kure.*
	Malabar,	*Vidu, manei, illam, akam.*
	Sinhalese,	*Geya.*

	Types.	
Inflecting.	SANSKRIT,	*Kshudh.*
	ARABIC,	*Júaa.*
Compounding.	BASK,	*Gose, ami.*
	FINNIC,	*Nalka.*
	MAGYAR,	*Ehseg.*
	TURKISH,	*Caret.*
	CIRCASSIAN,	*Caret.*
	GEORGIAN,	*Caret.*
	MONGOLIAN,	*Ülosgolang.*
	MANTSHU,	*Yatahushara.*
	JAVANESE, Ngoko,	*Luve.*
	JAVANESE, Krama,	*Ngeléh.*
	MALAY,	*Lápar.*
Isolating.	CHINESE, Nankin,	*T'ú-ngo.*
	CHINESE, Pekin,	*T'ú-o.*
	CHINESE, Canton,	*T'ò-ngo.*
	CHINESE, Shanghai,	*Tu-li-ngu.*
	AMOY, Colloquial,	*Iau.*
	JAPANESE,	*Haragaheru.*
	Brahuí,	*Bingun.*
Chinese Frontier & Tibet.	Gyámi,	*O-ti, wo-ti.*
	Gyárung,	*Tomos.*
	Tákpa,	*Caret.*
	Mányak,	*Vitengne.*
	Thochú,	*Ashpitch.*
	Sokpa,	*Wolúso.*
	Horpa,	*Namjongsi.*
	Tibetan (*written*),	*Ltogs.*
	Tibetan (*spoken*),	*Tok.*
Nepal (east to west).	Serpa,	*Tokúng.*
	Súnwár,	*Amaija.*
	Gúrung,	*Phokre.*
	Múrmi,	*Phoïdang.*
	Magar,	*Tukresya.*
	Thaksya,	*Phothanji.*
	Pákhya,	*Bhok-lágyo.*
	Newár,	*Pitya.*
	Limbu,	*Sá-lah-ma.*
Kiranti Group (East Nepal).	Kiránti,	*Sá-á.*
	Rodong,	*Sáká.*
	Rúngchenbung,	*Sá-á, súng-sá-wáa.*
	Chhingtángya,	*Sangsáwá.*
	Náchhereng,	*Saká-á.*
	Wáling,	*Sáangsawá.*
	Yákha,	*Sák.*
	Chourásya,	*Kremkho.*
	Kulungya,	*Sáká.*
	Thulungya,	*Krúim.*
	Báhingya,	*Solimi.*
	Lohorong,	*Sák'.*
	Lambichhong,	*Sák.*
	Báláli,	*Ságe.*
	Sáng-páng,	*Sáka.*
	Dúmi,	*So-a.*
	Kháling,	*So-o.*
	Dungmáli,	*Ságá.*
Broken Tribes of Nepal.	Dárhi,	*Bhukhas.*
	Denwár,	*Bhúk.*
	Pahri,	*Ha, he-nu.*
	Chepáng,	*Caret.*
	Bhrámu,	*U'yangkehe.*
	Váyu,	*Soksa, suk'sa.*
	Kuswar,	*Bhok.*
	Kusunda,	*Idáng.*
	Tháru,	*Bhok.*
	Lepcha (Sikkim),	*Tidok, kridok.*
	Bhútáni v. Lhopa,	*To-ki.*
N.-E. Bengal.	Bodo,	*U'nkwi-dung, uki-dong.*
	Dhimál,	*Mhitú.*
	Kocch,	*Bhúk.*
	Garo,	*Máyú-phitwá.*
	Káchári,	*Guki-dung.*
Eastern Frontier of Bengal.	Munipuri,	*Caret.*
	Míthán Nágá,	*Ram-rio.*
	Tablung Nágá,	*Ram-rio.*
	Khári Nágá,	*Caret.*
	Angámi Nágá,	*Caret.*
	Námsáng Nágá,	*Ramrio.*
	Nowgong Nágá,	*Yatür.*
	Tengsa Nágá,	*Chulale.*
	Abor Miri,	*Kinong.*
	Sibságar Miri,	*Konóng.*
	Deoria Chutia,	*Caret.*
	Singpho,	*Kosiu.*
Arrakan & Burmah.	Burman (*written*),	*Chhá-ngat.*
	Burman (*spoken*),	*Sá-ngat, ngat-mot-khyen.*
	Khyeng v. Shou,	*Bu-lan-a-dú-i.*
	Kámi,	*Búk-ma-khang.*
	Kúmi,	*Be-ou-lám.*
	Mrú v. Toung,	*Caret.*
	Sák,	*Caret.*
Siam & Tenasserim.	Talain v. Mon,	*Ka-lo-hpyo.*
	Sgau-karen,	*Caret.*
	Pwo-karen,	*Caret.*
	Toungh-thu,	*Ha-kho.*
	Shán,	*Ok-pyat.*
	Annamitic,	*Doi.*
	Siamese,	*Aotrat.*
	Ahom,	*Caret.*
	Khámti,	*Caret.*
	Laos,	*Caret.*
Central India.	Ho (Kol),	*Renga.*
	Kol (Singhbhum),	*Renge.*
	Santáli,	*Rengeh, ckenah, rengeláih* (adjectives).
	Bhúmij,	*Renge.*
	Urdon,	*Kéra.*
	Mundala,	*Ringat.*
	Rájmahali,	*Kire.*
	Gondi,	*Karu, karusátur.*
	Gayeti,	*Caret.*
	Rutluk,	*Caret.*
	Naikude,	*Caret.*
	Kolami,	*Caret.*
	Mádi,	*Caret.*
	Mádia,	*Caret.*
	Kuri,	*Caret.*
	Keikádi,	*Caret.*
	Khond,	*Chatanganki, pannenju.*
	Sávara,	*Dolejan.*
	Gadaba,	*Kuddu.*
	Yerukala,	*Soda, peruntsu.*
	Chentsu,	*Bhúk, bhoku.*
Southern India.	Tamil, anc.,	*Caret.*
	Tamil, mod.,	*Pasi.*
	Malayálma, anc.,	*Caret.*
	Malayálma, mod.,	*Viśappa.*
	Telugu,	*A'kali.*
	Karnátaka, anc.,	*Caret.*
	Karnátaka, mod.,	*Has'ivu.*
	Tuluva,	*Paduvu.*
	Kurgi,	*Caret.*
	Toduva, } Toda, }	*Caret.* *Bir-erthti.*
	Kóta,	*Petti-hoje.*
	Badaga,	*Hasu.*
	Kurumba,	*Hasu.*
	Irula,	*Passi.*
	Malabar,	*Pasi.*
	Sinhalese,	*Badaginni.*

Group	*Types.*	
Inflecting.	SANSKRIT,	*Loha.*
	ARABIC,	*Hadid.*
Compounding.	BASK,	*Burni, burdin.*
	FINNIC,	*Rauta.*
	MAGYAR,	*Vas.*
	TURKISH,	*Demir.*
	CIRCASSIAN,	*Ghutshey.*
	GEORGIAN,	*Rkina.*
	MONGOLIAN,	*Temor, temur.*
	MANTSHU,	*Sele.*
	JAVANESE, Ngoko,	*Wési.*
	JAVANESE, Krama,	*Tossan.*
	MALAY,	*Basi.*
Isolating.	CHINESE, Nankin,	*T'ieh.*
	CHINESE, Pekin,	*T'ich.*
	CHINESE, Canton,	*T'it.*
	CHINESE, Shanghai,	*T'ih.*
	AMOY, Colloquial,	*T'ih.*
	JAPANESE,	*Tetsu.*
	Brahuí,	*Ahin.*
Chinese Frontier & Tibet.	Gyámi,	*The.*
	Gyárung,	*Shom.*
	Tákpa,	*Lekh.*
	Mányak,	*Shi.*
	Thochú,	*Sormo.*
	Sokpa,	*Thúmár.*
	Horpa,	*Chú.*
	Tibetan (*written*),	*Lchags.*
	Tibetan (*spoken*),	*Chhyá.*
Nepal (east to west).	Serpa,	*Chhyá.*
	Súnwár,	*Wá-akli.*
	Gúrung,	*Pai.*
	Múrmi,	*Phai.*
	Magar,	*Phalám.*
	Tháksya,	*Phre.*
	Pákhya,	*Khaḍar.*
	Newár,	*Na.*
	Limbu,	*Phenje.*
Kiranti Group (East Nepal).	Kiránti,	*Phalám.*
	Rodong,	*Phalám.*
	Rúngchenbung,	*Phalám.*
	Chhingtángya,	*Bánchhúwa.*
	Náchhereng,	*Phalám.*
	Wáling,	*Phalám.*
	Yákha,	*Chek chi.*
	Chourásya,	*Phalám.*
	Kulungya,	*Sel.*
	Thulungya,	*Sel.*
	Báhingya,	*Syál.*
	Lohorong,	*Chyak'-chi.*
	Lambichhong,	*Chyak' chi.*
	Báláli,	*Phálám.*
	Sáng-páng,	*Sel, syel.*
	Dúmi,	*Sel.*
	Kháling,	*Caret.*
	Dungmáli,	*Caret.*
Broken Tribes of Nepal.	Dárhi,	*Phalám.*
	Denwár,	*Phalám.*
	Pahri,	*Ne.*
	Chepáng,	*Phalám.*
	Bhrámu,	*Phalám.*
	Váyu,	*Kak-ching, khak-chhing-mi.*
	Kuswar,	*Phalám.*
	Kusunda,	*Phalám.*
	Tháru,	*Loha.*
	Lepcha (Sikkim),	*Panjing.*
	Bhúṭáni v. Lhopa,	*Chyá.*

N.-E. Bengal.	Bodo,	*Chúrr, shúrr.*
	Dhimál,	*Chirr.*
	Kocch,	*Loha.*
	Garo,	*Shúrr.*
	Káchári,	*Sorr.*
Eastern Frontier of Bengal.	Munipuri,	*Yot.*
	Míthán Nágá,	*Jian.*
	Tablung Nágá,	*Yan.*
	Khári Nágá,	*Ayin.*
	Angámi Nágá,	*Je.*
	Námsáng Nágá,	*Ján.*
	Nowgong Nágá,	*Yin.*
	Tengsa Nágá,	*Yen.*
	Abor Miri,	*Yagurah.*
	Sibságar Miri,	*Yogir.*
	Deoria Chutia,	*Sung.*
	Singpho,	*Mpri.*
Arrakan & Burmah.	Burman (*written*),	*Sán.*
	Burman (*spoken*),	*Thán.*
	Khyeng v. Shou,	*Thi.*
	Kámi,	*S'hein.*
	Kúmi,	*Ta-mhu.*
	Mrú v. Toung,	*Loung-ha.*
	Sák,	*Thein.*
Siam & Tenasserim.	Talain v. Mon,	*Kasway.*
	Sgau-karen,	*Tah, htá.*
	Pwo-karen,	*Tah.*
	Toungh-thu,	*Say-thi.*
	Shán,	*Leit.*
	Annamitic,	*Sat.*
	Siamese,	*Lit, lek.*
	Ahom,	*Lik.*
	Khámti,	*Lek.*
	Laos,	*Lek.*
Central India.	Ho (Kol),	*Med.*
	Kol (Singhbhum),	*Meḍh.*
	Santáli,	*Meṇheh, meḍhad.*
	Bhúmij,	*Merhd, medhd (?).*
	Uráon,	*Paná.*
	Mundala,	*Marhan, maḍhan (?).*
	Rájmahali,	*Lohá.*
	Goṇḍi,	*Kachchi.*
	Gayeti,	*Kachchi.*
	Rutluk,	*Kachi.*
	Naikude,	*Yinamu.*
	Kolami,	*Lokand.*
	Mádi,	*Kachi.*
	Mádia,	*Kachi.*
	Kuri,	*Loha.*
	Keikádi,	*Ilmu.*
	Khoṇḍ,	*Luharigá.*
	Sávara,	*Lomá.*
	Gadaba,	*Vonchani.*
	Yerukala,	*Yerumbu.*
	Chentsu,	*Loho.*
Southern India.	Tamiḷ, anc.,	*Karumbon.*
	Tamiḷ, mod.,	*Irumbu.*
	Malayáḷma, anc.,	*Caret.*
	Malayáḷma, mod.,	*Irimba.*
	Telugu,	*Inumu.*
	Karṇáṭaka, anc.,	*Caret.*
	Karṇáṭaka, mod.,	*Kabbiṇa.*
	Tuḷuva,	*Karba.*
	Kurgi,	*Caret.*
	Toḍuva, }	*Caret.*
	Toḍa, }	*Kabbuṇ.*
	Kóta,	*Ibbe.*
	Baḍaga,	*Kabbuṇa.*
	Kurumba,	*Kabbuṇa.*
	Iruḷa,	*Irumbu.*
	Malabar,	*Irumbu.*
	Sinhalese,	*Yakaḍa.*

Group	Types.	
Inflecting.	SANSKRIT,	*Patra.*
	ARABIC,	*Waraḳ.*
Compounding.	BASK,	*Osto, ostro, orri.*
	FINNIC,	*Lehti.*
	MAGYAR,	*Level.*
	TURKISH,	*Yaprak.*
	CIRCASSIAN,	*Dshass.*
	GEORGIAN,	*Potḥoli.*
	MONGOLIAN,	*Nebtschi, nabchi.*
	MANTSHU,	*Abdaha, abtakha.*
	JAVANESE, Ngoko,	*Godong.*
	JAVANESE, Krama,	*Dáon.*
	MALAY,	*Dáwun.*
Isolating.	CHINESE, Nankin,	*Yeh.*
	CHINESE, Pekin,	*Ye.*
	CHINESE, Canton,	*I'p.*
	CHINESE, Shanghai,	*Zuyeh.*
	AMOY, Colloquial,	*Hioh.*
	JAPANESE,	*Ha.*
	Brahuí,	*Caret.*
Chinese Frontier & Tibet.	Gyámi,	*Yecha.*
	Gyárung,	*Taimek.*
	Tákpa,	*Blap.*
	Mányak,	*Nipcheḥ.*
	Thochú,	*Thrompi.*
	Sokpa,	*Nái.*
	Horpa,	*Bálah.*
	Tibetan (*written*),	*Lomá.*
	Tibetan (*spoken*),	*Hyomá.*
Nepal (east to west).	Serpa,	*Hyomap.*
	Súnwár,	*Saphá.*
	Gúrung,	*Lau.*
	Múrmi,	*Lápte.*
	Magar,	*Lhá.*
	Tháksya,	*Lhá.*
	Pákhya,	*Pát.*
	Newár,	*Lapte, hau.*
	Limbu,	*Pellá.*
Kiranti Group (East Nepal).	Kiránti,	*U' báva.*
	Rodong,	*Lábo.*
	Rúngchenbung,	*Ubáwa euchha.*
	Chhingtángya,	*Laphowa.*
	Náchhereng,	*Sam, saa-ma.*
	Wáling,	*Sung' phák, ba.*
	Yákha,	*Súm-phák.*
	Chourásya,	*Sáphá, moli.*
	Kulungya,	*Siba, la, um boa.*
	Thulungya,	*Se blám.*
	Báhingya,	*Sopho, sápha.*
	Lohorong,	*Singbak'.*
	Lambichhong,	*Láphák.*
	Báláli,	*Singbák', bák'.*
	Sáng-páng,	*Sáṅbá.*
	Dúmi,	*Sapam, sapho.*
	Kháling,	*Sapang, saphung.*
	Dungmáli,	*Sum-pha.*
Broken Tribes of Nepal.	Dárhi,	*Pát.*
	Denwár,	*Páta.*
	Pahri,	*Lati.*
	Chepáng,	*Lo.*
	Bhrámu,	*Sou.*
	Váyu,	*Lo.*
	Kuswar,	*Páta.*
	Kusunda,	*Hák.*
	Thárú,	*Pátá.*
	Lepcha (Sikkim),	*Lpo.*
	Bhúṭáni v. Lhopa,	*Syoma, dáma.*

N.-E. Bengal.	Bodo,	*Lai, bilai.*
	Dhimál,	*Lháwá, lhábá.*
	Kocch,	*Pát.*
	Garo,	*Lechak.*
	Káchári,	*Bilai.*
Eastern Frontier of Bengal.	Munipuri,	*Maná.*
	Míthán Nágá,	*Pan chak.*
	Tablung Nágá,	*Phum yak.*
	Khári Nágá,	*Tuwá.*
	Angámi Nágá,	*Ponye.*
	Námsáng Nágá,	*Nyáp.*
	Nowgong Nágá,	*A'm.*
	Tengsa Nágá,	*A'm.*
	Abor Miri,	*Anne.*
	Sibságar Miri,	*Ekamane.*
	Deoria Chutia,	*Chiá.*
	Singpho,	*Láp.*
Arrakan & Burmah.	Burman (*written*),	*Kwak.*
	Burman (*spoken*),	*Yuet, ayuet.*
	Khyeng v. Shou,	*She.*
	Kámi,	*Laháng.*
	Kúmi,	*Ngám.*
	Mrú v. Toung,	*Arám.*
	Sák,	*Pwinták.*
Siam & Tenasserim.	Talain v. Mon,	*Kanahtsu.*
	Sgau-karen,	*Lah, thela.*
	Pwo-karen,	*Lah.*
	Toungh-thu,	*Lay.*
	Shán,	*Moungmán.*
	Annamitic,	*Lá.*
	Siamese,	*Pihuma, bai.*
	Ahom,	*Bou.*
	Khámti,	*Maü.*
	Laos,	*Bai.*
Central India.	Ho (Kol),	*Sukám.*
	Kol (Singhbhum),	*Sákam.*
	Santáli,	*Sákam.*
	Bhúmij,	*Sikkam.*
	Uráon,	*A'tkhá.*
	Mundala,	*Sikam.*
	Rájmahali,	*A'tge.*
	Goṇḍi,	*A'ki.*
	Gayeti,	*Caret.*
	Rutluk,	*A'ki.*
	Naikude,	*Caret.*
	Kolami,	*Yegul.*
	Mádi,	*A'ki.*
	Mádia,	*A'ki, maka.*
	Kuri,	*Chakam.*
	Keikádi,	*Yela.*
	Khoṇḍ,	*A'ka.*
	Sávara,	*Olá.*
	Gadaba,	*Vollá.*
	Yerukala,	*Yale, yaláku.*
	Chentsu,	*Pát.*
Southern India.	Tamiḷ, anc.,	*Aḍei.*
	Tamiḷ, mod.,	*Ilei.*
	Malayáḷma, anc.,	*Caret.*
	Malayáḷma, mod.,	*Ila, ola.*
	Telugu,	*A'ku.*
	Karṇáṭaka, anc.,	*Caret.*
	Karṇáṭaka, mod.,	*Ele.*
	Tuḷuva,	*Ire.*
	Kurgi,	*Elakanḍ, toppu.*
	Toḍuva, }	*Err.*
	Toḍa, }	*Ersh.*
	Kóta,	*Yelle.*
	Baḍaga,	*Yelle.*
	Kurumba,	*Yelle.*
	Iruḷa,	*Yele.*
	Malabar,	*Ilei.*
	Sinhalese,	*Kole.*

	Types.	
Inflecting.	SANSKRIT,	*Jyotis.*
	ARABIC,	*Nour.*
Compounding.	BASK,	*Argi.*
	FINNIC,	*Walo.*
	MAGYAR,	*Vilag.*
	TURKISH,	*Caret.*
	CIRCASSIAN,	*Nefnoy.*
	GEORGIAN,	*Natheni.*
	MONGOLIAN,	*Gheghegheh (gegegen).*
	MANTSHU,	*Elden.*
	JAVANESE, Ngoko,	*Těrang.*
	JAVANESE, Krama,	*Těrang.*
	MALAY,	*Tărang.*
Isolating.	CHINESE, Nankin,	*Kwang.*
	CHINESE, Pekin,	*Kwang.*
	CHINESE, Canton,	*Kwong.*
	CHINESE, Shanghai,	*Leángkwong.*
	AMOY, Colloquial,	*Kng.*
	JAPANESE,	*Akari.*
	Brahuí,	*Caret.*
Chinese Frontier & Tibet.	Gyámi,	*Reyai.*
	Gyárung,	*Caret.*
	Tákpa,	*Wot.*
	Mányak,	*Wúh.*
	Thochú,	*Uik.*
	Sokpa,	*Caret.*
	Horpa,	*Spho.*
	Tibetan (*written*),	*Hod.*
	Tibetan (*spoken*),	*Hwe, eu.*
Nepal (east to west).	Serpa,	*Rhip, eu.*
	Súnwár,	*Hángo.*
	Gúrung,	*Bhla.*
	Múrmi,	*U'jálo.*
	Magar,	*Tyáwongcho, ráp.*
	Tháksya,	*Muthnangmu.*
	Pákhya,	*Urt-bátti.*
	Newár,	*Jala.*
	Limbu,	*O't, thorú.*
Kiránti Group (East Nepal).	Kiránti,	*U'lawa chámi.*
	Rodong,	*Námchha, kha wíya.*
	Rúngchenbung,	*Uláwachhámi, sam.*
	Chhingtángya,	*Khálámthá.*
	Náchhereng,	*Wújyálo.*
	Wáling,	*Wújyálo, khádái.*
	Yákha,	*Wap'na.*
	Chourásya,	*Dwám somo.*
	Kulungya,	*Kodáta, námchhowa, miwal'ma.*
	Thulungya,	*Hwah'wáya, sam.*
	Báhingya,	*Hwa.*
	Lohorong,	*Námwoge, námde.*
	Lambichhong,	*Kháte yú.*
	Báláli,	*Namoh'wa.*
	Sáng-páng,	*Khásema.*
	Dúmi,	*U'nel.*
	Kháling,	*Háhám.*
	Dungmáli,	*Khou, sam.*
Broken Tribes of Nepal.	Dárhi,	*U'jung.*
	Denwár,	*U'jat.*
	Pahri,	*Jala.*
	Chepáng,	*Samo, angho, angha.*
	Bhrámu,	*Caret.*
	Váyu,	*Dangdang.*
	Kuswar,	*Johan.*
	Kusunda,	*Jina ïkya.*
	Tháru,	*Anjoriyo.*
	Lepcha (Sikkim),	*A'om, achár.*
	Bhúṭáni v. Lhopa,	*Eu, dam.*

N.-E. Bengal.	Bodo,	*Churáng, shráng.*
	Dhimál,	*Sáneká, jolka.*
	Kocch,	*Jyoti.*
	Garo,	*Klángklang.*
	Káchári,	*Sorang.*
Eastern Frontier of Bengal.	Munipuri,	*Mangál.*
	Mithán Nágá,	*Rangai.*
	Tablung Nágá,	*Nining.*
	Khári Nágá,	*Snaugo.*
	Angámi Nágá,	*Ngukwi.*
	Námsáng Nágá,	*Rangvo.*
	Nowgong Nágá,	*Tsángurh.*
	Tengsa Nágá,	*Sangagho.*
	Abor Miri,	*Piuáng.*
	Sibságar Miri,	*Püáda.*
	Deoria Chutia,	*Dákári.*
	Singpho,	*Ningthoi.*
Arrakan & Burmah.	Burman (*written*),	*Lang.*
	Burman (*spoken*),	*Len, aleng.*
	Khyeng v. Shou,	*Caret.*
	Kámi,	*Avándagá.*
	Kúmi,	*Caret.*
	Mrú v. Toung,	*Watái.*
	Sák,	*Caret.*
Siam & Tenasserim.	Talain v. Mon,	*Ateng, rá.*
	Sgau-karen,	*Tahk'paw, tagopau.*
	Pwo-karen,	*Tserpan.*
	Toungh-thu,	*Lita-lay.*
	Shán,	*Alen.*
	Annamitic,	*Ngò' i.*
	Siamese,	*Psawon, sawang.*
	Ahom,	*Leng.*
	Khámti,	*Leng.*
	Laos,	*Leng, tseng.*
Central India.	Ho (Kol),	*Marsal.*
	Kol (Singhbhum),	*Maskal.*
	Santáli,	*Setong* (glare).
	Bhúmij,	*Tetaytura.*
	Uráon,	*Billi.*
	Mundala,	*Marsa* (?).
	Rájmahali,	*A'veli.*
	Goṇḍi,	*Berachi, vedchi.*
	Gayeti,	*Vedchi.*
	Rutluk,	*Beijianjor.*
	Naikude,	*Vektin, walang.*
	Kolami,	*Velang.*
	Mádi,	*Ves.*
	Mádia,	*Hujaláhur.*
	Kuri,	*Ujawaro.*
	Keikádi,	*Paymaro.*
	Khoṇḍ,	*Vujwálá.*
	Sávara,	*Tambá.*
	Gadaba,	*Tarádutu.*
	Yerukala,	*Valuku.*
	Chentsu,	*Díp, vujjait.*
Southern India.	Tamiḷ, anc.,	*Oḷi.*
	Tamiḷ, mod.,	*Veḷichcham.*
	Malayāḷma, anc.,	*Caret.*
	Malayāḷma, mod.,	*Veḷichcham.*
	Telugu,	*Veluturu, velugu.*
	Karṇáṭaka, anc.,	*Caret.*
	Karṇáṭaka, mod.,	*Beḷaku.*
	Tuḷuva,	*Bhoksha.*
	Kurgi,	*Bellá.*
	Toḍuva, }	*Pelch.*
	Toḍa, }	*Velaku.*
	Kóta,	*Belaku.*
	Baḍaga,	*Divige.*
	Kuṛumba,	*Dipa.*
	Iruḷa,	*Valaku.*
	Malabar,	*Velicham.*
	Sinhalese,	*Eliya.*

	Types.	
Inflecting.	SANSKRIT,	*Manu, manush, manushya.*
	ARABIC,	*Rajol.* [(vir).
Compounding.	BASK,	*Guizon* (homo et vir); *guizar*
	FINNIC,	*Ihmeno* (homo), *mies* (vir).
	MAGYAR,	*Ferfi.*
	TURKISH,	*Er.*
	CIRCASSIAN,	*Tsiffey, adam,* genaht.**
	GEORGIAN,	*Katsi.*
	MONGOLIAN,	*Era, ere, kümün, kömon, bya.*‖
	MANTSHU,	*Khakha, niyalma, oydzah.**
	JAVANESE, Ngoko,	*Wong.*
	JAVANESE, Krama,	*Tiyang.*
	MALAY,	*Orang.*
Isolating.	CHINESE, Nankin,	*Jin.*
	CHINESE, Pekin,	*Jan.*
	CHINESE, Canton,	*Yan.*
	CHINESE, Shanghai,	*Niang.*
	AMOY, Colloquial,	*Lâng, jîn.*
	JAPANESE,	*Hito.*
	Brahuí,	*Narína.*
Chinese Frontier & Tibet.	Gyámi,	*Rin.*
	Gyárung,	*Tirmi.*
	Tákpa,	*Mih.*
	Mányak,	*Chhoh.*
	Thochú,	*Náh.*
	Sokpa,	*Khún.*
	Horpa,	*Vzih.*
	Tibetan (*written*),	*Mi.*
	Tibetan (*spoken*),	*Mi.*
Nepal (east to west).	Serpa,	*Mi.*
	Súnwár,	*Múrú.*
	Gúrung,	*Mhi.*
	Múrmi,	*Mi.*
	Magar,	*Bharmi.*
	Tháksya,	*Mli.*
	Pákhya,	*Manchha.*
	Newár,	*Mano, mi-jang.*
	Limbu,	*Yapmi, yembecha.*
Kiranti Group (East Nepal).	Kiránti,	*Maná.*
	Rodong,	*Mina.*
	Rúngchenbung,	*Mána, maana.*
	Chhingtángya,	*Mápmi, mali'mi.*
	Náchhereng,	*Mina, min.*
	Wáling,	*Mana, mina.*
	Yákha,	*Yáp'mi.*
	Chourásya,	*Múyo.*
	Kulungya,	*Mis.*
	Thulungya,	*Michyu.*
	Báhingya,	*Múri.*
	Lohorong,	*Mina.*
	Lambichhong,	*Máli'mi, mali'mi-chi.*
	Báláli,	*Mina-chi.*
	Sáng-páng,	*Mina.*
	Dúmi,	*Has.*
	Kháling,	*Hash.*
	Dungmáli,	*Mina.*
Broken Tribes of Nepal.	Dárhi,	*Mánus.*
	Denwár,	*Mánus.*
	Pahri,	*Manche.*
	Chepáng,	*Pursi.*
	Bhrámu,	*Bal, bar.*
	Váyu,	*Singtong, loncho.*
	Kuswar,	*Gokchai, cháwái.*
	Kusunda,	*Mih'yák.*
	Tháru,	*Manhai.*
	Lepcha (Sikkim),	*Maro, tagri.*
	Bhútáni v. Lhopa,	*Mi.*

N.-E. Bengal.	Bodo,	*Hiwá, mánshi.*
	Dhimál,	*Wával, diáng, dayáng.*
	Kocch,	*Mánushi, betáchoá.*
	Garo,	*Miva.*
	Káchári,	*Mansui.*
Eastern Frontier of Bengal.	Munipuri,	*Minipa.*
	Míthán Nágá,	*Mi.*
	Tablung Nágá,	*Sauniak.*
	Khári Nágá,	*Ami.*
	Angámi Nágá,	*Theme.*
	Námsáng Nágá,	*Minyán.*
	Nowgong Nágá,	*Nyesung.*
	Tengsa Nágá,	*Mesung.*
	Abor Miri,	*Amie.*
	Sibságar Miri,	*A'mme.*
	Deoria Chutia,	*Mosi.*
	Singpho,	*Singpho.*
Arrakan & Burmah.	Burman (*written*),	*Lú.*
	Burman (*spoken*),	*Lú.*
	Khyeng v. Shou,	*Kláng.*
	Kámi,	*Kami.*
	Kúmi,	*Kumi.*
	Mrú v. Toung,	*Mrú.*
	Sák,	*Lú.*
Siam & Tenasserim.	Talain v. Mon,	*Karu.*
	Sgau-karen,	*Pgahk'nyaw, pakanyau.*
	Pwo-karen,	*Herplong, hplun.*
	Toungh-thu,	*Lan.*
	Shán,	*Konputrihn.*
	Annamitic,	*Ngu'ò'i.*
	Siamese,	*Hpuhtso, khon.*
	Ahom,	*Kun.*
	Khámti,	Kun, *khun.*
	Laos,	*Khon.*
Central India.	Ho (Kol),	*Ho, horo.*
	Kol (Singhbhum),	*Ho.*
	Santáli,	*Hạd, hoḍh, horh, heḍel,*
	Bhúmij,	*Horro.* [*(herel?), koḍa, mánio.*
	Uráon,	*Alla.*
	Mundala,	*Horl.*
	Rájmahali,	*Mále.*
	Goṇḍi,	*Máne, mánwál maurdsal.*
	Gayeti,	*Mánwál.*
	Rutluk,	*Mánwol.*
	Naikude,	*Mas.*
	Kolami,	*Pedda.*
	Mádi,	*Manei, koitar.*
	Mádia,	*Manei, gaita.*
	Kuri,	*Koro.*
	Keikádi,	*Managi.*
	Khoṇḍ,	*Lokká.*
	Sávara,	*Manḍra.*
	Gadaba,	*Lokko.*
	Yerukala,	*Munasam.*
	Chentsu,	*Mánús.*
Southern India.	Tamiḷ, anc.,	*Magan.*
	Tamiḷ, mod.,	*A'ḷ, manidan.*
	Malayáḷma, anc.,	*Caret.*
	Malayáḷma, mod.,	*A'ḷ.*
	Telugu,	*Manishi.*
	Karṇáṭaka, anc.,	*Caret.*
	Karṇáṭaka, mod.,	*A'ḷu.*
	Tuḷuva,	*A'l.*
	Kurgi,	*Mánus, manusu.*
	Toḍuva, }	*A'l.*
	Toḍa, }	*A'l.*
	Kóta,	*A'le, manijou.*
	Baḍaga,	*Manija, alu.*
	Kuṛumba,	*Manisha, alu.*
	Iruḷa,	*Manisha, alu*
	Malabar,	*Manushen, ádaven.*
	Sinhalese,	*Miniha.*

Group	Language	Monkey
	Types.	
Inflecting.	SANSKRIT,	*Kapi, markaṭa, vánara.*
	ARABIC,	*Nisnás, ḳird.*
Compounding.	BASK,	*Chimu, chimino.*
	FINNIC,	*Marakatti.*
	MAGYAR,	*Caret.*
	TURKISH,	*Caret.*
	CIRCASSIAN,	*Caret.*
	GEORGIAN,	*Caret.*
	MONGOLIAN,	*Bitschin.*
	MANTSHU,	*Bonio.*
	JAVANESE, Ngoko,	*Kĕṭek.*
	JAVANESE, Krama,	*Kĕṭek.*
	MALAY,	*Múñit.*
Isolating.	CHINESE, Nankin,	*Hautsze.*
	CHINESE, Pekin,	*Hautsze.*
	CHINESE, Canton,	*Málau.*
	CHINESE, Shanghai,	*Singsing.*
	AMOY, Colloquial,	*Kau.*
	JAPANESE,	*Saru.*
	Brahuí,	*Caret.*
Chinese Frontier & Tibet.	Gyámi,	*Khouch.*
	Gyárung,	*Shepri, ti.*
	Tákpa,	*Prá.*
	Mányak,	*Miyaháh.*
	Thochú,	*Wáissi.*
	Sokpa,	*Mechi.*
	Horpa,	*Zumdeḥ.*
	Tibetan (*written*),	*Sprebú.*
	Tibetan (*spoken*),	*Tyú.*
Nepal (east to west).	Serpa,	*Rhú.*
	Súnwár,	*Moro.*
	Gúrung,	*Timyú.*
	Múrmi,	*Máng.*
	Magar,	*Báner.*
	Tháksya,	*Pángdar.*
	Pákhya,	*Bádar.*
	Newár,	*Máko.*
	Limbu,	*Sobá.*
Kiranti Group (East Nepal).	Kiránti,	*Heláwá.*
	Rodong,	*Tong bhú, no i.*
	Rúngchenbung,	*Heláwa.*
	Chhingtángya,	*Heláwa.*
	Náchhereng,	*Popa.*
	Wáling,	*Heláwa.*
	Yákha,	*Pubáng.*
	Chourásya,	*Pokú.*
	Kulungya,	*Púpwa.*
	Thulungya,	*Núk syu.*
	Báhingya,	*More, muryo.*
	Lohorong,	*Púbáng.*
	Lambichhong,	*Kúbáng.*
	Bálálí,	*Púbáng.*
	Sáng-páng,	*Popáṇ.*
	Dúmi,	*Nús, muksu.*
	Kháling,	*Nús.*
	Dungmálí,	*Násá.*
Broken Tribes of Népal.	Dárhi,	*Banker.*
	Denwár,	*Bandar.*
	Pahri,	*Múga.*
	Chepáng,	*Yúk.*
	Bhrámu,	*Payúk.*
	Váyu,	*Phoka.*
	Kuswar,	*Báner.*
	Kusunda,	*Ugu.*
	Tháru,	*Bánar.*
	Lepcha (Sikkim),	*Sahen.*
	Bhúṭáni v. Lhopa,	*Pyá.*
N.-E. Bengal.	Bodo,	*Mokhara.*
	Dhimál,	*Nhoyá, húlmán.*
	Kocch,	*Bándor, húlmán.*
	Garo,	*Kouwe.*
	Káchári,	*Caret.*
Eastern Frontier of Bengal.	Munipuri,	*Yong.*
	Míthán Nágá,	*Mainuk.*
	Tablung Nágá,	*Simai.*
	Khári Nágá,	*Kishá.*
	Angámi Nágá,	*Takwi.*
	Námsáng Nágá,	*Veh.*
	Nowgong Nágá,	*Shitsü.*
	Tengsa Nágá,	*Suchi.*
	Abor Miri,	*Sibeh.*
	Sibságar Miri,	*Shibe.*
	Deoria Chutia,	*Iku.*
	Singpho,	*Woe.*
Arrakan & Burmah.	Burman (*written*),	*Myok.*
	Burman (*spoken*),	*Myauk.*
	Khyeng v. Shou,	*Young.*
	Kámi,	*Kalai.*
	Kúmi,	*Kala.*
	Mrú v. Toung,	*Tayút.*
	Sák,	*Kawuk.*
Siam & Tenasserim.	Talain v. Mon,	*Kamoi.*
	Sgau-karen,	*Tahen, tao.*
	Pwo-karen,	*Tseroke.*
	Toungh-thu,	*Khyag.*
	Shán,	*Lein.*
	Annamitic,	*Khi.*
	Siamese,	*Lenn, ling.*
	Ahom,	*Laling.*
	Khámti,	*Ling.*
	Laos,	*Wok, ling.*
Central India.	Ho (Kol),	*Gye.*
	Kol (Singhbhum),	*Sarrha, gáḍi.*
	Santáli,	*Gaḍi.*
	Bhúmij,	*Gáḍi.*
	Uráon,	*Bandra.*
	Mundala,	*Bandra.*
	Rájmahali,	*Muge.*
	Goṇḍi,	*Bandara, kove.*
	Gayeti,	*Mujal.*
	Rutluk,	*Kevi, pwal.*
	Naikude,	*Mui.*
	Kolami,	*Mui.*
	Mádi,	*Mungu, mus.*
	Mádia,	*Mujal.*
	Kuri,	*Sara.*
	Keikádi,	*Kwoti.*
	Khoṇḍ,	*Koju.*
	Sávara,	*Karoyi.*
	Gadaba,	*Gusá.*
	Yerukala,	*Kote.*
	Chentsu,	*Mákaḍ.*
Southern India.	Tamiḷ, anc.,	*Kaḍuvan.*
	Tamiḷ, mod.,	*Kurangu.*
	Malayáḷma, anc.,	*Caret.*
	Malayáḷma, mod.,	*Kuranga.*
	Telugu,	*Koti.*
	Karṇáṭaka, anc.,	*Caret.*
	Karṇáṭaka, mod.,	*Kōḍaga, manga.*
	Tuḷuva,	*Mange.*
	Kurgi,	*Caret.*
	Toḍuva, }	*Kodan.*
	Toḍa, }	*Turuni, kodan, pershk.*
	Kóta,	*Korte.*
	Baḍaga,	*Korangu.*
	Kuṛumba,	*Korangu.*
	Iruḷa,	*Korangu.*
	Malabar,	*Kurangku, manthi.*
	Sinhalese,	*Wandurá.*

Group	Types.	
Inflecting.	SANSKRIT,	*Chandra, chandramas.*
	ARABIC,	*Ḳamr.*
Compounding.	BASK,	*Illargi, ilargi, argizaita.*
	FINNIC,	*Huomen.*
	MAGYAR,	*Hold.*
	TURKISH,	*Ay.*
	CIRCASSIAN,	*Maathi.*
	GEORGIAN,	*Mthoware.*
	MONGOLIAN,	*Ssera, ssara, nienkareli,‡*
	MANTSHU,	*Biya. murun.‖*
	JAVANESE, Ngoko,	*Sasi.*
	JAVANESE, Krama,	*Wúlan.*
	MALAY,	*Búlan.*
Isolating.	CHINESE, Nankin,	*Yueh'.*
	CHINESE, Pekin,	*Yüeh.*
	CHINESE, Canton,	*Üt.*
	CHINESE, Shanghai,	*Müih.*
	AMOY, Colloquial,	*Geh.*
	JAPANESE,	*Bsüki.*
	Brahuí,	*Caret.*
Chinese Frontier & Tibet.	Gyámi,	*Yoliáng.*
	Gyárung,	*Tsile, chileh.*
	Tákpa,	*Leḥ.*
	Mányak,	*Lheḥ.*
	Thochú,	*Chháḥ.*
	Sokpa,	*Sárá.*
	Horpa,	*Slikno.*
	Tibetan (*written*),	*Zláva.*
	Tibetan (*spoken*),	*Dáwá.*
Nepal (east to west).	Serpa,	*Oulá.*
	Súnwár,	*Láto-sí.*
	Gúrung,	*Laugni.*
	Múrmi,	*Lhá-ni.*
	Magar,	*Gyá-hút.*
	Tháksya,	*Láti-gná.*
	Pákhya,	*Chan' dramabel'.*
	Newár,	*Two-mila, túyú-mila.*
	Limbu,	*Láva.*
Kiranti Group (East Nepal).	Kiránti,	*Lá-dima.*
	Rodong,	*Ládipa.*
	Rúngchenbung,	*Ládima.*
	Chhingtángya,	*Láthiba.*
	Náchhereng,	*Lánima.*
	Wáling,	*Ládima.*
	Yákha,	*Lá.*
	Chourásya,	*Twasyál, tosyal.*
	Kulungya,	*Lá.*
	Thulungya,	*Khlye, khle.*
	Báhingya,	*Lá.*
	Lohorong,	*Lá.*
	Lambichhong,	*Láḍiba.*
	Báláli,	*La.*
	Sáng-páng,	*La.*
	Dúmi,	*Lúmyámtú.*
	Kháling,	*Lyá.*
	Dungmáli,	*Ládima, ládipma.*
Broken Tribes of Nepal.	Dárhi,	*Jánhá, jánhá.*
	Denwár,	*Jyún.*
	Pahri,	*Nhibá.*
	Chepáng,	*Lahe, lame.*
	Bhrámu,	*Chalawani, chalawan.*
	Váyu,	*Cholo.*
	Kuswar,	*Jún.*
	Kusunda,	*Jun.*
	Tháru,	*Chand' ramajún.*
	Lepcha (Sikkim),	*Lavo.*
	Bhúṭáni v. Lhopa,	*Dau.*

N.-E. Bengal.	Bodo,	*Nokhábir.*
	Dhimál,	*Táli.*
	Kocch,	*Chánd.*
	Garo,	*Rángret.*
	Káchári,	*Nakaphor, nakabor.*
Eastern Frontier of Bengal.	Munipuri,	*Thá.*
	Míthán Nágá,	*Letnu.*
	Tablung Nágá,	*Le.*
	Khári Nágá,	*Leta.*
	Angámi Nágá,	*Kharr.*
	Námsáng Nágá,	*Dá.*
	Nowgong Nágá,	*Yitá.*
	Tengsa Nágá,	*Lutá.*
	Abor Miri,	*Palo.*
	Sibságar Miri,	*Polo.*
	Deoria Chutia,	*Yah.*
	Singpho,	*Sitá.*
Arrakan & Burmah.	Burman (*written*),	*La.*
	Burman (*spoken*),	*Lá.*
	Khyeng v. Shou,	*Khlau.*
	Kámi,	*Lá.*
	Kúmi,	*Hlo.*
	Mrú v. Toung,	*Púlá.*
	Sák,	Thattá.
Siam & Tenasserim.	Talain v. Mon,	*Khatu.*
	Sgau-karen,	*Lah, lháh.*
	Pwo-karen,	*Lah.*
	Toungh-thu,	*Lu.*
	Shán,	*Len.*
	Annamitic,	*Trang.*
	Siamese,	*Hpya-htit, tawan.*
	Ahom,	*Den.*
	Khámti,	*Lün.*
	Laos,	*Deun.*
Central India.	Ho (Kol),	*Chandú.*
	Kol (Singhbhum),	*Chándu.*
	Santáli,	*Kunami* (full), *guindáchándo* [(night-sun).
	Bhúmij,	*Chandu.*
	Uráon,	*Chando.*
	Mundala,	*Chandu.*
	Rájmahali,	*Bilpe.*
	Goṇḍi,	*Chandal, chanda, nalej.*
	Gayeti,	*Nalej.*
	Rutluk,	*Nalej, jagon.*
	Naikude,	*Nela.*
	Kolami,	*Nela.*
	Mádi,	*Nelanjiu.*
	Mádia,	*Chandanlej* (*chand, anlej ?*).
	Kuri,	*Gumong, chando.*
	Keikádi,	*Nalou.*
	Khoṇḍ,	*Layiḍi.*
	Sávara,	*Vongá.*
	Gadaba,	*Arke.*
	Yerukala,	*Tarra.*
	Chentsu,	*Másu.*
Southern India.	Tamiḷ, anc.,	*Piṛei.*
	Tamiḷ, mod.,	*Tingal, nela, sandiran.*
	Malayáḷma, anc.,	*Tinkal.*
	Malayáḷma, mod.,	*Anbiḷi.*
	Telugu,	(anc.) *Nela, jábilli, vennela.*
	Karṇáṭaka, anc.,	*Caret.*
	Karṇáṭaka, mod.,	*Tingaḷu.*
	Tuḷuva,	*Tingalu.*
	Kurgi,	*Caret.*
	Toḍuva, }	*Caret.*
	Toḍa, }	*Tiggal.*
	Kóta,	*Tiggule.*
	Baḍaga,	*Tiggalu.*
	Kurumba,	*Chandra, tingla.*
	Iruḷa,	*Nálavu.*
	Malabar,	*Melavú, chananderan.*
	Sinhalese,	*Sanda.*

Group	Types.	
Inflecting.	SANSKRIT,	*Maśaka.*
	ARABIC,	*Barghash.*
Compounding.	BASK,	*Elcho, eltzo* (gnat).
	FINNIC,	*Caret.*
	MAGYAR,	*Szunyog.*
	TURKISH,	*Sivrisinek.*
	CIRCASSIAN,	*Caret.*
	GEORGIAN,	*Caret.*
	MONGOLIAN,	*Bükona, bükoona* (gnat).
	MANTSHU,	*Kalman* (gnat).
	JAVANESE, Ngoko,	*Lamuk.*
	JAVANESE, Krama,	*Lamuk.*
	MALAY,	*Nyámuk.*
Isolating.	CHINESE, Nankin,	*Wa.*
	CHINESE, Pekin,	*Caret.*
	CHINESE, Canton,	*Caret.*
	CHINESE, Shanghai,	*Mangtsz'.*
	AMOY, Colloquial,	*Báng.*
	JAPANESE,	*Ka.*
	Brahuí,	*Caret.*
Chinese Frontier & Tibet.	Gyámi,	*Wocha.*
	Gyárung,	*Caret.*
	Tákpa,	*Pholi.*
	Mányak,	*Bimo.*
	Thochú,	*Beup.*
	Sokpa,	*Khokhwe.*
	Horpa,	*Ivasa.*
	Tibetan (*written*),	*Srínbú, mchurings.*
	Tibetan (*spoken*),	*Syedongma.*
Nepal (east to west).	Serpa,	*Dángma.*
	Súnwár,	*Lám-khútia.*
	Gúrung,	*Chwe.*
	Múrmi,	*Lám-khútia.*
	Magar,	*Lám-khútia.*
	Tháksya,	*Polorinaba.*
	Pákhya,	*Pokha.*
	Newár,	*Patl.*
	Limbu,	*Lámjonkhi.*
Kiránti Group (East Nepal).	Kiránti,	*Lámkhútia.*
	Rodong,	*Túngkáma.*
	Rúngchenbung,	*Lámkhútya.*
	Chhingtángya,	*Twang gyomma.*
	Náchhereng,	*Súpyál.*
	Wáling,	*Súpyál, tokli.*
	Yákha,	*Thokthoki-láng.*
	Chourásya,	*Gang'gayúmo.*
	Kulungya,	*Kwongtholi.*
	Thulungya,	*Mas.*
	Báhingya,	*Seupyel, sipyel.*
	Lohorong,	*Bhúsuná.*
	Lambichhong,	*Tonggengwa.*
	Báláli,	*Khasuk'ma, lamkhútia.*
	Sáng-páng,	*Toklihán, bahauma.*
	Dúmi,	*Sapal.*
	Kháling,	*Sapal.*
	Dungmáli,	*Kong kon'gma.*
Broken Tribes of Nepal.	Dárhi,	*Konkonya.*
	Denwár,	*Ghúsuná.*
	Pahri,	*Pati.*
	Chepáng,	*Caret.*
	Bhrámu,	*Amín.*
	Váyu,	*Eks'amek, kánánáng.*
	Kuswar,	*Pipsa, bhunsi.*
	Kusunda,	*Caret.*
	Tháru,	*Mas.*
	Lepcha (Sikkim),	*Mang-kong.*
	Bhútáni v. Lhopa,	*Zendong.*

N.-E. Bengal.	Bodo,	*Thámphoï-gangjang.*
	Dhimál,	*Jáhá, jáhán.*
	Kocch,	*Mosho.*
	Garo,	*Sotsá.*
	Káchári,	*Caret.*
Eastern Frontier of Bengal.	Munipuri,	*Kang.*
	Míthán Nágá,	*Caret.*
	Tablung Nágá,	*Caret.*
	Khári Nágá,	*Mrilá.*
	Angámi Nágá,	*Viru.*
	Námsáng Nágá,	*Mang-dong.*
	Nowgong Nágá,	*Merila.*
	Tengsa Nágá,	*Anjang.*
	Abor Miri,	*Songgou.*
	Sibságar Miri,	*Tamig.*
	Deoria Chutia,	*Dáṇ.*
	Singpho,	*Tsigrong.*
Arrakan & Burmah.	Burman (*written*),	*Khyang.*
	Burman (*spoken*),	*Khyen, khyin.*
	Khyeng v. Shou,	*Youngyán.*
	Kámi,	*Kánsaká.*
	Kúmi,	*Chánráng.*
	Mrú v. Toung,	*Tatsáng.*
	Sák,	*Pichí.*
Siam & Tenasserim.	Talain v. Mon,	*Khameet.*
	Sgau-karen,	*P'so, pettso.*
	Pwo-karen,	*Tserpoe.*
	Toungh-thu,	*Takhra.*
	Shán,	*You.*
	Annamitic,	*Ruôi.*
	Siamese,	*You, yung.*
	Ahom,	*Phreng.*
	Khámti,	*Yung.*
	Laos,	*Yung.*
Central India.	Ho (Kol),	*Pichu, siking.*
	Kol (Singhbhum),	*Siki.*
	Santáli,	*Sikiḍing, sikri.*
	Bhúmij,	*Luti.*
	Uráon,	*Bhusendi.*
	Mundala,	*Bhusundi.*
	Rájmahali,	*Minko.*
	Goṇḍi,	*Misi* (*visi* = fly).
	Gayeti,	(*Visi* = fly.)
	Rutluk,	*Caret.*
	Naikude,	(*Ningal* = fly.)
	Kolami,	(*Ningá* = fly.)
	Máli,	(*Visi, visu, nule* = fly.)
	Mádia,	*Caret.*
	Kuri,	(*Ruku* = fly.)
	Keikádi,	(*Yi* = fly.)
	Khoṇḍ,	*Viháṇgá.*
	Sávara,	*Abubbo.*
	Gadaba,	*Kirigi.*
	Yerukala,	*Yeyyi.*
	Chentsu,	*Musso.*
Southern India.	Tamiḷ, anc.,	*Caret.*
	Tamiḷ, mod.,	*Kosugu.*
	Malayáḷma, anc.,	*Caret.*
	Malayáḷma, mod.,	*Kotuka, piṟukka.*
	Telugu,	*Doma.*
	Karṇáṭaka, anc.,	*Caret.*
	Karṇáṭaka, mod.,	*Solle, chukkáḍi.*
	Tuḷuva,	*Caret.*
	Kurgi,	*Caret.*
	Toḍuva, }	*Caret.*
	Toḍa, }	*Chikattu.*
	Kóta,	*Chukattu.*
	Baḍaga,	*Chukattu.*
	Kurumba,	*Súgane.*
	Iruḷa,	*Jolle.*
	Malabar,	*Visei melvisei.*
	Sinhalese,	*Maduruo.*

Group	Types.	
Inflecting.	SANSKRIT,	*Mátṛi.*
	ARABIC,	*Omm.*
Compounding.	BASK,	*Ama.*
	FINNIC,	*Aiti.*
	MAGYAR,	*Anya.*
	TURKISH,	*Ana.*
	CIRCASSIAN,	*Tian, yan.*
	GEORGIAN,	*Deda.*
	MONGOLIAN,	*Eghe, eke.*
	MANTSHU,	*Eniye, eme.*
	JAVANESE, Ngoko,	*Biyang.*
	JAVANESE, Krama,	*Ibu.*
	MALAY,	*Ibu.*
Isolating.	CHINESE, Nankin,	*Muts'in.*
	CHINESE, Pekin,	*Muts'in.*
	CHINESE, Canton,	*Mots'an.*
	CHINESE, Shanghai,	*Niáng, áhmá.*
	AMOY, Colloquial,	*Bú.*
	JAPANESE,	*Haha.*
	Brahuí,	*Lummà.*
Chinese Frontier & Tibet.	Gyámi,	*Má.*
	Gyárung,	*Tomo.*
	Tákpa,	*Ama.*
	Mányak,	*Amá.*
	Thochú,	*Ou.*
	Sokpa,	*A'khi, yekhi.*
	Horpa,	*Ama.*
	Tibetan (*written*),	*Ama.*
	Tibetan (*spoken*),	*A'má.*
Nepal (east to west).	Serpa,	*A'má.*
	Súnwár,	*Amai.*
	Gúrung,	*A'mo.*
	Múrmi,	*Amma.*
	Magar,	*Má.*
	Tháksya,	*A'má.*
	Pákhya,	*A'má.*
	Newár,	*Mang.*
	Limbu,	*Amma.*
Kiranti Group (East Nepal).	Kiránti,	*Oma, euma.*
	Rodong,	*Ma, uma.*
	Rúngchenbung,	*O'ma, uma.*
	Chhingtángya,	*U'ma.*
	Náchhereng,	*U'mma.*
	Wáling,	*A'má.*
	Yákha,	*I'ma.*
	Chourásya,	*A'mo.*
	Kulungya,	*Ummá.*
	Thulungya,	*Mám, umam.*
	Báhingya,	*A'mo.*
	Lohorong,	*Umma.*
	Lambichhong,	*Ima.*
	Báláli,	*Uma.*
	Sáng-páng,	*Umma.*
	Dúmi,	*Myám, umyam.*
	Kháling,	*Mám, úmám.*
	Dungmáli,	*U'ma, umma.*
Broken Tribes of Népal.	Dárhi,	*U'yá.*
	Denwár,	*Ambái.*
	Pahri,	*Mi.*
	Chepáng,	*Amai.*
	Bhrámu,	*Amai.*
	Váyu,	*Ume, úmu.*
	Kuswar,	*Amái.*
	Kusunda,	*Mái.*
	Tháru,	*Mahatári.*
	Lepcha (Sikkim),	*Amo.*
	Bhúṭáni v. Lhopa,	*A'i.*
N.-E. Bengal.	Bodo,	*B'ma, bama, áyá.*
	Dhimál,	*Amá.*
	Kocch,	*Má.*
	Garo,	*Ama.*
	Káchári,	*Aie.*
Eastern Frontier of Bengal.	Munipuri,	*Imá.*
	Míthán Nágá,	*Annu.*
	Tablung Nágá,	*Onu.*
	Khári Nágá,	*Tü.*
	Angámi Nágá,	*Azo.*
	Námsáng Nágá,	*Ingyong.*
	Nowgong Nágá,	*Uchá.*
	Tengsa Nágá,	*A'pü.*
	Abor Miri,	*Namu.*
	Sibságar Miri,	*Náná.*
	Deoria Chutia,	*Tsimá.*
	Singpho,	*Nú.*
Arrakan & Burmah.	Burman (*written*),	*Ami.*
	Burman (*spoken*),	*Ami.*
	Khyeng v. Shou,	*Nú.*
	Kámi,	*Naúi.*
	Kúmi,	*Anvnú.*
	Mrú v. Toung,	*Aú.*
	Sák,	*Anú.*
Siam & Tenasserim.	Talain v. Mon,	*Ya.*
	Sgau-karen,	*Mo, amo.*
	Pwo-karen,	*Mo.*
	Toungh-thu,	*Men.*
	Shán,	*Amyá.*
	Annamitic,	*Me.*
	Siamese,	*Má, me.*
	Ahom,	*Me.*
	Khámti,	*Me.*
	Laos,	*Me.*
Central India.	Ho (Kol),	*Enga.*
	Kol (Singhbhum),	*Eáng.*
	Santáli,	*Gngá, áyo ! iyo !*
	Bhúmij,	*Mai.*
	Uráon,	*Ayyo.*
	Mundala,	*Engan.*
	Rájmahali,	*Aya.*
	Goṇḍi,	*Aval, ya, ma, bau.*
	Gayeti,	*Dai.*
	Rutluk,	*Dai, ouwal.*
	Naikude,	*Amma.*
	Kolami,	*Amma.*
	Mádi,	*Yali, awa.*
	Mádia,	*Maiyal.*
	Kuri,	*Aya, ma.*
	Keikádi,	*Amma.*
	Khoṇḍ,	*Ayyá*
	Sávara,	*Yo.*
	Gadaba,	*Penamma.*
	Yerukala,	*Táyi.*
	Chentsu,	*Má.*
Southern India.	Tamiḷ, anc.,	*I'ṇṛál.*
	Tamiḷ, mod.,	*Táy, áyi.*
	Malayáḷma, anc.,	*Caret.*
	Malayáḷma, mod.,	*Amma, taḷḷa.*
	Telugu,	*Talli, amma.*
	Karṇáṭaka, anc.,	*Caret.*
	Karṇáṭaka, mod.,	*Táyi, avva, amma.*
	Tuḷuva,	*Appe.*
	Kurgi,	*Avva.*
	Toḍuva,	*Caret.*
	Toḍa,	*Avv.*
	Kóta,	*Avve.*
	Baḍaga,	*Avve, tai.*
	Kurumba,	*A'vve.*
	Iruḷa,	*A'vve.*
	Malabar,	*Thai, matha, annei.*
	Sinhalese,	*Ammá.*

	Types.	
Inflecting.	SANSKRIT,	*Parvata, giri.*
	ARABIC,	*Jabal.*
Compounding.	BASK,	*Mendi.*
	FINNIC,	*Wuori.*
	MAGYAR,	*Hegy, domb.*
	TURKISH,	*Dagh, tepe.*
	CIRCASSIAN,	*Meyzi.*
	GEORGIAN,	*Mtha, gori.*
	MONGOLIAN,	*Aghola, agola, dab'agan, dir-* [*laran.*
	MANTSHU,	*Dabaga, alin.*
	JAVANESE, Ngoko,	*Gúnung.*
	JAVANESE, Krama,	*Rĕdi.*
	MALAY,	*Búkit, gúnung.*
Isolating.	CHINESE, Nankin,	*Shán.*
	CHINESE, Pekin,	*Shán.*
	CHINESE, Canton,	*Shán.*
	CHINESE, Shanghai,	*San.*
	AMOY, Colloquial,	*Soan.*
	JAPANESE,	*Yama.*
	Brahuí,	*Mash.*
Chinese Frontier & Tibet.	Gyámi,	*San, syan.*
	Gyárung,	*Tavet'.*
	Tákpa,	*Ri.*
	Mányak,	*Mbi.*
	Thochú,	*Spyáh.*
	Sokpa,	*Túvá.*
	Horpa,	*Rihrap.*
	Tibetan (*written*),	*Ri.*
	Tibetan (*spoken*),	*Rí.*
Nepal (east to west).	Serpa,	*Rí.*
	Súnwár,	*Dáṇḍá.*
	Gúrung,	*Kwoṇ.*
	Múrmi,	*Gang.*
	Magar,	*Dándá.*
	Tháksya,	*Yedadhyu.*
	Pákhya,	*Páhár.*
	Newár,	*Gún.*
	Limbu,	*Toksong.*
Kiranti Group (East Nepal).	Kiránti,	*Bhar.*
	Rodong,	*Dáṇda.*
	Rúngchenbung,	*Bhar.*
	Chhingtángya,	*Bour.*
	Náchhereng,	*Dáṇḍa.*
	Wáling,	*Dáṇda.*
	Yákha,	*Kwángu.*
	Chourásya,	*Kwáma.*
	Kulungya,	*Tám' him.*
	Thulungya,	*Bro.*
	Báhingya,	*Serte, koogkú.*
	Lohorong,	*Sani, kongku.*
	Lambichhong,	*Sánggú.*
	Bálálí,	*Yákphú.*
	Sáng-páng,	*Bhúri.*
	Dúmi,	*Caret.*
	Kháling,	*Udhám.*
	Dungmáli,	*Caret.*
Broken Tribes of Nepal.	Dárhi,	*Dáṇḍa.*
	Denwár,	*Pákhá.*
	Pahri,	*Tólhá.*
	Chepáng,	*Riás.*
	Bhrámu,	*Dáṇḍa.*
	Váyu,	*Chyájú, wane.*
	Kuswar,	*Pahár.*
	Kusunda,	*Parbat.*
	Tháru,	*Par'bat.*
	Lepcha (Sikkim),	*Rok.*
	Bhúṭáni v. Lhopa,	*Rong.*

N.-E. Bengal.	Bodo,	*Hájo, khro* (top), *geger* (side).
	Dhimál,	*Ra, púring* (top).
	Kocch,	*Parbot, málhi* (top), *májha* [(side).
	Garo,	*Há-chúr.*
	Káchári,	*Hajo.*
Eastern Frontier of Bengal.	Munipuri,	*Ching.*
	Míthán Nágá,	*Caret.*
	Tablung Nágá,	*Caret.*
	Khári Nágá,	*Apih.*
	Angámi Nágá,	*Chaju.*
	Námsáng Nágá,	*Háho.*
	Nowgong Nágá,	*Min-áram.*
	Tengsa Nágá,	*Masan.*
	Abor Miri,	*A'di.*
	Sibságar Miri,	*A'di.*
	Deoria Chutia,	*Asú.*
	Singpho,	*Bum.*
Arrakan & Burmah.	Burman (*written*),	*Tong.*
	Burman (*spoken*),	*Taung.*
	Khyeng v. Shou,	*Taung.*
	Kámi,	*Takún.*
	Kúmi,	*Moi.*
	Mrú v. Toung,	*S'hung, t'ung.*
	Sák,	*Tako.*
Siam & Tenasserim.	Talain v. Mon,	*Khalonkhyan.*
	Sgau-karen,	*K'sir, kutchhu.*
	Pwo-karen,	*Kulaung.*
	Toungh-thu,	*Koung.*
	Shán,	*Patouk.*
	Annamitic,	*Núi.*
	Siamese,	*Khanta, pukhau.*
	Ahom,	*Doi.*
	Khámti,	*Noi.*
	Laos,	*Loi.*
Central India.	Ho (Kol),	*Búru.*
	Kol (Singhbhum),	*Buru.*
	Santáli,	*Buru.*
	Bhúmij,	*Buru.*
	Uráon,	*Partá.*
	Mundala,	*Buru.*
	Rájmahali,	*Toke.*
	Goṇḍi,	*Dongar, mattá.*
	Gayeti,	*Matta.*
	Rutluk,	*Mata.*
	Naikude,	*Seppa.*
	Kolami,	*Met.*
	Mádi,	*Metta.*
	Mádia,	*Madhá.*
	Kuri,	*Katadi.*
	Keikádi,	*Gutta.*
	Khoṇḍ,	*Soru.*
	Sávara,	*Baru.*
	Gadaba,	*Koṇḍá.*
	Yerukala,	*Geṭṭu.*
	Chentsu,	*Parvat.*
Southern India.	Tamiḷ, anc.,	*Varei.*
	Tamiḷ, mod.,	*Malei.*
	Malayáḷma, anc.,	*Caret.*
	Malayáḷma, mod.,	*Mala.*
	Telugu,	*Koṇḍa, guṭṭa.*
	Karṇáṭaka, anc.,	*Male.*
	Karṇáṭaka, mod.,	*Guḍḍa, male, beṭṭa.*
	Tuḷuva,	*Guḍḍe.*
	Kurgi,	*Caret.*
	Toḍuva,	*Pann.*
	Toḍa,	*Bana, dalta, mársh.*
	Kóta,	*Vettume.*
	Baḍaga,	*Beṭṭa.*
	Kuṟumba,	*Beṭṭu.*
	Iruḷa,	*Mele.*
	Malabar,	*Malei, vetpu, meru.*
	Sinhalese,	*Kanda.*

Types.

Group	Language	Mouth
Inflecting.	SANSKRIT	*Mukha.*
	ARABIC	*Famm.*
Compounding.	BASK	*Ao, abo, au.*
	FINNIC	*Kuukausi.*
	MAGYAR	*Szaj.*
	TURKISH	*Aghz.*
	CIRCASSIAN	*Shey, moli,* koko.**
	GEORGIAN	*Piri, damna.**
	MONGOLIAN	*Aman, nang,‡ niuruchta.‖*
	MANTSHU	*Angga.*
	JAVANESE, Ngoko	*Changkem.*
	JAVANESE, Krama	*Tutuk.*
	MALAY	*Múlut.*
Isolating.	CHINESE, Nankin	*K'au.*
	CHINESE, Pekin	*K'au.*
	CHINESE, Canton	*Hau.*
	CHINESE, Shanghai	*Keu.*
	AMOY, Colloquial	*Ch' úi.*
	JAPANESE	*Kuchi.*
	Brahuí	*Caret.*
Chinese Frontier & Tibet.	Gyámi	*Chwe.*
	Gyárung	*Tikhe.*
	Tákpa	*Khá.*
	Mányak	*Yebá.*
	Thochú	*Dzúkh.*
	Sokpa	*A'má.*
	Horpa	*Ya.*
	Tibetan (*written*)	*Khá.*
	Tibetan (*spoken*)	*Khá.*
Nepal (east to west).	Serpa	*Khá.*
	Súnwár	*So.*
	Gúrung	*Sóng.*
	Múrmi	*Súng.*
	Magar	*Gner.*
	Tháksya	*Sung.*
	Pákhya	*Múkha.*
	Newár	*Mhútú.*
	Limbu	*Múrá.*
Kiránti Group (East Nepal).	Kiránti	*Doh.*
	Rodong	*Dyo.*
	Rúngchenbung	*Do.*
	Chhingtángya	*Thurum.*
	Náchhereng	*Gnocho.*
	Wáling	*Two, do.*
	Yákha	*Múláphu.*
	Chourásya	*Dúli.*
	Kulungya	*Gno.*
	Thulungya	*Si.*
	Báhingya	*Syeu.*
	Lohorong	*Yá.*
	Lambichhong	*Yási.*
	Báláli	*Yá.*
	Sáng-páng	*Gno.*
	Dúmi	*Kwom, kom.*
	Kháling	*Kwom.*
	Dungmáli	*Two.*
Broken Tribes of Nepal.	Dárhi	*Múhún.*
	Denwár	*Múhún.*
	Pahri	*Mhur.*
	Chepáng	*Motong.*
	Bhrámu	*Anám.*
	Váyu	*Múkchu.*
	Kuswar	*Múhú.*
	Kusunda	*Birgyád, birgyang.*
	Tháru	*Múkha.*
	Lepcha (Sikkim)	*Abong.*
	Bhútáni v. Lhopa	*Khá.*
N.-E. Bengal.	Bodo	*Khouga.*
	Dhimál	*Nuï.*
	Kocch	*Mukh.*
	Garo	*Hotong.*
	Kácharí	*Kuga.*
Eastern Frontier of Bengal.	Munipuri	*Chil.*
	Míthán Nágá	*Tun.*
	Tablung Nágá	*Chusim.*
	Khári Nágá	*Tabaun.*
	Angámi Nágá	*Amii.*
	Námsáng Nágá	*Tun.*
	Nowgong Nágá	*Tepang.*
	Tengsa Nágá	*Tabáng.*
	Abor Miri	*Napang.*
	Sibságar Miri	*Napüng.*
	Deoria Chutia	*Dumju.*
	Singpho	*Ninggup.*
Arrakan & Burmah.	Burman (*written*)	*Nhup.*
	Burman (*spoken*)	*Nhok, pazat, nhup.*
	Khyeng v. Shou	*Hakkau.*
	Kámi	*Amaká.*
	Kúmi	*Liboung.*
	Mrú v. Toung	*Naur.*
	Sák	*A'ngsi.*
Siam & Tenasserim.	Talain v. Mon	*Khamoupan.*
	Sgau-karen	*Tahko.*
	Pwo-karen	*Nok.*
	Toungh-thu	*Proung.*
	Shán	*Htsot.*
	Annamitic	*Mièng.*
	Siamese	*Pat, pák.*
	Ahom	*Sup.*
	Khámti	*Sop.*
	Laos	*Pák.*
Central India.	Ho (Kol)	*A'.*
	Kol (Singhbhum)	*A'.*
	Santáli	*Mochá.*
	Bhúmij	*Alang.*
	Uráon	*Bái.*
	Mundala	*Mocha.*
	Rájmahali	*Soro.*
	Goṇḍi	*Udi* (*mishang* = moustache).
	Gayeti	*Michhe* (moustache).
	Rutluk	*Micchegam* (moustache).
	Naikude	*Misal* (id.).
	Kolami	*Misal* (id.).
	Mádi	*Misa* (id.).
	Mádia	*Mishal* (id.).
	Kuri	*Mache, musar* (id.).
	Keikádi	*Misou* (id.).
	Khoṇḍ	*Súḍḍa.*
	Sávara	*Amúká.*
	Gadaba	*Tummo.*
	Yerukala	*Váyi.*
	Chentsu	*Mú.*
Southern India.	Tamiḷ, anc.	*Caret.*
	Tamiḷ, mod.	*Váy.*
	Malayáḷma, anc.	*Caret.*
	Malayáḷma, mod.	*Váya.*
	Telugu	*Nóru.*
	Karṇáṭaka, anc.	*Caret.*
	Karṇáṭaka, mod.	*Báyi.*
	Tuḷuva	*Bayi.*
	Kurgi	*Bayi.*
	Toḍuva	*Páyi.*
	Toḍa	*Boi.*
	Kóta	*Vai.*
	Baḍaga	*Bai.*
	Kurumba	*Bai.*
	Iruḷa	*Vai.*
	Malabar	*Vái.*
	Sinhalese	*Kaṭa.*

Types.		
Inflecting.	SANSKRIT,	*Náman.*
	ARABIC,	*Ism.*
Compounding.	BASK,	*Izen.*
	FINNIC,	*Nimi.*
	MAGYAR,	*Nev.*
	TURKISH,	*Ad.*
	CIRCASSIAN,	*Caret.*
	GEORGIAN,	*Sakhelo.*
	MONGOLIAN,	*Nera, nere.*
	MANTSHU,	*Gebu, tsolo.*
	JAVANESE, Ngoko,	*Aran.*
	JAVANESE, Krama,	*Wasta.*
	MALAY,	*Náma.*
Isolating.	CHINESE, Nankin,	*Ming.*
	CHINESE, Pekin,	*Ming.*
	CHINESE, Canton,	*Ming.*
	CHINESE, Shanghai,	*Mingdeu.*
	AMOY, Colloquial,	*Mian̤.*
	JAPANESE,	*Na.*
	Brahuí,	*Caret.*
Chinese Frontier & Tibet.	Gyámi,	*Miun.*
	Gyárung,	*Tirming.*
	Tákpa,	*Myeng.*
	Mányak,	*Ming.*
	Thochú,	*Rmáḥ.*
	Sokpa,	*Ner.*
	Horpa,	*Smen.*
	Tibetan (*written*),	*Ming.*
	Tibetan (*spoken*),	*Ming.*
Nepal (east to west).	Serpa,	*Min.*
	Súnwár,	*Ne.*
	Gúrung,	*Ming.*
	Múrmi,	*Min.*
	Magar,	*Ming.*
	Tháksya,	*Min.*
	Pákhya,	*Náu.*
	Newár,	*Náng.*
	Limbu,	*Ming.*
Kiránti Group (East Nepal).	Kiránti,	*Náng.*
	Rodong,	*Nang.*
	Rúngchenbung,	*Nang.*
	Chhingtángya,	*Nang.*
	Náchhereng,	*Na.*
	Wáling,	*Nang.*
	Yákha,	*Ning.*
	Chourásya,	*Di.*
	Kulungya,	*Ning.*
	Thulungya,	*Nang.*
	Báhingya,	*Ning.*
	Lohorong,	*Ning.*
	Lambichhong,	*Ning.*
	Báláli,	*Nang.*
	Sáng-páng,	*Nan̤.*
	Dúmi,	*Nang.*
	Kháling,	*Nang.*
	Dungmáli,	*Nang.*
Broken Tribes of Nepal.	Dárhi,	*Náyám.*
	Denwár,	*Náú.*
	Pahri,	*Nung.*
	Chepáng,	*Myeng.*
	Bhrámu,	*Min.*
	Váyu,	*Ming.*
	Kuswar,	*Nou.*
	Kusunda,	*Giji.*
	Thárú,	*Ná-u, ji.*
	Lepcha (Sikkim),	*Abriáng.*
	Bhúṭáni v. Lhopa,	*Ming.*

N.-E. Bengal.	Bodo,	*Múng.*
	Dhimál,	*Ming.*
	Kocch,	*Nám.*
	Garo,	*Múng.*
	Káchári,	*Mámo.*
Eastern Frontier of Bengal.	Munipuri,	*Caret.*
	Míthán Nágá,	*Man.*
	Tablung Nágá,	*Min.*
	Khári Nágá,	*Achu.*
	Angámi Nágá,	*Nzá.*
	Námsáng Nágá,	*Min.*
	Nowgong Nágá,	*Tenung.*
	Tengsa Nágá,	*Tenying.*
	Abor Miri,	*A'min.*
	Sibságar Miri,	*A'min.*
	Deoria Chutia,	*Mu.*
	Singpho,	*Ming.*
Arrakan & Burmah.	Burman (*written*),	*Amiṇ.*
	Burman (*spoken*),	*Amí.*
	Khyeng v. Shou,	*Namí.*
	Kámi,	*Amin.*
	Kúmi,	*Amin.*
	Mrú v. Toung,	*Emi.*
	Sák,	*Tú.*
Siam & Tenasserim.	Talain v. Mon,	*Yámu.*
	Sgau-karen,	*Amyi, ami, mi.*
	Pwo-karen,	*Maing.*
	Toungh-thu,	*Min.*
	Shán,	*Tsu.*
	Annamitic,	*Tēn.*
	Siamese,	*Htso, chü.*
	Ahom,	*Chu.*
	Khámti,	*Tsu.*
	Laos,	*Tsü.*
Central India.	Ho (Kol),	*Nutum, numu.*
	Kol (Singhbhum),	*Nutum.*
	Santáli,	*Gnutum.*
	Bhúmij,	*Numu.*
	Uráon,	*Nám.*
	Mundala,	*Natum.*
	Rájmahali,	*Námi.*
	Goṇḍi,	*Batti, parol, pallo.*
	Gayeti,	*Caret.*
	Rutluk,	*Caret.*
	Naikude,	*Caret.*
	Kolami,	*Caret.*
	Mádi,	*Caret.*
	Mádia,	*Caret.*
	Kuri,	*Caret.*
	Keikádi,	*Caret.*
	Khoṇḍ,	*Padda.*
	Sávara,	*Vonueman.*
	Gadaba,	*Nenimmede.*
	Yerukala,	*Andu.*
	Chentsu,	*Ná.*
Southern India.	Tamiḷ, anc.,	*Caret.*
	Tamiḷ, mod.,	*Pĕr.*
	Malayáḷma, anc.,	*Caret.*
	Malayáḷma, mod.,	*Per.*
	Telugu,	*Pēru.*
	Karṇáṭaka, anc.,	*Pesaru.*
	Karṇáṭaka, mod.,	*Hesaru.*
	Tuḷuva,	*Pudar.*
	Kurgi,	*Peda.*
	Toḍuva, }	*Per.*
	Toḍa, }	*Per.*
	Kóta,	*Per.*
	Baḍaga,	*Hesaru.*
	Kuṛumba,	*Hessaru, peru.*
	Iruḷa,	*Hessuru.*
	Malabar,	*Per, namam.*
	Sinhalese,	*Nama.*

Group	Types.	
Inflecting.	SANSKRIT,	*Nak* (Vedic), *rátri.*
	ARABIC,	*Leil.*
Compounding.	BASK,	*Gau, arrats, zaro.*
	FINNIC,	*Yo.*
	MAGYAR,	*Ej.*
	TURKISH,	*Gejeh.*
	CIRCASSIAN,	*Kaysh͏ey, tsheytshi.*
	GEORGIAN,	*Ghame, gutzilli.**
	MONGOLIAN,	*Ssuni.*
	MANTSHU,	*Dobori.*
	JAVANESE, Ngoko,	*Wengi.*
	JAVANESE, Krama,	*Dálu.*
	MALAY,	*Málam.*
Isolating.	CHINESE, Nankin,	*Ye.*
	CHINESE, Pekin,	*Ye.*
	CHINESE, Canton,	*Ye.*
	CHINESE, Shanghai,	*Yá, yáli.*
	AMOY, Colloquial,	*Min.*
	JAPANESE,	*Yoru.*
	Brahuí,	*Caret.*
Chinese Frontier & Tibet.	Gyámi,	*Khelo.*
	Gyárung,	*Todú, tongmor.*
	Tákpa,	*Senti.*
	Mányak,	*Kwakah.*
	Thochú,	*A'shá.*
	Sokpa,	*Sú.*
	Horpa,	*Spha.*
	Tibetan (*written*),	*Mtshanmo.*
	Tibetan (*spoken*),	*Chenmo.*
Nepal (east to west).	Serpa,	*Chemo.*
	Súnwár,	*Nado.*
	Gúrung,	*Mhois.*
	Múrmi,	*Mon.*
	Magar,	*Námbik.*
	Tháksya,	*Mun.*
	Pákhya,	*Ráti.*
	Newár,	*Chá.*
	Limbu,	*Kusen, sendik.*
Kiranti Group (East Nepal).	Kiránti,	*Khákwe.*
	Rodong,	*Khosai.*
	Rúngchenbung,	*Ukhákhwái, ukháko.*
	Chhingtángya,	*Ukha khúit.*
	Náchhereng,	*Umsyápa.*
	Wáling,	*Umkhakhú, akhakhwi.*
	Yákha,	*Seh'ni.*
	Chourásya,	*Domsá, dwáng príme.*
	Kulungya,	*Sepa.*
	Thulungya,	*Dum'ma, dungma.*
	Báhingya,	*Tyúgnáchi.*
	Lohorong,	*Sen.*
	Lambichhong,	*Isembá, semba.*
	Báláli,	*Setta.*
	Sáng-páng,	*Sepá, umsepá.*
	Dúmi,	*U'senyám.*
	Kháling,	*U' senám.*
	Dungmáli,	*U'mkhákhú, khákhúi.*
Broken Tribes of Nepal.	Dárhi,	*Ráto.*
	Denwár,	*Ráting.*
	Pahri,	*Chánáko, chauko.*
	Chepáng,	*Yá.*
	Bhrámu,	*Caret.*
	Váyu,	*Eksá, yeksa.*
	Kuswar,	*Ráthi.*
	Kusunda,	*Ing-gai.*
	Tháru,	*Ráti.*
	Lepcha (Sikkim),	*Sanap.*
	Bhútáni v. Lhopa,	*Phirú, nammo.*

N.-E. Bengal.	Bodo,	*Hor.*
	Dhimál,	*Nhishing.*
	Kocch,	*Ráth.*
	Garo,	*Phar.*
	Káchári,	*Hor.*
Eastern Frontier of Bengal.	Munipuri,	*Ahing.*
	Míthán Nágá,	*Rang nak.*
	Tablung Nágá,	*Vang niak.*
	Khári Nágá,	*A'yáh.*
	Angámi Nágá,	*Tizi.*
	Námsáng Nágá,	*Rangpan.*
	Nowgong Nágá,	*Aunu.*
	Tengsa Nágá,	*A'sangdi.*
	Abor Miri,	*Kamogah.*
	Sibságar Miri,	*Kammo.*
	Deoria Chutia,	*Siri.*
	Singpho,	*Siná.*
Arrakan & Burmah.	Burman (*written*),	*Nyín, nya.*
	Burman (*spoken*),	*Nyin, nyá.*
	Khyeng v. Shou,	*Ayán.*
	Kámi,	*Makhún.*
	Kúmi,	*Wadúm.*
	Mrú v. Toung,	*Wár.*
	Sák,	*Hanáhe.*
Siam & Tenasserim.	Talain v. Mon,	*Khatan.*
	Sgau-karen,	*Nah, páthi.*
	Pwo-karen,	*Munah.*
	Toungh-thu,	*Moha.*
	Shán,	*Ka khán.*
	Annamitic,	*Dêm.*
	Siamese,	*Thankhen, khün.*
	Ahom,	*Dam.*
	Khámti,	*Khün.*
	Laos,	*Khün.*
Central India.	Hȯ (Kol),	*Nida.*
	Kol (Singhbhum),	*Nindhá.*
	Santáli,	*Gnindá.*
	Bhúmij,	*Nidhá.*
	Urάon,	*Mákhá.*
	Mundala,	*Nidak.*
	Rájmahali,	*Máke.*
	Goṇḍi,	*Narka, narkaḍt.*
	Gayeti,	*Narka.*
	Rutluk,	*Narka.*
	Naikude,	*Ale.*
	Kolami,	*Andhar.*
	Mádi,	*Narka.*
	Mádia,	*Narka.*
	Kuri,	*Ráti.*
	Keikádi,	*Namar.*
	Khoṇḍ,	*Caret.*
	Sávara,	*Togolo.*
	Gadaba,	*Tungol.*
	Yerukala,	*Ravu, nàvàru.*
	Chentsu,	*Ráyit.*
Southern India.	Tamiḷ, anc.,	*Al.*
	Tamiḷ, mod.,	*Irá, iruḷ.*
	Malayáḷma, anc.,	*Caret.*
	Malayáḷma, mod.,	*Iruḷ.*
	Telugu,	*Réyi, rátri, mápu.*
	Karṇáṭaka, anc.,	*Iraṭu.*
	Karṇáṭaka, mod.,	*Iraḷu.*
	Tuḷuva,	*Iral.*
	Kurgi,	*Iraḷ, beiṭu.*
	Toḍuva, }	*Caret.*
	Toḍa, }	*Kaggár.*
	Kóta,	*Kattale.*
	Baḍaga,	*Iru, kattale.*
	Kuṛumba,	*Iru.*
	Iruḷa,	*Riṭṭu.*
	Malabar,	*Iravu, irattiri, al.*
	Sinhalese,	*Ræ.*

Types.

Group	Language	Oil
Inflecting.	SANSKRIT,	*Taila.*
	ARABIC,	*Zeit.*
Compounding.	BASK,	*Olio.*
	FINNIC,	*Oljy.*
	MAGYAR,	*Olaj.*
	TURKISH,	*Caret.*
	CIRCASSIAN,	*Caret.*
	GEORGIAN,	*Zethi.*
	MONGOLIAN,	*Toson.*
	MANTSHU,	*Nimenggi, imenggi.*
	JAVANESE, Ngoko,	*Lenga.*
	JAVANESE, Krama,	*Lisah.*
	MALAY,	*Miñak.*
Isolating.	CHINESE, Nankin,	*Yú.*
	CHINESE, Pekin,	*Yú.*
	CHINESE, Canton,	*Yau.*
	CHINESE, Shanghai,	*Yeu.*
	AMOY, Colloquial,	*Iû.*
	JAPANESE,	*Abura, abua.*
	Brahuí,	*Caret.*
Chinese Frontier & Tibet.	Gyámi,	*Eue, yú.*
	Gyárung,	*Chinswi* (from mustard).
	Tákpa,	*Kyamar.*
	Mányak,	*I'chirá, ltira.*
	Thochú,	*Chingyú.*
	Sokpa,	*Máchinthoso.*
	Horpa,	*Marnak.*
	Tibetan (*written*),	*Hbrúmár.*
	Tibetan (*spoken*),	*Núm.*
Nepal (east to west).	Serpa,	*Núm.*
	Súnwár,	*Gyo.*
	Gúrung,	*Chúgú.*
	Múrmi,	*Chigú.*
	Magar,	*Sidí.*
	Tháksya,	*Chhigu.*
	Pákhya,	*Tel.*
	Newár,	*Chikang.*
	Limbu,	*Ninge.*
Kiranti Group (East Nepal).	Kiránti,	*A'wá.*
	Rodong,	*Beli*
	Rúngchenbung,	*A'h' wa.*
	Chhingtángya,	*Kiya.*
	Náchhereng,	*Tel.*
	Wáling,	*A'h' wá.*
	Yákha,	*Kiwa.*
	Chourásya,	*Tilyám.*
	Kulungya,	*Khilám.*
	Thulungya,	*Tel.*
	Báhingya,	*Gyáwa.*
	Lohorong,	*Kewa.*
	Lambichhong,	*Kiya.*
	Báláli,	*A'h' wá.*
	Sáng-páng,	*Khil' lam.*
	Dúmi,	*Khilem.*
	Kháling,	*Khilam.*
	Dungmáli,	*A'h'wá.*
Broken Tribes of Nepal.	Dárhi,	*Tel.*
	Denwár,	*Tel.*
	Pahri,	*Sú.*
	Chepáng,	*Sáte, liko.*
	Bhrámu,	*Asá.*
	Váyu,	*Ki.*
	Kuswar,	*Tel.*
	Kusunda,	*Jing.*
	Tháru,	*Tela.*
	Lepcha (Sikkim),	*Nam.*
	Bhúṭáni v. Lhopa,	*Mákhú.*

Group	Language	Oil
N.-E. Bengal.	Bodo,	*Thou.*
	Dhimál,	*Chúúti.*
	Kocch,	*Túri, til, tisi, enda* (from [plants of same names).
	Garo,	*Tel.*
	Káchári,	*Tao.*
Eastern Frontier of Bengal.	Munipuri,	*Caret.*
	Mithán Nágá,	*Mangá.*
	Tablung Nágá,	*Mangá.*
	Khári Nágá,	*Tutsú.*
	Angámi Nágá,	*Kakizu.*
	Námsáng Nágá,	*Tánthi.*
	Nowgong Nágá,	*Totsú.*
	Tengsa Nágá,	*Mángá.*
	Abor Miri,	*Tuláng.*
	Sibságar Miri,	*Tuláng.*
	Deoria Chutia,	*Tu.*
	Singpho,	*Nam-án.*
Arrakan & Burmah.	Burman (*written*),	*Achhi.*
	Burman (*spoken*),	*S'hi.*
	Khyeng v. Shou,	*To.*
	Kámi,	*S'hi.*
	Kúmi,	*Sarou.*
	Mrú v. Toung,	*S'hi.*
	Sák,	*Sidák.*
Siam & Tenasserim.	Talain v. Mon,	*Kalihn.*
	Sgau-karen,	*Tho.*
	Pwo-karen,	*Thu.*
	Toungh-thu,	*Núman.*
	Shán,	*Naman.*
	Annamitic,	*Dâu.*
	Siamese,	*Namân, nam, man.*
	Ahom,	*Man ngá.*
	Khámti,	*Nam, man.*
	Laos,	*Nam, man.*
Central India.	Ho (Kol),	*Sunum.*
	Kol (Singhbhum),	*Sunum.*
	Santáli,	*Sunum, kade* (oil-cake).
	Bhúmij,	*Sunum.*
	Uráon,	*Issum.*
	Mundala,	*Sunam.*
	Rájmahali,	*Isgne.*
	Goṇḍi,	*Ning, ni.*
	Gayeti,	*Ni.*
	Rutluk,	*Ni.*
	Naikude,	*Nane.*
	Kolami,	*Nune.*
	Mádi,	*Ni, nai, niyu.*
	Mádia,	*Nei.*
	Kuri,	*Sunúm.*
	Keikádi,	*Yana.*
	Khoṇḍ,	*Niju.*
	Sávara,	*Miyyalo.*
	Gadaba,	*Sol.*
	Yerukala,	*Rganna, vanna.*
	Chentsu,	*Tel.*
Southern India.	Tamiḷ, anc.,	*Néyam.*
	Tamiḷ, mod.,	*Eṇṇei, nei, niṇam.*
	Malayáḷma, anc.,	*Caret.*
	Malayáḷma, mod.,	*Eṇṇa.*
	Telugu,	*Núne.*
	Karṇáṭaka, anc.,	*Caret.*
	Karṇáṭaka, mod.,	*Eṇṇe.*
	Tuḷuva,	*Enne.*
	Kurgi,	*Yuṇṇe.*
	Toḍuva, }	*Enn.*
	Toḍa, }	*Eṇṇei.*
	Kóta,	*Yeṇṇe.*
	Baḍaga,	*Yeṇṇe.*
	Kuṛumba,	*Yeṇṇe.*
	Iruḷa,	*Eṇṇe.*
	Malabar,	*Ennei, thylam.*
	Sinhalese,	*Tel.*

Types.		
Inflecting.	SANSKRIT	*Kadali.*
	ARABIC	*Lisánilḥamal.*
Compounding.	BASK	*Zainbelar.*
	FINNIC	*Caret.*
	MAGYAR	*Caret.*
	TURKISH	*Caret.*
	CIRCASSIAN	*Caret.*
	GEORGIAN	*Caret.*
	MONGOLIAN	*Caret.*
	MANTSHU	*Caret.*
	JAVANESE, Ngoko	*Gidang.*
	JAVANESE, Krama	*Pisang.*
	MALAY	*Pisang.*
Isolating.	CHINESE, Nankin	*Tsiaou.*
	CHINESE, Pekin	*Chiaou.*
	CHINESE, Canton	*Tsúi.*
	CHINESE, Shanghai	*Caret.*
	AMOY, Colloquial	*Geñgchio.*
	JAPANESE	*Obako.*
	Brahuí	*Caret.*
Chinese Frontier & Tibet.	Gyámi	*Máchouker.*
	Gyárung	*Caret.*
	Tákpa	*Lamrep.*
	Mányak	*Caret.*
	Thochú	*Sarmi.*
	Sokpa	*Caret.*
	Horpa	*Caret.*
	Tibetan (*written*)	*Caret.*
	Tibetan (*spoken*)	*Grálá, gnálá.*
Népal (east to west).	Serpa	*Langasi.*
	Súnwár	*Mújhi.*
	Gúrung	*Kala.*
	Múrmi	*Moche.*
	Magar	*Mocha.*
	Tháksya	*Tatung-ro.*
	Pákhya	*Kela.*
	Newár	*Mwai.*
	Limbu	*Láseh'.*
Kiránti Group (East Népal).	Kiránti	*Gnáksi.*
	Rodong	*Gnosí.*
	Rúngchenbung	*Gnaksí.*
	Chhingtángya	*Gnáklási.*
	Náchhereng	*Li-gnáksi.*
	Wáling	*Gnáksi.*
	Yákha	*Chemokla.*
	Chourásya	*Balchi.*
	Kulungya	*Li-gnoksi.*
	Thulungya	*Le-gnoksi.*
	Báhingya	*Grámuchi.*
	Lohorong	*Chángmak'.*
	Lambichhong	*Gnáklábu.*
	Bálálí	*Gnáklási.*
	Sáng-páng	*Gnálasi.*
	Dúmi	*Legnási.*
	Kháling	*Legnáksi.*
	Dungmáli	*Gnáksi.*
Broken Tribes of Népal.	Dárhi	*Kera.*
	Denwár	*Kera.*
	Pahri	*Mosyi, mozyi.*
	Chepáng	*Mlesai, maise.*
	Bhrámu	*Ungsye.*
	Váyu	*Risá.*
	Kuswar	*Kera.*
	Kusunda	*Mochá.*
	Tháru	*Kera.*
	Lepcha (Sikkim)	*Karding.*
	Bhúṭáni v. Lhopa	*Gnálá.*

N.-E. Bengal.	Bodo	*Thálit, laipháng.*
	Dhimál	*Yúmphi.*
	Kocch	*Kollo.*
	Garo	*Laktai.*
	Káchári	*Tali.*
Eastern Frontier of Bengal.	Munipuri	*Lapoi.*
	Míthán Nágá	*Caret.*
	Tablung Nágá	*Caret.*
	Khári Nágá	*Mango.*
	Angámi Nágá	*Tekwasi.*
	Námsáng Nágá	*Kieke.*
	Nowgong Nágá	*Samum.*
	Tengsa Nágá	*Mongo.*
	Abor Miri	*Kopagii.*
	Sibságar Miri	*Kopage.*
	Deoria Chutia	*Tuzu.*
	Singpho	*Lungu.*
Arrakan & Burmah.	Burman (*written*)	*Nghakpyo.*
	Burman (*spoken*)	*Nghetpyo.*
	Khyeng v. Shou	*Nhámpau.*
	Kámi	*Kati.*
	Kúmi	*Kúti.*
	Mrú v. Toung	*Dengkúi.*
	Sák	*Tsaú.*
Siam & Tenasserim.	Talain v. Mon	*Hpyat.*
	Sgau-karen	*Thkwi, thakwi.*
	Pwo-karen	*Thakwi.*
	Toungh-thu	*Gnd.*
	Shán	*Kwá.*
	Annamitic	*Shuôi.*
	Siamese	*Kalway, klue.*
	Ahom	*Kui.*
	Khámti	*Kúe.*
	Laos	*Kue.*
Central India.	Ho (Kol)	*Kadal.*
	Kol (Singhbhum)	*Kodal.*
	Santáli	*Kaëra.*
	Bhúmij	*Kodal.*
	Uráon	*Kera.*
	Mundala	*Kela.*
	Rájmahali	*Kalvi.*
	Goṇḍi	*Ker, kera* (*keréng*, pl.).
	Gayeti	*Ker.*
	Rutluk	*Kera.*
	Naikude	*Kela.*
	Kolami	*Kor.*
	Mádi	*Kedi, dugadi.*
	Mádia	*Caret.*
	Kuri	*Kete* (*thora* = wild).
	Keikádi	*Walasadi.*
	Khoṇḍ	*Táḍi.*
	Sávara	*Kinte.*
	Gadaba	*Vusubullu.*
	Yerukala	*Nivále.*
	Chentsu	*Koḍel, sodail.*
Southern India.	Tamiḷ, anc.	*Caret.*
	Tamiḷ, mod.	*Vázhei.*
	Malayáḷma, anc.	*Caret.*
	Malayáḷma, mod.	*Vázha.*
	Telugu	*Araṭi, araṭi-paṇḍu.*
	Karṇáṭaka, anc.	*Caret.*
	Karṇáṭaka, mod.	*Báḷe.*
	Tuḷuva	*Bále.*
	Kurgi	*Báḷe.*
	Toḍuva, }	*Caret.*
	Toḍa, }	*Párom.*
	Kóta	*Váhaṇṇe.*
	Baḍaga	*Bláchaṇṇu.*
	Kuṛumba	*Palehaṇṇu.*
	Iruḷa	*Pálepámbu.*
	Malabar	*Válei.*
	Sinhalese	*Kesel.*

Group	Language	River
	Types.	
Inflecting.	SANSKRIT,	*Nadī.*
	ARABIC,	*Nahr.*
Compounding.	BASK,	*Ibai, errio.*
	FINNIC,	*Kymi.*
	MAGYAR,	*Folyam.*
	TURKISH,	*Chay.*
	CIRCASSIAN,	*Tshai.*
	GEORGIAN,	*Mdinare.*
	MONGOLIAN,	*Ghol, ghool.*
	MANTSHU,	*Eyen, bira, biragán, sekiyen.*
	JAVANESE, Ngoko,	*Kali.*
	JAVANESE, Krama,	*Lepen.*
	MALAY,	*Sŭngei.*
Isolating.	CHINESE, Nankin,	*Ho, kiang.*
	CHINESE, Pekin,	*Ho, chiang.*
	CHINESE, Canton,	*Ho, kong.*
	CHINESE, Shanghai,	*ū.*
	AMOY, Colloquial,	*Kang, ho.*
	JAPANESE,	*Kawa.*
	Brahuí,	*Daryáv.*
Chinese Frontier & Tibet.	Gyámi,	*Shúi.*
	Gyárung,	*Tichi.*
	Tákpa,	*Chhi.*
	Mányak,	*Dyáḥ.*
	Thochú,	*Chabráḥ.*
	Sokpa,	*Wassú, úsú.*
	Horpa,	*Hráh.*
	Tibetan (*written*),	*Gtsang po.*
	Tibetan (*spoken*),	*Cháng po.*
Nepal (east to west).	Serpa,	*Hyúng.*
	Súnwár,	*Likú.*
	Gúrung,	*Khwong.*
	Múrmi,	*Syong.*
	Magar,	*Kholá.*
	Tháksya,	*Umdakyu.*
	Pákhya,	*Khola.*
	Newár,	*Khúsi.*
	Limbu,	*Chua, wohong.*
Kiranti Group (East Nepal).	Kiránti,	*Hongkú.*
	Rodong,	*Wá hwái.*
	Rúngchenbung,	*Hongkú.*
	Chhingtángya,	*Wáhok' ma.*
	Náchhereng,	*Húng kw'ama.*
	Wáling,	*Hong'ma.*
	Yákha,	*Hong'ma.*
	Chourásya,	*Gúlo.*
	Kulungya,	*Yowá.*
	Thulungya,	*Kúrkú.*
	Báhingya,	*Gúlo.*
	Lohorong,	*Yúwa, hong'ma.*
	Lambichhong,	*Wáyá.*
	Bálali,	*Hong'ma.*
	Sáng-páng,	*Hokoma, hongkoma.*
	Dúmi,	*Rú.*
	Kháling,	*Yo, káwá.*
	Dungmáli,	*Hongma.*
Broken Tribes of Nepal.	Dárhi,	*Kholá.*
	Denwár,	*Lári.*
	Pahri,	*Khárá.*
	Chepáng,	*Kyú, goro.*
	Bhrámu,	*Gúdúl.*
	Váyu,	*Gang, bimbo, bingmu.*
	Kuswar,	*Kosi.*
	Kusunda,	*Gimmekoná.*
	Tháru,	*Kholá.*
	Lepcha (Sikkim),	*Ongkyong.*
	Bhúṭáni v. Lhopa,	*Chhukyong.*

Group	Language	River
N.-E. Bengal.	Bodo,	*Doï* (water), *doïgedet, doïsha.*
	Dhimál,	*Chi* (water), *badkachi,* [*mhoikachi.*
	Kocch,	*Nodi, tarang.*
	Garo,	*Chi.*
	Káchári,	*Daisa, daima.*
Eastern Frontier of Bengal.	Munipuri,	*Turel.*
	Míthán Nágá,	*Lhua.*
	Tablung Nágá,	*Yang nú.*
	Khári Nágá,	*Atsü.*
	Angámi Nágá,	*Kharr.*
	Námsáng Nágá,	*Joan.*
	Nowgong Nágá,	*Tsülatsü.*
	Tengsa Nágá,	*Tülá.*
	Abor Miri,	*Asi.*
	Sibságar Miri,	*Abunge.*
	Deoria Chutia,	*Jimaji.*
	Singpho,	*Khá.*
Arrakan & Burmah.	Burman (*written*),	*Mrach.*
	Burman (*spoken*),	*Myit.*
	Khyeng v. Shou,	*Haloung.*
	Kámi,	*Kavá.*
	Kúmi,	*Kawú.*
	Mrú v. Toung,	*Au.*
	Sák,	*Pisi.*
Siam & Tenasserim.	Talain v. Mon,	*Pi.*
	Sgau-karen,	*Tiklo, klo.*
	Pwo-karen,	*Tikluk.*
	Toungh-thu,	*Nhrong.*
	Shán,	*Nánhouk.*
	Annamitic,	*Sông.*
	Siamese,	*Mayna, menam.*
	Ahom,	*Khe.*
	Khámti,	*Khyenam.*
	Laos,	*Namme.*
Central India.	Ho (Kol),	*Garra, gaḍa* (?).
	Kol (Singhbhum),	*Garra.*
	Santáli,	*Nái, sakaḍa, gáḍa* (?), *munḍu.*
	Bhúmij,	*Garra.*
	Uráon,	*Khár, khaḍ* (?).
	Mundala,	*Garra.*
	Rájmahali,	*Caret.*
	Goṇḍi,	*Dondá, jhodi, dhoda.*
	Gayeti,	*Jhodi.*
	Rutluk,	*Kurergangá.*
	Naikude,	*Peni.*
	Kolami,	*Peni.*
	Mádi,	*Bereridota.*
	Mádia,	(*Per* = water.)
	Kuri,	*Gada.*
	Keikádi,	*A'r.*
	Khoṇḍ,	*Joḍi.*
	Sávara,	*Náyi.*
	Gadaba,	*Roggilu.*
	Yerukala,	*A'ru.*
	Chentsu,	*Loddi, ladi.*
Southern India.	Tamiḷ, anc.,	*Varupunal.*
	Tamiḷ, mod.,	*A'ṟu.*
	Malayáḷma, anc.,	*Caret.*
	Malayáḷma, mod.,	*Puzha, áṟa.*
	Telugu,	*E'ru.*
	Karṇáṭaka, anc.,	*Poḷe.*
	Karṇáṭaka, mod.,	*Hoḷe.*
	Tuḷuva,	*Tude.*
	Kurgi,	*Poḷe.*
	Toḍuva, }	*Pá.*
	Toḍa, }	*Pa.*
	Kóta,	*Peye, pevi.*
	Baḍaga,	*Halla, holla.*
	Kuṟumba,	*Nirú.*
	Iruḷa,	*Palla.*
	Malabar,	*Yáru, kangei.*
	Sinhalese,	*Ganga.*

Types.

Inflecting.
| SANSKRIT, | Márga, pathin. |
| ARABIC, | Tarík, darb. |

Compounding.
BASK,	Bide, kamio.
FINNIC,	Tie.
MAGYAR,	Ut.
TURKISH,	Yol.
CIRCASSIAN,	Oghogu.
GEORGIAN,	Gza.
MONGOLIAN,	Tergheghur, zam.
MANTSHU,	Doro, dshugôn, giya.
JAVANESE, Ngoko,	Chalan.
JAVANESE, Krama,	Margi.
MALAY,	Jálan.

Isolating.
CHINESE, Nankin,	Lu.
CHINESE, Pekin,	Lu.
CHINESE, Canton,	Lo.
CHINESE, Shanghai,	Lu.
AMOY, Colloquial,	Lo.
JAPANESE,	Michi.

Brahuí, ... Kasar.

Chinese Frontier & Tibet.
Gyámi,	Lú.
Gyárung,	Tri.
Tákpa,	Lemdaug.
Mányak,	Ráḥ.
Thochú,	Griḥ.
Sokpa,	Chám.
Horpa,	Cheḥ.
Tibetan (written),	Lam.
Tibetan (spoken),	Lami.

Nepal (east to west).
Serpa,	Lam.
Súnwár,	Lá.
Gúrung,	Kyán.
Múrmi,	Ghyami.
Magar,	Lám.
Tháksya,	Ghyám.
Pákhya,	Báto.
Newár,	Lon.
Limbu,	Lám.

Kiranti Group (East Nepal).
Kiránti,	Lám.
Rodong,	Lám.
Rúngchenbung,	Lám.
Chhingtángya,	Lámbo.
Náchhereng,	Lám.
Wáling,	Lám.
Yákha,	Lám' bu.
Chourásya,	Lám.
Kulungya,	Lám.
Thulungya,	Lám.
Báhingya,	Lám.
Lohorong,	Lám, lámphú.
Lambichhong,	Lámbo.
Báláli,	Lám.
Sáng-páng,	Lám.
Dúmi,	Lámdaú.
Kháling,	Lámdo.
Dungmáli,	Lám.

Broken Tribes of Nepal.
Dárhi,	Pánya.
Denwár,	Bát.
Pahri,	Long.
Chepáng,	Lyám.
Bhrámu,	U'mmá.
Váyu,	Loh.
Kuswar,	Bát.
Kusunda,	Wou.
Tháru,	Rastá.

Lepcha (Sikkim), . . Laum.
Bhútáni v. Lhopa, . . Lám.

N.-E. Bengal.
Bodo,	Lámá.
Dhimál,	Dámá.
Kocch,	Pod, sorok.
Garo,	Lam.
Káchári,	Lama.

Eastern Frontier of Bengal.
Munipuri,	Caret.
Míthán Nágá,	Lam.
Tablung Nágá,	Lam.
Khári Nágá,	Ndí.
Angámi Nágá,	Cháḥ.
Námsáng Nágá,	Lam.
Nowgong Nágá,	Lemang.
Tengsa Nágá,	Unglan.
Abor Miri,	Lambeú.
Sibságar Miri,	Lámte.
Deoria Chutia,	Tságu.
Singpho,	Lám.

Arrakan & Burmah.
Burman (written),	Lam.
Burman (spoken),	Lán, lám.
Khyeng v. Shou,	Lám.
Kúmi,	Láng.
Kúmi,	Lám.
Mrú v. Toung,	Tamá.
Sák,	Láng.

Siam & Tenasserim.
Talain v. Mon,	Khapann.
Sgau-karen,	Klai, khle.
Pwo-karen,	Pungthah.
Toungthu,	Klaytantha.
Shán,	Tán.
Annamitic,	Dàng.
Siamese,	Hontán, tháng.
Ahom,	Táng.
Khámti,	Táng.
Laos,	Tang.
Ho (Kol),	Horá.
Kol (Singhbhum),	Horra.

Central India.
Santáli,	Har, dahár.
Bhúmij,	Horren.
Uráon,	Dáhári.
Mundala,	Horah.
Rájmahali,	Sarke.
Goṇḍi,	Sarri.
Gayeti,	Caret.
Rutluk,	Caret.
Naikude,	Caret.
Kolami,	Caret.
Mádi,	Caret.
Mádia,	Caret.
Kuri,	Caret.
Keikádi,	Caret.
Khoṇḍ,	Páhori.
Sávara,	Tangora.
Gadaba,	Kungoru.
Yerukala,	Yeṛi.
Chentsu,	Báṭ.

Southern India.
Tamil, anc.,	Neṛi.
Tamil, mod.,	Vazhi.
Malayáḷma, anc.,	Caret.
Malayáḷma, mod.,	Vazhi.
Telugu,	Dári, dôva, báṭa.
Karṇáṭaka, anc.,	Pádi.
Karṇáṭaka, mod.,	Hádi.
Tujuva,	Sádi.
Kurgi,	Baṭṭe.
Toḍuva,⎫	Morg.
Toḍa, ⎭	A'ldár.
Kóta,	A'láre.
Daḍaga,	Dári.
Kurumba,	Dari.
Irula,	Beii, daḍḍa.
Malabar,	Theru, vithi, vulei.
Sinhalese,	Mátvata.

Types.		
Inflecting.	SANSKRIT,	*Lavaṇa.*
	ARABIC,	*Milḥ.*
Compounding.	BASK,	*Gatz.*
	FINNIC,	*Suola.*
	MAGYAR,	*So.*
	TURKISH,	*Tuz.*
	CIRCASSIAN,	*Zogho, shugu.*
	GEORGIAN,	*Marili.*
	MONGOLIAN,	*Daboson, dabusun.*
	MANTSHU,	*Debsun, dabsun.*
	JAVANESE, Ngoko,	*Uyah.*
	JAVANESE, Krama,	*Sarim.*
	MALAY,	*Gáram.*
Isolating.	CHINESE, Nankin,	*Yen.*
	CHINESE, Pekin,	*Yen.*
	CHINESE, Canton,	*I'm.*
	CHINESE, Shanghai,	*Yeṇ.*
	AMOY, Colloquial,	*Iam.*
	JAPANESE,	*Liwo.*
	Brahuí,	*Be.*
Chinese Frontier & Tibet.	Gyámi,	*Yan.*
	Gyárung,	*Chhe.*
	Tákpa,	*Tsá.*
	Mányak,	*Cheḥ.*
	Thochú,	*Cheḥ.*
	Sokpa,	*Távoso.*
	Horpa,	*Chháḥ.*
	Tibetan (*written*),	*Tshá.*
	Tibetan (*spoken*),	*Chhá.*
Nepal (east to west).	Serpa,	*Chhá.*
	Súnwár,	*Yúsi.*
	Gúrung,	*Cháchá.*
	Múrmi,	*Cháchá.*
	Magar,	*Chá.*
	Tháksya,	*Chacha.*
	Pákhya,	*Nún.*
	Newár,	*Chhi.*
	Limbu,	*Yúm.*
Kiranti Group (East Nepal).	Kiránti,	*Yúm.*
	Rodong,	*Rúm.*
	Rúngchenbung,	*Yúm.*
	Chhingtángya,	*Yúm.*
	Náchhereng,	*Ram.*
	Wáling,	*Yúm.*
	Yákha,	*Yúm.*
	Chourásya,	*Yok' si.*
	Kulungya,	*Gúm.*
	Thulungya,	*Yo.*
	Báhingya,	*Yúk' si.*
	Lohorong,	*Yúm.*
	Lambichhong,	*Yúm.*
	Báláli,	*Yúm.*
	Sáng-páng,	*Rúm.*
	Dúmi,	*Ram.*
	Kháling,	*Ram.*
	Dungmáli,	*Yúm.*
Broken Tribes of Nepal.	Dárhi,	*Nún.*
	Denwár,	*Nún.*
	Pahri,	*Chihá.*
	Chepáng,	*Se.*
	Bhrámu,	*Chhá.*
	Váyu,	*Chia, jikhom.*
	Kuswar,	*Nún.*
	Kusunda,	*Huk vi.*
	Tháru,	*Nún.*
	Lepcha (Sikkim),	*Vom.*
	Bhúṭáni v. Lhopa,	*Chhá.*
N.-E. Bengal.	Bodo,	*Shyúngkáre, sayúngkri, sankhri.*
	Dhimál,	*Dese.*
	Kocch,	*Nún* (*jaikhat* = saltpetre).
	Garo,	*Syang.*
	Kácháṛi,	*Shoonkri.*
Eastern Frontier of Bengal.	Munipuri,	*Thúm.*
	Míthán Nágá,	*Hum.*
	Tablung Nágá,	*Hum.*
	Khári Nágá,	*Machi.*
	Angámi Nágá,	*Matse.*
	Námsáng Nágá,	*Sum.*
	Nowgong Nágá,	*Matsü.*
	Tengsa Nágá,	*Machi.*
	Abor Miri,	*A'lu.*
	Sibságar Miri,	*A'llo.*
	Deoria Chutia,	*Süṇ.*
	Singpho,	*Jum.*
Arrakan & Burmah.	Burman (*written*),	*Chhá.*
	Burman (*spoken*),	*S'há.*
	Khyeng v. Shou,	*Tsi.*
	Kámi,	*Maloi.*
	Kúmi,	*Piloi.*
	Mrú v. Toung,	*Wis' há.*
	Sák,	*Súng.*
Siam & Tenasserim.	Talain v. Mon,	*Po.*
	Sgau-karen,	*Ithah.*
	Pwo-karen,	*Tilah.*
	Toungh-thu,	*Tá.*
	Shán,	*Ko.*
	Annamitic,	*Muôi.*
	Siamese,	*Ká lo, kleüa.*
	Ahom,	*Klu.*
	Khámti,	*Kü.*
	Laos,	*Keu, kem.*
Central India.	Ho (Kol),	*Bulung.*
	Kol (Singhbhum),	*Bulung.*
	Santáli,	*Bulung, khárá* (adj.).
	Bhúmij,	*Bulung.*
	Uráon,	*Bekh.*
	Mundala,	*Bulang.*
	Rájmahali,	*Beke.*
	Goṇḍi,	*Sabbar, sawod.*
	Gayeti,	*Sawod.*
	Rutluk,	*Sawor.*
	Naikude,	*Sup.*
	Kolami,	*Sup.*
	Mádi,	*A'wori, howar.*
	Mádia,	*Howar.*
	Kuri,	*Bulum.*
	Keikádi,	*Upu.*
	Khoṇḍ,	*Vuppanga.*
	Sávara,	*Basi.*
	Gadaba,	*Bitti.*
	Yerukala,	*Sonava.*
	Chentsu,	*Nún.*
Southern India.	Tamiḷ, anc.,	*Caret.*
	Tamiḷ, mod.,	*Uppu.*
	Malayáḷma, anc.,	*Caret.*
	Malayáḷma, mod.,	*Uppa.*
	Telugu,	*Uppu.*
	Karṇáṭaka, anc.,	*Caret.*
	Karṇáṭaka, mod.,	*Uppu.*
	Tuḷuva,	*Upp.*
	Kurgi,	*Uppu.*
	Toḍuva,	*Uppu.*
	Toḍa,	*Uppu.*
	Kóta,	*Uppu.*
	Baḍaga,	*Uppu.*
	Kurumba,	*Uppu.*
	Iruḷa,	*Uppu.*
	Malabar,	*Uppu, lavanam.*
	Sinhalese,	*Lunu.*

	Types.	
Inflecting.	SANSKṚIT,	*Charman.*
	ARABIC,	*Jild, ḳishr.*
Compounding.	BASK,	*Larru, narru.*
	FINNIC,	*Nahka.*
	MAGYAR,	*Bor.*
	TURKISH,	*Dereh.*
	CIRCASSIAN,	*Shuway.*
	GEORGIAN,	*Kani.*
	MONGOLIAN,	*Arison.*
	MANTSHU,	*Feri.*
	JAVANESE, Ngoko,	*Kulit.*
	JAVANESE, Krama,	*Kulit.*
	MALAY,	*Kulit.*
Isolating.	CHINESE, Nankin,	*P'i.*
	CHINESE, Pekin,	*P'i.*
	CHINESE, Canton,	*P'i.*
	CHINESE, Shanghai,	*Bi.*
	AMOY, Colloquial,	*P'ê.*
	JAPANESE,	*Kawa.*
	Brahuí,	*Caret.*
Chinese Frontier & Tibet.	Gyámi,	*Phicha.*
	Gyárung,	*Tidri.*
	Tákpa,	*Phyekh.*
	Mányak,	*Graḥ.*
	Thochú,	*Rápi.*
	Sokpa,	*Sárú.*
	Horpa,	*Gla.*
	Tibetan (*written*),	*Págspa.*
	Tibetan (*spoken*),	*Págpa.*
Nepal (east to west).	Serpa,	*Koppa.*
	Súnwár,	*Kúsyúl.*
	Gúrung,	*Dhí.*
	Múrmi,	*Dibhi.*
	Magar,	*Chála.*
	Tháksya,	*Dhi.*
	Pákhya,	*Chhála.*
	Newár,	*Syú, chegú.*
	Limbu,	*Horik, saho.*
Kiranti Group (East Nepal).	Kiránti,	*U'hok bá.*
	Rodong,	*Húlepá.*
	Rúngchenbung,	*Hokwa, sahokwa.*
	Chhingtángya,	*Sáhok'wa.*
	Náchhereng,	*Sáhok.*
	Wáling,	*Sáhok.*
	Yákha,	*Sáho wárik.*
	Chourásya,	*Kwak'te, kok'te.*
	Kulungya,	*Soko wári.*
	Thulungya,	*Kwok'si, kok'si, kokte.*
	Báhingya,	*Kok'si, koksyu.*
	Lohorong,	*Sáhok.*
	Lambichhong,	*Sáhok'wa.*
	Báláli,	*Sáho'.*
	Sáng-páng,	*Sáhok'wa.*
	Dúmi,	*Sáká.*
	Kháling,	*Saká.*
	Dungmáli,	*Hokwa, umhokwa, sahokwa.*
Broken Tribes of Nepal.	Dárhi,	*Chála.*
	Denwár,	*Chála.*
	Pahri,	*Chúgra.*
	Chepáng,	*Caret.*
	Bhrámu,	*Caret.*
	Váyu,	*Kokcho.*
	Kuswar,	*Chála.*
	Kusunda,	*Gitán.*
	Tháru,	*Chám.*
	Lepcha (Sikkim),	*Athún kombo.*
	Bhúṭáni v. Lhopa,	*Páko, kompo.*

N.-E. Bengal.	Bodo,	*Bigúr.*
	Dhimál,	*Dhále.*
	Kocch,	*Chamra.*
	Garo,	*Holop.*
	Kácházi,	*Caret.*
Eastern Frontier of Bengal.	Munipuri,	*Ul.*
	Míthán Nágá,	*Khoan.*
	Tablung Nágá,	*Soh.*
	Khári Nágá,	*Tagap.*
	Angámi Nágá,	*Bikhr.*
	Námsáng Nágá,	*A'khuon.*
	Nowgong Nágá,	*Takap.*
	Tengsa Nágá,	*Takap.*
	Abor Miri,	*Dumoer.*
	Sibságar Miri,	*Asüg.*
	Deoria Chutia,	*Chikuṇ.*
	Singpho,	*Phi.*
Arrakan & Burmah.	Burman (*written*),	*Sáre.*
	Burman (*spoken*),	*Thảye, axá.*
	Khyeng v. Shou,	*Wún.*
	Kámi,	*Aphú.*
	Kúmi,	*Pe.*
	Mrú v. Toung,	*Pí.*
	Sák,	*Mi-lak.*
Siam & Tenasserim.	Talain v. Mon,	*Nan.*
	Sgau-karen,	*Tahpi, aphe.*
	Pwo-karen,	*Tserpate.*
	Toungh-thu,	*Phro.*
	Shán,	*Nann.*
	Annamitic,	*Da.*
	Siamese,	*Nann, nang.*
	Ahom,	*Plek.*
	Khámti,	*Nang.*
	Laos,	*Nang.*
Central India.	Ho (Kol),	*Caret.*
	Kol (Singhbhum),	*Ur.*
	Santáli,	*Hártá.*
	Bhúmij,	*Ur.*
	Uráon,	*Chapta.*
	Mundala,	*Harta.*
	Rájmahali,	*Cháme.*
	Goṇḍi,	*Tol.*
	Gayeti,	*Tol.*
	Rutluk,	*Caret.*
	Naikude,	*Tolka.*
	Kolami,	*Tol.*
	Mádi,	*Tol.*
	Mádia,	*Tol.*
	Kuri,	*Katre.*
	Keikádi,	*Tolu.*
	Khoṇd,	*Pándá.*
	Sávara,	*Wusál.*
	Gadaba,	*Artá.*
	Yerukala,	*Tálu.*
	Chentsu,	*Chamaḍá.*
Southern India.	Tamiḷ, anc.,	*Adal.*
	Tamiḷ, mod.,	*Tol.*
	Malayáḷma, anc.,	*Caret.*
	Malayáḷma, mod.,	*Tol.*
	Telugu,	*Tōlu.*
	Karṇáṭaka, anc.,	*Caret.*
	Karṇáṭaka, mod.,	*Tovalu, togalu.*
	Tuḷuva,	*Tolu.*
	Kurgi,	*Caret.*
	Toḍuva,	*Torra.*
	Toḍa,	*Tuvarsh.*
	Kóta,	*Tuval.*
	Baḍaga,	*Tolu.*
	Kuṛumba,	*Tolu.*
	Iruḷa,	*Tolu.*
	Malabar,	*Thol, tholi.*
	Sinhalese,	*Hama.*

Types.

Inflecting.
| SANSKRIT, ... | Div, ákás'a. |
| ARABIC, ... | Samá, falak. |

Compounding.
BASK, ...	Zeru.
FINNIC, ...	Taiwas.
MAGYAR, ...	Eg.
TURKISH, ...	Geuk.
CIRCASSIAN, ...	Caret.
GEORGIAN, ...	Tsa.
MONGOLIAN, . . .	Okhdarghoi, noae,‡ gdadu.§
MANTSHU, ...	Abkha.
JAVANESE, Ngoko, . .	Langit.
JAVANESE, Krama, . .	Langit.
MALAV, ...	Langit.

Isolating.
CHINESE, Nankin, . .	T'ien.
CHINESE, Pekin, . .	T'ien.
CHINESE, Canton, . .	T'in.
CHINESE, Shanghai, .	T'ien-k'ung, t'in-kúng.
AMOY, Colloquial, . .	T'iŋ.
JAPANESE, ...	Sora.

| Brahuí, | Caret. |

Chinese Frontier & Tibet.
Gyámi, ...	Khen.
Gyárung, ...	Tumon, teumeun.
Tákpa, ...	Namding.
Mányak, ...	Maḥ.
Thochú, ...	Mahto.
Sokpa, ...	Thenggre.
Horpa, ...	Koḥ.
Tibetan (written), . .	Nam-kháh.
Tibetan (spoken), . .	Nam.

Nepal (east to west).
Serpa, ...	Nam.
Súnwár, ...	Sarángi.
Gúrung, ...	Túndi, mún.
Múrmi, ...	Mú.
Magar, ...	Sarang.
Tháksya, ...	Mu.
Pákhya, ...	Sarga.
Newár, ...	Sarag.
Limbu, ...	Temsákpá.

Kiranti Group (East Nepal).
Kiránti, ...	Nam-cho.
Rodong, ...	Nám.
Rúngchenbung, . . .	Námchok.
Chhingtángya, . . .	Námchhuru.
Náchhereng, ...	Námchho.
Wáling, ...	Sag'ra.
Yákha, ...	Táng-khyáng.
Chourásya, ...	Dwám.
Kulungya, ...	Chhúburi, netwa neto.
Thulungya, ...	Dwámu.
Báhingya, ...	Dwámún.
Lohorong, ...	Námtríngma.
Lambichhong, . . .	A'tto, námchhiri.
Báláli, ...	Nám.
Sáng-páng, ...	Nindmbobi, nanumámchho.
Dúmi, ...	Námtú.
Kháling, ...	Dhám.
Dungmáli, ...	Nám.

Broken Tribes of Nepal.
Dárhi, ...	Sárág.
Denwár, ...	Sárág.
Pahri, ...	Sárág.
Chepáng, ...	Sárág.
Bhrámu, ...	Caret.
Váyu, ...	Nomo.
Kuswar, ...	Sáráng.
Kusunda, ...	Lágái.
Tháru, ...	Caret.

| Lepcha (Sikkim), . . | Talláng. |
| Bhútáni v. Lhopa, . . | Nam. |

N. E. Bengal.
Bodo, ...	Nokhoráng.
Dhimál, ...	Sorgi.
Kocch, ...	Sworg.
Garo, ...	Sorg.
Káchári, ...	Nokorangsa.

Eastern Frontier of Bengal.
Munipuri, ...	Nidhoripak.
Míthán Nágá, . . .	Caret.
Tablung Nágá, . . .	Caret.
Khári Nágá, ...	Aning.
Angámi Nágá, . . .	Thi.
Námsáng Nágá, . .	Rángtung.
Nowgong Nágá, . .	Mabat.
Tengsa Nágá, . . .	Phumching.
Abor Miri, ...	Teong.
Sibságar Miri, . . .	Domür.
Deoria Chutia, . . .	Pichoni.
Singpho, ...	Mu.

Arrakan & Burmah.
Burman (written), . .	Mogh.
Burman (spoken), . .	Mo.
Khyeng v. Shou, . .	Hanmhi.
Kámi, ...	Khau, khú.
Kúmi, ...	Kanl.
Mrú v. Toung, . . .	Mú.
Sák, ...	Kounggounglak.

Siam & Tenasserim.
Talain v. Mon, . . .	Parwai.
Sgau-karen, ...	Mu'k'polo, muhko.
Pwo-karen, ...	Trerpohpain.
Toungh-thu, ...	Mo.
Shán, ...	Hpa.
Annamitic, ...	Trǒ'i.
Siamese, ...	Akat, fa.
Ahom, ...	Fa.
Khámti, ...	Fa.
Laos, ...	Fafon.

Central India.
Ho (Kol), ...	Caret.
Kol (Singhbhum), . .	Sirma.
Santáli, ...	Chat, sermá, rimil (clouds).
Bhúmij, ...	Rimmil.
Urdon, ...	Mirkha.
Mundala, ...	Irma.
Rájmahali, ...	Saránge.
Gondi, ...	Bádur (?), abhar.
Gayeti, ...	Abhar.
Rutluk, ...	Sargam.
Naikude, ...	A'kásh.
Kolami, ...	Abhár, paiti.
Mádi, ...	A'bú, moyule.
Mádia, ...	Caret.
Kuri, ...	Agas, badrájá.
Keikádi, ...	Máná.
Khoṇḍ, ...	Mudengi.
Sávara, ...	Agásá.
Gadaba, ...	Koṇḍá.
Yerukala, ...	Menu.
Chentsu, ...	Sarg.

Southern India.
Tamil, anc., ...	Viṇ.
Tamil, mod., ...	Vánam.
Malayáḷma, anc., . .	Caret.
Malayáḷma, mod., . .	Vánam.
Telugu, ...	Minnu, ákás'amu.
Karṇátaka, anc., . .	Mugilu, bán, bánu.
Karṇátaka, mod., . .	Elarvaṭṭe.
Tuḷuva, ...	Caret.
Kurgi, ...	Caret.
Toḍuva,}	Pone.
Toḍa, }	Ban.
Kóta, ...	Vaname.
Baḍaga, ...	Banu.
Kurumba, ...	Bana.
Iruḷa, ...	Vanu.
Malabar, ...	Vánam.
Sinhalese, ...	Ahasa.

	Types.	
Inflecting.	SANSKRIT,	*Ahi, sarpa.*
	ARABIC,	*Heyyat.*
Compounding.	BASK,	*Suge.*
	FINNIC,	*Karmet.*
	MAGYAR,	*Kigyo.*
	TURKISH,	*Yilan.*
	CIRCASSIAN,	*Bley.*
	GEORGIAN,	*Gweli.*
	MONGOLIAN,	*Moghar, mogai.*
	MANTSHU,	*Mogai, meike, meikhe.*
	JAVANESE, Ngoko,	*Ula.*
	JAVANESE, Krama,	*Sawĕr.*
	MALAY,	*Ular.*
Isolating.	CHINESE, Nankin,	*Shie.*
	CHINESE, Pekin,	*She.*
	CHINESE, Canton,	*She.*
	CHINESE, Shanghai,	*Tsáng-zo.*
	AMOY, Colloquial,	*Chôa.*
	JAPANESE,	*Hebi, febi.*
	Brahuí,	*Caret.*
Chinese Frontier & Tibet.	Gyámi,	*Shre.*
	Gyárung,	*Khabri.*
	Tákpa,	*Mrüi.*
	Mányak,	*Brú.*
	Thochú,	*Brigi.*
	Sokpa,	*Thole.*
	Horpa,	*Phri.*
	Tibetan (*written*),	*Sbrúl.*
	Tibetan (*spoken*),	*Deu.*
Nepal (east to west).	Serpa,	*Drúl.*
	Súnwár,	*Búsa.*
	Gúrung,	*Bhugúri.*
	Múrmi,	*Púkúri.*
	Magar,	*Búl.*
	Tháksya,	*Pudhi.*
	Pákhya,	*Sápa.*
	Newár,	*Bi.*
	Limbu,	*Osek.*
Kiranti Group (East Nepal).	Kiránti,	*Pachám.*
	Rodong,	*Púchho.*
	Rúngchenbung,	*Púchhám.*
	Chhingtángya,	*Púchhá.*
	Náchhereng,	*Pu-ú.*
	Wáling,	*Puchháp, púchham.*
	Yákha,	*Púchák.*
	Chourásya,	*Bisa.*
	Kulungya,	*Pu.*
	Thulungya,	*Phú chyú.*
	Báhingya,	*Búsá.*
	Lohorong,	*Púse, pusema.*
	Lambichhong,	*Pu.*
	Báláli,	*Pú.*
	Sáng-páng,	*Pú.*
	Dúmi,	*Bheï.*
	Kháling,	*Bheï.*
	Dungmáli,	*Púchháp.*
Broken Tribes of Nepal.	Dárhi,	*Sámp.*
	Denwár,	*Sámp.*
	Pahri,	*Bi.*
	Chepáng,	*Lú.*
	Bhrámu,	*Púigu.*
	Váyu,	*Hobu.*
	Kuswar,	*Sámp.*
	Kusunda,	*Tou.*
	Tháru,	*Sápa.*
	Lepcha (Sikkim),	*Beu.*
	Bhútáni v. Lhopa,	*Beu.*

N.-E. Bengal.	Bodo,	*Jibo.*
	Dhimál,	*Púnhá.*
	Kocch,	*Sámp (gohoma*=cobra).
	Garo,	*Dúpú.*
	Káchári,	*Jibu.*
Eastern Frontier of Bengal.	Munipuri,	*Lil.*
	Míthán Nágá,	*Pu.*
	Tablung Nágá,	*Pu.*
	Khári Nágá,	*Ahü.*
	Angámi Nágá,	*Thinhye.*
	Námsáng Nágá,	*Pú.*
	Nowgong Nágá,	*Pürr.*
	Tengsa Nágá,	*Phalü.*
	Abor Miri,	*Caret.*
	Sibságar Miri,	*Tábbe.*
	Deoria Chutia,	*Dubu.*
	Singpho,	*Lapú.*
Arrakan & Burmah.	Burman (*written*),	*Mrwe.*
	Burman (*spoken*),	*Myue, mywa.*
	Khyeng v. Shou,	*Phol.*
	Kámi,	*Makhúi.*
	Kúmi,	*Púwi.*
	Mrú v. Toung,	*Taroa (tadoa ?).*
	Sák,	*Kapú.*
Siam & Tenasserim.	Talain v. Mon,	*Tharun (tadun ?).*
	Sgau-karen,	*Ghu, gu, mgu.*
	Pwo-karen,	*Ghu.*
	Toungh-thu,	*H'm.*
	Shán,	*Ngu.*
	Annamitic,	*Ran.*
	Siamese,	*Ngu, ngú.*
	Ahom,	*Ngo.*
	Khámti,	*Ngú.*
	Laos,	*Ngu.*
Central India.	Ho (Kol),	*Bing.*
	Kol (Singhbhum),	*Bing.*
	Santáli,	*Bing.*
	Bhúmij,	*Bing.*
	Uráon,	*Nir.*
	Mundala,	*Bing.*
	Rájmahali,	*Ner.*
	Gondi,	*Tadás (taras ?).*
	Gayeti,	*Tadas.*
	Rutluk,	*Tadas.*
	Naikude,	*Caret.*
	Kolami,	*Pam.*
	Mádi,	*Tadas, tadasi.*
	Mádia,	*Caret.*
	Kuri,	*Bing.*
	Keikádi,	*Pamu.*
	Khond,	*Lorâse.*
	Sávara,	*Ja.*
	Gadaba,	*Budubu.*
	Yerukala,	*Tüna.*
	Chentsu,	*Sáp.*
Southern India.	Tamil, anc.,	*Kadsevi.*
	Tamil, mod.,	*Pámbu.*
	Malayálma, anc.,	*Caret.*
	Malayálma, mod.,	*Pámba.*
	Telugu,	*Pámu.*
	Karnátaka, anc.,	*Pávu.*
	Karnátaka, mod.,	*Hávu.*
	Tuluva,	*Parapunu.*
	Kurgi,	*Pambu.*
	Toduva, }	*Pab.*
	Toda, }	*Páb.*
	Kóta,	*Pábe.*
	Badaga,	*Hávu, pámbu.*
	Kurumba,	*Havu.*
	Irula,	*Pámbu.*
	Malabar,	*Pámbu.*
	Sinhalese,	*Sarpaya.*

Group	Language	Star
	Types.	
Inflecting.	SANSKRIT,	*Tárá.*
	ARABIC,	*Nijm, kaukab.*
Compounding.	BASK,	*Izar.*
	FINNIC,	*Tahti.*
	MAGYAR,	*Czillagzat.*
	TURKISH,	*Yildiz.*
	CIRCASSIAN,	*Ushago, dshogha.*
	GEORGIAN,	*Warskulavi.*
	MONGOLIAN,	*Odon, fottagi.*‡
	MANTSHU,	*Usikha.*
	JAVANESE, Ngoko,	*Lintang.*
	JAVANESE, Krama,	*Lintang.*
	MALAY,	*Bintang.*
Isolating.	CHINESE, Nankin,	*Sing.*
	CHINESE, Pekin,	*Hsing.*
	CHINESE, Canton,	*Sing.*
	CHINESE, Shanghai,	*Sing.*
	AMOY, Colloquial,	*Ch'in.*
	JAPANESE,	*Hoshi.*
	Brahuí,	*Istár.*
Chinese Frontier & Tibet.	Gyámi,	*Singhsyú.*
	Gyárung,	*Tsini.*
	Tákpa,	*Karma.*
	Mányak,	*Kraḥ.*
	Thochú,	*Ghada.*
	Sokpa,	*Caret.*
	Horpa,	*Sgre.*
	Tibetan (*written*),	*Skarma.*
	Tibetan (*spoken*),	*Karma.*
Nepal (east to west).	Serpa,	*Karma.*
	Súnwár,	*Sorú.*
	Gúrung,	*Pirá, tárgya.*
	Múrmi,	*Karchin.*
	Magar,	*Bhúga.*
	Tháksya,	*Sar.*
	Pákhya,	*Tárá.*
	Newár,	*Nagú.*
	Limbu,	*Kheseva.*
Kiranti Group (East Nepal).	Kiránti,	*Sángyen.*
	Rodong,	*Pitipya, pitappa.*
	Rúngchenbung,	*Sáng-gen.*
	Chhingtángya,	*Chok chongi.*
	Náchhereng,	*Sanggeʳ wa.*
	Wáling,	*Sanggen-ma.*
	Yákha,	*Chokchigi.*
	Chourásya,	*Soru.*
	Kulungya,	*Sángger.*
	Thulungya,	*Swar.*
	Báhingya,	*Sorú.*
	Lohorong,	*Sánge, sánggemmá.*
	Lambichhong,	*Chokchonggi.*
	Báláli,	*Súngemmá.*
	Sáng-páng,	*Sanggeuṇ.*
	Dúmi,	*Songger.*
	Kháling,	*Songgar.*
	Dungmáli,	*Sanggenmá.*
Broken Tribes of Nepal.	Dárhi,	*Tirya, tirya.*
	Denwár,	*Tárái.*
	Pahri,	*Núnggi, nunggni.*
	Chepáng,	*Kar.*
	Bhrámu,	*Caret.*
	Váyu,	*Khwámen.*
	Kuswar,	*Táraï.*
	Kusunda,	*Inggai.*
	Thárú,	*Caret.*
	Lepcha (Sikkim),	*Suhor.*
	Bhúṭáni v. Lhopa,	*Kám.*
N.-E. Bengal.	Bodo,	*Háthotkhi.*
	Dhimál,	*Phúro.*
	Kocch,	*Tárá.*
	Garo,	*Laitan.*
	Káchári,	*Haturki* (pl.).
Eastern Frontier of Bengal.	Munipuri,	*Thomucha.*
	Míthán Nágá,	*Lethi.*
	Tablung Nágá,	*Cháhá.*
	Khári Nágá,	*Peti.*
	Angámi Nágá,	*Themü.*
	Námsáng Nágá,	*Merik.*
	Nowgong Nágá,	*Pitinu.*
	Tengsa Nágá,	*Lutingting.*
	Abor Miri,	*Tákár.*
	Sibságar Miri,	*Tákár.*
	Deoria Chutia,	*Jiti.*
	Singpho,	*Sigan.*
Arrakan & Burmah.	Burman (*written*),	*Kre.*
	Burman (*spoken*),	*Kye, kyay.*
	Khyeng v. Shou,	*A'ashe.*
	Kámi,	*As'hí.*
	Kúmi,	*Kasí.*
	Mrú v. Toung,	*Kirek.*
	Sák,	Th*ageingthi.*
Siam & Tenasserim.	Talain v. Mon,	*Noung.*
	Sgau-karen,	*Tsah, htsah.*
	Pwo-karen,	*Tsah.*
	Toungh-thu,	*H'sa.*
	Shán,	*Loung.*
	Annamitic,	*Tinh.*
	Siamese,	*Touk, dáu.*
	Ahom,	*Dau.*
	Khámti,	*Naú.*
	Laos,	*Láu.*
Central India.	Ho (Kol),	*I'pil.*
	Kol (Singhbhum),	*Epil.*
	Santáli,	*Ipil, bhúraká.*
	Bhúmij,	*Ipil.*
	Uráon,	*Binká.*
	Mundala,	*Ipil.*
	Rájmahali,	*Bindeke.*
	Goṇḍi,	*Sukú, sukum.*
	Gayeti,	*Sukum.*
	Rutluk,	*Sukum.*
	Naikude,	*Sukha.*
	Kolami,	*Chukka.*
	Mádi,	*Uko, huku.*
	Mádia,	*Hukam.*
	Kuri,	*Epal, idiu.*
	Keikádi,	*Chukka.*
	Khoṇḍ,	*Sukálá.*
	Sávara,	*Tute.*
	Gadaba,	*Tsukka.*
	Yerukala,	*Tsukka.*
	Chentsu,	*Bhuḍaká.*
Southern India.	Tamiḷ, anc.,	*Viṇmín.*
	Tamiḷ, mod.,	*Vánmin, táragei.*
	Malayáḷma, anc.,	*Caret.*
	Malayáḷma, mod.,	*Mín.*
	Telugu,	*Chukka.*
	Karṇáṭaka, anc.,	*Minu.*
	Karṇáṭaka, mod.,	*Chukki.*
	Tuḷuva,	*Dáráya.*
	Kurgi,	*Caret.*
	Toḍuva, } Toḍa, }	*Pone-min.*
		Min.
	Kóta,	*Mine.*
	Baḍaga,	*Minu.*
	Kurumba,	*Minu.*
	Iruḷa,	*Vánu minu.*
	Malabar,	*Natchetheram, velli.*
	Sinhalese,	*Taruwa, tárukáwa.*

Group	Language	Stone
	Types.	
Inflecting.	SANSKRIT,	*Aśman, prastara, páshána.*
	ARABIC,	Hajr.
Compounding.	BASK,	*Arri, lapitz.*
	FINNIC,	*Kiwi.*
	MAGYAR,	*Kö.*
	TURKISH,	*Tash.*
	CIRCASSIAN,	*Müshey.*
	GEORGIAN,	*Kwa.*
	MONGOLIAN,	*Tsiloghon, chilaghon.*
	MANTSHU,	*Wekhe.*
	JAVANESE, Ngoko,	*Wátu.*
	JAVANESE, Krama,	*Sela.*
	MALAY,	*Bátu.*
Isolating.	CHINESE, Nankin,	*Shih.*
	CHINESE, Pekin,	*Shih.*
	CHINESE, Canton,	*Shik.*
	CHINESE, Shanghai,	*Sah-deu.*
	AMOY, Colloquial,	*Chioh.*
	JAPANESE,	*Ishi.*
	Brahuí,	*Khall.*
Chinese Frontier & Tibet.	Gyámi,	*Huthou.*
	Gyárung,	*Rúgú.*
	Tákpa,	*Gorr.*
	Mányak,	*Wobi.*
	Thochú,	*Gholopi.*
	Sokpa,	*Chhilo.*
	Horpa,	*Rgáme.*
	Tibetan (*written*),	*Rdo.*
	Tibetan (*spoken*),	*Do.*
Nepal (east to west).	Serpa,	*Doh.*
	Súnwár,	*Phúnglú.*
	Gúrung,	*Yúma.*
	Múrmi,	*Yúmbá.*
	Magar,	*Lhúng.*
	Tháksya,	*Caret.*
	Pákhya,	*Caret.*
	Newár,	*Lohong.*
	Limbu,	*Lúng.*
Kiranti Group (East Nepal).	Kiránti,	*Lúngtá.*
	Rodong,	*Lúngto.*
	Rúngchenbung,	*Lúngta.*
	Chhingtángya,	*Lúnggwakwa.*
	Náchhereng,	*Lún.*
	Wáling,	*Lúngtak.*
	Yákha,	*Lúngkhokwa.*
	Chourásya,	*Lúng.*
	Kulungya,	*Lúng.*
	Thulungya,	*Lúng.*
	Báhingya,	*Lúng.*
	Lohorong,	*Lúngkong'wa, lingkawa.*
	Lambichhong,	*Lúng, lúngo, lungokwa.*
	Báláli,	*Lu'ko'wa.*
	Sáng-páng,	*Lúng.*
	Dúmi,	*Lúng.*
	Kháling,	*Lúng.*
	Dungmáli,	*Lúngtá.*
Broken Tribes of Nepal.	Dárhi,	*Páthár.*
	Denwár,	*Dohkho.*
	Pahri,	*Lhonggo, lhonggno.*
	Chepáng,	*Báng.*
	Bhrámu,	*Kúngbá.*
	Váyu,	*Lúnphu.*
	Kuswar,	*Pathár.*
	Kusunda,	*Caret.*
	Tháru,	*Caret.*
	Lepcha (Sikkim),	*Long.*
	Bhútáni v. Lhopa,	*Doh.*

Group	Language	Stone
N.-E. Bengal.	Bodo,	*Onthai.*
	Dhimál,	*U'nthúr.*
	Kocch,	*Páthar.*
	Garo,	*Long.*
	Káchári,	*Untai.*
Eastern Frontier of Bengal.	Munipuri,	*Núng.*
	Míthán Nágá,	*Long.*
	Tablung Nágá,	*Yong.*
	Khári Nágá,	*Along.*
	Angámi Nágá,	*Kache.*
	Námsáng Nágá,	*Long.*
	Nowgong Nágá,	*Lungzük.*
	Tengsa Nágá,	*Lungmanggo.*
	Abor Miri,	*Iling.*
	Sibságar Miri,	*Ilüng.*
	Deoria Chutia,	*Yatiri.*
	Singpho,	*Nlung.*
Arrakan & Burmah.	Burman (*written*),	*Kyok.*
	Burman (*spoken*),	*Kyauk.*
	Khyeng v. Shou,	*Lún.*
	Kámi,	*Kalún.*
	Kúmi,	*Lúns'houng.*
	Mrú v. Toung,	*Tawhá.*
	Sák,	*Talon.*
Siam & Tenasserim.	Talain v. Mon,	*Kamau.*
	Sgau-karen,	*Ler, hlui.*
	Pwo-karen,	*Láng.*
	Toungh-thu,	*Lung.*
	Shán,	*Mahein.*
	Annamitic,	*Dá.*
	Siamese,	*Hi, hin.*
	Ahòm,	*Frá.*
	Khámti,	*Hin.*
	Laos,	*Hin.*
Central India.	Ho (Kol),	*Dirri.*
	Kol (Singhbhum),	*Dirri.*
	Santáli,	*Kháp, dhiri.*
	Bhúmij,	*Dirri.*
	Uráon,	*Pakhna.*
	Mundala,	*Diri.*
	Rájmahali,	*Chaihe.*
	Gondi,	*Tongi, kal.*
	Gayeti,	*Kal.*
	Rutluk,	*Kal, patu.*
	Naikude,	*Gund.*
	Kolami,	*Dop.*
	Mádi,	*Kal.*
	Mádia,	*Kal.*
	Kuri,	*Degá.*
	Keikádi,	*Kal.*
	Khond,	*Viddi.*
	Sávara,	*Arregna.*
	Gadaba,	*Birel.*
	Yerukala,	*Kellu.*
	Chentsu,	*Paththar.*
Southern India.	Tamil, anc.,	*Kan.*
	Tamil, mod.,	*Kal.*
	Malayálma, anc.,	*Caret.*
	Malayálma, mod.,	*Kalla.*
	Telugu,	*Ráyi, kallu.*
	Karnátaka, anc.,	*Caret.*
	Karnátaka, mod.,	*Kallu.*
	Tuluva,	*Kalla.*
	Kurgi,	*Caret.*
	Toduva,	*Kall.*
	Toda,	*Kall.*
	Kóta,	*Kallu.*
	Badaga,	*Kallu.*
	Kurumba,	*Kallu.*
	Irula,	*Kallu.*
	Malabar,	*Kallu.*
	Sinhalese,	*Gala.*

Group	Types.	
Inflecting.	SANSKRIT,	*Súrya.*
	ARABIC,	*Shams.*
Compounding.	BASK,	*Eguzki, eki.*
	FINNIC,	*Paiva (païwa).*
	MAGYAR,	*Nap.*
	TURKISH,	*Gunesh.*
	CIRCASSIAN,	*Tygha, gede,* susi.**
	GEORGIAN,	*Mze, schialla.†*
	MONGOLIAN,	*Neran, naran, kou,‡ dellizin,§*
	MANTSHU,	*Shun.* [*tzingga.*‖
	JAVANESE, Ngoko,	*Srengenge.*
	JAVANESE, Krama,	*Srengenge.*
	MALAY,	*Máta-ari.*
Isolating.	CHINESE, Nankin,	*Jih.*
	CHINESE, Pekin,	*Jih.*
	CHINESE, Canton,	*Yat.*
	CHINESE, Shanghai,	*Nieh-deu.*
	AMOY, Colloquial,	*Jit.*
	JAPANESE,	*Hi.*
	Brahuí,	*Dey.*
Chinese Frontier & Tibet.	Gyámi,	*Rethou.*
	Gyárung,	*Kini.*
	Tákpa,	*Pláng.*
	Mányak,	*Nyima.*
	Thochú,	*Mún.*
	Sokpa,	*Nára.*
	Horpa,	*Gna.*
	Tibetan (*written*),	*Nyimá.*
	Tibetan (*spoken*),	*Nyimá.*
Nepal (east to west).	Serpa,	*Nimo.*
	Súnwár,	*Ná.*
	Gúrung,	*Dhini.*
	Múrmi,	*Dini.*
	Magar,	*Námkhán.*
	Tháksya,	*Ghaṇgni, saughini.*
	Pákhya,	*Ghánia.*
	Newár,	*Sújá.*
	Limbu,	*Nam.*
Kiranti Group (East Nepal).	Kiránti,	*Nam.*
	Rodong,	*Námlíya, nám.*
	Rúngchenbung,	*Nám.*
	Chhingtángya,	*Nám.*
	Náchhereng,	*Nám.*
	Wáling,	*Namchhowa.*
	Yákha,	*Nám.*
	Chourásya,	*Dwám.*
	Kulungya,	*Nám.*
	Thulungya,	*Nepsúng, nem.*
	Báhingya,	*Nám.*
	Lohorong,	*Nám.*
	Lambichhong,	*Nám.*
	Bálálí,	*Nám.*
	Sáng-páng,	*Lonpá.*
	Dúmi,	*Nám.*
	Kháling,	*Nám.*
	Dungmálí,	*Námchhoúgwá.*
Broken Tribes of Nepal.	Dárhi,	*Gámá.*
	Denwár,	*Gámá.*
	Pahri,	*Suje.*
	Chepáng,	*Nyám.*
	Bhrámu,	*Uní.*
	Váyu,	*Nomo, numa.*
	Kuswar,	*Súraj.*
	Kusunda,	*Ing.*
	Tháru,	*Raüda.*
	Lepcha (Sikkim),	*Sachak.*
	Bhútáni v. Lhopa,	*Nyim.*
N.-E. Bengal.	Bodo,	*Shán.*
	Dhimál,	*Belá.*
	Kocch,	*Belá.*
	Garo,	*Sán, rasán.*
	Káchári,	*Sang-dong.*
Eastern Frontier of Bengal.	Munipuri,	*Númit.*
	Mithán Nágá,	*Ranghán.*
	Tablung Nágá,	*Wanghi.*
	Khári Nágá,	*Suhih.*
	Angámi Nágá,	*Nakhi.*
	Námsáng Nágá,	*Sán.*
	Nowgong Nágá,	*A'nnü.*
	Tengsa Nágá,	*Tinglü.*
	Abor Miri,	*Dunie.*
	Sibságar Miri,	*Doanye.*
	Deoria Chutia,	*Sáṇh.*
	Singpho,	*Ján.*
Arrakan & Burmah.	Burman (*written*),	*Ne.*
	Burman (*spoken*),	*Ne, ná.*
	Khyeng v. Shou,	*Konhi.*
	Kámi,	*Kani.*
	Kúmi,	*Kani.*
	Mrú v. Toung,	*Tanin.*
	Sák,	*Sami.*
Siam & Tenasserim.	Talain v. Mon,	*Tangway.*
	Sgau-karen,	*Mu, muh.*
	Pwo-karen,	*Mumai.*
	Toungh-thu,	*Mu.*
	Shán,	*Kawon.*
	Annamitic,	*Măt-trờ'i.*
	Siamese,	*Kawon, tawan.*
	Ahom,	*Bán.*
	Khámti,	*Wan.*
	Laos,	*Kangwan.*
Central India.	Ho (Kol),	*Singi.*
	Kol (Singhbhum),	*Singi.*
	Santáli,	*Beḍa, chándo, singmarsal.*
	Bhúmij,	*Singi.*
	Uráon,	*Dharmi.*
	Mundala,	*Singi.*
	Rájmahali,	*Beḍ.*
	Goṇḍi,	*Suraj, suryal, din.*
	Gayeti,	*Suryál, din.*
	Rutluk,	*Surajá.*
	Naikude,	*Suryátali.*
	Kolami,	*Podh.*
	Mádi,	*Porde, hodudu, yadde.*
	Mádia,	*Pod.*
	Kuri,	*Gomoi.*
	Keikádi,	*Surya.*
	Khoṇḍ,	*Belá.*
	Sávara,	*Vuyu.*
	Gadaba,	*Singi.*
	Yerukala,	*Proddu, beruli.*
	Chentsu,	*Belá.*
Southern India.	Tamiḷ, anc.,	*Carat.*
	Tamiḷ, mod.,	*Pagalon, súriyan.*
	Malayáḷma, anc.,	*Caret.*
	Malayáḷma, mod.,	*Súrya.*
	Telugu,	*Poddu, súryuḍu.*
	Karṇáṭaka, anc.,	*Pallili.*
	Karṇáṭaka, mod.,	*Hottu.*
	Tuḷuva,	*Polutu.*
	Kurgi,	*Bedu.*
	Toḍuva, }	*Caret.*
	Toḍa, }	*Birsh.*
	Kóta,	*Potte.*
	Baḍaga,	*Hottu.*
	Kurumba,	*Hottu.*
	Iruḷa,	*Podu.*
	Malabar,	*Veyil, poluthu.*
	Sinhalese,	*Súrya.*

	Types.	
Inflecting.	SANSKRIT,	*Pipásá.*
	ARABIC,	*Aaṭash.*
Compounding.	BASK,	*Egarri, edagale, egartzu.*
	FINNIC,	*Jano.*
	MAGYAR,	*Szomjuság.*
	TURKISH,	*Caret.*
	CIRCASSIAN,	*Caret.*
	GEORGIAN,	*Caret.*
	MONGOLIAN,	*Ümdagaskolang.*
	MANTSHU,	*Kanghara.*
	JAVANESE, Ngoko,	*Kasátan.*
	JAVANESE, Krama,	*Ngelát.*
	MALAY,	*Dhága.*
Isolating.	CHINESE, Nankin,	*K'au-k'oh.*
	CHINESE, Pekin,	*K'au-ho.*
	CHINESE, Canton,	*Keng-hot.*
	CHINESE, Shanghai,	*Ken-li'kiuŋ.*
	AMOY, Colloquial,	*Chúita* (mouth dry).
	JAPANESE,	*Nodo kawaku.*
	Brahuí,	*Malás.*
Chinese Frontier & Tibet.	Gyámi,	*Khángti.*
	Gyárung,	*Taskom'.*
	Tákpa,	*Caret.*
	Mányak,	*Depsyá.*
	Thochú,	*Tirpitch.*
	Sokpa,	*Uleso.*
	Horpa,	*Nasyá.*
	Tibetan (*written*),	*Skom.*
	Tibetan (*spoken*),	*Khákúm.*
Nepal (east to west).	Serpa,	*Khákum.*
	Súnwár,	*Páng-dati.*
	Gúrung,	*Kwiphi.*
	Múrmi,	*Kwiphúi.*
	Magar,	*Disona.*
	Tháksya,	*Kejuphiji.*
	Pákhya,	*Pámitis.*
	Newár,	*Piás.*
	Límbu,	*Wámikma.*
Kiranti Group (East Nepal).	Kiránti,	*Waitmá.*
	Rodong,	*Wáimá.*
	Rúngchenbung,	*Wáitmá, wámitmá.*
	Chhingtángya,	*Wáikmá.*
	Náchhereng,	*Wámimá.*
	Wáling,	*Wáikmá.*
	Yákha,	*Wáitmáng.*
	Chourásya,	*Dakkho.*
	Kulungya,	*Wammá.*
	Thulungya,	*Kodá.*
	Báhingya,	*Bwakudwaktu.*
	Lohorong,	*Wait'ma.*
	Lambichhong,	*Wait' ma.*
	Báláli,	*Waime.*
	Sáng-páng,	*Wám'ma.*
	Dúmi,	*Kumána.*
	Kháling,	*Kunur', kunun'.*
	Dungmáli,	*Cháomit' ma.*
Broken Tribes of Nepal.	Dárhi,	*Pias.*
	Denwár,	*Tirkha.*
	Pahri,	*Pyáhá.*
	Chepáng,	*Caret.*
	Bhrámu,	*A'wáphang.*
	Váyu,	*Tidaksa.*
	Kuswar,	*Tirkha.*
	Kusunda,	*Tápyáu.*
	Tháru,	*Pipás.*
	Lepcha (Sikkim),	*U'ngno.*
	Bhúṭáni v. Lhopa,	*Khákom.*

N.-E. Bengal.	Bodo,	*Gángdúng.*
	Dhimál,	*Chiámli.*
	Kocch,	*Piás.*
	Garo,	*Chíka láng noitwa.*
	Káchári,	*Caret.*
Eastern Frontier of Bengal.	Munipuri,	*Caret.*
	Míthán Nágá,	*Caret.*
	Tablung Nágá,	*Caret.*
	Khári Nágá,	*Caret.*
	Angámi Nágá,	*Caret.*
	Námsáng Nágá,	*Khamlán.*
	Nowgong Nágá,	*Tukula, seratür.*
	Tengsa Nágá,	*Chebale, chuale.*
	Abor Miri,	*Tuling.*
	Sibságar Miri,	*Tüliing.*
	Deoria Chutia,	*Caret.*
	Singpho,	*Pháng-gerá.*
Arrakan & Burmah.	Burman (*written*),	*Rengat.*
	Burman (*spoken*),	*Yengát, yai'natkhyer.*
	Khyeng v. Shou,	*T'wilanadúi.*
	Kámi,	*Túi-makháng.*
	Kúmi,	*Túanhei.*
	Mrú v. Toung,	*Caret.*
	Sák,	*Caret.*
Siam & Tenasserim.	Talain v. Mon,	*Htantikh.*
	Sgau-karen,	*Caret.*
	Pwo-karen,	*Caret.*
	Toungh-thu,	*H'taenk'ti.*
	Shán,	*Ratnan.*
	Annamitic,	*Khat.*
	Siamese,	*Ratnan.*
	Ahom,	*Caret.*
	Khámti,	*Caret.*
	Laos,	*Caret.*
Central India.	Ho (Kol),	*Tetangteá.*
	Kol (Singhbhum),	*Totángtanna.*
	Santáli,	*Tetángte* (verb), *totángtanna.*
	Bhúmij,	*Totángtanna.*
	Uráon,	*Amun kala.*
	Mundala,	*Titang.*
	Rájmahali,	*Amkirva.*
	Goṇḍi,	*Yetaksátur, wutki wusta.*
	Gayeti,	*Caret.*
	Rutluk,	*Caret.*
	Naikude,	*Caret.*
	Kolami,	*Caret.*
	Mádi,	*Caret.*
	Mádia,	*Caret.*
	Kuri,	*Caret.*
	Keikádi,	*Caret.*
	Khoṇḍ,	*Yesengepekmanenju.*
	Sávara,	*Araga.*
	Gadaba,	*Yide.*
	Yerukala,	*Dagga, dappikonu.*
	Chentsu,	*Pyaslagi, pyas.*
Southern India.	Tamiḷ, anc.,	*Caret.*
	Tamiḷ, mod.,	*Nirveṭkei.*
	Malayáḷma, anc.,	*Caret.*
	Malayáḷma, mod.,	*Taṇṇirdáham.*
	Telugu,	*Dappi.*
	Karṇáṭaka, anc.,	*Caret.*
	Karṇáṭaka, mod.,	*Niradike.*
	Tuḷuva,	*Bajil.*
	Kurgi,	*Caret.*
	Toḍuva, Toḍa,	*Nikhosti. Nirchásti.*
	Kóta,	*Arthoje.*
	Baḍaga,	*Arupu.*
	Kuṛumba,	*Arupu.*
	Iruḷa,	*Veke.*
	Malabar,	*Thakam.*
	Sinhalese,	*Pipása.*

	Types.	
Inflecting.	SANSKRIT,	*Vyághra.*
	ARABIC,	*Nimr.*
Compounding.	BASK,	*Katamotz.*
	FINNIC,	*Caret.*
	MAGYAR,	*Caret.*
	TURKISH,	*Caret.*
	CIRCASSIAN,	*Caret.*
	GEORGIAN,	*Caret.*
	MONGOLIAN,	*Irbiss.*
	MANTSHU,	*Taskha.*
	JAVANESE, Ngoko,	*Machan.*
	JAVANESE, Krama,	*Sima.*
	MALAY,	*Arimau.*
Isolating.	CHINESE, Nankin,	*Láou-hu.*
	CHINESE, Pekin,	*Láou-hu.*
	CHINESE, Canton,	*Lo-fú.*
	CHINESE, Shanghai,	*Lau-hu.*
	AMOY, Colloquial,	*Ho.*
	JAPANESE,	*Tora.*
	Brahuí,	*Caret.*
Chinese Frontier & Tibet.	Gyámi,	*Khú.*
	Gyárung,	*Kong.*
	Tákpa,	*Tee.*
	Mányak,	*Lephe.*
	Thochú,	*Khoḥ.*
	Sokpa,	*Pár.*
	Horpa,	*Sták.*
	Tibetan (*written*),	*Stag.*
	Tibetan (*spoken*),	*Tak.*
Nepal (east to west).	Serpa,	*Jik.*
	Súnwár,	*Gúpsa.*
	Gúrung,	*Cheṇ.*
	Múrmi,	*Chyan.*
	Magar,	*Rânghú.*
	Tháksya,	*Ná.*
	Pákhya,	*Bágha.*
	Newár,	*Dhúṇ.*
	Limbu,	*Keh'va.*
Kiránti Group (East Nepal).	Kiránti,	*Kiwá.*
	Rodong,	*Chábhá.*
	Rúngchenbung,	*Kiwa.*
	Chhingtángya,	*Kibha.*
	Náchhereng,	*Dhmg' trá.*
	Wáling,	*Dhina rá, dhinra.*
	Yákha,	*Kiba.*
	Chourásya,	*Gúpso.*
	Kulungya,	*Nári.*
	Thulungya,	*Gúpsyú.*
	Báhingya,	*Gúpsá.*
	Lohorong,	*Kiba.*
	Lambichhong,	*Kiba.*
	Bálálí,	*Keuba.*
	Sáng-páng,	*Kipa.*
	Dúmi,	*Nyor.*
	Kháling,	*Nyor.*
	Dungmáli,	*Kibhá.*
Broken Tribes of Nepal.	Dárhi,	*Bág.*
	Denwár,	*Bág.*
	Pahri,	*Dhúṇ.*
	Chepáng,	*Jákela, ja.*
	Bhrámu,	*Búmáng.*
	Váyu,	*Bilo, bilu.*
	Kuswar,	*Bághi.*
	Kusunda,	*Dájá káúli.*
	Tháru,	*Bágha.*
	Lepcha (Sikkim),	*Sathong.*
	Bhúṭáni v. Lhopa,	*Táh.*
N.-E. Bengal.	Bodo,	*Mochá.*
	Dhimál,	*Khúṇá.*
	Kocch,	*Bág.*
	Garo,	*Matsá.*
	Kácháii,	*Moosá, misa.*
Eastern Frontier of Bengal.	Munipuri,	*Kei.*
	Míthán Nágá,	*Chianú.*
	Tablung Nágá,	*Sahnu.*
	Khári Nágá,	*Akhü.*
	Angámi Nágá,	*Takhu.*
	Námsáng Nágá,	*Sá.*
	Nowgong Nágá,	*Kayi.*
	Tengsa Nágá,	*Khü.*
	Abor Miri,	*Simiü.*
	Sibságar Miri,	*Sümyo.*
	Deoria Chutia,	*Mesá.*
	Singpho,	*Sirong.*
Arrakan & Burmah.	Burman (*written*),	*Kyá.*
	Burman (*spoken*),	*Kyá.*
	Khyeng v. Shou,	*Kyi.*
	Kámi,	*Takái.*
	Kúmi,	*Takái.*
	Mrú v. Toung,	*Tapri.*
	Sák,	*Kaṭhá.*
Siam & Tenasserim.	Talain v. Mon,	*Kala.*
	Sgau-karen,	*Bautho, ka, hkhe.*
	Pwo-karen,	*Khay.*
	Toungh-thu,	*Ka.*
	Shán,	*Htso.*
	Annamitic,	*Hum-beo.*
	Siamese,	*Tso, süa.*
	Ahom,	*Sú.*
	Khámti,	*Sü.*
	Laos,	*Seu.*
Central India.	Ho (Kol),	*Kulá.*
	Kol (Singhbhum),	*Garúmkúla.*
	Santáli,	*Kula, bágáhi, háḍgar.*
	Bhúmij,	*Kula.*
	Uráon,	*Lakhra.*
	Mundala,	*Kulah.*
	Rájmahali,	*Sad.*
	Goṇḍi,	*Pulli.*
	Gayeti,	*Burkál.*
	Rutluk,	*Pulial, bagheli.*
	Naikude,	*Pul.*
	Kolami,	*Pul.*
	Mádi,	*Burkal, dual.*
	Mádia,	*Burkal.*
	Kuri,	*Kula.*
	Keikádi,	*Puli.*
	Khoṇḍ,	*Kroḍi.*
	Sávara,	*Kina.*
	Gadaba,	*Yekkili.*
	Yerukala,	*Náhugáḍi.*
	Chentsu,	*Bág.*
Southern India.	Tamiḷ, anc.,	*Pul.*
	Tamiḷ, mod.,	*Puli.*
	Malayáḷma, anc.,	*Caret.*
	Malayáḷma, mod.,	*Puli, kaṭuvá.*
	Telugu,	*Puli.*
	Karṇáṭaka, anc.,	*Puli.*
	Karṇáṭaka, mod.,	*Huli.*
	Tuḷuva,	*Pili.*
	Kurgi,	*Nari.*
	Toḍuva,	*Pirri.*
	Toḍa,	*Bürsh.*
	Kóta,	*Pujje.*
	Baḍaga,	*Huli.*
	Kuṛumba,	*Huli.*
	Iruḷa,	*Pulli.*
	Malabar,	*Puli, vengei.*
	Sinhalese,	*Koṭiyá.*

	Types.	
Inflecting.	SANSKṚIT,	*Dat, danta.*
	ARABIC,	*Sinn.*
Compounding.	BASK,	*Ortz.*
	FINNIC,	*Hammas.*
	MAGYAR,	*All.*
	TURKISH,	*Dish.*
	CIRCASSIAN,	*Tsey.*
	GEORGIAN,	*Kbili.*
	MONGOLIAN,	*Ssidon, shidon.*
	MANTSHU,	*Weihe, weikhe.*
	JAVANESE, Ngoko,	*Untu.*
	JAVANESE, Krama,	*Untu.*
	MALAY,	*Gigi.*
Isolating.	CHINESE, Nankin,	*Yá.*
	CHINESE, Pekin,	*Yá.*
	CHINESE, Canton,	*Ngá.*
	CHINESE, Shanghai,	*Ngá-tsz'.*
	AMOY, Colloquial,	*Ch'úiki.*
	JAPANESE,	*Ha.*
	Brahuí,	*Dandán.*
Chinese Frontier & Tibet.	Gyámi,	*Yá.*
	Gyárung,	*Tiswè.*
	Tákpa,	*Wáḥ.*
	Mányak,	*Phwiḥ.*
	Thochú,	*Sweḥ.*
	Sokpa,	*Syúchi.*
	Horpa,	*Syo.*
	Tibetan (*written*),	*So.*
	Tibetan (*spoken*),	*So.*
Nepal (east to west).	Serpa,	*Lo.*
	Súnwár,	*Kryú.*
	Gúrung,	*Sak.*
	Múrmi,	*Swá.*
	Magar,	*Syak.*
	Thákysa,	*Gyo.*
	Pákhya,	*Dáta.*
	Newár,	*Wá.*
	Limbu,	*Hebo.*
Kiránti Group (East Nepal).	Kiránti,	*Kang.*
	Rodong,	*King.*
	Rúngchenbung,	*Kang.*
	Chhingtángya,	*Keng.*
	Náchhereng,	*Ka a.*
	Wáling,	*Kang.*
	Yákha,	*Ha, hachi.*
	Chourásya,	*Glun'so.*
	Kulungya,	*Káng.*
	Thulungya,	*Lyú.*
	Báhingya,	*Khleú.*
	Lohorong,	*Keng.*
	Lambichhong,	*Keng.*
	Bálálí,	*Keng.*
	Sáng-páng,	*Káṇ.*
	Dúmi,	*Guilo, anglo.*
	Kháling,	*Gnálu.*
	Dungmáli,	*Kang.*
Broken Tribes of Nepal.	Dárhi,	*Dánt.*
	Denwár,	*Dánt.*
	Pahri,	*Wá.*
	Chepáng,	*Srek.*
	Bhrámu,	*Súa, swá.*
	Váyu,	*Lú.*
	Kuswar,	*Dant.*
	Kusunda,	*Toho.*
	Tháru,	*Dáta.*
	Lepcha (Sikkim),	*Apho.*
	Bhúṭáni v. Lhopa,	*Soh.*

N.-E. Bengal.	Bodo,	*Hathai.*
	Dhimál,	*Sitong.*
	Kocch,	*Dánt.*
	Garo,	*Phá-tong.*
	Káchári,	*Hatai* (pl.).
Eastern Frontier of Bengal.	Munipuri,	*Yá.*
	Mithán Nágá,	*Vá.*
	Tablung Nágá,	*Phá.*
	Khári Nágá,	*Taphá.*
	Angámi Nágá,	*Uhu.*
	Námsáng Nágá,	*Pá.*
	Nowgong Nágá,	*Tabu.*
	Tengsa Nágá,	*Taphu.*
	Abor Miri,	*I'páng.*
	Sibságar Miri,	*A'ie.*
	Deoria Chutia,	*Háti.*
	Singpho,	*Wá.*
Arrakan & Burmah.	Burman (*written*),	*Swá.*
	Burman (*spoken*),	Thwá, *ṭhwáu.*
	Khyeng v. Shou,	*Kahau.*
	Kámi,	*Afhá.*
	Kúmi,	*Ho.*
	Mrú v. Toung,	*Yún.*
	Sák,	*Aṭhawá.*
Siam & Tenasserim.	Talain v. Mon,	*Nget.*
	Sgau-karen,	*Maï.*
	Pwo-karen,	*Mai.*
	Toungh-thu,	*Tagná.*
	Shán,	*Khyo.*
	Annamitic,	*Rang.*
	Siamese,	*Thohn, fan, khian.*
	Ahom,	*Khiu.*
	Khámti,	*Khiu.*
	Laos,	*Khiau.*
Central India.	Ho (Kol),	*Danta.*
	Kol (Singhbhum),	*Dátha.*
	Santáli,	*Dátá.*
	Bhúmij,	*Dátta.*
	Uráon,	*Pál.*
	Mundala,	*Dáta.*
	Rájmahali,	*Pál.*
	Goṇḍi,	*Palk, palapalk* (pl.).
	Gayeti,	*Palk* (pl.).
	Rutluk,	*Palak* (pl.).
	Naikude,	*Palku* (pl.).
	Kolami,	*Palkul* (pl.).
	Mádi,	*Pal, palku* (pl.).
	Mádia,	*Palaku* (pl.).
	Kuri,	*Tiding.*
	Keikádi,	*Pal.*
	Khoṇḍ,	*Ahámu.*
	Sávara,	*Ajágna.*
	Gadaba,	*Ginná.*
	Yerukala,	*Pallam, pelivelu.*
	Chentsu,	*Dát.*
Southern India.	Tamiḷ, anc.,	*Eyiṛu.*
	Tamiḷ, mod.,	*Pal, palgaḷ* (pl.).
	Malayáḷma, anc.,	*Caret.*
	Malayáḷma, mod.,	*Palla.*
	Telugu,	*Pallu.*
	Karṇáṭaka, anc.,	*Pallu.*
	Karṇáṭaka, mod.,	*Hallu.*
	Tuḷuva,	*Kúli.*
	Kurgi,	*Pall.*
	Toḍuva, Toḍa, }	*Caret.*
		Pársh.
	Kóta,	*Palle.*
	Baḍaga,	*Hallu.*
	Kuṛumba,	*Hallu.*
	Iruḷa,	*Pallu.*
	Malabar,	*Pallu.*
	Sinhalese,	*Datha.*

	Types.	
Inflecting.	SANSKṚIT	*Vṛiksha, taru, druma.*
	ARABIC	*Shajar.*
Compounding.	BASK	*Arbola, arecha, zuhaitz.*
	FINNIC	*Puu.*
	MAGYAR	*Fak, pa.**
	TURKISH	*Aghaj.*
	CIRCASSIAN	*Frah.*
	GEORGIAN	*Khe.*
	MONGOLIAN	*Modon, modun, pu,*† *gilgada.*‖
	MANTSHU	*Mo, moo.*
	JAVANESE, Ngoko	*Wit.*
	JAVANESE, Krama	*Wit.*
	MALAY	*Pohun, pokok.*
Isolating.	CHINESE, Nankin	*Shú, muh.*
	CHINESE, Pekin	*Shú, mú.*
	CHINESE, Canton	*Shü, muk.*
	CHINESE, Shanghai	*Zü.*
	AMOY, Colloquial	*Ch'iu.*
	JAPANESE	*Ki.*
	Brahuí	*Darakht.*
Chinese Frontier & Tibet.	Gyámi	*Hrú.*
	Gyárung	*Shi.*
	Tákpa	*Sheng dong.*
	Mányak	*Sápoḥ.*
	Thochú	*Gwozosi.*
	Sokpa	*Moto.*
	Horpa	*Nah.*
	Tibetan (*written*)	*Ljonshing.*
	Tibetan (*spoken*)	*Shindong, shingdong.*
Nepal (east to west).	Serpa	*Dongo.*
	Súnwár	*Kawa.*
	Gúrung	*Sindú.*
	Múrmi	*Dhong.*
	Magar	*Sing.*
	Tháksya	*Ghyung.*
	Pákhya	*Rukha.*
	Newár	*Simá.*
	Limbu	*Sing.*
Kiránti Group (East Nepal).	Kiránti	*Sangtáng.*
	Rodong	*Song-púwa.*
	Rúngchenbung	*Sang-táng.*
	Chhingtángya	*Sang.*
	Náchhereng	*Sá-a.*
	Wáling	*Sang u.*
	Yákha	*Ing tháp, sing gaitháp.*
	Chourásya	*Sing.*
	Kulungya	*Thouám.*
	Thulungya	*Dhak'sa.*
	Báhingya	*Sing, dhyáksí.*
	Lohorong	*Sin'g tángdák, simmak.*
	Lambichhong	*Sin'gitangli.*
	Báláli	*Sin'tenda.*
	Sáng-páng	*Tupsáng.*
	Dúmi	*Topshú.*
	Khálíng	*Dhyáksá.*
	Dungmáli	*San'gpu.*
Broken Tribes of Nepal.	Dárhi	*Rúk.*
	Denwár	*Gátch.*
	Pahri	*Simá.*
	Chepáng	*Sing, singtak.*
	Bhrámu	*Simma.*
	Váyu	*Singphung.*
	Kuswar	*Gátch.*
	Kusunda	*I'.*
	Tháru	*Gáchh.*
	Lepcha (Sikkim)	*Kúng.*
	Bhúṭáni v. Lhopa	*Shing.*

N.-E. Bengal.	Bodo	*Pháng, bonpháng.*
	Dhimál	*Shing, sing.*
	Kocch	*Gácch, ped.*
	Garo	*Pan.*
	Kácharí	*Bon phang.*
Eastern Frontier of Bengal.	Munipuri	*Upál.*
	Míthán Nágá	*Pan.*
	Tablung Nágá	*Peh.*
	Khári Nágá	*Sundong.*
	Angámi Nágá	*Si.*
	Námsáng Nágá	*Bang.*
	Nowgong Nágá	*Santung.*
	Tengsa Nágá	*Sangtung.*
	Abor Miri	*Esing.*
	Sibságar Miri	*Ising.*
	Deoria Chutia	*Popoṇ.*
	Singpho	*Phun.*
Arrakan & Burmah.	Burman (*written*)	*Apang.*
	Burman (*spoken*)	*Apen.*
	Khyeng v. Shou	*Thin.*
	Kámi	*Akún.*
	Kúmi	*Dinkoung.*
	Mrú v. Toung	*Tsingdúng.*
	Sák	*Púngpáng.*
Siam & Tenasserim.	Talain v. Mon	*Kanoung.*
	Sgau-karen	*Thay.*
	Pwo-karen	*Thaing.*
	Toungh-thu	*Thingmu.*
	Shán	*Ton.*
	Annamitic	*Kâi.*
	Siamese	*Ton.*
	Ahom	*Tun.*
	Khámti	*Tun.*
	Laos	*Ton.*
Central India.	Ho (Kol)	*Daru.*
	Kol (Singhbhum)	*Dáru.*
	Santáli	*Dáre, ladá, budá* (shrub);
	Bhúmij	*Dárú.* [*bir* (forest).
	Uráon	*Man.*
	Mundala	*Dáru.*
	Rájmahali	*Man.*
	Goṇḍi	*Mare, mará.*
	Gayeti	*Mada.*
	Rutluk	*Mara.*
	Naikude	*Chet.*
	Kolami	*Mot.*
	Mádi	*Mara.*
	Mádia	*Bhanda.*
	Kuri	*Sing.*
	Keikádi	*Maro.*
	Khoṇḍ	*Mránu.*
	Sávara	*Anebagna.*
	Gadaba	*Sunabbo.*
	Yerukala	*Cheḍe, marom.*
	Chentsu	*Gáts.*
Southern India.	Tamiḷ, anc.	*Caret.*
	Tamiḷ, mod.	*Seḍi, maram.*
	Malayáḷma, anc.	*Caret.*
	Malayáḷma, mod.	*Cheḍi, maram.*
	Telugu	*Cheṭṭu.*
	Karṇáṭaka, anc.	*Caret.*
	Karṇáṭaka, mod.	*Giḍa, mara.*
	Tuḷuva	*Mara.*
	Kurgi	*Mara.*
	Toḍuva, }	*Men.*
	Toḍa, }	*Maen.*
	Kóta	*Marame.*
	Baḍaga	*Mora.*
	Kuṛumba	*Mara.*
	Iruḷa	*Mara.*
	Malabar	*Maram.*
	Sinhalese	*Gaha.*

Group	Language	Village
Types.		
Inflecting.	SANSKṚIT,	*Gráma.*
	ARABIC,	*Dayaah.*
Compounding.	BASK,	*Erri, iri, uri.*
	FINNIC,	*Kyla.*
	MAGYAR,	*Talu.*
	TURKISH,	*Keui, aoghl.*
	CIRCASSIAN,	*Zouytshil.*
	GEORGIAN,	*Sul, daba.*
	MONGOLIAN,	*Poskho, balgasun.*
	MANTSHU,	*Falan, tokso.*
	JAVANESE, Ngoko,	*Desa.*
	JAVANESE, Krama,	*Dusun.*
	MALAY,	*Kampong, dusun.*
Isolating.	CHINESE, Nankin,	*Hiang.*
	CHINESE, Pekin,	*Hsiang.*
	CHINESE, Canton,	*Heong.*
	CHINESE, Shanghai,	*Hiáng-tsang.*
	AMOY, Colloquial,	*Hiuṇ-siá.*
	JAPANESE,	*Mura.*
	Brahuí,	*Shahar.*
Chinese Frontier & Tibet.	Gyámi,	*Twángcha.*
	Gyárung,	*Wokhyú, túkhyú.*
	Tákpa,	*Yú.*
	Mányak,	*Hú.*
	Thochú,	*Wekhá.*
	Sokpa,	*Hoto.*
	Horpa,	*Rhava.*
	Tibetan (*written*),	*Yúl-tsho.*
	Tibetan (*spoken*),	*Thong.*
Nepal (east to west).	Serpa,	*Yúl.*
	Súnwár,	*Gáuṇ.*
	Gúrung,	*Nása.*
	Múrmi,	*Namso.*
	Magar,	*Lánghá.*
	Tháksya,	*Hál.*
	Pákhya,	*Gáu.*
	Newár,	*De, gang.*
	Limbu,	*Bángphe.*
Kiranti Group (East Nepal).	Kiránti,	*Teng.*
	Rodong,	*Tūngmá.*
	Rúngchenbung,	*Teng.*
	Chhingtángya,	*Ten.*
	Náchhereng,	*Tyál.*
	Wáling,	*Teng.*
	Yákha,	*Ten.*
	Chourásya,	*Del.*
	Kulungya,	*Tel.*
	Thulungya,	*Del.*
	Báhingya,	*Dyal.*
	Lohorong,	*Gáṇ-wá.*
	Lambichhong,	*Ten.*
	Báláli,	*Ten.*
	Sáng-páng,	*Te.*
	Dúmi,	*Del.*
	Kháling,	*Del.*
	Dungmáli,	*Ten.*
Broken Tribes of Nepal.	Dárhi,	*Gáoṇ.*
	Denwár,	*Gáoṇ.*
	Pahri,	*Goṇ.*
	Chepáng,	*Caret.*
	Bhrámu,	*Háng dúng.*
	Váyu,	*Mulung.*
	Kuswar,	*Gáoṇ.*
	Kusunda,	*Láháng.*
	Tháru,	*Ga-woṇ.*
	Lepcha (Sikkim),	*Kyong.*
	Bhúṭáni v. Lhopa,	*Kyong.*

Group	Language	Village
N.-E. Bengal.	Bodo,	*Phárá.*
	Dhimál,	*Derá.*
	Kocch,	*Gáon, bondor.*
	Garo,	*Song.*
	Káchári,	*Caret.*
Eastern Frontier of Bengal.	Munipuri,	*Khul.*
	Mithán Nágá,	*Ting.*
	Tablung Nágá,	*Tying.*
	Khári Nágá,	*Ayim.*
	Angámi Nágá,	*Arame.*
	Námsáng Nágá,	*Há.*
	Nowgong Nágá,	*Yüm.*
	Tengsa Nágá,	*Yam.*
	Abor Miri,	*Dulong.*
	Sibságar Miri,	*Dolüng.*
	Deoria Chutia,	*A'tigu.*
	Singpho,	*Mereng.*
Arrakan & Burmah.	Burman (*written*),	*Rwá.*
	Burman (*spoken*),	*Yuá.*
	Khyeng v. Shou,	*Nám.*
	Kámi,	*Váng.*
	Kúmi,	*Aváng.*
	Mrú v. Toung,	*Kwá.*
	Sák,	*Thing.*
Siam & Tenasserim.	Talain v. Mon,	*Koh.*
	Sgau-karen,	*T'wau, kau.*
	Pwo-karen,	*Twan.*
	Toungh-thu,	*Dung.*
	Shán,	*Mann.*
	Annamitic,	*Láng.*
	Siamese,	*Pann, ban.*
	Ahom,	*Bán.*
	Khámti,	*Mán.*
	Laos,	*Ban.*
Central India.	Ho (Kol),	*Hattu.*
	Kol (Singhbhum),	*Hattu.*
	Santáli,	*A'to, haḍakundia, rásidto* (town).
	Bhúmij,	*Hathúje.*
	Uráon,	*Padda.*
	Mundala,	*Hátu.*
	Rájmahali,	*Kep.*
	Goṇḍi,	*Nár, nák* (pl.).
	Gayeti,	*Nár.*
	Rutluk,	*Caret.*
	Naikude,	*Ur.*
	Kolami,	*Ur.*
	Mádi,	*Náru, nágu.*
	Mádia,	*Nár.*
	Kuri,	*Gawa.*
	Keikádi,	*Uru.*
	Khoṇḍ,	*Náju.*
	Sávara,	*Gorajáng, ḍa.*
	Gadaba,	*Yiugoma.*
	Yerukala,	*Náḍu.*
	Chentsu,	*Gá.*
Southern India.	Tamiḷ, anc.,	*Pakkaṇam.*
	Tamiḷ, mod.,	*U'r.*
	Malayáḷma, anc.,	*Caret.*
	Malayáḷma, mod.,	*Kara, grámam.*
	Telugu,	*U'ru.*
	Karṇáṭaka, anc.,	*Paḷḷi.*
	Karṇáṭaka, mod.,	*Haḷḷi, uru.*
	Tuḷuva,	*U'ru.*
	Kurgi,	*Caret.*
	Toḍuva, Toḍa,	*Moḍḍ, mort. Haṭṭi, úr.*
	Kóta,	*Paṭṭi.*
	Baḍaga,	*Haṭṭi.*
	Kuṛumba,	*U'ru.*
	Iruḷa,	*U'ru.*
	Malabar,	*Kurichi, keramam.*
	Sinhalese,	*Gama.*

Group	Types.	
Inflecting.	SANSKRIT,	*Ap, vári, jala.*
	ARABIC,	*Ma.*
Compounding.	BASK,	*Ur.*
	FINNIC,	*Wesi.*
	MAGYAR,	*Viz.*
	TURKISH,	*Su.*
	CIRCASSIAN,	*Psi, psu, kinsi,* shin.**
	GEORGIAN,	*Tsgali, tszün.**
	MONGOLIAN,	*Oson, usun, üth,* gadar.*‖
	MANTSHU,	*Muke.*
	JAVANESE, Ngoko,	*Bannu.*
	JAVANESE, Krama,	*Toya.*
	MALAY,	*Ayar.*
Isolating.	CHINESE, Nankin,	*Shwui.*
	CHINESE, Pekin,	*Shui.*
	CHINESE, Canton,	*Shui.*
	CHINESE, Shanghai,	*S'.*
	AMOY, Colloquial,	*Chúi, súi.*
	JAPANESE,	*Mizzu.*
	Brahuí,	*Dír.*
Chinese Frontier & Tibet.	Gyámi,	*Shúi.*
	Gyárung,	*Tichí.*
	Tákpa,	*Chhí.*
	Mányak,	*Dyáḥ.*
	Thochú,	*Chah.*
	Sokpa,	*Wassú, úsú.*
	Horpa,	*Hraḥ.*
	Tibetan (*written*),	*Chhú.*
	Tibetan (*spoken*),	*Chhú.*
Nepal (east to west).	Serpa,	*Chhú.*
	Súnwár,	*Pankhu.*
	Gúrung,	*Kyú.*
	Múrmi,	*Kwí.*
	Magar,	*Dí.*
	Tháksya,	*Kya.*
	Pákhya,	*Páni.*
	Newár,	*Law, lá.*
	Limbu,	*Chúa.*
Kiranti Group (East Nepal).	Kiránti,	*Cháwá.*
	Rodong,	*Wa.*
	Rúngchenbung,	*Cháwá.*
	Chhingtángya,	*Chú-wá.*
	Náchhereng,	*Kaä-wá.*
	Wáling,	*Cha-wá.*
	Yákha,	*Mang chúwa.*
	Chourásya,	*Kákú.*
	Kulungya,	*Káu.*
	Thulungya,	*Kú.*
	Báhingya,	*Pwá-ku, bwá-pu.*
	Lohorong,	*Yowá.*
	Lambichhong,	*Chúwá.*
	Báláli,	*Kúngwá.*
	Sáng-páng,	*Wá, kánwá.*
	Dúmi,	*Kú.*
	Kháling,	*Kú.*
	Dungmáli,	*Cháliwá.*
Broken Tribes of Nepal.	Dárhi,	*Pati.*
	Denwár,	*Kyú.*
	Pahri,	*Lúkhú.*
	Chepáng,	*Ti.*
	Bhrámu,	*A'wá.*
	Váyu,	*Ti.*
	Kuswar,	*Páni.*
	Kusunda,	*Táng.*
	Tháru,	*Páni.*
	Lepcha (Sikkim),	*Ong.*
	Bhúṭáni v. Lhopa,	*Chhú.*

N.-E. Bengal.	Bodo,	*Doï.*
	Dhimál,	*Chí.*
	Kocch,	*Jál.*
	Garo,	*Chiká.*
	Kácharí,	*Doi, dai.*
Eastern Frontier of Bengal.	Munipuri,	*Ishing.*
	Mithán Nágá,	*Ti.*
	Tablung Nágá,	*Riang.*
	Khári Nágá,	*Atsü.*
	Angámi Nágá,	*Zü.*
	Námsáng Nágá,	*Jo.*
	Nowgong Nágá,	*Tsü.*
	Tengsa Nágá,	*Tü.*
	Abor Miri,	*A'ssi.*
	Sibságar Miri,	*A'che.*
	Deoria Chutia,	*Ji.*
	Singpho,	*Ntsin.*
Arrakan & Burmah.	Burman (*written*),	*Re.*
	Burman (*spoken*),	*Ye, ya.*
	Khyeng v. Shou,	*Túi.*
	Kámi,	*Túi.*
	Kúmi,	*Túi.*
	Mrú v. Toung,	*Túi.*
	Sák,	*O.*
Siam & Tenasserim.	Talain v. Mon,	*Dhihk.*
	Sgau-karen,	*Ti, thi, hti.*
	Pwo-karen,	*Ti.*
	Toungh-thu,	*HTi.*
	Shán,	*Náu.*
	Annamitic,	*Nu'ó'k.*
	Siamese,	*Nan, nam.*
	Ahom,	*Nam.*
	Khámti,	*Nam.*
	Laos,	*Nam.*
Central India.	Ho (Kol),	*Dah.*
	Kol (Singhbhum),	*Dáh.*
	Santáli,	*Dáh, ḍheo* (waves).
	Bhúmij,	*Dáh.*
	Uráon,	*Um, chëip.*
	Mundala,	*Dha.*
	Rájmahali,	*Am.*
	Goṇḍi,	*Yer.*
	Gayeti,	*Yer.*
	Rutluk,	*Er.*
	Naikude,	*Ir.*
	Kolami,	*Ir.*
	Mádi,	*Er, gegu.*
	Mádia,	*Per.*
	Kuri,	*Da.*
	Keikádi,	*Tanni.*
	Khoṇḍ,	*Srídrú.*
	Sávara,	*Dá.*
	Gadaba,	*Deyyá.*
	Yerukala,	*Tanni.*
	Chentsu,	*Páni.*
Southern India.	Tamiḷ, anc.,	*Punal.*
	Tamiḷ, mod.,	*Taṇṇír, nír.*
	Malayáḷma, anc.,	*Caret.*
	Malayáḷma, mod.,	*Veḷḷam, nír.*
	Telugu,	*Níllu.*
	Karṇáṭaka, anc.,	*Caret.*
	Karṇáṭaka, mod.,	*Níru.*
	Tuḷuva,	*Nír.*
	Kurgi,	*Níru.*
	Toḍuva, }	*Caret.*
	Toḍa, }	*Nír.*
	Kóta,	*Níre.*
	Baḍaga,	*Níru.*
	Kuṛumba,	*Níru.*
	Iruḷa,	*Dani.*
	Malabar,	*Thannír, nír, salam.*
	Sinhalese,	*Watura.*

	Types.	
Inflecting.	SANSKṚIT,	*S'rama.*
	ARABIC,	*Taab, aaná.*
Compounding.	BASK,	*Neke, neka, arika, laa, una [unasun, auno.*
	FINNIC,	*Tyo.*
	MAGYAR,	*Faradsag.*
	TURKISH,	*Yorghun.*
	CIRCASSIAN,	*Caret.*
	GEORGIAN,	*Caret.*
	MONGOLIAN,	*Ükseregu.*
	MANTSHU,	*Shodara.*
	JAVANESE, Ngoko,	*Chape.*
	JAVANESE, Krama,	*Chape.*
	MALAY,	*Lalah.*
Isolating.	CHINESE, Nankin,	*Pi-kiuen.*
	CHINESE, Pekin,	*P'i-chüan.*
	CHINESE, Canton,	*Kau-kün.*
	CHINESE, Shanghai,	*Sá-du.*
	AMOY, Colloquial,	*Sián, iá.*
	JAPANESE,	*Kutabuleru.*
	Brahuí,	*Caret.*
Chinese Frontier & Tibet.	Gyámi,	*Sphwá-leu.*
	Gyárung,	*Disdúk.*
	Tákpa,	*Caret.*
	Mányak,	*Ná-brida.*
	Thochú,	*Darvatch.*
	Sokpa,	*Yátava.*
	Horpa,	*Nerthá.*
	Tibetan (*written*),	*Caret.*
	Tibetan (*spoken*),	*Gyák.*
Nepal (east to west).	Serpa,	*Yeche.*
	Súnwár,	*Dati.*
	Gúrung,	*Bhlá.*
	Múrmi,	*Blap-chi.*
	Magar,	*Mhúncho.*
	Tháksya,	*Bhalápji.*
	Pákhya,	*Galelágyo.*
	Newár,	*Tyanu.*
	Limbu,	*Nama.*
Kiranti Group (East Nepal).	Kiránti,	*Hotáng.*
	Rodong,	*Hosá.*
	Rúngchenbung,	*Hottáng.*
	Chhingtángya,	*U'hottáng.*
	Náchhereng,	*Haya.*
	Wáling,	*U'hottáng.*
	Yákha,	*Yáksyángná.*
	Chourásya,	*Bál-me.*
	Kulungya,	*Gúmo.*
	Thulungya,	*Griúm-dá.*
	Báhingya,	*Bál.*
	Lohorong,	*Yáktáng.*
	Lambichhong,	*Sua.*
	Báláli,	*Yák'ta, yak.*
	Sáng-páng,	*Ho-yáṇ.*
	Dúmi,	*Ghrum'ma.*
	Kháling,	*Ghrima.*
	Dungmáli,	*Miho.*
Broken Tribes of Nepal.	Dárhi,	*Thákin.*
	Denwár,	*Hadyaila.*
	Pahri,	*Nelnu, ngalnu.*
	Chepáng,	*Caret.*
	Bhrámu,	*Kitukhwi.*
	Váyu,	*Job.*
	Kuswar,	*Caret.*
	Kusunda,	*Balangba.*
	Tháru,	*Thákali.*
	Lepcha (Sikkim),	*Pel.*
	Bhúṭáni v. Lhopa,	*Tháng-chhe.*

N.-E. Bengal.	Bodo,	*Mengbai, myengdúng.*
	Dhimál,	*Máïka.*
	Kocch,	*Thakáï.*
	Garo,	*Rewe kou.*
	Káchári,	*Caret.*
Eastern Frontier of Bengal.	Munipuri,	*Caret.*
	Míthán Nágá,	*Caret.*
	Tablung Nágá,	*Caret.*
	Khári Nágá,	*Caret.*
	Angámi Nágá,	*Caret.*
	Námsáng Nágá,	*Boau.*
	Nowgong Nágá,	*A'nyoko.*
	Tengsa Nágá,	*Ngüchaho.*
	Abor Miri,	*Caret.*
	Sibságar Miri,	*Amírse, molámak.*
	Deoria Chutia,	*Caret.*
	Singpho,	*Báhá.*
Arrakan & Burmah.	Burman (*written*),	*Mo, pangban.*
	Burman (*spoken*),	*Mo, penbán, anyoung.*
	Khyeng v. Shou,	*Rauo.*
	Kámi,	*Másá.*
	Kúmi,	*Akom.*
	Mrú v. Toung,	*Caret.*
	Sák,	*Caret.*
Siam & Tenasserim.	Talain v. Mon,	*Kawon.*
	Sgau-karen,	*Caret.*
	Pwo-karen,	*Caret.*
	Toungh-thu,	*Táwa.*
	Shán,	*Kon.*
	Annamitic,	*Nhok.*
	Siamese,	*Mai.*
	Ahom,	*Caret.*
	Khámti,	*Caret.*
	Laos,	*Caret.*
Central India.	Ho (Kol),	*Tagauteá.*
	Kol (Singhbhum),	*Esub lagiena.*
	Santáli,	*Lángáte* (verb), *lángiena, [dakhal* (adj.).
	Bhúmij,	*Laga jouále.*
	Uráon,	*Kháridkar.*
	Mundala,	*Thakana.*
	Rájmahali,	*Caret.*
	Goṇḍi,	*Dikmandatúr.*
	Gayeti,	*Caret.*
	Rutluk,	*Itore* (weak).
	Naikude,	*Caret.*
	Kolami,	*Sadamtarikam* (weak).
	Mádi,	*Caret.*
	Mádia,	*Caret.*
	Kuri,	*Bangbal* (weak).
	Keikádi,	*Dila* (weak).
	Khoṇḍ,	*Lahite.*
	Sávara,	*Caret.*
	Gadaba,	*Burre.*
	Yerukala,	*Ayyosu.*
	Chentsu,	*Haran, vusiki.*
Southern India.	Tamiḷ, anc.,	*Ayarvu.*
	Tamiḷ, mod.,	*Iḷeippu.*
	Malayáḷma, anc.,	*Caret.*
	Malayáḷma, mod.,	*Taḷarcha.*
	Telugu,	*Alupu.*
	Karṇáṭaka, anc.,	*Caret.*
	Karṇáṭaka, mod.,	*Daṇuvu.*
	Tuḷuva,	*Caret.*
	Kurgi,	*Caret.*
	Toḍuva, }	*Caret.*
	Toḍa, }	*Caret.*
	Kóta,	*Salupu.*
	Baḍaga,	*Salupu.*
	Kurumba,	*Salupu.*
	Iruḷa,	*Salipu.*
	Malabar,	*Ileittha, kalaittha.*
	Sinhalese,	*Wehesa.*

	Types.	
Inflecting.	SANSKṚIT,	*A'lu, madhumúlam.*
	ARABIC,	*Caret.*
Compounding.	BASK,	*Caret.*
	FINNIC,	*Caret.*
	MAGYAR,	*Caret.*
	TURKISH,	*Caret.*
	CIRCASSIAN,	*Caret.*
	GEORGIAN,	*Caret.*
	MONGOLIAN,	*Caret.*
	MANTSHU,	*Caret.*
	JAVANESE, Ngoko,	*Uwi.*
	JAVANESE, Krama,	*Uwi.*
	MALAY,	*Ubi, ubi-bangala.*
Isolating.	CHINESE, Nankin,	*Ta-shú.*
	CHINESE, Pekin,	*Ta-shú.*
	CHINESE, Canton,	*Tai-shü.*
	CHINESE, Shanghai,	*Saṇ-yáh.*
	AMOY, Colloquial,	*Toa-chû, ô.*
	JAPANESE,	*Imo, tsu-kemono.*
	Brahuí,	*Caret.*
Chinese Frontier & Tibet.	Gyámi,	*Yáng-sú.*
	Gyárung,	*Seten.*
	Tákpa,	*Khe.*
	Mányak,	*Zgwaḥ.*
	Thochú,	*Jyah.*
	Sokpa,	*Caret.*
	Horpa,	*Zo.*
	Tibetan (*written*),	*Dová.*
	Tibetan (*spoken*),	*Thomá.*
Nepal (east to west).	Serpa,	*Dhoa.*
	Súnwár,	*Rebe.*
	Gúrung,	*Taya.*
	Múrmi,	*Teme.*
	Magar,	*Námi.*
	Tháksya,	*Hmau dau.*
	Pákhya,	*Caret.*
	Newár,	*Hi.*
	Limbu,	*Khe.*
Kiranti Group (East Nepal).	Kiránti,	*Sáki.*
	Rodong,	*Soki.*
	Rúngchenbung,	*Sáki.*
	Chhingtángya,	*Khi-sú-wa.*
	Náchhereng,	*Khi-yok'sa.*
	Wáling,	*Sa-khi, yak.*
	Yákha,	*Khe, súchigwa.*
	Chourásya,	*Rang'jabí.*
	Kulungya,	*Khe.*
	Thulungya,	*Bálak'pu.*
	Báhingya,	*Rebe, swokokti.*
	Lohorong,	*Námkhe, sua, khibre.*
	Lambichhong,	*Nángkhi.*
	Báláli,	*Khú.*
	Sáng-páng,	*Khi.*
	Dúmi,	*Ki.*
	Kháling,	*Sásros.*
	Dungmáli,	*Sakhi.*
Broken Tribes of Nepal.	Dárhi,	*Pindlu.*
	Denwár,	*Cho-yán.*
	Pahri,	*Sági.*
	Chepáng,	*Goí.*
	Bhrámu,	*Yák.*
	Váyu,	*Rápí, chopi.*
	Kuswar,	*Geti, bhyágar.*
	Kusunda,	*Byalongolandán.*
	Tháru,	*Kanmul.*
	Lepcha (Sikkim),	*Buk.*
	Bhúṭáni v. Lhopa,	*Kyu.*

N.-E. Bengal.	Bodo,	*Thá.*
	Dhimál,	*Ling.*
	Kocch,	*A'lú.*
	Garo,	*Han.*
	Káchári,	*Caret.*
Eastern Frontier of Bengal.	Munipuri,	*Há.*
	Míthán Nágá,	*Caret.*
	Tablung Nágá,	*Caret.*
	Khári Nágá,	*Caret.*
	Angámi Nágá,	*Caret.*
	Námsáng Nágá,	*Há-khuon.*
	Nowgong Nágá,	*Shi.*
	Tengsa Nágá,	*Chu.*
	Abor Miri,	*Ngunü.*
	Sibságar Miri,	*A'lie.*
	Deoria Chutia,	*Caret.*
	Singpho,	*Nai.*
Arrakan & Burmah.	Burman (*written*),	*Myok.*
	Burman (*spoken*),	*Myauk.*
	Khyeng v. Shou,	*Bahá.*
	Kámi,	*Khá.*
	Kúmi,	*Ho.*
	Mrú v. Toung,	*Mau.*
	Sák,	*Kángkú.*
Siam & Tenasserim.	Talain v. Mon,	*Kawa.*
	Sgau-karen,	*Nwai, noe.*
	Pwo-karen,	*Nwá.*
	Toungh-thu,	*Nwá.*
	Shán,	*Ho-mau.*
	Annamitic,	*Caret.*
	Siamese,	*Mau, man-dom.*
	Ahom,	*Caret.*
	Khámti,	*Man.*
	Laos,	*Hoa-man.*
Central India.	Ho (Kol),	*Caret.*
	Kol (Singhbhum),	*Merumtosang.*
	Santáli,	*Sáng, sáṇ, gaṇa, kápu, kolo.*
	Bhúmij,	*Sángá.*
	Uráon,	*A'lu.*
	Mundala,	*A'ru.*
	Rájmahali,	*Caret.*
	Goṇḍi,	*Naska-kangda.*
	Gayeti,	*Caret.*
	Rutluk,	*Caret.*
	Naikude,	*Caret.*
	Kolami,	*Caret.*
	Mádi,	*Caret.*
	Mádia,	*Caret.*
	Kuri,	*Caret.*
	Keikádi,	*Caret.*
	Khoṇḍ,	*Gánḍikúna.*
	Sávara,	*Gane.*
	Gadaba,	*Dampu.*
	Yerukala,	*Aluvele.*
	Chentsu,	*Sarú, sakar kanda.*
Southern India.	Tamiḷ, anc.,	*Caret.*
	Tamiḷ, mod.,	*Vaḷḷi, kizhangu.*
	Malayáḷma, anc.,	*Caret.*
	Malayáḷma, mod.,	*Kizhangu, káchil.*
	Telugu,	*Peṇḍalamu.*
	Karṇáṭaka, anc.,	*Caret.*
	Karṇáṭaka, mod.,	*Caret.*
	Tuḷuva,	*Caret.*
	Kurgi,	*Caret.*
	Toḍuva, }	*Caret.*
	Toḍa, }	*Caret.*
	Kóta,	*Caret.*
	Baḍaga,	*Mulinge.*
	Kuṛumba,	*Caret.*
	Iruḷa,	*Caret.*
	Malabar,	*Kilangu.*
	Sinhalese,	*Ala.*

	Types.	
Inflecting.	SANSKRIT,	*Dushta, asat, nirguṇa.*
	ARABIC,	*Sharrír, radí.*
Compounding.	BASK,	*Gaizto, gesto, donge, deunge, [deunga.*
	FINNIC,	*Paha.*
	MAGYAR,	*Rosz.*
	TURKISH,	*Fena.*
	CIRCASSIAN,	*Bzaghey.*
	GEORGIAN,	*Tsughi.*
	MONGOLIAN,	*Ekel.*
	MANTSHU,	*Ekhe.*
	JAVANESE, Ngoko,	*Hala.*
	JAVANESE, Krama,	*Hawon.*
	MALAY,	*Jáhat, ta'baik.*
Isolating.	CHINESE, Nankin,	*Ngoh.*
	CHINESE, Pekin,	*O.*
	CHINESE, Canton,	*Ok.*
	CHINESE, Shanghai,	*Ch'eu; veh-hau* (not good).
	AMOY, Colloquial,	*P'áiṇ.*
	JAPANESE,	*Warui.*
	Brahuí,	*Gando.*
Chinese Frontier & Tibet.	Gyámi,	*Hou-ti-myú.*
	Gyárung,	*Makasne.*
	Tákpa,	*Lihúmani.*
	Mányak,	*Mánda.*
	Thochú,	*Ghái, ghé, mari.*
	Sokpa,	*Má-bene.*
	Horpa,	*Gáyenyer.*
	Tibetan (*written*),	*Nángpo.*
	Tibetan (*spoken*),	*Dúkpo.*
Nepal (east to west).	Serpa,	*Ma-lemú.*
	Súnwár,	*Marin-noso.*
	Gúrung,	*A'saba.*
	Múrmi,	*Ajába.*
	Magar,	*Mágyepche.*
	Thaksya,	*Na-ásba.*
	Pákhya,	*Ghatiya, behor.*
	Newár,	*Ma-bhing.*
	Limbu,	*Phem-ba, khepembo.*
Kiránti Group (East Nepal).	Kiránti,	*Auva.*
	Rodong,	*Ise, iseko.*
	Rúngchenbung,	*Enwo, ánúninko, cuttko.*
	Chhingtángya,	*It'no.*
	Náchhereng,	*Is'da.*
	Wáling,	*Noúdhoi, aitpa.*
	Yákha,	*Nu-nin-ha.*
	Chourásya,	*A'ḍúcho.*
	Kulungya,	*Man'noi, manno.*
	Thulungya,	*Minyúpa.*
	Báhingya,	*Mányúba.*
	Lohorong,	*Isa, phenni.*
	Lambichhong,	*Núyuk ninkha.*
	Bálálí,	*I'sáno, isa'p núnine.*
	Sáng-páng,	*I'si.*
	Dúmi,	*Múnlpa, mumyúpa.*
	Kháling,	*Mányúpa.*
	Dungmáli,	*I; ichle;*[1] *mayi.*[2]
Broken Tribes of Nepal.	Dárhi,	*Bontha.*
	Denwár,	*Bonsajha.*
	Pahri,	*Mabhingguhma.*
	Chepáng,	*Pilo.*
	Bhrámu,	*Mado.*
	Váyu,	*Maningnuhkamo.*
	Kuswar,	*Nakhaja.*
	Kusunda,	*Kaingbarai.*
	Tháru,	*Tniman.*
	Lepcha (Sikkim),	*Azyen, zyembo.*
	Bhúṭáni v. Lhopa,	*Ma-lem.*
N.-E. Bengal.	Bodo,	*Hamma.*
	Dhimál,	*Máelká.*
	Kocch,	*Mondo.*
	Garo,	*Sarchá.*
	Káchári,	*Húmma.*
Eastern Frontier of Bengal.	Munipuri,	*Phutte.*
	Míthán Nágá,	*Manmai.*
	Tablung Nágá,	*Yemei.*
	Khári Nágá,	*Maro.*
	Angámi Nágá,	*Sowe.*
	Námsáng Nágá,	*Achi.*
	Nowgong Nágá,	*Matsong.*
	Tengsa Nágá,	*Machong.*
	Abor Miri,	*Aimang.*
	Sibságar Miri,	*Aima.*
	Deoria Chutia,	*Chani.*
	Singpho,	*Ngaiá.*
Arrakan & Burmah.	Burman (*written*),	Chho.
	Burman (*spoken*),	S'*ho, makaung.*
	Khyeng v. Shou,	*Poya.*
	Kámi,	*S'hau.*
	Kúmi,	*Hauio.*
	Mrú v. Toung,	*Caret.*
	Sák,	*Caret.*
Siam & Tenasserim.	Talain v. Mon,	*Hakhá.*
	Sgau-karen,	*Er, aohh.*
	Pwo-karen,	*Ung.*
	Toungh-thu,	*Kay.*
	Shán,	*Mali.*
	Annamitic,	*Xâu.*
	Siamese,	*Chua, maidi, mali.*
	Ahom,	*Khyá.*
	Khámti,	*Mani.*
	Laos,	*Hái, bodi.*
Central India.	Ho (Kol),	*Etka.*
	Kol (Singhbhum),	*Etka.*
	Santáli,	*Báḍih, baḍiena.*
	Bhúmij,	*Júdajanna.*
	Uráon,	*Maldau.*
	Mundala,	*Káhesá.*
	Rájmahali,	*Báná.*
	Goṇḍi,	*Buromanda, kharab.*
	Gayeti,	*A'nemátal.*
	Rutluk,	*Buro.*
	Naikude,	*Nasadin.*
	Kolami,	*Karáb.*
	Mádi,	*Ládgor, lágo.*
	Mádia,	*Caret.*
	Kuri,	*Karáb.*
	Keikádi,	*Kettá.*
	Khoṇḍ,	*Nekkánju áye.*
	Sávara,	*Seḍele.*
	Gadaba,	*Nimmakávo.*
	Yerukala,	*Keṭṭa, keṭṭasu.*
	Chentsu,	*Kharáb.*
Southern India.	Tamiḷ, anc.,	*Caret.*
	Tamiḷ, mod.,	*Keṭṭa.*
	Malayáḷma, anc.,	*Caret.*
	Malayáḷma, mod.,	*Chitta, keṭṭa.*
	Telugu,	*Cheḍḍa.*
	Karṇáṭaka, anc.,	*Caret.*
	Karṇáṭaka, mod.,	*Keṭṭa.*
	Tuḷuva,	*Pedikaṭṭano.*
	Kurgi,	*Kuṭṭad.*
	Toḍuva, }	*Caret.*
	Toḍa, }	*Vollade.*
	Kóta,	*A'ga.*
	Baḍaga,	*Holla.*
	Kurumba,	*Keṭṭa.*
	Iruḷa,	*Polla.*
	Malabar,	*Akátha.*
	Sinhalese,	*Naraka.*

Group	Language	Bitter
	Types.	
Inflecting.	SANSKRIT,	Tikta.
Inflecting.	ARABIC,	Murr.
Compounding.	BASK,	Miñ, min, samiñ, samin, karmin, kuarats.
Compounding.	FINNIC,	Haikia.
Compounding.	MAGYAR,	Keserü.
Compounding.	TURKISH,	Aji.
Compounding.	CIRCASSIAN,	Diggi.
Compounding.	GEORGIAN,	Mtsare.
Compounding.	MONGOLIAN,	Gasigun.
Compounding.	MANTSHU,	Amtan, goshihun.
Compounding.	JAVANESE, Ngoko,	Pahit.
Compounding.	JAVANESE, Krama,	Pahit.
Compounding.	MALAY,	Páhit.
Isolating.	CHINESE, Nankin,	K'ü.
Isolating.	CHINESE, Pekin,	K'ú.
Isolating.	CHINESE, Canton,	Fú.
Isolating.	CHINESE, Shanghai,	Ku.
Isolating.	AMOY, Colloquial,	Kö.
Isolating.	JAPANESE,	Karai.
	Brahuí,	Kharen.
Chinese Frontier & Tibet.	Gyámi,	Khúti.
Chinese Frontier & Tibet.	Gyárung,	Kúchchék.
Chinese Frontier & Tibet.	Tákpa,	Khákbó.
Chinese Frontier & Tibet.	Mányak,	Dákhá.
Chinese Frontier & Tibet.	Thochú,	Khák.
Chinese Frontier & Tibet.	Sokpa,	Caret.
Chinese Frontier & Tibet.	Horpa,	Snésné.
Chinese Frontier & Tibet.	Tibetan (*written*),	Caret.
Chinese Frontier & Tibet.	Tibetan (*spoken*),	Kháko.
Nepal (east to west).	Serpa,	Khakti.
Nepal (east to west).	Súnwár,	Kaso.
Nepal (east to west).	Gúrung,	Kámba.
Nepal (east to west).	Múrmi,	Kámba.
Nepal (east to west).	Magar,	Khácho.
Nepal (east to west).	Tháksya,	Kambá.
Nepal (east to west).	Pákhya,	Tito.
Nepal (east to west).	Newár,	Khaiyú.
Nepal (east to west).	Limbu,	Kekhikpa.
Kiránti Group (East Nepal).	Kiránti,	Khákko.
Kiránti Group (East Nepal).	Rodong,	Khi-ke.
Kiránti Group (East Nepal).	Rúngchenbung,	Khá-kwa, khako.
Kiránti Group (East Nepal).	Chhingtángya,	Khak'no.
Kiránti Group (East Nepal).	Náchhereng,	Khik'da.
Kiránti Group (East Nepal).	Wáling,	Khak.
Kiránti Group (East Nepal).	Yákha,	Khika, khigha.
Kiránti Group (East Nepal).	Chourásya,	Khácho.
Kiránti Group (East Nepal).	Kulungya,	Khike.
Kiránti Group (East Nepal).	Thulungya,	Khépa.
Kiránti Group (East Nepal).	Báhingya,	Kába; -daäsi;[1] -daä.[2]
Kiránti Group (East Nepal).	Lohorong,	Khikta, khik'ka.
Kiránti Group (East Nepal).	Lambichhong,	Khik'yukha.
Kiránti Group (East Nepal).	Báláli,	Khyukúp, kheukup.
Kiránti Group (East Nepal).	Sáng-páng,	Khiki.
Kiránti Group (East Nepal).	Dúmi,	Khepa.
Kiránti Group (East Nepal).	Kháling,	Khápa.
Kiránti Group (East Nepal).	Dungmáli,	Khak, khak-chie,[1] makhák.[2]
Broken Tribes of Nepal.	Dárhi,	Tita.
Broken Tribes of Nepal.	Denwár,	Tita.
Broken Tribes of Nepal.	Pahri,	Khakhadha.
Broken Tribes of Nepal.	Chepáng,	Caret.
Broken Tribes of Nepal.	Bhrámu,	Kyakhai.
Broken Tribes of Nepal.	Váyu,	Khachim.
Broken Tribes of Nepal.	Kuswar,	Tito.
Broken Tribes of Nepal.	Kusunda,	Katuk.
Broken Tribes of Nepal.	Tháru,	Tin.
	Lepcha (Sikkim),	Akrim, krimbo.
	Bhúṭáni v. Lhopa,	Khákó.

Group	Language	Bitter
N.-E. Bengal.	Bodo,	Gakhá.
N.-E. Bengal.	Dhimál,	Khákká.
N.-E. Bengal.	Kocch,	Kaduva.
N.-E. Bengal.	Garo,	Háni.
N.-E. Bengal.	Káchári,	Goká.
Eastern Frontier of Bengal.	Munipuri,	Akhába.
Eastern Frontier of Bengal.	Míthán Nágá,	Khá.
Eastern Frontier of Bengal.	Tablung Nágá,	Khá.
Eastern Frontier of Bengal.	Khári Nágá,	Khá.
Eastern Frontier of Bengal.	Angámi Nágá,	Chási.
Eastern Frontier of Bengal.	Námsáng Nágá,	Akhá.
Eastern Frontier of Bengal.	Nowgong Nágá,	Paklá.
Eastern Frontier of Bengal.	Tengsa Nágá,	Paklá.
Eastern Frontier of Bengal.	Abor Miri,	Kónam.
Eastern Frontier of Bengal.	Sibságar Miri,	Kodák.
Eastern Frontier of Bengal.	Deoria Chutia,	Kai.
Eastern Frontier of Bengal.	Singpho,	Khá.
Arrakan & Burmah.	Burman (*written*),	Khá.
Arrakan & Burmah.	Burman (*spoken*),	Khá, chháthi.
Arrakan & Burmah.	Khyeng v. Shou,	Khau.
Arrakan & Burmah.	Kámi,	Khá.
Arrakan & Burmah.	Kúmi,	Akho.
Arrakan & Burmah.	Mrú v. Toung,	Caret.
Arrakan & Burmah.	Sák,	Caret.
Siam & Tenasserim.	Talain v. Mon,	Ka-tau.
Siam & Tenasserim.	Sgau-karen,	Kah, kha.
Siam & Tenasserim.	Pwo-karen,	Khah.
Siam & Tenasserim.	Toungh-thu,	Khu.
Siam & Tenasserim.	Shán,	Khon.
Siam & Tenasserim.	Annamitic,	Dang.
Siam & Tenasserim.	Siamese,	Khóm, khon.
Siam & Tenasserim.	Ahom,	Khum.
Siam & Tenasserim.	Khámti,	Khóm.
Siam & Tenasserim.	Laos,	Khóm.
Central India.	Ho (Kol),	Moroia.
Central India.	Kol (Singhbhum),	Hárdá.
Central India.	Santáli,	Haḍhat.
Central India.	Bhúmij,	Harrada.
Central India.	Uráon,	Harkhá.
Central India.	Mundala,	Harpand.
Central India.	Rájmahali,	Karkeh.
Central India.	Goṇḍi,	Kaḍúta, kaitá.
Central India.	Gayeti,	Keiemul.
Central India.	Rutluk,	Keitá.
Central India.	Naikude,	Send.
Central India.	Kolami,	Chendu.
Central India.	Mádi,	Kahitá.
Central India.	Mádia,	Keile.
Central India.	Kuri,	Katik.
Central India.	Keikádi,	Kachu.
Central India.	Khoṇḍ,	Pittáyine.
Central India.	Sávara,	Asa.
Central India.	Gadaba,	Vusám.
Central India.	Yerukala,	Ketstsu.
Central India.	Chentsu,	Titto.
Southern India.	Tamiḷ, anc.,	Caret.
Southern India.	Tamiḷ, mod.,	Kasanda, kasappu.
Southern India.	Malayáḷma, anc.,	Caret.
Southern India.	Malayáḷma, mod.,	Kaippuḷḷa.
Southern India.	Telugu,	Chédu.
Southern India.	Karṇáṭaka, anc.,	Caret.
Southern India.	Karṇáṭaka, mod.,	Khayyi.
Southern India.	Tuḷuva,	Khayipe.
Southern India.	Kurgi,	Kaipal.
Southern India.	Toḍuva,	Kachchatt.
Southern India.	Toḍa,	Káthti.
Southern India.	Kóta,	Kaju.
Southern India.	Badaga,	Káhi.
Southern India.	Kuṟumba,	Káhi.
Southern India.	Iruḷa,	Késape.
Southern India.	Malabar,	Kasappu.
Southern India.	Sinhalese,	Titta.

Group	Types.	
Inflecting.	SANSKṚIT,	*Kṛishṇa, śyáma, kála.*
	ARABIC,	*Aswad.*
Compounding.	BASK,	*Beltz, belch, baltz, balch.*
	FINNIC,	*Musta.*
	MAGYAR,	*Fekete.*
	TURKISH,	*Kara.*
	CIRCASSIAN,	*Shudzah.*
	GEORGIAN,	*Shavi.*
	MONGOLIAN,	*Khara.*
	MANTSHU,	*Sakhaliyan.*
	JAVANESE, Ngoko,	*Hirĕng.*
	JAVANESE, Krama,	*Chemeng.*
	MALAY,	*Hitam.*
Isolating.	CHINESE, Nankin,	*Heh.*
	CHINESE, Pekin,	*He.*
	CHINESE, Canton,	*Hak.*
	CHINESE, Shanghai,	*Hah.*
	AMOY, Colloquial,	*O.*
	JAPANESE,	*Kuroi.*
	Brahuí,	*Mon.*
Chinese Frontier & Tibet.	Gyámi,	*Khidi.*
	Gyárung,	*Kanak.*
	Tákpa,	*Nak-po.*
	Mányak,	*Dáná.*
	Thochú,	*Nyik.*
	Sokpa,	*Caret.*
	Horpa,	*Nyá-nyá.*
	Tibetan (*written*),	*Nágpo.*
	Tibetan (*spoken*),	*Nákpo.*
Nepal (east to west).	Serpa,	*Nakpo.*
	Súnwár,	*Kerá.*
	Gúrung,	*Mlongyá.*
	Múrmi,	*Mlángai.*
	Magar,	*Chik chi dancho.*
	Tháksya,	*Maláng.*
	Pákhya,	*Kálo.*
	Newár,	*Hákú.*
	Limbu,	*Kúmaklá.*
Kiranti Group (East Nepal).	Kiránti,	*Mákachakwa.*
	Rodong,	*Makchúma.*
	Rúngchenbung,	*Mak-chakmá.*
	Chhingtángya,	*Mákkachúkma.*
	Náchhereng,	*Mokchibpa.*
	Wáling,	*Mákchúma, makchakchak.*
	Yákha,	*Makhrúna.*
	Chourásya,	*Khúchy'amo.*
	Kulungya,	*Gúgrúpa.*
	Thulungya,	*Kekema.*
	Báhingya,	*Kyákyám.*
	Lohorong,	*Maik'ye, maiye.*
	Lambichhong,	*Mayukkha.*
	Bálálí,	*Makthropa.*
	Sáng-páng,	*Mao, makachik'pa.*
	Dúmi,	*Mak'chupu.*
	Khálíng,	*Kekem.*
	Dungmáli,	*Mákchácha, makchak',*[2] *chak chiye.*[1]
Broken Tribes of Nepal.	Dárhi,	*Kajráro.*
	Denwár,	*Kárda.*
	Pahri,	*Hákuguhona.*
	Chepáng,	*Galto.*
	Bhrámu,	*Chiling.*
	Váyu,	*Khakchingmi.*
	Kuswar,	*Kalda.*
	Kusunda,	*Pángsing.*
	Tháru,	*Kariyá.*
	Lepcha (Sikkim),	*Anok.*
	Bhúṭáni v. Lhopa,	*Nákpo.*

N.-E. Bengal.	Bodo,	*Gatcham, gotchom.*
	Dhimál,	*Dáaká.*
	Kocch,	*Kála.*
	Garo,	*Penck.*
	Káchári,	*Kán-s'ibai* (darkness).
Eastern Frontier of Bengal.	Munipuri,	*Amuba.*
	Míthán Nágá,	*Nak.*
	Tablung Nágá,	*Niak.*
	Khári Nágá,	*Nak.*
	Angámi Nágá,	*Kati.*
	Námsáng Nágá,	*Anyak.*
	Nowgong Nágá,	*Tanak.*
	Tengsa Nágá,	*Nyakla.*
	Abor Miri,	*Yákár.*
	Sibságar Miri,	*Yákádák.*
	Deoria Chutia,	*Sakokoi.*
	Singpho,	*Cháng.*
Arrakan & Burmah.	Burman (*written*),	*Nak.*
	Burman (*spoken*),	*Net, maithí.*
	Khyeng v. Shou,	*Kán.*
	Kámi,	*Manún.*
	Kúmi,	*Kanúm.*
	Mrú v. Toung,	*Caret.*
	Sák,	*Caret.*
Siam & Tenasserim.	Talain v. Mon,	*Katsau.*
	Sgau-karen,	*Thu, athu.*
	Pwo-karen,	*Thung.*
	Toungh-thu,	*Phren.*
	Shán,	*Lan.*
	Annamitic,	Den.
	Siamese,	*Dam, lan.*
	Ahom,	*Dam.*
	Khámti,	*Nam.*
	Laos,	*Dam, nin.*
Central India.	Ho (Kol),	*Hende.*
	Kol (Singhbhum),	*Hende.*
	Santáli,	*Heṇḍe, káṇáng-káṇáng* (dark), *hende.*
	Bhúmij,	*Hende.*
	Uráon,	*Mokharo.*
	Mundala,	*Hendi.*
	Rájmahali,	*Márgo.*
	Goṇḍi,	*Kariyal.*
	Gayeti,	*Kadiyal.*
	Rutluk,	*Kariyal.*
	Naikude,	*Mulludi.*
	Kolami,	*Dowdankari.*
	Mádi,	*Kariyál, jurtor, karkál.*
	Mádia,	*Kariyál.*
	Kuri,	*Kende.*
	Keikádi,	*Karupu.*
	Khoṇḍ,	*Káláján á.*
	Sávara,	*Je.*
	Gadaba,	*Yiḍe.*
	Yerukala,	*Kaleḍe.*
	Chentsu,	*Kallá, kalḷṭa.*
Southern India.	Tamiḷ, anc.,	*Kariya.*
	Tamiḷ, mod.,	*Kaṛutta, kaṛuppána.*
	Malayáḷma, anc.,	*Caret.*
	Malayáḷma, mod.,	*Kaṛutta.*
	Telugu,	*Nalla, nalupu.*
	Karṇáṭaka, anc.,	*Caret.*
	Karṇáṭaka, mod.,	*Kari.*
	Tuḷuva,	*Khappa.*
	Kurgi,	*Kartad.*
	Toḍuva, }	*Kapp.*
	Toḍa, }	*Kárthti.*
	Kóta,	*Kari.*
	Baḍaga,	*Kari, kappu.*
	Kuṛumba,	*Koppu.*
	Iruḷa,	*Kari.*
	Malabar,	*Karuppu.*
	Sinhalese,	*Kalu.*

	Types.	
Inflecting.	SANSKRIT,	*S'ita, s'ítala.*
	ARABIC,	*Bárid, bardán.*
Compounding.	BASK,	*Otz.*
	FINNIC,	*Kylinä.*
	MAGYAR,	*Hideg.*
	TURKISH,	*Söuk.*
	CIRCASSIAN,	*Tshi-et-sha.*
	GEORGIAN,	*Grili.*
	MONGOLIAN,	*Ködun.*
	MANTSHU,	*Shakhorun.*
	JAVANESE, Ngoko,	*Hadem.*
	JAVANESE, Krama,	*Hasrĕp.*
	MALAY,	*Dingin, sujok, salismah.*
Isolating.	CHINESE, Nankin,	*Lang, tung.*
	CHINESE, Pekin,	*Lang, tung.*
	CHINESE, Canton,	*Láng, tung.*
	CHINESE, Shanghai,	*Láng.*
	AMOY, Colloquial,	*Kóan.*
	JAPANESE,	*Samui.*
	Brahuí,	*Yakhí.*
Chinese Frontier & Tibet.	Gyámi,	*Sidi.*
	Gyárung,	*Kavandro, kamishta.*
	Tákpa,	*Krangmo.*
	Mányak,	*Phemphe.*
	Thochú,	*Styú.*
	Sokpa,	*Khouthún.*
	Horpa,	*Kúrkú.*
	Tibetan (*written*),	*Grángpo.*
	Tibetan (*spoken*),	*Thammo.*
Nepal (east to west).	Serpa,	*Thyángmo.*
	Súnwár,	*Chiso.*
	Gúrung,	*Simba.*
	Múrmi,	*Simba.*
	Magar,	*Ringcho.*
	Thaksya,	*Sim.*
	Pákhya,	*Chiso.*
	Newár,	*Khwá-won.*
	Limbu,	*Kesemba, semba.*
Kiranti Group (East Nepal).	Kiránti,	*Kengyong.*
	Rodong,	*Chiso.*
	Rúngchenbung,	*Kengko, kengmangwa.*
	Chhingtángya,	*Remno.*
	Náchhereng,	*Chhik'da.*
	Wáling,	*Wache'yang.*
	Yákha,	*Chiha.*
	Chourásya,	*Chiso.*
	Kulungya,	*Chhike, chia.*
	Thulungya,	*Chhákpa.*
	Báhingya,	*Chhikba.*
	Lohorong,	*Yepse, yempa.*
	Lambichhong,	*Chiyúkha.*
	Bálali,	*Ipchhiyúne.*
	Sáng-páng,	*Chhiki.*
	Dúmi,	*Chhú.*
	Kháling,	*Chhak'pa.*
	Dungmáli,	*Keng, keng'che,*[1] *mákeng.*[2]
Broken Tribes of Nepal.	Dárhi,	*Chiso.*
	Denwár,	*Chiso.*
	Pahri,	*Khukhudha.*
	Chepáng,	*Yesto.*
	Bhrámu,	*Chiso.*
	Váyu,	*Khemta.*
	Kuswar,	*Chiso.*
	Kusunda,	*Kháng-go.*
	Tháru,	*Thandá.*
	Lepcha (Sikkim),	*Ahyúm, hyumbo.*
	Bhútáni v. Lhopa,	*Khyú-mo.*
N.-E. Bengal.	Bodo,	*Gúshú.*
	Dhimál,	*Tirká.*
	Kocch,	*Thanda.*
	Garo,	*Chikrop.*
	Káchári,	*Gosha.*
Eastern Frontier of Bengal.	Munipuri,	*Ayingba.*
	Míthán Nágá,	*Ráng-kham.*
	Tablung Nágá,	*Wang-sam.*
	Khári Nágá,	*Aiyang.*
	Angámi Nágá,	*Si.*
	Námsáng Nágá,	*Aki.*
	Nowgong Nágá,	*Kádsütá.*
	Tengsa Nágá,	*A'chikab.*
	Abor Miri,	*Ansinge.*
	Sibságar Miri,	*Ansinge, sikkire.*
	Deoria Chutia,	*Chepepe.*
	Singpho,	*Katsí.*
Arrakan & Burmah.	Burman (*written*),	*Khyam, e.*
	Burman (*spoken*),	*Khyán, e, chyannthí.*
	Khyeng v. Shou,	*Kayoung.*
	Kámi,	*De, di.*
	Kúmi,	*Siwái.*
	Mrú v. Toung,	*Caret.*
	Sák,	*Caret.*
Siam & Tenasserim.	Talain v. Mon,	*Ba.*
	Sgau-karen,	*Gho.*
	Pwo-karen,	*Tser gaung.*
	Toungh-thu,	*Khwá.*
	Shán,	*Kat.*
	Annamitic,	*Lañ.*
	Siamese,	*Yen, náu, kaun.*
	Ahom,	*Khye, náu.*
	Khámti,	*Yen.*
	Laos,	*Náu, yen.*
Central India.	Ho (Kol),	*Rabang.*
	Kol (Singhbhum),	*Rabang.*
	Santáli,	*Rábáng, hemaol, rátáng* [(frost).
	Bhúmij,	*Rabang.*
	Uráon,	*Ekh.*
	Mundala,	*Reártana.*
	Rájmahali,	*Paniai.*
	Gondi,	*Mudungtá, múragtá.*
	Gayeti,	*Mudungtal.*
	Rutluk,	*Marustá.*
	Naikude,	*Igam.*
	Kolami,	*Pani.*
	Mádi,	*Dalangtá, kinda, keringtá.*
	Mádia,	*Caret.*
	Kuri,	*Chamrabáng, rarang.*
	Keikádi,	*Idá.*
	Khond,	*Jilliminju.*
	Sávara,	*Sayi vudede.*
	Gadaba,	*Tsallari.*
	Yerukala,	*Musunu.*
	Chentsu,	*Sittalá.*
Southern India.	Tamil, anc.,	*Tanniya.*
	Tamil, mod.,	*Kulirnda, sidalamana.*
	Malayálma, anc.,	*Caret.*
	Malayálma, mod.,	*Tanutta.*
	Telugu,	*Challani.*
	Karnátaka, anc.,	*Caret.*
	Karnátaka, mod.,	*Tampu.*
	Tuluva,	*Ch'hali.*
	Kurgi,	*Kultat.*
	Toduva, }	*Pillele.*
	Toda, }	*Perthti, kuorthti.*
	Kóta,	*Jalli.*
	Badaga,	*Jalli, koravu.*
	Kurumba,	*Jei.*
	Irula,	*Jalli.*
	Malabar,	*Kulirmei.*
	Sinhalese,	*Sitala.*

	Types.	
Inflecting.	SANSKRIT,	*Vakra, kuṭila.*
	ARABIC,	*Aaway.*
Compounding.	BASK,	*Makur.*
	FINNIC,	*Wäära.*
	MAGYAR,	*Gürbe.*
	TURKISH,	*Egri, eyri.*
	CIRCASSIAN,	*Bittey.*
	GEORGIAN,	*Mrudi.*
	MONGOLIAN,	*Bökedör, beyedei.*
	MANTSHU,	*Mudangga.*
	JAVANESE, Ngoko,	*Beng-kong.*
	JAVANESE, Krama,	*Beng-kong.*
	MALAY,	*Bangkok.*
Isolating.	CHINESE, Nankin,	*Wáu-k'iuh.*
	CHINESE, Pekin,	*Wáu-chü.*
	CHINESE, Canton,	*Huk.*
	CHINESE, Shanghai,	*K'öh, giöh.*
	AMOY, Colloquial,	*Oai.*
	JAPANESE,	*Magalu.*
	Brahuí,	*Caret.*
Chinese Frontier & Tibet.	Gyámi,	*Tingdimyú.*
	Gyárung,	*Makas'to.*
	Tákpa,	*Kyok-po.*
	Mányak,	*Kho-kho.*
	Thochú,	*Jaggra, jablá-give.*
	Sokpa,	*Caret.*
	Horpa,	*Gúngú.*
	Tibetan (*written*),	*Sgúrbo, túdpo.*
	Tibetan (*spoken*),	*Kákpo.*
Nepal (east to west).	Serpa,	*Kok-lok.*
	Súnwár,	*Bángo.*
	Gúrung,	*Kúding.*
	Múrmi,	*Kokteng.*
	Magar,	*Gúmcho.*
	Tháksya,	*Yeba.*
	Pákhya,	*Báng-go.*
	Newár,	*Beko.*
	Limbu,	*Koktú.*
Kiránti Group (East Nepal).	Kiránti,	*U'dungú twon tong.*
	Rodong,	*Bánggo, koko dyú pa.*
	Rúngchenbung,	*Yektu, ukudak dak.*
	Chhingtángya,	*Byángkruk.*
	Náchhereng,	*Bánggo.*
	Wáling,	*Bánggo.*
	Yákha,	*Yegekna, yekyang.*
	Chourásya,	*Ulgúmcho.*
	Kulungya,	*Mantwáipa.*
	Thulungya,	*Mijotgpa.*
	Báhingya,	*Madyom'ba, gung-gung-me.*
	Lohorong,	*Khokho, O'ok'ye.*
	Lambichhong,	*O'krik'pa, bang'krik-pa.*
	Báláli,	*Khok-khokpugu.*
	Sáng-páng,	*Toh' noná.*
	Dúmi,	*Khráda.*
	Kháling,	*Gúnggúng-ma.*
	Dungmáli,	*Okrokrak'chi.*
Broken Tribes of Nepal.	Dárhi,	*Kwonkáro.*
	Denwár,	*Bánko.*
	Pahri,	*Pharasogumna.*
	Chepáng,	*Dongto.*
	Bhrámu,	*Bángo.*
	Váyu,	*Kokolángmo.*
	Kuswar,	*Bángo.*
	Kusunda,	*Wáng-káng.*
	Tháru,	*Tat.*
	Lepcha (Sikkim),	*Mandng.*
	Bhúṭáni v. Lhopa,	*Tyokkú.*

N.-E. Bengal.	Bodo,	*Khúngkrá, khongkra.*
	Dhimál,	*Kyoká.*
	Kocch,	*Beka.*
	Garo,	*Kákroï.*
	Káchári,	*Caret.*
Eastern Frontier of Bengal.	Munipuri,	*Khoye.*
	Míthán Nágá,	*Kom.*
	Tablung Nágá,	*Kom.*
	Khári Nágá,	*Tikihang.*
	Angámi Nágá,	*Krewi.*
	Námsáng Nágá,	*Akuang.*
	Nowgong Nágá,	*Tikrak.*
	Tengsa Nágá,	*Koikolo.*
	Abor Miri,	*Muwat, gado.*
	Sibságar Miri,	*Gudák.*
	Deoria Chutia,	*Kekurai.*
	Singpho,	*Mágo.*
Arrakan & Burmah.	Burman (*written*),	*Kok.*
	Burman (*spoken*),	*Kauk, kaukthi.*
	Khyeng v. Shou,	*Kolák.*
	Kámi,	*Tako.*
	Kúmi,	*Akwe.*
	Mrú v. Toung,	*Caret.*
	Sák,	*Caret.*
Siam & Tenasserim.	Talain v. Mon,	*Tanouk.*
	Sgau-karen,	*Ká, t'blir.*
	Pwo-karen,	*Kaing.*
	Toungh-thu,	*Ngáken.*
	Shán,	*Kot.*
	Annamitic,	*Vay.*
	Siamese,	*Ngo, kot.*
	Ahom,	*Ke, ngok.*
	Khámti,	*Ngok.*
	Laos,	*Kom, kot.*
Central India.	Ho (Kol),	*Caret.*
	Kol (Singhbhum),	*Kochamocha.*
	Santáli,	*Lungkambeh.*
	Bhúmij,	*Hessú bánka.*
	Uráon,	*Bengko.*
	Mundala,	*Kekúndo.*
	Rájmahali,	*Sero.*
	Goṇḍi,	*Teḍho, hekodal.*
	Gayeti,	*Waritá.*
	Rutluk,	*Wariál.*
	Naikude,	*Wánkade.*
	Kolami,	*Sarase.*
	Mádi,	*Waktá, adám, wadeg.*
	Mádia,	*A'daphi.*
	Kuri,	*Kwocha.*
	Keikádi,	*Wánká.*
	Khoṇḍ,	*Baukaḍḍjúne.*
	Sávara,	*Kokkade.*
	Gadaba,	*Dairoyi.*
	Yerukala,	*Vankara.*
	Chentsu,	*Banko.*
Southern India.	Tamiḷ, anc.,	*Koḍiya.*
	Tamiḷ, mod.,	*Kóṇiya, kóṇalána.*
	Malayáḷma, anc.,	*Caret.*
	Malayáḷma, mod.,	*Valanga.*
	Telugu,	*Vankara.*
	Karṇáṭaka, anc.,	*Caret.*
	Karṇáṭaka, mod.,	*Soṭṭa.*
	Tuḷuva,	*Mont.*
	Kurgi,	*Caret.*
	Toḍuva,	*Caret.*
	Toḍa,	*Balug.*
	Kóta,	*Kenke.*
	Baḍaga,	*Gokke.*
	Kuṛumba,	*Gokke.*
	Iruḷa,	*Kokki.*
	Malabar,	*Konal.*
	Sinhalese,	*Äda.*

Group	Types.	
Inflecting.	SANSKṚIT,	*Pivara, pína, pushṭa.*
	ARABIC,	*Náṣiḥ, samín.*
Compounding.	BASK,	*Gizen, lodi.*
	FINNIC,	*Lihawa.*
	MAGYAR,	*Kövér.*
	TURKISH,	*Semiz.*
	CIRCASSIAN,	*Tsheh.*
	GEORGIAN,	*Caret.*
	MONGOLIAN,	*Boghisa.*
	MANTSHU,	*Tchalukha.*
	JAVANESE, Ngoko,	*Lĕmu.*
	JAVANESE, Krama,	*Lĕma.*
	MALAY,	*Gamúk.*
Isolating.	CHINESE, Nankin,	*Fi.*
	CHINESE, Pekin,	*Fei.*
	CHINESE, Canton,	*Fi.*
	CHINESE, Shanghai,	*Ts'ong.*
	AMOY, Colloquial,	*Púi.*
	JAPANESE,	*Futotoru.*
	Brahuí,	*Caret.*
Chinese Frontier & Tibet.	Gyámi,	*Houti.*
	Gyárung,	*Kwipan.*
	Tákpa,	*Gyák-pa.*
	Mányak,	*Dachúḥ.*
	Thochú,	*Charwá.*
	Sokpa,	*Yokhwe-the.*
	Horpa,	*Kalbo, galvo.*
	Tibetan (*written*),	*Rgyagspo.*
	Tibetan (*spoken*),	*Tho-thombo.*
Nepal (east to west).	Serpa,	*Gyámo.*
	Súnwár,	*Dúmso.*
	Gúrung,	*Choba.*
	Múrmi,	*Choba.*
	Magar,	*Dhesho.*
	Tháksya,	*Dhumlwa.*
	Pákhya,	*Moto.*
	Newár,	*Lhong.*
	Limbu,	*Mehrú.*
Kiranti Group (East Nepal).	Kiránti,	*Tok-páṇ.*
	Rodong,	*Lete.*
	Rúngchenbung,	*Leyángko, tokpang, chhuwo.*
	Chhingtángya,	*U'sámtáno.*
	Náchhereng,	*U'mdhep pálidda.*
	Wáling,	*Chipto, badhepo, lebyang.*
	Yákha,	*Yemnúbá.*
	Chourásya,	*Kholbo.*
	Kulungya,	*Leipá.*
	Thulungya,	*Senipá.*
	Báhingya,	*Seneúba.*
	Lohorong,	*Yámmuye.*
	Lambichhong,	*Isamtai mekha.*
	Báláli,	*Yámtnu dhepa.*
	Sáng-páng,	*Litiko.*
	Dúmi,	*Leï.*
	Kháling,	*Senupá.*
	Dungmáli,	*Dhi.*
Broken Tribes of Nepal.	Dárhi,	*Moto.*
	Denwár,	*Moto.*
	Pahri,	*Lhonghmo.*
	Chepáng,	*Caret.*
	Bhrámu,	*Kichho.*
	Váyu,	*Lonta.*
	Kuswar,	*Moto.*
	Kusunda,	*Biji.*
	Tháru,	*Mot.*
	Lepcha (Sikkim),	*Asyúm, syumbo.*
	Bhúṭáni v. Lhopa,	*Gyámo.*

N.-E. Bengal.	Bodo,	*Gúphúng.*
	Dhimál,	*Dhámká, chopka.*
	Kocch,	*Mota.*
	Garo,	*Kánentwa.*
	Káchári,	*Caret.*
Eastern Frontier of Bengal.	Munipuri,	*Caret.*
	Míthán Nágá,	*Chong.*
	Tablung Nágá,	*Nittan.*
	Khári Nágá,	*Tabiti.*
	Angámi Nágá,	*Pomoja.*
	Námsáng Nágá,	*Atat.*
	Nowgong Nágá,	*Tabok.*
	Tengsa Nágá,	*Tabok.*
	Abor Miri,	*Udo.*
	Sibságar Miri,	*Juiname.*
	Deoria Chutia,	*Mejirini.*
	Singpho,	*Phúm.*
Arrakan & Burmah.	Burman (*written*),	*Wa, tup.*
	Burman (*spoken*),	*Wa, tok, wauthi.*
	Khyeng v. Shou,	*Thoi.*
	Kámi,	*Len.*
	Kúmi,	*Len.*
	Mrú v. Toung,	*Caret.*
	Sák,	*Caret.*
Siam & Tenasserim.	Talain v. Mon,	*Kara.*
	Sgau-karen,	*Caret.*
	Pwo-karen,	*Caret.*
	Toungh-thu,	*Pay.*
	Shán,	*Payi.*
	Annamitic,	*Day.*
	Siamese,	*Awen, sai, man.*
	Ahom,	*Pi.*
	Khámti,	*Pi.*
	Laos,	*Pi, tui.*
Central India.	Ho (Kol),	*Rota.*
	Kol (Singhbhum),	*Kiriená.*
	Santáli,	*Legesáḥ, saraïh-leko, járiḍang-sánghi.*
	Bhúmij,	*Barai, mota.*
	Uráon,	*Mota.*
	Mundala,	*Mota.*
	Rájmahali,	*Gandi tarve.*
	Goṇḍi,	*Khodavinch, tajo, moto.*
	Gayeti,	*Kodavij.*
	Rutluk,	*Korbis, karal.*
	Naikude,	*Koru.*
	Kolami,	*Korau, kubamon.*
	Mádi,	*Koduwasku, kosela, berpor, mendul.*
	Mádia,	*Caret.*
	Kuri,	*Charbi, bedeka.*
	Keikádi,	*Nono, todu.*
	Khoṇḍ,	*Gellu ayininju.*
	Sávara,	*Kovvudele.*
	Gadaba,	*Bhirúgu.*
	Yerukala,	*Kovvitsu, nenamu.*
	Chentsu,	*Telubhariya, tellaraṭa.*
Southern India.	Tamiḷ, anc.,	*Vaḷatta.*
	Tamiḷ, mod.,	*Kozhuppána, vaḷappamána, koḷuppu.*
	Malayáḷma, anc.,	*Caret.*
	Malayáḷma, mod.,	*Kozhutta.*
	Telugu,	*Kovvina, kovvu, balinina.*
	Karṇáṭaka, anc.,	*Caret.*
	Karṇáṭaka, mod.,	*Kobbina.*
	Tuḷuva,	*Thora.*
	Kurgi,	*Caret.*
	Toḍuva,	*Pekkam.*
	Toḍa,	*Bechiti.*
	Kóta,	*Porále.*
	Baḍaga,	*Kobbu.*
	Kuṟumba,	*Gobbu.*
	Iruḷa,	*Kolupu.*
	Malabar,	*Koluttha, thúlitha.*
	Sinhalese,	*Tara.*

	Types.	
Inflecting.	SANSKRIT, ...	*Sama, samána, sapáṭa.*
	ARABIC, ...	*Basíṭ, musaṭṭaḥ.*
Compounding.	BASK, ...	*Zelai, lauba, naba, planu.*
	FINNIC, ...	*Tasa.*
	MAGYAR, ...	*Sik.*
	TURKISH, ...	*Duz.*
	CIRCASSIAN, ...	*Caret.*
	GEORGIAN, ...	*Pḷgeli, sada.*
	MONGOLIAN, ...	*Khaptagai.*
	MANTSHU, ...	*Khalfiyan.*
	JAVANESE, Ngoko, . .	*Rata.*
	JAVANESE, Krama, . .	*Rachin.*
	MALAY, ...	*Ráta.*
Isolating.	CHINESE, Nankin, . .	*P'ing.*
	CHINESE, Pekin, . .	*P'ing.*
	CHINESE, Canton, . .	*P'ing.*
	CHINESE, Shanghai, .	*Bing.*
	AMOY, Colloquial, . .	*Piṇ.*
	JAPANESE, ...	*Hilatai.*
	Brahuí, ...	*Caret.*
Chinese Frontier & Tibet.	Gyámi, ...	*Caret.*
	Gyárung, ...	*Caret.*
	Tákpa, ...	*Caret.*
	Mányak, ...	*Caret.*
	Thochú, ...	*Caret.*
	Sokpa, ...	*Caret.*
	Horpa, ...	*Caret.*
	Tibetan (*written*), . .	*Caret.*
	Tibetan (*spoken*), . . .	*Caret.*
Nepal (east to west).	Serpa, ...	*Liblib.*
	Súnwár, ...	*Caret.*
	Gúrung, ...	*Phlébá.*
	Múrmi, ...	*Caret.*
	Magar, ...	*Caret.*
	Tháksya, ...	*Pabapilhe.*
	Pákhya, ...	*Pátalo.*
	Newár, ...	*Pati.*
	Limbu, ...	*Kuphella.*
Kiranti Group (East Nepal).	Kiránti, ...	*Caret.*
	Rodong, ...	*Phlempá.*
	Rúngchenbung, . . .	*Phemdagwa, phedu'wa,*
	Chhingtángya, . . .	*Phempedepmá.* [*phebdapma.*
	Náchhereng, ...	*Phremphremya.*
	Wáling, ...	*Phimpichichi.*
	Yákha, ...	*Phekphekuá.*
	Chourásya, ...	*Plemplimme.*
	Kulungya, ...	*Phemphempa.*
	Thulungya, ...	*Plemplemmá.*
	Báhingya, ...	*Plem-plem'me.*
	Lohorong, ...	*Phekphek'-ma.*
	Lambichhong, . . .	*Ranrankha.*
	Báláli, ...	*Phek phek pa.*
	Sáng-páng, ...	*Phem phem'-ko.*
	Dúmi, ...	*Phlemphlem'-me.*
	Kháling, ...	*Phemphemme.*
	Dungmáli, ...	*Phepchidákda.*
Broken Tribes of Nepal.	Dárhi, ...	*Chepto.*
	Denwár, ...	*Chepto.*
	Pahri, ...	*Pherchyakyengu.*
	Chepáng, ...	*Caret.*
	Bhrámu, ...	*Nimbule.*
	Váyu, ...	*Tengteng.*
	Kuswar, ...	*Sambh.*
	Kusunda, ...	*Chyáugkáng.*
	Thárü, ...	*Pánarabangpánang.*
	Lepcha (Sikkim), . .	*Asap, sapbo, alep, lepbo.*
	Bhúṭáni v. Lhopa, . .	*Le-blep, sab-them.*

N.-E. Bengal.	Bodo, ...	*Sománni.*
	Dhimál, ...	*Sáriká.*
	Kocch, ...	*Samán.*
	Garo, ...	*Gakshan.*
	Kácharí, ...	*Caret.*
Eastern Frontier of Bengal.	Munipuri, ...	*Caret.*
	Mithán Nágá, . . .	*Caret.*
	Tablung Nágá, . . .	*Caret.*
	Khári Nágá, ...	*Caret.*
	Angámi Nágá, . . .	*Caret.*
	Námsáng Nágá, . . .	*Tode.*
	Nowgong Nágá, . .	*Matam.*
	Tengsa Nágá, . . .	*Madamka.*
	Abor Miri, ...	*Neing-sudó.*
	Sibságar Miri, . . .	*Omandák.*
	Deoria Chutia, . . .	*Caret.*
	Singpho, ...	*Ram.*
Arrakan & Burmah.	Burman (*written*), . .	*Pyá.*
	Burman (*spoken*), . . .	*Pyá, pyathi.*
	Khyeng v. Shou, . .	*Pe.*
	Kámi, ...	*Phádá.*
	Kúmi, ...	*Kampo.*
	Mrú v. Toung, . . .	*Caret.*
	Sák, ...	*Caret.*
Siam & Tenasserim.	Talain v. Mon, . . .	*Khataithi.*
	Sgau-karen, ...	*Caret.*
	Pwo-karen, ...	*Caret.*
	Toungh-thu, ...	*Sau-pyay.*
	Shán, ...	*Pyí.*
	Annamitic, ...	*Bang.*
	Siamese, ...	*Hpen.*
	Ahom, ...	*Caret.*
	Khámti, ...	*Caret.*
	Laos, ...	*Caret.*
Central India.	Ho (Kol), ...	*Caret.*
	Kol (Singhbhum), . .	*Mitaungia.*
	Santáli, ...	*Mih-sáung, chápada;*
	Bhúmij, ...	*Morsom.* *kárahá-te* and
	Uráon, ...	*Chapti.* *bhát-äute* (to
	Mundala, ...	*Chaptia.* level).
	Rájmahali, ...	*Barábar.*
	Goṇḍi, ...	*Naphúral maṇḍánur, neli.*
	Gayeti, ...	*Caret.*
	Rutluk, ...	*Nicho* (low).
	Naikude, ...	*Dubrak* (low).
	Kolami, ...	*Utten* (low).
	Mádi, ...	*Pedal* (low).
	Mádia, ...	*Caret.*
	Kuri, ...	*Ita* (low).
	Keikádi, ...	*Gidda* (low).
	Khoṇḍ, ...	*Rosarola.*
	Sávara, ...	*Samangaḍele.*
	Gadaba, ...	*Sadunngádulta.*
	Yerukala, ...	*Sadanu.*
	Chentsu, ...	*Chekuno, chakkakini.*
Southern India.	Tamiḷ, anc., ...	*Aḍara.*
	Tamiḷ, mod., ...	*Taṭṭaiyána.*
	Malayáḷma, anc., . .	*Caret.*
	Malayáḷma, mod., . .	*Paranna.*
	Telugu, ...	*Taṭṭena.*
	Karṇáṭaka, anc., . .	*Caret.*
	Karṇáṭaka, mod., . .	*Chappaṭe.*
	Tuḷuva, ...	*Caret.*
	Kurgi, ...	*Caret.*
	Toḍuva, }	*Caret.*
	Toḍa, }	*Caret.*
	Kóta, ...	*Caret.*
	Baḍaga, ...	*Caret.*
	Kuṟumba, ...	*Caret.*
	Iruḷa, ...	*Caret.*
	Malabar, ...	*Shattei.*
	Sinhalese, ...	*Pätali.*

Group	*Types.*	
Inflecting.	SANSKRIT,	*Sádhu, bhadra, áryya s'ubha.*
	ARABIC,	*Tayyib, kheir.*
Compounding.	BASK,	*On.*
	FINNIC,	*Hywä.*
	MAGYAR,	*Jo.*
	TURKISH,	*Eyi.*
	CIRCASSIAN,	*Souy-yey.*
	GEORGIAN,	*Kargi.*
	MONGOLIAN,	*Ssain.*
	MANTSHU,	*Sain.*
	JAVANESE, Ngoko,	*Běchik.*
	JAVANESE, Krama,	*Sahe.*
	MALAY,	*Báyik.*
Isolating.	CHINESE, Nankin,	*Háou.*
	CHINESE, Pekin,	*Háou.*
	CHINESE, Canton,	*Ho.*
	CHINESE, Shanghai,	*Hau.*
	AMOY, Colloquial,	*Ho.*
	JAPANESE,	*Yoi.*
	Brahuí,	*Sharo.*
Chinese Frontier & Tibet.	Gyámi,	*Houkhou, houti.*
	Gyárung,	*Kasne.*
	Tákpa,	*Lihúni.*
	Mányak,	*Deundaḥ.*
	Thochú,	*Náï.*
	Sokpa,	*Chháng-bene.*
	Horpa,	*Gáye-gnor.*
	Tibetan (*written*),	*Bazángpo.*
	Tibetan (*spoken*),	*Yappo.*
Nepal (east to west).	Serpa,	*Lemú.*
	Súnwár,	*Rimso.*
	Gúrung,	*Saba.*
	Múrmi,	*Jába.*
	Magar,	*Gyepche.*
	Tháksya,	*A'sbá.*
	Pákhya,	*Báhiya, niko.*
	Newár,	*Bhing.*
	Limbu,	*Nohba, kenohba.*
Kiranti Group (East Nepal).	Kiránti,	*Nuhva.*
	Rodong,	*Nyo, kregne.*
	Rúngchenbung,	*Nuwo, nuwochi.*
	Chhingtángya,	*Núno.*
	Náchhereng,	*Nada, nat, natkni.*
	Wáling,	*Nu, khupunu, amwa, i.*
	Yákha,	*Núha.*
	Chourásya,	*Ducho.*
	Kulungya,	*No, noi, noyu.*
	Thulungya,	*Nyupa.*
	Báhingya,	*Nyúba.*
	Lohorong,	*Núye, nukchia;*[1] *nukmiha.*[2]
	Lambichhong,	*Núyu-kha.*
	Báláli,	*Núne, nup.*
	Sáng-páng,	*Ni.*
	Dúmi,	*Nyúpa.*
	Kháling,	*Nyúpa.*
	Dungmáli,	*Nú; nuehle;*[1] *númau'nu.*[2]
Broken Tribes of Nepal.	Dárhi,	*Niko.*
	Denwár,	*Sajhá.*
	Pahri,	*Bhingguhma.*
	Chepáng,	*Pito.*
	Bhrámu,	*Gádo.*
	Váyu,	*Nuh'kámo, nuh'kamo.*
	Kuswar,	*Bhala.*
	Kusunda,	*Waiyaki.*
	Tháru,	*Niman, badhai.*
	Lepcha (Sikkim),	*Aryúm, ryumbo.*
	Bhútáni v. Lhopa,	*Lemo.*

N.-E. Bengal.	Bodo,	*Gham, ghám.*
	Dhimál,	*Elká.*
	Kocch,	*Bhála.*
	Garo,	*Penem.*
	Káchári,	*Gahum, gham.*
Eastern Frontier of Bengal.	Munipuri,	*Aphabá.*
	Mithán Nágá,	*Maile.*
	Tablung Nágá,	*Mailunke.*
	Khári Nágá,	*Aro'.*
	Angámi Nágá,	*Viwe.*
	Námsáng Nágá,	*Asan.*
	Nowgong Nágá,	*Tatsong.*
	Tengsa Nágá,	*Chongkolo.*
	Abor Miri,	*Aidu.*
	Sibságar Miri,	*Aida.*
	Deoria Chutia,	*Churini.*
	Singpho,	*Gajá.*
Arrakan & Burmah.	Burman (*written*),	*Kong.*
	Burman (*spoken*),	*Kaung, ḳaungthi.*
	Khyeng v. Shou,	*Be.*
	Kámi,	*Húi.*
	Kúmi,	*Haui.*
	Mrú v. Toung,	*Caret.*
	Sák,	*Caret.*
Siam & Tenasserim.	Talain v. Mon,	*Khá.*
	Sgau-karen,	*Gha.*
	Pwo-karen,	*Ghi.*
	Toungh-thu,	*Heu.*
	Shán,	*Liyau.*
	Annamitic,	*Tôt.*
	Siamese,	*Dí, liyouk.*
	Ahom,	*Dí.*
	Khámti,	*Ní.*
	Laos,	*Dí.*
Central India.	Ho (Kol),	*Bugi.*
	Kol (Singhbhum),	*Búgi, bháge, bhugi, manják, siráh-báráh.*
	Santáli,	*Búgi.*
	Bhúmij,	*Búgi.*
	Uráon,	*Besri.*
	Mundala,	*Bogi.*
	Rájmahali,	*Cru.*
	Goṇḍi,	*Besmanda, chokat.*
	Gayeti,	*Caret.*
	Rutluk,	*Tisa.*
	Naikude,	*Berindod.*
	Kolami,	*Dadam.*
	Mádi,	*Besh, nehena, neinatu.*
	Mádia,	*Nehana.*
	Kuri,	*Awal.*
	Keikádi,	*Nalla.*
	Khoṇḍ,	*Nekkánju.*
	Sávara,	*Ampase.*
	Gadaba,	*Jalem.*
	Yerukala,	*Nalla.*
	Chentsu,	*Achháye, bhálá.*
Southern India.	Tamiḷ, anc.,	*Caret.*
	Tamiḷ, mod.,	*Nalla.*
	Malayáḷma, anc.,	*Caret.*
	Malayáḷma, mod.,	*Nana, nallam.*
	Telugu,	*Manchi, chokáṭamu, bágu.*
	Karṇáṭaka, anc.,	*Caret.*
	Karṇaṭaka, mod.,	*Oḷḷe, cheluva.*
	Tuḷuva,	*Eddattano.*
	Kurgi,	*Nallad.*
	Toḍuva,	*Caret.*
	Toḍa,	*Vulti.*
	Kóta,	*Volle.*
	Baḍaga,	*Volle.*
	Kuṛumba,	*Volle.*
	Iruḷa,	*Nálla.*
	Malabar,	*Nalla.*
	Sinhalese,	*Honda.*

Group	Types.	
Inflecting.	SANSKṚIT,	*Mahat, vṛihat, pṛithu;*
	ARABIC,	*Kabír.* [*bahu* (many).
Compounding.	BASK,	*Andi, aundi, larri, eskerge,*
	FINNIC,	*Suuri.* [*ordongo.*
	MAGYAR,	*Nagy.*
	TURKISH,	*Leuyuk.*
	CIRCASSIAN,	*Asudet, bahsh.*
	GEORGIAN,	*Didi.*
	MONGOLIAN,	*Seghe.*
	MANTSHU,	*Amba.*
	JAVANESE, Ngoko,	*Gĕḍe.*
	JAVANESE, Krama,	*Hageng.*
	MALAY,	*Basár.*
Isolating.	CHINESE, Nankin,	*Ta.*
	CHINESE, Pekin,	*Ta.*
	CHINESE, Canton,	*Tái.*
	CHINESE, Shanghai,	*Tu.*
	AMOY, Colloquial,	*Toá.*
	JAPANESE,	*Oki.*
	Brahuí,	*Caret.*
Chinese Frontier & Tibet.	Gyámi,	*Tá-ti.*
	Gyárung,	*Kahti'.*
	Tákpa,	*Thenbo.*
	Mányak,	*Kah-kah.*
	Thochú,	*Pwi-tha.*
	Sokpa,	*I'khi.*
	Horpa,	*Kamthú.*
	Tibetan (*written*),	*Chhenpo, ṣbombo.*
	Tibetan (*spoken*),	*Bombo.*
Nepal (east to west).	Serpa,	*Girbú.*
	Súnwár,	*Kol-sotu.*
	Gúrung,	*Thebá.*
	Múrmi,	*Gnájáng.*
	Magar,	*Kráncho.*
	Thâksya,	*Theba.*
	Pákhya,	*Thúlo.*
	Newár,	*Taugo, ta-gu.*
	Limbu,	*Yomba.*
Kiránti Group (East Nepal).	Kiránti,	*U'toyáng.*
	Rodong,	*Ko, mahipmá, mahippa.*
	Rúngchenbung,	*Utokpang, utwapang.*
	Chhingtángya,	*Thekhá.*
	Náchhereng,	*U'mdheppa, yetikholcho.*
	Wáling,	*Atok'pa.*
	Yákha,	*Mákna.*
	Chourásya,	*Khol bo.*
	Kulungya,	*Dheppa.*
	Thulungya,	*Dokpu.*
	Báhingya,	*Gnolo.*
	Lohorong,	*Dheá, deha, dhechia, miha.*
	Lambichhong,	*Theuyuk'kha, theuyuk.*
	Báláli,	*Dhepa.*
	Sáng-páng,	*Umdhep'pa.*
	Dúmi,	*Gholpa.*
	Khâling,	*Ghálpa.*
	Dungmáli,	*Dhigo, dhi; dhichi;*[1] *mad-* [*hik-chi.*[2]
Broken Tribes of Nepal.	Dárhi,	*Caret.*
	Denwár,	*Caret.*
	Pahri,	*Caret.*
	Chepáng,	*Caret.*
	Bhrámu,	*Caret.*
	Váyu,	*Caret.*
	Kuswar,	*Caret.*
	Kusunda,	*Wogonrái.*
	Tháru,	*Mot.*
	Lepcha (Sikkim),	*Atim, timbo.*
	Bhútáni v. Lhopa,	*Bombo.*

N.-E. Bengal.	Bodo,	*Mahat.*
	Dhimál,	*Dhamká.*
	Kocch,	*Baḍa.*
	Garo,	*Godá.*
	Káchári,	*Gidet.*
Eastern Frontier of Bengal.	Munipuri,	*Caret.*
	Mithán Nágá,	*Achung, nau.*
	Tablung Nágá,	*Yong-nong.*
	Khári Nágá,	*Tahpetiau.*
	Angámi Nágá,	*Jopür.*
	Námsáng Nágá,	*Adong.*
	Nowgong Nágá,	*Talulu.*
	Tengsa Nágá,	*Tape.*
	Abor Miri,	*Bote.*
	Sibságar Miri,	*A'ttadák.*
	Deoria Chutia,	*Am-chá-dini.*
	Singpho,	*Gubá.*
Arrakan & Burmah.	Burman (*written*),	Krí.
	Burman (*spoken*),	Kyí, *kyokthi.*
	Khyeng v. Shou,	*Len.*
	Kámi,	*Leng.*
	Kúmi,	*Len.*
	Mrú v. Toung,	*Caret.*
	Sák,	*Caret.*
Siam & Tenasserim.	Talain v. Mon,	*Thanot.*
	Sgau-karen,	*Caret.*
	Pwo-karen,	*Caret.*
	Toungh-thu,	*Tan.*
	Shán,	*Youhk.*
	Annamitic,	*Lön.*
	Siamese,	*Kalohn, luang, yai.*
	Ahom,	*Long.*
	Khámti,	*Lung, yaü.*
	Laos,	*Luang, yai.*
Central India.	Ho (Kol),	*Marang.*
	Kol (Singhbhum),	*Márang.*
	Santáli,	*Márang, nápaḍá, hápaḍá.*
	Bhúmij,	*Hisso márang.*
	Uráon,	*Kohá.*
	Mundala,	*Márang.*
	Rájmahali,	*Bevo.*
	Gonḍi,	*Fada, paror, mota.*
	Gayeti,	*Sajor.*
	Rutluk,	*Jetan.*
	Naikude,	*Dahud, dodo.*
	Kolami,	*Gubanda.*
	Mádi,	*Bedha, beraha, perama.*
	Mádia,	*Caret.*
	Kuri,	*Kat, gad.*
	Keikádi,	*Bardu.*
	Khonḍ,	*Deranju.*
	Sávara,	*Gogo.*
	Gadaba,	*Mudo.*
	Yerukala,	*Berudu.*
	Chentsu,	*Badaká.*
Southern India.	Tamiḷ, anc.,	*Caret.*
	Tamiḷ, mod.,	*Periya.*
	Malayáḷma, anc.,	*Caret.*
	Malayáḷma, mod.,	*Valiya, periya.*
	Telugu,	*Pedda.*
	Karṇáṭaka, anc.,	*Caret.*
	Karṇáṭaka, mod.,	*Doḍḍa.*
	Tuḷuva,	*Mallow.*
	Kurgi,	*Caret.*
	Toḍuva,	*Caret.*
	Toḍa,	*Etud.*
	Kóta,	*Daḍḍa.*
	Baḍaga,	*Daḍḍa.*
	Kuṟumba,	*Doḍḍa.*
	Iruḷa,	*Doḍḍa.*
	Malabar,	*Peria.*
	Sinhalese,	*Mahat.*

Group	Language	Green
Types.		
Inflecting.	SANSKRIT, ...	*Harit, hari, palāśa.*
	ARABIC, ...	*Akhḍar.*
Compounding.	BASK, ...	*Berde, ferde.*
	FINNIC, ...	*Viheriä.*
	MAGYAR, ...	*Zöld.*
	TURKISH, ...	*Yeshil.*
	CIRCASSIAN, ...	*Shkhantey.*
	GEORGIAN, ...	*Mtsvani.*
	MONGOLIAN, ...	*Nogon.*
	MANTSHU, ...	*Niokhon.*
	JAVANESE, Ngoko, . .	*Hijo.*
	JAVANESE, Krama, . .	*Hijĕm.*
	MALAY, ...	*Hijau.*
Isolating.	CHINESE, Nankin, . .	*Luh.*
	CHINESE, Pekin, . .	*Lü.*
	CHINESE, Canton, . .	*Luk.*
	CHINESE, Shanghai, .	*Lŏh.*
	AMOY, Colloquial, . .	*Lek.*
	JAPANESE, ...	*Aui.*
	Brahuí, ...	*Caret.*
Chinese Frontier & Tibet.	Gyámi, ...	*Ligdi.*
	Gyárung, ...	*Karmyák.*
	Tákpa, ...	*Chángú.*
	Mányak, ...	*Chúgindo.*
	Thochú, ...	*Zyángkú.*
	Sokpa, ...	*Kho-kho.*
	Horpa, ...	*Jhángú.*
	Tibetan (*written*), . .	*Hjángkhú.*
	Tibetan (*spoken*), . .	*Jhángú.*
Nepal (east to west).	Serpa, ...	*Númmo.*
	Súnwár, ...	*Gigi.*
	Gúrung, ...	*U'rkyá.*
	Múrmi, ...	*Pingai.*
	Magar, ...	*Phiphi dancho.*
	Tháksya, ...	*Phin.*
	Pákhya, ...	*Hariyo.*
	Newár, ...	*Wáwon.*
	Limbu, ...	*Lehla.*
Kiranti Group (East Nepal).	Kiránti, ...	*Chakla.*
	Rodong, ...	*Hariyo.*
	Rúngchenbung, . . .	*Hariyo.*
	Chhingtángya, . . .	*Chak'la.*
	Náchhereng, ...	*Hariyo.*
	Wáling, ...	*Chak'la.*
	Yákha, ...	*Phina.*
	Chourásya, ...	*Sisijokcho, sisijoma.*
	Kulungya, ...	*Gigipa.*
	Thulungya, ...	*Gigim.*
	Báhingya, ...	*Gigim.*
	Lohorong, ...	*Phiye.*
	Lambichhong, . . .	*Caret.*
	Báláli, ...	*Phiphipa.*
	Sáng-páng, ...	*Caret.*
	Dúmi, ...	*Wálu.*
	Kháling, ...	*Gigima.*
	Dungmáli, ...	*Mak'po keke, mak'pokeka, kachi.**
Broken Tribes of Nepal.	Dárhi, ...	*Haryo.*
	Denwár, ...	*Harro.*
	Pahri, ...	*Womwondha.*
	Chepáng, ...	*Phelto.*
	Bhrámu, ...	*Siksik.*
	Váyu, ...	*Girúngmi.*
	Kuswar, ...	*Hardiálo.*
	Kusunda, ...	*Hariyo.*
	Tháru, ...	*Hariyer.*
	Lepcha (Sikkim), . .	*Phúng-phong.*
	Bhúṭáni v. Lhopa, . .	*Nhyambo.*

Group	Language	Green
N.-E. Bengal.	Bodo, ...	*Samsram, khángshur.*
	Dhimál, ...	*Nelpá.*
	Kocch, ...	*Hara.*
	Garo, ...	*Heng jeleng.*
	Káchári, ...	*Goshum* (blue).
Eastern Frontier of Bengal.	Munipuri, ...	*Napú.*
	Míthán Nágá, . . .	*Caret.*
	Tablung Nágá, . . .	*Caret.*
	Khári Nágá, . . .	*Shim-puluk.*
	Angámi Nágá, . . .	*Kapaje.*
	Námsáng Nágá, . . .	*Ahing.*
	Nowgong Nágá, . . .	*Tacham.*
	Tengsa Nágá, . . .	*Tacham.*
	Abor Miri, ...	*Caret.*
	Sibságar Miri, . . .	*Gedák.*
	Deoria Chutia, . . .	*Pijoni.*
	Singpho, ...	*Ketsing.*
Arrakan & Burmah.	Burman (*written*), . .	*Chim.*
	Burman (*spoken*), . .	*Sering, tseinthi.*
	Khyeng v. Shou, . .	*Nau.*
	Kámi, ...	*Maeinsin.*
	Kúmi, ...	*Kanhein.*
	Mrú v. Toung, . . .	*Caret.*
	Sák, ...	*Caret.*
Siam & Tenasserim.	Talain v. Mon, . . .	*Hnentanyit.*
	Sgau-karen, ...	*Lah.*
	Pwo-karen, ...	*Yi.*
	Toungh-thu, ...	*Ling.*
	Shán, ...	*Chyo.*
	Annamitic, ...	*Xañ.*
	Siamese, ...	*Khayo, kheau.*
	Ahom, ...	*Kyi.*
	Khámti, ...	*Khyen.*
	Laos, ...	*Kheau.*
Central India.	Ho (Kol), ...	*Gáde.*
	Kol (Singhbhum), . .	*Gadesosang.*
	Santáli, ...	*Háli, hariyar.*
	Bhúmij, ...	*Gade sosang.*
	Uráon, ...	*Harria.*
	Mundala, ...	*Harriár.*
	Rájmahali, ...	*Kenkajro.*
	Goṇḍi, ...	*Haro, hirawa.*
	Gayeti, ...	*Kache.*
	Rutluk, ...	*Hariro.*
	Naikude, ...	*Pachaná.*
	Kolami, ...	*Pachchi.*
	Mádi, ...	*Arta, artana.*
	Mádia, ...	*Hariyal.*
	Kuri, ...	*Hara.*
	Keikádi, ...	*Pasuru.*
	Khoṇḍ, ...	*Caret.*
	Sávara, ...	*Volámbidldakuvu.*
	Gadaba, ...	*Volempatstsa.*
	Yerukala, ...	*Yalátstsággo.*
	Chentsu, ...	*Harihjal, sabuniya.*
Southern India.	Tamiḷ, anc., ...	*Caret.*
	Tamiḷ, mod., ...	*Pachchei, pasu.*
	Malayáḷma, anc., . .	*Caret.*
	Malayáḷma, mod., . .	*Pachcha.*
	Telugu, ...	*A'kupachcha, pachcha.*
	Karṇáṭaka, anc., . .	*Caret.*
	Karṇáṭaka, mod., . .	*Hasuru.*
	Tuḷuva, ...	*Pachche.*
	Kurgi, ...	*Caret.*
	Toḍuva, ...	*Caret.*
	Toḍa, ...	*Paje.*
	Kóta, ...	*Paje.*
	Baḍaga, ...	*Hase.*
	Kuṟumba, ...	*Hase.*
	Iruḷa, ...	*Páje.*
	Malabar, ...	*Pachei.*
	Sinhalese, ...	*Kolapáṭa.*

	Types.	
Inflecting.	SANSKṚIT,	*Surúpa, rúpavat, sugátra.*
	ARABIC,	*Jamíl.*
Compounding.	BASK,	*Eder, galant, polit, ficho.*
	FINNIC,	*Kaunis.*
	MAGYAR,	*Szep.*
	TURKISH,	*Guzel.*
	CIRCASSIAN,	*Dahshey.*
	GEORGIAN,	*Lamasi.*
	MONGOLIAN,	*Isala.*
	MANTSHU,	*Amballingu.*
	JAVANESE, Ngoko,	*Bagus.*
	JAVANESE, Krama,	*Bagus.*
	MALAY,	*Elok.*
Isolating.	CHINESE, Nankin,	*Háou-yangwoh.*
	CHINESE, Pekin,	*Háou-yangwoh.*
	CHINESE, Canton,	*Hò-yeong-tsze.*
	CHINESE, Shanghai,	*Ch'ü-hau-küṇ.*
	AMOY, Colloquial,	*Súi.*
	JAPANESE,	*Kireni.*
	Brahuí,	*Zabro.*
Chinese Frontier & Tibet.	Gyámi,	*Houti.*
	Gyárung,	*Kúmchúr.*
	Tákpa,	*Lihúmi, gnománo.*
	Mányak,	*Phyún phú.*
	Thochú,	*Rkwi.*
	Sokpa,	*Cháng-bene.*
	Horpa,	*Kamsyúr.*
	Tibetan (*written*),	*Dsesmo, stúgpo.*
	Tibetan (*spoken*),	*Jebo.*
Nepal (east to west).	Serpa,	*Lemo, simbu.*
	Súnwár,	*Rimso.*
	Gúrung,	*Saba.*
	Múrmi,	*Brot-khába.*
	Magar,	*Shecheja.*
	Tháksya,	*Bastu, mhikyahepá.*
	Pákhya,	*Rámro.*
	Newár,	*Bánlá.*
	Limbu,	*Nohva, kenohva.*
Kiranti Group (East Nepal).	Kiránti,	*Khánúhwo.*
	Rodong,	*Khannyá, sangnya.*
	Rúngchenbung,	*Kháng-núwo.*
	Chhingtángya,	*Uchunúno.*
	Náchhereng,	*Khan-náda.*
	Wáling,	*Khang'nú.*
	Yákha,	*Ichchúnúna.*
	Chourásya,	*Rácho.*
	Kulungya,	*Gnali núpa.*
	Thulungya,	*Jyopa.*
	Dáhingya,	*Rim'ba, -daäsi,*[1] *-daä.*[2]
	Lohorong,	*Kamnúye.*
	Lambichhong,	*U'chunúyukha.*
	Báláli,	*Khennung.*
	Sáng-páng,	*Khánni.*
	Dúmi,	*Bhan'gpa.*
	Kháling,	*Bhang'pa.*
	Dungmáli,	*Khánnu, khannu-chú.*[1]
Broken Tribes of Nepal.	Dárhi,	*Rámro.*
	Denwár,	*Caret.*
	Pahri,	*Banglaguhma.*
	Chepáng,	*Dyangto.*
	Bhrámu,	*Kusyen.*
	Váyu,	*Bing.*
	Kuswar,	*Banaila.*
	Kusunda,	*Waiyaimyá-bák.*
	Tháru,	*Besmanai.*
	Lepcha (Sikkim),	*Aryum, ryumbo.*
	Bhúṭáni v. Lhopa,	*Lemo.*
N.-E. Bengal.	Bodo,	*Majáng, mojáng.*
	Dhimál,	*Remká, elka (?).*
	Kocch,	*Songot.*
	Garo,	*Nemá.*
	Káchári,	*Moöjung.*
Eastern Frontier of Bengal.	Munipuri,	*Aphujaba.*
	Míthán Nágá,	*Caret.*
	Tablung Nágá,	*Caret.*
	Khári Nágá,	*Kubaitaro.*
	Angámi Nágá,	*Visu.*
	Námsáng Nágá,	*Asaná.*
	Nowgong Nágá,	*Kángatsong.*
	Tengsa Nágá,	*Chongthang.*
	Abor Miri,	*Kampodo.*
	Sibságar Miri,	*Kángkáne.*
	Deoria Chutia,	*Ichubare.*
	Singpho,	*Jásoi.*
Arrakan & Burmah.	Burman (*written*),	*Lha.*
	Burman (*spoken*),	*Lhá, hlathi.*
	Khyeng v. Shou,	*Paui.*
	Kámi,	*Anon.*
	Kúmi,	*Hoi.*
	Mrú v. Toung,	*Caret.*
	Sák,	*Caret.*
Siam & Tenasserim.	Talain v. Mon,	*Gau.*
	Sgau-karen,	*A'khwibah, p'kwahghá.*
	Pwo-karen,	*Khwilah.*
	Toungh-thu,	*Tárá.*
	Shán,	*Hanlin.*
	Annamitic,	*Săk.*
	Siamese,	*Ngám, hanlau.*
	Ahom,	*Khyeng.*
	Khámti,	*Ngám.*
	Laos,	*Ngám.*
Central India.	Ho (Kol),	*Búgí nelloteá.*
	Kol (Singhbhum),	*Búgilika.*
	Santáli,	*Jantar, máhil, manják, soghoḍ, ḍol.*
	Bhúmij,	*Búgikúri.*
	Uráon,	*Besre.*
	Mundala,	*Bes.*
	Rájmahali,	*Crúgáre.*
	Goṇḍi,	*Sajari.*
	Gayeti,	*Caret.*
	Rutluk,	*Nehen, lachkut.*
	Naikude,	*Dadapata.*
	Kolami,	*Dadápan.*
	Mádi,	*Beshmwkhami, karkal.*
	Mádia,	*Nehana.*
	Kuri,	*Chajar.*
	Keikádi,	*Nalla.*
	Khoṇḍ,	*Caret.*
	Sávara,	*Ambasanate.*
	Gadaba,	*Limmokká.*
	Yerukala,	*Nalla.*
	Chentsu,	*Bhalláṭi, sundor.*
Southern India.	Tamiḷ, anc.,	*Azhakiya (aḷakiya).*
	Tamiḷ, mod.,	*Azhakána, saundariyamána.*
	Malayáḷma, anc.,	*Caret.*
	Malayáḷma, mod.,	*Azhakuḷḷa.*
	Telugu,	*Andamaina, chakkani.*
	Karṇáṭaka, anc.,	*Caret.*
	Karṇáṭaka, mod.,	*Cheluva.*
	Tuḷuva,	*Eddattano.*
	Kurgi,	*Caret.*
	Toḍuva,	*Narradodi.*
	Toḍa,	*Nárthti.*
	Kóta,	*Pasane, singara.*
	Baḍaga,	*Singara.*
	Kuṛumba,	*Singara.*
	Iruḷa,	*Alagu.*
	Malabar,	*Alahu, alahána.*
	Sinhalese,	*Lakshana.*

Group	Types.	
Inflecting.	SANSKṚIT,	*Ushṇa, chaṇḍa, santapta, tápi.*
	ARABIC,	*Hárr, ḥámi.*
Compounding.	BASK,	*Bero, berotsu, beroti, berodun.*
	FINNIC,	*Palawa.*
	MAGYAR,	*Forro.*
	TURKISH,	*Sijak.*
	CIRCASSIAN,	*Pahbey.*
	GEORGIAN,	*Datskha.*
	MONGOLIAN,	*Khalaghen.*
	MANTSHU,	*Khalkhon.*
	JAVANESE, Ngoko,	*Pannas.*
	JAVANESE, Krama,	*Pannas.*
	MALAY,	*Angat.*
Isolating.	CHINESE, Nankin,	*Jeh, nwan.*
	CHINESE, Pekin,	*Jo, nwan.*
	CHINESE, Canton,	*It, nün.*
	CHINESE, Shanghai,	*Nieh.*
	AMOY, Colloquial,	*Joáh.*
	JAPANESE,	*Atsui.*
	Brahuí,	*Basuní.*
Chinese Frontier & Tibet.	Gyámi,	*Redi.*
	Gyárung,	*Kassi, kavassi.*
	Tákpa,	*Gromo.*
	Mányak,	*Cheche.*
	Thochú,	*Si.*
	Sokpa,	*Hálon.*
	Horpa,	*Cheche.*
	Tibetan (written),	*Tshápo, dropo.*
	Tibetan (spoken),	*Chábo.*
Nepal (east to west).	Serpa,	*Tenmo.*
	Súnwár,	*Hoso.*
	Gúrung,	*Kro-ba.*
	Múrmi,	*Lepá.*
	Magar,	*Khan-cho.*
	Tháksya,	*Lhap.*
	Pákhya,	*Táto.*
	Newár,	*Khwá.*
	Limbu,	*Kego-ba.*
Kiranti Group (East Nepal).	Kiránti,	*Kúyáng.*
	Rodong,	*Kúrekwa, kúreko.*
	Rúngchenbung,	*Kúko, kúmangwa.*
	Chhingtángya,	*Kú-no.*
	Náchhereng,	*Semi wa.*
	Wáling,	*Kúyang.*
	Yákha,	*Kú-ha.*
	Chourásya,	*Táto.*
	Kulungya,	*Hoke.*
	Thulungya,	*Glyoglem.*
	Báhingya,	*Gleglem, -daäsi;[1] -daa.[2]*
	Lohorong,	*Kúse, ku, kukchia.*
	Lambichhong,	*Kúyu, kúyúkha.*
	Báláli,	*Kúne, kú.*
	Sáng-páng,	*Háki, púti.*
	Dúmi,	*Wál, hai.*
	Kháling,	*Glogloma.*
	Dungmáli,	*Ku, kúchie,[1] makú.[2]*
Broken Tribes of Nepal.	Dárhi,	*Táto.*
	Denwár,	*Táto.*
	Pahri,	*Kwáguhma.*
	Chepáng,	*Dháto.*
	Bhrámu,	*U'dúm.*
	Váyu,	*Jeta.*
	Kuswar,	*Táto.*
	Kusunda,	*Bhrok.*
	Tháru,	*Chuhan.*
	Lepcha (Sikkim),	*Arhúm, rhumbo.*
	Bhúṭáni v. Lhopa,	*Teu mo.*
N.-E. Bengal.	Bodo,	*Gúdúng.*
	Dhimál,	*Chákâ, sááka.*
	Kocch,	*Gorom.*
	Garo,	*Gútúng.*
	Káchári,	*Gudung.*
Eastern Frontier of Bengal.	Munipuri,	*Asába.*
	Mithán Nágá,	*Kham.*
	Tablung Nágá,	*Shem.*
	Khári Nágá,	*Tetsá.*
	Angámi Nágá,	*Khakwu.*
	Námsáng Nágá,	*Akhám.*
	Nowgong Nágá,	*Tatsok.*
	Tengsa Nágá,	*Lamme.*
	Abor Miri,	*Gudorong.*
	Sibságar Miri,	*Gundme.*
	Deoria Chutia,	*Kaiṇi.*
	Singpho,	*Káthet.*
Arrakan & Burmah.	Burman (written),	*Pú.*
	Burman (spoken),	*Pú, puthi.*
	Khyeng v. Shou,	*Kholeik.*
	Kámi,	*Bi.*
	Kúmi,	*Bi.*
	Mrú v. Toung,	*Caret.*
	Sák,	*Caret.*
Siam & Tenasserim.	Talain v. Mon,	*Kata.*
	Sgau-karen,	*Ko.*
	Pwo-karen,	*Tserku.*
	Toungh-thu,	*Kheu.*
	Shán,	*Meik.*
	Annamitic,	*Nóng.*
	Siamese,	*Ron, met.*
	Ahom,	*Ran, lut.*
	Khámti,	*Hon, mai, lüt.*
	Laos,	*Hon.*
Central India.	Ho (Kol),	*Lolo.*
	Kol (Singhbhum),	*Lolo.*
	Santáli,	*Lolo, setong, uragum.*
	Bhúmij,	*Gumár.*
	Uráon,	*Bidáh.*
	Mundala,	*Balhaltan.*
	Rájmahali,	*Kúrni.*
	Goṇḍi,	*Kástai, kastá.*
	Gayeti,	*Kastal.*
	Rutluk,	*Kasta.*
	Naikude,	*Ukhadá.*
	Kolami,	*Situr.*
	Mádi,	*Kasta, kasinta.*
	Mádia,	*Kasta.*
	Kuri,	*Lolor.*
	Keikádi,	*Udku.*
	Khoṇḍ,	*Rumúrumam.*
	Sávara,	*Toggayi.*
	Gadaba,	*Geehem.*
	Yerukala,	*Vuḍuku.*
	Chentsu,	*Joru, ṭapta.*
Southern India.	Tamiḷ, anc.,	*Veyya.*
	Tamiḷ, mod.,	*Súṭa, kaivuḷḷa, veppamána.*
	Malayáḷma, anc.,	*Caret.*
	Malayáḷma, mod.,	*Chúṭa.*
	Telugu,	*Veḍi, uḍuku.*
	Karṇáṭaka, anc.,	*Caret.*
	Karṇáṭaka, mod.,	*Bisi.*
	Tuḷuva,	*Sekhe.*
	Kurgi,	*Bekkel.*
	Toḍuva,	*Caret.*
	Toḍa,	*Kásti, kásviji.*
	Kóta,	*U'ri.*
	Baḍaga,	*Uri, bisse.*
	Kurumba,	*Bisse.*
	Iruḷa,	*Kája.*
	Malabar,	*Súdu.*
	Sinhalese,	*U'sne.*

Types.

Inflecting.	SANSKRIT,	*Dîrgha.*
	ARABIC,	*Táwîl.*
Compounding.	BASK,	*Luze.*
	FINNIC,	*Pitkä.*
	MAGYAR,	*Hosszu.*
	TURKISH,	*Uzoen.*
	CIRCASSIAN,	*Kakha.*
	GEORGIAN,	*Gridzali.*
	MONGOLIAN,	*Urtu.*
	MANTSHU,	*Gulmin.*
	JAVANESE, Ngoko,	*Dawa.*
	JAVANESE, Krama,	*Panjang.*
	MALAY,	*Panjang.*
Isolating.	CHINESE, Nankin,	*Ch'ang.*
	CHINESE, Pekin,	*Ch'ang.*
	CHINESE, Canton,	*Ch'eong.*
	CHINESE, Shanghai,	*Dzáng.*
	AMOY, Colloquial,	*Tñg.*
	JAPANESE,	*Nagai.*
	Brahuí,	*Gwand.*
Chinese Frontier & Tibet.	Gyámi,	*Thángti.*
	Gyárung,	*Kasri.*
	Tákpa,	*Ringbo.*
	Mányak,	*Shásha.*
	Thochú,	*Drithú.*
	Sokpa,	*U'r thú.*
	Horpa,	*Kachi.*
	Tibetan (*written*),	*Ringpo.*
	Tibetan (*spoken*),	*Rimbo.*
Nepal (east to west).	Serpa,	*Rimbo.*
	Súnwár,	*Joso.*
	Gúrung,	*Rhimba.*
	Múrmi,	*Rengba.*
	Magar,	*Lotcho.*
	Thaksya,	*Hrimba.*
	Pákhya,	*Lámo.*
	Newár,	*Taha, taha.*
	Limbu,	*Kemba.*
Kiranti Group (East Nepal).	Kiránti,	*Mentá.*
	Rodong,	*Kile.*
	Rúngchenbung,	*Akibang, amyetpang, metta.*
	Chhingtángya,	*Kemek'no.*
	Náchhereng,	*Báipa, repa.*
	Wáling,	*Badhemet, rhiṇbo.*
	Yákha,	*Kena.*
	Chourásya,	*Hik'bo, yotihicho.*
	Kulungya,	*Wadbháipa.*
	Thulungya,	*Dhyúpa.*
	Báhingya,	*Jhoíba.*
	Lohorong,	*Keye, kibe.*
	Lambichhong,	*Keyuk, keyuk'kha.*
	Báláli,	*Kepa.*
	Sáng-páng,	*Máipa.*
	Dúmi,	*Songpa.*
	Kháling,	*Song'pa.*
	Dungmáli,	*Ki, kichago,[1] makigachie.[2]*
Broken Tribes of Nepal.	Dárhi,	*Lámo.*
	Denwár,	*Lámo.*
	Pahri,	*Táhágu.*
	Chepáng,	*Caret.*
	Bhrámu,	*Kúvo, alhok.*
	Váyu,	*Phlinta.*
	Kuswar,	*Lámo.*
	Kusunda,	*Hwang gai.*
	Thárú,	*Lambá.*
	Lepcha (Sikkim),	*Arhen, rhenbo.*
	Bhútáni v. Lhopa,	*Rimbú.*
N.-E. Bengal.	Bodo,	*Galou.*
	Dhimál,	*Rhinká.*
	Kocch,	*Lámba.*
	Garo,	*Pillo.*
	Káchári,	*Gojo.*
Eastern Frontier of Bengal.	Munipuri,	*Ashangba.*
	Míthán Nágá,	*Lo.*
	Tablung Nágá,	*Lau.*
	Khári Nágá,	*Tilhaum.*
	Angámi Nágá,	*Josü.*
	Námsáng Nágá,	*A'lo.*
	Nowgong Nágá,	*Talang.*
	Tengsa Nágá,	*Lángkolo.*
	Abor Miri,	*Baddolo.*
	Sibságar Miri,	*Aiárdák.*
	Deoria Chutia,	*Lui.*
	Singpho,	*Gálú.*
Arrakan & Burmah.	Burman (*written*),	*Rhiṇ.*
	Burman (*spoken*),	*She, shakthi.*
	Khyeng v. Shou,	*Sou.*
	Kámi,	*Sá.*
	Kúmi,	*Asouk.*
	Mrú v. Toung,	*Caret.*
	Sák,	*Caret.*
Siam & Tenasserim.	Talain v. Mon,	*Kalein.*
	Sgau-karen,	*'Taw.*
	Pwo-karen,	*'Lau.*
	Toungh-thu,	*H'to.*
	Shán,	*Young.*
	Annamitic,	*Dai.*
	Siamese,	*Young, yáu.*
	Ahom,	*Lejau.*
	Khámti,	*Yáu.*
	Laos,	*Yáu.*
Central India.	Ho (Kol),	*Jilling.*
	Kol (Singhbhum),	*Jilling.*
	Santáli,	*Jeleng, jhaila.*
	Bhúmij,	*Baroa, jilling.*
	Uráon,	*Digha.*
	Mundala,	*Jiling.*
	Rájmahali,	*Digaro.*
	Goṇḍi,	*Lamba, leior.*
	Gayeti,	*Caret.*
	Rutluk,	*Leior.*
	Naikude,	*Podam.*
	Kolami,	*Pudam.*
	Mádi,	*Lakhu, lati.*
	Mádia,	*Caret.*
	Kuri,	*Giling.*
	Keikádi,	*Wasara.*
	Khoṇḍ,	*Lambájámu.*
	Sávara,	*Jelo.*
	Gadaba,	*Tiyyár.*
	Yerukala,	*Vasaram, aragam.*
	Chentsu,	*Vuncho, namoṭá.*
Southern India.	Tamiḷ, anc.,	*Niliya.*
	Tamiḷ, mod.,	*Niṇḍa, neḍu.*
	Malayáḷma, anc.,	*Caret.*
	Malayáḷma, mod.,	*Niṇḍa.*
	Telugu,	*Niḍupu, poḍugu.*
	Karṇáṭaka, anc.,	*Caret.*
	Karṇáṭaka, mod.,	*Udda.*
	Tuḷuva,	*Udda.*
	Kurgi,	*Caret.*
	Toḍuva,	*Caret.*
	Toḍa,	*Nirigiti.*
	Kóta,	*Uddame.*
	Badaga,	*Udda.*
	Kuṛumba,	*Udda.*
	Iruḷa,	*Uddya.*
	Malabar,	*Nedia ninda.*
	Sinhalese,	*Diga.*

	Types.	
Inflecting.	SANSKṚIT,	*A'ma, apakva.*
	ARABIC,	*Fajj.*
Compounding.	BASK,	*Gordin, gordiñ.*
	FINNIC,	*Uusi.*
	MAGYAR,	*Azöröś.*
	TURKISH,	*Kham.*
	CIRCASSIAN,	*Tzinney.*
	GEORGIAN,	*Medli.*
	MONGOLIAN,	*Tohükei.*
	MANTSHU,	*Magdakha-akho.*
	JAVANESE, Ngoko,	*Mĕntah.*
	JAVANESE, Krama,	*Mĕntah.*
	MALAY,	*Mantah.*
Isolating.	CHINESE, Nankin,	*Sang.*
	CHINESE, Pekin,	*Shang.*
	CHINESE, Canton,	*Shang.*
	CHINESE, Shanghai,	*Sáng, veh-zōh.*
	AMOY, Colloquial,	*Chiṇ.*
	JAPANESE,	*Nama.*
	Brahuí,	*Caret.*
Chinese Frontier & Tibet.	Gyámi,	*Myúphú.*
	Gyárung,	*Makasmán.*
	Tákpa,	*Machoso.*
	Mányak,	*Demámi.*
	Thochú,	*Amin.*
	Sokpa,	*Chhikthe.*
	Horpa,	*Númálúmsi.*
	Tibetan (*written*),	*Caret.*
	Tibetan (*spoken*),	*Zyembo.*
Nepal (east to west).	Serpa,	*Zyenba.*
	Súnwár,	*Cheri pla.*
	Gúrung,	*A'mîva.*
	Múrmi,	*Chinga.*
	Magar,	*Mibil.*
	Tháksya,	*A'tehebá.*
	Pákhya,	*Kácho.*
	Newár,	*Kachi.*
	Limbu,	*Kúlehla.*
Kiranti Group (East Nepal).	Kiránti,	*U'chîva.*
	Rodong,	*Mo, ummo.*
	Rúngchenbung,	*Wománg, umáng.*
	Chhingtángya,	*U máng.*
	Náchhereng,	*Mápe.*
	Wáling,	*Umpáwa.*
	Yákha,	*Nusúmha.*
	Chourásya,	*Krábo.*
	Kulungya,	*Mamtumkhapa, mamdupa.*
	Thulungya,	*Uchákhli.*
	Báhingya,	*Achekhli.*
	Lohorong,	*Mentúmpa, mákampa.*
	Lambichhong,	*Hingli, hingli-kha.*
	Báláli,	*Mátupti.*
	Sáng-páng,	*Man'dú, mausetnáchi.*
	Dúmi,	*U'súta.*
	Kháling,	*U'súta.*
	Dungmáli,	*Ummáng.*
Broken Tribes of Nepal.	Dárhi,	*Kácho.*
	Denwár,	*Caret.*
	Pahri,	*Kazhignhma.*
	Chepáng,	*Caret.*
	Bhrámu,	*Pon.*
	Váyu,	*Chalamo.*
	Kuswar,	*Kácho.*
	Kusunda,	*Ben.*
	Tháru,	*Kácha.*
	Lepcha (Sikkim),	*Azeu, zeubo.*
	Bhúṭáni v. Lhopa,	*Máchobo.*
N.-E. Bengal.	Bodo,	*Gatháng.*
	Dhimál,	*Sinkhá.*
	Kocch,	*Káchha, kancha.*
	Garo,	*Piting.*
	Káchári,	*Gotung.*
Eastern Frontier of Bengal.	Munipuri,	*Asungba.*
	Míthán Nágá,	*Caret.*
	Tablung Nágá,	*Caret.*
	Khári Nágá,	*Tachim.*
	Angámi Nágá,	*Memo.*
	Námsáng Nágá,	*A'hing.*
	Nowgong Nágá,	*Mátok, tazzu.*
	Tengsa Nágá,	*Tái.*
	Abor Miri,	*Caret.*
	Sibságar Miri,	*Leda.*
	Deoria Chutia,	*Pijo.*
	Singpho,	*Ketsing.*
Arrakan & Burmah.	Burman (*written*),	*Chim.*
	Burman (*spoken*),	*Seing, tsenthi.*
	Khyeng v. Shou,	*Tein.*
	Kámi,	*Kás'hl.*
	Kúmi,	*Kánghei.*
	Mrú v. Toung,	*Caret.*
	Sák,	*Caret.*
Siam & Tenasserim.	Talain v. Mon,	*Tsentsangeet.*
	Sgau-karen,	*Thi'k'sa), atsi.*
	Pwo-karen,	*Athaing.*
	Toungh-thu,	*Tathit.*
	Shán,	*Chyo.*
	Annamitic,	*Sông.*
	Siamese,	*Dip, chyo.*
	Ahom,	*Lip.*
	Khámti,	*Nip.*
	Laos,	*Dip.*
Central India.	Ho (Kol),	*Caret.*
	Kol (Singhbhum),	*Baral.*
	Santáli,	*A'sára, kásá, gádár.*
	Bhúmij,	*Baral.*
	Uráon,	*Khena, arha.*
	Mundala,	*Beral.*
	Rájmahali,	*Kene.*
	Goṇḍi,	*Kachchomanda, hivwo, kai.*
	Gayeti,	*Kái.*
	Rutluk,	*Kacho.*
	Naikude,	*Caret.*
	Kolami,	*Keik.*
	Mádi,	*Kodukela, kaiar, kai.*
	Mádia,	*Káyá.*
	Kuri,	*Kách.*
	Keikádi,	*Kai.*
	Khoṇḍ,	*Saḍáde.*
	Sávara,	*Amegna.*
	Gadaba,	*Broluká.*
	Yerukala,	*Pasuru.*
	Chentsu,	*Kancho, káchoṭá.*
Southern India.	Tamiḷ, anc.,	*Pozháda.*
	Tamiḷ, mod.,	*Pachchei, káy.*
	Malayáḷma, anc.,	*Caret.*
	Malayáḷma, mod.,	*Pachcha.*
	Telugu,	*Pachchi, káya.*
	Karṇáṭaka, anc.,	*Caret.*
	Karṇáṭaka, mod.,	*Hasi, káyáda.*
	Tuḷuva,	*Paje.*
	Kurgi,	*Pachche.*
	Toḍuva,	*Caret.*
	Toḍa,	*Paji.*
	Kóta,	*Paje.*
	Baḍaga,	*Háse.*
	Kuṛumba,	*Hásu.*
	Iruḷa,	*Paje.*
	Malabar,	*Pachei.*
	Sinhalese,	*Amu.*

Types.		
Inflecting.	SANSKṚIT,	*Rakta, lohita, rohita.*
	ARABIC,	*Aḥmar.*
Compounding.	BASK,	*Gorri.*
	FINNIC,	*Punainen.*
	MAGYAR,	*Veres.*
	TURKISH,	*Kizil.*
	CIRCASSIAN,	*Tlishi.*
	GEORGIAN,	*Tsiṭheli.*
	MONGOLIAN,	*Ulagan.*
	MANTSHU,	*Fulgiyan.*
	JAVANESE, Ngoko,	*Habang.*
	JAVANESE, Krama,	*Habrit.*
	MALAY,	*Merah.*
Isolating.	CHINESE, Nankin,	*Hung.*
	CHINESE, Pekin,	*Hung.*
	CHINESE, Canton,	*Hung.*
	CHINESE, Shanghai,	*Hung.*
	AMOY, Colloquial,	*Añg.*
	JAPANESE,	*Akai.*
	Brahuí,	*Khisun.*
Chinese Frontier & Tibet.	Gyámi,	*Khongdi.*
	Gyárung,	*Kaver'ni.*
	Tákpa,	*Leu.*
	Mányak,	*Dani.*
	Thochú,	*Shidzi.*
	Sokpa,	*Ulán.*
	Horpa,	*Gingi.*
	Tibetan (*written*),	*Smúkpo.*
	Tibetan (*spoken*),	*Márpo.*
Nepal (east to west).	Serpa,	*Morpo.*
	Súnwár,	*Lala.*
	Gúrung,	*Wolkya.*
	Múrmi,	*Bála.*
	Magar,	*Gyácho.*
	Tháksya,	*Walá.*
	Pákhya,	*Ráto.*
	Newár,	*Hyoun.*
	Limbu,	*Kúhella.*
Kiranti Group (East Nepal).	Kiránti,	*Hálá láwá.*
	Rodong,	*Hípakima.*
	Rúngchenbung,	*Halalá-mang, hala-chakma.*
	Chhingtángya,	*Halachekma.*
	Náchhereng,	*Halalápa.*
	Wáling,	*Hárchhokma, halachakchak.*
	Yákha,	*Phána.*
	Chourásya,	*Lakachima.*
	Kulungya,	*Halalápa.*
	Thulungya,	*Lálám.*
	Báhingya,	*Lálám.*
	Lohorong,	*Har'rá, -chia,*[1] *-miha.*[2]
	Lambichhong,	*Wárawába.*
	Báláli,	*Halápa.*
	Sáng-páng,	*Halalápa.*
	Dúmi,	*Halála.*
	Kháling,	*Halálám.*
	Dungmáli,	*Harchhop'chho.*
Broken Tribes of Nepal.	Dárhi,	*Raktaro.*
	Denwár,	*Raktaro.*
	Pahri,	*Sidhagu.*
	Chepáng,	*Dúto.*
	Bhrámu,	*Pháya.*
	Váyu,	*Langchingmi.*
	Kuswar,	*Pilla.*
	Kusunda,	*Bánubá.*
	Tháru,	*Lál.*
	Lepcha (Sikkim),	*A'heur.*
	Bhúṭáni v. Lhopa,	*Mábo.*
N.-E. Bengal.	Bodo,	*Gajá, gatchá.*
	Dhimál,	*I'ká, jika.*
	Kocch,	*Lál.*
	Garo,	*Pisak.*
	Kácharí,	*Caret.*
Eastern Frontier of Bengal.	Munipuri,	*Angangba.*
	Míthán Nágá,	*Caret.*
	Tablung Nágá,	*Caret.*
	Khári Nágá,	*Tamüram.*
	Angámi Nágá,	*Mrí.*
	Námsáng Nágá,	*Achak.*
	Nowgong Nágá,	*Maram.*
	Tengsa Nágá,	*Malamla.*
	Abor Miri,	*Yalung.*
	Sibságar Miri,	*Lüdák.*
	Deoria Chutia,	*Saru.*
	Singpho,	*Khyeng.*
Arrakan & Burmah.	Burman (*written*),	*Nī.*
	Burman (*spoken*),	*Nī, nithī.*
	Khyeng v. Shou,	*Sen.*
	Kámi,	*E'.*
	Kúmi,	*Kanlein.*
	Mrú v. Toung,	*Caret.*
	Sák,	*Caret.*
Siam & Tenasserim.	Talain v. Mon,	*Hpakit.*
	Sgau-karen,	*Ghaw, gáu.*
	Pwo-karen,	*Wauh.*
	Toungh-thu,	*Tánya.*
	Shán,	*Len.*
	Annamitic,	Do.
	Siamese,	*Taí, deng.*
	Ahom,	*Deng.*
	Khámti,	*Neng.*
	Laos,	*Deng, kam.*
Central India.	Ho (Kol),	*Arra.*
	Kol (Singhbhum),	*Hessú árá.*
	Santáli,	*A'ráh, sindur, jarang-jarang, garlá* (purple).
	Bhúmij,	*Baṛaranga.*
	Uráon,	*Khenso.*
	Mundala,	*Arrah.*
	Rájmahali,	*Keso.*
	Goṇḍi,	*Lal.*
	Gayeti,	*Bulal.*
	Rutluk,	*Sundi.*
	Naikude,	*Yerodi.*
	Kolami,	*Yerrodi.*
	Mádi,	*Netrali, rengal, pekieli.*
	Mádia,	*Lal.*
	Kuri,	*Ratta.*
	Keikádi,	*Yerpu.*
	Khoṇḍ,	*Gerú.*
	Sávara,	*Soyipu.*
	Gadaba,	*Beraiḍuttu.*
	Yerukala,	*Yarraḍekirá.*
	Chentsu,	*Goriya, gorinṭa.*
Southern India.	Tamiḷ, anc.,	*Seyya.*
	Tamiḷ, mod.,	*Sivanda, sivappu.*
	Malayáḷma, anc.,	*Caret.*
	Malayáḷma, mod.,	*Chuvanna.*
	Telugu,	*Erra, yerupu.*
	Karṇáṭaka, anc.,	*Caret.*
	Karṇáṭaka, mod.,	*Kempu.*
	Tuḷuva,	*Kempu.*
	Kurgi,	*Chondad.*
	Toḍuva, }	*Caret.*
	Toḍa, }	*Kebbu.*
	Kóta,	*Kembu.*
	Baḍaga,	*Kebbu.*
	Kuṛumba,	*Kempu.*
	Iruḷa,	*Jevve.*
	Malabar,	*Sivantha.*
	Sinhalese,	*Ratu.*

Types.

Inflecting.	SANSKRIT,	*Pakva.*
	ARABIC,	*Mustawi.*
Compounding.	BASK,	*Eldu, zori, sasoitu, humo.*
	FINNIC,	*Kypsi.*
	MAGYAR,	*E'rett.*
	TURKISH,	*Olmush.*
	CIRCASSIAN,	*Caret.*
	GEORGIAN,	*Caret.*
	MONGOLIAN,	*Bolbason.*
	MANTSHU,	*Magdakha.*
	JAVANESE, Ngoko,	*Matěng.*
	JAVANESE, Krama,	*Matěng.*
	MALAY,	*Másak.*
Isolating.	CHINESE, Nankin,	*Shuh.*
	CHINESE, Pekin,	*Shú.*
	CHINESE, Canton,	*Shuk.*
	CHINESE, Shanghai,	*Zŏh.*
	AMOY, Colloquial,	*Sek.*
	JAPANESE,	*Caret.*
	Brahuí,	*Caret.*
Chinese Frontier & Tibet.	Gyámi,	*Phúti.*
	Gyárung,	*Kasmán.*
	Tákpa,	*Choso.*
	Mányak,	*Demi.*
	Thochú,	*An, min.*
	Sokpa,	*Bálchhen.*
	Horpa,	*Núlúmsi.*
	Tibetan (*written*),	*Sminbo.*
	Tibetan (*spoken*),	*Chembo.*
Nepal (east to west).	Serpa,	*Chobo.*
	Súnwár,	*Miso.*
	Gúrung,	*Miva.*
	Múrmi,	*Minba.*
	Magar,	*Mincho.*
	Tháksya,	*Tyáhcjiba.*
	Pákhya,	*Páko.*
	Newár,	*Nhingú.*
	Limbu,	*Kúsongva.*
Kiranti Group (East Nepal).	Kiránti,	*Dau va.*
	Rodong,	*Tupsako, mattákowa.*
	Rúngchenbung,	*Túmawo.*
	Chhingtángya,	*Uthubáï.*
	Náchhereng,	*Dú wák.*
	Wáling,	*Sumsa, tupsa bhangsa.*
	Yákha,	*Usáha, tupsáha.*
	Chourásya,	*Thicho.*
	Kulungya,	*Tumkhápa, dúpa.*
	Thulungya,	*Thikta, thokta.*
	Báhingya,	*Ming'ta, jita, mimba, jiba.*
	Lohorong,	*Dumem'pa, tumempa.*
	Lambichhong,	*Thuyuyukha, thuyu.*
	Báláli,	*Túmáp, túmpa.*
	Sáng-páng,	*Setnáchi, túmako, dúwako.*
	Dúmi,	*Mis'te.*
	Kháling,	*Dhami'pa.*
	Dungmáli,	*Tum'sá, tumsachie,[1] [matumsa.[2]*
Broken Tribes of Nepal.	Dárhi,	*Páko.*
	Denwár,	*Caret.*
	Pahri,	*Búgu.*
	Chepáng,	*Caret.*
	Bhrámu,	*Kiming.*
	Váyu,	*Minmo.*
	Kuswar,	*Páko.*
	Kusunda,	*Pakog.*
	Tháru,	*Pákal.*
	Lepcha (Sikkim),	*Amyen, myeubo.*
	Bhútáni v. Lhopa,	*Chochopo.*

N.-E. Bengal.	Bodo,	*Gamang.*
	Dhimál,	*Minká.*
	Kocch,	*Pakka.*
	Garo,	*Papman.*
	Káchári,	*Caret.*
Eastern Frontier of Bengal.	Munipuri,	*Amunba.*
	Míthán Nágá,	*Jum.*
	Tablung Nágá,	*Yim.*
	Khári Nágá,	*Tenhing.*
	Angámi Nágá,	*Me.*
	Námsáng Nágá,	*A'chúm.*
	Nowgong Nágá,	*Táman.*
	Tengsa Nágá,	*Táman.*
	Abor Miri,	*Mindo.*
	Sibságar Miri,	*Minda.*
	Deoria Chutia,	*Munom.*
	Singpho,	*Min.*
Arrakan & Burmah.	Burman (*written*),	*Mhiṇ, rang.*
	Burman (*spoken*),	*Mhe, yen, mhaithi.*
	Khyeng v. Shou,	*Mhin.*
	Kámi,	*Min.*
	Kúmi,	*Mhún.*
	Mrú v. Toung,	*Caret.*
	Sák,	*Caret.*
Siam & Tenasserim.	Talain v. Mon,	*Tú.*
	Sgau-karen,	*Me, amhi.*
	Pwo-karen,	*Amaing.*
	Toungh-thu,	*Hma.*
	Shán,	*Ahtsol.*
	Annamitic,	*Shin.*
	Siamese,	*Súk, wen.*
	Ahom,	*Rung, suk.*
	Khámti,	*Súk.*
	Laos,	*Súk.*
Central India.	Ho (Kol),	*Caret.*
	Kol (Singhbhum),	*Biriena.*
	Santáli,	*Bele, pákaṭ.*
	Bhúmij,	*Ihsinjanna.*
	Uráon,	*Panja.*
	Mundala,	*Bilia.*
	Rájmahali,	*Panjeke.*
	Goṇḍi,	*Pútá, pandatál.*
	Gayeti,	*Pandatá.*
	Rutluk,	*Pandi.*
	Naikude,	*Panditin.*
	Kolami,	*Pannu.*
	Mádi,	*Muitá, pandi.*
	Mádia,	*Padale.*
	Kuri,	*Biliye.*
	Keikádi,	*Pala, pagdu.*
	Khoṇḍ,	*Mránnutangi sendijaninju.*
	Sávara,	*Agúcunate.*
	Gadaba,	*Mágegisá, bullo.*
	Yerukala,	*Mágisu, paṇḍisu.*
	Chentsu,	*Mugilá, pakká.*
Southern India.	Tamiḷ, anc.,	*Kaninda.*
	Tamiḷ, mod.,	*Pazhutta (paḷutta).*
	Malayáḷma, anc.,	*Caret.*
	Malayáḷma, mod.,	*Pazhutta (paḷutta).*
	Telugu,	*Mágina, paṇḍu.*
	Karṇáṭaka, anc.,	*Caret.*
	Karṇáṭaka, mod.,	*Mágida.*
	Tuḷuva,	*Paranda.*
	Kurgi,	*Caret.*
	Toḍuva, } Toḍa, }	*Caret.*
		Caret.
	Kóta,	*Caret.*
	Baḍaga,	*Caret.*
	Kuṛumba,	*Caret.*
	Iruḷa,	*Caret.*
	Malabar,	*Caret.*
	Sinhalese,	*Idunu.*

Group	*Types.*	
Inflecting.	SANSKRIT,	*Varttula, golákára,*
	ARABIC,	*Mudawwar.* [*chakrákára.*
Compounding.	BASK,	*Boill, biribill.*
	FINNIC,	*Ympyriäinen.*
	MAGYAR,	*Kerek.*
	TURKISH,	*Deghirmi.*
	CIRCASSIAN,	*Khurahi.*
	GEORGIAN,	*Rekwali.*
	MONGOLIAN,	*Bügarönggui.*
	MANTSHU,	*Mugheliye.*
	JAVANESE, Ngoko,	*Bundĕr.*
	JAVANESE, Krama,	*Bundĕr.*
	MALAY,	*Búlat.*
Isolating.	CHINESE, Nankin,	*Yuen.*
	CHINESE, Pekin,	*Yuen.*
	CHINESE, Canton,	*Ün.*
	CHINESE, Shanghai,	*Yüṇ.*
	AMOY, Colloquial,	*I'ṇ.*
	JAPANESE,	*Marui.*
	Brahuí,	*Caret.*
Chinese Frontier & Tibet.	Gyámi,	*Eangdi, yángdi.*
	Gyárung,	*Kálárlar.*
	Tákpa,	*Birhi.*
	Mányak,	*Wáḥ-waḥ.*
	Thochú,	*Ashyara.*
	Sokpa,	*Caret.*
	Horpa,	*Lolo.*
	Tibetan (*written*),	*Zlumpo.*
	Tibetan (*spoken*),	*Riri.*
Nepal (east to west).	Serpa,	*Girmo.*
	Súnwár,	*Kúl-kúl.*
	Gúrung,	*Phal-dong.*
	Múrmi,	*Rilto.*
	Magar,	*Dallo.*
	Tháksya,	*Bhumrlba, ghighirbá.*
	Pákhya,	*Dallo, bátulo.*
	Newár,	*Gogú, gogu.*
	Limbu,	*Kúgakma.*
Kiránti Group (East Nepal).	Kiránti,	*Aubo.*
	Rodong,	*Búplúngmá.*
	Rúngchenbung,	*Boptitiwo, bopiriri, hitriri.*
	Chhingtángya,	*Kalabok'bo.*
	Náchhereng,	*U'mkoldu, púpúlpa.*
	Wáling,	*Kalabokbok.*
	Yákha,	*Kákliktíkara, púkpúkna.*
	Chourásya,	*Khitiriri, dolo.*
	Kulungya,	*Júmjúmpa, púlpúlpa.*
	Thulungya,	*Púpúlma.*
	Báhingya,	*Pupul'me.*
	Lohorong,	*Pumpumma, pumpumye.*
	Lambichhong,	*Kák'liklikkha.*
	Báláli,	*Puklukluk.*
	Sáng-páng,	*Phuphul'ko, pupul'ko.*
	Dúmi,	*Pupul'mu.*
	Kháling,	*Papal'ma.*
	Dungmáli,	*Umpop.*
Broken Tribes of Nepal.	Dárhi,	*Dallo.*
	Denwár,	*Dúmro.*
	Pahri,	*Gonágu.*
	Chepáng,	*Caret.*
	Bhrámu,	*Dallo.*
	Váyu,	*Kúlkúl.*
	Kuswar,	*Dallo.*
	Kusunda,	*Dallo, mang gni.*
	Tháru,	*Dhela, gola.*
	Lepcha (Sikkim),	*Rer-rerbo.*
	Bhúṭáni v. Lhopa,	*Gouto yeupo.*

N.-E. Bengal.	Bodo,	*Dúllútni, tolotni.*
	Dhimál,	*Gúrmaká, gotaka.*
	Kocch,	*Gol.*
	Garo,	*Goglot-ni.*
	Kácházi,	*Caret.*
Eastern Frontier of Bengal.	Munipuri,	*Caret.*
	Míthán Nágá,	*Caret.*
	Tablung Nágá,	*Caret.*
	Khári Nágá,	*Meketang.*
	Angámi Nágá,	*Khruhi.*
	Námsáng Nágá,	*A'túm.*
	Nowgong Nágá,	*Tarang.*
	Tengsa Nágá,	*Litükpu.*
	Abor Miri,	*Caret.*
	Sibságar Miri,	*A'tumdák.*
	Deoria Chutia,	*Tumoru.*
	Singpho,	*Dindin.*
Arrakan & Burmah.	Burman (*written*),	*Lun.*
	Burman (*spoken*),	*Long, ḷun, ḷonthí.*
	Khyeng v. Shou,	*Púlú.*
	Kámi,	*Púlún.*
	Kúmi,	*Caret.*
	Mrú v. Toung,	*Caret.*
	Sák,	*Caret.*
Siam & Tenasserim.	Talain v. Mon,	*Khatoung.*
	Sgau-karen,	*Caret.*
	Pwo-karen,	*Caret.*
	Toungh-thu,	*Tunglung.*
	Shán,	*Mon.*
	Annamitic,	*Tron.*
	Siamese,	*Htsí, klom.*
	Ahom,	*Klom, pán.*
	Khámti,	*Mon.*
	Laos,	*Kom.*
Central India.	Ho (Kol),	*Goṭa* (*gota?*).
	Kol (Singhbhum),	*Dingurúgia.* [*pákáḍ* (adv.).
	Santáli,	*Gulánta, righi* (noun),
	Bhúmij,	*Golándia, goṭagia.*
	Uráon,	*Golgol.*
	Mundala,	*Goṭá.*
	Rájmahali,	*Golė.*
	Goṇḍi,	*Gola, gol.*
	Gayeti,	*Wátarál.*
	Rutluk,	*Caret.*
	Naikude,	*Natore.*
	Kolami,	*Gundu.*
	Mádi,	*Gomma.*
	Mádia,	*Gula.*
	Kuri,	*Gol.*
	Keikádi,	*Gundra.*
	Khoṇḍ,	*Caret.*
	Sávara,	*Gudi, solágundu.*
	Gadaba,	*Biregunḍu.*
	Yerukala,	*Guṇdu.*
	Chentsu,	*Chatan, goṭyaṭi.*
Southern India.	Tamiḷ, anc.,	*Servána.*
	Tamiḷ, mod.,	*Tiraṇḍa, uraṇḍayána.*
	Malayáḷma, anc.,	*Caret.*
	Malayáḷma, mod.,	*Urunḍa.*
	Telugu,	*Gunḍu, gunḍrani.*
	Karṇáṭaka, anc.,	*Caret.*
	Karṇáṭaka, mod.,	*Gunḍu.*
	Tuḷuva,	*Uruṭṭu.*
	Kurgi,	*Caret.*
	Toḍuva, }	*Caret.*
	Toḍa, }	*Caret.*
	Kóta,	*Mudde.*
	Baḍaga,	*Uruṭu.*
	Kuṛumba,	*Uruṭe.*
	Iruḷa,	*Ruṭṭe.*
	Malabar,	*Vattippu.*
	Sinhalese,	*Waṭa, guli.*

Types.		
Inflecting.	SANSKṚIT,	*Hraswa, alpatanu, kshudratanu.*
	ARABIC,	*Kaṣir.*
Compounding.	BASK,	*Chiki, tipi.*
	FINNIC,	*Wăhă.*
	MAGYAR,	*Rövid.*
	TURKISH,	*Kissah.*
	CIRCASSIAN,	*Kĕhtshey.*
	GEORGIAN,	*Mokli.*
	MONGOLIAN,	*Odoï.*
	MANTSHU,	*Osohun, etchige.*
	JAVANESE, Ngoko,	*Chilik.*
	JAVANESE, Krama,	*Halit.*
	MALAY,	*Pendek.*
Isolating.	CHINESE, Nankin,	*Twan, yai.*
	CHINESE, Pekin,	*Twan, ai.*
	CHINESE, Canton,	*Ai.*
	CHINESE, Shanghai,	*Tüṇkuh, áhtsz'.*
	AMOY, Colloquial,	*Oe.*
	JAPANESE,	*Sei no hi kui hito.*
	Brahuí,	*Caret.*
Chinese Frontier & Tibet.	Gyámi,	*Titi.*
	Gyárung,	*Kachin.*
	Tákpa,	*Zúgthung.*
	Mányak,	*Dridrá.*
	Thochú,	*Kthátha.*
	Sokpa,	*Caret.*
	Horpa,	*Gáde.*
	Tibetan (*written*),	*Caret.*
	Tibetan (*spoken*),	*Mábo.*
Nepal (east to west).	Serpa,	*Mámo.*
	Súnwár,	*Hocho.*
	Gúrung,	*Cheúnbo.*
	Múrmi,	*Meba.*
	Magar,	*Temcho.*
	Tháksya,	*Putulu.*
	Pákhya,	*Hocho.*
	Newár,	*Chigdhi, bágo, chikidhi.*
	Limbu,	*Tángba.*
Kiranti Group (East Nepal).	Kiránti,	*Simtá.*
	Rodong,	*Inang-kile, pa-kile.*
	Rúngchenbung,	*Simta, simyang.*
	Chhingtángya,	*Unno.*
	Náchhereng,	*Yeterepa, yetebhaipa.*
	Wáling,	*Dúiyang.*
	Yákha,	*Lúklúkna.*
	Chourásya,	*A'rocho, arobo.*
	Kulungya,	*Chireppa.*
	Thulungya,	*Dokhonyepa.*
	Báhingya,	*Dyákholába, dekholába.*
	Lohorong,	*Taksye, mim'mu, múk'nu.*
	Lambichhong,	*Wuṇyuk'kha, waṇyuk.*
	Báláli,	*Táksip'.*
	Sáng-páng,	*Uttuchheripiko.*
	Dúmi,	*Tibichyom.*
	Kháling,	*Dokháisong'pa.*
	Dungmáli,	*Tungo.*
Broken Tribes of Nepal.	Dárhi,	*Nanar.*
	Denwár,	*Hocho.*
	Pahri,	*Khoso.*
	Chepáng,	*Caret.*
	Bhrámu,	*Anyak.*
	Váyu,	*Thothi.*
	Kuswar,	*Hocho.*
	Kusunda,	*Poktok.*
	Tháru,	*Nicha.*
	Lepcha (Sikkim),	*Aman, maubo.*
	Bhúṭáni v. Lhopa,	*Mhámten, mhour.*
N.-E. Bengal.	Bodo,	*Gahai.*
	Dhimál,	*Bángraká.*
	Kocch,	*Choto.*
	Garo,	*Bandok.*
	Káchári,	*Mudai.*
Eastern Frontier of Bengal.	Munipuri,	*Tele.*
	Míthán Nágá,	*Caret.*
	Tablung Nágá,	*Caret.*
	Khári Nágá,	*Orejute.*
	Angámi Nágá,	*Kharuo.*
	Námsáng Nágá,	*Amienpa.*
	Nowgong Nágá,	*Tatsü.*
	Tengsa Nágá,	*A'nanglá.*
	Abor Miri,	*Adedi.*
	Sibságar Miri,	*A'ndudák.*
	Deoria Chutia,	*Patigaini.*
	Singpho,	*Kutún.*
Arrakan & Burmah.	Burman (*written*),	*Nim.*
	Burman (*spoken*),	*Neing, puthi.*
	Khyeng v. Shou,	*Caret.*
	Kámi,	*Doi.*
	Kúmi,	*Caret.*
	Mrú v. Toung,	*Caret.*
	Sák,	*Caret.*
Siam & Tenasserim.	Talain v. Mon,	*Kwa.*
	Sgau-karen,	*Pu, aphu.*
	Pwo-karen,	*Pu.*
	Toungh-thu,	*Pú.*
	Shán,	*Pauk.*
	Annamitic,	*Ño.*
	Siamese,	*Tì, tam-boa.*
	Ahom,	*Tam.*
	Khámti,	*Tam.*
	Laos,	*Tam.*
Central India.	Ho (Kol),	*Imiting.*
	Kol (Singhbhum),	*Hessu imitingia.*
	Santáli,	*Khaṭo, gáṇṭhiá, kungja* (stooping).
	Bhúmij,	*Baḍa bángarba.*
	Uráon,	*Natúá.*
	Mundala,	*Húḍing.*
	Rájmahali,	*Chápo.*
	Goṇḍi,	*Chundúrmanda.*
	Gayeti,	*Caret.*
	Rutluk,	*Caret.*
	Naikude,	*Caret.*
	Kolami,	*Caret.*
	Mádi,	*Caret.*
	Mádia,	*Caret.*
	Kuri,	*Caret.*
	Keikádi,	*Caret.*
	Khoṇḍ,	*Caret.*
	Sávara,	*Doyina.*
	Gadaba,	*Poṭṭe.*
	Yerukala,	*Ardullá.*
	Chentsu,	*Khaṭoṭi.*
Southern India.	Tamiḷ, anc.,	*Caret.*
	Tamiḷ, mod.,	*Kuṛiya.*
	Malayáḷma, anc.,	*Caret.*
	Malayáḷma, mod.,	*Kuṛiya, kuḷḷa.*
	Telugu,	*Poṭṭi.*
	Karṇáṭaka, anc.,	*Caret.*
	Karṇáṭaka, mod.,	*Giḍḍa, kuru.*
	Tuḷuva,	*Caret.*
	Kurgi,	*Caret.*
	Toḍuva,	*Kullol.*
	Toḍa,	*Kuruḍa moch.*
	Kóta,	*Moḍ ále.*
	Baḍaga,	*Moncava.*
	Kuṛumba,	*Kúle alu.*
	Iruḷa,	*Kúle manisha.*
	Malabar,	*Kullan.*
	Sinhalese,	*Miṭi.*

Group	Language	Word
	Types.	
Inflecting.	SANSKRIT,	*Hraswa, alpa, kshudra.*
	ARABIC,	*Kaṣîr, ḳalîl.*
Compounding.	BASK,	*Labur, escas.*
	FINNIC,	*Lyhyt.*
	MAGYAR,	*Rövid.*
	TURKISH,	*Kisseh.*
	CIRCASSIAN,	*Kehtshey.*
	GEORGIAN,	*Mokli.*
	MONGOLIAN,	*Akhor.*
	MANTSHU,	*Hafirahun.*
	JAVANESE, Ngoko,	*Chĕṇḍak.*
	JAVANESE, Krama,	*Chĕṇḍak.*
	MALAY,	*Singkat.*
Isolating.	CHINESE, Nankin,	*Twan.*
	CHINESE, Pekin,	*Twan.*
	CHINESE, Canton,	*Tün.*
	CHINESE, Shanghai,	*Tüṇ.*
	AMOY, Colloquial,	*Te.*
	JAPANESE,	*Mishigai.*
	Brahuí,	*Caret.*
Chinese Frontier & Tibet.	Gyámi,	*Thongti.*
	Gyárung,	*Kachan.*
	Tákpa,	*Thongpo.*
	Mányak,	*Dridrá.*
	Thochú,	*Wongchithá.*
	Sokpa,	*Caret.*
	Horpa,	*Kalge.*
	Tibetan (*written*),	*Thúngpo.*
	Tibetan (*spoken*),	*Thúndúng.*
Nepal (east to west).	Serpa,	*Thinmo.*
	Súnwár,	*Túpah.*
	Gúrung,	*Rúiba.*
	Múrmi,	*Túmba.*
	Magar,	*Túncho.*
	Tháksya,	*Rimba.*
	Pákhya,	*Chhoto.*
	Newár,	*Chíhá, chiha.*
	Limbu,	*Tángba.*
Kiranti Group (East Nepal).	Kiránti,	*Dúngtá.*
	Rodong,	*Inang-kile, pákile.*
	Rúngchenbung,	*Adúngpang, dúngta.*
	Chhingtángya,	*Báunno.*
	Náchhereng,	*Yetebaipá, chichhábaipa.*
	Wáling,	*Achimet.*
	Yákha,	*Lúklúk na.*
	Chourásya,	*Ahikbo, amsihicho.*
	Kulungya,	*Chibhái ipa.*
	Thulungya,	*Dokhondhyúpa.*
	Báhingya,	*Dyakhojholba,-daasi,[1] -daa.[2]*
	Lohorong,	*Takś'ye, tyáksu.*
	Lambichhong,	*Wuṇ yuk, wuṇ yuk'kha.*
	Báláli,	*Teksip.*
	Sáng-páng,	*Duïpa, dwipa.*
	Dúmi,	*Tibichyám.*
	Kháling,	*Dokháisongpá.*
	Dúngmáli,	*Tun, tunchle,[1] matun' gochie.[2]*
Broken Tribes of Nepal.	Dárhi,	*Choti.*
	Denwár,	*Kháto.*
	Pahri,	*Pútihagu.*
	Chepáng,	*Caret.*
	Bhrámu,	*Anyak.*
	Váyu,	*Mamphinta.*
	Kuswar,	*Choto.*
	Kusunda,	*Poktok.*
	Tháru,	*Chhot.*
	Lepcha (Sikkim),	*A'tán, tanbo.*
	Bhúṭáni v. Lhopa,	*Thúmbú.*
N.-E. Bengal.	Bodo,	*Gúchúng.*
	Dhimál,	*Totoká (notoka !).*
	Kocch,	*Choto.*
	Garo,	*Bandok.*
	Káchári,	*Caret.*
Eastern Frontier of Bengal.	Munipuri,	*Tele.*
	Míthán Nágá,	*Mau.*
	Tablung Nágá,	*Soh.*
	Khári Nágá,	*Tütsizau.*
	Angámi Nágá,	*Jü.*
	Námsáng Nágá,	*Atún.*
	Nowgong Nágá,	*Tatsü.*
	Tengsa Nágá,	*A'nanglá.*
	Abor Miri,	*Adedi.*
	Sibságar Miri,	*A'ndüdák.*
	Deoria Chutia,	*Sutugai.*
	Singpho,	*Kutún.*
Arrakan & Burmah.	Burman (*written*),	*To.*
	Burman (*spoken*),	*To, tothi.*
	Khyeng v. Shou,	*Twe.*
	Kámi,	*Doi.*
	Kúmi,	*Do.*
	Mrú v. Toung,	*Caret.*
	Sák,	*Caret.*
Siam & Tenasserim.	Talain v. Mon,	*Kali.*
	Sgau-karen,	*Pu, aphu.*
	Pwo-karen,	*Pu.*
	Toungh-thu,	*Deng.*
	Shán,	*Tot.*
	Annamitic,	*Ngăn.*
	Siamese,	*Tsánn, san.*
	Ahom,	*Lot.*
	Khámti,	*Lot.*
	Laos,	*San, hun.*
Central India.	Ho (Kol),	*Dungúi.*
	Kol (Singhbhum),	*Dungúya.*
	Santáli,	*Kháṭo.*
	Bhúmij,	*Kándia.*
	Uráon,	*Phúdá.*
	Mundala,	*Húding.*
	Rájmahali,	*Jokka.*
	Goṇḍi,	*Chúndur, chodor.*
	Gayeti,	*Caret.*
	Rutluk,	*Chudur, abado.*
	Naikude,	*Mota.*
	Kolami,	*Moda.*
	Mádi,	*Kande, daktir.*
	Mádia,	*Caret.*
	Kuri,	*Kodar.*
	Keikádi,	*Giddu.*
	Khoṇḍ,	*Koggári.*
	Sávara,	Do*yina.*
	Gadaba,	D*ille.*
	Yerukala,	*Kuratsa.*
	Chentsu,	*Khaṭa.*
Southern India.	Tamiḷ, anc.,	*Caret.*
	Tamiḷ, mod.,	*Kuṛiya, kuṭṭamána, kuṭṭamána.*
	Malayáḷma, anc.,	*Caret.*
	Malayáḷma, mod.,	*Kuṛiya, kuṛu.*
	Telugu,	*Kurucha, kuru, poṭṭi.*
	Karṇáṭaka, anc.,	*Caret.*
	Karṇáṭaka, mod.,	*Giḍḍa.*
	Tuḷuva,	*Kuḍḍya.*
	Kurgi,	*Caret.*
	Toḍuva, }	*Caret.*
	Toḍa, }	*Kurigiti.*
	Kóta,	*Mone.*
	Baḍaga,	*Mone.*
	Kurumba,	*Mone, kúle.*
	Iruḷa,	*Kúle.*
	Malabar,	*Kattei, kurukal.*
	Sinhalese,	*Luhuṇḍu, koṭa.*

	Types.	
Inflecting.	SANSKṚIT,	*Alpa, kshudra.*
	ARABIC,	*Saghír.*
Compounding.	BASK,	*Chiki, tipi, mendre, chume, nimiño.*
	FINNIC,	*Wähä.*
	MAGYAR,	*Kis.*
	TURKISH,	*Kuchuk, ufak.*
	CIRCASSIAN,	*Bughuzay.*
	GEORGIAN,	*Patara.*
	MONGOLIAN,	*Ütshogen.*
	MANTSHU,	*Osokhon.*
	JAVANESE, Ngoko,	*Chiyut.*
	JAVANESE, Krama,	*Chiyut.*
	MALAY,	*Kachil.*
Isolating.	CHINESE, Nankin,	*Siaou.*
	CHINESE, Pekin,	*Hsiaou.*
	CHINESE, Canton,	*Siú, sai.*
	CHINESE, Shanghai,	*Siau.*
	AMOY, Colloquial,	*Soè.*
	JAPANESE,	*Sei no dsi sai hito.*
	Brahuí,	*Caret.*
Chinese Frontier & Tibet.	Gyámi,	*Syouti.*
	Gyárung,	*Kachhaî.*
	Tákpa,	*Chúngbo, prú.*
	Mányak,	*Yú.*
	Thochú,	*Bratsi-tha.*
	Sokpa,	*Bágá.*
	Horpa,	*Kamma.*
	Tibetan (*written*),	*Chhúng, phra.*
	Tibetan (*spoken*),	*Chún-chúng.*
Nepal (east to west).	Serpa,	*Tippe.*
	Súnwár,	*The baba.*
	Gúrung,	*Chúmba.*
	Múrmi,	*Jájá.*
	Magar,	*Márcho.*
	Tháksya,	*Chyángba.*
	Pákhya,	*Sánu.*
	Newár,	*Chígo, chigu.*
	Limbu,	*Chúkpa.*
Kiránti Group (East Nepal).	Kiránti,	*U'chú yáng.*
	Rodong,	*Inangko.*
	Rúngchenbung,	*U'chúkpáng.*
	Chhingtángya,	*Mikhá.*
	Náchhereng,	*A'msikholcho.*
	Wáling,	*Achokpa.*
	Yákha,	*Mik'na.*
	Chourásya,	*Yokka.*
	Kulungya,	*Chisma.*
	Thulungya,	*Kíchem.*
	Báhingya,	*Kachim.*
	Lohorong,	*Misyúma, misup'pa.*
	Lambichhong,	*Michi-yuk'kha, michiyuk.*
	Bálálí,	*Mepachhá.*
	Sáng-páng,	*Tuchheppa.*
	Dúmi,	*Tibichyom.*
	Kháling,	*Tibichem, yakhe.*
	Dungmáli,	*Umchuk'pang.*
Broken Tribes of Nepal.	Dárhi,	*Náni.*
	Denwár,	*Chotke.*
	Pahri,	*Chljagu, chigidhagu.*
	Chepáng,	*Maito, mayo.*
	Bhrámu,	*A'mi.*
	Váyu,	*Choh'mi.*
	Kuswar,	*I'bra.*
	Kusunda,	*Hungkoi.*
	Tháru,	*Chhot.*
	Lepcha (Sikkim),	*Achim, chimbo.*
	Bhúṭáni v. Lhopa,	*Chúngbo.*
N.-E. Bengal.	Bodo,	*Múdúi.*
	Dhimál,	*Mhoiká.*
	Kocch,	*Choto.*
	Garo,	*Pamar.*
	Kácharí,	*Gohai.*
Eastern Frontier of Bengal.	Munipuri,	*Caret.*
	Míthán Nágá,	*Ahipia.*
	Tablung Nágá,	*Sui.*
	Khári Nágá,	*Minghaji.*
	Angámi Nágá,	*Kanachapo.*
	Námsáng Nágá,	*A'ring.*
	Nowgong Nágá,	*Tilala.*
	Tengsa Nágá,	*Tesu.*
	Abor Miri,	*Angido.*
	Sibságar Miri,	*A'medák.*
	Deoria Chutia,	*Suru suroni.*
	Singpho,	*Katsi.*
Arrakan & Burmah.	Burman (*written*),	*Nge.*
	Burman (*spoken*),	*Nge, ngaythí.*
	Khyeng v. Shou,	*Ndo.*
	Kámi,	*Spi.*
	Kúmi,	*Athám.*
	Mrú v. Toung,	*Caret.*
	Sák,	*Caret.*
Siam & Tenasserim.	Talain v. Mon,	*Dhot.*
	Sgau-karen,	*Caret.*
	Pwo-karen,	*Caret.*
	Toungh-thu,	*Pá.*
	Shán,	*Leikh.*
	Annamitic,	*Bé.*
	Siamese,	*Let, lek, noi.*
	Ahom,	*Noi.*
	Khámti,	*Lek, on.*
	Laos,	*Lek, noi.*
Central India.	Ho (Kol),	*Húding.*
	Kol (Singhbhum),	*Hurung.*
	Santáli,	*Huring, kaṭih, gálác, jakár.*
	Bhúmij,	*Huringia, kato.*
	Uráon,	*Sanka.*
	Mundala,	*Huring.*
	Rájmahali,	*Caret.*
	Goṇḍi,	*Chudor, toro, pataro.*
	Gayeti,	*Chudor.*
	Rutluk,	*Chudor.*
	Naikude,	*Chinná.*
	Kolami,	*Chinnam.*
	Mádi,	*Hudiká, udilo.*
	Mádia,	*Hudili.*
	Kuri,	*Sang, sani.*
	Keikádi,	*Chinna.*
	Khoṇḍ,	*Caret.*
	Sávara,	*Sonna.*
	Gadaba,	*Mengen.*
	Yerukala,	*Chinnakerum, siruváyan.*
	Chentsu,	*Khopati.*
Southern India.	Tamiḷ, anc.,	*Vaṛidána.*
	Tamiḷ, mod.,	*Siṛiya, sinna.*
	Malayáḷma, anc.,	*Caret.*
	Malayáḷma, mod.,	*Cheṛiya.*
	Telugu,	*Chinna.*
	Karṇáṭaka, anc.,	*Caret.*
	Karṇáṭaka, mod.,	*Saṇṇa, chikka.*
	Tuḷuva,	*Kennu.*
	Kurgi,	*Cheriyadu.*
	Toḍuva,	*Caret.*
	Toḍa,	*Caret.*
	Kóta,	*Caret.*
	Baḍaga,	*Caret.*
	Kuṛumba,	*Caret.*
	Iruḷa,	*Caret.*
	Malabar,	*Siria, sinna.*
	Sinhalese,	*Punchi.*

Types.		
Inflecting.	SANSKRIT,	*Amla, śukta.*
	ARABIC,	*Hámoḍ.*
Compounding.	BASK,	*Gazi, min, lach, garrach.*
	FINNIC,	*Hapain.*
	MAGYAR,	*Savanju.*
	TURKISH,	*Ekshi.*
	CIRCASSIAN,	*Shegho.*
	GEORGIAN,	*Mkave.*
	MONGOLIAN,	*Kutsideï.*
	MANTSHU,	*Dshushughun.*
	JAVANESE, Ngoko,	*Hasĕm.*
	JAVANESE, Krama,	*Hasĕm.*
	MALAY,	*A'sam.*
Isolating.	CHINESE, Nankin,	*Swan.*
	CHINESE, Pekin,	*Swan.*
	CHINESE, Canton,	*Sün.*
	CHINESE, Shanghai,	*Su.*
	AMOY, Colloquial,	*Sng.*
	JAPANESE,	*Sui.*
	Brahuí,	*Kharen.*
Chinese Frontier & Tibet.	Gyámi,	*Láti.*
	Gyárung,	*Kúchchúr.*
	Tákpa,	*Kyúrpú.*
	Mányak,	*Dachá.*
	Thochú,	*Chak.*
	Sokpa,	*Ammahálon.*
	Horpa,	*S gúsgo.*
	Tibetan (*written*),	*Caret.*
	Tibetan (*spoken*),	*Caret.*
Népal (east to west).	Serpa,	*Caret.*
	Súnwár,	*Dúso.*
	Gúrung,	*Soba.*
	Múrmi,	*Caret.*
	Magar,	*Thúpcho.*
	Tháksya,	*Kimbá.*
	Pákhya,	*A'milo.*
	Newár,	*Phakú.*
	Limbu,	*Menlim mina.*
Kiranti Group (East Népal).	Kiránti,	*Súvo.*
	Rodong,	*Súre.*
	Rúngchenbung,	*Sún chakwa.*
	Chhingtángya,	*Súntá.*
	Náchhereng,	*Chochárpa.*
	Wáling,	*Súnta.*
	Yákha,	*Suá, súha.*
	Chourásya,	*Júrcho.*
	Kulungya,	*Jujur.*
	Thulungya,	*Jyurpa.*
	Báhingya,	*Jyúrba, -daäsi;[1] -daa.[2]*
	Lohorong,	*Sún'ta, limni.*
	Lambichhong,	*Súyukha.*
	Báláli,	*Sít'tu.*
	Sáng-páng,	*Chúri.*
	Dúmi,	*Júgúr.*
	Kháling,	*Jhár'pa.*
	Dungmáli,	*Sun; sunchie;[1] masun.[2]*
Broken Tribes of Népal.	Dárhi,	*Syisye.*
	Denwár,	*Koro.*
	Pahri,	*Palugu.*
	Chepáng,	*Nimlo.*
	Bhrámu,	*Kyáso.*
	Váyu,	*Sokim, sokim.*
	Kuswar,	*Nágúlyo.*
	Kusunda,	*Daur tan.*
	Tháru,	*Khattá.*
	Lepcha (Sikkim),	*Krop.*
	Bhúṭáni v. Lhopa,	*Tekpo.*
N.-E. Bengal.	Bodo,	*Gaphá, gakhoï.*
	Dhimál,	*Dakká.*
	Kocch,	*Títá.*
	Garo,	*Phakká.*
	Káchári,	*Gokai.*
Eastern Frontier of Bengal.	Munipuri,	*Asinba.*
	Míthán Nágá,	*Shí.*
	Tablung Nágá,	*Sí.*
	Khári Nágá,	*Tehsan.*
	Angámi Nágá,	*Khye.*
	Námsáng Nágá,	*Así.*
	Nowgong Nágá,	*Túsan.*
	Tengsa Nágá,	*Senla.*
	Abor Miri,	*Kune.*
	Sibságar Miri,	*Kudák.*
	Deoria Chutia,	*Sitotoi.*
	Singpho,	*Khrí.*
Arrakan & Burmah.	Burman (*written*),	*Khyiṇ.*
	Burman (*spoken*),	*Khyin, khyinthí.*
	Khyeng v. Shou,	*To.*
	Kámi,	*Tho.*
	Kúmi,	*Ahto.*
	Mrú v. Toung,	*Caret.*
	Sák,	*Caret.*
Siam & Tenasserim.	Talain v. Mon,	*Hpya.*
	Sgau-karen,	*Se, tse.*
	Pwo-karen,	*Tsaing.*
	Toungh-thu,	*H'sya.*
	Shán,	*Htsol.*
	Annamitic,	*Shua.*
	Siamese,	*Som, preo, htso.*
	Ahom,	*Sum.*
	Khámti,	*Som.*
	Laos,	*Som.*
Central India.	Ho (Kol),	*Jojo.*
	Kol (Singhbhum),	*Jojo.*
	Santáli,	*Maraïh, kású.*
	Bhúmij,	*Jojo.*
	Uráon,	*Tissa.*
	Mundala,	*Jojou.*
	Rájmahali,	*Tise.*
	Goṇḍi,	*Chúk manda, savitá.*
	Gayeti,	*Savitál.*
	Rutluk,	*Nagul.*
	Naikude,	*Caret.*
	Kolami,	*Tirre.*
	Mádi,	*Wovita, weita, pulla.*
	Mádia,	*Dhirdhira.*
	Kuri,	*Kataye.*
	Keikádi,	*Pulpu.*
	Khoṇḍ,	*Trahane.*
	Sávara,	*Aragna.*
	Gadaba,	*Susoká.*
	Yerukala,	*Pulladikkiri.*
	Chentsu,	*Ammuto.*
Southern India.	Tamiḷ, anc.,	*Caret.*
	Tamiḷ, mod.,	*Puḷitta, puḷippu.*
	Malayáḷma, anc.,	*Caret.*
	Malayáḷma, mod.,	*Puḷi.*
	Telugu,	*Pullani, pullaṭi.*
	Karṇáṭaka, anc.,	*Caret.*
	Karṇáṭaka, mod.,	*Huḷi.*
	Tuḷuva,	*Puli.*
	Kurgi,	*Caret.*
	Toḍuva, }	*Pilba.*
	Toḍa, }	*Pülthati.*
	Kóta,	*Pulsa.*
	Baḍaga,	*Hulli.*
	Kuṟumba,	*Hulli.*
	Iruḷa,	*Pulli.*
	Malabar,	*Puḷippu.*
	Sinhalese,	*Ambul.*

Group	Types.	
Inflecting.	SANSKRIT,	*Chaturasra, chatush-koṇa.*
	ARABIC,	*Murabbaa.*
Compounding.	BASK,	*Lauki, laurki.*
	FINNIC,	*Neljäs = kulmainen.*
	MAGYAR,	*Caret.*
	TURKISH,	*Ghyùnya.*
	CIRCASSIAN,	*Caret.*
	GEORGIAN,	*Caret.*
	MONGOLIAN,	*Tepker.*
	MANTSHU,	*Hoshongko.*
	JAVANESE, Ngoko,	*Pasági.*
	JAVANESE, Krama,	*Pasági.*
	MALAY,	*Barsikusiku.*
Isolating.	CHINESE, Nankin,	*Fang.*
	CHINESE, Pekin,	*Fang.*
	CHINESE, Canton,	*Fong.*
	CHINESE, Shanghai,	*Fong.*
	AMOY, Colloquial,	*Li-kak.*
	JAPANESE,	*Shi-kaku.*
	Brahuí,	*Caret.*
Chinese Frontier & Tibet.	Gyámi,	*Pyángdi.*
	Gyárung,	*Zhirdo.*
	Tákpa,	*Túpzhi.*
	Mányak,	*Drazo.*
	Thochú,	*Ghzirú.*
	Sokpa,	*Caret.*
	Horpa,	*Súr-zhi.*
	Tibetan (*written*),	*Grúb-zhi* (angles four).
	Tibetan (*spoken*),	*Thúzi* (angles four).
Nepal (east to west).	Serpa,	*Túpchi.*
	Súnwár,	*Chár-pátya.*
	Gúrung,	*Kona-pli.*
	Múrmi,	*Kúni-pli.*
	Magar,	*Chou-khá-nya.*
	Tháksya,	*Bhilirchhowa.*
	Pákhya,	*Chárapálo.*
	Newár,	*Pekúngla.*
	Limbu,	*Kuyok túve lish.*
Kiranti Group (East Nepal).	Kiránti,	*Pheb dába, lea kona.*
	Rodong,	*Plangpáchimá.*
	Rúngchenbung,	*La-ákúná.*
	Chhingtángya,	*Cháraupátyá.*
	Náchhereng,	*Phepheya.*
	Wáling,	*Layá khúktáng.*
	Yákha,	*Lichina yúsúk.*
	Chourásya,	*Charkune.*
	Kulungya,	*Lih khonglá.*
	Thulungya,	*Khikerma.*
	Báhingya,	*Lepataye.*
	Lohorong,	*Rik'sukye.*
	Lambichhong,	*Caret.*
	Báláli,	*Caret.*
	Sáng-páng,	*Likapáta.*
	Dúmi,	*Caret.*
	Kháling,	*Bhálchyusko.*
	Dungmáli,	*Rik'tum.*
Broken Tribes of Nepal.	Dárhi,	*Charkonya.*
	Denwár,	*Caret.*
	Pahri,	*Pekúnglagu.*
	Chepáng,	*Caret.*
	Bhrámu,	*Chárpatya.*
	Váyu,	*Caret.*
	Kuswar,	*Chárpatya.*
	Kusunda,	*Chárapáte.*
	Tháru,	*Chárakunabate.*
	Lepcha (Sikkim),	*Ton kyong phali.*
	Bhúṭáni v. Lhopa,	*Duzhi yeupo.*

Group		
N.-E. Bengal.	Bodo,	*Konámanbreni.*
	Dhimál,	*Dia-thúnika* (angles four).
	Kocch,	*Chou-konia.*
	Garo,	*Koná bri ni.*
	Káchári,	*Caret.*
Eastern Frontier of Bengal.	Munipuri,	*Caret.*
	Míthán Nágá,	*Caret.*
	Tablung Nágá,	*Caret.*
	Khári Nágá,	*Caret.*
	Angámi Nágá,	*Caret.*
	Námsáng Nágá,	*Caret.*
	Nowgong Nágá,	*Tangakáku.*
	Tengsa Nágá,	*Tangik.*
	Abor Miri,	*Caret.*
	Sibságar Miri,	*Caret.*
	Deoria Chutia,	*Caret.*
	Singpho,	*Caret.*
Arrakan & Burmah.	Burman (*written*),	*Lethong.*
	Burman (*spoken*),	*Ledhaung, ḷaihtouknaithi.*
	Khyeng v. Shou,	*Kyilhi.*
	Kámi,	*Atikimli.*
	Kúmi,	*Taki.*
	Mrú v. Toung,	*Caret.*
	Sák,	*Caret.*
Siam & Tenasserim.	Talain v. Mon,	*Ponkalan.*
	Sgau-karen,	*Caret.*
	Pwo-karen,	*Caret.*
	Toungh-thu,	*Sitseng.*
	Shán,	*Pyay.*
	Annamitic,	*Vuông.*
	Siamese,	*Htsilen.*
	Ahom,	*Caret.*
	Khámti,	*Caret.*
	Laos,	*Caret.*
Central India.	Ho (Kol),	*Chepéd.*
	Kol (Singhbhum),	*Upúnkocha.*
	Santáli,	*Girite, murcháute* (verbs).
	Bhúmij,	*Upúnkou.*
	Urdon,	*Chárkona.*
	Mundala,	*Gotá.*
	Rájmahali,	*Caret.*
	Goṇḍi,	*Nálukhúnt, charkuntya.*
	Gayeti,	*Caret.*
	Rutluk,	*Khutul.*
	Naikude,	*Caret.*
	Kolami,	*Okesarase.*
	Mádi,	*Caret.*
	Mádia,	*Caret.*
	Kuri,	*Charkutya* (*charkuntya ?*).
	Keikádi,	*Choukunta.*
	Khoṇḍ,	*Taṭṭu.*
	Sávara,	*Onjimúlalankabagná, sagná-*
	Gadaba,	*Duttu.* [*daku.*
	Yerukala,	*Tsadaram.*
	Chentsu,	*Sadunúta, chakkata.*
Southern India.	Tamiḷ, anc.,	*Caret.*
	Tamiḷ, mod.,	*Saduramána, chatukkamána.*
	Malayáḷma, anc.,	*Caret.*
	Malayáḷma, mod.,	*Chaturamáyuḷḷa.*
	Telugu,	*Chadaramu, chaukamu.*
	Karṇáṭaka, anc.,	*Caret.*
	Karṇáṭaka, mod.,	*Chauka.*
	Tuḷuva,	*Chauka.*
	Kurgi,	*Caret.*
	Toḍuva, }	*Caret.*
	Toḍa, }	*Caret.*
	Kóta,	*Saṭṭe.*
	Baḍaga,	*Jauka.*
	Kurumba,	*Jauka.*
	Iruḷa,	*Javuka.*
	Malabar,	*Sathuramana.*
	Sinhalese,	*Satarás.*

Group	Language	Word
	Types.	
Inflecting.	SANSKRIT,	*Sarala, riju.*
	ARABIC,	*Mustakim.*
Compounding.	BASK,	*Zuzen, chushen, artez, margo.*
	FINNIC,	*Suora.*
	MAGYAR,	*Egyenes.*
	TURKISH,	*Doghru.*
	CIRCASSIAN,	*Caret.*
	GEORGIAN,	*Marjeni.*
	MONGOLIAN,	*Bototoi.*
	MANTSHU,	*Godokhon.*
	JAVANESE, Ngoko,	*Bĕnnĕr.*
	JAVANESE, Krama,	*Lĕrĕs.*
	MALAY,	*Batúl.*
Isolating.	CHINESE, Nankin,	*Pih-chih.*
	CHINESE, Pekin,	*Pi-chih.*
	CHINESE, Canton,	*Chik.*
	CHINESE, Shanghai,	*Zah.*
	AMOY, Colloquial,	*Tit.*
	JAPANESE,	*Masugu.*
	Brahuí,	*Caret.*
Chinese Frontier & Tibet.	Gyámi,	*Tingdi.*
	Gyárung,	*Kakas'to.*
	Tákpa,	*Tráng bo.*
	Mányak,	*Chú chú.*
	Thochú,	*Kasth.*
	Sokpa,	*Caret.*
	Horpa,	*Kathong.*
	Tibetan (*written*),	*Dránpo.*
	Tibetan (*spoken*),	*Thángbo.*
Nepal (east to west).	Serpa,	*Tángo.*
	Súnwár,	*Shejo.*
	Gúrung,	*Kyún.*
	Múrmi,	*Thácho.*
	Magar,	*Dhingcho.*
	Tháksya,	*Tananphirphai.*
	Pákhya,	*Tersai.*
	Newár,	*Tapyong.*
	Limbu,	*Toudo.*
Kiranti Group (East Nepal).	Kiránti,	*U'dúngtwongtong.*
	Rodong,	*Sojho.*
	Rúngchenbung,	*Sojho.*
	Chhingtángya,	*Chángno.*
	Náchhereng,	*Sejho.*
	Wáling,	*Sejho.*
	Yákha,	*Sojho.*
	Chourásya,	*Sojho.*
	Kulungya,	*Twáipa.*
	Thulungya,	*Jongpa.*
	Báhingya,	*Dyom'ba.*
	Lohorong,	*Lungkúye, chengye.*
	Lambichhong,	*Sori, sorikha.*
	Báláli,	*Lúngku.*
	Sáng-páng,	*Toh'no.*
	Dúmi,	*Danta.*
	Kháling,	*Dhvaipa.*
	Dungmáli,	*Cháng.*
Broken Tribes of Nepal.	Dárhi,	*Sojho.*
	Denwár,	*Solar.*
	Pahri,	*Tipyungguhma.*
	Chepáng,	*Dhimto.*
	Bhrámu,	*Caret.*
	Váyu,	*Chengchengmo.*
	Kuswar,	*Sojho.*
	Kusunda,	*Caret.*
	Thárú,	*Sojh.*
	Lepcha (Sikkim),	*Náng.*
	Bhútáni v. Lhopa,	*Thángbo*
N.-E. Bengal.	Bodo,	*Thúngjúng, gothong.*
	Dhimál,	*Ghenká.*
	Kocch,	*Sidhá.*
	Garo,	*Preng den.*
	Káchári,	*Caret.*
Eastern Frontier of Bengal.	Munipuri,	*Chume.*
	Míthán Nágá,	*Caret.*
	Tablung Nágá,	*Caret.*
	Khári Nágá,	*Mathunjau.*
	Angámi Nágá,	*Thekhá.*
	Námsáng Nágá,	*A'ling.*
	Nowgong Nágá,	*Tumutum.*
	Tengsa Nágá,	*Matungkolo.*
	Abor Miri,	*Pundu.*
	Sibságar Miri,	*Guyokdak.*
	Deoria Chutia,	*Pune.*
	Singpho,	*Preng.*
Arrakan & Burmah.	Burman (*written*),	*Phrong.*
	Burman (*spoken*),	*Phyaung, hpaungthí.*
	Khyeng v. Shou,	*Klún.*
	Kámi,	*To.*
	Kúmi,	*Tau.*
	Mrú v. Toung,	*Caret.*
	Sák,	*Caret.*
Siam & Tenasserim.	Talain v. Mon,	*Touk.*
	Sgau-karen,	*Lo, blir.*
	Pwo-karen,	*Laung.*
	Toungh-thu,	*Tsone.*
	Shán,	*Tsú.*
	Annamitic,	*Ngay.*
	Siamese,	*Trong, sű, htso.*
	Ahom,	*U'.*
	Khámti,	*Nan.*
	Laos,	*Caret.*
Central India.	Ho (Kol),	*Caret.*
	Kol (Singhbhum),	*Múli.*
	Santáli,	*Sajhete* (verb).
	Bhúmij,	*Búgisaj.*
	Uráon,	*U'jgo.*
	Mundala,	*Sojhia.*
	Rájmahali,	*Jákro.*
	Goṇḍi,	*Tukvá, sarko.*
	Gayeti,	*Kasnu.*
	Rutluk,	*Kasum.*
	Naikude,	*Dadapad.*
	Kolami,	*Andidadam.*
	Mádi,	*Kasumi, kasomue.*
	Mádia,	*Soj.*
	Kuri,	*Korá.*
	Keikádi,	*Sukágá.*
	Khoṇḍ,	*Soddemanne.*
	Sávara,	*Barídako.*
	Gadaba,	*Lakoḍuttu.*
	Yerukala,	*Sadunu.*
	Chentsu,	*Sorichhaiyye, sorikaráhache.*
Southern India.	Tamiḷ, anc.,	*Ozhungána.*
	Tamiḷ, mod.,	*Nerána.*
	Malayáḷma, anc.,	*Caret.*
	Malayáḷma, mod.,	*Nere, chovve.*
	Telugu,	*Sariggá-uṇḍe, chakkagá.*
	Karṇáṭaka, anc.,	*Caret.*
	Karṇáṭaka, mod.,	*Sariyáda, neṭṭage.*
	Tuḷuva,	*Sarta.*
	Kurgi,	*Nere.*
	Toḍuva,	*Caret.*
	Toḍa,	*Caret.*
	Kóta,	*Hasia, neṭṭu.*
	Baḍaga,	*Neṭṭage.*
	Kuṛumba,	*Neṭṭage.*
	Iruḷa,	*Neṭṭe.*
	Malabar,	*Nere.*
	Sinhalese,	*Kelin.*

	Types.	
Inflecting.	SANSKRIT,	*Swádu, madhura.*
	ARABIC,	*Helú.*
Compounding.	BASK,	*Gozo, ezti.*
	FINNIC,	*Makia.*
	MAGYAR,	*Edes.*
	TURKISH,	*Tatlu.*
	CIRCASSIAN,	*Ezshu, ezrey.*
	GEORGIAN,	*Tkbili.*
	MONGOLIAN,	*Amdaï.*
	MANTSHU,	*Tchantchuhun.*
	JAVANESE, Ngoko,	*Lĕgi.*
	JAVANESE, Krama,	*Lĕgi.*
	MALAY,	*Mánis.*
Isolating.	CHINESE, Nankin,	*T'ien.*
	CHINESE, Pekin,	*T'ien.*
	CHINESE, Canton,	*T'im.*
	CHINESE, Shanghai,	*Tien.*
	AMOY, Colloquial,	*Tin.*
	JAPANESE,	*Amai.*
	Brahuí,	*Hanen.*
Chinese Frontier & Tibet.	Gyámi,	*Syángdi.*
	Gyárung,	*Kamgnar'.*
	Tákpa,	*Nyokpa.*
	Mányak,	*Debi.*
	Thochú,	*Jam.*
	Sokpa,	*Amthethe.*
	Horpa,	*Thúthú.*
	Tibetan (*written*),	*Caret.*
	Tibetan (*spoken*),	*Gnármo.*
Nepal (east to west).	Serpa,	*Gnormo.*
	Súnwár,	*Jiji.*
	Gúrung,	*Gnába.*
	Múrmi,	*Kekeba.*
	Magar,	*Jyúcho.*
	Tháksya,	*Koghibá.*
	Pákhya,	*Guliyo.*
	Newár,	*Chakú.*
	Limbu,	*Kelimba.*
Kiranti Group (East Nepal).	Kiránti,	*Lemko.*
	Rodong,	*Lam chho, walye.*
	Rúngchenbung,	*Lemko, lemchi.*
	Chhingtángya,	*Lem'no.*
	Náchhereng,	*Lemda.*
	Wáling,	*Lem, lemya.*
	Yákha,	*Limha.*
	Chourásya,	*Jijilúcho.*
	Kulungya,	*Lema.*
	Thulungya,	*Jijin.*
	Báhingya,	*Jijim; -daäsi;[1] -daä.[2]*
	Lohorong,	*Lim'-pa, limte.*
	Lambichhong,	*Limyukha, lemyú.*
	Bálâli,	*Lim.*
	Sáng-páng,	*Limi.*
	Dúmi,	*Lem.*
	Kháling,	*Lempá.*
	Dungmáli,	*Lem, lem'chie;[1] malem.[2]*
Broken Tribes of Nepal.	Dárhi,	*Gúre.*
	Denwár,	*Gúryo.*
	Pahri,	*Chággu.*
	Chepáng,	*Nimto.*
	Bhrámu,	*Kyosyá.*
	Váyu,	*Chinjimo.*
	Kuswar,	*Gulyo.*
	Kusunda,	*A'hál.*
	Tháru,	*Mithá.*
	Lepcha (Sikkim),	*Akliam, kliambo.*
	Bhútáni v. Lhopa,	*Gnámo.*

N.-E. Bengal.	Bodo,	*Gadoï.*
	Dhimál,	*Táaka.*
	Kocch,	*Mitha.*
	Garo,	*Shamá.*
	Káchári,	*Godai.*
Eastern Frontier of Bengal.	Munipuri,	*Athúmba.*
	Míthán Nágá,	*Ti.*
	Tablung Nágá,	*Urang.*
	Khári Nágá,	*Miang.*
	Angámi Nágá,	*Che.*
	Námsáng Nágá,	*A'tú.*
	Nowgong Nágá,	*Tánang.*
	Tengsa Nágá,	*Tánang.*
	Abor Miri,	*Tido.*
	Sibságar Miri,	*Tidák.*
	Deoria Chutia,	*Jiri.*
	Singpho,	*Dúi.*
Arrakan & Burmah.	Burman (*written*),	*Khyo.*
	Burman (*spoken*),	*Khyo, chyathi.*
	Khyeng v. Shou,	*Túi.*
	Kámi,	*Tú.*
	Kúmi,	*Túi.*
	Mrú v. Toung,	*Caret.*
	Sák,	*Caret.*
Siam & Tenasserim.	Talain v. Mon,	*Tat,*
	Sgau-karen,	*Sir, tser.*
	Pwo-karen,	*Tsung.*
	Toungh-thu,	*Neu.*
	Shán,	*Tron.*
	Annamitic,	*Ngot.*
	Siamese,	*Wán.*
	Ahom,	*Oi.*
	Khámti,	*Wán.*
	Laos,	*Wán.*
Central India.	Ho (Kol),	*Ibilla.*
	Kol (Singhbhum),	*Sibila.*
	Santáli,	*Sebel, hengnem.*
	Bhúmij,	*Sibila.*
	Uráon,	*Tini.*
	Mundala,	*Sibil.*
	Rájmahali,	*Embe.*
	Goṇḍi,	*Mingatá, mingul.*
	Gayeti,	*Mingul.*
	Rutluk,	*Mithomi.*
	Naikude,	*Tirre.*
	Kolami,	*Send.*
	Mádi,	*Mingta, mirangul.*
	Mádia,	*Milgale.*
	Kuri,	*Simel.*
	Keikádi,	*Tipu.*
	Khoṇḍ,	*Sendijáninju.*
	Sávara,	*Mana.*
	Gadaba,	*Sabbulká.*
	Yerukala,	*Teyyanikkiri.*
	Chentsu,	*Mithá.*
Southern India.	Tamiḷ, anc.,	*Iniya.*
	Tamiḷ, mod.,	*Tittitta, tittippu.*
	Malayáḷma, anc.,	*Caret.*
	Malayáḷma, mod.,	*Swádulla.*
	Telugu,	*Tiyyani, tipu.*
	Karṇáṭaka, anc.,	*Caret.*
	Karṇáṭaka, mod.,	*S'í.*
	Tuḷuva,	*Tipe.*
	Kurgi,	*Mantal.*
	Toḍuva, }	*Caret.*
	Toḍa, }	*Dijati.*
	Kóta,	*Se.*
	Baḍaga,	*Si.*
	Kuṛumba,	*Si.*
	Iruḷa,	*Rúse.*
	Malabar,	*Inippu.*
	Sinhalese,	*Mihiri.*

Group	Language	Word
	Types.	
Inflecting.	SANSKRIT,	*Tuṅga, uchchadeha.*
	ARABIC,	*Táwíl.*
Compounding.	BASK,	*Andi, aundi.*
	FINNIC,	*Pitkä.*
	MAGYAR,	*Magas.*
	TURKISH,	*U'zun.*
	CIRCASSIAN,	*Kakha.*
	GEORGIAN,	*Gridzali.*
	MONGOLIAN,	*Öndor.*
	MANTSHU,	*Ten.*
	JAVANESE, Ngoko,	*Duwur, duhur.*
	JAVANESE, Krama,	*Hinggil.*
	MALAY,	*Renjong.*
Isolating.	CHINESE, Nankin,	*Káou, ch'ang.*
	CHINESE, Pekin,	*Káou, ch'ang.*
	CHINESE, Canton,	*Kò.*
	CHINESE, Shanghai,	*Dzáng-kuh, dzáng-niang, dzáng-tsz.*
	AMOY, Colloquial,	*Koâiṇ.*
	JAPANESE,	*Sei no takai hito.*
	Brahui,	*Caret.*
Chinese Frontier & Tibet.	Gyámi,	*Kouti.*
	Gyárung,	*Kasri.*
	Tákpa,	*Zúgring.*
	Mányak,	*Hra-hra.*
	Thochú,	*Bráthá.*
	Sokpa,	*U'ndúr.*
	Horpa,	*Gakhye.*
	Tibetan (*written*),	*Caret.*
	Tibetan (*spoken*),	*Thombo.*
Nepal (east to west).	Serpa,	*Thenbo.*
	Súnwár,	*Laiso.*
	Gúrung,	*Kuhba.*
	Múrmi,	*Nohba.*
	Magar,	*Ghiángcho.*
	Tháksya,	*Bauchhenba.*
	Pákhya,	*A'go.*
	Newár,	*Tadhi.*
	Limbu,	*Kemba.*
Kiranti Group (East Nepal).	Kiránti,	*Kontá.*
	Rodong,	*Kile, run'de.*
	Rúngchenbung,	*Kiyang, kongyang, kwangla.*
	Chhingtángya,	*Keno.*
	Náchhereng,	*Bháipa, repa.*
	Wáling,	*Kiyáng.*
	Yákha,	*Kená.*
	Chourásya,	*Robo, rocho.*
	Kulungya,	*Wadreppa.*
	Thulungya,	*Yepa.*
	Báhingya,	*Lába.*
	Lohorong,	*Keye.*
	Lambichhong,	*Keyuk, keyuk'kha.*
	Bálálí,	*Kibyep.*
	Sáng-páng,	*Ottoripiko.*
	Dúmi,	*Song'pa.*
	Kháling,	*Song'pa. [bádhememekachi.[2]*
	Dungmáli,	*Badhemego, badhemechágo,[1]*
Broken Tribes of Nepal.	Dárhi,	*Dhenga.*
	Denwár,	*Algo.*
	Pahri,	*Thaso.*
	Chepáng,	*Caret.*
	Bhrámu,	*Alhok.*
	Váyu,	*Jongta.*
	Kuswar,	*Algo.*
	Kusunda,	*Phiyong.*
	Tháru,	*Uchcha.*
	Lepcha (Sikkim),	*Atho, thobo.*
	Bhútáni v. Lhopa,	*Thembo, tho.*
N.-E. Bengal.	Bodo,	*Gajon.*
	Dhimál,	*Dhángáká.*
	Kocch,	*Uccha.*
	Garo,	*Pillo.*
	Kácharí,	*Gojo.*
Eastern Frontier of Bengal.	Munipuri,	*Caret.*
	Míthán Nágá,	*Choak.*
	Tablung Nágá,	*Tau.*
	Khári Nágá,	*Oregu.*
	Angámi Nágá,	*Karkhre.*
	Námsáng Nágá,	*Achuong.*
	Nowgong Nágá,	*Talángka.*
	Tengsa Nágá,	*Lángla.*
	Abor Miri,	*Caret.*
	Sibságar Miri,	*Aidrdáh.*
	Deoria Chutia,	*Suini.*
	Singpho,	*Tsode.*
Arrakan & Burmah.	Burman (*written*),	*Mrang.*
	Burman (*spoken*),	*Myen, myinthi.*
	Khyeng v. Shou,	*Lhún.*
	Kámi,	*Kasá.*
	Kúmi,	*Caret.*
	Mrú v. Toung,	*Caret.*
	Sák,	*Caret.*
Siam & Tenasserim.	Talain v. Mon,	*Thalon.*
	Sgau-karen,	*'Tau.*
	Pwo-karen,	*Tongtang.*
	Toungh-thu,	*H'to.*
	Shán,	*Tson.*
	Annamitic,	*Kao.*
	Siamese,	*Thohn, súng.*
	Ahom,	*Sung.*
	Khámti,	*Sung.*
	Laos,	*Sung.*
Central India.	Ho (Kol),	*Sangali.*
	Kol (Singhbhum),	*Batari salangi.*
	Santáli,	*Usul.*
	Bhúmij,	*Baraisangaluma.*
	Uráon,	*Micha.*
	Mundala,	*Jiling.*
	Rájmahali,	*Digaro.*
	Goṇḍi,	*Jhangchomanda.*
	Gayeti,	*Caret.*
	Rutluk,	*Caret.*
	Naikude,	*Caret.*
	Kolami,	*Caret.*
	Mádi,	*Caret.*
	Mádia,	*Caret.*
	Kuri,	*Caret.*
	Keikádi,	*Caret.*
	Khoṇḍ,	*Caret.*
	Sávara,	*Lanka.*
	Gadaba,	*Tiyyár.*
	Yerukala,	*Vasaram.*
	Chentsu,	*Namo.*
Southern India.	Tamiḻ, anc.,	*Caret.*
	Tamiḻ, mod.,	*Uyarnda.*
	Malayáḻma, anc.,	*Caret.*
	Malayáḻma, mod.,	*Uyarnna.*
	Telugu,	*Poḍugáṭi.*
	Karṇáṭaka, anc.,	*Caret.*
	Karṇáṭaka, mod.,	*Ucha.*
	Tuḷuva,	*Caret.*
	Kurgi,	*Caret.*
	Toḍuva, } Toda, }	*Niraka, neragatti.* *Nirigiál.*
	Kóta,	*Uddaman.*
	Baḍaga,	*Uddava.*
	Kurumba,	*Uddalu.*
	Iruḷa,	*Udda-manishu.*
	Malabar,	*Uyarnthavan.*
	Sinhalese,	*Usa.*

Group	Types.	
Inflecting.	SANSKRIT,	*Tanu, kshiṇa.*
	ARABIC,	*Raḳiḳ, rafiaa.*
Compounding.	BASK,	*Flako, argal, erbal, maskel* [*santar, hebain.*
	FINNIC,	*Laiha.*
	MAGYAR,	*Nyulank.*
	TURKISH,	*Erk.*
	CIRCASSIAN,	*Wedd.*
	GEORGIAN,	*Sudoli.*
	MONGOLIAN,	*Nimeghen.*
	MANTSHU,	*Torha.*
	JAVANESE, Ngoko,	*Tipis, kuru.*
	JAVANESE, Krama,	*Tipis, kĕra.*
	MALAY,	*Kúrus.*
Isolating.	CHINESE, Nankin,	*Sau.*
	CHINESE, Pekin,	*Sau.*
	CHINESE, Canton,	*Shau.*
	CHINESE, Shanghai,	*Seu.*
	AMOY, Colloquial,	*Poh.*
	JAPANESE,	*Yasetoru.*
	Brahuí,	*Caret.*
Chinese Frontier & Tibet.	Gyámi,	*Syouti.*
	Gyárung,	*Kwichem.*
	Tákpa,	*Kámrháng.*
	Mányak,	*Kári.*
	Thochú,	*Charghe.*
	Sokpa,	*O'khúnáe.*
	Horpa,	*Chú chú.*
	Tibetan (*written*),	*Srobbo, ridpo.*
	Tibetan (*spoken*),	*Mábo* (?).
Nepal (east to west).	Serpa,	*Nenma.*
	Súnwár,	*Gyeso.*
	Gúrung,	*Jhenba.*
	Múrmi,	*Jeutpá.*
	Magar,	*Rúcho.*
	Tháksya,	*Jyalba.*
	Pákhya,	*Háriyáko.*
	Newár,	*Gonsi.*
	Limbu,	*Yoshú.*
Kiránti Group (East Nepal).	Kiránti,	*Yom.*
	Rodong,	*Pálete, simámyo.*
	Rúngchenbung,	*Yomyangko, ropyangko.*
	Chhingtángya,	*Rongsi.*
	Náchhereng,	*Ramdá.*
	Wáling,	*Rongyang, achitpo.*
	Yákha,	*Hächigokná.*
	Chourásya,	*Yokká.*
	Kulungya,	*Gamsipá.*
	Thulungya,	*Jerpá.*
	Báhingya,	*Kachim, ryam'ba.*
	Lohorong,	*Yámisa.*
	Lambichhong,	*Keksu reksukha.*
	Bálálí,	*Mepachá.*
	Sáng-páng,	*Romiko.*
	Dúmi,	*Rom.*
	Kháling,	*Jyor'pa.*
	Dungmáli,	*Chuk.*
Broken Tribes of Nepal.	Dárhi,	*Dúbro.*
	Denwár,	*Dúbro.*
	Pahri,	*Gangsihma.*
	Chepáng,	*Caret.*
	Bhrámu,	*Máchho.*
	Váyu,	*Gerṭa.*
	Kuswar,	*Khengralo.*
	Kusunda,	*Gharáu.*
	Tháru,	*Dabar.*
	Lepcha (Sikkim),	*Achim, chimbo.*
	Bhúṭáni v. Lhopa,	*Byeko.*

Group		
N.-E. Bengal.	Bodo,	*Gaham.*
	Dhimál,	*Syenká, mhoïka.*
	Kocch,	*Sukna.*
	Garo,	*Jotkreng.*
	Káchári,	*Caret.*
Eastern Frontier of Bengal.	Munipuri,	*Caret.*
	Míthán Nágá,	*Caret.*
	Tablung Nágá,	*Caret.*
	Khári Nágá,	*Achi.*
	Angámi Nágá,	*Soponoru.*
	Námsáng Nágá,	*Achá.*
	Nowgong Nágá,	*Apoprr.*
	Tengsa Nágá,	*Apo.*
	Abor Miri,	*Caret.*
	Sibságar Miri,	*Gidák.*
	Deoria Chutia,	*Dugumjini.*
	Singpho,	*Lasi.*
Arrakan & Burmah.	Burman (*written*),	*Lhyá.*
	Burman (*spoken*),	*Shyá, penthi.*
	Khyeng v. Shou,	*Pám.*
	Kámi,	*Tapá.*
	Kúmi,	*Tháin.*
	Mrú v. Toung,	*Caret.*
	Sák,	*Caret.*
Siam & Tenasserim.	Talain v. Mon,	*Tharai.*
	Sgau-karen,	*Caret.*
	Pwo-karen,	*Caret.*
	Toungh-thu,	*Hyeng.*
	Shán,	*Raung.*
	Annamitic,	*Mong, mañ.*
	Siamese,	*Hpohn, maiman.*
	Ahom,	*Heng.*
	Khámti,	*Yom.*
	Laos,	*Caret.*
Central India.	Ho (Kol),	*Battri.*
	Kol (Singhbhum),	*Bátaria.*
	Santáli,	*Etáng, nánhá chiribiti,*
	Bhúmij,	*Baraiúsú.* [*chámaṭiá* (of a woman).
	Uráon,	*Serñá.*
	Mundala,	*U'sú.*
	Rájmahali,	*Gandi.*
	Goṇḍi,	*Sirsi hattúr.*
	Gayeti,	*Chudor* (small).
	Rutluk,	*Chudor* (small).
	Naikude,	*Chinná* (small).
	Kolami,	*Chinnam* (small).
	Mádi,	*Hudilá* (small).
	Mádia,	*Hudili* (small).
	Kuri,	*Sang* (small).
	Keikádi,	*Chinna* (small).
	Khoṇḍ,	*Banda ayininju.*
	Sávara,	*Palapalasan.*
	Gadaba,	*Palasanadulta.*
	Yerukala,	*Bakkadu.*
	Chentsu,	*Saruvoti, sakunaṭa.*
Southern India.	Tamiḷ, anc.,	*Melliya.*
	Tamiḷ, mod.,	*Melinda.*
	Malayáḷma, anc.,	*Caret.*
	Malayáḷma, mod.,	*Meliñña.*
	Telugu,	*Paluchani.*
	Karṇáṭaka, anc.,	*Caret.*
	Karṇáṭaka, mod.,	*Teḷḷána.*
	Tuḷuva,	*Sabara.*
	Kurgi,	*Caret.*
	Toḍuva, }	*Caret.*
	Toḍa, }	*Kinud.*
	Kóta,	*Vottale.*
	Baḍaga,	*Kuna.*
	Kuṟumba,	*Melle.*
	Iruḷa,	*Vaḍage.*
	Malabar,	*Melintha, mellia.*
	Sinhalese,	*Tuni.*

Group	Language	Word
Types.		
Inflecting.	SANSKṚIT,	*Kurúpa, virúpa, rúpahína.*
	ARABIC,	Kabîḥ, *basheaa.*
Compounding.	BASK,	*Itsusi, ichusi, ezañ, kemenge.*
	FINNIC,	*Ruma.*
	MAGYAR,	*Caret.*
	TURKISH,	*Chirkin.*
	CIRCASSIAN,	*Eyceh.*
	GEORGIAN,	*Pilsi.*
	MONGOLIAN,	*Oroöda.*
	MANTSHU,	*Botsikhe.*
	JAVANESE, Ngoko,	*Halarupa.*
	JAVANESE, Krama,	*Hawonwarni.*
	MALAY,	*U'duh.*
Isolating.	CHINESE, Nankin,	*Ch'au-yang-uoh.*
	CHINESE, Pekin,	*Ch'au-yang-uoh.*
	CHINESE, Canton,	*Ch'au-yeong.*
	CHINESE, Shanghai,	*Veh-hau-küṇ.*
	AMOY, Colloquial,	*K'iap-sì.*
	JAPANESE,	*Mi-to-monai.*
	Brahuí,	*Caret.*
Chinese Frontier & Tibet.	Gyámi,	*Houtimyú.*
	Gyárung,	*Makumchhúr.*
	Tákpa,	*Lihúmáni, gnomámano.*
	Mányak,	*Mámphyu.*
	Thochú,	*Márkwi.*
	Sokpa,	*Mábcne.*
	Horpa,	*Memsyùr.*
	Tibetan (*written*),	*Midsesma, mistúgpo.*
	Tibetan (*spoken*),	*Men jebo.*
Nepal (east to west).	Serpa,	*Malemu, masimba.*
	Súnwár,	*Marimnoso.*
	Gúrung,	*A'saba.*
	Múrmi,	*Brotá khába.*
	Magar,	*Másecho.*
	Tháksya,	*Mhi-ákyáhopá.*
	Pákhya,	*Caret.*
	Newár,	*Bámala.*
	Limbu,	*Phemlá.*
Kiranti Group (East Nepal).	Kiránti,	*Khángúvo.*
	Rodong,	*Khäïse.*
	Rúngchenbung,	*Khán euttko, khau genwo.*
	Chhingtángya,	*Uchik'no, uchuino.*
	Náchhereng,	*Khäïsada.*
	Wáling,	*Kháni.*
	Yákha,	*Ichchúgnána.*
	Chourásya,	*A'rancho.*
	Kulungya,	*Gnáli-ipa.*
	Thulungya,	*Mijyopa.*
	Báhingya,	*Márim'ba, -daäsi;*[1] *-daä.*[2]
	Lohorong,	*Kamisa.*
	Lambichhong,	*U'chu núyuk nin.*
	Báláli,	*Khek'yúg, khenninung.*
	Sáng-páng,	*Kháisi.*
	Dúmi,	*Múbhángpa.*
	Kháling,	*Mábhán'gpa.*
	Dungmáli,	*Khaikhaik'pu.*
Broken Tribes of Nepal.	Dárhi,	*Injeramro.*
	Denwár,	*Caret.*
	Pahri,	*Bamalaguhma.*
	Chepáng,	*Pilo.*
	Bhrámu,	*Masyon.*
	Váyu,	*Mambing.*
	Kuswar,	*Nakhaja.*
	Kusunda,	*A'ingbarai.*
	Tháru,	*Bauramani.*
	Lepcha (Sikkim),	*Maryúnne.*
	Bhúṭáni v. Lhopa,	*Málem.*

Group	Language	Word
N.-E. Bengal.	Bodo,	*Chapma.*
	Dhimál,	*Máremká, máelka.*
	Kocch,	*Baiya.*
	Garo,	*Sarchá.*
	Káchári,	*Caret.*
Eastern Frontier of Bengal.	Munipuri,	*Sukthiba.*
	Míthán Nágá,	*Caret.*
	Tablung Nágá,	*Caret.*
	Khári Nágá,	*Maro.*
	Angámi Nágá,	*Shopur.*
	Námsáng Nágá,	*Pangtsi.*
	Nowgong Nágá,	*Matsong.*
	Tengsa Nágá,	*Machong.*
	Abor Miri,	*Caret.*
	Sibságar Miri,	*Aimang.*
	Deoria Chutia,	*Üchini.*
	Singpho,	*Samnáng.*
Arrakan & Burmah.	Burman (*written*),	*Arupchho.*
	Burman (*spoken*),	*Ayokṣho, ayupṣ'ho.*
	Khyeng v. Shou,	*Asií.*
	Kámi,	*Akhesung.*
	Kúmi,	*Hoïo.*
	Mrú v. Toung,	*Caret.*
	Sák,	*Caret.*
Siam & Tenasserim.	Talain v. Mon,	*Hen.*
	Sgau-karen,	*T'khibah.*
	Pwo-karen,	*Lahung.*
	Toungh-thu,	*Caret.*
	Shán,	*Hantichk.*
	Annamitic,	*Xâu.*
	Siamese,	*Rái, houhikh.*
	Ahom,	*Khye plá.*
	Khámti,	*Háng hai.*
	Laos,	*Hai.*
Central India.	Ho (Kol),	*Kabúgi.*
	Kol (Singhbhum),	*Esúctkalika.*
	Santáli,	*Tamboḍḍi, saṇḍa-maṇḍa, pa-karakah-sáhing.*
	Bhúmij,	*Utea neloa.*
	Uráon,	*Málá.*
	Mundala,	*Kaihes.*
	Rájmahali,	*Caret.*
	Goṇḍi,	*Búrotá-manda, chokat-hilli.*
	Gayeti,	*Caret.*
	Rutluk,	*Buro.*
	Naikude,	*Caret.*
	Kolami,	*Wadinasatti.*
	Mádi,	*Lagor, kattá.*
	Mádia,	*Banomyo.*
	Kuri,	*Caret.*
	Keikádi,	*Gidadu.*
	Khoṇḍ,	*Sonjabosdhe.*
	Sávara,	*Ambaste.*
	Gadaba,	*Nimmokávord.*
	Yerukala,	*Nalladillá.*
	Chentsu,	*Kharáb.*
Southern India.	Tamiḷ, anc.,	*Payirpána.*
	Tamiḷ, mod.,	*Aruvaruppána, andakeḍáma.*
	Malayáḷma, anc.,	*Caret.*
	Malayáḷma, mod.,	*Veṛupuḷḷa.*
	Telugu,	*Vikáramaina.*
	Karṇáṭaka, anc.,	*Caret.*
	Karṇáṭaka, mod.,	*Andagéḍi.*
	Tuḷuva,	*Padikettano.*
	Kurgi,	*Caret.*
	Toḍuva, }	*Oḍeda.*
	Toḍa, }	*A'dádi.*
	Kóta,	*Máse.*
	Baḍaga,	*Holla.*
	Kuṛumba,	*Hola.*
	Iruḷa,	*Polla.*
	Malabar,	*Avalatchana.*
	Sinhalese,	*Kata.*

Group	Language	White
	Types.	
Inflecting.	SANSKRIT,	*S'ukla, s'weta, dhavala, sita,* [*s'uchi, s'ubhra.*
	ARABIC,	*Abyaḍ.*
Compounding.	BASK,	*Zuri, churi.*
	FINNIC,	*Walkia.*
	MAGYAR,	*Feher.*
	TURKISH,	*Ak.*
	CIRCASSIAN,	*Pihshey.*
	GEORGIAN,	*Thethri.*
	MONGOLIAN,	*Chagan.*
	MANTSHU,	*Shangiyan.*
	JAVANESE, Ngoko,	*Putih.*
	JAVANESE, Krama,	*Pĕṭak.*
	MALAY,	*Putih.*
Isolating.	CHINESE, Nankin,	*Peh.*
	CHINESE, Pekin,	*Pai.*
	CHINESE, Canton,	*Pák.*
	CHINESE, Shanghai,	*Pah.*
	AMOY, Colloquial,	*Peh.*
	JAPANESE,	*Sirvi.*
	Brahuí,	*Piún.*
Chinese Frontier & Tibet.	Gyámi,	*Pidi.*
	Gyárung,	*Kaprom.*
	Tákpa,	*Kherú.*
	Mányak,	*Dallú.*
	Thochú,	*Phyokh.*
	Sokpa,	*Chhágán.*
	Horpa,	*Phrú-phrú.*
	Tibetan (*written*),	*Dkárpo.*
	Tibetan (*spoken*),	*Kárpo.*
Nepal (east to west).	Serpa,	*Karpo.*
	Súnwár,	*Bwisye.*
	Gúrung,	*Tárkya.*
	Múrmi,	*Tára.*
	Magar,	*Bocho.*
	Tháksya,	*Tarpa.*
	Pákhya,	*Seto.*
	Newár,	*Túyú.*
	Limbu,	*Kúphora.*
Kiranti Group (East Nepal).	Kiránti,	*U'mpi yáng wa.*
	Rodong,	*Páyoṇma, umpayonyon.*
	Rúngchenbung,	*Omko, womyáng, wopi* [*yangma.*
	Chhingtángya,	*Bathrúna.*
	Náchhereng,	*Umlok'pa.*
	Wáling,	*Bothrúma, wompichichi.*
	Yákha,	*Phúna.*
	Chourásya,	*Búbjoma.*
	Kulungya,	*Womlopa.*
	Thulungya,	*Búbúm.*
	Báhingya,	*Búbúm.*
	Lohorong,	*Bihá, biye.*
	Lambichhong,	*Omyukkha, omyuk.*
	Báláli,	*Beyepa.*
	Sáng-páng,	*Ombaṇloṇpa.*
	Dúmi,	*Búbúm.*
	Kháling,	*Búbúm.*
	Dungmáli,	*Om; omchi;*[1] *maongache.*[2]
Broken Tribes of Nepal.	Dárhi,	*Goro.*
	Denwár,	*Goro.*
	Pahri,	*Túyúguhma.*
	Chepáng,	*Bhámto.*
	Bhrámu,	*A'bo.*
	Váyu,	*Dawángmi.*
	Kuswar,	*Pándal.*
	Kusunda,	*A'sai.*
	Tháru,	*Ujar.*
	Lepcha (Sikkim),	*A'dúm.*
	Bhúṭáni v. Lhopa,	*Kápo.*

Group	Language	White
N.-E. Bengal.	Bodo,	*Gúphút.*
	Dhimál,	*Jeéká, jeika.*
	Kocch,	*Dhoula.*
	Garo,	*Bokláng.*
	Káchári,	*Caret.*
Eastern Frontier of Bengal.	Munipuri,	*Angouba.*
	Míthán Nágá,	*Thoh.*
	Tablung Nágá,	*Heng.*
	Khári Nágá,	*Mesing.*
	Angámi Nágá,	*Kacha.*
	Námsáng Nágá,	*Apo.*
	Nowgong Nágá,	*Tamasong.*
	Tengsa Nágá,	*Masang.*
	Abor Miri,	*Asido.*
	Sibságar Miri,	*Kámpodák.*
	Deoria Chutia,	*Puri.*
	Singpho,	*Phrong.*
Arrakan & Burmah.	Burman (*written*),	*Phrú.*
	Burman (*spoken*),	*Phyú, hpyúthí.*
	Khyeng v. Shou,	*Búk.*
	Kámi,	*Alún.*
	Kúmi,	*Kanlúm.*
	Mrú v. Toung,	*Caret.*
	Sák,	*Caret.*
Siam & Tenasserim.	Talain v. Mon,	*Hpatihn.*
	Sgau-karen,	*Wah.*
	Pwo-karen,	*Bwah.*
	Toungh-thu,	*Bwá.*
	Shán,	*Khoung.*
	Annamitic,	*Trang.*
	Siamese,	*Khoung, kháu.*
	Ahom,	*Phok.*
	Khámti,	*Kháu, phuk.*
	Laos,	*Kháu, pheuk.*
Central India.	Ho (Kol),	*Pundi.*
	Kol (Singhbhum),	*Pundi.*
	Santáli,	*Esel, poṇḍa, galái, belkeng.*
	Bhúmij,	*Hissú punia.*
	Uráon,	*Pandrú.*
	Mundala,	*Pundi.*
	Rájmahali,	*Jimpro.*
	Goṇḍi,	*Panguro, pandari.*
	Gayeti,	*Pandari.*
	Rutluk,	*Pandaro.*
	Naikude,	*Touda.*
	Kolami,	*Telodi.*
	Mádi,	*Pandari, viditor.*
	Mádia,	*Padaral.*
	Kuri,	*Pulung.*
	Keikádi,	*Vella.*
	Khoṇḍ,	*Sukkáre.*
	Sávara,	*Palu.*
	Gadaba,	*Tatár.*
	Yerukala,	*Valeḍá.*
	Chentsu,	*Vujula, savarniṭa.*
Southern India.	Tamiḷ, anc.,	*Veḷḷiya.*
	Tamiḷ, mod.,	*Veḷutta, velley.*
	Malayáḷma, anc.,	*Caret.*
	Malayáḷma, mod.,	*Veḷutta.*
	Telugu,	*Tella, telupu.*
	Karṇáṭaka, anc.,	*Caret.*
	Karṇaṭaka, mod.,	*Biḷi.*
	Tuḷuva,	*Bollane.*
	Kurgi,	*Baltad.*
	Toḍuva,	*Pelpam.*
	Toḍa,	*Belpu.*
	Kóta,	*Velape.*
	Baḍaga,	*Belapu.*
	Kuṛumba,	*Bole.*
	Iruḷa,	*Velle.*
	Malabar,	*Venmei.*
	Sinhalese,	*Sudu.*

Group	Language	Word
	Types.	
Inflecting.	SANSKRIT,	*Jágri, budh.*
	ARABIC,	*Isteiķaza.*
Compounding.	BASK,	*Esnatu, ernatu, irazarri.*
	FINNIC,	*Herăän.*
	MAGYAR,	*Caret.*
	TURKISH,	*Caret.*
	CIRCASSIAN,	*Caret.*
	GEORGIAN,	*Waghkidseb.*
	MONGOLIAN,	*Serigulgu.*
	MANTSHU,	*Getene.*
	JAVANESE, Ngoko,	*Tangi.*
	JAVANESE, Krama,	*Tangi.*
	MALAY,	*Zága.*
Isolating.	CHINESE, Nankin,	*Sing.*
	CHINESE, Pekin,	*Hsing.*
	CHINESE, Canton,	*Sing.*
	CHINESE, Shanghai,	*Kau-chi-le, kau-tseņ-le.*
	AMOY, Colloquial,	*Ch'iņ.*
	JAPANESE,	*Okiteru, wokoshi.*
	Brahuí,	*Bashkabota.*
Chinese Frontier & Tibet.	Gyámi,	*Khile.*
	Gyárung,	*Tarwas.*
	Tákpa,	*Láng.*
	Mányak,	*Dougwáḥ.*
	Thochú,	*Toron.*
	Sokpa,	*Pos.*
	Horpa,	*Taryen.*
	Tibetan (written),	*Caret.*
	Tibetan (spoken),	*Caret.*
Nepal (east to west).	Serpa,	*Caret.*
	Súnwár,	*Bok.*
	Gúrung,	*Red.*
	Múrmi,	*Caret.*
	Magar,	*Swon.*
	Tháksya,	*Reto.*
	Pákhya,	*U'tha.*
	Newár,	*Don.*
	Limbu,	*Phoke.*
Kiránti Group (East Nepal).	Kiránti,	*Caret.*
	Rodong,	*Púkalenda, khrupsa.*
	Rúngchenbung,	*Púwalonta, chi,[1] nin.[2]*
	Chhingtángya,	*Pogák.*
	Náchhereng,	*Poka.*
	Wáling,	*Thing'ta.*
	Yákha,	*Cheng'da.*
	Chourásya,	*Búkdtá, sáistá.*
	Kulungya,	*Poka.*
	Thulungya,	*Báka.*
	Báhingya,	*Bokko, bokse,[1] bokine.[2]*
	Lohorong,	*Cheno, poge, poglente.*
	Lambichhong,	*Poga, pogachi,[1] poga ni.[2]*
	Bálálí,	*Polit, politachi,[1] polita nin.[2]*
	Sáng-páng,	*Thittáchi,[1] -ni.[2]*
	Dúmi,	*Phúge.*
	Kháling,	*Phúk'ye.*
	Dungmáli,	*Phúge.*
Broken Tribes of Nepal.	Dárhi,	*Chetas, chetas.*
	Denwár,	*U'th.*
	Pahri,	*Doņ.*
	Chepáng,	*Tyokche, tyoksa.*
	Bhrámu,	*Sowa.*
	Váyu,	*Tháimche, sis'che.*
	Kuswar,	*U'thou, uthou.*
	Kusunda,	*Blengwoto.*
	Tháru,	*Uthali, jagal.*
	Lepcha (Sikkim),	*Sí.*
	Bhúṭáni v. Lhopa,	*Lhong.*
N.-E. Bengal.	Bodo,	*Jakháng, sidimanno* (pass.).
	Dhimál,	*Chetam* (pass.), *lhopá* (act.).
	Kocch,	*Jágibar.*
	Garo,	*Sarai.*
	Kácharí,	*Caret.*
Eastern Frontier of Bengal.	Munipuri,	*Hougolo.*
	Míthán Nágá,	*Caret.*
	Tablung Nágá,	*Caret.*
	Khári Nágá,	*Sishaugo.*
	Angámi Nágá,	*Sirte.*
	Námsáng Nágá,	*Chingo.*
	Nowgong Nágá,	*Ula.*
	Tengsa Nágá,	*Phayá.*
	Abor Miri,	*Emüaipü.*
	Sibságar Miri,	*Dárdoku.*
	Deoria Chutia,	*Harnamani.*
	Singpho,	*Dúmu.*
Arrakan & Burmah.	Burman (written),	*No.*
	Burman (spoken),	*No.*
	Khyeng v. Shou,	*Kakák.*
	Kámi,	*Thá.*
	Kúmi,	*Anthá.*
	Mrú v. Toung,	*Caret.*
	Sák,	*Caret.*
Siam & Tenasserim.	Talain v. Mon,	*Ngu.*
	Sgau-karen,	*Puthinaw.*
	Pwo-karen,	*Nang-tang.*
	Toungh-thu,	*Ting.*
	Shán,	*Ten.*
	Annamitic,	*Thŭ'k.*
	Siamese,	*Teln, tün.*
	Ahom,	*Teng.*
	Khámti,	*Tün.*
	Laos,	*Tün.*
Central India.	Ho (Kol),	*Eneted.*
	Kol (Singhbhum),	*Birman.*
	Santáli,	*Ebhenohte.*
	Bhúmij,	*Rúárman.*
	Uráon,	*Amhakhaudara.*
	Mundala,	*Adágya.*
	Rájmahali,	*Ejra.*
	Goṇḍi,	*Jagemán, chaitoana.*
	Gayeti,	*Caret.*
	Rutluk,	*Caret.*
	Naikude,	*Caret.*
	Kolami,	*Caret.*
	Mádi,	*Caret.*
	Mádia,	*Caret.*
	Kuri,	*Caret.*
	Keikádi,	*Yedi.*
	Khoṇḍ,	*Ningáḍahámu.*
	Sávara,	*Dímego.*
	Gadaba,	*Moḍukusudukka.* [ḍuyiru.
	Yerukala,	*Teligayirukku, dindugun*
	Chentsu,	*Jáglero, jágaleraho.*
Southern India.	Tamiḷ, anc.,	*Caret.*
	Tamiḷ, mod.,	*Vizhittal.*
	Malayáḷma, anc.,	*Caret.*
	Malayáḷma, mod.,	*Unaru.*
	Telugu,	*Mêlukonu.*
	Karṇáṭaka, anc.,	*Caret.*
	Karṇáṭaka, mod.,	*Echchattiru.*
	Tuḷuva,	*Echchirigiḍupuna.*
	Kurgi,	*Caret.*
	Toḍuva,	*Caret.* [yecharichagir.
	Toḍa,	*Eḍaderth bini, vorigadi,*
	Kóta,	*Mekikene, yecharagiru.*
	Baḍaga,	*Yleddane, yecharike iru.*
	Kuṛumba,	*Yecharikeagiru.*
	Iruḷa,	*Yelke, nenevá girave.*
	Malabar,	*Villippu.*
	Sinhalese,	*Pubudinavá.*

Group	Language	Word
	Types.	
Inflecting.	SANSKRIT,	*A'ní, ní.*
	ARABIC,	*Jába.*
Compounding.	BASK,	*Ekarri.*
	FINNIC,	*Tuon.*
	MAGYAR,	*Hoz.*
	TURKISH,	*Getir.*
	CIRCASSIAN,	*Kakh.*
	GEORGIAN,	*Caret.*
	MONGOLIAN,	*Atcharakho.*
	MANTSHU,	*Gatchime.*
	JAVANESE, Ngoko,	*Hanggáwa.*
	JAVANESE, Krama,	*Hambekta.*
	MALAY,	*Báwa.*
Isolating.	CHINESE, Nankin,	*Pá-lai.*
	CHINESE, Pekin,	*Pá-lai.*
	CHINESE, Canton,	*Nim-loi.*
	CHINESE, Shanghai,	*Tan-le.*
	AMOY, Colloquial,	*T'eh-lái.*
	JAPANESE,	*Mote-koi.*
	Brahuí,	*Halbo, hatbo.*
Chinese Frontier & Tibet.	Gyámi,	*Lále.*
	Gyárung,	*Kopet.*
	Tákpa,	*Rotá.*
	Mányak,	*Trúlhe.*
	Thochú,	*Dzila.*
	Sokpa,	*A'hbatáhira.*
	Horpa,	*Wákhye.*
	Tibetan (*written*),	*Hkhyon, skyeh.*
	Tibetan (*spoken*),	*Básyo.*
Nepal (east to west).	Serpa,	*Gyap.*
	Súnwár,	*Pit.*
	Gúrung,	*Pog.*
	Múrmi,	*Bou.*
	Magar,	*Ráko.*
	Tháksya,	*Bhakau.*
	Pákhya,	*Lyályá.*
	Newár,	*Haki.*
	Limbu,	*Pheppe.*
Kiranti Group (East Nepal).	Kiránti,	*Páang.*
	Rodong,	*Baizyú, baidyu.*
	Rúngchenbung,	*Báttuki bana.*
	Chhingtángya,	*Thápta.*
	Náchhereng,	*Beh'yu.*
	Wáling,	*Báttu.*
	Yákha,	*Ap'tu.*
	Chourásya,	*Phittá.*
	Kulungya,	*Bák'yu.*
	Thulungya,	*Phída.* [*ladapamno.*[2]
	Báhingya,	*Pityo, rato, pitise,*[1] *pitine,*[2]
	Lohorong,	*Ládúppo, ladappe, ladapche.*[1]
	Lambichhong,	*Thápta.*
	Bálálí,	*Dáppu, yangdáppu.*
	Sáng-páng,	*Báhyu.*
	Dúmi,	*Pide.*
	Kháling,	*Pide, pichle,*[1] *pisnaye.*[2]
	Dungmálí,	*Tág'we, tagwechle,*[1] [*tagnumye.*[2]
Broken Tribes of Nepal.	Dárhi,	*Anak.*
	Denwár,	*A'nhik'.*
	Pahri,	*Búyá.*
	Chepáng,	*Caret.*
	Bhrámu,	*Khái.*
	Váyu,	*Pishto.*
	Kuswar,	*Anik.*
	Kusunda,	*A'i.*
	Tháru,	*Lyáre, leáre.*
	Lepcha (Sikkim),	*Búdi.*
	Bhútáni v. Lhopa,	*Básyo.*
N.-E. Bengal.	Bodo,	*Lábo.*
	Dhimál,	*Chúmá, chúmlengleli.*
	Kocch,	*Leásibar.*
	Garo,	*Láphá.*
	Káchári,	*Labau.*
Eastern Frontier of Bengal.	Munipuri,	*Púrúo.*
	Míthán Nágá,	*Láhai.*
	Tablung Nágá,	*Yakei.*
	Khári Nágá,	*Heneratli.*
	Angámi Nágá,	*Scyawe.*
	Námsáng Nágá,	*Vanro.*
	Nowgong Nágá,	*A'nyaung.*
	Tengsa Nágá,	*Khaluang.*
	Abor Miri,	*Bombipu.*
	Sibságar Miri,	*Bomkuka.*
	Deoria Chutia,	*Larini.*
	Singpho,	*Láu.*
Arrakan & Burmah.	Burman (*written*),	*Yúkhe.*
	Burman (*spoken*),	*Yúghe.*
	Khyeng v. Shou,	*Caret.*
	Kámi,	*Mahái.*
	Kúmi,	*Lo.*
	Mrú v. Toung,	*Caret.*
	Sák,	*Caret.*
Siam & Tenasserim.	Talain v. Mon,	*Kitnen.*
	Sgau-karen,	*Halso, haitso.*
	Pwo-karen,	*Ghaitsoh.*
	Toungh-thu,	*Htútone.*
	Shán,	*Oungma.*
	Annamitic,	Demđên.
	Siamese,	*Oungman, aumá.*
	Ahom,	*A'nmá.*
	Khámti,	*Aumá.*
	Laos,	*Aumá.*
Central India.	Ho (Kol),	*Awiteá.*
	Kol (Singhbhum),	*Dá.*
	Santáli,	*Gemerate, águite, idiáguite.*
	Bhúmij,	*Daigoágueman.*
	Uráon,	*Ondrá.*
	Mundala,	*A'gomen.*
	Rájmahali,	*Ondrá.*
	Gondi,	*Tarángá, táttana.*
	Gayeti,	*Caret.*
	Rutluk,	*Caret.*
	Naikude,	*Caret.*
	Kolami,	*Caret.*
	Mádi,	*Caret.*
	Mádia,	*Caret.*
	Kuri,	*Caret.*
	Keikádi,	*Kunda.*
	Khond,	*Támu.*
	Sávara,	*Pangayiba.*
	Gadaba,	*Yindre.*
	Yerukala,	*Yittikondu.*
	Chentsu,	*A'ne, diyá.*
Southern India.	Tamil, anc.,	*Koná.*
	Tamil, mod.,	*Konduvá, kondá.*
	Malayálma, anc.,	*Caret.*
	Malayálma, mod.,	*Konduvaru.*
	Telugu,	*Techchu, tisuka.*
	Karnátaka, anc.,	*Caret.*
	Karnátaka, mod.,	*Taru, tá.*
	Tuluva,	*Caret.*
	Kurgi,	*Caret.*
	Toduva,	*Caret.*
	Toda,	*Tashken.*
	Kóta,	*Kadube.*
	Badaga,	*Tanane.*
	Kurumba,	*Tanane.*
	Irula,	*Tarke.*
	Malabar,	*Konduvá.*
	Sinhalese,	*Genenavá.*

Group	Types.	
Inflecting.	SANSKRIT,	A'gam, e, áyá.
	ARABIC,	Já'a, áta.
Compounding.	BASK,	Etorri, eldu izan.
	FINNIC,	Tulen.
	MAGYAR,	Jo.
	TURKISH,	Gel.
	CIRCASSIAN,	Kahkuyey.
	GEORGIAN,	Mokad.
	MONGOLIAN,	Irekho.
	MANTSHU,	Dohime.
	JAVANESE, Ngoko,	Těka.
	JAVANESE, Krama,	Datěng.
	MALAY,	Dátang.
Isolating.	CHINESE, Nankin,	Lái.
	CHINESE, Pekin,	Lái.
	CHINESE, Canton,	Loi.
	CHINESE, Shanghai,	Le.
	AMOY, Colloquial,	Lâi.
	JAPANESE,	Kuru, kitari.
	Brahuí,	Barak.
Chinese Frontier & Tibet.	Gyámi,	Le.
	Gyárung,	Kapún, papún.
	Tákpa,	Syo.
	Mányak,	Lemo.
	Thochú,	Hai.
	Sokpa,	Ire.
	Horpa,	Kwilhen.
	Tibetan (written),	Hóng, s-byon.
	Tibetan (spoken),	Syo.
Nepal (east to west).	Serpa,	Syok.
	Súnwár,	Pyú.
	Gúrung,	Kho.
	Múrmi,	Khou, jyangou.
	Magar,	Ráni.
	Tháksya,	Khau.
	Pákhya,	A'ija.
	Newár,	Wá.
	Limbu,	Phere.
Kiránti Group (East Nepal).	Kiránti,	Báná.
	Rodong,	Bóna.
	Rúngchenbung,	Bána.
	Chhingtángya,	Thába.
	Náchhereng,	Táwa.
	Wáling,	Bána.
	Yákha,	A'ba.
	Chourásya,	Pikátá.
	Kulungya,	Bána.
	Thulungya,	Bika.
	Báhingya,	Piwo, ráwo, pi-se,[1] pi-ne.[2]
	Lohorong,	Dábe, dache,[1] da-ne.[2]
	Lambichhong,	Thába, thábachi,[1] thabani.[2]
	Báláli,	Dába, dabachi,[1] dabanin.[2]
	Sáng-páng,	Báná-chi,[1] -ni.[2]
	Dúmi,	Pú.
	Kháling,	Paúye.
	Dungmáli,	Tábe.
Broken Tribes of Nepal.	Dárhi,	A'úk.
	Denwár,	An.
	Pahri,	Lá.
	Chepáng,	Caret.
	Bhrámu,	Tháyá.
	Váyu,	Phí.
	Kuswar,	A'be.
	Kusunda,	Agga.
	Tháru,	A'wá, yáuha.
	Lepcha (Sikkim),	Di.
	Bhútáni v. Lhopa,	Syó.

Group	Language	Word
N.-E. Bengal.	Bodo,	Phoi.
	Dhimál,	Lo, le.
	Kocch,	A'sibar.
	Garo,	Phoi.
	Káchári,	Phai.
Eastern Frontier of Bengal.	Munipuri,	Lao.
	Míthán Nágá,	Ráhai.
	Tablung Nágá,	Ongkoi.
	Khári Nágá,	Hinnerang.
	Angámi Nágá,	Akiphirche.
	Námsáng Nágá,	Káro.
	Nowgong Nágá,	Arung.
	Tengsa Nágá,	Ahalü.
	Abor Miri,	Giküpü.
	Sibságar Miri,	Kápü.
	Deoria Chutia,	Nangkwá.
	Singpho,	Sáu.
Arrakan & Burmah.	Burman (written),	Lá, rok.
	Burman (spoken),	Lá, yauk.
	Khyeng v. Shou,	Lo.
	Kámi,	Va.
	Kúmi,	You.
	Mrú v. Toung,	Caret.
	Sák,	Caret.
Siam & Tenasserim.	Talain v. Mon,	Kalonra.
	Sgau-karen,	Hal.
	Pwo-karen,	Ghay.
	Toungh-thu,	Lone.
	Shán,	Mha.
	Annamitic,	Dên, lai.
	Siamese,	Má.
	Ahom,	Má.
	Khámti,	Má.
	Laos,	Má.
Central India.	Ho (Kol),	Hujuteá, setreteá.
	Kol (Singhbhum),	Hújúman.
	Santáli,	Dáráite, hejuhte.
	Bhúmij,	Hijúman.
	Uráon,	Báná.
	Mundala,	Déla hájúm.
	Rájmahali,	Bárá.
	Goṇḍi,	Báránigá, wara.
	Gayeti,	Caret.
	Rutluk,	Caret.
	Naikude,	Caret.
	Kolami,	Caret.
	Mádi,	Caret.
	Mádia,	Caret.
	Kuri,	Caret.
	Keikádi,	Wango.
	Khoṇḍ,	Ninju.
	Sávara,	Jáyeba.
	Gadaba,	Phinge.
	Yerukala,	Vá, várá.
	Chentsu,	Asibo, asili.
Southern India.	Tamiḷ, anc.,	Caret.
	Tamiḷ, mod.,	Vá.
	Malayáḷma, anc.,	Caret.
	Malayáḷma, mod.,	Varu.
	Telugu,	Vachchu, chéru.
	Karṇáṭaka, anc.,	Caret.
	Karṇáṭaka, mod.,	Baru, bá.
	Tuḷuva,	Barapuna.
	Kurgi,	Caret.
	Toḍuva,	Caret.
	Toḍa,	It-va.
	Kóta,	It-va, vágc.
	Baḍaga,	Ite-ba.
	Kuṟumba,	Ite-ba, ba.
	Iruḷa,	Iti-ba, barave.
	Malabar,	Vá.
	Sinhalese,	Waren, enavá.

Group	Language	Drink
	Types.	
Inflecting.	SANSKRIT, ...	*Pá* (*pivati*).
	ARABIC, ...	*Sharaba.*
Compounding.	BASK, ...	*Edan.*
	FINNIC, ...	*Juon.*
	MAGYAR, ...	*I'n.*
	TURKISH, ...	*I'ch.*
	CIRCASSIAN, ...	*Yeshwey.*
	GEORGIAN, ...	*Wsmwad* (*swam*).
	MONGOLIAN, ...	*Ughucho.*
	MANTSHU, ...	*Omime.*
	JAVANESE, Ngoko, . .	*Ngombé.*
	JAVANESE, Kraina, . .	*Ngunjuk.*
	MALAY, ...	*Minom.*
Isolating.	CHINESE, Nankin, . .	*K'oh.*
	CHINESE, Pekin, . .	*Ho.*
	CHINESE, Canton, . .	*Yam.*
	CHINESE, Shanghai, .	*Heh, ch'ah* (eat or drink).
	AMOY, Colloquial, . .	*Nomu.*
	JAPANESE, ...	*Lim, nomi.*
	Brahuí, ...	*Dir kunakh.*
Chinese Frontier & Tibet.	Gyámi, ...	*Khwá.*
	Gyárung, ...	*Tamot.*
	Tákpa, ...	*Thong.*
	Mányak, ...	*Gnachhoh.*
	Thochú, ...	*A'thi.*
	Sokpa, ...	*Wúo.*
	Horpa, ...	*Wathi.*
	Tibetan (*written*), . .	*Hthúng.*
	Tibetan (*spoken*), . . .	*Thúng.*
Nepal (east to west).	Serpa, ...	*Thúng.*
	Súnwár, ...	*Túng.*
	Gúrung, ...	*Thúnñ.*
	Múrmi, ...	*Thúng.*
	Magar, ...	*Gau.*
	Tháksya, ...	*Piu.*
	Pákhya, ...	*Piu.*
	Newár, ...	*Ton.*
	Limbu, ...	*Thungne.*
Kiránti Group (East Nepal).	Kiránti, ...	*Dúng.*
	Rodong, ...	*Dúgno, dúgnu.*
	Rúngchenbung, . . .	*Dúgno, dugnachu,*[1] *dugna-num.*[2]
	Chhingtángya, . . .	*Thúwa, thúa.*
	Náchhereng, ...	*Dúngo.*
	Wáling, ...	*Dúgno.*
	Yákha, ...	*U'gnú.*
	Chourásya, ...	*Túkátá.*
	Kulungya, ...	*Dúng'gnu.*
	Thulungya, ...	*Dúgná.*
	Báhingya, ...	*Túgnotungo, tuse,*[1] *tune.*[2]
	Lohorong, ...	*Dunge, dungeche,*[1] *dungane.*[2]
	Lambichhong, . . .	*Thúgná, thugnachu.*[1]
	Báláli, ...	*Dúgno, dagnachi.*[1]
	Sáng-páng, ...	*Dugnu, dúgnúchu,*[1] *dugna-num.*[2]
	Dúmi, ...	*Tingne.*
	Kháling, ...	*Tyung'ye.*
	Dungmáli, ...	*Túgne.*
Broken Tribes of Nepal.	Dárhi, ...	*Pyú.*
	Denwár, ...	*Kháik.*
	Pahri, ...	*Toin.*
	Chepáng, ...	*Túmche, tumsá.*
	Bhrámu, ...	*Syánga.*
	Váyu, ...	*Túngche, tungko.*
	Kuswar, ...	*Kháik.*
	Kusunda, ...	*Túng-gonong.*
	Tháru, ...	*Piyal, piláyaba.*
	Lepcha (Sikkim), . .	*Thong.*
	Bhútáni v. Lhopa, . .	*Thong.*

Group	Language	Drink
N.-E. Bengal.	Bodo, ...	*Lúng.*
	Dhimál, ...	*A'm.*
	Kocch, ...	*Píbár.*
	Garo, ...	*Lúng.*
	Káchári, ...	*Lang.*
Eastern Frontier of Bengal.	Munipuri, ...	*Thouo.*
	Míthán Nágá, . . .	*Singhá.*
	Tablung Nágá, . . .	*Yang ying shi.*
	Khári Nágá, ...	*Atsiong.*
	Angámi Nágá, . . .	*Dzükretowe.*
	Námsáng Nágá, . . .	*Joko.*
	Nowgong Nágá, . .	*Chajamti.*
	Tengsa Nágá, . . .	*Tünun.*
	Abor Miri, ...	*Taipü.*
	Sibságar Miri, . . .	*Tüpu.*
	Deoria Chutia, . . .	*Jinime.*
	Singpho, ...	*Lun.*
Arrakan & Burmah.	Burman (*written*), . .	*Sok.*
	Burman (*spoken*), . . .	Thauk.
	Khyeng v. Shou, . .	*U'e.*
	Kámi, ...	*Nei.*
	Kúmi, ...	*Nei.*
	Mrú v. Toung, . . .	*Caret.*
	Sák, ...	*Caret.*
Siam & Tenasserim.	Talain v. Mon, . . .	*Thou.*
	Sgau-karen, ...	*Owrau, aúh.*
	Pwo-karen, ...	*Aw.*
	Toungh-thu, ...	*Nwa.*
	Shán, ...	*Kyen.*
	Annamitic, ...	*Uōng.*
	Siamese, ...	*Deum, kenn.*
	Ahom, ...	*Kleu.*
	Khámti, ...	*Kinnam.*
	Laos, ...	*Kinnam.*
Central India.	Ho (Kol), ...	*Mooiteá.*
	Kol (Singhbhum), . .	*Núeman.*
	Santáli, ...	*Gnuite.*
	Bhúmij, ...	*Nayman.*
	Urāon, ...	*U'nāh.*
	Mundala, ...	*Noimi.*
	Rájmahali, ...	*Oná.*
	Gondi, ...	*Yerú undkar, undana.*
	Gayeti, ...	*Caret.*
	Rutluk, ...	*Caret.*
	Naikude, ...	*Caret.*
	Kolami, ...	*Caret.*
	Mádi, ...	*Caret.*
	Mádia, ...	*Caret.*
	Kuri, ...	*Caret.*
	Keikádi, ...	*Kudi.*
	Khond, ...	*Punamu.*
	Sávara, ...	*Góba.*
	Gadaba, ...	*Yidu.*
	Yerukala, ...	*Kudi.*
	Chentsu, ...	*Pí, piyer.*
Southern India.	Tamil, anc., ...	*Caret.*
	Tamil, mod., ...	*Kudi.*
	Malayálma, anc., . .	*Caret.*
	Malayálma, mod., . .	*Kudikka.*
	Telugu, ...	*Tágu.*
	Karnátaka, anc., . . .	*Caret.*
	Karnátaka, mod., . .	*Kudi.*
	Tuluva, ...	*Parapuna.*
	Kurgi, ...	*Caret.*
	Toduva, ...	*Caret.*
	Toda, ...	*U'nu, udth-bini.*
	Kóta, ...	*U'ne, unikiene.*
	Badaga, ...	*Kudi, kudidane.*
	Kurumba, ...	*Kudi.*
	Irula, ...	*Kudidukove, kudidukoveko, tinke.*
	Malabar, ...	*Kudi.*
	Sinhalese, ...	*Bonawa.*

Types.		
Inflecting.	SANSKRIT,	*Khád, bhaksh, bhuj.*
	ARABIC,	*A'kala.*
Compounding.	BASK,	*Jan, yan.*
	FINNIC,	*Syön.*
	MAGYAR,	*En.*
	TURKISH,	*Ye.*
	CIRCASSIAN,	*Teshesht.*
	GEORGIAN,	*Jamad* (*cham*).
	MONGOLIAN,	*Ideku.*
	MANTSHU,	*Dsheme.*
	JAVANESE, Ngoko,	*Mangan.*
	JAVANESE, Krama,	*Neḍa.*
	MALAY,	*Mákan.*
Isolating.	CHINESE, Nankin,	*K'Ih.*
	CHINESE, Pekin,	*Ch'ih.*
	CHINESE, Canton,	*Shik.*
	CHINESE, Shanghai,	*Ch'ah.*
	AMOY, Colloquial,	*Chiáh.*
	JAPANESE,	*Taberu, kurai.*
	Brahuí,	*Kunakh.*
Chinese Frontier & Tibet.	Gyámi,	*Thye, khye.*
	Gyárung,	*Tazo.*
	Tákpa,	*Zo.*
	Mányak,	*Gnajeu.*
	Thochú,	*Adz.*
	Sokpa,	*Ethe.*
	Horpa,	*Nangi.*
	Tibetan (*written*),	*Zo.*
	Tibetan (*spoken*),	*So.*
Nepal (east to west).	Serpa,	*Se, so.*
	Súnwár,	*Jau.*
	Gúrung,	*Chad.*
	Múrmi,	*Chou.*
	Magar,	*Jeú.*
	Thákysa,	*Lhila.*
	Pákhya,	*Gáu, khúwa.*
	Newár,	*Na.*
	Limbu,	*Che.*
Kiranti Group (East Nepal).	Kiránti,	*Cho.*
	Rodong,	*Cho.*
	Rúngchenbung,	*Cho, chacheu, chachi*[1] (*cha-*
	Chhingtángya,	*Choha, choa.* [*num*).[2]
	Náchhereng,	*Chúu.*
	Wáling,	*Cho.*
	Yákha,	*Cho.*
	Chourásya,	*Jákátá.*
	Kulungya,	*Cho.*
	Thulungya,	*Pe.*
	Báhingya,	*Báwo, jáwo, jase,*[1] *jane.*[2]
	Lohorong,	*Chae, choye, chaiche,*[1] *chainc.*[2]
	Lambichhong,	*Cho, chasachu,*[1] *chasanum.*[2]
	Báláli,	*Cho, chachi,*[1] *chanin.*[2]
	Sáng-páng,	*Cho, chochu,*[1] *chanum.*[2]
	Dúmi,	*Jyu.*
	Kháling,	*Jyúye, kúye.*
	Dungmáli,	*Choye.*
Broken Tribes of Nepal.	Dárhi,	*Khou.*
	Denwár,	*Kháik.*
	Pahri,	*Ne.*
	Chepáng,	*Jeche, jhísa.*
	Bhrámu,	*Chá.*
	Váyu,	*Jáche, jako.*
	Kuswar,	*Kháik.*
	Kusunda,	*A'm.*
	Tháru,	*Khai.*
	Lepcha (Sikkim),	*Zo, thá.*
	Bhúṭáni v. Lhopa,	*Sah.*
N.-E. Bengal.	Bodo,	*Já.*
	Dhimál,	*Chá.*
	Kocch,	*Khábar.*
	Garo,	*Sá.*
	Káchári,	*Caret.*
Eastern Frontier of Bengal.	Munipuri,	*Cháo.*
	Míthán Nágá,	*Sáhá.*
	Tablung Nágá,	*Háchi.*
	Khári Nágá,	*Tsaung.*
	Angámi Nágá,	*Chiliche.*
	Námsáng Nágá,	*Cháo.*
	Nowgong Nágá,	*Chijong.*
	Tengsa Nágá,	*Tyu.*
	Abor Miri,	*Dolanka.*
	Sibságar Miri,	*Dolangka.*
	Deoria Chutia,	*Harini.*
	Singpho,	*Sháu.*
Arrakan & Burmah.	Burman (*written*),	Chá.
	Burman (*spoken*),	Sá.
	Khyeng v. Shou,	*E.*
	Kámi,	*Tsá.*
	Kúmi,	*Tsá.*
	Mrú v. Toung,	*Caret.*
	Sák,	*Caret.*
Siam & Tenasserim.	Talain v. Mon,	*Tsi.*
	Sgau-karen,	*Anw, au.*
	Pwo-karen,	*Awng.*
	Toungh-thu,	*Am.*
	Shán,	*Kyen.*
	Annamitic,	*Ăn.*
	Siamese,	*Kenn, kin.*
	Ahom,	*Kin.*
	Khámti,	*Kin.*
	Laos,	*Kin.*
Central India.	Ho (Kol),	*Jometeá.*
	Kol (Singhbhum),	*Júmeman.*
	Santáli,	*Jomate, tápágate, lápehte.*
	Bhúmij,	*Júmiábo.*
	Uráon,	*Mokháh.*
	Mundala,	*Jamemi.*
	Rájmahali,	*Lápá, mokámina.*
	Goṇḍi,	*Báratil, tindana.*
	Gayeti,	*Caret.*
	Rutluk,	*Caret.*
	Naikude,	*Caret.*
	Kolami,	*Caret.*
	Mádi,	*Caret.*
	Mádia,	*Caret.*
	Kuri,	*Caret.*
	Keikádi,	*Tin.*
	Khoṇḍ,	*Tinumu.*
	Sávara,	*Gába, jombá.*
	Gadaba,	*Som.*
	Yerukala,	*Vunu, kulla.*
	Chentsu,	*Khá, khayye.*
Southern India.	Tamiḷ, anc.,	*Caret.*
	Tamiḷ, mod.,	*Tin.*
	Malayáḷma, anc.,	*Caret.*
	Malayáḷma, mod.,	*Tinnu, uṇṇu.*
	Telugu,	*Tinu.*
	Karṇáṭaka, anc.,	*Caret.*
	Karṇáṭaka, mod.,	*Tinnu.*
	Tuḷuva,	*Tinupuna.*
	Kurgi,	*Unn.*
	Toḍuva, }	*Caret.*
	Toḍa, }	*Thedth-bine, tennu.*
	Kóta,	*Tiggene, tinnu.*
	Baḍaga,	*Tinane, tinnu.*
	Kuṛumba,	*Tinnu.*
	Iruḷa,	*Tinke, tinnave, tinduko.*
	Malabar,	*Thin, sappedu.*
	Sinhalese,	*Bonavá.*

	Types.	
Inflecting.	SANSKṚIT	*Dá, yam (yachchhati), dad.*
	ARABIC	*Aaṭa, wahaba.*
Compounding.	BASK	*Eman, emon.*
	FINNIC	*Annan.*
	MAGYAR	*Ad.*
	TURKISH	*Ver.*
	CIRCASSIAN	*Yetteh.*
	GEORGIAN	*Wadzleb (dzl).*
	MONGOLIAN	*Ökkü.*
	MANTSHU	*Bume.*
	JAVANESE, Ngoko	*Haweh.*
	JAVANESE, Krama	*Suka.*
	MALAY	*Bri, kasi.*
Isolating.	CHINESE, Nankin	*Kih.*
	CHINESE, Pekin	*Kei.*
	CHINESE, Canton	*Pi.*
	CHINESE, Shanghai	*Peh.*
	AMOY, Colloquial	*Ho.*
	JAPANESE	*Yaru, ataye.*
	Brahuí	*Ety.*
Chinese Frontier & Tibet.	Gyámi	*Kí, yoho.*
	Gyárung	*Davong, davo.*
	Tákpa	*Be, bin.*
	Mányak	*Wakhi, takhi.*
	Thochú	*Dagsh, kwúgsh.*
	Sokpa	*Wúg, euk.*
	Horpa	*Túkhye, túkhong.*
	Tibetan (*written*)	H*búh, phul, thong.*
	Tibetan (*spoken*)	*Phin, babak.*
Nepal (east to west).	Serpa	*Bin.*
	Súnwár	*Gi.*
	Gúrung	*Pin.*
	Múrmi	*Pin.*
	Magar	*Láni.*
	Tháksya	*Pino.*
	Pákhya	*Deu.*
	Newár	*Byú, ti.*
	Limbu	*Pire, pirangne.*
Kiranti Group (East Nepal).	Kiránti	*Páäng, púi.*
	Rodong	*I'dong, ídu.*
	Rúngchenbung	*Púáng, chang,*[1] *nang.*[2]
	Chhingtángya	*Púang, pú.*
	Náchhereng	*Píawa, píyo.*
	Wáling	*Puáng, pú.*
	Yákha	*Kapyáng, piang pi.*
	Chourásya	*Gaká, goktá.*
	Kulungya	*Piyá, piyú.*
	Thulungya	*Gwáäng, gwáka.*
	Báhingya	*Giyi giwo, gise,*[1] *gine.*[2]
	Lohorong	*Pígne, pitte, pigache,*[1] *pigane.*[2]
	Lambichhong	*Piráng.*
	Báláli	*Pigná, pittu.*
	Sáng-páng	*Píán.*
	Dúmi	*Bigná, bi.*
	Kháling	*Bignáye.*
	Dungmáli	*Píyángye, piye.*
Broken Tribes of Nepal.	Dárhi	*Dihik.*
	Denwár	*Dhik.*
	Pahri	*Bichhon.*
	Chepáng	*Büï.*
	Bhrámu	*Pyú.*
	Váyu	*Hâto.*
	Kuswar	*Deik.*
	Kusunda	*A'i.*
	Tháru	*Dada.*
	Lepcha (Sikkim)	*Bo, bi.*
	Bhúṭáni v. Lhopa	*Náng, bábak.*

N.-E. Bengal.	Bodo	*Hot.*
	Dhimál	*Pi.*
	Kocch	*Dánkonu, dibár.*
	Garo	*Há.*
	Káchári	*Caret.*
Eastern Frontier of Bengal.	Munipuri	*Pio.*
	Míthán Nágá	*Lahai.*
	Tablung Nágá	*Yakhu.*
	Khári Nágá	*Khiugo.*
	Angámi Nágá	*Süwawe.*
	Námsáng Nágá	*Ku.*
	Nowgong Nágá	*Kwáng.*
	Tengsa Nágá	*Khalang.*
	Abor Miri	*Bípü.*
	Sibságar Miri	*Sopá.*
	Deoria Chutia	*Larini.*
	Singpho	*Yáu.*
Arrakan & Burmah.	Burman (*written*)	*Pekhya.*
	Burman (*spoken*)	*Pekhyá, pe.*
	Khyeng v. Shou	*Pege.*
	Kámi	*Napú.*
	Kúmi	*Pei.*
	Mrú v. Toung	*Caret.*
	Sák	*Caret.*
Siam & Tenasserim.	Talain v. Mon	*Ka.*
	Sgau-karen	*Halaw, ha.*
	Pwo-karen	*Pilong.*
	Toungh-thu	*Pha.*
	Shán	*Pan.*
	Annamitic	*Sho.*
	Siamese	*Hihn, hai.*
	Ahom	*Heu.*
	Khámti	*Haü.*
	Laos	*Hü.*
Central India.	Ho (Kol)	*Emetcá.*
	Kol (Singhbhum)	*Immaiman.*
	Santáli	*Emate, gataüte.*
	Bhúmij	*U'maiman.*
	Uráon	*Chhiá.*
	Mundala	*Dá.*
	Rájmahali	*Katá.*
	Goṇḍi	*Sí, siana.*
	Gayeti	*Caret.*
	Rutluk	*Caret.*
	Naikuḍe	*Caret.*
	Kolami	*Caret.*
	Mádi	*Caret.*
	Mádia	*Caret.*
	Kuri	*Caret.*
	Keikádi	*Kuḍu.*
	Khoṇḍ	*Siyáuinju.*
	Sávara	*Tilisibba.*
	Gadaba	*Cheḍive.*
	Yerukala	*Tá, vanko.*
	Chentsu	*Nediyo.*
Southern India.	Tamiḷ, anc.	*Caret.*
	Tamiḷ, mod.	*Koḍu.*
	Malayáḷma, anc.	*Caret.*
	Malayáḷma, mod.	*Koṭukka, taru.*
	Telugu	*Ichchu.*
	Karṇáṭaka, anc.	*I'.*
	Karṇáṭaka, mod.	*Koḍu.*
	Tuḷuva	*Koḍupuna.*
	Kurgi	*Tá.*
	Toḍuva	*Caret.*
	Toḍa	*Tashken, ta, kor.*
	Kóta	*Kaḍube, ta.*
	Baḍaga	*Tanane, ta, koḍu.*
	Kuṛumba	*Tanane, koḍu.*
	Iruḷa	*Tarke, tarave.*
	Malabar	*Thákoḍu.*
	Sinhalese	*Diyan, denavá.*

Group	Types.	
Inflecting.	SANSKRIT,	*Gam, yá, sṛi (sarati), chal, char, pad.*
	ARABIC,	*Ráḥa.*
Compounding.	BASK,	*Joan, jun, gan.*
	FINNIC,	*Menen.*
	MAGYAR,	*Men.*
	TURKISH,	*Git.*
	CIRCASSIAN,	*Yago, mago.*
	GEORGIAN,	*Slwad (twal).*
	MONGOLIAN,	*Odkho.*
	MANTSHU,	*Geneme.*
	JAVANESE, Ngoko,	*Lunga.*
	JAVANESE, Krama,	*Kesah.*
	MALAY,	*Pargi.*
Isolating.	CHINESE, Nankin,	*K'ü.*
	CHINESE, Pekin,	*Ch'ü.*
	CHINESE, Canton,	*Hü.*
	CHINESE, Shanghai,	*Chi.*
	AMOY, Colloquial,	*K'ì.*
	JAPANESE,	*Iku, yuki.*
	Brahuí,	*Hinak.*
Chinese Frontier & Tibet.	Gyámi,	*Chhi.*
	Gyárung,	*Yeyen, dachin.*
	Tákpa,	*Gai.*
	Mányak,	*Yú.*
	Thochú,	*Dákan.*
	Sokpa,	*Yá bú (?).*
	Horpa,	*Tashin, washin.*
	Tibetan (written),	*Song, gro, gyu.*
	Tibetan (spoken),	*Gyo, song.*
Nepal (east to west).	Serpa,	*Gyok.*
	Súnwár,	*Lau.*
	Gúrung,	*Yád.*
	Múrmi,	*Nyú, syego.*
	Magar,	*Nú ni.*
	Tháksya,	*Hero.*
	Pákhya,	*Báija.*
	Newár,	*Hoṇ.*
	Limbu,	*Bege.*
Kiranti Group (East Nepal).	Kiránti,	*Khárá.*
	Rodong,	*A'ta, pung'sa.*
	Rúngchenbung,	*Khára,[1] -chinin.[2]*
	Chhingtángya,	*Khàda.*
	Náchhereng,	*Khàta.*
	Wáling,	*Khára.*
	Yákha,	*Khyá.*
	Chourásya,	*Levástá.*
	Kulungya,	*Khàta.*
	Thulungya,	*Dak'sa.*
	Báhingya,	*Láwo, láse,[1] láne.[2]*
	Lohorong,	*Kháḍe, khache,[1] khane.[2]*
	Lambichhong,	*Kháḍa, kháḍachi,[1] khaḍani.[2]*
	Bálálì,	*Kheda, khedachi,[1] kheda nin.[2]*
	Sáng-páng,	*Khátá,[1] chini.[2]*
	Dúmi,	*Khochche.*
	Kháling,	*Khoche.*
	Dungmálì,	*Kháde.*
Broken Tribes of Nepal.	Dárhi,	*Jáák.*
	Denwár,	*Já.*
	Pahri,	*Lásoṇ.*
	Chepáng,	*Caret.*
	Bhrámu,	*Yengá, yenga.*
	Váyu,	*Lák'lá.*
	Kuswar,	*Ná, náhin.*
	Kusunda,	*Dá.*
	Tháru,	*Jájá.*
	Lepcha (Sikkim),	*Non.*
	Bhúṭáni v. Lhopa,	*Song.*

N.-E. Bengal.	Bodo,	*Tháng.*
	Dhimál,	*Hade.*
	Kocch,	*Jábár.*
	Garo,	*Loi.*
	Káchári,	*Tung.*
Eastern Frontier of Bengal.	Munipuri,	*Chulo.*
	Míthán Nágá,	*Tong.*
	Tablung Nágá,	*Angsi.*
	Khári Nágá,	*Wá.*
	Angámi Nágá,	*Totache.*
	Námsáng Nágá,	*Káo.*
	Nowgong Nágá,	*Tsu, wang.*
	Tengsa Nágá,	*Chennang.*
	Abor Miri,	*Gupü gikangka.*
	Sibságar Miri,	*Sá.*
	Deoria Chutia,	*A'kená.*
	Singpho,	*Wán.*
Arrakan & Burmah.	Burman (written),	*Swá, kwya.*
	Burman (spoken),	*Thwá, kyuạ.*
	Khyeng v. Shou,	*Tsit.*
	Kámi,	*Lá.*
	Kúmi,	*Lá.*
	Mrú v. Toung,	*Caret.*
	Sák,	*Caret.*
Siam & Tenasserim.	Talain v. Mon,	*Aara.*
	Sgau-karen,	*Laì, le.*
	Pwo-karen,	*Lay.*
	Toungh-thu,	*Lway.*
	Shán,	*Kwa.*
	Annamitic,	*Di.*
	Siamese,	*Pihk, pai.*
	Ahom,	*Ká.*
	Khámti,	*Ká.*
	Laos,	*Pai, men.*
Central India.	Ho (Kol),	*Senotcá, olted.*
	Kol (Singhbhum),	*Sanoam.*
	Santáli,	*Chalahman.*
	Bhúmij,	*Sanoman.*
	Uráon,	*Kálá.*
	Mundala,	*Dásenámi.*
	Rájmahali,	*Eká, kálá.*
	Goṇḍi,	*Hannogalma, handana.*
	Gayeti,	*Caret.*
	Rutluk,	*Caret.*
	Naikude,	*Caret.*
	Kolami,	*Caret.*
	Mádi,	*Caret.*
	Mádia,	*Caret.*
	Kuri,	*Caret.*
	Keikádi,	*Ponga.*
	Khoṇḍ,	*Nallákanju.*
	Sávara,	*Maba.*
	Gadaba,	*Voyináyare.*
	Yerukala,	*Po.*
	Chentsu,	*Jáyivi, já.*
Southern India.	Tamiḷ, anc.,	*Caret.*
	Tamiḷ, mod.,	*Pó.*
	Malayáḷma, anc.,	*Caret.*
	Malayáḷma, mod.,	*Po.*
	Telugu,	*Povu, veḷḷu.*
	Karṇáṭaka, anc.,	*Caret.*
	Karṇáṭaka, mod.,	*Hógu.*
	Tuḷuva,	*Popuna.*
	Kurgi,	*Po.*
	Toḍuva,	*Caret.*
	Toḍa,	*At fo.*
	Kóta,	*At hogu.*
	Badaga,	*A'te hogu.*
	Kuṟumba,	*A'te hogu.*
	Iruḷa,	*Bho.*
	Malabar,	*Po.*
	Sinhalese,	*Yanavá.*

Group	Language	Word
	Types.	
Inflecting.	SANSKRIT, ...	*S'ru, ákarṇ.*
	ARABIC, ...	*Samaa.*
Compounding.	BASK, ...	*Aditu, entzun.*
	FINNIC, ...	*Kuulen.*
	MAGYAR, ...	*Hall.*
	TURKISH, ...	*Ishit.*
	CIRCASSIAN, ...	*Yaydoh.*
	GEORGIAN, ...	*Smenad.*
	MONGOLIAN, ...	*Sonoskhö.*
	MANTSHU, ...	*Dontshime.*
	JAVANESE, Ngoko, . .	*Ngrungu.*
	JAVANESE, Krama, . .	*Mireng.*
	MALAY, ...	*Dangar.*
Isolating.	CHINESE, Nankin, . .	*T'ing-kien.*
	CHINESE, Pekin, . .	*T'ing-chien.*
	CHINESE, Canton, . .	*T'ing-k'in.*
	CHINESE, Shanghai, .	*T'ing.*
	AMOY, Colloquial, . .	*T'iaṇ.*
	JAPANESE, ...	*Kiku.*
	Brahui, ...	*Khafto, bingak.*
Chinese Frontier & Tibet.	Gyámi, ...	*Thyen.*
	Gyárung, ...	*Karnyou.*
	Tákpa, ...	*Nyan.*
	Mányak, ...	*Khabe ni.*
	Thochú, ...	*Kokshustan.*
	Sokpa, ...	*Súnú.*
	Horpa, ...	*Wul min.*
	Tibetan (*written*), . .	*Nyan, gson.*
	Tibetan (*spoken*), . .	*Nyen.*
Nepal (east to west).	Serpa, ...	*Nyen.*
	Súnwár, ...	*Nyen.*
	Gúrung, ...	*Thed.*
	Múrmi, ...	*Gnán.*
	Magar, ...	*Thanáso.*
	Tháksya, ...	*Nagnino.*
	Pákhya, ...	*Suna.*
	Newár, ...	*Nyo.*
	Limbu, ...	*Khepse, khepse.*
Kiranti Group (East Nepal).	Kiránti, ...	*Yenú.*
	Rodong, ...	*Yenyú.*
	Rúngchenbung, . .	*Yenu, enu, enachu,[1] enanum.[2]*
	Chhingtángya, . . .	*Khem sa.*
	Náchhereng, ...	*Yena.*
	Wáling, ...	*Yenu.*
	Yákha, ...	*Khep'su.*
	Chourásya, ...	*Thokátá.*
	Kulungya, ...	*Yenu.*
	Thulungya, ...	*Thyosa.*
	Báhingya, ...	*Nino, ninishe,[1] ninne.[2]*
	Lohorong, ...	*Kheme; khemache;[1] khemamne.[2]*
	Lambichhong, . . .	*Khemsa.*
	Báláli, ...	*Yenu.*
	Sáng-páng, ...	*Yenu.*
	Dúmi, ...	*Ni.*
	Khálíng, ...	*Niye; niiye;[1] na niye.[2]*
	Dungmáli, ...	*Yene; yen'che;[1] yenanum'ye.[2]*
Broken Tribes of Nepal.	Dárhi, ...	*Súnkare.*
	Denwár, ...	*Sún.*
	Pahri, ...	*Nyá.*
	Chepáng, ...	*Sái.*
	Bhrámu, ...	*Asoyo.*
	Váyu, ...	*Hánko, tháko.*
	Kuswar, ...	*Sunou.*
	Kusunda, ...	*Mang'bo.*
	Thàru, ...	*Suna.*
	Lepcha (Sikkim), . .	*Nyen.*
	Bhútáni v. Lhopa, . .	*Nyen.*

Group	Language	Word
N.-E. Bengal.	Bodo, ...	*Khaná chong.*
	Dhimál, ...	*Hin.*
	Kocch, ...	*Caret.*
	Garo, ...	*Natám.*
	Kácháari, ...	*Caret.*
Eastern Frontier of Bengal.	Munipuri, ...	*Tao.*
	Míthán Nágá, . . .	*Athak.*
	Tablung Nágá, . . .	*Chai ha.*
	Khári Nágá, ...	*Jaugo.*
	Angámi Nágá, . . .	*Silowe.*
	Námsáng Nágá, . . .	*Táto.*
	Nowgong Nágá, . .	*Aáshu.*
	Tengsa Nágá, . . .	*Angáng.*
	Abor Miri, ...	*Tadtrapü.*
	Sibságar Miri, . . .	*Táttoka.*
	Deoria Chutia, . . .	*Kanatori.*
	Singpho, ...	*Nángu.*
Arrakan & Burmah.	Burman (*written*), . .	*Krá.*
	Burman (*spoken*), . . .	*Kyá, nahtounthi.*
	Khyeng v. Shou, . .	*Kayauk.*
	Kámi, ...	*Thái.*
	Kúmi, ...	*Thái.*
	Mrú v. Toung, . . .	*Caret.*
	Sák, ...	*Caret.*
Siam & Tenasserim.	Talain v. Mon, . . .	*Kalan.*
	Sgau-karen, ...	*Nahhu.*
	Pwo-karen, ...	*Nahgung.*
	Toungh-thu, ...	*Heung.*
	Shán, ...	*Htanlá.*
	Annamitic, ...	*Nghe.*
	Siamese, ...	*Htawlon, dai yin.*
	Ahom, ...	*Nyin.*
	Khámti, ...	*Ngin.*
	Laos, ...	*Nyin.*
Central India.	Ho (Kol), ...	*Ayumteá.*
	Kol (Singhbhum), . .	*Jaimman.*
	Santáli, ...	*Jyúmman.*
	Bhúmij, ...	*Jyúmmanmego.*
	Uráon, ...	*Mijnka.*
	Mundala, ...	*Jyoumemi.*
	Rájmahali, ...	*Mená.*
	Goṇḍi, ...	*Keinjana.*
	Gayeti, ...	*Caret.*
	Rutluk, ...	*Caret.*
	Naikude, ...	*Caret.*
	Kolami, ...	*Caret.*
	Mádi, ...	*Caret.*
	Mádia, ...	*Caret.*
	Kuri, ...	*Caret.*
	Keikádi, ...	*Kar, wei.*
	Khoṇḍ, ...	*Venjámu.*
	Sávara, ...	*Andángá.*
	Gadaba, ...	*Vovo.*
	Yerukala, ...	*Keru, keṭu.*
	Chentsu, ...	*Sún.*
Southern India.	Tamiḷ, anc., ...	*Caret.*
	Tamiḷ, mod., ...	*Kêḷ.*
	Malayáḷma, anc., . .	*Caret.*
	Malayáḷma, mod., . .	*Keḷ.*
	Telugu, ...	*Vinu.*
	Karṇáṭaka, anc., . .	*Caret.*
	Karṇáṭaka, mod., . .	*Keḷu.*
	Tuḷuva, ...	*Caret.*
	Kurgi, ...	*Caret.*
	Toḍuva, }	*Caret.*
	Toḍa, }	*Kelth bine, vonatth bine, voraṭir.*
	Kóta, ...	*Vorutabe, voruṭṭulle.*
	Badaga, ...	*Kretine, voradine, kṭe.*
	Kurumba, ...	*Kretine, voradine, kelu.*
	Iruḷa, ...	*Kelke, keṭukove.*
	Malabar, ...	*Kel.*
	Sinhalese, ...	*Ahanavá.*

Group	Language	Word
Types.		
Inflecting.	SANSKRIT,	*Han, badh, mṛi (márayati).*
	ARABIC,	*Katala.*
Compounding.	BASK,	*Il, eriotu, eriokatu, sarbaskitu.*
	FINNIC,	*Tapan.*
	MAGYAR,	*Caret.*
	TURKISH,	*Euldur.*
	CIRCASSIAN,	*Uikkey.*
	GEORGIAN,	*Wklav [kl].*
	MONGOLIAN,	*Alakho.*
	MANTSHU,	*Wame.*
	JAVANESE, Ngoko,	*Matenni.*
	JAVANESE, Krama,	*Mejahhi.*
	MALAY,	*Búnoh.*
Isolating.	CHINESE, Nankin,	*Sháh.*
	CHINESE, Pekin,	*Shá.*
	CHINESE, Canton,	*Shát.*
	CHINESE, Shanghai,	*Sah.*
	AMOY, Colloquial,	*T'ài.*
	JAPANESE,	*Korosú, koroshi.*
	Brahuí,	*Kasbo.*
Chinese Frontier & Tibet.	Gyámi,	*Sá.*
	Gyárung,	*Náse.*
	Tákpa,	*Sotá.*
	Mányak,	*Nasya.*
	Thochú,	*Tasch.*
	Sokpa,	*Caret.*
	Horpa,	*Tashe.*
	Tibetan (*written*),	*Shig sod, hgúm.*
	Tibetan (*spoken*),	*Se.*
Nepal (east to west).	Serpa,	*Syet.*
	Súnwár,	*Sat.*
	Gúrung,	*Thod, sed.*
	Múrmi,	*Sát.*
	Magar,	*Gnáp.*
	Tháksya,	*Caret.*
	Pákhya,	*Márideú.*
	Newár,	*Syá.*
	Limbu,	*Sere.*
Kiranti Group (East Nepal).	Kiránti,	*Serú.*
	Rodong,	*Setyú.*
	Rúngchenbung,	*Seru, sera chu,[1] sera num.[2]*
	Chhingtángya,	*Sera.*
	Náchhereng,	*Situ.*
	Wáling,	*Seru.*
	Yákha,	*Chenu, sisu.*
	Chourásya,	*Syáttá.*
	Kulungya,	*Setu, khoksyu.*
	Thulungya,	*Seda.*
	Báhingya,	*Sáto, satishe,[1] satine.[2]*
	Lohorong,	*Sede, sedache,[1] sedamne,[2] thapta.*
	Lambichhong,	*Sera.*
	Báláli,	*Sedú.*
	Sáng-páng,	*Situ.*
	Dúmi,	*Sede.*
	Kháling,	*Sede, se chi,[1] se snaye.[2]*
	Dungmáli,	*Sede, sedechie,[1] sernumye.[2]*
Broken Tribes of Nepal.	Dárhi,	*Káti-ik.*
	Denwár,	*Márik'.*
	Pahri,	*Páli.*
	Chepáng,	*Caret.*
	Bhrámu,	*Sáto, aprito, aprito.*
	Váyu,	*Sishto, yúkto.*
	Kuswar,	*Hirkaik.*
	Kusunda,	*Wagdágo.*
	Tháru,	*Már.*
	Lepcha (Sikkim),	*Sot.*
	Bhúṭáni v. Lhopa,	*Seh.*

Group	Language	Word
N.-E. Bengal.	Bodo,	*Shothát.*
	Dhimál,	*Se, sheli.*
	Kocch,	*Máriaphaláná.*
	Garo,	*Toktat.*
	Káchári,	*Shitang, shithatno, watno.*
Eastern Frontier of Bengal.	Munipuri,	*Hato-o.*
	Míthán Nágá,	*Langdau.*
	Tablung Nágá,	*Toi chi.*
	Khári Nágá,	*Yaksitogo.*
	Angámi Nágá,	*Dukhiawe.*
	Námsáng Nágá,	*Rikváto.*
	Nowgong Nágá,	*A'soko.*
	Tengsa Nágá,	*A'seko, siyang.*
	Abor Miri,	*Púpu.*
	Sibságar Miri,	*Dingketo.*
	Deoria Chutia,	*Botechiro.*
	Singpho,	*Satu.*
Arrakan & Burmah.	Burman (*written*),	*Sat.*
	Burman (*spoken*),	*Thát.*
	Khyeng v. Shou,	*Túe.*
	Kámi,	*Dúrhummale.*
	Kúmi,	*Pukhou.*
	Mrú v. Toung,	*Caret.*
	Sák,	*Caret.*
Siam & Tenasserim.	Talain v. Mon,	*Tsa.*
	Sgau-karen,	*Mathi.*
	Pwo-karen,	*Mathi.*
	Toungh-thu,	*Mathay.*
	Shán,	*Outtihn.*
	Annamitic,	*Shem.*
	Siamese,	*Outtihn, khá, au tai.*
	Ahom,	*Potai.*
	Khámti,	*Au tai.*
	Laos,	*Khá.*
Central India.	Ho (Kol),	*Goiteá.*
	Kol (Singhbhum),	*Margojokai.*
	Santáli,	*Goidapalsmon.*
	Bhúmij,	*Margagojiman.*
	Uráon,	*Pitalchia.*
	Mundala,	*Márgoji.*
	Rájmahali,	*Pittá.*
	Goṇḍi,	*Jakstvaústi, jukkana.*
	Gayeti,	*Caret.*
	Rutluk,	*Caret.*
	Naikude,	*Caret.*
	Kolami,	*Caret.*
	Mádi,	*Caret.*
	Mádia,	*Caret.*
	Kuri,	*Caret.*
	Keikádi,	*Pranamedu.*
	Khoṇḍ,	*Vesámáhudu.*
	Sávara,	*Kílisibba.*
	Gadaba,	*Abboye.*
	Yerukala,	*Kolusu, kollu.*
	Chentsu,	*Marepheló, morevaleyo.*
Southern India.	Tamiḷ, anc.,	*Caret.*
	Tamiḷ, mod.,	*Kollu.*
	Malayáḷma, anc.,	*Caret.*
	Malayáḷma, mod.,	*Kolla.*
	Telugu,	*Champu.*
	Karṇáṭaka, anc.,	*Caret.*
	Karṇáṭaka, mod.,	*Kollu.*
	Tuḷuva,	*Caret.*
	Kurgi,	*Kollu.*
	Toḍuva,	*Caret.*
	Toḍa,	*Besht vers bini, birshkir, koddu.*
	Kóta,	*Taverigábe, tavarsidade.*
	Baḍaga,	*Koddane, kodd hoku.*
	Kurumba,	*Koddane, kondu hoku.*
	Iruḷa,	*Kolluke, adidukove, kondukove.*
	Malabar,	*Kollu.*
	Sinhalese,	*Maranavá.*

Group	Language	Word
	Types.	
Inflecting.	SANSKRIT,	*Has, smi, kakk.*
	ARABIC,	*Daḥeka.*
Compounding.	BASK,	*Farraegin, barreegin, irriegin.*
	FINNIC,	*Nauran.*
	MAGYAR,	*Nevet.*
	TURKISH,	*Geul.*
	CIRCASSIAN,	*Wiguzay.*
	GEORGIAN,	*Sitsili* [*tsil*].
	MONGOLIAN,	*Inyakho.*
	MANTSHU,	*Indsheme.*
	JAVANESE, Ngoko,	*Gumúyu.*
	JAVANESE, Krama,	*Gemújeng.*
	MALAY,	*Tertáva.*
Isolating.	CHINESE, Nankin,	*Siaou.*
	CHINESE, Pekin,	*Hsiaou.*
	CHINESE, Canton,	*Siú.*
	CHINESE, Shanghai,	*Sian.*
	AMOY, Colloquial,	*Ch'io.*
	JAPANESE,	*Waräu.*
	Brahuí,	*Makhebo.*
Chinese Frontier & Tibet.	Gyámi,	*Syo.*
	Gyárung,	*Kándre.*
	Tákpa,	*Gye.*
	Mányak,	*Narir.*
	Thochú,	*Daran.*
	Sokpa,	*Enna.*
	Horpa,	*Khákhe.*
	Tibetan (*written*),	*Bgad.*
	Tibetan (*spoken*),	*Gá.*
Nepal (east to west).	Serpa,	*Gwet.*
	Súnwár,	*Ris.*
	Gúrung,	*Nyed.*
	Múrmi,	*Nyet.*
	Magar,	*Ret.*
	Tháksya,	*Gneto.*
	Pákhya,	*Hás.*
	Newár,	*Nhyú.*
	Limbu,	*Yere.*
Kiránti Group (East Nepal).	Kiránti,	*I'yá.*
	Rodong,	*Riya, rya.*
	Rúngchenbung,	*I'yá, isa.*
	Chhingtángya,	*Reta.*
	Náchhereng,	*Bhesa.*
	Wáling,	*I'ya.*
	Yákha,	*Yúttucháya.*
	Chourásya,	*Rendá restá.*
	Kulungya,	*Gesa.*
	Thulungya,	*Rísá.*
	Báhingya,	*Riso, rische,*[1] *risini.*[2]
	Lohorong,	*Yichae, ichoye, ichare, ichache,*[1] *ichane.*[2]
	Lambichhong,	*Risa, risa chi,*[1] *risa ni.*[2]
	Báláli,	*Yúchá, yucha chi,*[1] *yucha nin.*[2]
	Sáng-páng,	*Ghísá, ghísáchi,*[1] *ghisá ni.*[2]
	Dúmi,	*Reche.*
	Kháling,	*Reche.*
	Dungmáli,	*Ríge.*
Broken Tribes of Nepal.	Dárhi,	*Hansuk.*
	Denwár,	*Bhyás, rhias.*
	Pahri,	*Nhili.*
	Chepáng,	*Nhische, nhisa.*
	Bhrámu,	*Núya.*
	Váyu,	*I'sche, yesche.*
	Kuswar,	*Háskou, haskou.*
	Kusunda,	*Nakyába.*
	Tháru,	*Káhasal.*
	Lepcha (Sikkim),	*Then.*
	Bhúṭáni v. Lhopa,	*Gá.*

Group	Language	Word
N.-E. Bengal.	Bodo,	*Mini.*
	Dhimál,	*Leng.*
	Kocch,	*Hásinu, muskihasinu* (to smile).
	Garo,	*Mini.*
	Kácharí,	*Miniyu mini thá dung.*
Eastern Frontier of Bengal.	Munipuri,	*Nu.*
	Míthán Nágá,	*Nile.*
	Tablung Nágá,	*Nichi.*
	Khári Nágá,	*Manitli.*
	Angámi Nágá,	*Nu.*
	Námsáng Nágá,	*Ngio.*
	Nowgong Nágá,	*Mannü.*
	Tengsa Nágá,	*Mannü.*
	Abor Miri,	*Nilodopü.*
	Sibságar Miri,	*Yirda.*
	Deoria Chutia,	*Hatukari.*
	Singpho,	*Maniu.*
Arrakan & Burmah.	Burman (*written*),	*Re.*
	Burman (*spoken*),	*Ye.*
	Khyeng v. Shou,	*Anwi.*
	Kámi,	*Manwi.*
	Kúmi,	*A'mnhwi.*
	Mrú v. Toung,	*Caret.*
	Sák,	*Caret.*
Siam & Tenasserim.	Talain v. Mon,	*Garihn.*
	Sgau-karen,	*Ne, nih.*
	Pwo-karen,	*Ni.*
	Toungh-thu,	*Nga.*
	Shán,	*Kho.*
	Annamitic,	*Ku'ò'i.*
	Siamese,	*Horau, hoaro.*
	Ahom,	*Khru.*
	Khámti,	*Kho.*
	Laos,	*Hán, khoa.*
Central India.	Ho (Kol),	*Landeiteá.*
	Kol (Singhbhum),	*Landaiman.*
	Santáli,	*Lándate, khetelándate* (loud),
	Bhúmij,	*Landai.* [*bhábahte* (titter).
	Uráon,	*Alkah.*
	Mundala,	*Caret.*
	Rájmahali,	*A'lká.*
	Goṇḍi,	*Kavitoni, kawana.*
	Gayeti,	*Caret.*
	Rutluk,	*Caret.*
	Naikude,	*Caret.*
	Kolami,	*Caret.*
	Mádi,	*Caret.*
	Mádia,	*Caret.*
	Kuri,	*Caret.*
	Keikádi,	*Sri.*
	Khoṇḍ,	*Kakkumu.*
	Sávara,	*Mágnába.*
	Gadaba,	*Luḍḍo.*
	Yerukala,	*Sirilá, chirike.*
	Chentsu,	*Hás.*
Southern India.	Tamiḷ, anc.,	*Nagu.*
	Tamiḷ, mod.,	*Nagai.*
	Malayáḷma, anc.,	*Caret.*
	Malayáḷma, mod.,	*Chiri.*
	Telugu,	*Navvu.*
	Karṇáṭaka, anc.,	*Caret.*
	Karṇáṭaka, mod.,	*Nagu.*
	Tuḷuva,	*Telepuna.*
	Kurgi,	*Caret.*
	Toḍuva,	*Caret.*
	Toḍa,	*Karth bini, kari.*
	Kóta,	*Karsibe, kárje.*
	Baḍaga,	*Naggedane, nege.*
	Kuṛumba,	*Nage.*
	Iruḷa,	*Jirike, girkáḍu.*
	Malabar,	*Sirippu.*
	Sinhalese,	*Hinahavenavá.*

Group	Language	Word
	Types.	
Inflecting.	SANSKRIT,	*Uttul, uchchhri.*
	ARABIC,	*Rafaa.*
Compounding.	BASK,	*Jaso, jasan, eregi, altza.*
	FINNIC,	*Nousen.*
	MAGYAR,	*Caret.*
	TURKISH,	*Kalkdir.*
	CIRCASSIAN,	*Ettey.*
	GEORGIAN,	*Caret.*
	MONGOLIAN,	*Ergögö.*
	MANTSHU,	*Tukiyeme.*
	JAVANESE, Ngoko,	*Jungjung.*
	JAVANESE, Krama,	*Jungjung.*
	MALAY,	*Angkat.*
Isolating.	CHINESE, Nankin,	*Kü ki-lai.*
	CHINESE, Pekin,	*Chü k'i-lai.*
	CHINESE, Canton,	*Kü hi-loi.*
	CHINESE, Shanghai,	*Kiü-chi-le.*
	AMOY, Colloquial,	*Kü kï-lai.*
	JAPANESE,	*Ageru, takaksuru.*
	Brahuí,	*Hef.*
Chinese Frontier & Tibet.	Gyámi,	*Máyú.*
	Gyárung,	*Tayok.*
	Tákpa,	*Longna.*
	Mányak,	*Dachi.*
	Thochú,	*Tachi.*
	Sokpa,	*Wúra.*
	Horpa,	*Rangke, rházi.*
	Tibetan (*written*),	*Hdegs, slon, ṣnyob.*
	Tibetan (*spoken*),	*Khúr.*
Nepal (east to west).	Serpa,	• *Khúr.*
	Súnwár,	*Pok.*
	Gúrung,	*Nod.*
	Múrmi,	*Púyo.*
	Magar,	*Bú.*
	Tháksya,	*Thithonko.*
	Pákhya,	*Bok.*
	Newár,	*Lhoṇ bu.*
	Limbu,	*Pokhe, poke.*
Kiranti Group (East Nepal).	Kiránti,	*Khuyú.*
	Rodong,	*Púku, sandyú.*
	Rúngchenbung,	*Thentu,*[1] *num.*[2]
	Chhingtángya,	*Khúrá, thedak.*
	Náchhereng,	*Thettu.*
	Wáling,	*Thentu.*
	Yákha,	*Khu, thendu.*
	Chourásya,	*Rottá.*
	Kulungya,	*Poka.*
	Thulungya,	*Phoká, kwaksá.*
	Báhingya,	*Rokto, roktise,*[1] *roktine.*[2]
	Lohorong,	*Thepoge, thelente, theache,*[1] *theamme.*[2]
	Lambichhong,	*Koba, koplota.*
	Báláli,	*Thettu.*
	Sáng-páng,	*Thettu.*
	Dúmi,	*Thende.*
	Kháling,	*Thende, thendechie,*[1] *thendes-naye.*[2]
	Dungmáli,	*Thende, thendechie,*[1] *then'de num ye.*[2]
Broken Tribes of Nepal.	Dárhi,	*Bokuk.*
	Denwár,	*Algáik.*
	Pahri,	*Búgno, bungo.*
	Chepáng,	*Caret.*
	Bhrámu,	*Uyogno, uyogo.*
	Váyu,	*Reko.*
	Kuswar,	*Algaik.*
	Kusunda,	*Túlinggwajo.*
	Tháru,	*Uthá o, lad.*
	Lepcha (Sikkim),	*Chún.*
	Bhúṭáni v. Lhopa,	*Thú.*
N.-E. Bengal.	Bodo,	*Bokháng, boklop.*
	Dhimál,	*Lhopá.*
	Kocch,	*Uthyakonu.*
	Garo,	*Paicho.*
	Káchári,	*Caret.*
Eastern Frontier of Bengal.	Munipuri,	*Thángalao.*
	Mithán Nágá,	*Lauko.*
	Tablung Nágá,	*Noh si.*
	Khári Nágá,	*Chungotso.*
	Angámi Nágá,	*Tupele.*
	Námsáng Nágá,	*Tuons.*
	Nowgong Nágá,	*Achongatong.*
	Tengsa Nágá,	*Aiyoang.*
	Abor Miri,	*Lássápü.*
	Sibságar Miri,	*Jowon.*
	Deoria Chutia,	*Lagaromni.*
	Singpho,	*Phonu.*
Arrakan & Burmah.	Burman (*written*),	*Mhrang, mhrok.*
	Burman (*spoken*),	*Mhyen, mhyauk.*
	Khyeng v. Shou,	*Youkke.*
	Kámi,	*Takhún.*
	Kúmi,	*Katán.*
	Mrú v. Toung,	*Caret.*
	Sák,	*Caret.*
Siam & Tenasserim.	Talain v. Mon,	*Katoung.*
	Sgau-karen,	*So'taw, heká.*
	Pwo-karen,	*Tsohtong.*
	Toungh-thu,	*Hya, young.*
	Shán,	*Hohkhen.*
	Annamitic,	*Len.*
	Siamese,	*Hounkhan, yok.*
	Ahom,	*Yok, tang.*
	Khámti,	*Yo, yong.*
	Laos,	*Yá.*
Central India.	Ho (Kol),	*Caret.*
	Kol (Singhbhum),	*Rúkúbman.*
	Santáli,	*Beredate, tulate, rákápate.*
	Bhúmij,	*U'thaibaitman.*
	Uráon,	*Chodá.*
	Mundala,	*Rimemi.*
	Rájmahali,	*Chivá.*
	Goṇḍi,	*Tehá.*
	Gayeti,	*Caret.*
	Rutluk,	*Caret.*
	Naikude,	*Caret.*
	Kolami,	*Caret.*
	Mádi,	*Caret.*
	Mádia,	*Caret.*
	Kuri,	*Caret.*
	Keikádi,	*Caret.*
	Khoṇḍ,	*Densumu.*
	Sávara,	*Lanka.*
	Gadaba,	*Leno.*
	Yerukala,	*Yeḍuḍu.*
	Chentsu,	*Tol.*
Southern India.	Tamiḷ, anc.,	*Merkol.*
	Tamiḷ, mod.,	*Eḍu.*
	Malayáḷma, anc.,	*Caret.*
	Malayáḷma, mod.,	*Eṭu.*
	Telugu,	*Ettu.*
	Karṇáṭaka, anc.,	*Caret.*
	Karṇáṭaka, mod.,	*Ettu.*
	Tuḷuva,	*Diripana.*
	Kurgi,	*Caret.*
	Toḍuva,	*Caret.*
	Toḍa,	*Túchs bine, mokversbine, túch.*
	Kóta,	*Yetti gabe, mekarse.*
	Baḍaga,	*Yettinetúkine, tuku, hi.*
	Kurumba,	*Yettinetúkine, túku.*
	Iruḷa,	*Yekkuke, túkove.*
	Malabar,	*Uyarthu, thúkku.*
	Sinhalese,	*Ussanavá.*

Group	Types.	
Inflecting.	SANSKRIT, ...	*Chal, sṛi, i, char, gam, kram.*
	ARABIC, ...	*Masha.*
Compounding.	BASK, ...	*Ibilli.*
	FINNIC, ...	*Käyn.*
	MAGYAR, ...	*Yar.*
	TURKISH, ...	*Yuru.*
	CIRCASSIAN, ...	*Caret.*
	GEORGIAN, ...	*Caret.*
	MONGOLIAN, ...	*Jabokho.*
	MANTSHU, ...	*Sutshume.*
	JAVANESE, Ngoko, . .	*Lumáku.*
	JAVANESE, Krama, . .	*Lumampah.*
	MALAY, ...	*Jálan.*
Isolating.	CHINESE, Nankin, . .	*Hing-tsau.*
	CHINESE, Pekin, . .	*Hsing-tsau.*
	CHINESE, Canton, . .	*Hang-lò.*
	CHINESE, Shanghai, .	*Dung, tseu.*
	AMOY, Colloquial, . .	*Kiâṇ.*
	JAPANESE, ...	*Aluku, aruki.*
	Brahui, ...	*Chiring.*
Chinese Frontier & Tibet.	Gyámi, ...	*Chú, chhi.*
	Gyárung, ...	*Yeyen, yachin.*
	Tákpa, ...	*Gai.*
	Mányak, ...	*Yú.*
	Thochú, ...	*Dákan.*
	Sokpa, ...	*A'hyar yábo.*
	Horpa, ...	*Tashin.*
	Tibetan (*written*), . .	*Hgro.*
	Tibetan (*spoken*), . . .	*Gyo.*
Nepal (east to west).	Serpa, ...	*Dong.*
	Súnwár, ...	*Gák.*
	Gúrung, ...	*Yáy.*
	Múrmi, ...	*Brou.*
	Magar, ...	*Wha ni.*
	Tháksya, ...	*Hero.*
	Pákhya, ...	*Hat.*
	Newár, ...	*Nyá, húṇ.*
	Limbu, ...	*Bege.*
Kiranti Group (East Nepal).	Kiránti, ...	*Biyá.*
	Rodong, ...	*Pong sa, lamtya.*
	Rúngchenbung, . . .	*Lám dúma, biya.*[1]
	Chhingtángya, . . .	*Phána.*
	Náchhereng, ...	*Lámdíma.*
	Wáling, ...	*Biya.*
	Yákha, ...	*Láma.*
	Chourásya, ...	*Háltá.*
	Kulungya, ...	*Lámdúma.*
	Thulungya, ...	*Lámdiya.* [*kine.*[2]
	Báhingya, ...	*Gwakko, gwakshe,*[1] *gwa-* [*ne.*[2]
	Lohorong, ...	*Lámdúme, lamdache,*[1] *lamda*
	Lambichhong, ...	*Phaua, laöma, phanachi,*[1]*-ni.*[2]
	Báláli, ...	*Dúma, dumachi,*[1] *duma nin.*[2]
	Sáng-páng, ...	*Londúma, bi, tandchini.*
	Dúmi, ...	*Lámthúlo.*
	Kháling, ...	*Lámthúye.*
	Dungmáli, ...	*Lámtúme.*
Broken Tribes of Nepal.	Dárhi, ...	*Hiḍuk.*
	Denwár, ...	*Chol.*
	Pahri, ...	*Go.*
	Chepáng, ...	*Whá, whása.*
	Bhrámu, ...	*Syo, jewa.*
	Váyu, ...	*Khokche.*
	Kuswar, ...	*Non.*
	Kusunda, ...	*Aban.*
	Tháru, ...	*Chal.*
	Lepcha (Sikkim), . .	*Non, di.*
	Bhúṭáni v. Lhopa, . .	*Dyú.*

Group	Language	Word
N.-E. Bengal.	Bodo, ...	*Tho, tháng, thábái.*
	Dhimál, ...	*Ti, hade.*
	Kocch, ...	*Cholinu.*
	Garo, ...	*Loï.*
	Káchári, ...	*Caret.*
Eastern Frontier of Bengal.	Munipuri, ...	*Chulo.*
	Míthán Nágá, . . .	*Tong, khá.*
	Tablung Nágá, . . .	*Angsi.*
	Khári Nágá, ...	*Rong chwa.*
	Angámi Nágá, . . .	*Tothe.*
	Námsáng Nágá, . .	*Choo, khuams.*
	Nowgong Nágá, . .	*Asámataur.*
	Tengsa Nágá, . . .	*Asambat.*
	Abor Miri, ...	*Iokoda.*
	Sibságar Miri, . . .	*Gümandak.*
	Deoria Chutia, . . .	*Kerurini.*
	Singpho, ...	*Thotu, damu.*
Arrakan & Burmah.	Burman (*written*), . .	*Le, kwya.*
	Burman (*spoken*), . . .	*Le, kyuá.*
	Khyeng v. Shou, . .	*Caret.*
	Kámi, ...	*Caret.*
	Kúmi, ...	*Caret.*
	Mrú v. Toung, . . .	*Caret.*
	Sák, ...	*Caret.*
Siam & Tenasserim.	Talain v. Mon, . . .	*Kyay.*
	Sgau-karen, ...	*Laitah, ghai.*
	Pwo-karen, ...	*Tsaing, ghai.*
	Toungh-thu, ...	*Lay.*
	Shán, ...	*Layyú.*
	Annamitic, ...	*Didao.*
	Siamese, ...	*Htaro, dün.*
	Ahom, ...	*Ká.*
	Khámti, ...	*Pai.*
	Laos, ...	*Men.*
Central India.	Ho (Kol), ...	*Senoteá.*
	Kol (Singhbhum), . .	*Sanoman.* [*senohte.*
	Santáli, ...	*Túḍámate, chálähte, ḍánáte,*
	Bhúmij, ...	*Dholábúsanoman.*
	Uráon, ...	*Gúcha.*
	Mundala, ...	*Sendmi.*
	Rájmahali, ...	*Sakrá* (?).
	Goṇḍi, ...	*Taká, takana.*
	Gayeti, ...	*Caret.*
	Rutluk, ...	*Caret.*
	Naikude, ...	*Caret.*
	Kolami, ...	*Caret.*
	Mádi, ...	*Caret.*
	Mádia, ...	*Caret.*
	Kuri, ...	*Caret.*
	Keikádi, ...	*Naḍu.*
	Khoṇḍ, ...	*Kujinámu.*
	Sávara, ...	*Yirba.*
	Gadaba, ...	*Vamsu.*
	Yerukala, ...	*Naḍá.*
	Chentsu, ...	*Tzo.*
Southern India.	Tamiḷ, anc., . . .	*Caret.*
	Tamiḷ, mod., . . .	*Naḍa.*
	Malayáḷma, anc., . .	*Caret.*
	Malayáḷma, mod., . .	*Naḍaiḷa.*
	Telugu, ...	*Naḍuchu.*
	Karṇáṭaka, anc., . .	*Caret.*
	Karṇáṭaka, mod., . .	*Naḍe.*
	Tuḷuva, ...	*Caret.*
	Kurgi, ...	*Caret.*
	Toḍuva, }	*Caret.*
	Toḍa, }	*Naḍedersh bini, at nar.*
	Kóta, ...	*Naḍegabe, naḍe.*
	Baḍaga, ...	*Naḍedane, naḍe.*
	Kuṛumba, ...	*Naḍedane, naḍe.*
	Iruḷa, ...	*Naḍake, naḍandu kove.*
	Malabar, ...	*Naḍamáduthal, naḍei.*
	Sinhalese, ...	*Ävindinavá.*

Group	Language	Run
	Types.	
Inflecting.	SANSKṚIT,	*Dháv, du, dru, rañh, śighrañ-chal.*
	ARABIC,	*Rakada.*
Compounding.	BASK,	*Eyatu, lasteregin, korri, eyakajoan.*
	FINNIC,	*Juoksen.*
	MAGYAR,	*Szalad.*
	TURKISH,	*Kosh.*
	CIRCASSIAN,	*Caret.*
	GEORGIAN,	*Galtsawad.*
	MONGOLIAN,	*Göyögö.*
	MANTSHU,	*Sudshume.*
	JAVANESE, Ngoko,	*Lumáyu.*
	JAVANESE, Krama,	*Lumajĕr.*
	MALAY,	*Lári.*
Isolating.	CHINESE, Nankin,	*P'áou.*
	CHINESE, Pekin,	*P'áou.*
	CHINESE, Canton,	*Tsau.*
	CHINESE, Shanghai,	*Pau.*
	AMOY, Colloquial,	*Cháu.*
	JAPANESE,	*Kakeru, fashiri.*
	Brahuí,	*Halmak.*
Chinese Frontier & Tibet.	Gyámi,	*Thewo.*
	Gyárung,	*Danargyúk.*
	Tákpa,	*Pshet.*
	Mányak,	*Tachimoyú.*
	Thochú,	*Dádran.*
	Sokpa,	*Thúr keng.*
	Horpa,	*Tamgyo.*
	Tibetan (*written*),	*Rgyúg.*
	Tibetan (*spoken*),	*Gyúge, chong.*
Nepal (east to west).	Serpa,	*Chong.*
	Súnwár,	*Plok.*
	Gúrung,	*Dhid.*
	Múrmi,	*Yár.*
	Magar,	*Yani.*
	Tháksya,	*Guinahero.*
	Pákhya,	*Phalála.*
	Newár,	*Bwá.*
	Limbu,	*Lokte, lokte.*
Kiranti Group (East Nepal).	Kiránti,	*Loyá.*
	Rodong,	*Wona.*
	Rúngchenbung,	*Lwáya, loya.*
	Chhingtángya,	*Ping'da.*
	Náchhereng,	*Bal'sa.*
	Wáling,	*Lora.*
	Yákha,	*Lúk'ta.*
	Chourásya,	*Prokátá.*
	Kulungya,	*Búlsa.*
	Thulungya,	*Wánda.*
	Báhingya,	*Wánno, wanshe,[1] wanne.[2]*
	Lohorong,	*Pine, pineache,[1] pinane.[2]*
	Lambichhong,	*Pin'da, pinchi,[1] -ni.[2]*
	Báláli,	*Phína, phinachi,[1] phinanin.[2]*
	Sáng-páng,	*Bhúsa, bhúsa,[1] chini.[2]*
	Dúmi,	*Ghúre.*
	Kháling,	*Ghúre.*
	Dungmáli,	*Rode.*
Broken Tribes of Nepal.	Dárhi,	*Dúgaruk.*
	Denwár,	*Dúgar.*
	Pahri,	*Kenggno, keingo, kenggo.*
	Chepáng,	*Kí kisa.*
	Bhrámu,	*Gegweya.*
	Váyu,	*Lúngche.*
	Kuswar,	*Dhou.*
	Kusunda,	*Gorgowoto.*
	Thâru,	*Dhába.*
	Lepcha (Sikkim),	*Deung.*
	Bhúṭáni v. Lhopa,	*Páṇ kyap.*
N.-E. Bengal.	Bodo,	*Khot, khát* (flee).
	Dhimál,	*Dháp, khat* (flee).
	Koech,	*Dowrinu, bhâginu* (flee).
	Garo,	*Talok.*
	Káchári,	*Caret.*
Eastern Frontier of Bengal.	Munipuri,	*Chelo.*
	Míthán Nágá,	*Rikle.*
	Tablung Nágá,	*Phal chi.*
	Khári Nágá,	*Semekwa.*
	Angámi Nágá,	*Mhathele.*
	Námsáng Nágá,	*Chuano.*
	Nowgong Nágá,	*Sámawaung.*
	Tengsa Nágá,	*A'ásambat.*
	Abor Miri,	*Dukpü.*
	Sibságar Miri,	*Dupdandak.*
	Deoria Chutia,	*Jononini.*
	Singpho,	*Gagátu.*
Arrakan & Burmah.	Burman (*written*),	*Pre.*
	Burman (*spoken*),	*Pye.*
	Khyeng v. Shou,	*Chone.*
	Kámi,	*Awhi.*
	Kúmi,	*Lei.*
	Mrú v. Toung,	*Caret.*
	Sák,	*Caret.*
Siam & Tenasserim.	Talain v. Mon,	*Garitaa.*
	Sgau-karen,	*Kha, hkhú.*
	Pwo-karen,	*Tsaingt'laing.*
	Toungh-thu,	*Law.*
	Shán,	*Lenkwa.*
	Annamitic,	*Shay.*
	Siamese,	*Wenpihu, wing pi.*
	Ahom,	*Paikhan.*
	Khámti,	*Len.*
	Laos,	*Len pai.*
Central India.	Ho (Kol),	*Nirteá.*
	Kol (Singhbhum),	*Nirìman.*
	Santáli,	*Daüdate, gatarate, khámas-düte* (causal).
	Bhúmij,	*Durman.*
	Uráon,	*Bonga.*
	Mundala,	*Lirmi.*
	Rájmahali,	*Bonga.*
	Goṇḍi,	*Vittana bittá.*
	Gayeti,	*Caret.*
	Rutluk,	*Caret.*
	Naikude,	*Caret.*
	Kolami,	*Caret.*
	Mádi,	*Caret.*
	Mádia,	*Caret.*
	Kuri,	*Caret.*
	Keikádi,	*Wodu.*
	Khoṇḍ,	*Gyáhamu.*
	Sávara,	*Nadam.*
	Gadaba,	*Dugga.*
	Yerukala,	*Vodu.*
	Chentsu,	*Beg.*
Southern India.	Tamiḷ, anc.,	*Caret.*
	Tamiḷ, mod.,	*Odu, woda.*
	Malayáḷma, anc.,	*Caret.*
	Malayáḷma, mod.,	*Otu.*
	Telugu,	*Parigettu, uruku.*
	Karṇáṭaka, anc.,	*Caret.*
	Karṇáṭaka, mod.,	*Wódu.*
	Tuḷuva,	*Páruna.*
	Kurgi,	*Wódu.*
	Toḍuva, Toḍa,	*Caret.*
	Toḍa,	*Vudu, vor.*
	Kóta,	*Vose, ate vodu.*
	Badaga,	*Vadu, vodu.*
	Kuṛumba,	*Vadu, vodu.*
	Iruḷa,	*Vodipoke, vodu.*
	Malabar,	*Oduthal.*
	Sinhalese,	*Duvanavá.*

Group	Language	Word
	Types.	
Inflecting.	SANSKṚIT,	*Túshṇím-bhú, maunam-kṛi.*
	ARABIC,	*Sakata.*
Compounding.	BASK,	*Isil, ijil, ijildu.*
	FINNIC,	*Waikenen.*
	MAGVAR,	*Caret.*
	TURKISH,	*Suz.*
	CIRCASSIAN,	*Caret.*
	GEORGIAN,	*Dadumebad* (*dum*).
	MONGOLIAN,	*Ssam baikho.*
	MANTSHU,	*Tchip bime.*
	JAVANESE, Ngoko,	*Mĕnnĕg.*
	JAVANESE, Krama,	*Kendĕl.*
	MALAV,	*Díam.*
Isolating.	CHINESE, Nankin,	*Puh-y'aou-ch'uh-shing.*
	CHINESE, Pekin,	*Mú-yáou-ch'ú-sheng.*
	CHINESE, Canton,	*Mok-ch'ut-sheng.*
	CHINESE, Shanghai,	*Veh-hiáng.*
	AMOY, Colloquial,	*Cheñg.*
	JAPANESE,	*Damateru.*
	Brahuí,	*Caret.*
Chinese Frontier & Tibet.	Gyámi,	*Quápotho.*
	Gyárung,	*Nák chún.*
	Tákpa,	*Thomá.*
	Mányak,	*Thathadyú.*
	Thochú,	*Rsgástan, dzúk kochin.*
	Sokpa,	*A'h má hopchhi.*
	Horpa,	*Yágúzi.*
	Tibetan (*written*),	*Khrog.*
	Tibetan (*spoken*),	*Chúm.*
Nepal (east to west).	Serpa,	*Khárá.*
	Súnwár,	*Pálo ma pau.*
	Gúrung,	*Táya pun.*
	Múrmi,	*Kúdyú.*
	Magar,	*Má chák.*
	Tháksya,	*Lhemthalo.*
	Pákhya,	*Chochira.*
	Newár,	*Súmú khá choṇ.*
	Limbu,	*Swáte.*
Kiranti Group (East Nepal).	Kiránti,	*Manchebda.*
	Rodong,	*Maichepda, chyoma.*
	Rúngchenbung,	*Wáiwáiyúgná, manchehádu.*
	Chhingtángya,	*Wáyeb.*
	Náchhereng,	*Wáhe.*
	Wáling,	*Wáyep.*
	Yákha,	*Swák wáya.*
	Chourásya,	*Lhá.*
	Kulungya,	*Wait wáya.*
	Thulungya,	*Líba.*
	Báhingya,	*Líbabwakko.*
	Lohorong,	*Chichúye, yonge.* [*nannin.*[2]
	Lambichhong,	*In'chenán, inchenanchi,*[1] *inche*
	Báláli,	*Chichuwet, chichuwetech.*[1]
	Sáng-páng,	*Waiwaitúwa.*
	Dúmi,	*Líbámo.*
	Kháling,	*Leba.*
	Dungmáli,	*Máncheptáye.*
Broken Tribes of Nepal.	Dárhi,	*Júnborauk.*
	Denwár,	*I'unsárhá.*
	Pahri,	*Sunánchoṇ.*
	Chepáng,	*Caret.*
	Bhrámu,	*Mápe, mákhale.*
	Váyu,	*Tháit, gyúngponche.*
	Kuswar,	*Mámáborou, mamaborou.*
	Kusunda,	*Abágánebin.*
	Tháru,	*Chupraho.*
	Lepcha (Sikkim),	*Sakmá.*
	Bhúṭáni v. Lhopa,	*Kháchúm.*
N.-E. Bengal.	Bodo,	*Srithá.*
	Dhimál,	*Chikápahi, mádop.*
	Kocch,	*Chuphonu.*
	Garo,	*Tápchilip tong.*
	KácháRi,	*Caret.*
Eastern Frontier of Bengal.	Munipuri,	*Caret.*
	Míthán Nágá,	*Caret.*
	Tablung Nágá,	*Caret.*
	Khári Nágá,	*Tukurá.*
	Angámi Nágá,	*Chasibale.*
	Námsáng Nágá,	*Caret.*
	Nowgong Nágá,	*Manakazong.*
	Tengsa Nágá,	*Ayoksulang.*
	Abor Miri,	*A'sopü.*
	Sibságar Miri,	*A'sopa.*
	Deoria Chutia,	*Turucha.*
	Singpho,	*Temdingau.*
Arrakan & Burmah.	Burman (*written*),	*Titchhitne.*
	Burman (*spoken*),	*Teiksheikne.*
	Khyeng v. Shou,	*Mhe.*
	Kámi,	*Onvo.*
	Kúmi,	*Caret.*
	Mrú v. Toung,	*Caret.*
	Sák,	*Caret.*
Siam & Tenasserim.	Talain v. Mon,	*Monkanoukkanouk.*
	Sgau-karen,	*Obwah.*
	Pwo-karen,	*Aukkser.*
	Toungh-thu,	*Hnging.*
	Shán,	*Yuhlsithlsit.*
	Annamitic,	*Ninlăng.*
	Siamese,	*Neurú, ning yú.*
	Ahom,	*Supmu.*
	Khámti,	*Yú tsip tsip.*
	Laos,	*Dak dak yú.*
Central India.	Ho (Kol),	*Happanted.*
	Kol (Singhbhum),	*Hápauman.*
	Santáli,	*Guḍamohte, koḍamoräihte.*
	Bhúmij,	*Hapiakanman.*
	Uráon,	*Amha kachnekrah.*
	Mundala,	*Happá.*
	Rájmahali,	*Aslúbehá.*
	Goṇḍi,	*Immakammeneman.*
	Gayeti,	*Caret.*
	Rutluk,	*Caret.*
	Naikude,	*Caret.*
	Kolami,	*Caret.*
	Mádi,	*Caret.*
	Mádia,	*Caret.*
	Kuri,	*Caret.*
	Keikádi,	*Caret.*
	Khoṇḍ,	*Kinni jáminnú.*
	Sávara,	*Kaḍangámá.*
	Gadaba,	*Vayisodukka.*
	Yerukala,	*Summa, tsummateyiru.*
	Chentsu,	*Tlsuperaho, tsupparo.*
Southern India.	Tamiḷ, anc.,	*Caret.*
	Tamiḷ, mod.,	*Summáviru, amai.*
	Malayáḷma, anc.,	*Caret.*
	Malayáḷma, mod.,	*Miṇḍáthiru, uriyáḍáthiru.*
	Telugu,	*Uraḍu.*
	Karṇáṭaka, anc.,	*Caret.*
	Karṇáṭaka, mod.,	*Summaneyira.*
	Tuḷuva,	*Manipantippuna.*
	Kurgi,	*Caret.*
	Toḍuva, }	*Caret.*
	Toḍa, }	*Bokkiru, bokir.*
	Kóta,	*Bheve, pakiru.*
	Baḍaga,	*Súmagiru, sappeniru, japa-*
	Kuṛumba,	*Symaniru, súmagiru.* [*niru.*
	Iruḷa,	*Summa iru, maniadeiru.*
	Malabar,	*Summayiru.*
	Sinhalese,	*Navatinavá.*

Group	Types.	
Inflecting.	SANSKRIT,	*A's, sad, upavis', nishad.*
	ARABIC,	*Jalasa.*
Compounding.	BASK,	*Eserri, jarri, jasarri.*
	FINNIC,	*Istun.*
	MAGYAR,	*Ül.*
	TURKISH,	*Obur.*
	CIRCASSIAN,	*Uskhansht.*
	GEORGIAN,	*Dajdomad (ziv).*
	MONGOLIAN,	*Sagokho.*
	MANTSHU,	*Teme.*
	JAVANESE, Ngoko,	*Lunggah.*
	JAVANESE, Krama,	*Lênggah.*
	MALAY,	*Dúduk.*
Isolating.	CHINESE, Nankin,	*Tso-hiá.*
	CHINESE, Pekin,	*Tso-hsiá.*
	CHINESE, Canton,	*Tso-há.*
	CHINESE, Shanghai,	*Zu-o-chi.*
	AMOY, Colloquial,	*Che.*
	JAPANESE,	*Swaru.*
	Brahuí,	*Tulluk.*
Chinese Frontier & Tibet.	Gyámi,	*Cho.*
	Gyárung,	*Nánen.*
	Tákpa,	*Zúk.*
	Mányak,	*Naijeu.*
	Thochú,	*Ajon.*
	Sokpa,	*So.*
	Horpa,	*Unzun, wanzún.*
	Tibetan (*written*),	*Hdúg.*
	Tibetan (*spoken*),	*Deh.*
Nepal (east to west).	Serpa,	*Det.*
	Súnwár,	*Bák.*
	Gúrung,	*Tidh.*
	Múrmi,	*Tyú.*
	Magar,	*Nú ná.*
	Thákysa,	*Túpa.*
	Pákhya,	*Basa.*
	Newár,	*Phe tú.*
	Limbu,	*Yúng ne.*
Kiranti Group (East Nepal).	Kiránti,	*Yúngá.*
	Rodong,	*Yúgna, higna.*
	Rúngchenbung,	*Yúgna.*
	Chhingtángya,	*Yúba.*
	Náchhereng,	*Tyúwa.*
	Wáling,	*Yúgna.*
	Yákha,	*Yúgna.*
	Chourásya,	*Bákstá.*
	Kulungya,	*Túwa.*
	Thulungya,	*Gaiṇsa.*
	Báhingya,	*Nisyo, nische,*[1] *nisine.*[2]
	Lohorong,	*Pene, pache,*[1] *pane.*[2]
	Lambichhong,	*Yúgná, yugnachi,*[1] *yugnani.*[2]
	Báláli,	*Pehyúsa, peyusachi,*[1] *peyusanin.*[2]
	Sáng-páng,	*Túwá, -chi,*[1] *-ni.*[2]
	Dúmi,	*Mo.*
	Kháling,	*Gnáche.*
	Dungmáli,	*Yúgne.*
Broken Tribes of Nepal.	Dárhi,	*Basuk.*
	Denwár,	*Bas.*
	Pahri,	*Kujungchoṇ.*
	Chepáng,	*Músche, musa.*
	Bhrámu,	*Múká.*
	Váyu,	*Mosche.*
	Kuswar,	*Basou.*
	Kusunda,	*Bhingwoto.*
	Tháru,	*Baith.*
	Lepcha (Sikkim),	*Gnán.*
	Bhúṭáni v. Lhopa,	*Deu.*

N.-E. Bengal.	Bodo,	*Jo, choö.*
	Dhimál,	*Yong.*
	Kocch,	*Bosinu.*
	Garo,	*Abak.*
	Káchári,	*Jhobaijonai.*
Eastern Frontier of Bengal.	Munipuri,	*Phumo.*
	Míthán Nágá,	*Ngodau.*
	Tablung Nágá,	*Umchi.*
	Khári Nágá,	*Manio.*
	Angámi Nágá,	*Bache.*
	Námsáng Nágá,	*Tongo.*
	Nowgong Nágá,	*Manákarü.*
	Tengsa Nágá,	*Mannang.*
	Abor Miri,	*Dúpü.*
	Sibságar Miri,	*Dutoka.*
	Deoria Chutia,	*Dudurini.*
	Singpho,	*Dúngu.*
Arrakan & Burmah.	Burman (*written*),	*Thaing.*
	Burman (*spoken*),	*Thaing, htihnthi.*
	Khyeng v. Shou,	*Ngúnge.*
	Kámi,	*Kanú.*
	Kúmi,	*Tat.*
	Mrú v. Toung,	*Caret.*
	Sák,	*Caret.*
Siam & Tenasserim.	Talain v. Mon,	*Khagyo.*
	Sgau-karen,	*'Sanaw, tshenoh.*
	Pwo-karen,	*Tsurnang.*
	Toungh-thu,	*Unglan.*
	Shán,	*Nanyú.*
	Annamitic,	*Ngôi.*
	Siamese,	*Nau, nang.*
	Ahom,	*Nang.*
	Khámti,	*Nang.*
	Laos,	*Nang.*
Central India.	Ho (Kol),	*Dúbteá.*
	Kol (Singhbhum),	*Dubman.*
	Santáli,	*Duḍapate, beṭhárate, eḍhchte* [(sit on haunches).
	Bhúmij,	*Dúrúbkanman.*
	Uráon,	*U'kha.*
	Mundala,	*Dumi.*
	Rájmahali,	*Oka.*
	Goṇḍi,	*Uddaniga, uddana.*
	Gayeti,	*Caret.*
	Rutluk,	*Caret.*
	Naikude,	*Caret.*
	Kolami,	*Caret.*
	Mádi,	*Caret.*
	Mádia,	*Caret.*
	Kuri,	*Caret.*
	Keikádi,	*Ukka.*
	Khoṇḍ,	*Kukkumu.*
	Sávara,	*Gobá.*
	Gadaba,	*Vaisá.*
	Yerukala,	*Vukká, vukkárinḍiri.*
	Chentsu,	*Bos.*
Southern India.	Tamiḷ, anc.,	*Uḍká.*
	Tamiḷ, mod.,	*Uḍkáru, uḷukkáru.*
	Malayáḷma, anc.,	*Caret.*
	Malayáḷma, mod.,	*Iḷachchu.*
	Telugu,	*Kúrchuṇḍu.*
	Karṇáṭaka, anc.,	*Caret.*
	Karṇáṭaka, mod.,	*Kútu koḷḷu.*
	Tuḷuva,	*Kullona.*
	Kurgi,	*Yeḷe.*
	Toḍuva, }	*Caret.*
	Toḍa, }	*Neshkir.*
	Kóta,	*Kúsure, kúkiru.*
	Baḍaga,	*Kuli, kútiru.*
	Kurumba,	*Kuli, kútiru, kutuko.*
	Iruḷa,	*Kukuve, ukandu kove.*
	Malabar,	*Iru.*
	Sinhalese,	*Indaganavá.*

Group	*Types.*	
Inflecting.	SANSKṚIT,	*Swap, nidrá, s'i, swapnam̃-kṛi.*
	ARABIC,	*Náma.*
Compounding.	BASK,	*Loegin, loakartu, loizan.*
	FINNIC,	*Makaan.*
	MAGYAR,	*Alud.*
	TURKISH,	*Uyu.*
	CIRCASSIAN,	*Tshlyah.*
	GEORGIAN,	*Mdsinaos (dzin).*
	MONGOLIAN,	*Umtacho.*
	MANTSHU,	*Amkhame.*
	JAVANESE, Ngoko,	*Turu.*
	JAVANESE, Krama,	*Tilem.*
	MALAY,	*Tidor.*
Isolating.	CHINESE, Nankin,	*Shwui-kiaou.*
	CHINESE, Pekin,	*Shui-chiaou.*
	CHINESE, Canton,	*Fan-kiú.*
	CHINESE, Shanghai,	*Kwan, kwang-kau.*
	AMOY, Colloquial,	*K'ùn.*
	JAPANESE,	*Nemu.*
	Brahuí,	*Khachak.*
Chinese Frontier & Tibet.	Gyámi,	*Swikyor.*
	Gyárung,	*Korman'.*
	Tákpa,	*Nyet.*
	Mányak,	*Khaiyaḥ.*
	Thochú,	*A'nan.*
	Sokpa,	*Wúmtha.*
	Horpa,	*Gúrgyún.*
	Tibetan (*written*),	*Nyan.*
	Tibetan (*spoken*),	*Nye.*
Nepal (east to west).	Serpa,	*Nyol.*
	Súnwár,	*I'p.*
	Gúrung,	*Rod.*
	Múrmi,	*Gnúng.*
	Magar,	*Mis.*
	Tháksya,	*Nhuko.*
	Pákhya,	*Saira.*
	Newár,	*Dyon.*
	Limbu,	*Ipse.*
Kiranti Group (East Nepal).	Kiránti,	*Imsá.*
	Rodong,	*Im'sa, imsanu.*
	Rúngchenbung,	*Im'sa.*
	Chhingtángya,	*Ip'sa.*
	Náchhereng,	*Im'sa.*
	Wáling,	*Im'sa.*
	Yákha,	*Ip'sa.*
	Chourásya,	*Glomtá.*
	Kulungya,	*Im'sa.*
	Thulungya,	*A'm'sa.*
	Báhingya,	*Ip'po, ipse,[1] ipine.[2]*
	Lohorong,	*I'me, imache,[1] immane.[2]*
	Lambichhong,	*Im'sa, imsachi,[1] imsani.[2]*
	Báláli,	*Ip'cha, ipchasi,[1] ipchanin.[2]*
	Sáng-páng,	*Ipsa, ipsachi,[1] ipsani.[2]*
	Dúmi,	*Am'si.*
	Kháling,	*Am'si.*
	Dungmáli,	*Im'se.*
Broken Tribes of Nepal.	Dárhi,	*Sútuk.*
	Denwár,	*Sút.*
	Pahri,	*Dyúṇ.*
	Chepáng,	*Emche, yemsa.*
	Bhrámu,	*Náwa.*
	Váyu,	*Im'che.*
	Kuswar,	*Sutou.*
	Kusunda,	*Iptu* (causal ?).
	Tháru,	*Sutali.*
	Lepcha (Sikkim),	*Dá.*
	Bhúṭáni v. Lhopa,	*Nye.*

Group	Language	Word
N.-E. Bengal.	Bodo,	*Múdúláng, múdú.*
	Dhimál,	*Jún.*
	Kocch,	*Sútibar.*
	Garo,	*Gúr.*
	Kácháti,	*Mudubai.*
Eastern Frontier of Bengal.	Munipuri,	*Hibo.*
	Míthán Nágá,	*Jipdau.*
	Tablung Nágá,	*Chunshi.*
	Khári Nágá,	*Ipigili.*
	Angámi Nágá,	*Zü.*
	Námsáng Nágá,	*Júpo.*
	Nowgong Nágá,	*Annanü.*
	Tengsa Nágá,	*Annü.*
	Abor Miri,	*Iddo.*
	Sibságar Miri,	*Yüm.*
	Deoria Chutia,	*Yumgarini.*
	Singpho,	*Yúpu.*
Arrakan & Burmah.	Burman (*written*),	*Ip.*
	Burman (*spoken*),	*Eik.*
	Khyeng v. Shou,	*I'p.*
	Kámi,	*I.*
	Kúmi,	*I.*
	Mrú v. Toung,	*Caret.*
	Sák,	*Caret.*
Siam & Tenasserim.	Talain v. Mon,	*Tet.*
	Sgau-karen,	*Mi, mih.*
	Pwo-karen,	*Mi.*
	Toungh-thu,	*Ping.*
	Shán,	*Nonn.*
	Annamitic,	*Ngu.*
	Siamese,	*Nona, lap.*
	Ahom,	*Non.*
	Khámti,	*Non, nap.*
	Laos,	*Non, lap.*
Central India.	Ho (Kol),	*Gititeá.*
	Kol (Singhbhum),	*Gitiman.*
	Santáli,	*Gitihte, jápihte, kukujohte, uskupuskuhte* (snooze).
	Bhúmij,	*Gitijúm.*
	Uráon,	*Khándara.*
	Mundala,	*Dúrong.*
	Rájmahali,	*Kándrá.*
	Goṇḍi,	*Sungji, narmana.*
	Gayeti,	*Caret.*
	Rutluk,	*Caret.*
	Naikude,	*Caret.*
	Kolami,	*Caret.*
	Máḍi,	*Caret.*
	Mádia,	*Caret.*
	Kuri,	*Caret.*
	Keikáḍi,	*Tungu.*
	Khoṇḍ,	*Dohumu.*
	Sávara,	*Dúnebá.*
	Gaḍaba,	*Eyyá.*
	Yerukala,	*Tugguḍayi, varugu.*
	Chentsu,	*Súl, sutiyár.*
Southern India.	Tamiḷ, anc.,	*Caret.*
	Tamiḷ, mod.,	*Túngu.*
	Malayáḷma, anc.,	*Caret.*
	Malayáḷma, mod.,	*Uṛangngu, tungngu.*
	Telugu,	*Tonguṇḍu.*
	Karṇáṭaka, anc.,	*Caret.*
	Karṇáṭaka, mod.,	*Nidde máḍu.*
	Tuḷuva,	*Nidriiḍupuna.*
	Kurgi,	*Varaku.*
	Toḍuva,	*Caret.*
	Toḍa,	*Vorchth bin, vorgine, vorẓ.*
	Kóta,	*Pat kene, voraga.*
	Baḍaga,	*Voragine, voragu.*
	Kuṛumba,	*Voragine, nidre madu.*
	Iruḷa,	*Rombuve, kaḍandukove, kuḍanduko.*
	Malabar,	*Nelthirei.*
	Sinhalese,	*Nidágannavá.*

	Types.	
Inflecting.	SANSKṚIT,	*Vach, vad, bhásh, álap.*
	ARABIC,	*Takallama.*
Compounding.	BASK,	*Itzegin, berbegin, mintzoizan.*
	FINNIC,	*Sanon.*
	MAGYAR,	*Beszelszol.*
	TURKISH,	*Søile.*
	CIRCASSIAN,	*Tighadshas.*
	GEORGIAN,	*Wlaparakob (ubn).*
	MONGOLIAN,	*Kelegu.*
	MANTSHU,	*Leoleme.*
	JAVANESE, Ngoko,	*Nutur.*
	JAVANESE, Krama,	*Wichanten.*
	MALAY,	*Káta.*
Isolating.	CHINESE, Nankin,	*Kiang.*
	CHINESE, Pekin,	*Chiang.*
	CHINESE, Canton,	*Kong.*
	CHINESE, Shanghai,	*Páh-wŏh.*
	AMOY, Colloquial,	*Kong.*
	JAPANESE,	*Hanasu, iu.*
	Brahuí,	*Párak.*
Chinese Frontier & Tibet.	Gyámi,	*Caret.*
	Gyárung,	*Tachen.*
	Tákpa,	*Syát.*
	Mányak,	*Thadyu.*
	Thochú,	*Kwor, kúrr.*
	Sokpa,	*Caret.*
	Horpa,	*Napsheh, tayin.*
	Tibetan (*written*),	*Brjod, smros.*
	Tibetan (*spoken*),	*Lap (sap ?).*
Nepal (east to west).	Serpa,	*Caret.*
	Súnwár,	*Bák.*
	Gúrung,	*Caret.*
	Múrmi,	*Caret.*
	Magar,	*Caret.*
	Thāksya,	*I'yáto.*
	Pákhya,	*Caret.*
	Newár,	*Nava.*
	Limbu,	*Páre.*
Kiranti Group (East Nepal).	Kiránti,	*Caret.*
	Rodong,	*Chewa, pul'sa.*
	Rúngchenbung,	*Chewá, khángmeu.*
	Chhingtángya,	*Chewa.*
	Náchhereng,	*Nina.*
	Wáling,	*Chewa.*
	Yákha,	*Chekta.*
	Chourásya,	*Bákstá.*
	Kulungya,	*Nēna.*
	Thulungya,	*Jesa.*
	Báhingya,	*Bo'ho, bwakko (-se,[1] -ine[2]).*
	Lohorong,	*Yammuse (-mache,[1] -mane[2]).*
	Lambichhong,	*Chega, chegachi,[1] chegani.[2]*
	Báláli,	*Púklús, puklusachi,[1] puklu- [sanin.[2]*
	Sáng-páng,	*Niná, -chi,[1] -ni.[2]*
	Dúmi,	*Je.*
	Kháling,	*Jeye.*
	Dungmáli,	*Chebe.*
Broken Tribes of Nepal.	Dárhi,	*Boráuk.*
	Denwár,	*Sarha.*
	Pahri,	*Lhá.*
	Chepáng,	*Nhosche, nhosa.*
	Bhrámu,	*Khaláwa.*
	Váyu,	*It' (ito); dawahot, bot (bo'to).*
	Kuswar,	*Barou, ghanou.*
	Kusunda,	*Pwáktoba.*
	Tháru,	*Bolai.*
	Lepcha (Sikkim),	*Lí.*
	Bhúṭáni v. Lhopa,	*Lap.*
N.-E. Bengal.	Bodo,	*Rai.*
	Dhimál,	*Dop.*
	Kocch,	*Bolinu.*
	Garo,	*Brot, borot.*
	Káchári,	*Caret.*
Eastern Frontier of Bengal.	Munipuri,	*Haio.*
	Míthán Nágá,	*Káh.*
	Tablung Nágá,	*Táh.*
	Khári Nágá,	*Aihushang.*
	Angámi Nágá,	*Pusiche.*
	Námsáng Nágá,	*Thú.*
	Nowgong Nágá,	*Shang.*
	Tengsa Nágá,	*Suang.*
	Abor Miri,	*Lüpü.*
	Sibságar Miri,	*Saluto.*
	Deoria Chutia,	*Icharini.*
	Singpho,	*Súu.*
Arrakan & Burmah.	Burman (*written*),	*Pro, chho.*
	Burman (*spoken*),	*Pyo, s'ho, pyauhtso.*
	Khyeng v. Shou,	*Háwe.*
	Kámi,	*Tape.*
	Kúmi,	*Thoi.*
	Mrú v. Toung,	*Caret.*
	Sák,	*Caret.*
Siam & Tenasserim.	Talain v. Mon,	*Hankai.*
	Sgau-karen,	*K'to, tathuthah.*
	Pwo-karen,	*Klaing.*
	Toungh-thu,	*Ungdau.*
	Shán,	*Sat.*
	Annamitic,	*Noi.*
	Siamese,	*Hutsa, phut.*
	Ahom,	*Bok.*
	Khámti,	*Wá.*
	Laos,	*Pak.*
Central India.	Ho (Kol),	*Kajiteá.*
	Kol (Singhbhum),	*Kajiman.*
	Santáli,	*Mente, radate khâĕkâĕte* (whisper), *gálammaráüte* (gossip).
	Bhúmij,	*Kajiman.*
	Uráon,	*Kachnekrah.*
	Mundala,	*Kajemi.*
	Rájmahali,	*Auda.*
	Goṇḍi,	*Bárámanke, wurkana.*
	Gayeti,	*Caret.*
	Rutluk,	*Caret.*
	Naikude,	*Caret.*
	Kolami,	*Caret.*
	Mádi,	*Caret.*
	Mádia,	*Caret.*
	Kuri,	*Caret.*
	Keikádi,	*Pesu.*
	Khoṇḍ,	*Katágehámu.*
	Sávara,	*Birdána.*
	Gadaba,	*Sammeva.*
	Yerukala,	*Vâtesula, vesetallá.*
	Chentsu,	*Kathháko, kathhá.*
Southern India.	Tamiḷ, anc.,	*Caret.*
	Tamiḷ, mod.,	*Pésu.*
	Malayáḷma, anc.,	*Caret.*
	Malayáḷma, mod.,	*Paṛaya, samsárikka.*
	Telugu,	*Mâṭláḍu.*
	Karṇáṭaka, anc.,	*Caret.*
	Karṇáṭaka, mod.,	*Mátáḍu.*
	Tuḷuva,	*Pater puna.*
	Kurgi,	*Takpare.*
	Toḍuva,	*Caret.*
	Toḍa,	*Eshth bini, arversh bini, [arvor.*
	Kóta,	*Mansbe, mánivo.*
	Badaga,	*Nudi ḍane, mátáḍine, nuḍi.*
	Kuṛumba,	*Mataḍu, nuḍi.*
	Iruḷa,	*Peshike, pesu.*
	Malabar,	*Pesu.*
	Sinhalese,	*Katháḱaranavá.*

Group	Types.	
Inflecting.	SANSKRIT,	*Daṇḍ, pádábhyáṁ-sthá, sthá,*
	ARABIC,	*Wakafa.* [(*tishthati*).
Compounding.	BASK,	*Ilki, jaiki.*
	FINNIC,	*Nousen.*
	MAGYAR,	*All.*
	TURKISH,	*Kalk.*
	CIRCASSIAN,	*Caret.*
	GEORGIAN,	*Caret.*
	MONGOLIAN,	*Tokhdakho.*
	MANTSHU,	*Ilime.*
	JAVANESE, Ngoko,	*Tangi.*
	JAVANESE, Krama,	*Tangi.*
	MALAY,	*Diri.*
Isolating.	CHINESE, Nankin,	*Chán ki-lái.*
	CHINESE, Pekin,	*Chán-ki-lái.*
	CHINESE, Canton,	*K'i-hi-shan.*
	CHINESE, Shanghai,	*Lok-chi-le.*
	AMOY, Colloquial,	*K'i.*
	JAPANESE,	*Tatsu, okosotatsu.*
	Brahuí,	*Bathmarak.*
Chinese Frontier & Tibet.	Gyámi,	*Chhile.*
	Gyárung,	*Taryup yachin.*
	Tákpa,	*Lang.*
	Mányak,	*Khanjeh.*
	Thochú,	*Toron.*
	Sokpa,	*Posth.*
	Horpa,	*Záryen.*
	Tibetan (*written*),	*Hchhar.*
	Tibetan (*spoken*),	*Long.*
Nepal (east to west).	Serpa,	*Long.*
	Súnwár,	*Bok.*
	Gúrung,	*Rádh.*
	Múrmi,	*Ráb.*
	Magar,	*Swoná.*
	Tháksya,	*Gnajurpa.*
	Pákhya,	*Utha.*
	Newár,	*Dong.*
	Limbu,	*Poge.*
Kiranti Group (East Nepal).	Kiránti,	*Yewá lúntá.*
	Rodong,	*Púkalenda, reta.*
	Rúngchenbung,	*Púwalonta.*
	Chhingtángya,	*Yeba.*
	Náchhereng,	*Repa.*
	Wáling,	*Ye wa.*
	Yákha,	*Púgá.*
	Chourásya,	*Yámstá.*
	Kulungya,	*Thorepa.*
	Thulungya,	*Yep'da.* [*pinc.*[2]
	Báhingya,	*Ráppo, rongso, rap'she,*[1] *ra-*
	Lohorong,	*Yebe, yepoge, yebache,*[1] *rebane.*[2]
	Lambichhong,	*Poklonda, yebá, yebachi,*[1] *ye-*
	Báláli,	*Yepok, yeba, yepoka-* [*bani.*[2]
	Sáng-páng,	*Ripáchi,*[1] *-ni.*[2] [*chi,*[1] *yepoká-*
	Dúmi,	*Ripha.* [*nin.*[2]
	Kháling,	*Repye.*
	Dungmáli,	*Rebe.*
Broken Tribes of Nepal.	Dárhi,	*U'thúk.*
	Denwár,	*U'th.*
	Pahri,	*Dáïngchoṇ.*
	Chepáng,	*Chingsa.*
	Bhrámu,	*So.*
	Váyu,	*Y'epche.*
	Kuswar,	*U'thou.*
	Kusunda,	*Loengwoto.*
	Tháru,	*Khaḍáho.*
	Lepcha (Sikkim),	*Lúk, ding.*
	Bhúṭáni v. Lhopa,	*Long.*

N.-E. Bengal.	Bodo,	*Gochong, jakháng.*
	Dhimál,	*Jáp.*
	Kocch,	*Thárubonu.*
	Garo,	*Chap.*
	Kāchári,	*Guchung dang.*
Eastern Frontier of Bengal.	Munipuri,	*Lebo.*
	Mithán Nágá,	*Ajong.*
	Tablung Nágá,	*Yong chi.*
	Khári Nágá,	*Hunligili.*
	Angámi Nágá,	*Thale.*
	Námsáng Nágá,	*Chapo.*
	Nowgong Nágá,	*Notak.*
	Tengsa Nágá,	*Septak.*
	Abor Miri,	*Dangküpü.*
	Sibságar Miri,	*Dárup.*
	Deoria Chutia,	*Tákarini.*
	Singpho,	*Tsapu, rotu.*
Arrakan & Burmah.	Burman (*written*),	*Tha, mat.*
	Burman (*spoken*),	*Thá, mat.*
	Khyeng v. Shou,	*Túne.*
	Kámi,	*Kado.*
	Kúmi,	*A'ngthou.*
	Mrú v. Toung,	*Caret.*
	Sák,	*Caret.*
Siam & Tenasserim.	Talain v. Mon,	*Monlet, khatau.*
	Sgau-karen,	*'Serter, tshethu.*
	Pwo-karen,	*Tsungtung.*
	Toungh-thu,	*Ughhung.*
	Shán,	*Tsotrü.*
	Annamitic,	*Dây.*
	Siamese,	*Roa, yün.*
	Ahom,	*Ti.*
	Khámti,	*Sau.*
	Laos,	*Song.*
Central India.	Ho (Kol),	*Tinguntea.*
	Kol (Singhbhum),	*Tingunman.*
	Santáli,	*Tingohte, ḍemachohte, berehte*
	Bhúmij,	*Tinguakanman.* [(rise).
	Uráon,	*I'lláhá.*
	Mundala,	*Tengunmi.*
	Rájmahali,	*Choiya.*
	Goṇḍi,	*Tedaníga, nittana.*
	Gayeti,	*Caret.*
	Rutluk,	*Caret.*
	Naikude,	*Caret.*
	Kolami,	*Caret.*
	Mádi,	*Caret.*
	Mádia,	*Caret.*
	Kuri,	*Caret.*
	Keikádi,	*Ninduko.*
	Khoṇḍ,	*Nistámu.*
	Sávara,	*Dedebá.*
	Gadaba,	*Tune ná.*
	Yerukala,	*Nikkebogu, ninḍrukonḍuyiru.*
	Chentsu,	*Thá doho.*
Southern India.	Tamiḷ, anc.,	*Caret.*
	Tamiḷ, mod.,	*Nil.*
	Malayáḷma, anc.,	*Caret.*
	Malayáḷma, mod.,	*Nilka.*
	Telugu,	*Niluchunḍu, niluchu.*
	Karṇáṭaka, anc.,	*Caret.*
	Karṇáṭaka, mod.,	*Nintu kollu.*
	Tuḷuva,	*Entuna.*
	Kurgi,	*Nillu.*
	Toḍuva, }	*Caret.*
	Toḍa, }	*Mklo.*
	Kóta,	*Nitulle, meke.*
	Baḍaga,	*Niddiru, lyettu.*
	Kurumba,	*Niddiru, yeddu.*
	Iruḷa,	*Nike, yendu kove.*
	Malabar,	*Nil.*
	Sinhalese,	*Hiṭinavá.*

Group	Language	Strike
Types.		
Inflecting.	SANSKRIT,	*Taḍ, han, tud.*
	ARABIC,	Daraba.
Compounding.	BASK,	*Jo, jazartu.*
	FINNIC,	*Picksen.*
	MAGYAR,	*Üb.*
	TURKISH,	*Vur.*
	CIRCASSIAN,	*Yeywan, yoh.*
	GEORGIAN,	*Wkhots.*
	MONGOLIAN,	*Göpsigö.*
	MANTSHU,	*Shasikalane.*
	JAVANESE, Ngoko,	*Hanggitik.*
	JAVANESE, Krama,	*Hanggitik.*
	MALAY,	*Púkul.*
Isolating.	CHINESE, Nankin,	*Tá.*
	CHINESE, Pekin,	*Tá.*
	CHINESE, Canton,	*Tá.*
	CHINESE, Shanghai,	*Táng.*
	AMOY, Colloquial,	*P'ah.*
	JAPANESE,	*Utsŭ.*
	Brahuí,	*Khalbo.*
Chinese Frontier & Tibet.	Gyámi,	*Tá.*
	Gyárung,	*Tatúp.*
	Tákpa,	*Dúngc.*
	Mányak,	*Danthá.*
	Thochú,	*Dagatch.*
	Sokpa,	*Chhok ka.*
	Horpa,	*Nazbi.*
	Tibetan (*written*),	Bdún, ṛdeg.
	Tibetan (*spoken*),	*Dúng.*
Nepal (east to west).	Serpa,	*Dúng.*
	Súnwár,	*Túp.*
	Gúrung,	*Tan.*
	Múrmi,	*Rob.*
	Magar,	*Dung.*
	Tháksya,	*Táü, thopáti.*
	Pákhya,	*Kút.*
	Newár,	*Dá.*
	Limbu,	*Hipte, hipte.*
Kiranti Group (East Nepal).	Kiránti,	*Mou.*
	Rodong,	*Chai zyú, chai dyú.*
	Rúngchenbung,	*Mou, moanum.*[1]
	Chhingtángya,	*Tena.*
	Náchhereng,	*Yop'sú.*
	Wáling,	*Mou.*
	Yákha,	*Mok'tu.*
	Chourásya,	*Túptá.*
	Kulungya,	*Keru.*
	Thulungya,	*Yalsa.*
	Báhingya,	*Tyúpo, tipo, tipshe,*[1] *tipine.*[2]
	Lohorong,	*Lome, lo mache,*[1] *lo mam ne.*[2]
	Lambichhong,	*Tena.*
	Báláli,	*Lomu.*
	Sáng-páng,	*Yosu, kiru, yop'su.*
	Dúmi,	*Klen'de.*
	Kháling,	*Yát'ye.*
	Dungmáli,	*Nore, norchie,*[1] *nornumye.*[2]
Broken Tribes of Nepal.	Dárhi,	*Thátháik.*
	Denwár,	*Márik.*
	Pahri,	*Dáchhoṇ.*
	Chepáng,	*Caret.*
	Bhrámu,	*Moto.*
	Váyu,	*Toh'po.*
	Kuswar,	*Thátháik.*
	Kusunda,	*Pungbogo.*
	Tháru,	*Már, maráu.*
	Lepcha (Sikkim),	*Bak.*
	Bhúṭáni v. Lhopa,	*Dúng.*

Group	Language	Strike
N.-E. Bengal.	Bodo,	*Sho.*
	Dhimál,	*Dánghai.*
	Kocch,	*Pitinu.*
	Garo,	*Tok.*
	Káchári,	*Bu dung.*
Eastern Frontier of Bengal.	Munipuri,	*Yaiyo.*
	Míthán Nágá,	*Maithun.*
	Tablung Nágá,	*Set chi.*
	Khári Nágá,	*Yakchau.*
	Angámi Nágá,	*Vashuwe.*
	Námsáng Nágá,	*Váto.*
	Nowgong Nágá,	*Tasungr, tatapsap.*
	Tengsa Nágá,	*Taphetoko.*
	Abor Miri,	*Pápü.*
	Sibságar Miri,	*Düto.*
	Deoria Chutia,	*Borini.*
	Singpho,	*Dúpu.*
Arrakan & Burmah.	Burman (*written*),	*Raik, put.*
	Burman (*spoken*),	*Yáik, pok.*
	Khyeng v. Shou,	*Mole.*
	Kámi,	*Male.*
	Kúmi,	*Pu khouorathum.*
	Mrú v. Toung,	*Caret.*
	Sák,	*Caret.*
Siam & Tenasserim.	Talain v. Mon,	*Tat.*
	Sgau-karen,	*Taw, patau.*
	Pwo-karen,	*Du.*
	Toungh-thu,	*Tway.*
	Shán,	*Pautihn.*
	Annamitic,	Dañ.
	Siamese,	*Pautihn, ti, bol.*
	Ahom,	*Dá, po.*
	Khámti,	*Po.*
	Laos,	*Tí, bup.*
Central India.	Ho (Kol),	*Rutcá.*
	Kol (Singhbhum),	*Goiman.*
	Santáli,	*Susárate kuhaüte dálate, c'heṭáhte, karáh-karahte.*
	Bhúmij,	*Magíman.*
	Uráon,	*Khorah.*
	Mundala,	*Dáli.*
	Rájmahali,	*Bája.*
	Goṇḍi,	*Júu, jiana.*
	Gayeti,	*Caret.*
	Rutluk,	*Caret.*
	Naikude,	*Caret.*
	Kolami,	*Caret.*
	Mádi,	*Caret.*
	Mádia,	*Caret.*
	Kuri,	*Caret.*
	Keikádi,	*Adi.*
	Khoṇḍ,	*Vetámu.*
	Sávara,	*Teda.*
	Gadaba,	*Buvo.*
	Yerukala,	*Mottu.*
	Chentsu,	*Már, maryo.*
Southern India.	Tamiḷ, anc.,	*Caret.*
	Tamiḷ, mod.,	*Aḍi.*
	Malayáḷma, anc.,	*Caret.*
	Malayáḷma, mod.,	*Aḍi, tallu.*
	Telugu,	*Koṭṭu.*
	Karṇáṭaka, anc.,	*Caret.*
	Karṇáṭaka, mod.,	*Hoḍe.*
	Tuḷuva,	*Caret.*
	Kurgi,	*Yeppu, eri.*
	Toḍuva,	*Caret.*
	Toḍa,	*Puis bini, buro.*
	Kóta,	*Puigabe, puiye.*
	Baḍaga,	*Huidane, hui.*
	Kuṛumba,	*Huidane, hui.*
	Iruḷa,	*A'ḍike, aḍi.*
	Malabar,	*Adi, thattu.*
	Sinhalese,	*Gahanavá.*

Types.

Group	Language	Word
Inflecting.	SANSKRIT,	*Grah, ádá, hṛi, dhṛi.*
	ARABIC,	*A'khaza.*
Compounding.	BASK,	*Artu, itsiki.*
	FINNIC,	*Otan.*
	MAGYAR,	*Vesz.*
	TURKISH,	*Al.*
	CIRCASSIAN,	*Tzirishch.*
	GEORGIAN,	*Wigheb [gheb].*
	MONGOLIAN,	*Abcho.*
	MANTSHU,	*Dshatame.*
	JAVANESE, Ngoko,	*Chěkěl.*
	JAVANESE, Krama,	*Chěpěng.*
	MALAY,	*Ambil.*
Isolating.	CHINESE, Nankin,	*Pá.*
	CHINESE, Pekin,	*Pá.*
	CHINESE, Canton,	*Nim.*
	CHINESE, Shanghai,	*Tan.*
	AMOY, Colloquial,	*T'eh.*
	JAPANESE,	*Toru, tori.*
	Brahuí,	*Halltak.*
Chinese Frontier & Tibet.	Gyámi,	*Rákwo.*
	Gyárung,	*Daven.*
	Tákpa,	*Yá, longá.*
	Mányak,	*Dango.*
	Thochú,	*Jádjh.*
	Sokpa,	*Caret.*
	Horpa,	*Gwonkhe, túshthú.*
	Tibetan (*written*),	*Blan, júng, hen.*
	Tibetan (*spoken*),	*Leng, yá.*
Nepal (east to west).	Serpa,	*Ling.*
	Súnwár,	*Hye.*
	Gúrung,	*Kinú.*
	Múrmi,	*Thob.*
	Magar,	*Leo.*
	Tháksya,	*Bhakáu.*
	Pákhya,	*La.*
	Newár,	*Ká, na.*
	Limbu,	*Le.*
Kiránti Group (East Nepal).	Kiránti,	*Bátú.*
	Rodong,	*Ne, púkji, púdyu.*
	Rúngchenbung,	*Ne, battu.*
	Chhingtángya,	*Khátta.*
	Náchhereng,	*Ne, beh yú.*
	Wáling,	*Ne, báttu.*
	Yákha,	*Kwe, áktu, kettu.*
	Chourásya,	*Ne, paistá.*
	Kulungya,	*Ne, kháú, kháyu.*
	Thulungya,	*Ne, briya.*
	Báhingya,	*Ne, láto, jápo, blawo.*
	Lohorong,	*Naye, labe.*
	Lambichhong,	*Ko, thepta.*
	Báláli,	*Ná, khettá.*
	Sáng-páng,	*Ne, kháyú.*
	Dúmi,	*Ne, kháta.*
	Kháling,	*Caret.*
	Dungmáli,	*Ne, kháye.*
Broken Tribes of Nepál.	Dárhi,	*Lehik.*
	Denwár,	*Leik.*
	Pahri,	*Háya.*
	Chepáng,	*Leï.*
	Bhrámu,	*Tháyo.*
	Váyu,	*Doko.*
	Kuswar,	*Neik.*
	Kusunda,	*Má.*
	Tháru,	*Lala.*
	Lepcha (Sikkim),	*Lyo.*
	Bhúṭáni v. Lhopa,	*Len nang.*
N.-E. Bengal.	Bodo,	*Lá, ná.*
	Dhimál,	*Rhú.*
	Kocch,	*Libár.*
	Garo,	*Lé, lau.*
	Káchári,	*Caret.*
Eastern Frontier of Bengal.	Munipuri,	*Lono.*
	Míthán Nágá,	*Paule.*
	Tablung Nágá,	*Yakei.*
	Khári Nágá,	*Hiraugo.*
	Angámi Nágá,	*Khriliwe.*
	Námsáng Nágá,	*Kapo.*
	Nowgong Nágá,	*Niagirr.*
	Tengsa Nágá,	*Chiokko, ánno.*
	Abor Miri,	*Lápü.*
	Sibságar Miri,	*Láto.*
	Deoria Chutia,	*Lario.*
	Singpho,	*Láu.*
Arrakan & Burmah.	Burman (*written*),	*Yú.*
	Burman (*spoken*),	*Yú.*
	Khyeng v. Shou,	*Si.*
	Kámi,	*Lá.*
	Kúmi,	*Lo.*
	Mrú v. Toung,	*Caret.*
	Sák,	*Caret.*
Siam & Tenasserim.	Talain v. Mon,	*Kit.*
	Sgau-karen,	*Hena, he.*
	Pwo-karen,	*Mahni.*
	Toungh-thu,	*Khone.*
	Shán,	*An.*
	Annamitic,	*Bat.*
	Siamese,	*Ouk, au, nap.*
	Ahom,	*Au.*
	Khámti,	*Au.*
	Laos,	*Au.*
Central India.	Ho (Kol),	*Telleitcá.*
	Kol (Singhbhum),	*Ne.*
	Santáli,	*Idíte, ne!*
	Bhúmij,	*Ne.*
	Uráon,	*Oánda.*
	Mundala,	*Ne.*
	Rájmahali,	*Kinda.*
	Goṇḍi,	*Tará, woutona, yetalle.*
	Gayeti,	*Caret.*
	Rutluk,	*Caret.*
	Naikude,	*Caret.*
	Kolami,	*Caret.*
	Mádi,	*Caret.*
	Mádia,	*Caret.*
	Kuri,	*Caret.*
	Keikádi,	*Yedutuko.*
	Khoṇḍ,	*Kúway.*
	Sávara,	*Yama.*
	Gadaba,	*Demá.*
	Yerukala,	*Váko, vánkemáṭe.*
	Chentsu,	*Niyyo, niyá.*
Southern India.	Tamiḷ, anc.,	*Ettukkol.*
	Tamiḷ, mod.,	*Eḍuttukkol, yeda.*
	Malayáḷma, anc.,	*Caret.*
	Malayáḷma, mod.,	*Eṭukka.*
	Telugu,	*Puchchukonu, tisukonu.*
	Karṇáṭaka, anc.,	*Caret.*
	Karṇáṭaka, mod.,	*Dukoḷḷu.*
	Tuḷuva,	*Caret.*
	Kurgi,	*Caret.*
	Toḍuva, } Toḍa, }	*Caret.*
		Tegi, yettfo.
	Kóta,	*Veḍe.*
	Baḍaga,	*Tegi.*
	Kuṛumba,	*Tegi.*
	Iruḷa,	*Bongu.*
	Malabar,	*Edu.*
	Sinhalese,	*Ganuavá.*

	Types.	
Inflecting.	SANSKṚIT,	*A'ní, apaní, apahṛi.*
	ARABIC,	*A'khaza.*
Compounding.	BASK,	*Kendu, edeki, ideki, idoki.*
	FINNIC,	*Otanpois.*
	MAGYAR,	*Elvesz.*
	TURKISH,	*Getur.*
	CIRCASSIAN,	*Caret.*
	GEORGIAN,	[*Zia.*]
	MONGOLIAN,	*Apgatchikho.*
	MANTSHU,	*Gaime.*
	JAVANESE, Ngoko,	*Hamet.*
	JAVANESE, Krama,	*Mendet.*
	MALAY,	*Angkat.*
Isolating.	CHINESE, Nankin,	*Pá-k'ü.*
	CHINESE, Pekin,	*Pá-ch'ü.*
	CHINESE, Canton,	*Ním-hü.*
	CHINESE, Shanghai,	*Tan-le.*
	AMOY, Colloquial,	*T'eh-k'i.*
	JAPANESE,	*Mote-ike.*
	Brahuí,	*Harfhin.*
Chinese Frontier & Tibet.	Gyámi,	*Láchhe.*
	Gyárung,	*Dicháng.*
	Tákpa,	*Khor.*
	Mányak,	*Túyú.*
	Thochú,	*Doukwa.*
	Sokpa,	*A'hbachhi.*
	Horpa,	*Wúmbe.*
	Tibetan (*written*),	Hkhúr, ḅkhyer.
	Tibetan (*spoken*),	*Bák song.*
Nepal (east to west).	Serpa,	*Khúr syop.*
	Súnwár,	*Lat.*
	Gúrung,	*Bhod.*
	Múrmi,	*Por.*
	Magar,	*A'rho.*
	Tháksya,	*Bhoro.*
	Pákhya,	*Láljá.*
	Newár,	*Yenki.*
	Limbu,	*Tere.*
Kiranti Group (East Nepal).	Kiránti,	*Khá tú.*
	Rodong,	*Pugzyú, púgdyú.*
	Rúngchenbung,	*Khátuki khára.*
	Chhingtángya,	*Kháttu khára, kháttu lonta.*
	Náchhereng,	*Khe yu.*
	Wáling,	*Kháttu.*
	Yákha,	*Khettu, yang khettu.*
	Chourásya,	*Lettá.*
	Kulungya,	*Kháyu.*
	Thulungya,	*Daú da.*
	Báhingya,	*Látyo, lá tojo, la tise,*[1] *latine.*[2]
	Lohorong,	*Lahette, lakhette, lakhettache.*[1]
	Lambichhong,	*Khátta, chikhette, yi khette,*
	Báláli,	*Yákhettu.* [*la khette.*
	Sáng-páng,	*Kháh'yu.*
	Dúmi,	*Khotte.* [*naye.*[2]
	Kháling,	*Khátte, khatte chie,*[1] *khos-*
	Dungmáli,	*Kháde, khádechie,*[1] *kháde-* [*ningye.*
Broken Tribes of Nepal.	Dárhi,	*Lejik.*
	Denwár,	*Legaik'.*
	Pahri,	*Búláson, búláson.*
	Chepáng,	*Caret.*
	Bhrámu,	*Yánggno, yango.*
	Váyu,	*Lákto, lakto.*
	Kuswar,	*Nehin.*
	Kusunda,	*Wá.*
	Tháru,	*Lejáre.*
	Lepcha (Sikkim),	*Bú non.*
	Bhúṭáni v. Lhopa,	*Bak song.*
N.-E. Bengal.	Bodo,	*Láng.*
	Dhimál,	*Chúngpú.*
	Kocch,	*Lejábár.*
	Garo,	*Leláng.*
	Káchári,	*Caret.*
Eastern Frontier of Bengal.	Munipuri,	*Pukho.*
	Míthán Nágá,	*Pai pau.*
	Tablung Nágá,	*Noh si.*
	Khári Nágá,	*Heneraugo.*
	Angámi Nágá,	*Satele.*
	Námsáng Nágá,	*Kapkáto.*
	Nowgong Nágá,	*Penruang.*
	Tengsa Nágá,	*Cheba chenang.*
	Abor Miri,	*Bomkang.*
	Sibságar Miri,	*Bomkang.*
	Deoria Chutia,	*Laromni.*
	Singpho,	*Láu wáu.*
Arrakan & Burmah.	Burman (*written*),	*Yúswá.*
	Burman (*spoken*),	*Yúthwá.*
	Khyeng v. Shou,	*Caret.*
	Kámi,	*Láhál.*
	Kúmi,	*Lode.*
	Mrú v. Toung,	*Caret.*
	Sák,	*Caret.*
Siam & Tenasserim.	Talain v. Mon,	*K'ítna.*
	Sgau-karen,	*Sokwi, ketcho, katso.*
	Pwo-karen,	*Tsohkwaik.*
	Toungh-thu,	*Htúlway.*
	Shán,	*Oungkwa.*
	Annamitic,	*Demdi.*
	Siamese,	*Oungkol, thü.*
	Ahom,	*Sung.*
	Khámti,	*Song.*
	Laos,	*Song, thü.*
Central India.	Ho (Kol),	*I'títeá, sabteá.*
	Kol (Singhbhum),	*I'díman.*
	Santáli,	*Iditaráite, dohte* (by force).
	Bhúmij,	*Idimengo.*
	Uráon,	*Honá.*
	Mundala,	*E'díme.*
	Rájmahali,	*Oiyá.*
	Goṇḍi,	*Oumaniga, wontona, woyalle.*
	Gayeti,	*Caret.*
	Rutluk,	*Caret.*
	Naikude,	*Caret.*
	Kolami,	*Caret.*
	Mádi,	*Caret.*
	Mádia,	*Caret.*
	Kuri,	*Caret.*
	Keikádi,	*Yedu.*
	Khoṇḍ,	*Ahánesamallmu.*
	Sávara,	*Pdgná lá yirba.*
	Gadaba,	*Sogusiyyá.*
	Yerukala,	*Yiṭṭikonḍupo, vakkondu-*
	Chentsu,	*Nikejá, niyá.* [*pomu.*
Southern India.	Tamiḷ, anc.,	*Koḍupó.*
	Tamiḷ, mod.,	*Konḍupó, yeḍuttupó.*
	Malayáḷma, anc.,	*Caret.*
	Malayáḷma, mod.,	*Konḍupó.*
	Telugu,	*Tisukapó.*
	Karṇáṭaka, anc.,	*Caret.*
	Karṇáṭaka, mod.,	*Oyyu.*
	Tuḷuva,	*Konḍattu popuna.*
	Kurgi,	*Caret.*
	Toḍuva, }	*Caret.*
	Toḍa, }	*Ett fo.*
	Kóta,	*Ett hogu.*
	Baḍaga,	*Yettiunḍ hogu.*
	Kuṛumba,	*Yettiunḍ hogu.*
	Iruḷa,	*Eḍedu konḍu poke.*
	Malabar,	*Eduttupodu.*
	Sinhalese,	*Ahakkaranavá.*

Group	Language	Word
	Types.	
Inflecting.	SANSKRIT,	*Kath, vad, nivid.*
	ARABIC,	*Kála, ḥaka.*
Compounding.	BASK,	*Esan, erran.*
	FINNIC,	*Juttun.*
	MAGYAR,	*Caret.*
	TURKISH,	*Caret.*
	CIRCASSIAN,	*Caret.*
	GEORGIAN,	*Wautskeb.*
	MONGOLIAN,	*Togotchilakho.*
	MANTSHU,	*Khendume.*
	JAVANESE, Ngoko,	*Nuturri.*
	JAVANESE, Krama,	*Hasanjang.*
	MALAY,	*Bilang.*
Isolating.	CHINESE, Nankin,	*Kiang kih-t'ing.*
	CHINESE, Pekin,	*Ching kei-t'ing.*
	CHINESE, Canton,	*Kong-t'ing.*
	CHINESE, Shanghai,	*Kau-su.*
	AMOY, Colloquial,	*Káikong.*
	JAPANESE,	*Mongatalu, uanasiworusu.*
	Brahuí,	*Parak.*
Chinese Frontier & Tibet.	Gyámi,	*Shro.*
	Gyárung,	*Tachen.*
	Tákpa,	*Syat.*
	Mányak,	*Thaidyú.*
	Thochú,	*Kúrr.*
	Sokpa,	*Khala.*
	Horpa,	*Tayin, napshe.*
	Tibetan (*written*),	*Bshod, ḥchhod.*
	Tibetan (*spoken*),	*Láp, chwe.*
Nepal (east to west).	Serpa,	*Lap.*
	Súnwár,	*Den.*
	Gúrung,	*Bid.*
	Múrmi,	*Syát.*
	Magar,	*Khangni.*
	Tháksya,	*Bhigo.*
	Pákhya,	*Kaha.*
	Newár,	*Koṇ.*
	Limbu,	*Chekhe, cheke.*
Kiranti Group (East Nepal).	Kiránti,	*Khang metu.*
	Rodong,	*Rág'na.*
	Rúngchenbung,	*Yeng mettu, khángmusa,*
	Chhingtángya,	*Chepta. [khangmettu.*
	Náchhereng,	*Púu.*
	Wáling,	*Khouj su.*
	Yákha,	*Yok'mettu.*
	Chourásya,	*Sokátá.*
	Kulungya,	*Poá.*
	Thulungya,	*Sing'da.*
	Báhingya,	*Sogno, sodi, sodo.*
	Lohorong,	*I'se, -ache,*[1] *-amne.*[2]
	Lambichhong,	*Tumlúsa.*
	Báláli,	*I'su.*
	Sáng-páng,	*Páyu.*
	Dúmi,	*Blet'te, blet'te. [sua.*[2]
	Kháling,	*Blátte, lat'te, blattechi,*[1] *blatte-*
	Dungmáli,	*Lúye, lúchle,*[1] *lunumye.*[2]
Broken Tribes of Nepal.	Dárhi,	*Káhuk.*
	Denwár,	*Sarha.*
	Pahri,	*Kyen.*
	Chepáng,	*Nhosche.*
	Bhrámu,	*Chisoyo.*
	Váyu,	*Ishito, bolito.*
	Kuswar,	*Ghanaiik.*
	Kusunda,	*Wongdágo.*
	Tháru,	*Kahare.*
	Lepcha (Sikkim),	*Dan.*
	Bhútáni v. Lhopa,	*Lap.*
N.-E. Bengal.	Bodo,	*Rai.*
	Dhimál,	*Dop.*
	Kocch,	*Bolinu.*
	Garo,	*Borot.*
	Káchári,	*Caret.*
Eastern Frontier of Bengal.	Munipuri,	*Caret.*
	Míthán Nágá,	*Caret.*
	Tablung Nágá,	*Caret.*
	Khári Nágá,	*Caret.*
	Angámi Nágá,	*Caret.*
	Námsáng Nágá,	*Ngáo.*
	Nowgong Nágá,	*Shiang.*
	Tengsa Nágá,	*Suang.*
	Abor Miri,	*Lüpü.*
	Sibságar Miri,	*Lubida.*
	Deoria Chutia,	*Caret.*
	Singpho,	*Súṇ.*
Arrakan & Burmah.	Burman (*written*),	*Chho, krá.*
	Burman (*spoken*),	*S'ho kyá, pyawthi.*
	Khyeng v. Shou,	*Caret.*
	Kámi,	*Caret.*
	Kúmi,	*Tho.*
	Mrú v. Toung,	*Caret.*
	Sák,	*Caret.*
Siam & Tenasserim.	Talain v. Mon,	*Hanmarai.*
	Sgau-karen,	*Taì.*
	Pwo-karen,	*Laubah.*
	Toungh-thu,	*Thouthan.*
	Shán,	*Lat.*
	Annamitic,	*Noi, kè.*
	Siamese,	*Lat, bok wá.*
	Ahom,	*Bok.*
	Khámti,	*Wá.*
	Laos,	*Wá.*
Central India.	Ho (Kol),	*Menteá.*
	Kol (Singhbhum),	*Kajiman.*
	Santáli,	*Raḍate, láḍite* (converse),
	Bhúmij,	*Kajiman. [páḍáute*(inform).
	Uráon,	*Káchana.*
	Mundala,	*Káji.*
	Rájmahali,	*Tenga.*
	Goṇḍi,	*Wurkana, kantána manje.*
	Gayeti,	*Caret.*
	Rutluk,	*Caret.*
	Naikude,	*Caret.*
	Kolami,	*Caret.*
	Mádi,	*Caret.*
	Mádia,	*Caret.*
	Kuri,	*Caret.*
	Keikádi,	*Caret.*
	Khoṇḍ,	*Vesámu.*
	Sávara,	*Appungá.*
	Gadaba,	*Tsúno.*
	Yerukala,	*Sonnu.*
	Chentsu,	*Ko.*
Southern India.	Tamiḷ, anc.,	*Caret.*
	Tamiḷ, mod.,	*Sol.*
	Malayáḷma, anc.,	*Caret.*
	Malayáḷma, mod.,	*Paṛaya.*
	Telugu,	*Cheppu.*
	Karṇáṭaka, anc.,	*Caret.*
	Karṇáṭaka, mod.,	*Hêḷu.*
	Tuḷuva,	*Panuppuna.*
	Kurgi,	*Pare.*
	Toḍuva, }	*Caret.*
	Toḍa, }	*Binduḍverth bine, esht.*
	Kóta,	*Peidibe, parrde.*
	Baḍaga,	*Hlegine, hlegu.*
	Kuṛumba,	*Hlegine, helu.*
	Iruḷa,	*Sollre, sollu.*
	Malabar,	*Sollu.*
	Sinhalese,	*Kiyápan.*

Group	Language	Word
	Types.	
Inflecting.	SANSKṚIT,	*Zñá (jánáti), budh (bodhati), vid.*
	ARABIC,	*Fahama.*
Compounding.	BASK,	*Endeglatu, iskidatu, aditu, gosartu.*
	FINNIC,	*Ymmarran.*
	MAGYAR,	*Erb.*
	TURKISH,	*Anna, akla.*
	CIRCASSIAN,	*Tzshghaga.*
	GEORGIAN,	*Caret.*
	MONGOLIAN,	*Ergitchegö.*
	MANTSHU,	*Ulkhimbe.*
	JAVANESE, Ngoko,	*Ngĕrti.*
	JAVANESE, Krama,	*Ngĕrtos.*
	MALAY,	*Mangárti.*
Isolating.	CHINESE, Nankin,	*Hiáou-tih.*
	CHINESE, Pekin,	*Hsiáou-te.*
	CHINESE, Canton,	*Hiú-tak.*
	CHINESE, Shanghai,	*Tung.*
	AMOY, Colloquial,	*Hiâu.*
	JAPANESE,	*Wakaru, kadensuru.*
	Brahuí,	*Tarak.*
Chinese Frontier & Tibet.	Gyámi,	*Syá.*
	Gyárung,	*Tisen.*
	Tákpa,	*Sem.*
	Mányak,	*Najinje.*
	Thochú,	*Akhchan.*
	Sokpa,	*Heriya.*
	Horpa,	*Sam tenchû.*
	Tibetan (*written*),	*Soms, go.*
	Tibetan (*spoken*),	*Som.*
Nepal (east to west).	Serpa,	*Syen.*
	Súnwár,	*Caret.*
	Gúrung,	*Mhádid.*
	Múrmi,	*Go.*
	Magar,	*Phero.*
	Thaksya,	*Ghau.*
	Pákhya,	*Bujha.*
	Newár,	*Sikí.*
	Limbu,	*Singnite, singte.*
Kiránti Group (East Nepal).	Kiránti,	*Sin tu.*
	Rodong,	*Kámmú, muï dyu.*
	Rúngchenbung,	*Mittu.*
	Chhingtángya,	*Pitta.*
	Náchhereng,	*Chí yu.*
	Wáling,	*Mittu.*
	Yákha,	*Mittu.*
	Chourásya,	*Bimstá.*
	Kulungya,	*Min'nu.*
	Thulungya,	*Mim'da.*
	Báhingya,	*Mimto, mimtise,[1] mimtine.[2]*
	Lohorong,	*Mitte, mitheache,[1] mitteamne.*
	Lambichhong,	*Mim'da.*
	Báláli,	*Mittu.*
	Sáng-páng,	*Mit'nu.*
	Dúmi,	*Momsi.*
	Kháling,	*Mam'de, mi miye,[1] mam naye.[2]*
	Dungmáli,	*Mih'ye, mih yechle,[1] mihyenum ye.[2]*
Broken Tribes of Nepal.	Dárhi,	*Bújhkare.*
	Denwár,	*Bújh.*
	Pahri,	*Thúí.*
	Chepáng,	*Caret.*
	Bhrámu,	*Búzdyû.*
	Váyu,	*Seko.*
	Kuswar,	*Bujhou.*
	Kusunda,	*Caret.*
	Tháru,	*Bujhare.*
	Lepcha (Sikkim),	*Ching.*
	Bhúṭáni v. Lhopa,	*Som tang, noh.*

Group	Language	Word
N.-E. Bengal.	Bodo,	*Bújìlá.*
	Dhimál,	*Bújhte rhú.*
	Kocch,	*Bujhinu.*
	Garo,	*Bújai.*
	Káchári,	*Caret.*
Eastern Frontier of Bengal.	Munipuri,	*Caret.*
	Míthán Nágá,	*Avan.*
	Tablung Nágá,	*Tau singpu.*
	Khári Nágá,	*Metechau.*
	Angámi Nágá,	*Siwe.*
	Námsáng Nágá,	*Ijáto.*
	Nowgong Nágá,	*Matürrmá.*
	Tengsa Nágá,	*Myangmang.*
	Abor Miri,	*Ken.*
	Sibságar Miri,	*Kintoka.*
	Deoria Chutia,	*Takarini.*
	Singpho,	*Choiu.*
Arrakan & Burmah.	Burman (*written*).	*Liṇ, si.*
	Burman (*spoken*),	*Le, ṭhi, nálaythí.*
	Khyeng v. Shou,	*Ne.*
	Kámi,	*Kanái.*
	Kúmi,	*Caret.*
	Mrú v. Toung,	*Caret.*
	Sák,	*Caret.*
Siam & Tenasserim.	Talain v. Mon,	*Tihtmara.*
	Sgau-karen,	*Nahpor.*
	Pwo-karen,	*Nahthi.*
	Toungh-thu,	*Thana.*
	Shán,	*Húlikh.*
	Annamitic,	*Hiêu.*
	Siamese,	*Húlet, rú.*
	Ahom,	*Hú.*
	Khámti,	*Hú, thom.*
	Laos,	*Rü, hü.*
Central India.	Ho (Kol),	*Ayumurumteá.*
	Kol (Singhbhum),	*Adaiman.*
	Santáli,	*A'njomoromatc* (understand from hearing).
	Bhúmij,	*Etwanachigiim.*
	Uráon,	*Bhújarka.*
	Mundala,	*Samújhai.*
	Rájmahali,	*Bújiá.*
	Goṇḍi,	*Pútte.*
	Gayeti,	*Caret.*
	Rutluk,	*Caret.*
	Naikude,	*Caret.*
	Kolami,	*Caret.*
	Mádi,	*Caret.*
	Mádia,	*Caret.*
	Kuri,	*Caret.*
	Keikádi,	*Caret.*
	Khoṇḍ,	*Anupumenju.*
	Sávara,	*Anḍángalayi.*
	Gadaba,	*Memyá avure.*
	Yerukala,	*Telentsu.*
	Chentsu,	*Málúm.*
Southern India.	Tamiḷ, anc.,	*Caret.*
	Tamiḷ, mod.,	*Aṛi.*
	Malayáḷma, anc.,	*Caret.*
	Malayáḷma, mod.,	*Tiri.*
	Telugu,	*Teli.*
	Karṇáṭaka, anc.,	*Caret.*
	Karṇáṭaka, mod.,	*Tiḷi.*
	Tuḷuva,	*Teriyunnupuna.*
	Kurgi,	*Ari.*
	Toḍuva, } Toḍa, }	*Caret.*
		Arth bine, aridir.
	Kóta,	*Arsibe, arsulle.*
	Baḍaga,	*Aridane, aridiru, aridutto.*
	Kuṛumba,	*Aridane, ariduko.*
	Iruḷa,	*Arike, arindiru.*
	Malabar,	*Vilangu.*
	Sinhalese,	*Tĕrunvenavá.*

Types.

Group	Language	Word
Inflecting.	SANSKRIT,	*Rud* (*rodati*), *krand.*
	ARABIC,	*Baka.*
Compounding.	BASK,	*Negaregin, nigaregin, negarrezariizan.*
	FINNIC,	*Itken.*
	MAGYAR,	*Caret.*
	TURKISH,	*Aghla.*
	CIRCASSIAN,	*Mehkueh.*
	GEORGIAN,	*Wastiri* (*tir*).
	MONGOLIAN,	*Uilacho.*
	MANTSHU,	*Soksime.*
	JAVANESE, Ngoko,	*Tangis.*
	JAVANESE, Krama,	*Muwun.*
	MALAY,	*Tángis.*
Isolating.	CHINESE, Nankin,	*Tí-kuh.*
	CHINESE, Pekin,	*Tí-k'u.*
	CHINESE, Canton,	*Hám.*
	CHINESE, Shanghai,	*K'öh.*
	AMOY, Colloquial,	*Lau-bak-sái* (let fall tears).
	JAPANESE,	*Naku.*
	Brahuí,	*Hagh.*
Chinese Frontier & Tibet.	Gyámi,	*Shúhrin.*
	Gyárung,	*Dakakrú.*
	Tákpa,	*Gnu.*
	Mányak,	*Dangwá.*
	Thochú,	*Arzan.*
	Sokpa,	*Wúnna.*
	Horpa,	*Nakabrá.*
	Tibetan (*written*),	*Nú, shúm.*
	Tibetan (*spoken*),	*Gno.*
Nepal (east to west).	Serpa,	*Gnúmi.*
	Súnwár,	*Gnák.*
	Gúrung,	*Krod.*
	Múrmi,	*Krájh.*
	Magar,	*Ráp.*
	Tháksya,	*Táko.*
	Pákhya,	*Sanchha.*
	Newár,	*Khwo.*
	Limbu,	*Hábe.*
Kiranti Group (East Nepal).	Kiránti,	*Khává.*
	Rodong,	*Khápa.*
	Rúngchenbung,	*Kháwa*
	Chhingtángya,	*Hába.*
	Náchhereng,	*Khápa.*
	Wáling,	*Khá wa.*
	Yákha,	*Hába.*
	Chourásya,	*Khráptá.*
	Kulungya,	*Khápa.*
	Thulungya,	*Khrápda.*
	Báhingya,	*Gnokko, gnokse,*[1] *gnokine.*[2]
	Lohorong,	*Hábe, habache,*[1] *habane.*[2]
	Lambichhong,	*Hába, habachi,*[1] *habani.*[2]
	Báláli,	*Khába, khabachi,*[1] *khabanin.*[2]
	Sáng-páng,	*Khápá, -chi,*[1] *-ni.*[2]
	Dúmi,	*Gnoke.*
	Kháling,	*Gnoke.*
	Dungmáli,	*Khábe.*
Broken Tribes of Nepal.	Dárhi,	*Rouk.*
	Denwár,	*Hán.*
	Pahri,	*Khwe.*
	Chepáng,	*Rhiasche, rhiasa.*
	Bhrámu,	*Hápá.*
	Váyu,	*O'kche.*
	Kuswar,	*Dakarou, dakarou.*
	Kusunda,	*Jhámao.*
	Tháru,	*Káröol.*
	Lepcha (Sikkim),	*Rhiop.*
	Bhútáni v. Lhopa,	*Gnú.*
N.-E. Bengal.	Bodo,	*Gáp.*
	Dhimál,	*Khár.*
	Kocch,	*Ronú.*
	Garo,	*Hep.*
	Káchári,	*Caret.*
Eastern Frontier of Bengal.	Munipuri,	*Kupbo.*
	Míthán Nágá,	*Saple.*
	Tablung Nágá,	*Saptike.*
	Khári Nágá,	*Chipli.*
	Angámi Nágá,	*Krá.*
	Námsáng Nágá,	*Sapo.*
	Nowgong Nágá,	*A'chaprr.*
	Tengsa Nágá,	*Chappale.*
	Abor Miri,	*Kappü.*
	Sibságar Miri,	*Kapda.*
	Deoria Chutia,	*Ugarini.*
	Singpho,	*Khrápu.*
Arrakan & Burmah.	Burman (*written*),	*Ngo.*
	Burman (*spoken*),	*Ngo.*
	Khyeng v. Shou,	*Akáp.*
	Kámi,	*Khá.*
	Kúmi,	*Awú.*
	Mrú v. Toung,	*Caret.*
	Sák,	*Caret.*
Siam & Tenasserim.	Talain v. Mon,	*Rán.*
	Sgau-karen,	*Haw, hauh.*
	Pwo-karen,	*Gang.*
	Toungh-thu,	*Ngen.*
	Shán,	*Hihk.*
	Annamitic,	*Khok.*
	Siamese,	*Raunghihn, ronghai.*
	Ahom,	*Hai.*
	Khámti,	*Hai.*
	Laos,	*Hai.*
Central India.	Ho (Kol),	*Raëteá.*
	Kol (Singhbhum),	*Raiman.*
	Santáli,	*Ráhte, kahabárate, khungsuh, khungsuhte* (sob).
	Bhúmij,	*Eyamman.*
	Uráon,	*Chinkháh.*
	Mundala,	*E'yamtemi.*
	Rájmahali,	*Olgá.*
	Gondi,	*Aráto, adana, arana.*
	Gayeti,	*Caret.*
	Rutluk,	*Caret.*
	Naikude,	*Caret.*
	Kolami,	*Caret.*
	Mádi,	*Caret.*
	Mádia,	*Caret.*
	Kuri,	*Caret.*
	Keikádi,	*Agu.*
	Khond,	*Caret.*
	Sávara,	*Kamyite.*
	Gadaba,	*Borryo.*
	Yerukala,	*Agulá, agu.*
	Chentsu,	*Kánd, kandiyár.*
Southern India.	Tamil, anc.,	*Caret.*
	Tamil, mod.,	*Azhu.*
	Malayálma, anc.,	*Caret.*
	Malayálma, mod.,	*Kezhu.*
	Telugu,	*E'dchu.*
	Karnátaka, anc.,	*Caret.*
	Karnátaka, mod.,	*Alu.*
	Tuluva,	*Alupuna.*
	Kurgi,	*Caret.*
	Toduva,	*Caret.*
	Toda,	*Atth bini, atthli.*
	Kóta,	*Attube, áge.*
	Badaga,	*A'ltáne, lau.*
	Kurumba,	*Alu, áltáne.*
	Irula,	*E'ke, aluve.*
	Malabar,	*Alukei.*
	Sinhalese,	*Andanavá.*

APPENDIX.

ENGLISH INDEX.

FRENCH INDEX.

GERMAN INDEX.

RUSSIAN INDEX.

LATIN INDEX.

www.ingramcontent.com/pod-product-compliance
Lightning Source LLC
Chambersburg PA
CBHW030408270326
41926CB00009B/1322
* 9 7 8 3 7 4 4 7 5 1 7 6 6 *